P9-CDJ-813

BEYOND
ENRICHMENT

Building Effective Arts Partnerships with Schools and Your Community

JANE REMER

ACA BOOKS
American Council for the Arts
New York, New York

Copyright © 1996 Jane Remer

All rights reserved. Copyright under Berne Copyright Convention, Universal Copyright Convention, and PanAmerican Copyright Convention. No part of this publication may be reproduced, stored in a retrieval system, or transmitted in any form, or by any means, electronic, photocopying, recording or otherwise, without prior written permission of the publisher.

Excerpt from THE PEOPLE, YES by Carl Sandburg, © 1936 by Harcourt Brace & Company and renewed 1964 by Carl Sandburg, reprinted by permission of the publisher.

Published by the American Council for the Arts
One East 53rd Street, New York, New York, 10022

Publications Editor: Daniel Jones

Author and Editor-in-Chief: Jane Remer
Managing Editor: Robert Porter
Book design by Blake Logan
Jacket design by Daniel Jones
Printing by Gilliland Printing, Inc.

Library of Congress Cataloging-in-Publication Data
Remer, Jane.
    Beyond enrichment : building effective arts partnerships with schools and
        your community / by Jane Remer
    p. cm.
  Includes bibliographical references and index.
  ISBN 1-879903-24-5
  1. Artists and community—United States. 2. Community art projects—
United States. 3. Artists as teachers—United States.
I. Title.
NX180.a77R46   1996
700'.7'073—dc20
1. Artists

This publication was made possible by the generous support of The Ahmanson Foundation, GE Fund, Botwinick-Wolfensohn Foundation, The BETA Fund, Capezio/Ballet Makers Dance Foundation Inc., and The Alexander Julian Foundation for Aesthetic Understanding & Appreciation.

Dedication

In Memoriam—Charles B. Fowler
"This Fragile Planet"

Charles Fowler completed the foreword to this book before it was actually written. He did so based on a detailed outline I sent him, a number of long conversations, and the 23 years we had spent as friends and colleagues. We originally planned to have him write the foreword as a first draft, finish writing his own book, *Strong Arts, Strong Schools*,[1] then revise the foreword and contribute another essay that we had discussed on school reform and the arts. To my great joy, he was able to finish his book; to my chagrin, he was unable to revise the foreword or to write the essay on school reform that I know would have been a dandy. To my great, great sorrow, he died of AIDS in June 1995. I have lost another friend. We have lost another champion. But the field has not lost the power of his singular voice.

We are lucky to have the legacy of Charles' incisive intelligence preserved in his many books, monographs and writings. Among his more important publications are *Can We Rescue the Arts for America's Children?* (American Council for the Arts, 1988), the high school textbook, *Music! Its Role and Importance in Our Lives* (Glencoe/Macmillan/McGraw-Hill, 1994), and *Strong Arts, Strong Schools* (Oxford University Press, in press). His relatively little-known but widely distributed booklet, *The Arts Process in Basic Education*, is probably the most concise description of the value of the arts, their place in the curriculum, and the ways in which they affect young people that anyone has written. It was prepared for the Pennsylvania Department of Education's Conference on the Arts in Basic Education in May 1973, with the advice and support of the JDR 3rd Fund. It was reprinted by the hundreds seven times in the seventies, and it is now out of print. I still have a copy and would love to see it revised because it is as valid today as it was in its final incarnation in 1977.

Charles' life was filled with passion for the arts in the education of all young people. He had a gift for communicating that passion more powerfully and more persuasively than almost anyone I have known. I had the opportunity to get to know and work closely with him for more than 20 years. We were fortunate to be in the arts-in-education generation just behind the pioneers of the sixties, and we had for mentors and role models arts and education leaders and visionaries like philanthropist John D. Rockefeller 3rd; JDR 3rd Fund Arts in Education Director Kathryn Bloom; Ford Foundation arts official W. McNeil "Mac" Lowry; the NEA's and the Kennedy Center's first Chairman Roger Stevens; Ford and then Rockefeller Foundation officer Junius Eddy; JDR 3rd Fund Associate Director Jack Morrison; writer and arts consultant Charles C. Mark; U.S. Office of Education Commissioners Frank Keppel and Harold "Doc" Howe II; educator-researcher John Goodlad, and many, many more.

In those days, the JDR 3rd Fund's Arts in Education program played a national role, hosting or cosponsoring important conferences, issuing numerous publications and forming two national networks of cities and states dedicated to the Fund's motto, "All the Arts for All the Children." Charles was instrumental in chronicling many of those important efforts, and he and I had the chance to write and edit as a team on several of the Fund's publications. After the Fund closed down, we saw less of each other but continued to work together on occasional projects or site visits for national organizations. This book, as it turns out, was to be our last joint venture.

I can think of no better way to pay tribute to Charles than by quoting from the last eloquent and unforgettable presentation he gave at the January 1995 Getty Center for the Arts conference on school reform in Washington, D.C. On the last day of the conference, Charles delivered a heart-rending and powerful multimedia presentation about the power of "the arts of AIDS" to educate by expressing the feelings of ordinary and extraordinary human beings from all over the globe. His speech was punctuated by musical excerpts, film clips, children's art—all underscoring the emotional and communicative power of the arts in our lives. It seems fitting to me that Charles should deliver his testament to the arts in his own inimitable words in this dedication:

> Why arts education? My thesis today is simple: The arts—creative writing and poetry, dance, media arts, music, theater and visual arts—serve as ways that we react to, record and share our impressions of the world. They tell us about people—how they thought and felt and what they valued. They help us to define ourselves and our times, as well as other people and other times. But more important, they are part of our search for a better life....
>
> What is the theme of this art? Tolerance and understanding, insight and compassion, sympathy and love. There is no more powerful way to bring this message to people than through the arts. And that is the human and essential dimension the arts bring to general education, a dimension of humanity sadly lacking in American schools today....

Establishing our utility as a subject is as essential to our existence as establishing the value of science is to maintaining its status as an educational priority. Over the years, we have suggested many practical rationales to justify our educational importance. Yes, let us go right on attempting to accumulate empirical evidence that high-quality arts experiences increase student motivation to learn, school attendance, achievement in basic subjects, creative/critical thinking, self-respect, and parental involvement, [while decreasing] discipline problems, drop-out rates, and student hostility. My own research tells me that these claims have some credibility.[2] But, first and foremost, let us justify our existence in general education based upon the primary and indigenous worth of the arts—their capacity as basic forms of human conceptualization and communication that help us understand who we are, that reveal our world as it is and was and might be, and that help us to know, appropriately, how to respond, particularly our capacity to care about other human beings, but most of all, to help us to better understand and live our lives....

In teaching the arts, we always teach their relationship to people, to purpose, and to meaning...[thousands of] years have come and gone, and we continue to try to find out what life is about, why we are here, the nature of the human condition, and our fate on this fragile planet. The arts are a compendium of much of the wisdom we have accumulated. What could possibly be more important?...[3]

Charles always celebrated change, although he was aware of its destructive tendencies, especially those that conspired to erase fragile institutional and individual memories. And so he believed in passing on the legacy of hard-earned experience and did more than most to establish and nourish that tradition. This book continues in that spirit because it is based on what we learned, over time, separately and together. It is written in honor of those who came before us to blaze the trail and for the generations to come who will, in turn, have their own stories to tell.

I shall certainly miss him, but it will be easy to remember all the good times, the trenchant wit, the searing honesty, and the hearty laughter.

Charles, this one's for you.

Jane Remer

March 1996

Notes

1. *Strong Arts, Strong Schools* (New York: Oxford University Press, in press).

2. *Understanding How the Arts Contribute to Excellent Education*, a report prepared for the National Endowment for the Arts (Philadelphia: Organization & Management Group, Inc. 1991).

3. "The Arts: Complementary Partners in General Education," Charles Fowler Presentation at the Getty Center for Education in the Arts' Conference "Beyond the Three Rs: Transforming Education with the Arts," Washington, D.C., January 14, 1995.

Contents

PART II

CHAPTER *6*
Determining Program and Instructional Effectiveness: Research, Evaluation, Assessment and Standards   357

CHAPTER *8*

Conclusion: The Oxymoronic Quest for Durable Change 495
Jane Remer

The People, Yes: Where To? What Next? Opportunity Knocks, Again: Are We Ready? Making a Difference: Building Arts Partnerships that Last; Critical Lessons Learned: Building the Local Infrastructure for More Durable Change; Avoiding the Godot Syndrome: A Framework for Immediate Action; The Journey Beyond Enrichment

APPENDICES

Foreword

In arts education today, we need all the help we can get. Recognizing the incredible resources we have at hand and making the most of them is what this book is all about. Certainly, one of the advantages of the arts, unlike most other subjects, is the vast array of community arts enterprises that have a vested interest in arts education, if not always the expertise or funds to excel at it. Working together, however, the schools and cultural agencies can exact a telling effect, bringing a rich and real dimension to education in the arts that neither could accomplish without the other.

This book is about connections and community. In his vast and thorough study of American schools published more than a decade ago, John I. Goodlad observed that "Education is no more confined exclusively to schools than is religion confined to churches, mosques, and synagogues.... The school is not and cannot be an institution apart. Nor is it, nor can it be, the exclusive provider in a community's educational system."[1] At its best, education is a collaboration between schools and other agencies, an "ecology of institutions" that includes the home, television, newspapers, religious institutions, museums and art galleries, colleges, libraries, performing arts organizations, businesses, and more. Schools need to attach themselves to these community assets for practical purposes—because the in-school programs are often inadequate and incomplete, and the realities of the community can teach that which the isolated school cannot.

But attaching schools and community agencies and getting them to work effectively together is not as simple as it might appear. Community agencies and schools tend to have different agendas, and they rarely understand each other's priorities, limitations, and potentials. To be successful and reap the maximum benefit, these associations must be interactive and collaborative. Just as the schools cannot do the whole job alone in the arts, they cannot do it all alone in any other subject. In the strategy of community connections, the arts are showing the way to the rest of education. This is an important dimension of educational reform, altering and enlarging the educational landscape and changing the vision of education in the process.

The interplay between in-school and out-of-school arts education may well have started as an act of desperation. For the sake of their long-term survival, there is hardly a cultural institution in the United States, whether a theater, museum, symphony orchestra, opera or dance company, library, or performing arts center, that doesn't count education among its functions. Educating the next generation of American youth to understand and value the arts is the only guarantee of continued existence, and the schools alone have not been able to manage the job. Nor can the cultural institutions by themselves fulfill the whole need. The galvanizing goals for both the schools and the cultural institutions are to widen access to the arts and to improve the quality of education in the arts. Together, these combined resources, however modest, can provide broader and richer dimensions and far greater impact on students.

There is a technique for building effective arts partnerships, and this is the focus of the treatise that follows. Cultural institutions regularly work within their sphere—community "outreach"—and just as regularly link up with the schools. These intersections take an almost infinite number of shapes, and many of these are explored here. There are special projects and programs, workshops for children, lectures and instruction, field trips, in-school and out-of-school performances, artists-in-residence, and festivals—the list could go on. These programs often reach out to teachers as well as students. When poets, storytellers, dancers, filmmakers, sculptors, potters, puppeteers, architects, designers, composers, and other artists work with students, they expand and enormously enrich the ongoing school arts program.

Many directors of education in our cultural institutions suffer from isolation, an inadequate budget, and low status. Ideally, they are part of their organization's senior administrative team. Where programs are most effective, the education director is included in the overall yearly planning process, has access to and support from top management, and has a workable budget. The in-school arts education staff can suffer some of the same difficulties—lack of understanding of how to identify, approach or use community resources effectively, and sometimes an ineptness at integrating these experiences into a consistent and comprehensive curricular framework. Often these efforts are viewed as above and beyond the demands and responsibilities that already stretch the arts and the classroom teacher to exhaustion.

So, there is much to be learned on both sides. This book explores the pitfalls and conveys the possibilities and the procedures that people have found to be successful in productively linking cultural opportunities with the schools. Fortunately, the arts have abundant resources to draw upon, and good sense tells us that we should capitalize on our strengths. Effective mobilization is the focus—how to plan, prepare, follow-up, and evaluate such utilization. The coordination of the work of outside organizations with the curricular-based arts and general education program is a promising way to augment and enhance arts experiences for all students, and, at the same time, show the reality of the professional art world, how it functions, and what it can contribute to the culture of the school and its inhabitants. Such efforts are mutually beneficial for the cultural institutions and the schools, and the wisdom that follows, born of hard-won expertise, can help others to take advantage of these opportunities.

Charles Fowler

Notes

1. John I. Goodlad, *A Place Called School: Prospects for the Future* (New York: McGraw-Hill, 1984), pp. 349-50.

Acknowledgments

This book started out on a grand scale and soon became a massive, intricate and rewarding enterprise—in a word, a partnership among many wonderful collaborators. It owes its life to the following institutions and individuals.

First, I would like to thank my financial partners, the funders: The GE Fund and especially Jane Polin, who was the first to come on board and has helped champion the cause; The Ahmanson Foundation, which also provided generous support for the revised and expanded second edition of *Changing Schools Through the Arts: How to Build on the Power of an Idea*; the Botwinick-Wolfensohn Foundation, which gave us a vote of confidence from Elaine and James D. Wolfensohn; The Alexander Julian Foundation for Aesthetic Understanding & Appreciation, and the backing of Alex Julian; The BETA Fund and the welcome initiative of Alexander Bernstein; and all the trustees of the Capezio/Ballet Makers Dance Foundation Inc.

To Robert Porter, my managing editor, a special thanks. This is the second book we have done together; Bob's long experience as a publisher, his critical eye, sharp intelligence and uncanny ability to catch windy rhetoric, inconsistencies and impenetrable jargon have been invaluable to the quality of the work we have produced. Blake Logan, the talented book designer, has been a pleasure to work with; she is a real artist as well as a craftswoman who caught the spirit of the work and designed the pages accordingly. To both Anna Lee and Karin Dando, my thanks for their production assistance.

Abundant thanks, too, to the fine people at ACA: Daniel Jones, the publications editor, who did the copy editing and coordinated the production; Virginia Rhodus, the general manager; Gigi Ledkovsky, director of development; and Sharon Maier, her assistant. They are all sensitive, stalwart and invaluable allies. While he is no longer with the organization, I must thank Luis R. Cancel, the former president, who immediately saw the potential value of the book for ACA and the field and agreed to publish it.

I want to thank all those distinguished colleagues across the country with whom it is a privilege to work, to think, to debate, to agree to disagree, and ultimately to come together in our commonly held belief in the importance of a quality education for all children that includes the arts. Many of these excellent people have spent untold hours outlining, shaping, writing and editing their thoughts and the lessons learned based on long, hard-earned experience. Some of them deserve my deepest gratitude for gracefully and graciously taking my, and later Bob Porter's, editorial suggestions and revising, revising and revising yet again until we had honed the pieces to our mutual satisfaction.

And finally, I am grateful to David Rockefeller, Jr. for his continuing personal support and confidence in my work in a field to which he and his uncle, John D. Rockefeller 3rd, have made such a significant and lasting contribution.

I had no idea what I was getting myself into when I began this learning journey three years ago. It has turned out to be another unforgettable experience. I am grateful to all the above for the opportunity to continue my education in such good company.

CHAPTER *1*

Introduction

From Enrichment
to Engagement

A Learning Journey

This book is about building arts partnerships that move the arts beyond enrichment—from the periphery of education into the muscle and sinew of the daily curriculum—and about those who are willing to become engaged in an often intense, symbiotic relationship to get them there. In this journey, partnerships are not the ends but the metaphorical means of transportation—the delivery system, in education jargon—for introducing and integrating a community's arts and cultural resources into the schools and behind the classroom door.

The book is also about the structural, operational and yes, even philosophical, overhauls that often take place within arts organizations and schools when they become deeply engaged in a reconsideration of their mission and in the process of developing a healthy, responsive relationship. Finally, it is about the struggle to produce and sustain the profound changes that can occur in teaching and learning for all children when artists, professional arts educators and classroom teachers determine how to pool their expertise to integrate arts instruction into the basic curriculum.

A study of more than 30 years of American arts in education history reveals cycles of boom and bust, periods full of rhetorical promise and bursts of activity followed by long stretches of dashed expectations, withdrawn support and in some instances, abrupt abandonment of promising projects, programs and initiatives. We appear to be in another one of t boom intervals. The challenge is to see whether we can take advantage of the opportunity to discover, together, how the profound changes we propose can become pervasive and enduring.

Lasting change—an oxymoron—within arts organizations and schools and the way they work together toward a larger purpose, is the quiet revolution we seek. If our quest is successful, the changes will ultimately bring the arts out of the extracurricular shadows. They will shake free of their status as mere enrichment, and put teeth into the rhetoric of our national educational goals. They will take their place alongside the other academic disciplines considered vital and worthy of serious study by all American students.

Systemic change, as you know, is an enormously difficult process, one that calls for often radical alterations in the way people think and do business—alone or especially in concert. But for those interested in seeing this change evolve and take root, it should by now have become painfully clear that we cannot afford to rely on quixotic federal or even sincere national leadership alone to get the job done. Widespread growth and stability in the arts-in-education field can develop slowly, but only when the primary impetus and support is grounded in the local schools and their community.

This book is, as Carol Ponder so nicely puts it, a "learning journey." Together we will find out how to cultivate local leadership and support for the arts in general education from our patrons, partners and the larger community. We will discover that we can accomplish this by creating a conducive climate, the professional capacity within the schools and the arts organizations, and an ardent constituency within each of our communities. How to do all this is the main subject of this book.

The Need for This Book

Years ago, after I finished the first edition of my book, *Changing Schools Through the Arts: The Power of an Idea*, I began making plans for another. The new book would deal with one of the themes that ran throughout *Changing Schools:* the importance of linking the schools with a community's arts and cultural resources. The thesis would be that community cultural organizations have an educative role to play in the lives of school children, and that effective arts partnerships can act as catalysts for instructional change and, under certain conditions, schoolwide improvement. My intention was to unpack and explore all the issues embedded in *Changing Schools* that dealt with this topic. I put together a prospectus, secured new or renewed funding commitments, and was prepared to begin when my editor at McGraw-Hill told me that the company, which had been a major publisher of arts and arts-in-education titles for a decade, was reorganizing and had changed its policy of support for the field. Disappointed but resigned, I filed the materials away for future reference.

Some ten years and a new publisher later, David O'Fallon, who was then on the education staff at the Kennedy Center for the Performing Arts, wrote an enthusiastic review of the revised, expanded and resubtitled edition of *Changing Schools Through the Arts: How to Build on the Power of an Idea*:

> This book is written from the perspective of a school-change agent, one who was comfortable with artists and arts organizations, yet viewed the world through the eyes of the professional educator and foundation officer. Leaders of arts organizations will have to look elsewhere for insights into dealing with the pitfalls and restrictions unique to their world. [1]

David's comment struck a responsive chord. Convinced that the climate was right, especially against the backdrop of a new cycle of educational reform at the national and state levels that included the arts as basics in general education for the first time, I dug out my old files, developed a new prospectus, and again secured some preliminary assurances of funding. My publisher, the American Council for the Arts, liked the idea and we were off on a new joint venture.

The Purpose of This Book

In addition to the perceived need in the field, the propitious climate of reform, and the renewed attention to the arts as part of schooling, I had several other reasons for undertaking this project.

First, during the last ten years or so, much of my work as a program advisor, staff and curriculum developer, strategic long-range planner and responsive evaluator has been with arts and cultural organizations, centers, agencies, foundations and individual artists. This has given me a wealth of firsthand experience and an in-depth perspective on the philosophical, institutional, programmatic and practical issues these groups face as they struggle to work effectively in a complex and constantly changing field. I have learned a lot of lessons along the way, and in the tradition of my mentors, principal among them Kathryn Bloom, former director of the JDR 3rd Fund, I believe part of my professional responsibility and my personal obligation is to pass them along to the next generation—orally, in print, formally in a university setting, and informally with graduate interns.

Second, and related to the first, I have worked in the field a long time. I have watched the arts gain and lose ground several times. I have lived through several cycles of educational rhetoric and reform. I have seen the public and philanthropic dollars wax, wane, wax and wane again in support of the arts and the arts in education. I have heard rationales for the arts in education and authored a few myself. The current climate, full of both ominous signs as well as promise, challenged me to confront some hard questions that inform almost every chapter in this book.

- After all these years of energy, expense and advocacy, why aren't the arts a tangible and permanent presence behind the classroom door in every school in this country?
- If indeed there is a "window of opportunity" to advance the cause of the arts in the education of every child, what must be done now that has never been done before to take advantage of it?
- What mistakes have we made over the years, what lessons have we learned from them, or apparently not yet learned, and what are the strategies that we have overlooked or not yet invented?
- What successes have we had, why have we had them, what are their characteristics, and what kinds of paradigms, guidelines and criteria can we construct and share to build success into every venture?
- What is the role of the arts and cultural community in this process, and how can its engagement benefit its own institutions or individual lives as well as all American children?

The Creative Process

As I was putting together my prospectus, I recognized the need for the experience and the voices of other professionals in the field. Originally, I had thought to ask a few colleagues to write on suggested topics. As I got further into the developmental process, and after a lot of conversations and correspondence, I found myself engaged in a dialectic that kept leading me from one question to its antithesis and then to the search for synthesis. Synthesis, or consensus, was hard to come by, and this in turn suggested the need for more perspectives, more points of view, and more experiential interpretations.

I ended up with more than 45 contributors and many thoughts and quotes from other practitioners addressing a multitude of issues, all clustered around certain dominant themes and subtopics. While this meant a monumental amount of time and energy devoted to organization, communication and editorial clarification, to shaping thoughts and issues, and to long hours on the telephone, fax and e-mail, I thought the final result would be worth it. I hoped we could demonstrate that the diversity of the arts-in-education community was part of its strength, that different voices could and should be heard on issues of concern to everyone, regardless of philosophy or approach. There is no single, simple answer to any of the questions we raise, and it is important to acknowledge that fact.

My role in the process has been a fluid one of architect, engineer, interior designer and carpenter. I designed the organization, selected the contextual issues and the content, identified the contributors, negotiated the nature and scope of their essays, and provided editorial guidance. I had to cajole, politely threaten, plead, praise and be infinitely patient with busy people who, for basically intrinsic reward, were working hard to meet my many deadlines. In the book, this role translates into main editor, primary writer, coach, facilitator and, I hope, synthesizer. While we are many voices in many rooms of the same house, for the moment it is my house, and I take full responsibility for the overall approach and point of view.

The voices include those of educators, arts administrators, artists and foundation executives. They include former U.S. education commissioners, school superintendents, principals, supervisors, college and university professors, and classroom and specialist teachers. They also include chief executive officers and education staff from national and local arts centers; national, state and local arts agencies; national and local arts-in-education programs; and arts-in-education institutes. In addition, perspectives are offered from British and American private and corporate foundations and associations, the American professional education associations, and from the professional research, evaluation and assessment communities. These people represent two countries and twelve states—more if you include the voices of those represented in the many examples of programs cited throughout the book.

Concept and Organization

My philosophical and theoretical assumptions underlying *Changing Schools* remain the same for *Beyond Enrichment*. I believe in the power and virtue of American public education for all children. I maintain that the individual school is the most effective unit for institutional and instructional change, and that networking and collaboration are the most effective strategies for building on and implementing the change process at the grassroots level. I am convinced that with proper support, both bottom up and top down, schools and the people in and around their local communities are capable of charting their own destinies. I also know that for change to occur and to last, those expected to carry it out must have a substantial stake in the action. And finally, I believe that every community, whether urban, suburban or rural, has a wealth of resources that can illuminate and bring to life many of the subjects and disciplines taught and learned behind the classroom door; that it makes good economic, cultural and social sense to link these resources systematically with the curriculum; and that children will benefit from these learning experiences because they are authentic and contemporary, grounded in an immediately recognizable reality.

In short, I believe that under certain conditions, schools are capable of positive change and that the community, especially the arts community, has a significant role to play in helping them navigate and enliven the process. Similarly, I know that the arts and cultural community stands to benefit in the short and long run from its thoughtful participation in and contribution to the schooling of the young people in its geographical sphere. I believe partnerships are one of the more effective ways of accomplishing desirable ends for everyone. But sound partnerships are easy to announce and hard to come by and sustain. Schooling, it turns out, is a messy business, and so, by the way, are the arts. How then do we create order and satisfaction from apparent chaos? How do we manage to bring together two entirely different cultures in a synergistic relationship? And how do we make this tenuous and miraculous merger last?

Embarking on Our Learning Journey

To answer these and many more detailed questions, I turned to friends, colleagues, acquaintances and others with considerable experience in the field. We begin by tackling the question of what schools are for and where the arts fit in. We then explore the relationship between the arts and school reform. From there we plunge into institutional partnerships and then classroom partnerships. After that we take on research and evaluation and the role of catalysts in prompting and sustaining collaborative community action. Bookending this journey is my introduction to set the stage and the conclusion to bring down the curtain. I think the book is best read straight through since it has been structured developmentally as well as thematically. However, for those who like side trips or prefer their own itinerary, there is no reason why you can't begin wherever you like and then jump back to where you left off or venture elsewhere to pick up another thread.

I have conceived of it as a kind of think piece and workbook crammed with essays, case studies, interviews, guidelines and criteria and other useful or provocative information. It poses questions and supplies many answers, few of them definitive. No teacher's guide is available to supply all the proper responses. I believe profoundly in the Socratic approach of inquiry-based learning, where questions beget more and often deeper, better questions.

My purpose is to help you begin or continue a dialogue with yourself, your staff or your colleagues so that you define your own site-specific questions and your own local answers, using this book as a resource and a guide. I also believe that the lessons we learn from people's failures or setbacks are as important as many of our unexamined successes—those we exuberantly accept and proclaim without sufficiently scrutinizing why things worked as well as they did. To this end, I have tried to encourage my colleagues to speak honestly about some of their less than glorious experiences so we all can profit from them.

We will explore how individual arts organizations, agencies and artists can work more effectively as learning resources to students, teachers, administrators, parents and other community members. We will study various types of effective programs and services that can be developed with and for schools and the local community.

We will address a cluster of questions such as:

- What are the aims of education and what is the case for the arts in schooling? What is school reform, and what effect does the most recent wave have on the arts, on artists and on your institution?

- Should your organization get involved in education, and what's in it for you? What factors should you consider? Who is your potential audience, and what are their needs? What are your resources (time, people, facilities, money)?

- What kinds of programs and services should you offer and where should they take place? What will be taught and learned, by whom and to what end? How can you best relate to today's young audiences and build bridges to understanding? With whom and how do you design these programs and services?

- Who shall teach the arts and what is your role as an outsider in the curriculum development and instructional process? What kind of professional and technical support services do you need to build and sustain these activities?

- Is this game really worth the candle? How will you evaluate the effectiveness of the purpose, structure and operation of your programs and their impact on teaching and learning? How will you determine the impact on your own organization?
- How can you decide whether and how to develop and sustain your collaborations and partnerships? To whom will you turn for leadership, support and inspiration at the national, state and local levels and what kind of assistance can you expect?

Learner Outcomes for the Reader

By the time the curtain comes down, I expect you will have shaped the answers, or at least the outlines of answers, to these and other questions we raise throughout the book. I think you will find affirmation, confirmation and provocative challenges that will stimulate further thought and then considered action. I know you will be aware of more local, state and national resources for your work and a number of people to whom you can turn for counsel or assistance.

Above all, I hope you will be able to consider your work in the arts in education through the filter of the essential questions that I raise and the provisional answers I have found for them in the course of my own reflective journey through these pages.

Q. After all these years of energy, expense and advocacy, why aren't the arts a tangible and permanent presence behind the classroom door in every school in this country?

A. We have not built the commitment, the climate, the capacity, the constituency or sufficient community support at the grassroots level.

Q. What can we do now that is different from what we have done for more than thirty years to create the commitment, the climate, the capacity, the constituency and the community support for change to endure at the grassroots level?

A. Let us find out together as we proceed on our learning journey.

Notes

1. Association of Performing Arts Presenters, *Bulletin*, May 1993.

CHAPTER 2

What Schools are For and the Case for the Arts in General Education

Coloring Outside the Lines
What Schools are For and Where the Arts Fit In

Featuring the Work and Writings of
John I. Goodlad and Ernest L. Boyer

Setting the Stage

This book raises questions about schools, schooling and the arts for which no one, including philosophers, educators, politicians, or reformers has found simple, definitive answers. What schools are for, who they are for and who should support them has always been contingent upon the society in which, and for which, they exist. It is axiomatic that schools reflect the values and the politics of the surrounding culture. At the same time, the place of the arts in public education has ridden the crests and shallows of various education reform waves during the last 40-odd years. When the arts are considered at all, the discussion usually revolves around teaching the arts for their own intrinsic worth or teaching the arts as instrumentalities—as means to other academic, social or political ends. With some notable exceptions, few of our current school reformers have wrestled with this issue. Even fewer seem to think it is an essential question.

To build effective arts partnerships between arts organizations and schools, the partners must know a good deal about the different institutional landscapes—their cultures, habits, politics and purposes. I believe it is important for arts organizations and artists to arrive at their own examined idea of the purpose of schools and the role of the arts in the education of our young. Without this philosophical inquiry, there is no solid foundation for the discussions of collaboration and partnership that will follow.

To help define the territory and to pose some of the guiding questions, I have asked several prominent educators to share their perspectives. This chapter will give you a range of views about the subject from two former U.S. commissioners of education, Ernest L. Boyer and Harold "Doc" Howe II; two active school superintendents, Anthony Alvarado and Richard Benjamin; and a practicing principal, Mae Kennerly.

The Purpose of Schools: Babysitting, Self-Esteem and the Status Quo

I teach a university arts-in-education course for practicing or potential arts administrators. One of the first things I do with my students is to brainstorm about the purpose of schools. I tell them that, since they have all had schooling, they are qualified as experts. Here is an example of what ended up on the chalkboard in one of these sessions:

What Schools Are For: Our Expectations of Schooling

Education	Self-image	Crime prevention
Learning	Vocational training	Violence reduction
Social skills	Discipline	Drug prevention
Basic skills	Sense of community	Assistance to unwed
Thinking	Respect for others	mothers
Babysitting	Greatest hits of	Solutions or antidotes to
Self-esteem	Western Literature	poverty and homelessness
Status-quo	Multiculturalism	Combat racism, bigotry,
Citizenship	Maturation and social	prejudice
Getting a job	responsibility	Self-realization

I usually follow this exercise with a discussion of the following questions:

Where are the arts in this list? They are not explicit; are they implied? You are all actual or would-be arts administrators. What does this tell us about American values, your own values, and your own school experience?

The conversation invariably turns to American values and to the American attitude about what educators call the affective side of learning—the emotional, the passionate, the sentimental, the intuitive, the expressive. In a word, feelings.

A Macho Society

In the next chapter on School Reform and the Arts, John Goodlad says flatly: "There are several reasons why the arts are still not a presence behind the classroom door and not part of the basic education of every child.... We are still, in some ways, a macho society...."

Picture this. An 11-year-old youngster—a sixth-grader—is at dinner with his family. His mother asks, "James, what did you do in school today?" James replies, "In language arts class, we read Hawthorne's *The Scarlet Letter* and got in touch with how it feels to be an outcast. In science we sorted out the shapes of different cells, categorized them and made beautiful color-coded drawings in our portfolios. In social studies we discussed Bizet's opera *Carmen* and talked about the cigarette girl's passion for personal freedom and why it ultimately led to her death. In physical education we did clog dances and the Virginia Reel to some of Mozart's contra dances. In the afternoon, we went to the historical museum and learned to quilt using geometric patterns based on stained glass windows. It was awesome." His father replies, sternly: "But what did you *learn* today? I certainly hope you get back to the basics tomorrow. No young man of mine is going to go soft on me with all this vague, artsy, feelings stuff!"

We *are* a macho society, but the problem is more complex. We come from a Puritanical tradition that holds feelings, emotions and passion suspect. Many of us are squeamish about these "soft" aspects of our humanity. We are afraid of their rampant consequences and uncomfortable with being "out of control." We are known abroad for our American know-how: we get things done; we build the better mousetrap; we are not regarded as meditative, reflective, contemplative and serene. We are too much in a hurry. We talk about cooperation, teamwork, respect for and identification with others, but we actually value competition, power, money and quick success. Is it any wonder, then, that the arts are hard to find at the top of most of our lists about schools, or perhaps on any of our lists at all?

What Schools Are For: John Goodlad's Perspective

In his book, *What Schools Are For*,[1] Dr. John I. Goodlad lists the various functions schools have historically served: creating the good person in the good society; socialization of immigrants; preparation of the young for jobs; keeping young people off the labor market; fostering patriotis..

relieving and freeing mothers from the chores of child rearing and supervision (babysitting); developing individual talents; teaching certain facts,
basic concepts, skills and processes; and reconstructing the social order.
He deals with three distinctly different ways of thinking about what
schools are for and asks these questions: What are schools expected or
asked to do? What do schools actually do? What should schools be doing?

Goodlad believes that much of what schools are expected to
contribute to society does not appear in local and state lists of educational
goals and that determining what various individuals and groups expect
from schools is a form of survey research; it is basically sociological, not
philosophical. Trying to determine what schools actually do, he maintains,
is an overwhelmingly complex task, especially when attempting to take
the experiences of those who live and work in the schools—students,
teachers, administrators and others—into account.

Goodlad certainly knows whereof he speaks; he has spent the better
part of his professional life working in and with schools and observing
them as one of the country's top educational researchers. For him, the
question of what schools *should* do boils down to whether they should be
used for ends other than, or in addition to, strictly educational ones, and
if so, whether these ends determine and justify the means. Here he is
referring to the separation of distinctly educative functions from the social,
economic and political problems the schools have been asked to help
solve—integration, poverty, drug and crime reduction and the like.

Goodlad sees education as a larger social and cultural enterprise than
the business of schooling. He explains his perspective this way:

> ...I write in praise of the common school...and education for the
> masses.... Today's schools are only marginally educational institu-
> tions.... I am all for alternatives to the traditional system of
> schooling, but if these are to be more viable educationally than
> what we presently have, they must be available to all....
>
> Lawrence Cremin's succinct definition suggests the nature and
> scope of education: "[Education is] the deliberate, systematic, and
> sustained effort to transmit or evoke knowledge, attitudes, values,
> skills and sensibilities." Education occurs in the individual; it
> involves the whole of the individual; it occurs in schools, homes,
> churches and other institutions as well as through the press, radio
> and television.... The prime role of our schools is the development
> of the full potential of each individual.... Their proper role is to do
> the educating not done or not done easily elsewhere in the culture....

...successful education is that which promotes successful problem solving, sensitive human relations, self-understanding, and the integration of one's total life experience.

Successful schooling is schooling that promotes such traits to the utmost. The evidence for this kind of success is found, first, in the quality of the educational experience and, ultimately, in the person.... the educational gap for the schools to fill has to do with contemplating, questioning, inquiring—activities that few employers pay for and that television allows little time for.... schools, to be educative, must possess the academic freedom necessary to deviate from many established ways.... Of critical importance is the use of resources in the larger educational ecology for developing individual talent.

Schools take on a special significance because they and they alone were created to assure that a deliberate, systematic and sustained process of educating would go on in our country [for the general population].... Schools provide a public service, paid for out of public tax monies and in accord with people's willingness and ability to pay.... Our public system of schooling is to a considerable degree a servant to its clients and dependent for support upon their understanding of and belief in education.... One of the major problems for all educational institutions is how they can satisfy the demands of their clients and still educate. The balance is a precarious one.

What makes the balance particularly delicate is the fact that education, properly conducted, is eminently practical. It prepares not for just one but many vocations; it prepares not just for society as it is but for a changing civilization; it provides not merely for present satisfactions but makes possible a lifetime of enjoyment....[2]

A Taxonomy of Goals for Schools

Goodlad presents what might be called a taxonomy of the data he and his colleagues gathered from the large sample of students, teachers and parents in schools selected for his ten-year, nationally recognized *Study of Schooling in the United States*. He explains that the evidence he gathered supports the importance of four general categories of goals (Figure 2.1). Moreover, he points out that, historically, schooling in the U.S. over more than three centuries has shifted from discipline honed by the classics and religion to civic, religious and vocational responsibility; to worthy membership in home, community, state and nation; to concern for justice and respect for others; to appreciation for democratic values; and to respect for self and development of individual talents. As shown below, Goodlad breaks the four broad categories into twelve goals for schooling based on an analysis and synthesis of over 100 statements by state and local boards of education in the U.S.

☞ Figure 2.1: The four basic categories of goals for schooling in the U.S.

1. Academic (functional literacy)
2. Vocational (readiness for productive work and economic responsibility)
3. Social and civic (socialization for participation in a complex society)
4. Personal (self-fulfillment)

The Twelve Goals of Schooling[3]

1. **Mastery of basic skills.** Students develop abilities to acquire ideas through reading and listening, to communicate ideas through writing and speaking, to understand and utilize mathematical concepts, to utilize available sources of information, and to read, write and manipulate basic arithmetic operations.

2. **Career and vocational education.** Students develop abilities to select an occupation, to build salable skills and specialized knowledge, and to acquire attitudes and habits that make them productive participants in economic life. They learn to form positive attitudes toward work, the necessity of making a living and an appreciation of the social value and dignity of work.

3. **Intellectual development.** Students develop abilities to think rationally, solve problems, and reason logically using different modes of inquiry. They learn to use and evaluate knowledge (i.e., critical and independent thinking), to make judgments and decisions in a wide variety of life roles and intellectual activities, and to accumulate a general fund of knowledge. They acquire concepts in mathematics, literature, natural science and social science, learn to use knowledge sources including technology to gain access to information, and develop positive attitudes toward intellectual activity, such as curiosity and a desire for further learning.

4. **Enculturation.** Students develop insights into the values and characteristics of one's civilization, awareness of one's cultural and historical

heritages, and familiarity with the ideas that have inspired and influenced mankind. They learn how past heritages influence the direction and values of society and acquire, examine and accept the norms, values, standards and traditions of the groups of which one is a member.

5. **Interpersonal relations.** Students develop a knowledge of opposing value systems, an understanding of how members of a family function, and skill in communicating effectively in groups. They acquire the ability to identify with and advance the goals and concerns of others and the ability to form productive and satisfying relations with others based on respect, trust, cooperation, consideration and caring.

6. **Autonomy.** Students develop a positive attitude toward learning, skill in selecting personal learning goals, skill in coping with and accepting continuing change, and skill in making decisions with purpose. They acquire the ability to plan and organize the environment in order to realize their goals and a willingness to accept responsibility for and the consequences of their own decisions.

7. **Citizenship.** Students develop a sense of historical perspective, a knowledge of the basic workings of government, a commitment to the values of liberty and government by the consent of the governed, and an attitude of inquiry to examine societal values. They acquire the ability to think productively about the improvement of society, skills in democratic action in large and small groups, a willingness to participate in the political life of the nation and community, a commitment to the fulfillment of humanitarian ideas everywhere, and a commitment to involve themselves in resolving social issues.

8. **Creativity and aesthetic perception.** Students develop the ability to motivate themselves to deal with new problems in original ways, to be sensitive to problems and tolerant of new ideas, to be flexible, to redefine skills, and to see an object from different points of view. They learn to enjoy and be willing to experience the act of creation, to understand the creative contributions of others and evaluate them, to communicate through creative work actively or perceptively as a creator or as a consumer, and to develop the commitment to enrich cultural and social life.

9. **Self-concept.** Students develop the ability to search for meaning in their activities, to build the self-confidence needed for confronting their assumptions and behavior, and to live with their limitations and strengths. They learn to acquire the general knowledge and interest in other human beings as a means of knowing themselves, to construct an internal framework by which they, as individuals, can organize the concept of "self," and to develop a knowledge of their own body and a positive attitude toward their own physical appearance.

10. **Emotional and physical well-being.** Students develop the willingness to receive new impressions and to expand affective sensitivity, the competence and skills for continuous adjustment and emotional stability, and the ability to control or release the emotions according to their values. They learn to use leisure time effectively, to develop positive attitudes toward health and physical fitness, and to develop physical fitness and psychomotor skills.

11. **Moral and ethical character.** Students develop the judgment to evaluate events and phenomena as good or evil, a commitment to truth and values, and the ability to utilize values in determining choices. They also develop moral integrity, an understanding of the necessity for moral conduct, and a desire to strengthen the moral fabric of society.

12. **Self-realization.** Students construct the idea that there is more than one way of being an effective and fulfilled human being and that efforts to develop a better self contribute to the development of a better society.

How Do I Fit into the Aims of Education: An Exercise for Potential Arts Partners

These twelve goals of schooling, along with a distillation of their accompanying characteristics, are offered as a planning device or as an evaluative tool. If you are currently collaborating with a school or other education partner, or if you are planning a partnership, invite your education colleagues into this discussion. It will go a long way toward helping you to create the trust and mutual respect that is essential to your enterprise. Do not be tempted to skip quickly to Goal 8. While at first glance it seems to be the only place where the arts have a direct and indisputable role to play, on closer inspection you will discover that the arts can help schools to reach each of the twelve educational purposes—directly or indirectly. I suggest that you proceed by asking the following questions:

- Which of these goals does the school or district espouse, and what language is used to describe them?
- Are the arts mentioned by name in the goals?
- Where do the arts and the arts processes seem to fit into the goals?
- Is education one of my goals or mentioned in the mission statement of my arts institution?
- What are my goals or the goals of my arts institution?
- Where do our goals fit with the school's goals?

- In what ways can the art forms, the programs and the services that my institution offers contribute to these school goals?
- What specific programs, services and strategies can we devise together that will better meet both the school's and our goals?

A note of caution: Be careful as you proceed through this discussion that, in your desire to help achieve educational ends, you don't view the arts exclusively as instrumental means. In other words, be sure to keep a balance between study in and about the arts with learning other knowledge, skills and abilities through the arts. And be doubly sure to build in safeguards for quality and, to the extent possible, sequential learning.

The next step in this exercise is to consider various rationales for the arts in education so that you can build your own persuasive case statement that describes the need for and benefit to participants. The fresh and powerful child-centered arguments below were offered by Dr. Ernest L. Boyer at a recent national conference.

Ernest L. Boyer: Coloring Outside the Lines

Until his untimely death on December 6, 1995, Dr. Ernest L. Boyer was the president of the Carnegie Foundation for the Advancement of Teaching. Before joining the foundation, he served as U.S. commissioner of education, and as chancellor of the State University of New York. Dr. Boyer also served as the chair of the New Jersey Literacy in the Arts Task Force in 1989, whose report, *Literacy in the Arts: An Imperative for New Jersey Schools* is must reading for anyone interested in a comprehensive, closely reasoned and systematic statewide approach to providing arts education for all of a state's children.[4]

I first met Ernie Boyer in the late seventies when he was commissioner in the Office of Education (the forerunner of the Department of Education) during President Jimmy Carter's administration. I have always enjoyed reading or listening to what he had to say about the arts, education, language and literacy. He said it more eloquently than almost anyone I know, so I have included excerpts from the keynote address he gave at the National Endowment for the Arts' Art-21 Conference in Chicago in April 1994. We will learn about his vision of the new school and the five essential reasons why the arts must play a critical role in the education of every child in that environment. With his blessing, I took the liberty of reorganizing his remarks for this chapter.[5] He is another pioneer in the field whose intelligence and persuasive voice will be sorely missed.

The Language of the Angels

It is my deep conviction—and it will be the simple proposition that I present to you this morning—that the arts are one of humankind's most vital forms of language. In most respects the human species is far less equipped than other creatures on this planet: We are no match for the lion in strength; we're outstripped by the ostrich in speed; we can't outswim the dolphin; we see less acutely than the hawk. And yet, as humans, we excel in the exquisite use of symbols, which empowers us to outdistance all other forms of life in what we see, and feel, and know. There is, in short, one incontrovertible conclusion to be reached. The arts are not a frill. They are deeply embedded in that which makes us truly human. Here are five essential reasons why the arts are crucial for lifelong learning.

The Arts Express Feelings and Ideas That Words Cannot Convey

Even with the beauty of the written and spoken word, language is incomplete. There remains, deeply buried in the bosom of the human spirit, those experiences that cannot be captured by the verbal utterances we call words. Words cannot portray sufficiently the joy of a spring morning or the fruits of a fall harvest or the grief and loneliness that mark the ending of a love relationship. For the most intimate and profound— most moving—experiences, we need more subtle sounds and more effective symbols. And so it is that men and women throughout history have used music, dance and the visual arts to express feelings words cannot convey.

Wouldn't it be wonderful if singing and painting and rhythm were woven into the fabric of every family? Wouldn't it be wonderful if every preschool and every day-care center was a place of beauty, with corridors filled with color? Wouldn't it be wonderful if every neighborhood had music and drama and painting and dance for little children? And wouldn't it be wonderful if we had a ready-to-learn cable channel with music and poetry and theater and painting, a channel dedicated exclusively to learning for young children?

The Arts Expand the Child's Way of Knowing and Bring Creativity to the Nation's Classrooms

Several years ago I heard a marvelous little story about a youngster who sat down to color with her aunt. The niece took the Crayolas and the coloring book, quickly leafed past 30 pages of uncolored pictures and began coloring on a blank page in the back. When asked why she chose to color where there was no picture, the five-year-old replied, "Outside the lines you can do anything you want." I am convinced we need art in every school from kindergarten to grade 12 to encourage all young students to continue to color, if I might say so heretically, "outside the lines."

The Arts Help Students Integrate Their Learning and Discover the Connectedness of Things

The harsh truth is that in today's fragmented academic world, students complete their "Carnegie units," an unhappy term that our foundation invented 70 years ago. It's based on seat time: you spend 135 hours in a seat, I'll give you a "Carnegie unit." I am convinced that children spend a lot of time in seats accumulating "Carnegie units," which they turn in like green stamps to get diplomas. But what they fail to gain, through all of the procedures, is a more coherent view of knowledge and a more integrated, more authentic view of life.

The harsh truth is that on most campuses and in most schools artists, educators, scientists, historians and everyone else live in separate worlds, kingdoms unto themselves, with no language that connects them. And so we reduce education to a trivial pursuit and ask students on tests to recall that which matters least. I suggest that the arts, with all of the elegance that they provide, have a profoundly essential function to perform in the nation's colleges and schools by helping our children and our young people to see connections, to have some sense of coherence in a fragmented and disjointed world in which we are preoccupied with the parts but never see the whole.

More than 50 years ago, Mark Van Doren wrote that the connectedness of things is what the educator contemplates to the limit of his capacity. I am convinced that connections across the disciplines can be accomplished most effectively through the arts.

The Arts in Education Help Children Who Are Emotionally and Physically Restricted and Motivate Young People Who Are Socially Alienated

I have seen time and time again how both children and adults, who are physically and linguistically restricted, communicate joyfully through painting and through dance, through sculpture and through weaving, because these media define their hopes and affirm who they are. They can make statements that give them presence in the larger social world through the miracle we call art.

During our study of the American high school, I became convinced that we have not only a school problem but also a youth problem in this country. Far too many teenagers feel unwanted, unneeded and unconnected to the larger world, and even in the school itself, many of them drift aimlessly and anonymously from class to class. I concluded that many drop out because no one noticed that they had in fact dropped in.

If I had just one wish, I would break up every school into units of no more than 500 students each. I'd assign every student to a family unit of no more than 20 and to meet with a mentor at the beginning of each day to know that someone truly cares. I would also like to see every student engage in a cause larger than themselves. In this new school, I would like to see every kid engaged in the arts throughout their schooling because it has been shown that troubled kids, especially, who participate in dance, drama, music and the visual arts become, almost overnight, less destructive and more creative. The tragedy for young people is not just the danger of random senseless death, it is also to die with commitments undefined, with convictions undeclared and with service unfulfilled. I'm convinced that the arts have a very special role to play in giving teenagers of this nation a larger sense of purpose.

We Need the Arts to Build Community Within and Beyond the School Walls

The arts help us to build community in neighborhoods, in different cultures, and across the generations. I know, of course, that art messages do not always build bridges of understanding. They also can create confusion, even confrontation, but I have an abiding faith that ultimately the arts will heal. They are, as one first-grader told me, the language of the angels. However, if the arts are to build community, not fear, we must celebrate diversity. We must be willing to listen to art language that we've not heard before, to try to discover the deeper understanding, and frankly to create cultural institutions in our cities that are themselves communities, not enclaves for the privileged.

And finally, I'm convinced the arts can build bridges not only across cultures, but across generations as well—connecting lives at their beginning and their ending. Margaret Mead wrote on one occasion that the health of any culture is sustained by three generations that vitally interact. A vertical culture. I am troubled that we're building in this country what might be described as a horizontal culture, with each age group living and dying all alone, speaking only to itself. I think in the later years, it's the time given to dreaming, to dancing, to storytelling that absolutely affirms the sacredness of life.

In conclusion, let me repeat that I am convinced that lifelong learning in the arts is a deeply satisfying journey that should never end, an expedition I believe crucial for five essential reasons:

First, we need the arts to express feelings and ideas that words cannot convey.

Second, we need the arts to stir creativity and enrich a student's way of knowing.

Third, we need the arts to integrate the fragments of academic life.

Fourth, we need the arts to empower the disabled and give hope to the disenchanted.

Fifth, and above all, we need the arts to create community and to build connections across the generations.

As James Agee once wrote, "With every child who is born, under no matter what circumstances, the potentiality of the human race is born again." In the end, then, it is through the arts that the life cycle comes full circle.

Developing A Rationale for the Arts in General Education

There have been many rationales developed for the arts in general education. In addition to Dr. Boyer's five essential reasons, you will find more explanations that can help to make a compelling case statement in *Why We Need the Arts: 8 Quotable Speeches by Leaders in Education, Government, Business and the Arts.*[6] You can also find many more statements in the arts-in-education literature of the last decade or so. I encourage you to do more research and to choose whichever rationale suits your particular purpose or, better yet, to craft your own "credo" so that it reflects your individual or institutional philosophy. Here are a few statements that I have written for different occasions over the years which may serve as examples to help you get started.

Rationale 1: A Practical Version with an Operational Definition[7]

Practical reasons for the arts in education. The place of the arts in education should need no justification. The arts are invigorating, life-giving, healing. They express our thoughts and feelings. They are nourishment for the spirit and the intellect. But since the arts do need defending behind the classroom door and in the school corridors, here are some practical reasons for the arts in education:

The arts are useful for the education of all children because they:

- are valuable and valid for their own sake (pure arts)
- illuminate other art forms (interarts)
- illuminate other subject areas and are illuminated by them (interdisciplinary)
- bring the community's cultural resources into the classroom (linkages)
- bring the students, their teachers and their parents out into the community (linkages)
- involve parents and guardians in school governance and volunteer activities (linkages)
- identify, respond to and serve the needs of special populations (gifted, talented, handicapped, etc.)
- provide a means, a common ground to break down racial stereotypes, barriers and prejudices (multiculturalism)
- provide the impetus and the content for positive changes in teaching and learning (curriculum and staff development)
- act as catalysts for comprehensive schoolwide improvement (change agents).

An Operational Definition of the Arts in Education. My current operational definition of the arts in education is based on the concept of "infusion" that Charles Fowler articulated so clearly in *The Arts Process in Basic Education*[8] in the section titled "The Place of the Arts in the Curriculum." Before offering this definition, it will be productive for us to explore the meaning of the term in Charles' own, inimitable language:

> The goal is the utilization of the arts process as an integral part of basic education. One prerequisite to attainment of this goal is to treat all the arts, collectively, as a content area that has the same status and educational responsibility as other major departments. The first step to accomplishing this goal is to view the arts *comprehensively*.

> The comprehensive view is advantageous. It immediately helps to organize the segmented, varied arts offerings in a school into one cohesive area of curriculum with unified goals and evaluative procedures. Properly conceived, the arts constitute a great integrating force in the school curriculum. To achieve such an end they must be viewed as a component of every discipline, for their subject matter is as broad as life itself.

The arts have always dealt with the vital concerns of contemporary man. To bring them into relation with the total curriculum is to assure that disciplines do not become divorced from the vital concerns of present-day society. Such an approach permits the arts to be viewed as alternative means of understanding subject matter or processes that at the same time complement and are integral to the total basic education program.

To understand the concept of the arts in basic education it is necessary to go one step further, to give attention to what is meant by the word "in"—the arts *in* basic education. The term "in" does not simply mean "as part of."...It means they are *infused* throughout the curriculum.

All the major subject-matter disciplines have aesthetic components that can provide bases for incorporation of the arts into basic education. Infuse, according to Webster's "implies the introducing into one thing of a second that gives life, vigor, or new significance." The idea of the arts in basic education means that the arts will be infused with other major areas of the curriculum in such a way that they mutually nourish one another to the benefit of all students. In other words, the arts ought to *permeate* the subject matter in the schools.[9]

Charles continues his discussion of infusion by describing what it is not (correlation/illustration, cursory attention by introduction of a song, a dance, a dramatized scene, a haiku poem or an occasional visit to a museum, theater or a concert). He continues:

Infusion signifies that the arts should be thought of and incorporated as interdisciplinary studies that are the responsibility of *all* teachers... through all the subject matter in the school [including] specialized arts courses that treat the subject matter of the arts as discrete disciplines.... The arts infuse into subject-matter teaching something so wholly new that teachers begin to ask students different kinds of questions and expect different kinds of products. The arts represent, by their nature, an interaction with other subject matters because their content spans all of life and touches every area of human existence. They can function as the means to integrate the entire basic education curriculum....

In the final analysis it is the *density* of the student's learning experience in the arts that will achieve the desired outcomes.[10]

In my operational definition of the arts in education, comprehensive arts-in-general-education programs have four modes of instruction that, taken together, infuse the arts in the general curriculum.

- *arts for arts' sake:* study of, about, and in the individual disciplines, including but not limited to music, visual arts, drama, dance, creative writing, poetry, film, video, architecture, etc.
- *arts at the service of other studies:* arts concepts, ideas, themes, material, strategies and processes introduced or integrated into the study of other (primary focus) disciplines serving to illuminate and reinforce other concepts, themes and ideas
- *other studies at the service of the arts:* educational concepts, ideas, material strategies and methodologies from other disciplines introduced or integrated into the study of one or several art forms
- *arts as an equal partner in a holistic, humanities/global education or multi-cultural approach:* the arts relate to, or correlate with the study of other topics, trends, movements in world history; as such they inform and are informed by this larger context

Rationale 2: A More Theoretical Approach[11]

Kathryn Bloom and I wrote the following statement in 1975; it continues to enjoy wide use nationally and abroad.

A Rationale for the Arts in Education. Many educators, as well as persons directly concerned with the arts, share the conviction that the arts are a means for expressing and interpreting human behavior and experience. It follows, therefore, that the education of children is incomplete if the arts are not part of the daily teaching and learning process. Arts-in-education programs are designed to make all of the arts integral to the general, or basic, education of every child in entire school systems.

Work with these programs demonstrates that changes take place in schools so that they become humane environments in which the arts are valued as tools for learning as well as for their own intrinsic sake. Experience further indicates that the arts are useful to educators in meeting some of their main goals—that is, providing a great variety of educational opportunities, distinguished by quality, for all children.

The following are specific ways that the arts can contribute to the general, or basic, education of every child:

1. The arts provide a medium for personal expression, a deep need experienced by children and adults alike. Children's involvement in the

arts can be a strong motivating force for improved communication through speaking and writing as well as through drawing or singing.

2. The arts focus attention and energy on personal observation and self-awareness. They can make children and adults more aware of their environment and help them develop a stronger sense of themselves and a greater confidence in their own abilities. Through increased self-knowledge, children are more likely to be able to command and integrate their mental, physical, and emotional faculties and cope with the world around them.

3. The arts are a universal human phenomenon and means of communication. Involvement in them, both as participant and observer, can promote a deeper understanding and acceptance of the similarities and differences among races, religions and cultural traditions.

4. The arts involve the elements of sound, movement, color, mass, energy, space, line, shape and language. These elements, singly or in combination, are common to the concepts underlying many subjects in the curriculum. For example, exploring solutions to problems in mathematics and science through the arts can increase the understanding of the process and the value of both.

5. The arts embody and chronicle the cultural, aesthetic and social development of the world's people. Through the arts, children can become more aware of their own cultural heritage in a broad historical context. Arts institutions, cultural organizations and artists have a vital role to play in the education of children, both in schools and in the community.

6. The arts are a tangible expression of human creativity, and as such reflect man's perceptions of his world. Through the arts, children and adults can become more aware of their own creative and human potential.

7. The various fields of the arts offer a wide range of career choices to young people. Arts-in-education programs provide opportunities for students to explore the possibility of becoming a professional actor, dancer, musician, painter, photographer, architect, filmmaker or teacher. There are also many lesser-known opportunities in arts-related technical areas such as lighting engineer, costumer in a theater, or a specialist in designing and installing exhibitions in museums. Other opportunities lie in administrative and educational work in arts organizations such as museums, performing arts groups and arts councils.

8. The arts can contribute substantially to special education. Educational programs emphasizing the arts and the creative process are being developed for students with learning disabilities, such as the mentally retarded and physically handicapped. These programs are

conceived as alternative approaches to learning for youngsters who may have problems in adjusting to more traditional classroom situations. The infusion of the arts into the general education of all children also encourages the identification of talented youngsters whose special abilities may otherwise go unnoticed or unrecognized.

9. The arts, as a means for personal and creative involvement by children and teachers, are a source of pleasure and mental stimulation. Learning as a pleasant, rewarding activity is a new experience for many young people and can be very important in encouraging positive attitudes toward schooling.

10. The arts are useful tools for everyday living. An understanding of the arts provides people with a broader range of choices about the environment in which they live, the lifestyle they develop, and the way they spend their leisure time.

Other Voices, Other Rooms: Our Contributors Speak

It is not the purpose of this chapter or this book to argue for or against a single rationale for the arts in education or one definition of education, schooling or arts education; my objective is quite the opposite. I operate on the principle of inclusion rather than exclusion: the contributors and I are much like an extended family—all in one house, with many voices in many rooms, to borrow from Truman Capote. We each have our own rationales and convictions informed by our own unique experiences. Sometimes we may respectfully or even noisily disagree, but more often than not, our values converge and our views coexist comfortably. I am convinced there is plenty of room for everyone's opinion, and the more dimensions we bring to the difficult issues the better. The point is, we need to keep the dialogue fresh and alive.

It is time to move on to some of the other rooms in our family home and hear the voices, thoughts and vision of Doc Howe, Tony Alvarado, Richard Benjamin and Mae Kennerly. We will find many echos and extensions of the ideas advanced in this introductory section.

Beyond Footnotes: Building a Constituency for the Arts

A Conversation with Harold (Doc) Howe II

I met Doc Howe in the mid-seventies when I worked at the JDR 3rd Fund's Arts in Education Program with Kathryn Bloom. He and a few other distinguished educators served as advisors to our program, and we met from time to time to discuss progress and new initiatives. Kathy had worked for Doc in the late sixties, when she headed the Arts and Humanities Program of the U.S. Office of Education and Doc was commissioner of education. Those were the days of President Lyndon B. Johnson's Great Society and of major educational legislation aimed at compensating for the damaging effects of poverty and disadvantage and at equalizing access and opportunity for all America's children. Those were also the days when the arts appeared on the federal stage for the first time since the WPA era of President Roosevelt, most notably in the Elementary and Secondary Education Act and in the enabling legislation for the National Endowments for the Arts and the Humanities.

I recently read Doc's fine book, *Thinking About Our Kids: An Agenda for American Education*,[12] and managed to track him down at the Harvard Graduate School of Education. He graciously agreed to an interview. One of Doc's basic themes is that arts folks should stop turning up with the "usual suspects" and preaching to the converted; they need to forge new and more imaginative alliances with other organizations concerned with children. They need to build a new political constituency for the arts in the lives of children to make any real progress toward the goal of "all the arts for all the children in all of our public schools."

Jane Remer: Doc, how, if at all, do the arts fit into your philosophy of what schools are for?

Doc Howe: I think about that through experience, rather than analytically, since I have had a certain amount of exposure to efforts to shove the arts into schools. I think the arts tend to be accepted somewhat in the earlier years of school and less so in the later years, particularly high school. In the later years, the schools narrow subjects into specific disciplines and allocate time in terms of a discipline's prestige. Schools see the arts as legitimate areas to cut to save money. They first get rid of the guidance counselors, then the librarians, and then the arts teachers.

Our society is building itself on a new base of technical communication, in which everyone can communicate with everyone all of the time. That produces a lot more interest in science, mathematics and mechanical literacy than it does in the arts. It is very easy for schools to forget that the broad spectrum of the arts provides probably the best record of human experience from which to draw some kind of wisdom for the values in our lives. It's a very sad situation, but you are fighting a large barrier of preference that is very tough to beat.

JR: What do you believe are the bisecting interests of the schools and the arts community? What advice would you give to the arts community about working with schools? What are some strategies that you would recommend?

DH: The arts can enhance the capacity of kids to develop confidence in their own learning ability. Having kids do everything from writing poetry, to painting pictures, to developing their own dramas, can be very powerful. Demonstrations by kids about what they have learned—they call them portfolios, which the arts actually invented—is ready-made for assessing the arts and for showing how the arts can express what they have learned in other fields.

The arts community doesn't argue the broad picture effectively. We have lots of advocates for the arts and lots of interventions to promote their interests—from the Arts Endowment, from a variety of privately funded activities. The biggest thing going is the Getty Center for Education in the Arts in California. These are all good, but they are minuscule in terms of making a real impact. If we want to make that impact, the arts have to pursue a couple of strategies.

One strategy is to link them to other fields thought to be significant. There is room for the arts in the fields of history, social studies, literature and, indeed, of the sciences and mathematics, if imaginatively translated. Schools now have some small interest in what you might call interdisciplinary education, and the arts to my knowledge are not taking as much advantage of that as they could. I think some very significant elements of meaning for kids are not conveyed by any instrument other than the arts. Education is diminished if these things aren't introduced in their historical sense and their social values sense. Understanding the music of blacks is a very important thing for people in this country to be able to do, yet it is not done very much.

I think we can find other ways to make more people recognize that the arts are significant. For instance, Howard Gardner's work is really catching on, and many schools are working with ideas based on his multiple intelligences concepts.[13] The arts can gain by embracing that kind of work and using it as a visible banner for finding their way into schools.

The general public needs help in understanding that the arts are not some kind of silly add-on that can easily be done away with. You will not win that argument by preaching, but I wonder to what extent we are using our new kinds of communication, particularly TV, to get into the minds of people that there are wonderful experiences for children in the arts that will help them overcome their nervousness about learning and their opposition to very academic types of learning. The arts can become a kind of intermediary between the kids' frustration with what goes on in schools and the possibility of turning that into something much more appealing.

Let me try to make this a little more specific. The idea that the individual classroom is the place that needs to change is one of the more powerful notions that we have in the schools today. Past critiques of the schools, like *A Nation at Risk*, asserted that kids are no good, teachers are no good, and that the problem can be fixed by making schools more rigorous—giving more tests and assuming you will be motivated by a fear of failure. Many people are beginning to see that as just so much baloney. The idea that has emerged distinguishes between what people call passive learning and active learning—the kind of thing about which Ted Sizer,[14] Jim Comer[15] and others are talking. Active learning says to the kids: "You are partly responsible for planning and carrying out your own learning." When kids try it, they find it is an interesting thing to do.

Teachers have to change their approaches to the classroom. A young Chinese girl is supposed to have said, "Tell me, and I forget. Show me and I remember. Involve me and I understand." There is a helluva lot of meaning in that, and the arts have the capacity to move to that involved mode a lot more easily than other subjects. The arts can involve kids in things that are exciting, things that have meaning, things that they create, and kids will love it. The arts will help kids who hate school not to do so. The business of changing classroom procedures to include the arts can become a strategy that will reach out to different subject fields.

Kids go through a psychological change in their middle-teen years. Their own self-consciousness makes them more inhibited, less open. The arts can help them open up—an important undergirding for the work to be done in the schools.

Mathematicians are back in the rut of the old factory-model school, whereas good arts teachers have broken away from that approach. They are looking for imagination, creativity—finding ways to stir up wonderful stuff, which comes out in painting, for example. The meaning of it for kids is significant, and it helps us determine more about the way kids think. I think these are the sorts of things that should be emphasized.

JR: Unfortunately, the arts don't seem to be a priority, or in some cases even an item on the agenda, of today's leading education reformers. What are some of the other barriers that come to mind?

DH: I agree that some reformers drag their feet about giving major attention to the arts, but Howard Gardner, for example, does not.

I think school boards to a large degree are blocking the way. I don't know of anyone who is taking them on about this subject in an organized fashion. Along with the superintendents, they control thinking about how to cut budgets, and I don't think they are very enlightened about the arts.

JR: Well, these days, most superintendents usually are not around long enough to become enlightened. They seem to change every two years.

DH: Paul Houston, a former superintendent in Arizona, now heads the American Association of School Administrators, and he would like to hear about your interest in these things. He is a liberal thinker about the schools, and I would try to get on his agenda about the school boards and the superintendents. School boards tend to think of schools as baby-sitting institutions: as long as a teacher is with a group of kids, they think a teacher is doing his or her job. If a teacher is not with a group of kids, they cannot imagine that a teacher is doing anything constructive. You need the superintendent to help school boards to appreciate the place of the arts in school programs.

JR: What about artists in schools as an old but proven strategy? You were a former principal; you have been in and around schools most of your life. Any advice for arts organizations, agencies and individual artists who are trying to work with schools?

Let's say that a group had been in residence and wanted to become a much more permanent guest. What would they have to prove to you to win your confidence?

DH: In the whole business of getting artists into schools, I have wondered whether anyone in the arts field has taken up the cudgels about "mentoring." There is quite a movement in the United States to give young people adult attention from people called mentors. This is nothing new, but it grows out of the fact that elementary and high school kids increasingly see less of adults. Their parents are working, commuting long distances, and the actual time available for kids to be with adults in a constructive way has been heavily eroded by television. Mentoring is an opportunity for a more balanced and constructive association of adults with kids, and arts groups can probably make a wonderful contribution in this arena. If adults with interests in kids and competencies in the arts wanted to move this idea along, it would be very useful. After school programs, particularly at the junior high school level, could be run very constructively by people connected with the arts. You could get a foot in the door in schools where they have heaved you out.

JR: I am dubious about relying on after-school programs to wedge the schoolhouse door open for the arts. The phrase "after school" says it all: extracurricular, not part of, not tested, doesn't count. As we know, what gets tested gets taught. Besides, I am concerned about all the kids, and after-school programs don't reach all of them. After-school programs are an excellent way to provide more intense study in the arts, to get deeply involved in special projects, but they don't get at the idea of the arts as basics for everyone.

DH: Yes, Jane, I see what you mean.

JR: Doc, it seems to me that whenever economics and politics rear their heads, things like the arts, libraries, and the other "soft" stuff never seems to make any headway. Do you agree with the statement, "Americans just do not value the arts?"

DH: The schools worship things that are academic, and to some degree, the arts are not at home in the academic scene because they don't deal in footnotes. The universities and colleges have people that they call "artists in residence," which means that this person really does not belong. That is a signal that performance in the arts is not acceptable as an academic endeavor.

You see, I think you have to look for agencies that are empathetic to kids but have never really thought about the arts as an important item to put on their agenda. I think you have to think about building a new constituency for the arts. For example, the National Coalition of Advocates for Students is an agency whose members are child advocate groups; then there's the Children's Defense Fund, and Designs for Change, for example, which emphasize the public services that are available to kids in poverty and from other cultures. These child advocate groups are politically active in public policy and locally active on the abuse of individual kids. Yet, I have never heard any of them add to their agenda that these kids are fenced off from the major field of human aspiration and motivation—the arts. The tendency is to think that all these kids need is arithmetic and food, and that you can ignore their spirits.

JR: Parents are interested in the basics—jobs, socialization, career advancement. They look you square in the eyes and say, "My kids don't have time for the arts; I want them to get the basics. They need to be able to compete, to get ahead, and to succeed. What good are the arts?"

DH: That attitude has to be fought, of course. Everyone knows about the Westinghouse awards for science, but I know of no comparable award for the arts with that kind of visibility.

JR: There are the Presidential Scholars and the National Association for Advancement in the Arts annual awards for outstanding accomplishment in the arts. But you're right, these don't get the same kind of press and publicity as the Westinghouse. It's the values issue, again.

DH: You see, the currency for determining value in schools, unfortunately, is the semester hour. And you cannot measure the arts by semester hour! Of *course* it is ridiculous that this is so; it is a crazy way to think of value. I think there is a kind of ferment going on in schools that is beginning to challenge the semester hour. One thing Ted Sizer is saying is that time ought to be a variable. It should not trap you. That makes room for the arts. Very interesting shifts are taking place around the land, but they are small scale.

JR: What do you think about the recent voluntary standards for the arts, and the National Assessment of Educational Progress' (NAEP's) projected arts assessment?

DH: I have not seen them yet, but I am worried about those voluntary national standards. As illustrated by the flack that is going on about the history standards, I really think that they are pushing the curriculum of the schools much too close to the political scene. Although the word "voluntary" was thrown in every two minutes in the legislation, schools are not as protected by that word as people may think. Political figures appoint the group charged with carrying out evaluation and changes in the standards.

There is a contradiction about these standards. These days, we are pushing strongly to try to develop what people call professional teachers. Yet, if people are really professional, they do not want the requirements for what they do to be run by the political process. *They* want to take the lead in deciding what those things will be. A profession is defined by a body of knowledge and a definition of good practice, and I see a tension—maybe even a confrontation—between the national standards and the idea of academic freedom.

The idea of academic freedom is rampant around the colleges and universities, but around the schools, no one talks about it at all. If people are to become professionals, they are going to require academic freedom. I think these standards will monopolize the scene and not give teachers the freedom to take the responsibilities they ought to have.

The mathematics standards moved along smoothly, but the history standards are not going well because of the organized right-wing Christians. They are going to fight for their thoughts in ways that are not the ways these things ought to be settled. I would be surprised if the arts do not get subjected to the same kind of issues and pressure.

JR: I work with people every day who are delighted about the arts standards, because they believe it has finally put the arts on the map.

DH: I would doubt that. As I have been pointing out, it will take more than voluntary standards to get the arts a permanent home in the curriculum.

JR: I agree. Let's talk about NAEP.

DH: It is a kind of dilemma. I doubt the assessment will give the arts the right kind of attention. It will tend to mechanize the arts and dampen creativity. I am troubled about that. The arts have this wonderful characteristic of freedom—to think anything and do anything you want—which creates a home for creativity. If creativity is going to happen among kids, it has to have that kind of place to live.

That is the really wonderful thing about civilization. It goes off in all directions and is best spoken for by the arts. If we are going to have any sense of the nature of civilization and its development for human beings, to ignore the arts is really like committing suicide.

JR: Anything else you'd like to add?

DH: There's one point I'd like to emphasize. I really think the arts community should look for allies in those nonarts social action groups that are advocates for children and have complementary agendas and power. I believe you will go a lot further in the educational arena if you build a more diverse political constituency for the arts.

Harold "Doc" Howe II has written and spoken widely about education issues related to both secondary schools and colleges. His most recent publication is Thinking About Kids: An Agenda for American Education *(The Free Press: New York, 1993). He is a former U.S. Commissioner of Education, serving from 1965-68 under President Lyndon Johnson. He was a Senior Lecturer at the Harvard University Graduate School of Education from 1981 until June 1994. From 1971-1981, he was Vice President for Education and Research for the Ford Foundation. Howe is a Yale graduate with an M.A. degree in history from Columbia University. He holds honorary degrees from Yale, Princeton and Notre Dame, among other universities. He began his distinguished career as a classroom teacher and has worked as both a principal and a school superintendent.*

Building Professional Capacity for the Arts in Education

A Conversation with Anthony Alvarado

Tony Alvarado and I go back to the seventies, when we both worked with the New York City Board of Education's Learning Cooperative. Tony was one of the Beacon Light School principals in a citywide network coordinated by the Coop, a reform effort under the direction of a visionary educator, Dr. Edythe J. Gaines. Beacon Light Schools were considered exemplars, and most of their principals were pioneers either in school redesign and organization, in curriculum and instruction, or in forging linkages with the community and its business and cultural resources.

Tony has been a trailblazer throughout his professional career as Community District 4 superintendent, the chancellor of the New York City Schools, and now, as a superintendent in Community District 2. He has been a staunch spokesman for and supporter of the arts in general education; we have spoken for years about collaborating in one of my books, and we finally seized the opportunity in this one.

Jane Remer: Let's begin with your thoughts about the current state of urban education and where you see the arts in the mix.

Anthony Alvarado: An important part of the big picture these days is decentralization and interdisciplinary teaching and learning. With massive decentralization, localized decision-making, and downsizing in the schools, we are returning in some respects to the way things were a long time ago. Back then, we did not have these two- and three-tier bureaucracies, and decisions about learning were made at the school level, rather than by a distant bureaucracy.

This decentralization—so good for the schools—unfortunately makes it difficult for arts organizations to gain simple access or entry to the schools. Things are quite different from the days when you could call one person—an arts supervisor, a curriculum coordinator—at the central district for all your school contacts and your arts program selections. Now you have to go to the schools one by one. That is time-consuming, labor-intensive and not always a very effective way of identifying appropriate school partners.

All this reform in education has created a bigger movement toward interdisciplinary teaching, so that the arts may have a wider instructional and curricular field in which to play. On the other hand, since the arts go off-kilter when some reasonable balance is not kept, we need to be vigilant in preserving study in the various art forms so that kids learn to play and compose music as compared with learning about music in a unit on Japan.

In New York, interdisciplinary work has had more support than the individual arts. You can walk into any elementary or junior high school and find kids with little or no formal experience in the arts. The key is finding ways for arts agencies to play a role in schools in both the formal teaching of the arts—to provide a module, to support or enhance music, theater, dance or art instruction, or to be part of an interdisciplinary planning group.

JR: Let's talk about the opportunities for arts organizations and artists.

AA: Because doors are now more open than in the past, especially in the cities, more arts organizations are in the schools than ever before—for one-shot deals, a few days a week, or as institutional players over the long haul. Most of us in the schools are no longer interested in arts institutions with short-term, often self-serving interests in the schools—the ones who want a contract to do one, small, short-lived service or performance with no instructional context or payoff. What we want and need is long-term commitment and evidence that the organization is interested in helping us make sure that kids are receiving quality arts instruction through the institution of the school.

In other words, we want to be assured that the organization is dedicated to being a resource to the schools, helping the schools build their own professional capacity in the arts. Yet since schools will never have all the arts resources they need—there are too many arts, too many different aspects to artistic and aesthetic learning, the arts organizations shouldn't worry about helping us to build our own capacity. They have resources and expertise we will always need, so they certainly don't have to fear planned obsolescence.

JR: Give me an example of an arts organization that has what you call an institutional role.

AA: Schools are starting to embrace the idea of focusing on the core of what the institution does well, and then farming out the rest to specialists. For example, I have a school where some kids go to the Elliot Feld Ballet and others go to Alvin Ailey to study modern dance. This came about because the building does not have the actual facilities or space for dance, and the current system does not allow for quality dance instruction, for the most part. In these instances, Feld and Ailey are providing the instruction that the institution cannot provide by itself.

JR: Talk to me a little about the current field of school reformers and the apparent lack of vision or enthusiasm for the arts.

AA: The real issue, reinforced by the current reform effort, is that the primary work of schools is intellectual. Like it or not, very little work is being done in the arts, although these education reformers are some of the country's leading progressives. The original America 2000, which became Goals 2000, left out the arts completely. It wasn't the reformers, it was the arts community and people with political clout who shouted, "Where are the arts? They must be included in the goals. We need some standards for the arts."

The reformers' omission of the arts is one among many reasons we have to make the case for the arts over and over—you see, they have never been fully accepted institutionally. There has always been some art and some music, but the time they are allotted, the way they are funded, and the way they are perceived keeps them on the periphery of what is considered basic instruction.

A million task forces and commissions have all tried to find a place for the arts. You do not see this happening with the other disciplines. It is second-class citizenship, perhaps, but the arts are not in the fiber of the American education system, and the current reformers are not helping the cause.

JR: I have been asking a number of people: What are schools for, and where do the arts fit in? And what advice would you have for arts organizations?

AA: Schools are institutions for developing human beings; they are a way to continue and expand civilization. The problem in America is that schools are asked to do so many things. The New York State Legislature has hundreds of laws about what schools should be teaching—communism, cruelty to animals, social ills, conflict resolution. You pick it, they think we should do it.

Schools have a bias toward intellectual work, one that I can understand and even accept. As we just finished saying, most reformers share the idea of intellectual work at the core of schooling, particularly now, when the work of schools is to get kids to think, to use their minds well, to develop good habits of mind, and to be able to analyze and apply. This insistence on the intellectual may create a bias against the arts, making them fight for a rightful place in the curriculum and the schools.

Yet the arts are their own unique way of knowing. Howard Gardner's seven intelligences lays it out rather nicely. They have a right to be on the plate because they do what we are talking about, just in another way. They address the issues of feelings, emotions, the spirit, aesthetics—things that are not dealt with particularly well by most schools. This area of child and adolescent development—the ability to experience passion, flights of fancy, beauty, and to be able to know oneself and other people through the arts—is something with which the other disciplines cannot grapple nearly as well or as naturally.

The intellectual bias obviously is continued when people measure what schooling does for kids. They rarely measure what the arts are particularly good at doing, and so the arts do not show up on the report card. Although people say the arts are important, they aren't counted. That is important because in schools, that which is assessed is ultimately what counts and gets taught.

JR: A colleague of mine recently wrote a thoughtful piece in which he almost exclusively emphasizes the intellectual and cognitive aspects of the arts. I wondered, where are emotion, feeling, creativity, imagination, and passion? In the rush to justify the arts on intellectual grounds, the very heart and soul of the arts are left out.

AA: It really should be the other way around. The argument should be made: why doesn't mathematics help someone do this, that, and the other with imagination and creativity? The great ones would say that new discoveries are full of creativity, imagination and beauty—and they would be right!

But the school is a political institution and reflects society over time—all of its biases, all of its demands and anxieties. From that societal attitude, the arts always get short shrift.

JR: I don't see any major changes of values and attitudes in the foreseeable future, but I continue to believe strongly that arts organizations have a great deal to contribute to schools and their community. What do you think about that?

AA: I think schools should relate to the outside world as a matter of course. To get the energy and the ideas, the thinking of society has to permeate what schools do in a useful way. Schools need this ferment, this relationship. They don't do well when they are run from ivory towers. Arts agencies are part of the social fabric of a community, and they need to be a part of the interrelationship with the schools.

There is a plethora of arts organizations now, and the problem is that schools do not know what to do with them. Schools are overwhelmed, since they weren't doing the arts well in the first place. You cannot be a good discriminator of arts agencies if you are somehow not doing the arts yourself. The more knowledgeable you are, the better consumer you are, and the better you can integrate something into what you do.

Yet the school setting has deteriorated. As things start to fall apart and other pressures start to come, the arts, which have never been at the center of schooling, start to fall off the plate. Interestingly, as we talk, the more convinced I am of how important it is to make the case for the arts, institutionally, as part of an educational philosophy and program for the schools. Until that is done successfully, we will always be fighting these rear-guard actions. It could very well be that this burgeoning group of arts agencies has not sufficiently understood how to make the case for the institution of schools to do the arts well.

JR: But, as you said, schools don't value that which they don't measure. If the arts don't show up on the report card, it becomes a Catch-22. As things become more decentralized, how does a community school district superintendent let this philosophy be known to his or her schools? What difference does that make anyway, when there is no carrot at the end of the stick to back it up?

AA: One thing to recognize is that schools are ritualistic. A few days before Thanksgiving, kids are coloring turkeys in every school in the nation.

JR: That is the holiday curriculum of the arts theory. Since we have the Greek calendar, the Jewish calendar, the Arabian calendar, the Muhammadan calendar, the Indian calendar and the English, to name a few, if we keep going, we'd have a holiday every day—ergo, a multicultural arts experience every day!

AA: Schools have their timing, their seasonal nature. Arts organizations have to understand this inner working of how kids and teachers proceed at school, especially at the elementary level, where it is more holistic. School people do not understand it, and the artists do not either. The right connections are hard to make.

Schools should offer the whole spectrum of what the arts can provide in schools—an ongoing formal arts program, the arts in interdisciplinary studies, and arts people selectively brought in to do one or two things where it fits (like the local baker, to talk about bread). This is what schools should use well and what arts organizations should try to make sure schools have access to. However, you have all these ongoing, competing institutional interests, both on the school and the arts organization level, that do not permit it to happen.

JR: In District 2, where do arts organizations go to talk about district-wide efforts or partnerships with individual schools?

AA: District 2 no longer has an arts coordinator. The organization is flatter, with resources being driven at the bottom. In high-involvement management, the top is supposed to focus folks on what they are supposed to do, and the bottom is supposed to have the resources, flexibility and the ability to make decisions according to their own perspectives. The city is in transition; we are not yet decentralized, but there is less coordination at the district level.

One thousand schools are now operating, each very differently, and arts organizations have to market their wares flexibly and responsively. That means they have to become a lot smarter about their business practices and about understanding their niche in a school system: What can they do? What can they do well? For whom? How can they get that money creatively without bastardizing their work, so that they are not teaching skydiving through oboes? How do they respond to a multicultural city? Do they need an integrated staff? What do they need to know about school culture, organization, curriculum, instruction and so on?

The pressures on arts agencies today are much stronger than ever in this rapidly changing world with growing needs. Today, schools are inventing curriculum units and their own courses of study, so arts organizations now have to come in to sit with that school and shape what they are doing to fit the schools' instructional plans. They cannot come in with their prepackaged deal anymore. Then they have to deal with all the gritty realities—how to get a contract, how to get a listing, how to get paid, how to get the business manager to follow up. Getting in the door and getting the contract is only part of the issue: they have to make sure to get the job done before their artists disappear. It can be a nightmare, I know.

Our middle schools, for example, are becoming very different institutions: inter-disciplinary teams have replaced departments. Where arts organizations once found working with the department heads useful, now they have to work with the team that is trying to put together a life for a kid that makes sense to the kid. That should suggest a whole new strategy for arts institutions.

JR: Let's say I represent a group of arts organizations, and I want to work out a partnership with you, the superintendent, so that all kids in the district will receive balanced exposure to, and engagement with, the arts as disciplines and as integrated into general school studies. If I don't want to go door to door, would I come to you and ask you to think through with me what the vision of this collaboration would be, what the framework would be, what its curriculum content is, what its instructional focus ought to be, and then figure out just how we should proceed with all these resources?

AA: Yes. We would put together some people from the schools who would work with you to tell you a bit about their lives and try to figure out with you how this would all fit together.

JR: Would you also include some people from the district level?

AA: Absolutely, but the action is at the school, which essentially has to invent what will happen. That part of the action is capacity building, so that the school is smart enough, skilled enough, and has enough knowledge to be able to come up with those responses, carry them out, evaluate them, and then carry on with an even stronger approach.

The old days were about the top telling the bottom what was good for them, but this new model is a mixed model. We are in transition: a few leftover authoritarian kings and queens still run their realms the old-fashioned way, though they are being besieged on all sides; and some schools at the far end of the spectrum are in total chaos and have no capacity to make good decisions. The reason the system hasn't responded to it yet is that some people are asking, "Do we really need districts?"

JR: And your response is?

AA: My response is that you need something above schools that creates glue, identifies and matches resources, and helps provide all those kinds of things such as technical assistance that the local school might need; however, it is not going to look like what we all thought a district looked like in the past. We have an absolute need for that "something" these days, because there is so little else to hold everything together—homes, family, religious institutions....

JR: There also needs to be some kind of central force or hub to pay attention to the equal distribution of services to all schools and kids.

AA: Yes, some would argue that you need someone to do the equity work. But a lot more has to happen. Let me describe the model of what the district does in literacy, for example.

We have a strong sense of what kids should be doing in literacy and what their capabilities are. We invest strongly in professional development; we have a lot of new learning in research and professional practice about important quality issues. I take 2.5 to 3 percent from my budget for professional development. Sometimes it is fought by the field, and most of it is being fought at the school level. Still, I believe you cannot choose not to grow; you cannot choose not to learn.

We have strong conversations, lots of networks, lots of putting everyone on the same wavelength, although the response may be very different. Because everyone is clear about what we want kids to be able to do, no one can give me a basal response. Everyone knows they can't, because they know that basals do not have the power to accomplish what we are trying to do.

You can't bull your way through professional development. We have a lot of conversation among teachers. We also have old-fashioned supervision, an expert going to the classroom and saying, "That doesn't look good. That's wrong. What are you going to do to fix that, that and that?" We hope the school has identified and is working on that same thing, but you need an outside force to be able to push a certain time frame.

The theory of all this is belief reinforced by practice. In high-involvement organizations, people are driven by accomplishing an end. Yet in most schools, they are not driven to do anything but get through the day. So one of the requirements of the new organization is very often not present in the schools. Choice and all that stuff do not really create that atmosphere. You really do need the mix—the networks—of principals....

JR: Networks across the district, I assume, not just by neighborhood....

AA: Both! Networks of teachers, of geography, of literacy goals/concerns. We have sixth-grade teachers; we have vertical networks. Wherever a need arises or the work is in common, then you try to involve others who are doing that, even those who aren't doing it, to make them more aware, more powerful.

JR: Who coordinates these networks? Is this done on a district or local level?

AA: Both—sometimes jointly. Take our work with principals, for example. We work individually with principals. We have principals' conferences that are all instructional, which no longer have anything to do with administration. The deputy superintendent and I visit principals, individually and together, and we talk to them one on one. Sometimes we put principals together so they can visit each other's schools to tell each other what is happening. Some principals have buddies who have nothing to do with the district with whom they can speak alone, quietly, and let it all hang out. On some issues we bring people together to solve a problem, and in solving that problem they may network with other people in the group. Others get together with the deputy superintendent in support groups once a month, and they all sit to solve problems or to focus on the initiative we are working on for the entire year. Thus, we create common threads within the district; we have strong dialogues and an abundance of knowledge about what is happening; and the work is discussed and publicly critiqued.

Then there is measurement, either by professional practice and professional observation or by hard or soft data. You look at kids' writing to find out if the writing is good, and when the second-grade writing looks like the first-grade writing, you have a problem. Then someone says, "What is second-grade writing supposed to look like?" and people have to answer that question. That is very different from ten years ago.

JR: That's an exciting model! My question now is, how do you make that wonderfully interactive model work for the arts? You have networking, professional development, peer counseling and leadership training all wrapped up into one!

AA: Absolutely. *And*, this looks a lot like the model we use for community agencies. We use individual consultants to work with us. We pay top people, with super knowledge and skills, top dollar; this is no longer working with some consultant for $50 or $100 a day. We thoughtfully work with universities, posing very specific questions about what knowledge and skill bases we want. New York University works with us on reading recovery: we have a professional development lab where teachers leave their classrooms for three weeks to spend time with a master teacher; then the master teacher goes back into the classroom to work with these teachers. We have professional development from people who have become professional developers; it is no longer like it used to be; these teachers are classroom-based.

Groups of teachers are working together where the grade conference and the staff development conference are actually done well; it is not like the old days where everyone used to dread going to a staff conference. We do massive summer work, some not new, but what goes on is different. If a school is ready, it goes off on a retreat to plan, sometimes with another school. This is what I mean by a plethora of activity.

I hear and understand your question about relating all of this to the arts—and I had not thought of doing it! Yet you are right. If we were doing the arts in this kind of model, then all these processes, all these mutually reinforcing dynamics would be involved—and this is after seven years' worth of work.

JR: You have in place this ferment of activity in the literacy area. I assume the same is true in the interdisciplinary arena. Wouldn't it be nice if we had the arts people at the table for both efforts? Would that work?

AA: That's an interesting question. I am convinced that what the model does, how it conceives of things, is 100 percent right. We did literacy because we thought that language, reading, and writing was the most important thing for all our kids—I am an English major—and we had the expertise to deal with it. Four or five years later, we started with mathematics, and a lot of writing goes on in math, too. You know, the whole language approach.

I don't know if the arts should have their own committee. Someone could argue that what I am doing are the disciplines, vertically, one by one. Is that a good model? I don't know, because then you are going to have many separate committees. The minute I put the arts people on a committee with the literacy people, I don't know what will happen. It would be interesting to try it.

In literacy, most of our work was poetry, novels—very little work with nonfiction. This year we are working on nonfiction—how you do research. We are starting to get some work in science, but it needs time. People like Sizer say that the disciplines stand in the way, and other people say the disciplines have a theoretical and conceptual base and a rationale. I guess I am old. I believe there is a place for the disciplines and a place for seeing them all interconnected.

JR: I don't know how you get interdisciplinary without strength in the individual disciplines.

AA: I agree, but strong intellectual arguments are going on. I guess I would have the arts, and then I would have to figure out what you do with this work. Part of this is a design problem—it is how to conceptualize it and fit it in within and across the curriculum. I think I would do all the arts in this initiative, and let it have its life—and that life would have to fit in with this other stuff.

The problem is money. Science, foreign language, you pick it. You can't do this Year I, Year II, Year III—a different discipline each year. It has taken me eight years to do the literacy, and I am just getting into math. In literature, we had to get the teachers to read books because they weren't reading anything. We had 270 teachers reading books and talking about them.

I think you're right—what we are doing about literacy is the right way to conceptualize things for the arts. Whether they are done separately or on an interdisciplinary basis, the arts are so susceptible politically to being taken off the map, I would have to find a way to do the arts.

The other issue is what has to happen at each level of the system: What is the role of the top? What is the role of the school? What is the role of the arts groups and of individual teachers? You have to get that right.

JR: Are you working in this fashion at the individual school level?

AA: Yes, we started with early childhood, which now is much stronger than upper elementary, which is stronger than the middle schools. Then we went to the middle schools; that level is difficult, but we are making progress in some places. If you visited most early childhood classrooms in the district, you would be impressed.

When the world begins to fractionalize, the issue becomes how to integrate, coordinate and get coherence. When I first came in here, I had a sign up saying, "Consult. (As distinct from go do a lot.)" But now it asks, "How do things fit so that you get synergy, and yet individual things work and reinforce one another?" That is very important.

For example, in literacy, we teach early childhood kids to make meaning out of print—it is expensive. One teacher works with four kids for 11 to 20 weeks. The goal at the end of the first grade is for kids to be readers; otherwise, they are lost. Yet just as important was the capacity building that I was doing at the school—the knowledge base that teachers were developing who were being trained. We did not see this as a program where teachers should be recycled. They go back to the classroom, and others go through the process. We do institution building, capacity building. How can teachers share their expertise, and how do we coordinate and integrate this with the other professional development going on in the building? We begin to see our lives as learners, so what we try to do is push, in a focused way, adult learning.

If you see what adults do in a school among themselves, you can almost predict what they are going to do with the kids. If the adult systems are not strong in professional development, then there will be weak systems with kids.

JR: What hard and soft data do you have about the kids?

AA: In certain selected places, we are starting to get strong. The other problem here was leadership; we replaced 26 principals in seven years. The lower-ranked schools especially have seen real movement.

The great man, great woman theory no longer applies: the problems we have now are ones of system, not whether we can get individual schools to be good. We have had lots of individual good schools, as you and I well remember. The question now is, how can we go to scale? How can we get the system to do it? One reason for fabulous schools is the individual, charismatic leader. However, you can't replicate that, so how do you get ordinary people to do extraordinary things?

The purpose of the organization is to focus people on what they do and create a sense of urgency, to focus the resources, and to figure out the design questions—professional development and issues of how the organization can help the individ. units achieve the ends of the larger organization.

JR: You have just described yet another template for the arts. I don't see it happening in the arts exclusively—unless you tell me that you are now going to pioneer this model with an initiative in the arts.

AA: That's interesting. What this conversation has done is raise that critical issue: The question is, how do we include the arts in the conceptual design in a way that can be translated into fluid practice?

You have to remember that you are always working hard to build capacity—of institutions and the people in them. The temptation is always—and this might be greater with the arts—to bring people in who can do it for you. Consequently, you end up with an institution that is dependent, that does not know anything about the arts and is held captive either by funding sources or by the relationships in the community. Ultimately, there is really no power...

JR: Creating yet another dependency.

AA: It's interesting to frame the question along that line. If you look at it historically, maybe one powerful reason the arts have never flown is that capacity building never occurred in school. You got a couple of individual, isolated specialists to do it, for only some of the kids, and never conceptualized it as an institutional responsibility.

JR: I have long maintained that unless artists and arts specialists help teachers become more comfortable with and more competent in the arts, we are missing an important link in the chain of capacity building, but more importantly, in the institutionalization of the arts.

AA: It is not only the teachers who need attention; you also have to look at the management and the organizational structure of the school culture. You have to look at how, when and where teachers talk, what they do when they get together, what their groupings are. Designing an organization is very important, or else the life of the organization that is run by its schedules and rituals will be giving a very different message from what the individual human beings will be saying. You have to be very sensitive to how the organization is run to make it happen at very high levels.

The arts model could have lots more players in it, so the relationships have to be even more sensitive. You would have to pay more attention to organizational and structural issues. It used to be that you only worried about how to get into the organization—how does the superintendent, principal, or teacher let me in to do what I am doing. You could forget about whether they were involved in the design.

JR: If I understand your literacy model, you are working simultaneously on structure, content, operation and methodology, the relationships of people, professional development....

AA: You cannot tell people, "This is the way you should be doing things," when the whole environment doesn't carefully give that message in every way that it operates.

JR: So you start working simultaneously with principals and teachers on leadership and professional development. That's hard. How do you do that?

AA: Part of it is a design question, and part of it is an art. That is why we still don't have the perfect model. I have made a whole batch of mistakes. It is why you can go to business school and come out not knowing how to run an actual business. It is not a menu of things. All these people behave in unique ways: the principal talks like this; the teachers do that; the school has always been such and such; this is who the kids are, the parents; and then, there are the arts agencies.

JR: Again, the role of the district is to provide leadership, the glue, the eyes and ears...

AA: And work on issues, structures, integrating people, coordinating—as you say, be the matchmaker, the hub...

JR: Capacity building.

AA: Yes, the watchword for reform, I believe—that and interactive, dynamic design.

JR: Tony, this has been simply delightful. Thank you for all your time and hard work.

AA: Jane, always a pleasure. I really have something to think about now—the arts model. We'll keep in touch.

Anthony J. Alvarado is a nationally recognized educational leader and has been Superintendent of Community School District 2 in New York City since 1987, where he is responsible for the education of more than 21,000 students in 43 elementary, middle and secondary schools and the administration of an $85 million budget. During his tenure, the district has become a model of systemic reform through a coherent and comprehensive professional development effort. Over the course of more than 30 years of experience in education, he has worked as a classroom teacher, principal, superintendent, and chancellor in the New York City Public Schools. He is a member of the Pew Forum on Education Reform, serves on the National Academy of Education panel on the NAEP Trial State Assessments and on the board of the Consortium for Policy Research in Education. He is the chair of the Advisory Board of the Institute for Learning of the Learning Research and Development Center at the University of Pittsburgh. He serves on the Carnegie Task Force on Learning in the Primary Grades, and he is a review team member for the ATLAS project at Harvard University and for the Rockefeller Foundation's professional development initiative. He has been a lecturer/adjunct professor at City College of New York, Long Island University, Pace, Hunter College and Teachers College, Columbia University.

The Arts, Artists and Arts Specialists Can Transform Education

A Conversation with Richard Benjamin

Dr. Richard C. Benjamin is the director of the Metropolitan Nashville Public Schools in Tennessee. A champion of the important role of public education in a democracy, he is equally ardent about the arts and their ability to help America transform the institution of public education so that it routinely and successfully challenges all students and helps them to meet high-level expectations. In my letter to him explaining a proposed interview, I framed the questions as follows:

> I am so glad that Carol Ponder of the Bernstein Center and the Nashville Institute was able to bring us together. I am equally delighted you have the time to answer a few questions about the arts and education. I was hoping you would discuss your definition of the purpose of schools and schooling and where you see the arts fitting in, either as basics or as disciplines that contribute to the general education of your students. Put differently, I would like to be able to ask you why the arts are important for your students? Would you also be willing to comment briefly on the role of the arts in school reform, if that seems appropriate to you and your district at this moment?

Jane Remer: Can you give me your definition of the purpose of schools and schooling?

Richard Benjamin: In the climate of school reform, I like to re-emphasize that aspect of the traditional mission of public education which deals with preparing young people for citizenship. For me, this strikes at the heart of one of the most important roles of public education in the United States—to prepare our students to maintain and extend democratic ideas and practices. Ours is perhaps the first nation to be born of ideals and principles involving the dignity of the individual—principles which are frequently examined closely and celebrated in the various art forms.

Specifically, I do not see the adventure in democracy as completed. Rather, I see that we have miles to go to live up to our creed and our national purpose. All of it depends on high quality and free public education. Mortimer Adler[16] has pointed out that when you want good government in a democratic setting, *every* citizen must have an education of the quality previously reserved only for princes.

Certainly, schools have other purposes, including preparing young people for lifelong learning and development as individuals and preparing them to earn a living. In our country these purposes require much greater success with *all* students. For me, this requires public education in America to be transformed into an institution that routinely and successfully challenges and assists all students to meet high-level expectations—in the arts and all the other subjects.

JR: Where do you see the arts fitting in, either as basics or as disciplines that contribute to the general education of your students?

RB: In the context of the three purposes of schooling: maintaining and extending democratic ideas and practices, preparing the young for lifelong learning, and preparing them for earning a living, I would focus on two of the several modes of instruction involving the arts. First of all, let's focus on art for art's sake. Teaching art for art's sake involves the employment and support of arts specialists. They plan and take primary responsibility for implementing a sequential curriculum leading to mastery of common student performance expectations in the arts. Many schools have such specialists, but all too many do not. This lack of institutionally based expertise is a fundamental flaw in the delivery of public education services and has very serious consequences for the arts education of all our students. It also has a detrimental impact on schooling, since we miss using the power of the arts to create that joyful and receptive climate for learning in which our students thrive.

The "arts for art's sake" approach provides many opportunities for enrichment from local community cultural resources. A very good example is one of our partnerships here in Nashville—the Nashville Institute for the Arts. This organization provides direct services to students in the form of classroom instruction and field visits to key arts events, along with classroom follow-up by trained professional local artists. A hallmark of this program is the extensive teacher training provided by many of these artists to volunteer teachers from area schools during the summer.

JR: Can you tell me about the role you see for the arts in school reform?

RB: I see the arts having a tremendous potential to help transform public education. We want to make use of the power of the arts individually and collectively to illuminate and reinforce learning both within the arts and in other areas. The best example here in Nashville is the promise of the Leonard Bernstein Center for Education through the Arts. A specific illustration is the use of *West Side Story* to teach lessons about prejudice, gangs, violence and conflict management. Another example is our partnership with the Songwriter's Showcase of the Country Music Hall of Fame. Here, students are taught to write songs on topics of their own choosing and then have their songs performed by noted personalities in the Nashville area. This program exemplifies two key elements in the transformation of schools: It helps students get in touch with their imaginative powers and creative abilities, and it connects them with the rich resources of their local communities.

The arts will become increasingly important in school reform for those schools and districts where equal attention will be paid not only to what is possible to do in the future, but also to what is desirable to do in the future. That is, as we as a society, as a democracy, become more technologically able, questions of what *should* be done will gain in importance for our students as against what *can* be done. Preparing students to engage in the discussion and successfully deliberate those questions will draw on the imaginative and problem-solving powers of the arts and the creative process. In helping students envisage what might and ought to be, I believe the arts will play a strong role in the transformation of American public education.

Dr. Richard C. Benjamin is Superintendent of Schools for metropolitan Nashville, TN, Public Schools, a system responsible for the education of 68,000 students. Prior to his current position, Dr. Benjamin served as Superintendent of Schools for Ann Arbor, MI, and as Associate Superintendent for planning and development for Fort Worth, TX, Independent School District. During the 1970s, he held various administrative posts in the Lansing, MI, School District. Dr. Benjamin received his B.A. from Michigan State University and his Ph.D. from the University of Michigan.

The Arts, Manners and More

A Conversation with Mae Kennerly

I am in Louisville, Kentucky on my first visit to Martin Luther King, Jr. Elementary, one of the Kentucky Center for the Arts' Creative Connections demonstration schools. I am with Education Director Debbie Shannon and Project Coordinator Jane Morgan Dudney. It is May and the program has been in operation for about eight months.

At the lobby entrance to the school, we are greeted by papier-mâché life-size figures of Martin Luther King, an African-American student at a desk, a young white artist with a beret and a paintbrush, another African American in a Nike sweatsuit with a peace sign, and a white girl dressed as a nurse (all somewhat stereotypical, come to think of it), with a high pile of books teetering near the "desk." The school receptionist tells me that someone from the extended art program helped the kids put this George Segal-esque living sculpture together. The books include the *Bible, Martin Luther King, Born to Rebel, A Black Manifesto, Othello, Tales Without Hate, Souls of Black Folk, The Kennedys, Pilgrim's Progress, Black in Selma, Malcolm X,* the *Koran, A Tale of Two Cities, Black Children, White Dreams, Institutional Racism, African Genesis, Stride Toward Freedom, Abraham Lincoln, Aristophanes, A Man for All Seasons,* Chaucer's *Canterbury Tales, The Ugly American, George Washington Carver, Black Poets,* and *Up From Slavery.*

King is part of the district's Options and Magnet program with a school focus on the visual and performing arts, gifted education and technology. An open enrollment school, it can draw from the entire county provided that 50 percent of the children are from the immediate neighborhood; the balance are accepted through application and audition. It is the home of the Fabulous Leopard Percussionists, a group of students who formed a rhythm band and have played to local and statewide acclaim and kudos. This is also the home of African-American principal Mae Kennerly, dedicated educator, nurturing caretaker, and tireless administrator. After a hearty welcome, Mae takes us on a walking tour of the circular, three-story building.

The arts are in action and evident everywhere: students are rehearsing their own scripted version of *The Lion King*; a visiting teenage orchestra (whose conductor is trying to recruit new players from King) plays Mozart for a rapt student audience in the cafeteria/auditorium; young sculptors covered in plaster of Paris dust are fashioning their own Pygmalions; the Fabs are rehearsing for an early evening performance. At one point Mae mentions that she is interested in adding sign language to her dance program, and Debbie and Jane say in unison: "Erin Delaney! Mae, we have just the artist for you. She incorporates signing into her dance workshops." Mae beams with delight at the new bounty of serendipity and partnerships.

As we walk through the school, Mae stops to say good afternoon to the teachers and the students she hadn't seen during the morning. Students' eyes light up when she enters a room. Some rush up to her and ask for hugs, which she gives. She knows everyone's name. The teachers are obviously at ease in her presence. The atmosphere is warm, safe and trusting.

We finish the tour and repair to Mae's office to talk about the school, the experience of the first year in Creative Connections, and the benefits of various arts partnerships for her faculty and students. As I listen to her, it becomes clear that Mae is defining her philosophy of education, what her school is for and the role the arts play in the education of all her students.

Jane Remer: How long have you been a principal, and how long at Martin Luther King?

Mae Kennerly: I have been a principal for six years, all here at King.

JR: Were you a classroom teacher before that?

MK: I was director of Head Start. Before that, I was an early childhood consultant for the district. I was a classroom teacher for about six of my 21 years.

JR: Tell me about King and your vision for the school.

MK: King has a very diverse school population, and we have something for everyone. It is a real hodgepodge. We have Head Start classes, learning-disabilities classes, behavior-disorder classes, a comprehensive program, an advanced program and a gifted-education program. We have a family resource center that connects the school with the community. And in our arts program, that's when we truly blend everyone together.

Mainly, we want our children to be exposed to as many arts areas as possible. We have an arts coordinator, arts teachers including creative dramatics, artist consultants and, of course, now Creative Connections! We are interested in doing more dance next year and, as I said earlier, we want to connect it to sign language, which we can now do with Erin Delaney's help. Another of our school goals is that all children be in front of a computer at least 15 minutes each day. Every teacher has technology in the classroom.

JR: What changes, if any, do you see in your school since the first meeting of the Creative Connections demonstration school network in October?

MK: I think the major thing that has happened to the King school as a result of being a part of the Creative Connections program is that we have had some time to plan. This is a piece of our puzzle that we have never had the opportunity to do.

Normally, we get or are given a project or a grant, and then plunge right in. We have so many things going on in the school that many times the artists who come in to work with our children have no idea of the other things going on. Often our classroom and arts teachers aren't aware of what's happening either.

We had a planning retreat that gave us an opportunity to bring everyone together, and it was like a first-time meeting because many of our artists don't know the teachers. For the first time, we were able to sit down together and talk about the direction we want to go with our school. We thought we were ready to go with a lot of things, but there is nothing like having time to sit and reflect with one another. It has been the high point of the project.

JR: So, you really found the retreat useful.

MK: Yes, we did. But we learned it would have been better to do it earlier in the school year. We also would have liked to have had the artists doing more warm-up activities with us rather than having a facilitator doing all the connecting. Other than that, as I said, it was a terrific planning opportunity.

You have to understand how we operate. When I came to King, we adopted a focus on the performing and visual arts. I get personal pleasure out of the arts, and I was excited. The teachers said, "What are you talking about?" I had just finished explaining my reasons for the arts focus when we then became a gifted-education center. So, we have usually planned everything after the district has offered us opportunities—our district is very progressive and comes up with many things for us to do.

That was the hard part for us with Creative Connections. We are used to getting things and then running with them, and with Creative Connections, we all had to stop and think a minute, and step back. We had to find out where we were headed to have some direction as a group, and I certainly appreciate that they slowed us down. It was good for the artists, and it was good for the limited staff (a member of each team in the building who then reported to teammates) who were able to come to the planning session.

One goal has been for each team to have a focus—for example, the percussion group, the creative dramatics group that also wants to go into some journalism and writing. It would be nice if every team would take an aspect of a large, integrated project: one team could write it; another could perform it; and another could produce it. It could become a school-wide project for the year. Another goal is to try to have as many teachers as possible go to the Kentucky Center for the Arts' Arts in Education Summer Institute, so that they will develop an appreciation and love for what they are doing.

JR: Where do you think you want to go with all of this?

MK: My goal is children are first and student success is first. I like children to be actively involved in things. I truly believe that the arts make students successful, because once they gain that confidence and build self-esteem, doing other things is easy. Another of our many goals is that children perform for someone at some point during the year. If you can stand before an audience and talk or demonstrate your talent, then that is half the battle of learning. We can all learn to read and to write once we have that confidence. That is the value of the arts for me.

We have some students who would be considered the reluctant learners or undesirable children that shine in the arts. That's why our arts program is so wonderful; we truly blend in all the children. Children from a behavior-disorder class can be standing right next to children from the gifted-education program, and when they are together like that, no one knows who's who. That often gives the student in the exceptional-child category an opportunity to shine. For example, a group of boys from the behavior-disorder class led our tap class, and it was so wonderful for them! They could finally do something for which they were recognized and praised. Their behavior, their whole world, changed. They worked hard because they knew they wanted to be a part of the group. That was part of the criteria—you had to earn the right to participate. It made it so much fun for them and so much easier on the adults.

The key to working with them is to find something to motivate them, and the arts are a motivator for everyone. Many parents send their children here because of the arts program. That is the draw. We have children from more than 30 different zip codes in the city. Two children actually pay to come here because they are crossing county lines—that is a compliment. Many parents send their children here because we offer things that many would have to pay for privately.

JR: What do you see as your next step for the Creative Connections program?

MK: I think we should continue to expand what we are doing and do some more in-service and pre-service activities for our staff. We are not 100 percent on board, and sometimes people have to experience things for themselves before it is meaningful. The time the program gives us to reflect is wonderful—people don't usually have time to get together to talk about what they are doing and to plan without interruption and distraction; it is just not built into the school year.

JR: How about staff development?

MK: I would also love to have our whole staff go through the Kentucky Center for the Arts' Arts in Education Institute. The teachers could see how much fun it is to learn. Usually, people who have fun bring it back and share it with others. Our goal is to get two teachers to go to the Center's Institute this year, and every year after that.

Meanwhile, we are having a three-day mini-institute for our parents and teachers this summer and another in February 1996. We are using the institute as a school-wide introductory activity and are trying to recruit at least two parents from each classroom. Out of the three focal points for the Creative Connections grant—professional development, curriculum development, and parent and community support—parent and community support was the area that our teachers selected, so that is how parent involvement in the institute came about. Parent involvement is part of our school-wide goal, as well. As you recall, several parents were involved in our retreat.

JR: Is teacher turnover an issue for you?

MK: No. Since I have been here, one person transferred, and one person retired. One teacher's been here for 20 years, another for ten.

JR: Then the plan to have two teachers go to the institute each year makes "cumulative" sense in a place like this. It wouldn't in a school where there is a lot of turnover or retirement. But it's a revolving door, isn't it? How do you make up for the loss of parents who move on and out of the school as their children get older?

MK: Many of the parents we are working with now have primary children, and that is our focus so we have something on which to build. They are the ones who are asking for things, and they are the ones we are pulling in. We have about ten parents who have rolled up their sleeves and are ready to get to work. That's good because they will be around for a while to help us recruit other parents. Our PTA president is enthusiastic, and she's here all the time. This core group is going to help with a writing project.

JR: Have artists worked in the classroom at King this year?

MK: Yes, quite a few. We have a number of resident artists and a number of resident arts specialists who are on contract. We have a two-hour awareness program on two days, and on the third day we have a talent program for kids who audition to come to King. We have manners and more, visual arts, creative dramatics, playwrights, gymnastics, keyboard, drama, tap, ballet, and martial arts.

JR: What is manners and more?

MK: We are trying to teach these children more about manners. It is like an etiquette class. They learn how to eat with a napkin, how to power walk, wear white gloves and ballroom dance. We did it with primary kids, and their parents were stunned watching their kids wipe their mouths with a napkin, not their shirt sleeves. I say, "please" and "thank you" and "you're welcome" to all the children. The new children coming in just look at me.

Unfortunately, some of our children don't come to school with the basic principles of manners, and eating is sometimes unreal. I ask them, "Can you sit and eat and talk without yelling across the table?" We take our kids out to lunch every grading period, and we go to a sit-down restaurant so we have to sit quietly, order, eat, figure out what forks to use. Those are basic survival skills that children really need. They all come from different backgrounds. Sometimes they are split between several homes, so we talk about school standards to be careful not to imply that the home is lacking or wrong.

JR: Have you observed any partnerships developing between Creative Connections artists and your teachers?

MK: Yes. You see, the Kentucky Center doesn't have to worry about busing, reading, math or things like that. We do. But they can be a tremendous resource to us in the arts. They have artists who teach at their institutes whom they have watched at work for weeks at a time. They audition and screen everyone who works with them. We don't have the time or the expertise to do that. It's not our main business. Many artists are out there that we don't know, so it is very important to have someone who can say, "You need to work with so and so, or see so and so." You saw it happen today when we made the connection between my needing a dancer who knows sign language and the Creative Connection's artist Erin Delaney. It helps to know each other's work and philosophy, so we can both take shortcuts. They have made good artistic matches for us.

The partnerships with Debbie and Jane have been wonderful, too. I think they're good facilitators and matchmakers—in a word, good connectors. Let me give you a couple of examples. We talked about our stage—how inadequate it is and how poor the sound system is. Debbie said, "Let me send Steve down to look at it." Steve is one of the main production guys at the Kentucky Center. I appreciate the small things that come from us being able to sit and talk. That's when they find out about some of our *real* needs.

Here's another example: part of our population takes Russian as a foreign language. Jane knew that, and so they sent the Russian Puppet Company here. The Russians had a wonderful time with the children, the food, and we were so thrilled that they showed up! That helped the school connect and bond.

Here's one more: the Fabulous Leopard Percussionists played at the General Electric Company's shareholders meeting, which was a big deal for us—the faculty, the students, our parents. Again, it was a result of the relationship that developed between our school and the Kentucky Center. It has given our school some great publicity and more exposure for our children. The unofficial things have been as wonderful as the official things. I call that a partnership.

JR: Do you have any other thoughts on expanding or deepening the program?

MK: I just think we need to take it slow and to try to implement some of the things we have talked about—get parents involved through the mini-institutes, get a couple of teachers involved in the Kentucky Center Institute every summer. That will be a major accomplishment for us.

When I talked with Mae in January 1996, she told me that arts activity was continuing apace at the school. She mentioned the upcoming Creative Connections staff development retreat; the fourth grade team's plans for a Renaissance Fair; the Primary Class' Christmas production which was performed for the school and then taken on the road for the community; the Fabs show for the Kentucky Music Educators Association, and the Show Choirs' planned production for the community during Black History Month (February). She was particularly enthusiastic about a new limestone carving with the school's name now prominently displayed at the lobby entrance near the papier-mâché figures. A parent volunteer had worked with the primary class to create this piece, and the children had learned to use drills, chisels and other tools of the trade in the process.

In Martin Luther King, Jr. Elementary in Louisville, Kentucky, the purpose of schooling is abundantly clear: Arts, manners, and much, much more.

Mae Kennerly is the Principal of Martin Luther King, Jr. Elementary School in Louisville, KY, a magnet school with a focus on gifted/talented education with a technology emphasis. As principal, Ms. Kennerly is responsible for overseeing the implementation of the Kentucky Education Reform Act (KERA). Previously, she has been a director of Head Start, a classroom teacher, and a kindergarten consultant. Ms. Kennerly was educated at Spalding University and Western Kentucky University.

Notes

1. John Goodlad, *What Schools Are For* (Phi Delta Kappa Educational Foundation, 1979) pp. 44; 46-52. (Reprinted with permission.)

2. Ibid.

3. Ibid. This is an abridged construction of Goodlad's discussion.

4. Available from the Alliance for Arts Education/New Jersey, P.O. Box 8176, Trenton, NJ 08650.

5. Full copies of the address may be obtained from the Public Affairs Division of the National Endowment for the Arts.

6. *Why We Need the Arts: 8 Quotable Speeches by Leaders in Education, Government, Business and the Arts* (New York: ACA Books, 1988).

7. From the second edition of *Changing Schools Through the Arts*, March 1990.

8. Charles B. Fowler, *The Arts Process in Basic Education* (Pennsylvania Department of Education, Harrisburg, first edition 1973; second edition 1977. Out of print.) This superb little booklet was reprinted seven times and hundreds of copies were published and distributed nationwide with financial assistance from the JDR 3rd Fund. Its contents include "Actions of the Arts Process," "The Arts Encompass the Entire Range of Art, Dance, Drama, Filmmaking, and Photography, Music and Writing," "Potentials of the Arts Process," "The Place of the Arts in the Curriculum," and two True/False sets of questions about a process-oriented arts program in the education of all students.

9. Ibid, page 19.

10. Ibid, pp. 20-21.

11. This rationale was originally written by Kathryn Bloom, executive director, Arts in Education Program, and myself for the New York City Public School's Arts in General Education Program. It later appeared in the January-February 1975 issue of *Principal Magazine*, and was included in the first and second editions of *Changing Schools*. Reprinted by permission, The JDR 3rd Fund © 1980.

12. The Free Press: New York, 1993.

13. Howard Gardner developed his theory of Multiple Intelligences (MI) at Project Zero, Harvard University. Originally described in his book, *Frames of Mind: The Theory of Multiple Intelligences* (New York: Basic Books, 1983), Gardner advances the concept that there are many different ways of knowing, actually seven different intelligences including musical, bodily-kinesthetic, logical-mathematical, linguistic, spacial, interpersonal and intrapersonal. Schools normally concentrate on only two of these avenues to learning, thus diminishing the opportunities for those who take in information in different ways. Gardner's theory has been put into practice in programs such as Arts PROPEL in Pittsburgh, PA. His MI theory has been incorporated into the Kentucky Education Reform Act and in the Basic Arts Program of the Kentucky Arts Council. The principles are widely adapted in many programs around the country, and Gardner's recent books describe some of these programs as well as classroom practice.

14. Theodore Sizer is a professor of history at Brown University, director of the national network known as the Coalition of Essential Schools, and the author of two important books on education: *Horace's Compromise* and *Horace's School*, both published in Boston by Houghton Mifflin in 1984 and 1992, respectively.

15. James Comer is a professor of psychiatry at Yale University's Child Development Center. His important work includes long-term partnerships with elementary schools in New Haven, Connecticut dedicated to restructuring by creating a harmonious learning community. In 1992, Dr. Comer joined Howard Gardner, Ted Sizer and Janet Whitla (Education Development Center, Newton, MA) in the design of a new "break-the-mold" school. Funded by the New American Schools Development Corporation, the design team created the ATLAS (Authentic Teaching, Learning and Assessment for all Students) project in three sites in Maine, Virginia and Maryland. The ATLAS model is based on five core beliefs:

- All students can and will achieve at high levels.
- Students acquire essential skills, habits and understandings within an authentic learning environment.
- Education is an evolving process
- Education requires a partnership among the schools, parents, and other key stake-holders in the community.
- Adults involved in the education of students need regular opportunities to continue their own learning.

The project in Prince George, Maryland involves a K-12 plan to reform education which includes a partnership with the local arts council. Music, dance, theater and visual arts are major components in this model project and local artists and arts organizations are important partnerships in this restructuring effort. [Source: National Assembly of Local Arts Agencies *Monographs*, Volume 4, Number 4, April 1995, pages 3 - 6]

16. Mortimer Adler, *We Hold These Truths: Understanding the Ideas and Ideals of the Constitution.* Adler is chairman of editors of *Encyclopedia Britannica*; honorary trustee of Apsen Institute; author of 38 books, and associate editor of *The Great Books of the Western World.*

CHAPTER *3*

School Reform
and the Arts

A Perspective on Reform

Our life is lived forward but only understood by looking backward.—Sören Kierkegaard

Looking Backward and Moving Forward

In Chapter Two, we explored what schools are for and where the arts fit into the process, and we learned that the answer depends in large measure on whom you ask the question. It became clear that while the arts have an important role to play in basic education, they are still essentially considered a marginal enterprise in the general business of schooling. Various reasons were advanced, among them a lack of professional capacity within the schools; no significant local, vocal constituency of support; the need for alliances with non-arts power blocs concerned with the welfare of children; the perceived non-academic nature of the content of the arts, and the plain fact that in today's world, a plethora of competing needs tends to drown out the claimed advantages they offer to improve motivation for and success in teaching and learning.

We also touched on recent promising developments in the continually unfolding saga of school reform to see what impact they might have on the arts locally. There is currently much talk about the transformation of general education and the power that the arts can lend to this difficult process. The topic of reform and the arts deserves more extensive investigation and we will pursue it further in this chapter.

Not every arts agency, organization or artist needs to be steeped in education theory or the various philosophies of school reform to engage in fruitful community work. Nor will everyone who reads this book decide to work directly with schools, much less become a full-fledged partner in the gradual, demanding and long-term change process. But I think everyone in the arts community can benefit from a general understanding of what's at stake in order to make a more informed choice about what role to play, if any, as a resource to schools.

This book proceeds from the belief that arts agencies, organizations and artists—and foundations and business—have an important role to play in moving the national rhetorical promise of reform to the local reality of school superintendents, principals, teachers, students and parents. I also contend that arts organizations can benefit enormously by making a conscious civic effort to become a vital part of the political, social and educative fabric of their local school community. Let us briefly examine current events through the filter of past experience so we may move forward with more information and confidence.

The Challenge: From National Rhetoric to Local Reality

It is tempting to regard the current flurry of national attention as a major turning point for the arts in American school reform. Professional arts educators, arts administrators, artists and philanthropists want to say: "Whew! At last! We can relax. We are finally on bedrock, and we can proceed with greater assurance with our own complementary agendas."

We must resist this temptation because, unless ways are found at the local level to systematically include and sustain the arts as basics in the redesign of American schooling, the arts will continue to play a largely marginal role in the general education of every child. It is true that Goals 2000 includes the arts for the first time in important federal education legislation; voluntary national standards now indicate what children should know and be able to do in each of four major art forms; a National Assessment for Educational Progress will evaluate the state of the arts at the eighth-grade level in certain American schools in 1997; the new Elementary and Secondary Education Act, known as the Improving America's Schools Act, includes the arts and makes them eligible for funding under certain titles of the legislation. None of this, however, guarantees that all our schools will offer arts instruction for all the children, kindergarten through grade 12, in every state and territory. Nor does it indicate what kind of instruction will be offered, the equality, frequency or sequence of opportunity, who will teach it, and who will pay for it. In our country, these are state and local matters, and federal education legislation does not ensure state and local compliance.

Obstacles to Change and the Need to Resist Complacency

Are we not better off with this new stir of activity that appears to include and finally dignify the place of the arts in the lives and schooling of children?

Yes, of course, and no, not yet.

Yes, because these events *are* breakthroughs, and they have a national imprimatur and federal support—for the political moment. Yes, because they promote, affirm and give credibility to the need for the arts as part of all children's basic education. Yes, because many states and localities have been encouraged to include the arts, some for the first time, in their comprehensive plans.

No, because:

- The legislation is motivated by political, economic and social agendas, not an overriding educational one. American history proves legislation of this kind to be short-lived and at the fickle mercy of the governing party's vision (or lack of it). In the last 30 years or so, I have lived through a succession of legislative acts that held glowing promise for the arts. They have almost all disappeared, along with their structures, their administrators and their money.

- State and local programs that are wholly or chiefly dependent on federal legislation and appropriations generally collapse without federal leadership and support. They usually lack the incentive or the mandate to command the allocation of scarce local resources for which there is genuine and fierce competition.

- Even if the political, social and economic winds were constant, nothing in the current legislation guarantees that the rhetoric will be transformed into reality behind the classroom door in every American school. School reform and educational change is a much harder, longer and infinitely more complex process, and as research has repeatedly shown, the status quo and entrenched attitudes resist change. For change to have a chance, the people most likely to be affected and held responsible for results must have a stake in the action and be engaged in the planning, design and implementation process—superintendents, principals, teachers and parents.

- Legislation, whether federal, state or local—mandated or voluntary—has for years called for the arts to take their place in general education, insisted on graduation requirements, courses for credit and the like. Yet research and experience have taught us that these requirements for the arts are frequently ignored, unenforced, and often fulfilled with equivalencies, such as computer science. Arts-in-education supporters can find only cold comfort here.

Other obstacles to change are rooted in the nature of school reform itself. Here are some of the lessons learned over the last 20 years. I have adapted them from an excellent source book, *From Risk to Renewal*,[1] and added those from my own experience over the years.

- Education must be valued as an end in itself for all citizens, not simply as a means to accomplishing national political and economic purposes, social engineering or the narrow agendas of special interest groups.

- Excellence, whether in the arts or other subjects, cannot be mandated, jolted, forced or threatened into being in our decentralized, democratic society.

- Complex social institutions resist change. Complex social animals do, too. Never underestimate the power of the status quo to prevail. People prefer the known to the unknown or unknowable. The schools reflect the values and the priorities of the society in which we live.

- Change requires a systemic, systematic, coherent design to prevail. It cannot proceed piecemeal, project by project. Most American reform efforts in recent memory have addressed only a piece of the puzzle.

- The United States has always been a nation with a strong anti-intellectual bent. It is also a society that grew out of the Puritan work ethic. Our national catchwords are competition, winning and profit. The arts do not necessarily flourish in this environment since they contribute little of value to the construct.

- Every school must become its own center of excellence. Government policies can provide the incentives, the framework and the environment needed to support good schools, but they can't create them.

- A cultural change is needed in the ways that we think about schools: we need to consider more than just how they operate. A first step in that direction is to rethink what we expect from our schools and have a sharp picture of what good schools look like.

- In our attempt to determine what students should know and be able to do, we must remember that no single blueprint exists for building the prototype school of tomorrow—one size *doesn't* fit all. A school that might thrive in Chicago would be unlikely to meet the needs of rural North Dakotans.

- A widening but by no means universal consensus is developing about what a "good school" should look like. It is child- and learning-centered; students take responsibility for constructing their own learning; teachers lecture less and coach more; critical thinking and problem solving, not rote memorization is the objective; learning is authentic, based on real-life and relevant situations, not textbook dominated; standardized, normative multiple-choice assessment is balanced with criterion-referenced, process-oriented, problem-solving measurement; and the entire task is dedicated to preparing the young for productive lifetime learning and earning. Perhaps most important, a good school is a place where decisions of governance, curriculum and instruction are made on site and as close to the heart of the educational enterprise as possible—in the classroom.

- Good schools and schooling cannot develop in isolation from the community's social and cultural institutions. Community partnerships—in the arts, culture, business, and the like—help build better schools, give students authentic experiences and build bridges between the schools and the larger social environment.

- The sheer size of the reform task is daunting: over 15,000 school districts, more than 85,000 public schools, 45 million and counting students, and 2.5 million teachers comprise the business of schooling in our country. For lasting change to occur, a huge need for professional development and leadership training must be fulfilled. On this scale, reform must be planned comprehensively and systemically but must proceed one school at a time, with district, state and federal support.

- The change must be bottom up, top down and horizontal and include local school boards and the community in the process.

John Goodlad: Lessons from Yesterday for Today...and Tomorrow

These days, Dr. John I. Goodlad is a professor of education and director of the Center for Educational Renewal at the University of Washington and president of the Institute for Educational Inquiry in Seattle. John and I worked together in the seventies when he was dean of the School of Education at UCLA and director of the Institute for Development of Educational Activities, a project of the Kettering Foundation. I was then the associate director of the Arts in Education Program at the JDR 3rd Fund in New York City. When I met John, he was deeply engaged in his comprehensive Study of Schooling in the United States, and we had the opportunity to join his research effort to the programmatic efforts under way at the JDR 3rd Fund, notably the League of Cities for the Arts in Education. John wrote the foreword for my *Changing Schools Through the Arts*, and we have kept in touch over the years.

As I began to tackle the daunting issue of educational reform and the arts, I naturally turned to him for his thoughts. What follows are excerpts from his writings and our recent correspondence.

As John has pointed out in his article, "Taking School Reform Seriously"[2]:

It becomes increasingly clear that there are two sets of school reform movements currently operating in the U.S. and that they are not joined. One, of which America 2000 [the predecessor to Goals 2000] is the most visible, is tied rhetorically to the national interest, international economic competitiveness, and corporate health. It is politically driven. The playing fields are federal executive and legislative halls of government, state capitols, and mayoral offices. Professional associations, the National School Boards Association, and the National Congress of Parents and Teachers strive valiantly to keep their constituencies informed [as do the national, state and local arts agencies and alliances with Goals 2000]. Occasionally, the major players in this movement nod in the direction of children, parents and teachers. The movement is driven by ideological appeal to that part of the nation's fabric dubbed by William James "the hard and tough."

The second movement exists in hundreds of localities. The focus is less on specific changes than on shifting greater authority and responsibility to individual school sites, nongraded primary or middle schools, productive use of technology, increased attention to mathematics and science or the ideas promulgated by educational leaders, such as James Comer, Howard Gardner, Henry Levin and Theodore Sizer.

Connections between these local efforts and the politically driven movement are not entirely missing. Notable examples are the Re: Learning project, sponsored by the Education Commission of the States in collaboration with Sizer's Coalition of Essential Schools, and the joining of the formerly educator-driven movement toward nongraded schools with state reform plans in Kentucky and Oregon.

As he said in *Arts and the Schools*[3]:

National education policy and practice is political, piecemeal and fashioned by people who do not work in schools; therefore, the most productive agenda for improvement of school arts programs will be built at the local level....

Although a good case probably can be made for direct transfer benefits, to justify the arts on the basis of what they contribute to student achievement in "basic" subjects is to gain only temporary socio-political benefits in policy formation.... In the long run the case for the arts is best argued on its own merits.

...The story of civilization can best be understood through studying the literature, drama, music, dance and visual arts of previous eras and by reinterpreting the human condition through contemporary participation in the arts.

And here are selections from our recent correspondence:

March 1995

Dear John:

I need your voice again in this new effort to bring historical perspective and refreshing candor. Can I ask you to dash off to me your thoughts on the current "reform" effort and the prospects you believe it holds for the arts "behind the classroom door?"

Many of my colleagues believe that if the current "window of opportunity"—a tired but accurate description—is ignored, the arts will have lost the chance for equality and equity forever. I don't share this view. I see a lot of rhetoric in high places and, so far, very little action at the local level, and precious little money trickling down to the schoolhouse for the arts. The arts are forever in a hopeless competition with more compelling social and political needs and forces.

Mind you, I do see incremental progress, in patches of course, nationwide. I continue to believe that whatever the political climate, and wherever the dollars come from (certainly fewer from the public arena in the foreseeable future), the arts will probably not be dislodged from the foothold they have gained in the schools beginning with the Johnson years. For private donors to the arts, education is still a very sexy draw. So even if we go back to a fifties climate, I am writing the new book for arts organizations, agencies and artists in the belief that they continue to have a vital contribution to make—and considerable satisfaction to be gained—if and when they learn how to collaborate with the schools for the benefit of all the kids.

What do you think about this? Can you whip up something I can include in the book?

I hope this finds you well and as abundantly productive as always. I look forward to hearing from you.

As always,

Jane

April 1995

Dear Jane:

I am delighted and encouraged by your tenacious advocacy of the arts. Although one might interpret optimistically some of the current rhetoric in high places, this is more like getting on the playing field as batboy rather than as outfielder. The rhetoric looks good only by contrast with what we have largely had since *A Nation At Risk*. Even the rhetoric is not yet back where it once was—and the rhetoric always has exceeded the implementation and action.

Like you, I am very depressed with what is happening in so many school districts. I thought I made it clear in *A Place Called School* [his report on the study of schooling] that we could have a full and rich curriculum that would include the arts in all of our elementary schools, for example, simply by getting 25 hours (instead of our documented 23.5 hours) out of the instructional week. This still leaves several hours for aimlessly messing around. Some of the schools, but not many, had attained or even gone beyond this goal, but most had not. I then went on to point out how this simple attainment might occur. But the political reformers were not interested in practical suggestions such as this.

In spite of this discouraging context, we must keep the flame burning. The arts and other components of the humanities always manage to have a small place on the stage, but only because a few people, like you, are willing to hang in there tenaciously.... I tend to keep recycling in regard to my central interests and commitments, so I probably will get back into arts education again, but this is not my present preoccupation. Clearly, the work in which I am now engaged—the simultaneous renewal of schooling and the education of educators—encompasses the arts in both schools and higher education.

With regards,

John

May 1995

Dear John:

I realize you are under crushing deadlines and that you never "dash" anything off, so I propose the following: either we make a telephone date or we try to find time for you to somehow give me your thoughts on the following questions. Your responses to these will "fast forward" us into the present, and since I envision making the piece a dialogue, I will probably use some connecting quotes from our recent correspondence.

Here are the questions I'd like to ask. You can respond to all, some, or better, ones of your own: [list of questions]

Let me know if this is do-able.

Warm regards,

Jane

July 1995

Response to My Specific Questions about the Arts and School Reform

Dear Jane:

Your request of me has been very much on my mind during this rather unsettled period of trying to get beyond administrative demand into a book I am writing (with deadlines staring me in the face).

In your memo of May 2, you raise several questions. Let me see what I can do with them.

1. Why do you think that after all these years of advocacy and activity, the arts are still not a presence behind the classroom door nor part of the basic education of every child?

1.0 There are several reasons why the arts are still not a presence behind the classroom door and not part of the basic education of every child. They include the following:

1.1 We are still in some ways a macho society. The pressures on the male children, in particular, are to be athletic. It is alright to be in the arts as an adult (when this peer pressure is off), but the arts are not encouraged during the formative years of the male child. When schools and school districts make a quantum leap in regard to the arts (as some were doing and perhaps are doing with substantial grant awards), and the arts become an encompassing activity for all children, much of this problem is mitigated.

1.2 Because we have equated education and schooling, and then made schooling instrumental primarily to individual and national economic advancement, the push for curricular expansion is in science and mathematics (with learning to read and write assumed). The arts are not regarded as having this instrumentality. In effect they become a kind of "add-on," a luxury after finishing work in the other subjects.

1.3 The world of school arts never has been well-integrated with the rest of schooling. There is a kind of self-fulfilling prophecy here: in order to get the arts established, there has been a special, somewhat compartmentalized, appeal, very much like the one that tends to have separated special from general education. To have to fight hard for something is also to establish an identity with boundaries that define the enterprise but also tend to segregate it. This problem is exacerbated by the degree to which teacher education in the arts (particularly music) is conducted quite separately from teacher education in general. To cap it off, the arts are then taught by specialists who tend to do their teaching during fixed periods of the week, to do it alone, and so tend not to be closely identified with the rest of the faculty. In effect, arts educators have failed to develop a larger professional constituency to support their work. When the arts are eliminated, most other teachers merely regret the absence of the specialist, but since they did not identify with the importance of the work, they often do not feel that children have lost that much.

What is rarely recognized by well-intentioned persons, even many arts specialists and others who serve for months on commissions for arts in schools, is that there is not a large and sympathetic army of educators ready and willing to march for the arts. "Army" is in many ways the relevant word, because the culture of the school, especially at the secondary level, is marked by competing factions for whom a subject specialty is a banner, and time for that specialty is what the fighting is all about. The arts in schools, for all their friends in the arts councils and junior leagues, have very few troops and fewer captains. School boards, which are political and have a limited knowledge base of the schools, rarely have established goals, and when they do, the arts are rarely included. Most superintendents are not arts supporters.

1.4 Finally—but, of course, there are additional reasons—the conversation conducted and promoted by arts educators tends to be almost a private conversation. I remember this problem coming to the forefront when we were doing that book on the arts that was supported by the JDR 3rd Fund.[4] The academic arts educators tended to argue over details of conducting the arts rather than addressing the problem of such conversation being worthless if the arts were not even in the curriculum.

There are divisive, ideological quarrels among arts educators that get in the way of presenting a common front to promote arts education.

2. What effect do you believe that recent legislation (Goals 2000, the voluntary national standards for the arts, the NAEP 1996 arts assessment, the new national arts research agenda, and inclusion of the arts in the new ESEA) will have at the grassroots level?

2.0 The legislation, development of standards, etc. to which you refer in this question are largely part of a political struggle regarding inclusion. This does not harm and certainly helps somewhat in regard to legitimating the arts (and probably increases the flow of public and private money). However, it does not go very far toward changing things at the grassroots level. There is nothing unique about this in regard to educational reform. Politically driven school reform is conducted by one group of actors, and these actors are only in very loose communication with actors at the grassroots level. And so, back on the ranch, things go on pretty much as they did before. Perhaps a few flags for the arts will be flown but this probably will produce not even a parade.

Two matters much closer to the grass roots do make a difference. One is the degree to which school boards think the arts are important—important enough to be protected during times of budget cutting. Unfortunately, with few superintendents even interested in the arts and the arts not well-represented among educators with power in the district, there is little outcry when the arts are cut. A second major factor can be the entrance requirements of universities. For example, the University of Washington had an impact when it required all applicants to have had at least one high school course in the arts—a drop in the bucket, perhaps, but an important message nonetheless.

3. What insight does your current work on renewing schools and the education of educators give you into the continued resistance or indifference to the arts in the schoolhouse?

3.0 I think I have answered most of this question in the above. One matter that looms large is the lack of a professional constituency for the arts. As stated above, programs for the preparation of educators in the arts tend to be separated from the rest of the teacher-education enterprise. In our research on teacher education, we found on the campuses of a couple of major research universities as many as six different schools and colleges conducting teacher-education programs, with little or no communication among them. This is particularly true at the secondary level, where teachers at many universities are prepared entirely outside of the school of education. This is as true for the preparation of secondary arts teachers as it is for the preparation of secondary math teachers.

Arts educators should get off the high ground that tends to convey to many people, including professional educators, an image of a very elite enterprise requiring highly talented people who must spend far more hours preparing in their field than do, for example, educators in mathematics. Take a look at the number of hours of music required to be a music specialist versus the number of hours required in any other field. I do not quarrel with the notion that it takes a long time to become competent in the field of music. But given this, what must be done in order to build the preparation of music educators into preparation programs more generally? Music educators appear to me to be quite content with their isolated status without recognizing the dire consequences in regard to the acceptance of the arts by other educators and the general public. I am suggesting that, in part, in regard to the problems of arts education, "We have met the enemy, and he is us."

4. Do you have any "lessons learned" about the arts as a result of your comprehensive study of schooling that you'd like to pass along to the new and next generation of arts educators, administrators and artists?

4.0 I think the lessons are all embedded in the above statements, which represent the things I have learned. I may sound a little cynical, but I am merely trying to recognize reality. I am as ardent an exponent of the arts as I ever was. Indeed, currently I am risking some of my leisure time to help with the arts in the community where I escape to do some writing.

Let me conclude with a suggestion. Clearly, the last dozen or so years of school reform have changed our expectations for schools toward things they cannot do— create better jobs and make us more competitive in the global economy. This is to invite failure, and school reform (not schools) clearly has failed. I do not anticipate a healthy climate for the arts in the near future. Indeed, there has not been a healthy climate throughout my entire career. Let us take note of the fact that, in making our schools so instrumental to things that they cannot do, we have reduced their educational power. Meanwhile, other educative agencies in the community are taking over. Why not join them?

The best arts program I have ever seen was in the community where Adelphi University was located. It was a college in those days (circa mid-1950s). The college and the community collaborated in a community Saturday-morning program in the arts. Children rotated through a series of experiences in the visual and graphic arts, music, drama and literature. Every Saturday morning, a child would participate in a three- or four-hour block in one of these and then rotate through all four throughout the academic year.

As I recall, there was no academic credit, and I do not believe that the college was the driving force, although the talent it represented was essential to the success of the venture. However, other sources of talent in the community were drawn upon. Perhaps community arts programs could ultimately become the driving force behind school-based arts programs. Please give some thought to this. For arts in schools to have made so little progress over so long a period of time may be telling us something about schools. You and I are so committed to public schooling that we may be wearing blinders...

With warm regards,

John

This is powerful stuff, indeed. It deserves serious discussion and analysis by all of us who continue to wage the campaign on behalf of the value of the arts for general education. I am particularly struck by Goodlad's emphasis on the need for the arts education field to make a concerted effort to develop a professional constituency within the schoolhouse and within the local district, especially the local school board and superintendent. He reminded me, too, that the general public still thinks of the arts as the province of the gifted and talented. This image of segre-gation—of the arts as an elite, isolated enterprise—plus the continuing perception of internal squabbling within the professional arts commu-nity, underscores the need for the field to continue its work together to dispel the notion that the arts are not important, rigorous academic endeavors for everyone. Is it any wonder, then, that the arts continue to battle for recognition and so often lose that battle at the local level at budget time?

While I may, as John suggests, have blinders on because of my com-mitment to public schooling, I have no reason to believe, as I remarked to Doc Howe in our conversation (see Chapter Two) that community arts programs will become a driving force for school-based programs. Many superb community programs have been around for years. Apart from the fact that they beg the question by serving "some," not "all," of the chil-dren, some of the time, they have had no visible effect on public schools programming. In fact, if anything, these excellent community programs, like model projects that do an exemplary job in scattered pockets around the country, generally have the unfortunate, opposite effect of letting public school officials off the hook. The thinking goes, "I don't need to spend my precious resources on the arts; they are being taken care of elsewhere." I remain stubbornly committed to all the arts for all the chil-dren, and since most of them are in the public schools, that is where I believe both public and private funds and efforts should be concentrated.

A Framework and Agenda for the Future

Now that you know, for a certainty, that the process of wedding the arts to constructive school change is a hard one, but assuming that you are still interested in working with schools as a resource to their reform efforts, what are some of the questions you might ask yourself and your colleagues as you move forward?

In the introduction to the guidelines published by the Goals 2000: Arts Education Partnerships, *The Arts and Education: Partners in Achieving Our National Education Goals*,[5] there is some strong language about systemic and instructional change in and through the arts that should offer you institutional comfort and personal inspiration. I have inserted some thoughts of my own in brackets.

> In this new environment, the task is not merely to look to the future but to create it neighborhood by neighborhood, school by school, state by state—to take new risks for our children's sake.

National and state education goals and standards offer a better way to think about the way we do education in this country. Their impact has the potential to reach to the very heart and mission of educational associations and arts organizations.... What is called for is not fitting new items on the existing agenda but finding ways to break away from old limitations and build successful models and processes for basic improvement.

Arts and education agencies, artists and educators, professional associations, business organizations, cultural and community institutions, decision makers and parent organizations will have to:

- revisit the mission [the history and the decision-making structure] of their own organizations and associations;
- reevaluate and reallocate their resources, both human and material;
- rethink staff time and priorities;
- reconfigure communications, publications, dissemination programs and strategies;
- engage in new strategic thinking and planning; and
- perhaps most important, take new [programmatic] risks...for our children's sake...for their future.

As the National Education Goals are implemented and the shape of education reform becomes clearer, new questions will arise.

- What core issues and concerns must be addressed?
- How do we keep the systemic focus of the reform effort alive?
- What teaching and learning advantages do the arts provide for education?
- What distinctive results do they deliver?
- What arts initiatives and program models seem to be working well in the reform context?
- How can these be replicated or adapted?
- What is not working and must be changed?

This passage sets the tone for the balance of this chapter and raises the fundamental questions that have guided the conceptual organization of this book. When combined with the concerns articulated by Tony Alvarado, John Goodlad, and Doc Howe, it is clear that we have a lot of hard work ahead of us. Since these themes will recur as we proceed, we will search for some of the solutions to the tough problems, although it is likely that we will discover more nagging questions than definitive answers. Still, we must continue the journey. Take heart. There are a lot of solid markers on the path.

Creative Connections

Linking the Kentucky Center for the Arts' Resources to Statewide Reform

A Case Study

Statewide Reform as a Context for School Partnerships

This case study will describe how an arts center with a statewide mandate has formed local school partnerships in response to the goals of comprehensive reform legislation and the needs of local schools. It is the story of the Kentucky Center for the Arts (KCA) and its Creative Connections program, a collaboration with the state department of education and several local schools; with state and local arts and cultural resources; and with the General Electric Fund and the staff and volunteers from GE's local plants and administrative offices.

Part of what makes this story so compelling is the way in which Kentucky's arts, education and business communities do business together; part of it also is the political, economic and social infrastructure that supports the arts in schools and in the life of the state. The rest of this story is about the creative energy and tireless hard work by the key players.

As a program and evaluation consultant to the GE Fund, I have had the opportunity to work with the KCA staff since 1993. I have also spent time with the Creative Connections school people, the teaching artists and many others in the community who are connected with the Kentucky Center and its education programs. A number of valuable lessons can be learned from the Kentucky Center's experience, and I offer the case study to illustrate several important points, among them: arts partnerships can be an effective spur and resource to education reform at the grassroots level; networking and collaboration can be effective strategies for building partnerships and for supporting school reform efforts; and dedicated, clear-visioned people in leadership positions from the arts, the education and the business communities play critical roles in building effective arts partnerships.

We will first take a brief look at Kentucky's reform act, move on to the Kentucky Center for the Arts, and then study the Creative Connections program. Finally, we will hear from the KCA staff about the lessons they have learned and their perspectives on partnerships.

The Kentucky Education Reform Act of 1990 (KERA)[6]

From a historical perspective, Kentucky was the first state to undertake a massive and comprehensive school reform effort that included the arts as basic subjects for all students. In fact, these efforts were begun several years before the arts became included in the national goals and the Goals 2000 legislation was passed.

In October 1988, the Kentucky Supreme Court held the system of common schools unconstitutional, and in response to this ruling, the Kentucky Education Reform Act of 1990 (KERA) was developed. It spelled out essential—and minimal—characteristics of an efficient system of common schools and defined an "adequate education" as one that helps all students to acquire seven capacities:

1. Communication skills necessary to function in a complex and changing civilization;
2. Knowledge to make economic, social and political choices;
3. Understanding of governmental processes as they affect the community, the state and the nation;
4. Sufficient self-knowledge and knowledge of one's mental and physical wellness;
5. **Sufficient grounding in the arts to enable each student to appreciate his or her cultural and historical heritage [emphasis added];**
6. Sufficient preparation to choose and pursue one's lifework intelligently; and
7. Skills to enable one to compete favorably with students in other states.

☞ Figure 3.1: Learning Under KERA: The Old Compared with the New

The Commonwealth of Kentucky altered its educational philosophy and strategy in 1990 through the Kentucky Education Reform Act. This educational approach is radically different from the previous educational system.

Learning under KERA is changing:

FROM	TO
Acquiring knowledge	Using knowledge, broadly defined, using more than one way of knowing
One right answer	The most appropriate answer or, in the arts, no single valid response
Scope and sequence	Revisiting skills and concepts at an increasingly complex level
Measuring aptitude	Assessing performance
Textbook as primary source	Textbook as only one of many resources
Exciting activities mainly for the talented	Exciting activities for all
Assessment as an artificial event	Assessment as a "dip stick" at given intervals in authentic contexts
Learning in separate disciplines	Learning across disciplines
Different standards for different students	High standards for all students
Teacher as dispenser of knowledge	Teacher as facilitator and coach

KERA and the Arts: Transformations— Kentucky's Curriculum Framework[7]

The centerpiece of Kentucky's education reform effort is found in *Transformations: Kentucky's Curriculum Framework*,[8] a two-volume document that contains the state's vision of what students should know and be able to do as a result of their school experience. More than 100 teachers, counselors, administrators, regional service center consultants, and university personnel were significantly engaged in the development of the framework. Representatives from the arts community were also deeply involved.

The Curriculum Framework has this to say about the arts:

> The Arts—Dance, Drama, Music, Visual Arts: The arts and humanities may often be used to facilitate and enrich the teaching of other subject matter. However, they must maintain their individual integrity in the curriculum and be taught for their own innate value.

And about national standards in the arts:

The information in this framework, combined with national content and achievement standards in music, visual arts, dance, drama, and second language, will provide teachers with the basis for designing local curriculum and assessments. Voluntary national standards in dance, drama, music, and visual arts are being developed by the National Committee for Standards in the Arts and will be available for review in mid-1993. The arts will be included in the 1996 National Assessment of Educational Progress.

Goals one and two of the curriculum framework mention the arts specifically. For example, here are the academic expectations that are arts-specific in goal two:

2.22   Students create products and make presentations that convey concepts and feelings.

2.23   Students analyze their own and others' artistic products and performances.

2.24   Students appreciate creativity and values of the arts and the humanities.

2.25   Through their productions and performances or interpretation, students show an understanding of the influence of time, place, personality, and society on the arts and humanities.

2.26   Students recognize differences and commonalities in the human experience through their productions, performances, or interpretations.

KERA as a National Landmark

KERA is significant school reform legislation. It is comprehensive, systemic, systematic and coherent. It does not take a piecemeal approach, nor does it depend heavily on federal or other transitory funds for support. It has built-in learner outcomes, standards and assessment as well as carrot-and-stick incentives for compliance. It has managed to translate the usual rhetoric into goals, expectations and strategies based on local reality and has found ways to both attract and enforce attention. This legislation is an excellent example of a top-down/bottom-up design that encourages curriculum design and development at the district and building level, local school-based decision-making and governance, and partnerships with the local community.

KERA calls for instruction in the arts for all children—as separate disciplines and as instruments for general teaching and learning. It also calls for the use of the community's arts and cultural resources. Professional development for in-service teachers is greatly needed, and the professional arts community in Kentucky is working collaboratively with the Kentucky Department of Education, higher education and others to help provide professional and technical assistance to schools and teachers. The challenge is to help teachers feel more comfortable in individual art forms, to learn about the art of instructional integration, and to recognize the importance of respect for and collaboration with school and district arts specialists.

The Kentucky Center for the Arts: Responding to the Needs of the Schools

History and Mission

Under the leadership of then-Chairman Gordon B. Davidson and Executive Director (now President) Marlow Burt, the Kentucky Center for the Arts opened to the public in 1983 and since that time has served the citizens of the commonwealth with a wide stylistic variety of performances, arts education opportunities and outreach programs. KCA has three theaters and five resident groups: Kentucky Opera, Louisville Ballet, the Louisville Orchestra, Louisville Theatrical Association and Stage One: The Louisville Children's Theatre. From its inception, the Kentucky Center has had a strong, institutional dedication to education as illustrated by its mission statement (Figure 3.2).

Figure 3.2: The Mission of the Kentucky Center for the Arts

The mission of the Kentucky Center for the Arts is to create an environment in which the artistic and economic vitality of Kentucky will be enhanced through the development, presentation, and promotion of programs that have a Kentucky, regional or national appeal, while employing the most efficient use of available resources. Specific goals are six-fold:

1. To encourage, support and showcase the performing arts activities of Louisville and Jefferson County arts organizations;

2. To present nationally and internationally prominent arts activities which will attract regional audiences;

3. To address the programmatic needs of the Commonwealth of Kentucky through the presentation of activities of Kentucky arts groups and the development of outreach programs and statewide television and radio broadcast capabilities;

4. **To establish comprehensive programs that strengthen Kentucky's educational system and provide new means of making the wide spectrum of the arts available to Kentucky's youth** [emphasis added];
5. To promote greater artistic diversity; and
6. To provide performance groups, be they national touring companies or small local troupes, with a technically excellent structure in which to operate.

The Center's Education Program

Since 1983, the Kentucky Center for the Arts has served nearly two million students and educators as a major arts education resource. It has demonstrated a serious commitment to arts education for all Kentucky students and teachers through its provision of a comprehensive array of programs and services. The initial program designs were based on a statewide needs assessment conducted by Dr. Patricia Goldberg, the KCA's first director of education, before the facility was opened in 1983.

Current KCA education programs are designed and carried out in the context of the KERA and fall into three categories:

1. Programs designed specifically for students;
2. Programs designed for teachers and administrators; and
3. Outreach programs and services such as bus and ticket subsidy for schools, and technical assistance for community centers

Programs designed for students have included: the Governor's School for the Arts, a highly successful summer residency program for artistically gifted students from across the Commonwealth of Kentucky; the Very Special Arts Festival, an all-day arts event for students with special needs, including mental and physical disabilities; the Outreach Youth Arts Festivals, which have helped to provide arts events for students in the far eastern parts of Kentucky; the Creative Connections demonstration project; and the Western High School partnership, funded by the GE Fund, which allowed KCA to work with this Jefferson County high school to design and establish an ongoing arts program.

Programs designed for teachers and administrators include: the Arts Education Showcases, which are day-long events at eight locations throughout Kentucky where more than a thousand teachers, educators and parents gain firsthand knowledge about arts education programs available to their students; and the Kentucky Institute for Arts in Education, a joint program of the Kentucky Center for the Arts, Eastern Kentucky University, Murray State University and the University of Louisville.

The institutes are two-week professional development summer seminars for small groups of teachers, administrators, parents and others interested in promoting and implementing arts in education.

In addition to subsidizing tickets and transportation, the Kentucky Center collaborates with other arts and cultural institutions around the state and provides consulting services and technical assistance.

Perspectives on Partnerships: A Conversation with Kentucky Center for the Arts' Staff—Marlow Burt, Michael Durham, Deborah Shannon, Susan Knight and Jane Dudney

From my perspective, arts education in Kentucky has never had a better opportunity than at this moment, and that also means a wonderful opportunity for the Kentucky Center for the Arts. KCA has taken on a new challenge as an arts center: It has become an on-site partner with local schools, serving as a resource to them in their efforts to adapt to KERA. The lessons KCA is learning will inform all its other programs. I had an opportunity to discuss this work and its impact on the Kentucky Center with key members of the staff. Participating in this exchange were Marlow Burt, president, Michael Durham, executive vice president, Debbie Shannon, director of education, Susan Knight, director of the Governor's School for the Arts, and Jane Morgan Dudney, Creative Connections coordinator.

Jane Remer: What do you see as the major obstacles to your collaborations or partnerships with schools and districts?

Debbie Shannon: The schools' needs don't always match our resources in intensity, purpose and timing. We will never have a staff large enough to have one-on-one relationships with all the schools in the state, so the question is: How do you build partnerships or provide critical services that can have a ripple effect?

JR: How *do* you?

DS: The Kentucky Center's response has been to continuously try to figure out how to plant the most fertile seeds. Our Arts in Education Showcases are one way. The Governor's School for the Arts (GSA) is very intense, life-changing. It takes many resources; an entire staff is dedicated to that program. We plant seeds in the Kentucky Institute for the Arts in Education—an intensive experience—for up to 120 teachers a year. We have three institutes and a maximum of 40 per institute—probably 75 schools. Some teachers have a profound experience at these institutes. Showcases offer a less intensive experience.

Susan Knight: From our experience at the GSA, partnerships between arts organizations and schools are not significantly different from other kinds of professional partnerships. Key ingredients are common objectives, mutual respect, willingness to share expertise and resources, excellent communications, commitment to planning and honest evaluations.

Marlow Burt: From my point of view, you need to develop values and priorities. Once you get someone who values the arts and values the relationships, the resources can be found.

Michael Durham: You have to learn to listen well because communication and listening are keys to any good partnership. In the Governor's School, we are discovering ways to bridge some of the gaps our audition process creates. We currently audition 1,400 students and take 164. With the process that we had set up—a two-tiered system using a regional and final audition—the vast majority of students didn't have a successful experience. We would go into the schools and say, "Please give us your gifted, your talented..." and then have to reject most of the applicants because of limited space. By listening to the teachers, families and students, we changed our priorities and the allocation of our resources. Rather than spend all those resources on two-tiered auditions, we have spread wider into the state, saving resources and finding new ones, to provide training workshops that prepare the applicants and give them the help they need. We particularly try to help students who wouldn't otherwise have those resources. The obstacles of time, space and distance are still there, but the real obstacle was that we were not listening well enough....

SK: GSA supports the schools by offering advanced training for a small but underserved population of students. Our niche is not large, but the service we provide is significant to the students, to the state and to the schools. Without us, the schools, except those in the more affluent urban areas, cannot possibly address the needs of these students.

JR: The Kentucky Center for the Arts is in a state that has the Kentucky Education Reform Act (KERA), a broad-based and cooperative statewide arts community, and a department of education that supports the legislation and the arts. People from the outside say, "Boy, have those Kentucky folks got it sweet! The mere existence of KERA should insure attention to and acceptance of the arts."

MB: I am not sure KERA has been fully accepted. The whole state has to accept KERA first, and that has not happened yet. Teachers are worried about the assessment.

DS: It was something born out of the political process...

MD: ...and mandated as well. Anything that comes down that path meets with resistance from some quarters, both within the school system and from parents, and then the politicians respond. On the other hand, it has created certain opportunities that we hope will remain. Like any legislation, KERA is far from perfect. Yet with respect to the arts being legislated as part of the curriculum, it does give us more opportunity as long as that is the law.

JR: What effect have Goals 2000, the voluntary national standards and other federal activity had on reinforcing KERA or giving credibility to KERA?

MB: It is a hook to hang your hat on. It allows you to say, "Look at what's happening nationally. What we're doing is in harmony with Goals 2000." Yet the unanswered question is how it translates in the classroom and to the school. For those of us who always hope that something is going to come along that will validate our interests in arts in education, it is a validation of sorts, as is KERA. But the practical challenge is getting it implemented, school by school, and then evaluated.

JR: What are some important lessons you have learned about initiating, developing and sustaining partnerships in Louisville and around the state? Let's assume that we had assembled a group of people interested in forming an arts center. What would you tell them?

MB: I think once you are convinced of the value of running an institution like this, establishing the fact that you are going to have an education program would probably be the first thing to consider. Then there are the practical questions: how do you make the programs work? How do you make sure that education is secure within your agenda? The key is to establish a sense of value that education is important, so that people will give you the resources to do the job. It is a constant process of trying to share with people the importance of the arts in education for young people—or anybody for that matter. It is about good communication—having the passion and developing a communication strategy for a continuing dialogue on behalf of education, on behalf of the students—and trying not to get discouraged. It does become discouraging, at times, but when you see the reaction of the other people who are involved, it becomes joyful. So the lesson is never to give up. Establish an internally shared value that this is the right thing to do and never waver.

JR: Education is prominent in the mission, yes?

MD: The official mission statement is rather long and rambling. We try to condense it and say, "to provide the best programs that complement existing programs, outreach efforts, professional development and programming for the state, and education." Among ourselves, we have said that education will probably be our priority for the next decade—*the* priority. If we change that, there will have to be some very good reasons.

JR: Do you get a fight from your board about education?

MB: No. We are proud of Debbie and Jane and the work they are doing; we are proud of our school relationships; we are proud about busing 100,000 kids a year in the state. Often, when you are running an institution, one side of you is the visionary and the high moral plane on which you want to operate the institution, and the other side is very practical—day-to-day, opportunistic, strategic.

JR: What are the characteristics of a good partnership?

MD: One lesson we have learned about partnerships, not just education partnerships, is that good partners make good partnerships. Consequently, we try to find good partners.

You must make sure you have common goals with a prospective partner. If you don't have the same motivation, a similar vision, the desire to achieve similar objectives, then you don't have enough in common and you are probably not going to succeed. It is common sense, but in cases when we have not identified those common characteristics, the partnerships have not worked. You need that synergy.

JR: How long does it usually take you to find that out?

MD: Our partnerships range from small to very large institutional ventures, and sometimes it takes several years to realize either that it is time to get out or that you have made it. We are always evaluating our partnerships, and we are always looking at various kinds of new partnerships. You cannot always know those things through an analytical process. You have to go out there, try it out, and see if it works. Listening is very important. We need to hear enough to understand what to do to find common ground—what their objectives are, where they are coming from. Otherwise, we are just knocking on the door again and pushing. Some of the best partnerships have been those where they have asked us to come in and help.

SK: It often falls to arts organizations that are committed to education to clearly identify what they can best offer to schools. From that point, it becomes a matching process. All too often, when collaborations do not turn out so well, it is because the needs of the schools and the capabilities of the arts organization were not properly assessed at the beginning. Sometimes arts organizations must take primary responsibility for educating school personnel about how student needs can be met by the arts.

JR: Marlow, as you look back at the education efforts, what would you have done differently?

MB: You would have to go back into the institution's history to understand the frustrations that exist within this organization's financing and the political nature of it. We started on a very difficult footing, because we never had a mandate that everyone in the state accepted. I don't know that we could have done anything differently, but I hope that any other institution approaching this sort of situation now would try to get a more universal agreement that the institution is valuable.

MD: One of the first things Marlow did after arriving in Louisville was to start collaborative education programs with our resident institutions. That worked to a certain degree with some, not so well with others. I don't know how we would have done it, but had we been able to put more resources into that effort from the beginning, we probably would have had a better head of steam by now.

MB: That's right. Since the governor and legislature were involved, we probably should have asked them to tell the state board of education: "You *will* use the KCA as a resource, there *will* be busing subsidies, there *will* be money for the various programs that we offer to teachers and artists around the state, because it affects the whole educational process in the state." When the building was being developed, we should have put into place some of the elements of support that we now require. But we were concerned about bricks and mortar, not programming. When I came, I brought concern about programming *and* bricks and mortar. Hindsight tells me that we should have reordered our priorities: we are not a building, we are a program. We should have put that in right from the start.

JR: I know from my Lincoln Center experience that you always have the tensions between bricks and mortar and programs, and a lot of fussing about turf and territoriality.

MB: In hindsight, our program mission needed a clearer definition. The Governor's School for the Arts started because I was trying to figure out how to kill some time in the summer. I saw a *New York Times* ad for an institute out in Long Island, and I said, "Aha! There it is." Now, it has turned into a great program, thanks to many very good people.

I don't want to take undue credit for this. What I do is recognize ideas and people's abilities to do things, and then say, "Go do it." I can't talk about education programs. Debbie's a wonderful administrator. She has got great ideas, does great things. I trust her, and that is it, "Go do it." The Governor's School was an idea, and I turned it over to someone like Susan Knight who can run it. You put a footprint on the institution and say, "You *will* have education." Then you find good people to do it, give them some resources, and they do good things.

JR: Susan has said she thinks that, because KCA is a presenting organization, it has both the luxury and the opportunity of doing education in a way that is not as easy for producing organizations.

MD: I think that *is* an advantage. It is certainly an advantage over a symphony or a ballet company that has to deal with the overhead of those art forms: they need to find an additional revenue stream to do education. But our advantage is also that we are an arts center with a statewide mission. We have partners of long standing now, people who are good friends around the state and within this immediate community. This puts us in a good position to accomplish things that others cannot.

MB: We do have power, persuasion and influence around the state, in many different ways. We have positioned ourselves well, people want to work with us, they listen to us. Over 12 years of operation, we have created a reputation for quality, sincerity and concern.

JR: So from other people's points of view, if they are looking for partners, KCA is a good place to start...

MB: We have been having an ongoing series of informal meetings with a loose-knit group of presenting institutions from across the state that have arts and education goals. These are institutions that have certain things in common which, by partnering, can accomplish more than they could alone. Some of them appear receptive to the idea of collaboration; others have some genuine concerns. Still, we feel that if we are to be effective in the arts in education over the next ten years, we will need the leverage of those kinds of partnerships to build a statewide network from the roots up. Then collectively we can leverage the support and money we need to get things done on a much larger scale.

JR: Thank you all for your time and for sharing your experience. You have provided some valuable insights into the nature of partnerships for others who may be considering similar ventures.

Creative Connections: Arts Partnerships as a Strategy for School Reform

Introduction[9]

In 1993, the Kentucky Center for the Arts embarked on an innovative demonstration project. Named "Creative Connections," this effort was launched as a partnership between the Kentucky Center, the GE Fund and, initially, a network of three pilot schools. Plans call for the network to grow gradually, with veteran schools acting as mentors for newcomers.

The purpose of Creative Connections is to design a program that demonstrates how the resources of an arts center can be used to help achieve school reform through the arts. Specifically, the project is designed to demonstrate how KCA, its education staff, a group of trained and highly skilled artists, local GE volunteers, and an array of supporting state institutions (including the Kentucky Department of Education and the Kentucky Arts Council), can work collaboratively with the schools to help them build instructional programs that incorporate the arts. KCA hopes that school principals and their site-based governing councils will strengthen internal staff capacity by helping teachers learn how to link Kentucky's arts and cultural resources to KERA goals.

The expected results include improved learning in and through the arts for students; positive attitudes and classroom innovation in and through the arts by teachers; greater parental involvement and advocacy; greater GE and community volunteer involvement in the schools; and a healthier, more vibrant climate and environment. In short, these are many of the acknowledged hallmarks of the "good school," in this case generated or facilitated by the arts.

Creative Connections: An Idea Born of Necessity is Put into Motion

While KERA mandates arts education as strongly as it does reading, math, science and other traditional subjects, most classroom teachers are not equipped to teach the arts as individual disciplines or across the curriculum. Kentucky educators and arts professionals alike have recognized that without quality, sustained professional development opportunities for teachers, many of the goals of KERA would not materialize—in the arts or any other subjects. Creative Connections was conceived as a response to these needs.

Early in 1994, KCA Education Director Debbie Shannon and I worked through a detailed program design and a request for proposal (RFP) that would be distributed to all the elementary schools in the four counties in which the General Electric Corporation has plants or offices. Using my book *Changing Schools Through the Arts* as a reference, drafts of all our work were shared with representatives from the Kentucky Department of Education, the Kentucky Arts Council and GE. We also developed a pre-planning and development time line that stretched from February through September 1994, during which time the design team would:[10]

- research the four districts, contact and involve the state education department and the Kentucky Arts Council;

- design and distribute the application forms to all elementary schools in the four districts;
- search for and hire a new program coordinator (half of whose salary would be paid from grant funds);
- review applications, select candidates for site visits, conduct site visits (a Kentucky Department of Education representative, a Kentucky Arts Council representative, a local principal from the arts council's Basic Arts Program, the local GE liaison, Debbie and I were involved in this process);
- select two schools (we increased the number to three since we had sufficient resources), notify them of acceptance, and set up fall launching and orientation meetings;

The long-range timetable was divided into the periods:

February - August 1994: Pre-planning design and development
September 1994 - February 1995: KCA education staff—planning with schools and districts
March - August 1995: First phase of implementation—selection of artists; evaluation
September 1995 - August 1996: Second phase of implementation—expansion, evaluation and plans for continuation beyond the initial grant period

The main strategies used to meet the program's goals included individual school planning and networking among the three schools. KCA staff and local and regional artists would function as resources to help the schools identify their needs based on the following three main program elements:

1. Professional Development
2. Curriculum Development
3. Parent/Community Involvement

Creative Connections: Linking KERA with Kentucky's Arts Resources

RFP's were sent to district superintendents, curriculum supervisors and principals. The covering letter said, in part:

> Enclosed is an application/information packet for Creative Connections: Linking KERA with Kentucky's Arts Resources, a new education program of the Kentucky Center for the Arts. KERA has established the arts as essential to the education of every child. The Kentucky Center, with the generous support of the

General Electric Fund and General Electric personnel, wants to work with two schools in the commonwealth to design a prototype or model process in which schools design their own programs and curriculum to meet this new and exciting mandate. The KCA will join forces with the Kentucky Arts Council and local and state arts resources to devise ways to help the schools accomplish this purpose. Activities will include professional development, curriculum development, in-school artist services, activities at cultural organizations locally and around the state, and evaluation and documentation....

Creative Connections will focus on two elementary schools selected from the General Electric Plant regions of Lexington, Louisville, Madisonville and Owensboro. This two-year pilot program will emphasize networking and partnerships among the KCA, the districts, the pilot schools and state and local arts resources in the implementation of KERA. The intention of the initiative is to create a "template" or process model that will serve as a demonstration to schools throughout Kentucky....

The RFP contained a program description and an application form:

Program Description and Application

Purpose: To develop a pilot program in two elementary schools in Kentucky to serve as model sites for use of state and local arts resources in the implementation of KERA.

Eligibility: Public elementary schools in the following Kentucky counties: Davies, Hopkins, Fayette and Jefferson

Program Period: July 1994 through August 1996

Application Postmark Deadline: Monday, May 2, 1994

Description: Creative Connections: Linking KERA With Kentucky's Arts Resources will be administered by the Kentucky Center for the Arts. Planning of the specific program elements will be a joint effort of the pilot schools, Kentucky Center for the Arts, and cooperating artists and cultural institutions. The chief strategies for building and extending this program will be networking and collaboration.

Program elements will include:

- Professional development for administrators, teachers and artists
- Development of curriculum and educational materials
- Schoolwide cultural resource planning
- Out-of-school performances
- In-school workshops and performances
- Visits to cultural institutions

- Artist residencies
- Family and community involvement
- Use of local GE volunteers

The school must provide:

- The site-based council, which will serve as the core planning group for this project, with the option of adding additional members to work on this program
- Teacher planning time
- A group of teachers to attend the Kentucky Institute for Arts in Education in the summer of 1995.... Noncredit fee is $135 and does not include lodging. If graduate credit is desired, current tuition at the university is to be paid.
- Funds for implementation of the Cultural Resource Plan. Amount will vary depending on the scope of the plan. The program will provide a base amount in cash, some artist time and possibly some tickets. Additional funds may be needed for buses, artist fees, tickets, etc.

Acting as the hub of the network, the Kentucky Center for the Arts would provide:[11]

- Coordination and facilitation of the network (individual school activities, group meetings and retreats, special events)
- A per capita allocation of program funds available to each school upon submission of appropriate requests and documentation
- On-site technical assistance to the network schools
- Identification, selection and training of artist teachers
- Identification of arts and cultural resources throughout the state
- Opportunities for demonstration schools to participate in KCA education events and workshops
- Publicity and promotion
- Documentation and evaluation services of outside professionals

Additional paragraphs described the deadline for the written application, the selection of finalists from these applications, the on-site interviews, and a notification timetable. The selection criteria included the following.

Preference will be given to schools that have:

- arts specialists
- a site-based council
- a history of using arts resources

- a demonstrated desire for the program
- a commitment of resources to the program
- the willingness and capacity to document the program planning and development process
- the willingness to participate in the project network (retreats, planning, evaluation meetings)
- an ongoing system of program evaluation and student assessment that includes the arts

The two-page application form asked for the school's vital statistics and demographics. It asked about the site-based team and who serves on it. There were questions about the use of arts resources over the past four years. An inquiry was made about the arts specialists employed in the school, the disciplines that they taught, and whether they were full time or part time. Information was sought on how much time each student spends weekly (on average) with arts specialists, by discipline. A key question asked about the amount of new and existing funds that the school could pledge to the program, which could include money already budgeted for teacher release time, buses for field trips, artist residencies or other funds available for cultural resources.

The final page of the application form required answers to defining questions on a separate sheet of paper and dated signatures by the superintendent, the principal, the parent-teacher organization or parent-teacher association (if applicable) and the site-based council. The open-ended questions were:

A. What is your school's educational mission and what is your philosophy about the place of the arts in education?

B. What kinds of arts resources do you currently work with in your schools? Are they local, state, professional, volunteer? What disciplines do they represent?

C. How do you currently evaluate your arts education programs, services and general studies?

D. How are student competencies, progress and accomplishments in the arts recognized on report cards and other school records?

E. Is interdisciplinary teaching and learning happening at your school? If so, what is the role of the arts and the arts specialists in this process?

F. In what way do you envision the Creative Connections initiative building on your current arts education efforts? How does that respond to the needs of your students?

G. List the members of your core team for this project and their current role in your school (e.g., Julie Smith, first-grade teacher and site-based council member; John Jones, parent).

The Current Network: Three Pilot Demonstration Schools

Three schools were selected from different parts of Jefferson County. All schools had subscribed to some form of site-based management, and all had arts specialists in one or more disciplines, either on staff or itinerant. Following is a brief profile of the three schools selected for the first phase of the Creative Connections project.

Fern Creek Elementary is located in southeastern Jefferson County and has a student population of 700. In their application to the program, they described themselves as a "meat and potatoes" school where the arts have been considered a dessert rather than a main course. During 1994-95, they held a two-day staff workshop retreat, engaged artists to conduct workshops for students and parents, and continued in-school professional development workshops for the faculty. Workshops included storytelling, drama, music, songwriting and journal writing, and visual art. During this first year, the school also established an arts resource center for teachers and students. For the 1995-96 school year, they have hired an artist as a part-time (three days a week) cultural resource facilitator. This artist has been hired through the Kentucky Center for the Arts and has a professional background in dance and theater arts and several years' experience as an educator. The cultural resource facilitator will be work-ing directly with teachers to provide workshops for students, assistance in arts planning and professional development opportunities, scheduling field trips and providing information on local cultural resource opportunities.

Martin Luther King, Jr. Elementary is in western Jefferson County and is a visual and performing arts-oriented school. Their 400-plus students come from 27 different zip codes. This wide geographic range represents parents who want to introduce their children to a variety of strong arts experiences. Their goals are to increase teacher capability across the arts and augment parent and community involvement.

During the 1994-95 school year, King held a successful planning re-treat and hosted the artists from the visiting Russian group Perm Puppet Theatre in a day of workshops and cultural exchange with the 150 chil-dren in King's Russian program. They also conducted a theme-based workshop in African dance for the entire school, a one-day residency for percussion and rhythm study for a grade-level team, and after-school work with the Fabulous Leopard Percussionists, a group of about 30 five- to nine-year-old King students whose performing skills had been recognized statewide long before the advent of Creative Connections. The group performed at one of GE's annual board meetings and, according to the GE Fund Program Manager Jane Polin, riveted the crowd's attention. Plans for 1995-96 include a teacher/parent arts workshop, a week-long percussion and rhythm residency that will include instrument-building, an extensive playwriting/drama activity for most of the first semester, and continued planning for the year with KCA. The Creative Connections committee intends to meet once a week to review activity requests and arts opportunities for students and faculty.

Watson Lane Elementary has more than 400 students and is located in the far southern portion of Jefferson County. In their application to the program, they described themselves as a school that is "physically and psychologically" isolated from central Louisville, which contains the majority of arts resources available in the area. The school is organized into teaching teams that use an instructional approach based on Howard Gardner's theory of multiple intelligences. The arts are an integral part of their instructional philosophy, and the faculty views this program as an opportunity to enhance their approach to holistic education.

When Watson Lane began the program in 1994-95, they had already identified curriculum and professional development as their top priorities. Their committee proposed to develop a series of units based on children's literature, incorporating the arts as a teaching method. Four professional artists were hired for spring 1995. The committee worked with these artists to select books for which the artists created lesson plans and prepared lists of materials and other resource information, which was made available to the entire faculty. Teacher participation was 100 percent; artists also conducted workshops for students and teachers based on the selected literature.

For the 1995-96 school year, each of the seven teaching teams has been allocated funds for arts projects, field trips, artists in residence, and project materials that fit in to their projects. The teachers may also apply for modest individual teacher grants, or partnership grants with a teacher from another team, for smaller projects, artist time, transportation and the like. All teams either have a specific plan in place or are working on ideas for arts-integrated, cross-curricular activities.

Network Meetings and Activities

In addition to the kick-off orientation meeting in October, the three demonstration schools have met three times; each meeting is hosted by a network school and attended by the Creative Connections committees. In addition to a tour of the school to see the program in action, the schools share their experiences about retreats, residencies, partnerships and future plans. Discussions focus on ideas to solve common problems and sharing newly-developed approaches to curriculum, instruction, and family and community involvement.

All of the demonstration schools sent teachers to the Louisville Institute for Arts in Education, the two-week professional development seminars in the arts organized by KCA and three universities that take place in Louisville and two other locations around the state. Teachers reported their excitement about discovering the "artist within" as a result of their immersion in music, dance, drama, visual arts and creative writing classes. They also had the opportunity to meet representatives from a number of arts and cultural organizations that offer resources and programs for schools, including: Kentucky Educational Television, the Kentucky Arts Council, Stage One: The Louisville Children's Theatre, the Heritage Consortium (historic homes, museums, river boats), Crane House's China Institute and Kente International, which represents African products, artifacts and culture.

How the Program Works

Creative Connections supports program designs that promote all the arts for all the children in entire schools. Creative Connections is a total school effort. It is not directed at a particular grade level, nor is it is only for the gifted and talented or those with special needs; it is intended to affect all the children in the three schools. These intentions can be honored because, first and foremost, each school has chosen to participate in the program; it has not been commanded to do so by any higher authority. It is also possible because of KERA mandates and statewide arts assessment practices, because the schools have chosen to organize into instructional teams or other configurations that foster flexibility, cooperation and bloc time-sharing, and because each school's schedule and budget is not dictated by the district. Decisions are site-based and can accommodate different community values, leadership styles, and learning needs.

Still, Creative Connections is young, and the schools are just beginning to be aware of the possibilities open to them. The process of change through the arts is generally best when it is thoughtful, incremental and systemic. This process has four basic stages of development: awareness of the arts and the value they have in the instruction and lives of all children; acceptance of this notion and an idea of how to plan for implementation and find the necessary resources (a process that sometimes involves taking three steps forward and two steps back); action—implementation of these plans; and frank evaluation of the results, with mid-course corrections along the way.

John Goodlad has called this process DDAE—a constant round of dialogue, decision-making, action and evaluation, which has been at the heart of his writings on school change and improvement over the years. He and others steeped in the experience and lore of school reform efforts warn that change is difficult, lonely and often thwarted at every turn. Fundamentally, no one really welcomes the prospect of change; it is threatening and conjures all the human fears of the unknown. Because the status quo is so much more familiar and comfortable, successful change efforts take time, patience, sustained leadership, collaboration, a sound plan of action and a solid infrastructure of support.[12]

Creative Connections rests on school-based decision-making for curriculum and instruction. The Creative Connections program has characteristics common to all the schools, but each school chooses the methods for student involvement and determines the kinds of professional and curriculum development activities that are needed. These include: introductory workshops led by artists; single art form, in-depth workshops; artists and teachers working together to develop curriculum; and professional development using the modeling approach (showing and explaining how something is done while you are doing it). Student and parent activities are hands-on and process oriented. Professional development is ongoing.

Absorbing one of the lessons learned from the area high school program, Creative Connections makes the schools responsible for identifying a site-based core planning group that may add members as the program develops. This group learns how to identify and use their local arts resources to serve their students better in meeting the KERA guidelines. Each school chooses one or more focus areas for curriculum development, professional training or parent and community involvement. They develop short- and long-range plans and determine the allocation of time and resources within the faculty. The schools also provide time for teacher planning in the program, participate in retreats and network meetings, send groups of teachers to the Kentucky Institute for Arts in Education each summer, and engage in documentation and evaluation activities. Each school also identifies new and existing funds from its budget for the program.

In Creative Connections, local artists are employed in residencies, professional development workshops, parent/student workshops, and as consultants for curriculum development (which in turn provides professional development opportunities to artists). Artists who work with the program are responsible for providing quality services related to the arts education aspects of the KERA reform effort. The demonstration schools are not looking for one-shot gigs or flashy assembly programs, but for actual hands-on experiences and activities that take learning across the curriculum. The artists are responsible not only for helping teachers and students to make the connections between arts and subjects historically labeled as "academic," but also for teaching in and about the art forms themselves. They are encouraged to seek out and work with school-based arts specialists in order to help build professional capacity and a constituency for the arts within each school.

Many teachers have chosen to work directly with artists to build professional skills. To determine areas in which teachers feel they would like help, a teacher survey revealed interests, skills and abilities and areas where they felt artistic resources would be valuable. The program attempts to build teacher comfort with and capacity in the arts, so that teachers can assume a greater responsibility for the arts in the curriculum of all their students. Teachers take an active role in this process by providing guidance and feedback on curricular suggestions offered by artists and administrators.

All fourth-grade students of the three Creative Connections schools have been surveyed about their interests in the arts. Naturally, they want *everything*. They want to go to more out-of-school performances and have opportunities to perform themselves. They want to dance, sing, write and generally express themselves in new and exciting ways. They are getting these opportunities.

The parents' role is to become advocates for arts education for their children. Typical advocacy activities include having students and teachers demonstrate/perform an arts event for the parents, which shows the "real life" skills necessary to complete the arts tasks. Student/parent workshops help the parents understand the significance of these lessons directly. Parents who are already advocates have been enlisted to help spread the word.

The Kentucky Center for the Arts is responsible for coordinating the program among the schools and for providing access to resources. In Kentucky, the current imperative for individual schools, their principals and their teachers is to create plans for the implementation of KERA. Comprehensive implementation includes the arts, which is where KCA steps in to assist. Through its network of individual artists, arts educators and arts institutions, the Kentucky Center can serve as the "bridge" for these schools, and the Creative Connections program is systematically developing effective approaches to planning this evolutionary interactive process.

Debbie Shannon and Jane Morgan Dudney spend considerable time in the schools providing advice, guidance and technical assistance on instruction, curriculum and parent-community involvement. They also work with each school's committee to provide support for long- and short-range program planning. Instructional units must all relate to the school's arts-in-education focus, to its Creative Connections plan and to the KERA instructional goals—no small feat. Once the schools' site-based committees decide how they want to approach program development possibilities, the KCA staff uses their experience to identify and select talented local artists who can fulfill the school's needs and requirements and also fit into its particular culture and environment.

The financial partnership between the GE Fund, KCA and the three elementary schools is a marriage of business philanthropy, arts dollars and education tax levy and other funds. The GE Fund made a three-year grant of $150,000 to KCA. Schools are responsible for an annual cash match, whose range depends on school enrollment and individual school resources. And in addition to staff support and services, KCA allocates funds from its education budget in direct support of the program.

Project Leadership, Management and Evaluation

Creative Connections is managed day to day by two of the Kentucky Center's four education department staff members: Education Director Debbie Shannon and Coordinator Jane Morgan Dudney. President Marlow Burt provides continuing accessible leadership, advocacy and personal support. Executive Vice President Michael Durham provides planning and program support.

Debbie Shannon spends approximately 25 percent of her time on the Creative Connections Program. She is a certified elementary and special education teacher and a professional arts administrator with prior experience as education director at the Kentucky Arts Council. She has a master of arts in teaching degree in the visual arts and has taught fourth grade and elementary visual arts. Jane Dudney, also a certified teacher, spends approximately 50-60 percent of her time on the program. She spends the balance of her time on the Arts Education Showcases, the Kentucky Institute for Arts in Education and other programs that directly benefit the Creative Connections schools.

Since the partnerships have been established with individual schools and not with a central district administration, the school management and coordination responsibilities are jointly shared by the principal and by a teacher whom the schools choose to act as a site coordinator.

Evaluation

Evaluation is key to the development and implementation of quality programs, and Vonnie Sanford serves as an evaluator on the program. Since 1981, Vonnie has reviewed and evaluated over one-third of the state arts agency education programs for the National Endowment for the Arts. As director of arts education programs for the Ohio Arts Council, Vonnie developed a wide variety of programs and services for pre-K through grade 12 education.

In January 1995, during a presentation to the three schools at a regular networking meeting, she outlined the evaluation processes available, solicited input from the group on the process to date, and set a timeline for the first six months. Baseline data is being collected on teacher, administrator, parent and student attitudes toward the arts. Current teaching practices and schoolwide approaches to arts education are being observed and documented.

Following is Vonnie's description of her approach to evaluation for Creative Connections:

> The evaluation will take a formative/interactive approach to serving the schools, the Kentucky Center, the artists and arts organizations—all those involved in shaping the program. The emphasis is on clarification of program goals, the implementation process, identification of strengths and weaknesses, and development of ways to improve as the program evolves. Regular roundtable discussions with each school's core planning group are already an integral part of the program. This provides participants with time for reflection and creative thought. Additionally, the evaluation will include ongoing observations of schoolwide planning processes: in-school activities, out-of-school performances/visits, professional development opportunities for teachers and artists, and an assessment of how all the components add to the program's total impact.
>
> Other data collection techniques include in-depth interviews with key stakeholders and other identified participants to gather anecdotal observations to help assess changes over time, and focus group meetings of other program participants as needed. Quantitative data will be collected from teachers and administrators through pre- and post-surveys and questionnaires.
>
> Finally, all data will be analyzed and synthesized, and the findings will be presented in a narrative and statistical form that will serve the program and the field. Included will be any problems encoun-

tered, all solutions developed and the lessons learned. Ultimately, the evaluation will define the essential ingredients of a successful partnership.

Anticipated Learner Outcomes

According to KCA education staff and Vonnie Sanford, as a result of the students' experiences in Creative Connections, they will know and be able to perform in varying degrees all of the academic expectations related to the arts in KERA. They will be more conversant with certain art forms and better equipped to face real-life decisions using their newly honed skills in problem solving, creative thinking and group interaction.

Classroom teachers will have a much higher comfort level with the arts, which is the first step in effective teaching in any area. In addition, teachers will have developed stronger respect for the role of the arts in the curriculum, will have learned how to partner with artists and arts specialists in instructional activities, and will have increased their skills in developing arts-related curriculum units.

Arts specialists will continue to serve on Creative Connections school councils, form partnerships with Creative Connections artists and work interactively with classroom teachers in various thematic units and schoolwide projects. Finally, artists will have learned new and more effective ways of working as part of curriculum design teams and how to develop partnerships with arts specialists and teachers in the classroom.

Early Lessons Learned

During a May 1995 visit to KCA, I talked to Debbie Shannon and Jane Dudney about the progress made in Creative Connections during its first year and some of the lessons they have learned. The following excerpts are from our conversation.

Professional and Curriculum Development

Debbie Shannon: We have learned lessons every step of the way this year, and so has each school. We were looking for opportunities to develop curriculum in the arts with them, but they don't yet have the tools to develop *any* curriculum,[13] much less in the arts. So we have changed Creative Connections' definition for curriculum development to "unit development."

Jane Remer: So, rather than scope and sequence over a whole year, you are talking unit by unit?

DS: It could be a short unit or for a semester; the school chooses. That is what teachers know how to do. They haven't been asked to do long-range, comprehensive curriculum development before this. We already have a statewide curriculum framework, but how does that translate into teachers developing curriculums? For 30 years, teachers have been told that curriculum is the state-approved textbook. I called the state department of education and the Jefferson County public schools, asking for resource materials, and they are still working on it. We are asking for something they cannot yet deliver in any subject area, let alone the arts.

Planning and Implementing the First Year of a School Partnership and Network

DS: We have been fairly consistent with the schools about having a schoolwide *program* plan as distinct from an instructional plan, but when we started, we had different definitions of words and concepts. We all needed to clarify what was meant by planning. As an institution, we are accustomed to doing long-range program planning. Schools generally, and teachers in particular, have very little experience in this area; their training for planning has been a *lesson plan* for a full week.

We have now designed an activity planning worksheet for them to fill out before any money is spent. The form asks for the program element addressed, by activity—professional development, curriculum development and/or parent/community support. It requires a description of the activity and its general goal. It also asks: What is the KERA objective? What are the academic expectations to be addressed? What are people's responsibilities, and who does what, when? What is the budget, and who pays for which expenses? We have basically said: "Here's a framework for program planning. Can you work together to complete it? If you need help, call us."

In the next go-round, I would narrow the focus. We should tell the schools what the first year will look like: we have a retreat, and this is what happens at the retreat; here are the people involved; these are the responsibilities.

We didn't do that at first because we didn't want to be too directive; we wanted them to have all kinds of freedom. The problem was that they didn't know what to do with that freedom, so I think I would start with more structure, guidance and technical assistance.

JR: In the first phase of this kind of school partnership—essentially one with major curricular and instructional changes—a definite need exists for a structure, guidelines, and a framework in which to operate. Since KCA initially conceived this partnership, you have had to provide more leadership and more initiative up front. You have had to "jump-start" the process. This particular partnership didn't start with a group of KCA and school people sitting around the table deciding they wanted to work together and then figuring out what, why and how. So the buy-in and a lot of the know-how have had to come later. You have to spend time helping to build professional capacity within the school staff and within the network of schools. That's part of the job of the network hub and of an arts partner who has that kind of expertise and time.

DS: Yes, but the new schools in the next round will benefit from the collective experience of Fern Creek, Watson Lane and Martin Luther King, Jr. KCA can come to the new schools with the three pilot schools and say: "Based on the lessons learned from our experience, here is what we propose to do." So the pilot schools have helped to develop the program during the first year of implementation, if not during the planning year. And they will be instrumental during the succeeding years of expansion.

JR: Of course, partnerships have to start somewhere. We know that the impetus for change can come from outside the school system, within the system, from among willing partners together. It doesn't really matter where you start, as long as these relationships develop trust, parity and collaboration—the characteristics that will ensure good performance and the ability to endure the vicissitudes of politics, economics and the other uncertainties of American educational life.

Jane Dudney: At the last all-school meeting, Martin Luther King, Jr. Principal Mae Kennerly stood up and said, "The best thing we have done to date is to have a retreat." She said, "We didn't think we had time or the need to plan, but we did." Now they are going to add a mini-institute for teachers and parents this summer.

Kentucky Artists, Artist Training and KERA

DS: When the Galef Institute's Collaborative for Elementary Learning staff was recruiting artists to apply for teacher training in their program, artists had to supply written materials showing they had some knowledge about education and how the arts fit in. The DWOK [Different Ways Of Knowing] people were astounded at the quality of our Kentucky artists' applications. The reason is that visionary types have been around over the years—at the department of education, the arts council, the Kentucky Center for the Arts—who have made sure that artists got this information and training. The artists are dedicated not only to their art form but also to arts education.

When KERA came about, it wasn't a new opportunity; the groundwork had been laid for years. One English teacher told me that the arts people were in a lot better shape than the English teachers; the English teachers don't have anybody to root for them. Arts groups are lobbying like crazy all over the state, whereas only one organization lobbies for English teachers. We always think of ourselves as the underdog, but we are really not. Who else has this kind of support system?

JR: Do the department of education, the arts council and the Kentucky Center have a unified approach to artist training?

DS: The department spreads the word, and the arts council has done some training on multiple intelligences (related to the Basic Arts Program). We are all pretty much agreed philosophically. For example, take the Kentucky Arts Council's technical assistance workshops this summer about how the artist should work to fit into KERA. What does KERA mean for artists, what do teachers want from artists now? The old expectations are changing, and more teachers now expect artists to serve as resources rather than 50-minute, isolated enrichments.

The Politics of Power and Money

JR: While each school has invested time and money in the project, KCA has considerable financial influence in this partnership. Tell me about the politics of power and money in Creative Connections.

DS: We have been able to stay the course because we manage the funds. Until we can see that the expenditure will fit into the goals, we won't write the check or contract with the artists. So the answer to the question, "Can we buy X?" is: "Maybe. If X somehow advances professional development, curriculum development or parental support in a plan that makes sense, then you can go buy X."

JR: This raises the issues of roles and functions in the partnership. One partner, KCA, has received funds from the GE Fund for specific purposes, so does KCA have the responsibility to put these conditions on the grant money?

DS: We are accountable to the funders. They are going to wonder why we bought certain items, too. This is not a struggle for control of the money. It is KCA trying to be accountable to a funding source that is investing in an entire process that models school change through the arts within the context of KERA in the state of Kentucky.

JR: I realize you make a lump-sum distribution to each school, but I'm still mulling over the power of the purse-strings issue. I guess it's similar to any partnership in which one partner is responsible for financial matters, but the difference is that presumably both partners have discussed and drawn up the criteria and guidelines together for acceptable and unacceptable expenditures. That hasn't been the case here.

JD: Watson Lane's plan came out of their May 9 committee meeting. Individual teacher grants will be possible once these teachers fill out their activity planning sheets and show us where the idea fits in the grand scheme of things. At Watson, the school requested that Debbie and I decide which grant requests would work. They did not want internal politics to interfere. They knew that for us to choose, it would be based on the quality of the activity and its relationship to the overall plan.

DS: They feel that we know what we are doing; it is our area of expertise. But they *don't* say, "You know what you're doing, give us a plan." It is the same situation when it comes to hiring artists: "You know artists better than we do." It is how we define roles and responsibilities. I think the fit here is just right. We are doing what is appropriate for us, they are doing likewise, and the partnership is evolving.

JR: Do you allocate an equal amount of money for each school?

DS: We base the budget loosely on an internal formula of student population. We then tell the schools about how much we have to spend. The first year each school got somewhere between $6,000 and $10,000; the amount will be doubled the second year.

Assessment
JR: Where is the KERA assessment this year? Remember, Lou DeLuca (director of the Kentucky Council on the Arts) said he expected the assessment to drive the curriculum reform?

DS: They did individual performance assessment in the arts. Much of that is in concert with the national standards. What the assessment has done is to say to people: "The arts are going to count."

JR: Moral of the story: What gets tested gets taught.

New Schools, New Sites: Structure,
Power and School Choice
DS: When we add new schools, we need to think about where we need structure and where the schools can make the choices. We could not have done this at the beginning; we needed experience to find this out. However, now we can say that schools need a planning retreat at the beginning of the year, and here is the reason.

We need to get the network functioning and hook up with the evolving statewide network of presenters. If things go as I anticipate, the presenters' network will be fully functioning by the time we are ready to look for more partners.

Questions for the Future

In fall 1995, I asked Debbie Shannon and Jane Dudney to gaze into their crystal ball and answer some questions about the future that I suspected would be on the mind of the reader.

I was interested in their plans for the continuing participation of current schools, expansion to new sites, and the process for ensuring systemic change. I also wanted to know what modifications they would make in the application process, how they planned to extend the current network and what use they would make of the pilot schools in the expansion process. I was also interested in their time line for expansion, the likelihood of statewide replication, and their prospects for funding. Here is their thoughtful reply:

As a performing arts center, we are very pleased with the lessons we have learned and the major strides made by the three original demonstration sites in the first year of the Creative Connections program. It is crucial to have the opportunity to continue and expand the program into the state to other school systems. In order to accomplish the goal of systemic change in the classroom, the program must be allowed to grow beyond these first pilot sites. Planning takes time, creating a trusting partnership and confident working environment takes time, and building a successful base for plan implementation takes time. The original three schools, having been through this process, will be able to act as a "network" of advisors to new schools upon the expansion of the program.

Trust is the cornerstone of a successful program. In order to compress the time for trust building, we want to work with regional partners in approaching and working with schools. The KCA has a long history of partnerships with local arts councils, performing arts centers and others interested in arts education. The selection of institutional partners will depend on a number of things, and the criteria of the potential funders is something to be considered. In the case of the GE Fund, for example, they support programs in areas where they have plant facilities. In Kentucky that means four specific counties are eligible for possible GE funding.

The details of the program will evolve as we continue to learn from the initial Creative Connections partners. The school teams will be consultants on the design and content of the application form and selection process for the new sites. The criteria for selection in the original application worked well; however, elements of the program, areas of responsibility and financial match would be spelled out in more detail in future applications.

Contingent on funding, we will seek applications in early spring 1996; select sites (probably two schools) in late spring 1996, and require schools to send participants to the Kentucky Institute for Arts in Education that summer. Current Creative Connections schools would be eligible for the second tier of the program. This will involve technical assistance, networking opportunities and matching funds for program implementation. Other elements will be added as the needs arise.

Ideally, the program will receive funds to continue and expand to other schools in partnership with a local arts organization/facility in that region of the state. Program expansion would provide an opportunity for the KCA to assist a partner center in creating a part-time position for an education coordinator who would act as the liaison between the KCA and the new Creative Connections schools. This "seed money" could stand alone or be matched by the partner center to create a full-time position, which would allow that center to work more closely with all the schools in their county, not just the designated Creative Connections sites. In addition to expansion into the state, matching funds would be available to the original Creative Connections schools for continuation of their plans. These schools would serve as advisors to the new schools, sharing their lessons learned, what worked and what didn't.

This scenario is the first phase of continuation and expansion. Once we can establish one partnership in which an arts center in the state focuses on connecting with the schools, other arts centers could follow in the same manner. It is feasible that Creative Connections and programs like it could expand to every county in the state, bringing together educators, artists and cultural organizations in a statewide arts education network.

School Development Through the Arts: The People, the Plan and the Support System

In the early seventies, I had the chance to meet and talk with Dr. Marcus A. Foster, an outstanding school superintendent of the Oakland School District. We were discussing his deep interest in the arts in general education and the likelihood of a partnership with the JDR 3rd Fund modeled on the formal relationship we had by then established with New York City and Minneapolis school districts. After I had described the nature of the plan and the partnerships that were evolving (into the League of [six] Cities for the Arts in Education, as it turned out), he said: "That's it. You've got it. The man (generically), the plan and the support system. The three essentials of a good school development program and a good partnership. Send me more materials, but count me in." Tragically, Foster was gunned down about a month later by local militants, and our partnership never materialized, but I never forgot the slogan. From my perspective, these three essentials—leadership, sound program design and a strong infrastructure—are present in Creative Connections.

The People

Creative Connections has done well in its first year of operation in the three pilot schools. School leadership is epitomized by the principals and the Creative Connections committees. There is vision, dedication to the arts for all their children, imagination and resourcefulness. KCA staff is clear-headed and energetic. In this situation, it is critical that both Debbie and Jane are certified teachers in addition to their strengths in the arts and as administrators. What impresses me is that a staff of three full-time people and a part-time assistant is able to manage and support such a diversity of statewide and local programs and still find the time, energy and clarity of purpose to relate individually to school people, artists and other program participants. It is equally impressive (and unique in my experience) that, in Kentucky, so many arts and education organizations appear to interact, partner and collaborate—very often with KCA at the heart of the ferment or as part of the hub of activity. Creative Connections benefits directly and indirectly from all of the above.

The Plan

The plan, which took about a year to conceptualize and design, appears to be working well. According to Debbie Shannon, it is providing schools with an opportunity to develop and assess a program that is specifically geared to the needs and interests of an individual school. With KERA, the notion of "time on task" (50 minutes of language arts, 50 minutes of social studies, etc.) no longer applies, so the arts must be integrated into the school day. The challenge is to maintain the teaching of the arts and other disciplines and to integrate the arts and arts concepts and process into other subjects.

The schools proceed and progress along these lines at different rates, of course, and in different thematic or structural directions. As KCA notes in a fall 1995 report to the GE Fund, they all appear to be "...working toward the long-term goal of systemic change in the classroom through the use of arts and cultural resources across the curriculum. Planning takes time, creating a trusting partnership and confident working environment takes time and building a successful base for plan implementation takes time. These schools have put in their time."

Thus, individual school development and curriculum reform within the powerful context of KERA are key to the success of this project. So is the interaction of an embryonic statewide Creative Connections network, with KCA acting as the hub. Network meetings are encouraging sharing and professional development among schools, an important strategy for growth. The future plans for sustaining the original demonstration schools, adding to them, using these schools as advisors for new network members, and ultimately decentralizing into local networks throughout the state is structurally and administratively sound. It is also a promising way to increase and intensify the grassroots constituency for and commitment to the arts in education statewide.

The plan incorporates all the elements I believe are essential to survival and growth. It builds professional capacity in educators, administrators and artists; it systematically creates a constituency for the arts; it builds deep roots in appropriate institutions within local communities; and it has made evaluation and dissemination integral to the program design.

The Support System

The support system is manifested in three interactive and interrelated "tiers": the KCA education staff support to the schools; the KCA administrative staff support to the education staff; and the Kentucky arts and cultural community network contribution to a climate and environment favorable to change. This dynamic system builds a kind of force field of security and insurance into the fragile, embryonic pilot period of the Creative Connections project.

The KCA staff, because of its connections locally and statewide, is ever on the alert to match resources to identified school needs. Mae Kennerly, principal of Martin Luther King, Jr. Elementary School, defined the effectiveness of the Creative Connections partnership as follows: "It's not just the 'official' (formal) aspects of the KCA-school partnership that are important; it's the 'unofficial' (informal) aspects that foster communication, trust and collegiality, all of which allow for frequent, casual conversations that often result in instant connections between school needs and arts resources." The conditions necessary for this symbiotic synergy are frequent, open communication, the ability to listen and hear, and the persistence and patience to go through the often difficult getting-to-know-you-and-trust-you stages.

The KCA administrative staff is committed to education as a priority of the institution. President Marlow Burt brings a wealth of experience, sets the tone, and establishes the vision. Executive Vice President Mike Durham, a leader in his own right, works in close concert with the education department staff and provides steady support. Debbie Shannon brings her perspective and energy to the mix. The fact that the education director is senior staff should not be overlooked; it completes the framework for responsibility, authority and support at key administrative levels. The fact that Jane Dudney was hired full-time with matching funds from the GE Fund provides additional concrete evidence of commitment and vision.

The community support is evidenced by two of many examples that point to an increased climate of support for the arts in the schools and to a promising future for the Creative Connections program in Kentucky.

Local Arts Centers. In 1995, KCA held informal meetings for a number of people from around the state who expressed interest in establishing or strengthening their own local arts centers and their education programs. The idea is to form a consortium of these groups so that resources, knowledge and expertise are shared, not competed for. The first meeting was well attended, and chances are good that the consortia may soon be underway. The implications for Creative Connections are huge. KCA envisions expanding the Creative Connections program to sites that have their own local arts centers, so that dependency on KCA resources, especially if geographically remote from the Kentucky Center, will be diminished.

They also envision a number of local school networks, with local centers acting as hubs across the state, all connected functionally to the KCA in a variety of ways. The sound idea of decentralizing and building broad acceptance and local capacity, while continuing the connection to KCA/Louisville, will further ensure the project's firm foundation. The climate for this type of expansion is ripe because the KCA artist showcases take place in eight different locations around the state, and a host of other arts and education resources work hand in glove statewide. And, to boot, they have the motivation of KERA.

Statewide Technical Assistance Workshop on the Arts and School Reform. During the summer of 1995, Executive Director Lou DeLuca and Assistant Director Dennis Horn of the Kentucky Arts Council collaborated with a group of arts and education organizations and individuals, including KCA staff, to conduct a remarkable (and I believe unique) two-day technical assistance workshop at KCA. One hundred and fifty Kentucky artists and arts and cultural organizations interested in education reform attended on a first-come, first-served basis. The workshop was designed to provide information on aspects of the state's education reform efforts that are pertinent to artists and to others who would like to improve their educational programs, materials, presentations and performances.

The agenda included topics such as: Building Bridges (multicultural projects); Arts Assessment; Kentucky's New Arts Content Guidelines and a panel discussing the fine new Kentucky Arts Council handbook, *KERA Opportunities for Artists and Craftspeople.* There were also a series of best practices sessions on thematic, integrated curriculum; learning and doing through the multiple intelligences; classroom models for optimum learning; and folk artists in education. The workshop was funded by the National Endowment for the Arts and a number of other partners and facilitated by experienced members of these partner groups. It delivered on its promise as a valuable experience, and several of the artists who work with Creative Connections attended. This event and others like it will also help to create a better climate for the arts in Kentucky education and provide needed skills and information to local artists. If the workshop expands to include more teachers, and if Creative Connections schools elect to participate, it may also strengthen the instructional impact of the project.

Hopes for the Future

Even at this early stage of development, Creative Connections has all the earmarks of a winner, and because its political, social, educational and cultural context is so rich, I ardently hope that it will escape the fate of so many other promising pilot/model/demonstration projects: to vanish without a trace after the initial pilot phase. If the lessons are heeded about building individual professional capacity, developing a vocal constituency for the arts within the individual schools, and constructing an interlocking network of strong local and vocal community support, then Creative Connections may well break the pattern and survive and thrive—with or *even possibly without* KERA.

At this juncture, KERA is a critical part of and impetus for the program. Should KERA, like other legislation of its kind over the years, be dismantled or should the arts suffer a reversal in the legislation, I hope even more fervidly that the local roots will have grown so deep that the schools' and communities' commitments to the program and its philosophy will live on.

Notes

1. *From Risk to Renewal: Charting a Course for Reform* by the editors of *Education Week* (Editorial Projects in Education, Inc., 1993). Written ten years after the National Commission on Excellence in Education issued its shocking report, *A Nation At Risk*, this book was underwritten by grants from the Pew Charitable Trusts and the Rockefeller Foundation. Project funds were contributed by the John D. and Catherine T. MacArthur Foundation. *A Nation At Risk* declared in martial metaphors that student achievement was in dire straits and that there was a "rising tide of mediocrity" in American schools. This prompted the so-called "back to basics" movement and an emphasis on doing more of the same (that appeared to be failing in the first place). As *From Risk to Renewal* explains:

> By the end of the 1980s, virtually every state had acted to impose the higher standards called for by the commission. Forty-two states had raised high school graduation requirements. Nearly every state had instituted a student-testing program. Three-fourths of high schools reported stricter attendance standards. And 70 percent set academic standards for athletics and extracurricular activities. But all of these efforts, however well-intentioned, have scarcely touched the classroom.

> The purpose of this special report has been to assess what has been learned over the past decade and to examine the key areas of the educational system that must be addressed if real change is to occur.

2. "Taking School Reform Seriously" appeared in the November 1992 issue of *Phi Delta Kappan*, pp. 232 - 238.

3. Jerome J. Hausman, ed., *Arts and the Schools* (New York: McGraw-Hill, 1980).

4. Ibid.

5. This thoughtful booklet was written by Bruce Boston and published in January 1995 with funds from the Coca Cola Foundation. Support for the planning process that produced the document was provided by The Thomas S. Kenan Institute for the Arts, Binney and Smith, Inc., the Music Educators National Conference, the U.S. Department of Education and the National Endowment for the Arts. Coordination and support services were provided by David O'Fallon and Bruce Boston. An abbreviated version supported by the GE Fund has been widely distributed to states and localities.

6. Information in this section is based on text in *Education Reform in Kentucky: A New Beginning* and several brochures and booklets published by the Commonwealth of Kentucky in Frankfort.

7. The material in this section is excerpted with the permission of the Kentucky Department of Education from *Transformations: Kentucky's Curriculum Framework, Volume I.*

8. The introduction to Volume I of *Transformations: Kentucky's Curriculum Framework* offers the assurance that a district's or school's curriculum should reflect local conditions, needs, and beliefs: "It is not mandatory that this curriculum framework be used; however, it does offer assistance as local curricula are designed to meet the state's 6 learning goals and 75 outcomes." The document itself has undergone a transformation since its inception and will continue to change as KERA progresses.

It then asks, "What is curriculum?"

The real curriculum is the one experienced by the student [author's note: as distinct from the one taught by the instructor]. It is, therefore, imperative that a written curriculum be a coherent, organized set of instructional opportunities which focuses on student learning. It must provide rich, engaging experiences connected to real-life situations.

It continues, "What is a curriculum framework?"

A framework presents parameters to assist in the development of curriculum. It is not a curriculum guide nor is it designed to be used as a tool for the delivery of instruction. It can serve as a major resource for the creation of districts' and schools' curricula, instruction, and performance assessments and for professional development.... This document is designed to

- provide direction to local teams of teachers, administrators, media/library specialists, students, parents, and community representatives as they develop curriculum unique to their districts and schools
- effect change by establishing capacity in districts and schools
- provide support as districts and schools plan and initiate activities that undergird the transformation process.

9. Portions of this section are based upon information in Kentucky Center for the Arts descriptive brochures and materials, reports to the GE Fund and a federal grant proposal.

10. In the 1970s, the League of Cities for the Arts in Education, coordinated by the John D. Rockefeller 3rd Fund's Arts in Education Program, developed an elaborate and effective approach to planning and implementing projects of this nature. The League's process model informed the planning of the Kentucky Center for the Art's Creative Connections project. The original design was formulated in New York City and subsequently adapted by Minneapolis, Seattle, Winston-Salem, Little Rock and Hartford, Connecticut, the original members of the League. In the 1980s, after the Fund had closed down, the New Orleans school district used the approach in its Arts Connection program. As coordinator

for the League in my days as associate director of the Fund's Program, I knew and understood the process firsthand. It is described in considerable detail in my book, *Changing Schools Through the Arts: How to Build on the Power of an Idea* (McGraw-Hill, 1982; ACA Books, 1990). This book, now replete with guidelines, criteria, checklists and other workbook tools, was distributed to the Creative Connections demonstration school principals and their staffs for the kick-off orientation meeting. It serves as a planning and reference guide for the project.

11. This section was not included in the original application. It is, however, a critical description of KCA's responsibility as a partner in the joint venture.

12. See the bibliography for useful references on Goodlad's work. See also *Changing Schools Through the Arts: How to Build on the Power of an Idea* (McGraw-Hill, 1982; ACA Books, 1990) for a detailed description of how Goodlad's research-based and validated change theory was wedded to the mission of the John D. Rockefeller 3rd Fund's Arts in Education Program and particularly the schools and districts participating in the League of Cities for the Arts in Education.

13. Curriculum: a *curriculum* consists of specific content to be taught at specific grade or age levels in a specific sequence. (See Note #8.)

CHAPTER 4

Arts Partnerships as a Strategy for Institutional Change

PART I
BEYOND ENRICHMENT: PROGRAMS AND SERVICES ON THE COLLABORATIVE CONTINUUM

Looking at Partnerships on the Collaborative Continuum

The arts can do more than enrich the education of all young people. They can contribute to their intellectual, social and emotional growth and development by providing new languages to speak, read and hear and new lenses through which to filter and refract the bewildering array of experiences in today's world. Partnerships between arts organizations, agencies, artists and schools can facilitate the conditions for this contribution.

In this section, we will take a brief look at the history of arts partnerships, explore an operational definition of the term, and then take a look at the continuum on which these collaborations occur. Finally, we will discuss how you can profitably use this information in your own work.

The Journey Beyond Enrichment: An Historical Perspective

Thirty or forty years ago, most arts organizations that worked with schools sent one or more abridged performances into a school auditorium, or received busloads of students, teachers and chaperones at their institutional venues: a museum, a gallery, a concert hall, a theater, an architectural landmark and so forth. These events were usually 50 minutes long (the length of a typical class period) and were sometimes preceded or followed up by study guides, which were prepared by the arts organization and distributed to the teachers and/or their students. Occasionally, if it was a performing arts event, the artists would engage in question-and-answer sessions or "curtain talks" with the student audiences after the show. Simple evaluation sheets, usually given to teachers, polled audience reactions and asked for suggested program improvements.

In the sixties, in an effort to intensify the arts experience, many organizations began sending an individual artist or groups of artists into the classroom to conduct workshops or demonstrations to augment the auditorium performances and visits to the arts institution. Single classroom visits soon evolved into a series of workshops, and the idea of the "artist in schools" emerged. Artist residencies sprang up all over the country, frequently sponsored by the National Endowment for the Arts, various state and local arts councils, and federal compensatory education programs. Varying in purpose, length, intensity and structure, these programs also varied in the degree to which they relied on collaborative planning, design, implementation, evaluation and funding.

In the seventies and eighties, as the Arts Endowment, the state and local arts councils and other organizations became more familiar with schools and schooling, residencies began to go beyond orientation meetings for participating teachers and administrators, master classes, clinics, student workshops and community performances. They began to add training for artists, occasional professional development opportunities for teachers, leadership training for principals and supervisors, and the development of curriculum materials and other instructional resources. From time to time, depending on the funding source, residencies were professionally documented and evaluated.

In the late eighties and the early nineties, often propelled by the national movement toward education reform, residencies and other in-school programs and services began to feature regular staff and curriculum development by teams of artists and teachers working together. Research and evaluation in the field gradually drew more attention and a few more dollars. In addition, documentation and dissemination of information began to pick up, especially with the advent of the Internet and the World Wide Web.

In another significant development, beginning in the late sixties with efforts by the John D. Rockefeller 3rd Fund's Arts in Education Program and continuing with the Getty Center for Education in the Arts, various programs were launched that promoted the arts both as content and as catalytic vehicles for structural and instructional change. Harvard Project Zero's Arts PROPEL project, and the many programs that have proliferated around the country based on Howard Gardner's theory of multiple intelligences, have begun to address the issues of curriculum design and instructional methodology incorporating the arts. The Kentucky Arts Council's Basic Arts Program is a recent example of this trend and is dealt with in detail in Chapter Six.

In less than 40 years, then, some arts organizations and agencies have moved from being simple service providers to full-fledged institutional partners. Others have moved beyond marketing the arts for audience development or as cultural enrichment to become providers of arts services as an impetus for instructional change and schoolwide reform. Of course, programs such as these exist only in pockets nationwide; they are the exception rather than the norm.

At this point, a word about enrichment is in order. In recent years, these types of events have been dismissed in some quarters as merely passive "arts exposure." This attitude is unfortunate because it overlooks two important points: first, some organizations only have the desire and the capability to provide introductory activities; and second, nothing is inherently wrong with exposure to the arts, provided that it is not a completely isolated event, and that the performance or exhibit is of first quality, skillfully crafted, affectingly delivered, and relevant and appropriate to the age and background of the student population. Of course, exposure is not sufficient by itself, and it is foolish to expect young children, let alone adults, to relate to a completely alien language or form of expression without adequate preparation. Nevertheless, to dismiss the value of encountering an art work is to short change the profoundly human and sometimes magical transactions that occur between an audience and the artistic experience.

Introductory experiences for children, youth and adults can be critical entry points to the arts. Many arts experiences also can stand on their own impressive merits—and there are those who insist they should. They can be instructive in and of themselves, depending on their content and form—lecture-demonstrations are a particularly felicitous and accessible way to be introduced to an art form.

Single performances or visits to galleries are not by themselves broadly educative, especially if they are unmediated. It is the purpose and the educative impact—what is consciously or subconsciously learned and then made available for reflection, extension and application—that best distinguishes the one- or several-shot arts experience from others that are more complex, intensely participatory and sustained over time. The point is, all these experiences are valuable if you look at them, as I do, as part of a developmental continuum.

Defining Partnerships

The *American Heritage Dictionary* defines "partnership" as a "legal contract entered into by two or more persons in which each agrees to furnish a part of the capital and labor for a business enterprise, and by which each shares a fixed proportion of profits and losses." While this is a suitable, albeit commercial, metaphor for many arts partnerships, a second definition is probably more appropriate in spirit: "a relationship between individuals or groups that is characterized by mutual cooperation and responsibility, as for the achievement of a specified goal."[1]

In his report, *Intersections: Community Arts and Education Collaborations*,[2] Craig Dreeszen defines arts partnerships as "the deliberate cooperation of community cultural organizations, school teachers and administrators, local arts agencies, and public and private funders to connect children with arts experiences and instruction in and out of schools."

I find all these definitions useful, but we need to take a step further. When I serve as an evaluator, I generally divide my work into an appraisal of the program design, structure and operation, and an assessment of learner outcomes. The two can be intertwined and synergistic, but arts partnerships without a solid program design rarely result in significant teaching and learning. For similar reasons, I find it expedient to divide partnerships into two broad subcategories: administrative and instructional.

Administrative partnerships are institutional collaborations. They deal with the form, structure and operation of a relationship. They address issues of organization, design, coordination, governance, overall roles and responsibilities, and evaluation of program effectiveness.

Instructional partnerships deal with the design, organization, content and methodology of the curriculum. They are about teaching and learning, and ultimately about the assessment of what the learner intuits, knows and is able to do as a result of engaging in the instructional process.

In reality, the administrative and instructional aspects of partnerships are not isolated phenomena; they are two modes in which the roles and functions of the people engaged in the process frequently overlap. In other words, they are subsets of a larger enterprise. For example, the partners who orchestrate the administrative collaboration may or may not be directly engaged in the instructional collaboration. Furthermore, these partnerships can begin as purely instructional collaborations and later add an administrative dimension, or vice versa. Some examples may help illustrate the point.

In one scenario, the educational partner might be a school and the arts partner a theater company. These partners might begin with an institutional collaboration by designing its purpose, administrative structure and operation. Alternatively, they might begin with an instructional program and then, depending upon the level of success and satisfaction, move to broaden and intensify the relationship by adding the "missing" administrative dimension. In this situation, the partners in each mode are the same.

In another scenario, the partners who design and coordinate the administrative collaboration are different from the players who are active in the instructional mode—they are not engaged in the teaching and learning process. In this situation, the administrative partnership might include a school district acting on behalf of several of its schools, and a state or local arts council acting as the coordinator and umbrella for a group of cooperating arts organizations. In the instructional mode of this collaboration, the education partners might be a group of schools and a university, and the arts partners might be the local symphony and art museum. These are only a few of the many possible combinations for arts-in-education partnerships.

Both the administrative and instructional partnership modes have certain features in common. They depend on people, require flexibility and are labor-intensive, dynamic and interactive. While developmental, their growth patterns do not necessarily follow a logical or predictable path. Both types of collaboration require a period of time to build trust and mutual respect and to define clearly articulated purposes, agreed-upon objectives, a clear notion of the partners' responsibilities, and concrete methods of evaluation and/or assessment.

This book discusses both kinds of partnerships and offers examples. Consequently, I think it will be useful to take a closer look at the anatomy of each so that you can develop a firm grasp of the architecture for these types of relationships.

Administrative Partnerships

In *Intersections*, Dreeszen presents a developmental chart that he titles "Growth of a Partnership."[3] It is shown in Table 4.1, with a few minor additions of my own, with his permission.

In my experience, this process is neither static nor linear once it begins. Most arts partnerships grow in a series of upward-spiraling (and occasionally downward-spiraling) cycles, more like the process John

Goodlad has described with the initials DDAE—dialogue, decision-making, action, evaluation. The cyclical nature allows for constant reevaluation of the course being followed and for any necessary intermediate corrections.

Table: 4.1: Growth of a Partnership

STAGE	KEY FEATURES	KEY TASKS
Get Ready	Get acquainted, build trust	Identify shared problem or opportunity [needs assessment, *my addition*]
Get Set	Plan	Identify leadership [and vision, *my addition*] Develop shared goals Establish structures [Define roles, functions, and responsibilities, *my addition*]
Go	Act	Implement programs
How Are We Doing?	Evaluate	Monitor & Evaluate

Dreeszen describes a Partnership Development Cycle, a six-stage process of partnership evolution from individual transaction to institutional collaboration.[4] He cautions that development is cumulative, all partnerships don't necessarily go from simple to complex, and they don't all go through each stage in the model. For me, his most important caveat is: "Increasingly complex intersections need not imply increasing quality of the arts education experience for individual school children." With the author's permission, I have adapted part of the six-stage process for this book.

The Partnership Development Cycle (abridged)

1. Simple transaction. An artist or an arts organization offers an arts program for a school's students, and a school purchases the arts program. The arts group is a vendor, and the school is a consumer. The school does not participate meaningfully in the design of the arts program, and the program provider does little or no needs assessment or adaptation of the program to the specific school site.

2. Joint venture. This is a more complex interaction. A school and an arts organization work together to define the students' needs and to design the arts education enrichment program. Even if this interaction is only a one-time event, this can be considered a joint venture. A succession of joint ventures may lead to an ongoing collaboration.

The remaining parts of the cycle focus on the development of linkages primarily within the arts community, including information networks, coordinated tasks, ongoing tasks and institutional collaborations. Since they do not directly address the formation of partnerships between schools and arts organizations, I will not go into further detail.[5]

I highly recommend reading *Intersections* from cover to cover to anyone serious about undertaking collaborative work, especially with other arts and community cultural organizations. One of the most useful instruments in the report is a page devoted to evaluating partnerships, because its questions address the key issues of administrative partnerships (Figure 4.1).

Figure 4.1: Assessing Partnerships[6]

1. To what problem or opportunity is the partnership working to respond?
2. Who are the partners?
3. What is the purpose of the partnership; does each partner understand the same purpose?
4. Who has the power and resources that may bear upon the problem?
5. What are each of the partner's self-interests in collaborating?
6. What differences between partners need to be negotiated?
7. How do partners communicate (face-to-face meeting, correspondence, phone calls)?
8. Who exercises leadership? Is the leader acknowledged by the other partners?
9. How are decisions made, i.e., by consensus, vote, by the leader?
10. Who implements decisions?
11. How is fulfillment of agreed-upon tasks monitored?
12. Is there a written agreement?
13. Is there a written budget or financial agreement?
14. Are actions evaluated? (*My addition:* Which ones, how, by whom, when? How are results shared among participants, sponsors and the general public?)

Instructional Partnerships: The Concept of the Beyond Enrichment Continuum

Instructional partnerships consist of activities and components of arts-in-education programs that range from the simple to the complex. I have designed a matrix to illustrate what I define as the six stages of these partnerships on what I call the Beyond Enrichment Continuum (Table 4.2). The number and the complexity of activities increase as you move across the continuum from left to right. The individual components of these stages are all variables, and you should think of the matrix as a checkerboard on which the pieces can be moved at will. The primary "target" population for these programs and services is the students. Secondary populations include teachers (classroom, subject area and specialists), parents, administrators and the general community.

The Beyond Enrichment Continuum attempts to demonstrate graphically how arts organizations, agencies and artists can begin to think about moving beyond enrichment and exposure activities to programs and services that address many of the essential concerns of educators. The first step is to locate where you think you are now; the second step is to locate where you believe you would like to be; and the third step, of course, is to work with your staff and your partners to figure out how to get there.

Theoretically, all programs and services along the spectrum of the continuum can be collaboratively designed and carried out; they can also relate to individual school needs and meet clearly identified instructional goals as defined by the schools and the arts organizations together. In my experience, the more complex the program, the more important it is to pay attention to these concerns. As you move across the continuum, the interactions among people and events are increasingly complex, the intensity of involvement is greater, and the impact of the instructional experience on the student (or adult) learner increases correspondingly. So do the margin for error and communication breakdown.

The more comprehensive the program, then, the greater the likelihood of its ability to help serve the identified instructional, emotional and social needs of the students. But it can do much more. It can address the concerns raised in earlier chapters by Anthony Alvarado, John Goodlad, and Harold "Doc" Howe II. It can help to create a climate of support and acceptance for the arts. It can build the capacity of the local school faculty in incorporating the arts into their curriculums, and build a larger constituency of teachers, administrators and parents for the arts within the school or district. Furthermore, if properly championed by local community leaders and publicized in the media, it can contribute substantially to local school board and other political support for the arts in the schools. These benefits can be doubled if the programs and services of the arts organizations, agencies and artists are perceived as an integral part of a districtwide, or schoolwide long-range plan that includes the arts as basics in the general curriculum. They can be tripled if there is a community development plan for the arts and culture.

Several words of caution: With rising intensity, expect to find a corresponding need for more resources and a greater commitment of time and energy. For those of you starting out either for the first time or on a completely new comprehensive venture with new partners, my advice to you is to think big for the long term but to start small. Starting small can mean launching and monitoring a pilot with all the program components in place in one site or one classroom. Or it can mean beginning with several of the basic components in one or two sites or classrooms and then layering in the other program elements as soon as your ongoing field testing indicates that you are on a steady and even keel. The important point here is to test the waters before moving to full scale; otherwise you and your partners risk being overwhelmed and making the inevitable mistakes from which it may be too difficult or too costly to recover.

A few more words of caution: The Beyond Enrichment Continuum assumes that the more comprehensive the program, the greater the *likelihood* of instructional impact. Do not assume that the continuum implies a guaranteed outcome anymore than intensity assures quality. Nor should it imply a value judgment that simple is acceptable, more is preferred and comprehensive is best. Value judgments can only be made when standards have criteria of excellence and measures of quality attached to them. In my definitions, I often imply criteria but I do not and cannot define what "good" means for you. That is a local decision. You may not agree with either the definitions or the criteria I offer, and I urge you to revise them accordingly or supply your own. In any event, please remember that in many instances, to borrow from Mies van der Rohe, less (of selective high-quality instruction) is definitely more (than a hodgepodge of lesser-quality instruction.)

Table 4.2: The Beyond Enrichment Continuum: Moving Beyond Enrichment
Six Stages of Instructional Partnerships—Find Yourself on the Continuum

Intensity of Instructional Impact	**Exposure, Participation** Simple Transaction: Relatively passive, informal and periodic enrichment experience(s); services are designed and provided by outside arts organization, artist, agency		**Exposure, Participation, Reflection** More Complex Transaction: Mixture of Passive and Participatory Activities	
Nature of Impact	Instruction is transmitted/Lowest Educational Impact		Instruction is transactive/Greater Educational Impact	
Needs, Planning			needs assessment	needs assessment, planning
Mode of Artistic and Instructional Experience	performances, museum exhibits, field trips, etc.	performances museum exhibits, field trips	performances museum exhibits, field trips	performances museum exhibits, field trips
		artist workshops for students	artist workshops for students	artist workshops for students
			residences	residencies
Artist Training				artist training
Professional and Staff Development		orientation for school staff	orientation for school and program staff	orientation for school and program staff
Curriculum Development				
Educational Resource Materials	educational resource materials	educational resource materials	educational resource materials	educational resource materials
Research and Development				
Documentation and Dissemination				
Program Evaluation and Student Assessment	program evaluation usually by arts organization	program evaluation usually by arts organization	program evaluation by partners (and outside consultant)	program evaluation by partners and outside consultant or agency

Lowest Educational Impact -> -

Least Expensive—in terms of resources and commitment ->

Success usually determined by quantity/numbers- ->

© Jane Remer

Exposure, Participation, Reflection, Internalization Comprehensive, Complex & Often Institutionalized Collaborations: Multilayered, interactive, interdependent; programs and services meet mutually defined educational and other social and emotional needs	
Instruction becomes transformative/Highest Impact	
needs assessment, planning	needs assessment, planning
performances, museum exhibits, field trips	performances, museum exhibits, field trips
artist workshops for students, parents	artist-teacher co-taught workshops for students, parents, the community
residencies	residencies (with co-teaching)
artist training	artist training (with teachers)
staff development for teachers	teacher and artist staff development (separately and together)
sequential instruction in an arts discipline; curriculum development by artists and teachers separately	sequential instruction in the arts disciplines; curriculum development by artists and teachers, separately and together
educational resource materials	educational resource materials developed by artists, teachers and curriculum experts
	research and development by outside professionals
documentation & dissemination	documentation, dissemination and diffusion
program evaluation and student assessment (both formative and summative) by partners and outside consultant or agency	program evaluation and student assessment (both formative and summative) by partners and outside consultant or agency

- - - - - - - - - - - - - - - - - -> - - - - - - - - - - - -> - - - - - - - -> **Highest Educational Impact**
- - - -> - - - - - - - - - - - - - - - - - > **Most Expensive—in terms of resources and commitment**
Success determined by quantity *and* quality instructional impact (but "more" is not always "better.")

Some Definitions of Terms

Rather than give you a tedious description of each stage of the continuum, column by column, I will offer some very brief definitions of the terms I use. I believe you can find your way through the diagram, which may be read vertically to identify instructional components and horizontally, from left to right, to trace the range of any given activity's intensity.

Performances include lecture demonstrations; abridged shows; fully staged versions of the classical, contemporary, popular and avant-garde repertory. They can take place in school or in the local community.

Museum Exhibits include blockbuster and small gallery showings in museums, galleries, artists' studios, storefronts and other alternative spaces of any of the visual, media and design arts.

Artist Workshops include one or more workshops for students (on one or more grade levels, the entire school, or selected according to interest or ability); can take place in or outside of school; can include study of an art form(s), study about an art form, study that connects the art form to other arts or academic disciplines, or the study of aesthetics, arts history and arts criticism; can consist of formal instruction or be improvisatory, creative, interpretive; can be theme or topic driven, curriculum driven, performance or artifact driven. Parents and the community may participate.

Residencies include master classes, performances, workshops, clinics and special social events for the community; they can range in duration from ten days to as long as a year and in participation from four or five classes to an entire school; parents and the community always participate.

Artist Training ranges from informal and occasional information-sharing sessions for artists to a year-long series of rigorous, formal staff development courses focusing on schools, schooling, education, curriculum, instruction, recent research and pedagogy, and all the elements of the art forms; may occur with artists alone or with artists and teachers (classroom, subject area and specialists) together.

Orientation, Staff Development ranges from simple project-wide meetings or conferences intended to cover "nuts and bolts" and introduce the "players," to year-long workshops or courses of study in individual art forms, interdisciplinary teaching and learning through the arts, multicultural and multi-arts instruction across the curriculum, and aesthetics, history and criticism; can include analytical encounters and reflection, creative, improvisatory and performance-based experiences.

Curriculum Development includes the development of simple lesson plans, more extensive units, courses of studies, and in rare instances a full curriculum (with scope and sequence across grade levels); can be developed by teachers (classroom, subject area and specialists) and artists working separately and together, assisted by professionals in the field.

Educational Resource Materials range from simple, single-sheet "playbill" information about the artist and the artwork to complex manuals, guides, workbooks and the like for students, teachers (classroom, subject area and specialists) and parents; can be designed by artists, teachers and curriculum specialists.

Research and Development generally is conducted by outside education professionals and related directly to investigation of certain aspects of the instructional and other goals and hypotheses implicit in the program design; can also be teacher designed and directed, with outside guidance and technical support (action research).

Documentation, Dissemination and Diffusion range from simple logs and "portfolio style" collections of program proposals, correspondence and instructional materials to sophisticated narrative accounts and case studies of program planning, design, implementation and evaluation; may be written by program staff and participants or an outside professional; may be published locally and informally, or more formally for distribution to a wide audience (participants, sponsors, community, the field, scholarly journals, press and the media); depending on research and evaluation results, may be "diffused"—transported to other locales for adaptation or replication through a combination of print, media and on-site technical assistance. Note: These activities can occur in both administrative and instructional partnerships.

Program Evaluation and Student Assessment can be undertaken by staff and participants using simple instruments, portfolios, questionnaires, some paper and pencil tests, interviews, focus groups and the like; an outside professional or team may use a similar or a much more sophisticated and rigorous approach, which should be closely coordinated with the research effort, if one is in place.

The term evaluation is generally used in connection with efforts to determine how well the program design, structure, management and operation worked to accomplish its stated aims. The term assessment is generally used in connection with student progress, achievement or competency. If resources are not a problem, you should conduct both a program evaluation and a student assessment; the former provides a context for the latter and enriches the portrayal of what learners know and are able to do.

Arts organizations have tended to make too many unrealistic claims for both their arts programs and their impact on students. Over-claiming is dangerous and ultimately self-defeating when there is no convincing evidence to substantiate the assertions. It is wiser to focus the goals and limit objectives narrowly, always in consultation with school partners regardless of where you are along the continuum.

Where Do You Fit on the Continuum?: How to Use this Information

While I consider the Beyond Enrichment Continuum a work in progress, I have designed it as a tool for your use for several reasons:

- to make the point that there are both less *and* more effective ways of serving the learning needs of young people, but that *all* ways on this continuum can be valid and reliable encounters with the arts;
- to emphasize that the more comprehensive and educative a program becomes, the more attention and resources it is likely to demand from you and your organization;
- to give you an opportunity to study the spectrum and see where you believe you are now and where you ultimately want to be;
- to urge you to analyze, discuss and, if you wish, completely redo the matrix to suit your own art form and your institutional or individual purposes; and
- to use it, in its current form or as you revise it, as a conceptual framework when reading about other programs in this book and elsewhere; it should also serve as a good planning tool for discussion among your peers, within your organization and with your education partners.

Arts Partnerships and Institutional Change

Comprehensive arts partnerships can result in significant change within an arts organization or an arts agency once the organization makes a serious commitment of time, energy and money to the enterprise. When education becomes an important item on the institutional agenda, priorities must be re-examined, existing resources reallocated and new resources identified. Often the entire structure and organization undergoes change to accommodate the new focus. Similarly, once schools make a serious commitment to the arts as part of the basic education of all their students, they too must re-examine their priorities, their structure and their scheduling to reflect the new philosophy. The more comprehensive the partnership, the more likely it is to affect the partners' usual way of doing business. These changes can prove to be unsettling as well as salutary.

Most of the discussion and examples offered in the essays that follow in this chapter deal with how to prepare for and establish administrative partnerships with schools based on the contributors' own experiences. In the case study about ArtsConnection that follows, and in the pieces by Arnold Aprill, Richard Bell, Joan Boyett, Mindy Garfinkel, and Mark Schubart, you will see vivid examples of local, regional and national programs that have had varying degrees of impact on both the arts institutions and the schools with which they work. You might want to use the Beyond Enrichment Continuum as you move about and through the book to test my hypothesis that, under certain conditions, more comprehensive programs result in greater institutional as well as instructional change. You also might want to notice what those conditions are from site to site and compare them to your own situation. The results should be useful to those of you interested in designing new initiatives or evaluating those that are ongoing.

Institutional Transformations
ArtsConnection's Journey from Service Provider to Instructional Partner

For the past 16 years, ArtsConnection, a private nonprofit organization dedicated exclusively to the arts in education, has worked to link children's learning needs with the cultural riches of New York City. It offers an informative example of how one institution is finding ways to move across the Beyond Enrichment Continuum from a service deliverer of arts exposure programs to a full-fledged partner in comprehensive arts-in-education initiatives. To accomplish this institutional transformation, ArtsConnection has come to realize that it must focus on the instructional infrastructure of professional staff and curriculum development, artist training, and research and evaluation. In the process, it is deepening and broadening its educational impact on the education community that it serves and intensifying the effectiveness of its advocacy efforts within the larger New York City community.

Each year, ArtsConnection's programs reach nearly 200,000 children in 100 of the city's schools. The numbers sound high until you realize that the city has more than a million students, some 60,000 teachers and more than 1,000 school buildings. ArtsConnection works throughout the city's five boroughs and maintains a diverse roster of more than 60 professional artist groups who present performances, lecture-demonstrations, workshops and residencies in the performing, visual, literary and media arts. These events represent many styles, genres, cultures and sensibilities. Artists are selected by a rigorous peer audition process and participate in training to learn about the culture of the schools, child development, curriculum design and instructional approaches.

ArtsConnection recently moved into the Jacqueline Kennedy Onassis High School for International Careers, a newly renovated building in midtown Manhattan, where it has established an ArtsConnection Center for performances and other participatory events throughout the year for school children and their families. In an unusual partnership with the New York City Board of Education, ArtsConnection maintains its administrative offices in the school and shares performance and classroom space for Center activities. In addition to the central Board of Education, 16 community school districts and five high school superintendents, ArtsConnection has formed partnerships with city and state agencies, including New York City's Department of Cultural Affairs and Division of Youth Services, and New York State's Division for Youth and Council on the Arts.

From Arts Provider to Arts Partner

ArtsConnection has occasionally revisited its mission statement and gone through several periods of restructuring and realignment. It has rethought the distribution of its resources and the qualifications and deployment of its program staff. It uses consultants in the arts and education to supply special expertise that may not exist within its diverse and highly gifted staff. Interestingly, the organization monitors its growth, tracks its development and consistently attempts to understand, apply and build on the institutional and programmatic lessons it learns. It is able to take these institutionally organic and developmental steps largely because of its leadership. Executive Director Steven Tennen is a tireless and committed worker with crystal clear vision and extensive arts and administrative experience, and the board, led by one of the local champions of change, Linda LeRoy Janklow, is professionally active, vocal and supportive.

In its early years, ArtsConnection developed a wide-ranging arts exposure program of workshops, performances and lecture-demonstrations in the performing and visual arts. Over the years and in response to the changing needs of the schools, the organization began to work with several districts and schools to develop programs and services of greater depth and dimension. Helped significantly by two National Endowment for the Arts Challenge Grants and two substantial U.S. Department of Education Jacob Javits Gifted and Talented Program Grants, ArtsConnection developed local initiatives that demonstrate how the arts can address a school's goals for all students and how the impact of an arts program can begin to spread throughout a school. These initiatives have included staff and curriculum development and an extensive research and evaluation component. They also have encouraged family involvement as participants and advocates for the arts in the schools.

The Young Talent Program, A.K.A. Talent Beyond Words and New Horizons

ArtsConnection's voyage across the continuum from a service provider to a full educational partner has been driven by the work of its Young Talent Program, one of the more valuable crucibles in its program development laboratory. The Young Talent Program initially offered dance classes in the schools and in various professional studios around the community to at-risk students who had been identified by ArtsConnection faculty after a one-day, in-school audition. The program's goal is to identify and develop the artistic talents of students and to help students use those talents to succeed in school and other areas of their lives. The Young Talent Program has always been guided by a populist and profoundly democratic philosophy: all children, including those considered "at-risk," have talents, and some of those talents are in the arts. A core premise of the program is that identifying potentially gifted students in dance, music and theater (whether or not they plan to become professionals) and nurturing their promise is sound educational practice.

The Young Talent Program, through nontraditional training and development in the various art forms, serves children who might otherwise have been written off. In fact, most of the students in the program are low-achievers in the standard curriculum and usually overlooked for programs of this nature. Teachers help to design and execute the entire program along with a host of ancillary services. Indeed, since many of the program's practices have broad application, teachers can apply what they learn in the staff and curriculum development components to *all* their students, in *all* their classes.

The program uses an innovative audition process to identify students. Under the creative leadership of Director of In-School Programs Barry Oreck, ArtsConnection has produced an extended talent identification and development process in dance, music and theater. This process relies on a series of weekly training workshops in the art form, auditions that take place over several weeks, a selection team of professional artists and the students' classroom teachers, and a sophisticated research and evaluation component directed by consultant Dr. Susan Baum. Additional program elements include regular dance training in professional studios, the tutoring and counseling of students in academic studies, family involvement in workshops and performances, and, during the last five years, a professional development and curriculum component.

The theoretical basis for the program includes the work of Drs. Joseph Renzulli and Howard Gardner. The Renzulli "triad" model of giftedness includes youngsters who exhibit a promising combination of above-average ability (not just the top one or two percent), task commitment and creativity. Gardner's theory advances the concept of multiple intelligences—seven different ways of knowing and comprehending the world—which include linguistic, spatial, mathematical/logical, bodily-kinesthetic, musical, interpersonal (understanding other people) and intrapersonal (understanding yourself).

In addition to these theories, the Young Talent Program embraces the idea of "self-regulation" and the notion of "arts processes." Self-regulation can be defined as an awareness of the behaviors that make us successful, such as good work habits and study skills, paying attention, persevering, problem solving, taking initiative, asking good questions, taking risks, cooperating, using feedback, and being prepared. ArtsConnection believes that study in and through the arts helps to cultivate and reinforce these skills, especially if arts-integrated curriculum is designed to emphasize them. ArtsConnection defines arts processes as basic skills in an arts discipline, improvisation, exploration of movement elements, playing and creating music, dramatization and group performance.

ArtsConnection's work in the Young Talent Program has far-reaching implications for all of its work. It extends the traditional narrow definition of intellectual giftedness and talent to apply to teaching and learning for all children. Their research indicates that teachers involved in this program have learned how to identify arts talent and potential in the "most unlikely" children. They are also learning how to connect all this abstract learning theory with the elusive fundamentals of the arts process and translate it into classroom practice. This helps teachers to deepen and expand their teaching repertoire and improve their ability to uncover, recognize and honor the special gifts and abilities of all of their students. Elements of the program design, especially those that include teachers observing their students engaged in the arts and developing new curriculum approaches, are being introduced in all ArtsConnection's in-school programs.

Zeroing In: Curriculum Development, Professional Training, Research and Evaluation

When writing about the arts in education, I believe it is useful to take the reader on a "visit" to a program—to get a sense of its dynamic and to listen to the voices of those closest to the action—so that we may learn more concretely from their experience. Following is a slice of life from ArtsConnection's Performing Arts Institute for Teachers, some thoughts from its staff and some reflections from one of its outstanding veteran teaching artists. We will focus on those elements that distinguish programs on the intensive end of the Beyond Enrichment Continuum—curriculum and staff development, research and evaluation—and on the lessons learned. Keep in mind that these elements are helping ArtsConnection to build professional capacity in its own institution and in the schools and to create a broader constituency for the arts within the schools and the community.

ArtsConnection's Performing Arts Institute for Teachers

The Schedule

It is August 28, 1995, the first day of ArtsConnection's Summer Performing Arts Institute for Teachers. As part of the original research and evaluation team, I have come for the "opening ceremonies." A quick look at the schedule reveals that this summer's institute runs four-and-a-half days, Monday to Friday, from 9 a.m. to 4 p.m in the theater and on the second and third floor of the Jacqueline Kennedy Onassis High School. School begins next week, so no kids are around, just a few teachers and administrators setting up.

Every day begins with coffee and continues with arts classes in dance, music, theater and an educational seminar. The instructors and topics for the week's seminars include: Barry Oreck and the teaching team on context and background; Susan Baum on learning styles; Kelly Hayes and Jessica Nicoll on discovery learning and transference; and Barry on talent identification in dance, music and theater. After a lunch break, two hours are devoted to curriculum-development projects and then a half-hour wrap-up. The final half day includes the arts classes, a curriculum-sharing activity, a culminating activity, and evaluation and wrap-up.

It is wonderful to see veteran and new teachers in attendance from the Young Talent Program and from other schools around the city. It is also good to see, for the first time, a mix of ArtsConnection staff, educational and research consultants, and the teaching/performing artists involved in the program. Everyone has an assigned role to play throughout the institute, and cross-fertilization and on-the-job professional development and training will undoubtedly occur as planned. Curriculum and instructional goals are clear; the process is laid out logically. The air is filled with anticipation.

For the first time, the institute will focus on building the instructional capacity of the teachers and the artists to work together, to develop arts-related curriculum and to assist in the construction of lesson plans for research purposes. Both teachers and artists will have opportunities to switch roles as instructors, as learners and as resources and facilitators. The arts classes will go beyond immersion in creative experiences for the teachers; they will provide each teacher with ample opportunity to develop his or her own dance, music or theater activities, lead them, ask for feedback on what did or didn't work, and get input and concrete suggestions from their peers and the artists. All teachers are expected to teach their arts activities in their own schools and to report back to ArtsConnection about the results. A large table is full of resource materials on teaching and learning in all the arts disciplines. There is enough handout material to fill a briefcase.

The institute is off to a good start. I return several times during the week to observe.

Quick Takes, Questions, Concerns and Satisfaction

- I watch a video of a science lesson on filtering water; as part of a demonstration of the hypothesis, students use movement to show how water molecules behave when frozen, at room temperature or hot. It probably makes the point about filtration, but I am concerned about the "dance." Where has it come from, where is it going, will "the dance" be developed? Using movement to vividly illustrate scientific principles is fine if there is parity and if the movement has integrity. I listen to the teachers and artists discussing the process. I talk with Jessica Nicoll, the dance instructor. She recognizes some of my concerns, but she also is delighted to see the imaginative use of dance to create dramatically new learning opportunities for the students. It is better than rote learning or dull workbook exercises, she insists.

- Jessica teaches everyone the difference between swinging and swaying. She adapts it to principles of physics. She explains how she has constructed the lesson: you present it; you explore (play with) the concept using different formations and group arrangements; and then you shape it into a swing and sway dance. She models the model and uses teacher volunteers to demonstrate the process. Kelly's guided group discussion indicates that the lesson was learned and absorbed. I see the principles translated into action by the teachers later in the week.

- The ArtsConnectors, teachers who have volunteered to participate in the research component, meet with the education consultants and the teaching artists. They work together to construct lessons that are "intended to elicit a variety of behaviors and intelligences and use processes that encourage active involvement and allow different individual strengths and learning styles to emerge." These lessons are constructed on printed forms with accompanying prompt sheets listing the self-regulatory behaviors, the Gardner intelligences and the arts processes. The teacher must create a scoring rubric for each lesson that assesses the student's achievement. Each student will have many ways to demonstrate what has been learned from each lesson. During the institute, each teacher will have the opportunity to simulate the lesson's arts process section to get feedback and to make modifications as necessary.

One teacher graciously lets me study his lessons about mapping, hemispheres, datelines, latitude and longitude, continents and oceans. Movement, dramatic and visual arts activities are woven effectively into his lessons. The teacher will have worked with his students in the various art forms to prepare them for these lessons. He feels more comfortable this year with some of the fundamentals in these art forms. I keep wishing a way could be found to integrate the few art and music specialists that still exist in these schools into the program and the institute. The chance to build that professional constituency within the school is tantalizing, and I know there are plans for these classroom teachers to act as "turnkeys" (sharers) of their information when they get back to school. I just wish it were more formalized.

- I watch Jessica Nicoll and Judith Samuel's dance class on Friday morning. A teacher is leading a sequenced series of very interesting movement exercises. The group settles down to discuss the process and the result. The teacher asks what she should do when parents talk, babies cry and other disturbances occur during a student performance. She says she has been trying, with some success, to teach her students how to behave at performances, and she is concerned that the parents' behavior (talking, laughing, making a fuss about the babies) contradicts and defeats her efforts. The answers fly thick and fast from the other teachers, the artists and the observers: "Get the parents involved as an audience by doing a simple, arm gesture sequence; students should make announcements before the show about expected audience behavior (in several languages); students might serve as ushers, 'policing the aisles' and 'reminding parents about appropriate audience behavior.'" Everyone agrees that assigning each student to teach an audience behavior lesson to his or her parents or care givers the night before the performance would be very effective.

- It is the final sharing session, and Linda Patterson-Weston, the administrator for curriculum initiatives (with primary responsibility for arts and cultural education), has been visiting from the New York City Board of Education. The group has been discussing some of the new teaching strategies they discovered during the week that they believe will help them transform learning and classroom practice. Asked if she would like to say a few words, Patterson-Weston rises and says, spontaneously:

> You are among the most important people in the system. Go back, educate your faculty and your administration. They think the arts are crayons and pencils; they have no concept of teaching in and through the arts. To "get it," they need to see the teaching strategies, to see changed behavior in our students. We need the support of all the teachers and the administrators in our schools.... You are the empowered population. I'm new; I just got a seat at the table; you are *my* source of power. It's your game; I'll learn the rules. We're going to win!

She gets a rousing ovation, naturally. The timing, of course, is perfect.

Serendipity strikes again.

Program Perspectives and Some Lessons Learned

To provide another dimension to this discussion, I asked Steven Tennen, Deputy Director for Programs Joanne Bernstein-Cohen, Barry Oreck and Jessica Nicoll for their thoughts and reflections on the institute and its ramifications for them, professionally, and for ArtsConnection as an institution.

Jane Remer: Jessica, can you give us some of your thoughts on the institute—the process, the problems and the prospects—from your perspective as a dance artist, a curriculum writer and a program documenter?

Jessica Nicoll: We began five years ago by asking teachers to immerse themselves in an artistic process. The question always loomed: What has this to do with our classrooms and our curriculum? For me, there was no doubt; an artistic process is a process of learning. Making and perceiving art cannot help but take a person deeper into their thinking, feeling and knowing selves. But this was too abstract. Ultimately we would have to translate this seemingly ephemeral artistic perspective into concrete strategies for teachers to teach. We couldn't, however, rush into that translation. We needed them to speak the language of the arts first. They created music and dance, improvised with the elements of rhythm, space, force and meaning within themselves. Watching each other, discussing their observations and experiences, the teachers developed a serious and articulate understanding of the artistic process.

The teachers in those first workshops astounded us with their sophisticated creations and perceptions. We asked them to take their skills back to the classroom to lead their students' artistic explorations. But we hadn't helped them find the tools to lead, only the tools to create. Some fell into frustratingly deep water trying to make *a dance, a song, a show*. They could see the value of the arts for themselves and for their students, but they were uncertain how to integrate an arts process with the demands of the school day.

We embarked on the next step: getting teachers to lead. They would need technical skills and confidence (how to set up a room, count off, jump in without a verbal introduction) that could only be gained by directing an activity themselves. This required the artists to give up control. We had to learn not to do it all for them; we had to help them guide student-motivated discovery rather than be the "one with the answers"; we had to give them a safe environment in which to try, to fail, to try again, and to succeed. In short, we had to model what we wanted them to do in their classrooms.

However, before teachers could use arts processes in their classrooms, they had to connect to their primary role: to teach the curriculum. As fully as they had embraced the arts activities led by artists, many still questioned the connection between the arts and their roles as teachers. One link was clearly curriculum connections: specifically, what can an arts process teach students about an academic subject? Artists and teachers together began to integrate the two. Curriculum, rather than being an end, became a beginning, a source of ideas to investigate and to explore.

Using the artistic process only as a means to learn curriculum could not, however, be the sole link in education. The second link was to encourage teachers to see the arts process as a way of learning. All arts processes require the learner to take an active role, to discover—rather than replicate—the answers (of which there may be more than one), and to find new questions in an atmosphere of spontaneity and trust. Putting creative explorations in the curriculum had gotten students moving, singing, exploring—thinking in new ways. We asked teachers to help students expand and develop those explorations into satisfying artistic experiences, to look with their students at the art they'd created and ask, "What do you see? How have we shaped it? What does it mean to you?"

JR: What are some of the lessons you have learned from this process?

JN: The first is about changing relationships, switching roles. The walls between artist as teacher and classroom teacher as student come down. In this institute, everyone is a learner at different moments. At times every day, each participant jumps out of his or her accustomed element and is asked to discover something new. We are bound together by the process—all learners, improvisors, discoverers, together.

Then there is the time paradox: "You can't run the third mile first." There is never enough time. We barely touch upon each idea—each layer that seems critical to the whole—and we must move on to the next. Yet it is the accumulated time, the years of working with these teachers, that has brought us all to the third mile. For example, improvisation—a key element in all three of our artistic disciplines—depends on spontaneity, following instincts and not "thinking" for too long. Yet developing the skills to improvise takes time—to explore, to observe, to respond and to cultivate. The time paradox: It takes time to be quick.

Finally, we have learned about the transformation process of teaching and learning. I use the one that Mary Joyce lays out[7]: (1) Present the idea. (2) Explore its possibilities. (3) Give it form. "Present, explore, form" is an artistic process, but I have found that it is also a process for all teaching and learning: scientific discovery, historical research, language arts, visual arts.... I think about the companion process most often used for the standard teaching of curriculum: (1) Present the idea. (2) Present it again, in test form. (3) Have students present the same idea back. I have seen the traditional process begin to change in the classrooms we work in. Our approach is full of promise.

JR: Barry, would you trace the origins and development of the institute, beginning with the Talent Beyond Words incarnation of the Young Talent Program?

Barry Oreck: As you know, the goal of the Young Talent Program is to identify and develop the artistic talents of students and to help students use those talents to succeed in school and other areas of their lives. We have seen many cases of students who have used their learning, communication and social skills, along with the discipline and task commitment developed in the arts, to improve their performance in school. Unfortunately, we found that this transfer was difficult and in many cases impossible without the involvement and cooperation of the classroom teacher. In order for students to use their artistic talents and interests in the classroom, the teacher has to recognize and appreciate these phenomena and allow the child to utilize their strengths to learn and communicate what they know.

The first step in this process was to involve the teacher directly in identifying the talents of their students. This required us to find criteria for a definition of talent that would be understandable and valid both to experts and novices. We also had to create a multi-session process that would allow for demonstration of a wide range of abilities and also allow time for the teachers and artists to meet and discuss the backgrounds and performances of the students. We began our staff development process with ten teachers from two schools in 1990 based on this talent identification model. Our research showed that after just four classes, teachers were able to recognize the talents of their students with the same ability as our artists. Over the next three years we expanded this training to include more than 75 teachers from ten schools in dance and music. We have now added a component in theater.

Once teachers were able to identify talented children, they told us they needed the tools to help students use these special abilities in other academic areas. This presented all of us with a much more difficult challenge. We organized after-school and Saturday workshops and week-long summer institutes from 1990-92 in which teachers had many opportunities to develop their own performing arts skills. They demonstrated tremendous creativity, a willingness to take risks and a strong desire to make their classrooms more active and artistic places. Observations showed, however, that little changed in the classroom. We found that it is a huge step from being an enthusiastic participant to feeling comfortable as a leader of arts activities. It was clear that many of the teachers had raised their opinion and expectations of students based on their artistic abilities, but at the same time, they lacked the experience or confidence to include movement, music or theater activities in the classroom.

The next phase of our staff development program began with our second Jacob Javits Gifted and Talented Program Grant in 1993. This project focuses specifically on teaching methods and support structures that can help students improve their performance in school. We are seeking to help teachers transform their classrooms into more active and inviting places so that artistically talented students—and most importantly, all students—can use their diverse strengths and "intelligences," as Gardner defines them, to succeed. This process involves many of the teachers who have attended all stages of the training as well as others who have just joined us in the past year.

Our current training model has two parts. First, and most critically, teachers need to learn specific techniques and methods for conducting classes on arts processes. We have repeatedly found that if the artistic element is short changed or poorly directed, then the students will not have a satisfying experience; in fact, all of the teacher's fears of creating chaos may quickly be realized. Without a safe atmosphere, a clear structure, and time for real discovery to take place, the process will neither inspire learning nor be satisfying or fun for the students. In the workshops, teachers work with artist mentors to try out their ideas, lead a variety of activities and get direct feedback on their attempts before they work with their own students. Ongoing mentoring and observation by professional artists and educators follows in the classroom. Teachers and artists also have the opportunity to co-teach and collaborate on arts-based curriculum projects.

The second part of the process is the adaptation of academic curricula and the transformation of the classroom to include arts activities. The teachers have discovered that not all arts activities and subject matter make a good match. They need to find learning objectives that call for discovery, higher-order thinking and problem solving to use the arts effectively. Learning facts or memorization, for instance, may be better taught through written work sheets or verbal drill. They also have found that they cannot spring arts activities on the students without adequate preparation and physical changes in the classroom. Our curriculum work includes designing learning objectives, preparatory activities, full lesson descriptions, support materials and space requirements, and assessment plans in all the major subject areas integrating movement, music and theater activities. The program's research component is studying the effectiveness of these approaches to determine the degree to which they allow students to use their artistic skills and self-regulatory behaviors to succeed in the classroom.

We hope that this ongoing process of teacher education can demonstrate the power of the arts to improve education for all children by revealing important elements of the artistic process that can reinforce good teaching and learning. We believe that this approach holds promise for maintaining the integrity of the artistic process while helping teachers and schools to reach their curricular goals.

JR: Joanne, you have often expressed concern about the need to make these instructional practices and services more widely available within the ArtsConnection schools and also a concern about quality, artistic balance and integrity. Can you share some of your thoughts on these matters with us?

Joanne Bernstein-Cohen: Now that ArtsConnection has initiated efforts to build its capacity for staff development, I am concerned about "next steps" in the process. These week-long institutes provide terrific opportunities for teachers to explore their own abilities as artists, to discuss the application of the arts process to the daily academic life of schools, and to participate in structured curriculum writing sessions with artists who are available as mentors and consultants. We know that participating teachers achieve substantial growth in music, dance and theater skills and that powerful arts-in-education models and strategies for classroom use are designed and developed. Day-long workshops during the school year are a good follow-up to this training; they further infuse these ideas and strategies into planning and teaching at the school level. These are critical steps in the staff development process.

On average, these institutes and workshops serve about 60 teachers from 16 schools during the summer and another 45 teachers from ten schools throughout the year. My concern, now that I have seen firsthand the powerful transformation of teachers in these staff development programs, is how do we reach teachers in the other 75-80 schools where we have programs so that we can extend the educational impact of these arts processes and partnerships to ArtsConnection's entire school community. Should we offer monthly staff development opportunities at the

ArtsConnection Center or multi-level summer institutes—one level for new teachers and several levels for veterans? Can we consider requiring staff development for each of our schools as part of an articulated relationship? Or should we do districtwide staff development days to begin to have greater impact on more of our schools? And at what point can teachers trained in our institute serve as on-site mentors for their colleagues?

Another concern is training our artists to develop the abilities to function in this staff development role. We now have several first-rate teams of artists with whom we have spent a lot of time on staff development models. We are aware that not all of the artists on our roster are suited for this task. If we are to increase our capacity to provide quality staff development and extend our work further into school communities, we will need to provide more training to artists to do this work.

The challenge for ArtsConnection is to deepen school partnerships by designing more in-depth programs based on the needs of schools. We must increase our staff capacity to help schools integrate these programs into their classrooms. To do this across all of our programs, we need dollars, time and personnel. We have learned that we must build and replicate these models slowly and carefully.

JR: Steve, can you say a few words about the institute and its significance to ArtsConnection's history, its present status and its future? Where does curriculum and staff development, research, evaluation and dissemination fit into the picture of an evolving institution?

Steven Tennen: It has been nearly 20 years since New York City's first fiscal crisis led to the elimination of so many of the music and art teachers from its public schools. In those days, the idea that children's needs depended upon outside service providers for any facet of their education was almost unheard of. In the mid-1990s, that dependence has become fact for the arts in New York City public schools. For an organization like ArtsConnection, that dependence creates growing responsibility. In the early days, our goals were to provide quality artists and arts experiences to schools and to ensure that those artists were on time and that the schools were prepared to receive them. This was not easy. We had to develop a comprehensive artist-selection process to ensure artistic quality and pedagogical understanding. We also had to build a complicated booking mechanism to ensure that artists knew where the schools were and when to get there, and that the schools in turn were expecting them. We were guests in their buildings.

We have all outgrown the guest/host relationship. We have also reached the stage where partnership must go beyond a buzzword to reality. Teachers bring one set of skills to the table, artists another. Working in tandem, with appropriate planning and sharing, we can create exceptional multidisciplinary educational opportunities. Creating the necessary dialogue between artists and educators, providing the forum for that exchange and the opportunities for experimentation—for the trial and error needed to develop successful curriculum and classroom experiences—must become our number one priority. It is why the development of ArtsConnection's Performing Arts Institute for Teachers has been so important.

It is popular to call this the age of school reform, but we are really in an age of school and societal revolution. The ground is shifting and the process is not going to be easy. This is a time when good programs and methods won't last very long if they can't justify their existence in terms of real educational results and prudent financial investment. But it is also a time when chances can be taken and creative opportunities seized. The arts can and should thrive in such an educational environment—if we can become a full partner at the educational table.

The arts will always have something special to say to children. Yet to get to the point where all children can benefit educationally from what the arts can give them, we need to improve our ability to share and to collaborate with our school colleagues.

The only concern I have is that, as we struggle internally to take the next institutional step, we keep the institutional picture in balance. We need to remind ourselves occasionally of the great distance we have already traveled and the great strides we have already taken, considering where ArtsConnection began 16 years ago.

An Institutional Perspective: Time, Patience and Evolutionary Change

It has taken ArtsConnection nearly five years to evolve its current approach to professional and curriculum development and to fine-tune its related research and evaluation methodology. The goals were clear from the start: to identify and provide sustained nurturing to at-risk children with artistic potential to help them succeed in school and outside; to develop teacher confidence and competence in the arts; to use the artist as instructor and resource; to integrate the arts into the curriculum; to involve parents and the community; to have an impact on the total school climate; to document the process; and to distribute the results widely, both locally and nationally. The ability to fund all of this has sometimes been elusive.

ArtsConnection staff has struggled for some time with the question of how to redesign its largest effort, the Arts Exposure Program, so that it will have greater educational impact on the students and teachers it reaches. In 1995, Arts Exposure began to offer extended and deepened arts instruction through new thematic program designs that place increased emphasis on collaborative planning and interdisciplinary teaching and learning among artists and teachers; teacher, artist and ArtsConnection staff training (both separate and together); improved curriculum resource materials; student assessment and program evaluation; and parent and family support activities. These and other program elements were added as a result of the staff's experience in the Young Talent Program. ArtsConnection now intends to transform its other programs and to increase their educational impact on a larger percentage of the student population in the schools and of the community it serves. It is a big job; it will take time and resources, but the commitment is there and the long-range plans are under way.

The organization's commitment to its mission has never wavered. federal money has been significant, but far from the whole financial story. Substantial public and private sources of support and some earned income have now been identified. Perhaps the most significant aspect of this evolutionary process is the degree to which the organization has attempted to institutionalize the lessons learned so that good practices are reflected in all of its ongoing programs and activities. This attitude toward progressive change and the growing number of comprehensive programs with instructional impact undoubtedly account for ArtsConnection's success in attracting and sustaining public, private, federal, state and local support. That, plus the child-centered mission and the vigilance exerted by the staff in protecting and improving the quality of its work complete the ever-changing picture of an institution that chooses to operate responsively for the benefit of children.

Perhaps this institutional responsiveness, this appetite (and stomach) for profound change is the most important organizational lesson of all. ArtsConnection is a good example of an institution impatient with the status quo. It appears to be savoring its journey across the Beyond Enrichment Continuum. This dimension of its work makes the lessons it is learning significant for the field.

The Chicago Arts Partnerships in Education (CAPE)

Building Bridges in the Tower of Babel

by Arnold Aprill

To form successful partnerships, educators and artists have to overcome both a language barrier and an anxiety barrier. They have different conceptual frameworks, so that one's rhetoric sounds like mystifying gibberish to the other. Educators and artists tend to use different languages to describe time structuring, discipline, student initiative, assessment and the relationship between affect, intuition and intellect. They often have different approaches to the tone, tempo, rhythm, and volume of instruction. Yet people were not talking babble in the Tower of Babel. They were energetically articulating coherent languages that were incomprehensible to each other.

The translation process between the education and the arts communities is further complicated by the fears and prejudices that each brings to the discussion. Most teachers and parents approach the arts with fear and shame, since their primary experience of the arts was childhood humiliation ("you can't sing, draw, act, dance..."), and most artists approach schools with suspicion and rebellion, since their primary experience of school was over-control.

Arts partnership programs can only succeed when a fertile discussion of ideas takes place among the partners. What structures can encourage a fruitful exchange of ideas, and what specific obstacles can hinder success? I will use the Chicago Arts Partnerships in Education (CAPE) as a case study to address some of these issues.

Rethinking Curriculum and Instruction in Community-based Arts Partnerships

CAPE is an ambitious curriculum-reform initiative devoted to rethinking the relationship of the arts to the teaching and learning process. It comprises 12 long-term, neighborhood-based partnerships between 53 professional arts organizations, 37 Chicago Public Schools and 27 community organizations. Each partnership typically has four arts organizations, three schools, and two community organizations, with one organization serving as the coordinator, or "anchor." Innovative approaches to teaching and learning are being developed by integrating the arts across the curriculum and by integrating in-school arts experiences with after-school and community-based learning experiences. The plan is to create a range of exemplary models of school improvement through the arts. These models will be used to serve the students and communities of the pioneering schools and to leverage new public understanding, policy and action concerning the essential nature of the arts in our schools and communities.

The initiative has been conceived as an opportunity for the schools and the arts organizations to examine the role and function of the arts in general school improvement. In seeking new approaches, they have reframed the problem to be solved. Instead of asking, "How can schools include more arts programming?" or "How can arts organizations increase attendance by schools at their performances and exhibitions?" they have posed the problem as "What are arts organizations and schools and community organizations going to do together to improve the educational experience for children?" Students are seen as more than the target of audience development plans. The focus has shifted from amassing large numbers of students "served" to developing ongoing relationships and multiple, connected experiences in the arts. In the process, the partners are attempting to move the arts from an enrichment/exposure model to a learner-centered curriculum integration model that includes student self-assessment. In this model, arts instruction is no longer prepackaged and delivered; it is co-planned by teachers, artists and parents.

Building Successful Partnerships: CAPE Tries a New Approach

CAPE is organized as a six-year project. The first year (school year 1993-94) was devoted to planning. At the end of the year, the partnerships each presented detailed five-year implementation plans. These plans reflected a commitment to arts education as a significant part of school improvement and an adherence to qualitative criteria adopted at the project's inception. The criteria include sequential instruction within comprehensive programs; recognition and support of the central roles of both classroom teachers and in-school arts specialists; curriculum integration that maintains artistic integrity; in-service training for artists on work in educational settings; training for educators in dance, music, theater and visual arts; ongoing planning; parent inclusion; assessment built into instruction; and the teaching of African, Latino, Asian, and Native American arts in equal status to European-derived art forms.

Implementation inside the schools will take place over the remaining five years of the project. Each school is expected to commit its own dollars to the program (a minimum of $5,000 during Year I of Implementation), and this amount is expected to increase each year. By the end of the sixth year, each school should be committing enough of its own budget to allow the arts-integrated curriculum to be institutionalized. Classroom teachers are expected to co-plan and co-teach with both in-school arts specialists and "outside" artists. CAPE promotes the idea of "artist as resource, not recess."

Funding is reviewed annually, with each partnership's support based upon the quality of ongoing implementation design and execution. Of the 14 partnerships that were initially funded for planning, 12 have passed the annual funder review into their second year of implementation. Each partnership typically received $25,000 for program support and $5,000 for technical assistance during the planning year, and $55,000 for implementation and $5,000 for technical assistance during Year I of Implementation. Implementation funds pay for ongoing planning between artists and teachers, artist fees for co-presenting with teachers in the classroom, staff development for teachers and artists, and the costs of community and parent programming.

Marshall Field's, a highly visible department store in Chicago, initiated CAPE after it commissioned a "needs and resource" assessment of arts education in Chicago Public Schools. Mitchell Korn of ArtsVision, who conceived CAPE and designed its structure, conducted the study. He then convened a series of public meetings, attended by artists, teachers, principals and parents, to discuss the findings of the report. The community's familiarity with Marshall Field's helped to develop public enthusiasm in a constituency unfamiliar with the philanthropic community and distrustful of the school bureaucracy.

Chicago's rich history of philanthropic discourse and collaboration through such organizations as the Donor's Forum and Chicago Women in Philanthropy afforded a fertile environment in which to launch a new initiative. Like many foundations and corporations around the country, those in the Chicago area for many years had been questioning the real impact on students of even the best arts exposure programs.

Marshall Field's worked with a consortium of 13 actively involved Chicago-based funders to develop CAPE.[8] The consortium announced a request for proposals in the daily newspapers in September 1992. Some partnerships had begun to form during the needs assessment process and the public meetings. The Chicago Music Alliance held a "Lonely Arts Club" session to help with partnership matchmaking. Schools, communities, and arts organizations drew on long-standing relationships that they now sought to deepen.

The request for proposal's demands for the first year of planning grants were so rigorous that only those partnerships that were able to collaborate from the beginning were capable of writing coherent proposals. The request required explicit goals, an articulated arts education philosophy from all participating schools and organizations, the delineation of partnership roles, and a detailed "plan to plan."

Because change is difficult, and because the process calls upon schools and arts organizations to change some of their basic operating principles, the program was constructed with several layers of technical assistance and accountability. A CAPE office was established to create a sense of collective action and advocacy. The office's two-person staff acts as a conduit between the funders' consortium and the partnerships; raises funds for the program; identifies quality technical assistance providers for the partnerships; organizes staff development sessions on arts integration, curriculum frameworks, and authentic assessment; and serves generally as a witness, cheerleader, and gadfly to the work in the schools. Site visits and feedback are provided by the funding consortium, the technical assistance providers, the program evaluation team and the executive director.

CAPE exists within the context of Chicago School Reform. Legislation in 1989 decentralized governance in Chicago Public Schools. At each school, a local school council of parents, teachers and community members makes budget decisions and hires and reviews principals. An active community of school-reform organizations provides advice and support on restructuring at the grass-roots level. The school-reform organizations are available to CAPE schools and arts organizations to help artists and educators understand school-change issues, and the CAPE initiative helps the school-reform community to understand the importance of the arts in learner-centered instruction (teaching focused on students assuming ownership of their own learning).

Curriculum and Instruction: Prospects and Polarities

Curriculum development is site-based, with an emphasis on arts integration and on access to arts experiences for all students. The CAPE office serves as a hub to partnership activity, coordinating in-service activities on curriculum, instruction and assessment. New understandings of both curriculum (the scope, sequence, content and structure of what is taught) and instruction (teaching methods) are developed through the creation of arts-integrated units. Implementation of these units is followed by reflection on how the units fit into the larger curriculum (Does the unit build on previously incorporated knowledge? Is it developmentally appropriate? Is it part of a coherent sequence of learning in the arts disciplines?) and on instructional success (Which teaching strategies worked? Which need to be revised? Which student competencies were actually developed?). This reflection process is facilitated by the technical assistance providers and/or the steering committees in each partnership and occurs within the context of the curriculum realignment going on in many Chicago schools. Several CAPE schools are incorporating inquiry-based approaches (organizing instruction around "essential questions") and thematic approaches (organizing instruction around such themes as "ecological issues" or "life in the future") as articulated by reformers such as Ted Sizer of the Coalition of Essential Schools and James Beane of the National Middle School Association.

A wide range of arts-integrated curriculum strands have already emerged from the project. With the additional support of an Illinois Arts Council grant, Chinese-American students at Robert Healy Elementary worked with professional singers and the Chicago Dance Medium to understand the Underground Railroad by reading about Harriet Tubman, creating dances that moved throughout the entire school, analyzing the paintings of Jacob Lawrence, singing songs of the period, and re-creating (and destroying) "Wanted" posters for runaway slaves. The participating classes had students who were easily distracted and had little engagement with schoolwork. The concentration, discipline, interest in historical content, leadership skills and the dance, writing and visual arts skills developed by the students during this arts-integrated unit impressed the teachers, the principal and the students themselves.

At John A. Walsh School in the Pilsen neighborhood, teachers were anxious to develop active learning materials focusing on the ancient cultures of the American Southwest, a history of special importance to the school's Mexican-American children. Artists and teachers attended seminars at the Oriental Institute and co-developed an arts-integrated unit in which students studied Mimbre culture, visited Mimbre artifacts at the Field Museum, made coil pots duplicating Mimbre ceramics and reproduced the traditional designs. The students shattered their pots and buried them in sand in the basement of the local park district building. Another class was engaged to conduct an archaeological expedition to unearth the artifacts and reconstruct them. The students catalogued the objects, curated their own museum display about the project, and scheduled themselves as docents to showcase their work to their peers and to the neighborhood. Their understanding of archaeology and their appreciation of ancient cultures became inseparable from their understanding of ceramics and painting.

Arts-integrated instruction being developed at other CAPE schools includes: studying Hispanic and African cultures through Afro-Caribbean music; exploring biological interdependence through music and dance; exploring sociology through playwriting in partnership with a suburban school; studying folktales by writing and designing "illuminated texts" modeled on Medieval calligraphy and book design; studying ceramics and biology by designing, sculpting and growing "chia pets"; studying city planning by building a scale model of the local school and the surrounding neighborhood; and bringing Greek myths to life by having students design and shoot their own animated films.

As educators move from being the lone deliverers of received curriculum to becoming co-constructors of new curriculum materials in dynamic interaction with other educators, artists and their students, a tension emerges between those educators and artists who are focused on adhering to state and local mandates and those educators and artists focused on developing new curriculum based on practice in the classroom. A similar tension exists between arts administrators, who tend to be content-based, and artists in residence, who tend to be process-based. The mandate-driven thinkers often show a tendency to become formal and formulaic, while the new-curriculum thinkers often show a tendency toward formlessness and a lack of rigor. These polarities embody two approaches to change—one being primarily top-down (with an emphasis on skills, standards, replicability and accountability) and the other being primarily bottom-up (with an emphasis on personal meaning, local contexts, site-specific choices and self-assessment). This tension (the problem of consensus-based change in a democracy) runs through the entire school-reform movement.

The CAPE partnerships typically went through extended honeymoon periods—characterized by naive and lofty assertions about the importance of art—during which idealized possibilities intoxicated the participants. This rhetorical period was essential to partnership development because it included parties who traditionally are excluded from policy development and from theoretical discussion. Yet this period seldom resulted in practical plans. An extended period of frustration usually followed the honeymoon: artists bemoaned the rigid practices of schools, schools bemoaned the self-absorption of artists, and everyone bemoaned the difficulty of making change in an underfunded bureaucracy.

Technical Assistance providers helped the partnerships through this period by providing information on divergent learning styles and teamwork strategies, but one of CAPE's primary strengths has been its monetary investment in planning and in the time needed for change. Frustration has played a valuable role in CAPE's development, and artists and educators were paid to tolerate their discomfort. The growth of the partnerships has followed a pattern similar to Piaget's model of cognitive development in children: experiencing dissonant systems of thought has forced the creation of new, more inclusive frames of reference. Enough trust and group cohesion had been formed during the honeymoon period to hold the partnerships together when they entered the Tower of Babel.

A common ground was developed through shared work and shared interest in children. Teachers and parents gained access to the artists' language through experiential training in the arts. Artists gained access to educators' language through training and planning sessions that illuminated educational theory, the responsibilities of teachers and the pressures on schools. New language was co-developed in joint workshops on curriculum, instruction and assessment. The executive director and workshop presenters spoke to school staffs, local school councils and arts organizations to communicate the importance of this joint venture.

Artists and arts specialists have been helpful in clarifying the importance of student initiative, risk taking and "mistakes" in the creative process. Teachers have been helpful in placing arts learning in the context of the whole curriculum and the development of the whole child, counterbalancing the tendency of arts organizations to construct their educational work around the marketing needs and implied world views of their collections/repertory, rather than connecting to the learning needs of students. The arts have been so marginalized throughout American culture that arts education advocates have a hard time remembering that their purpose is to encourage a diversity of thought and interest. Our task is to expand the educational palette, not to impose an arts palette. The position of the arts in education is not unlike that of the biblical Joseph. Although his visions empowered him in a foreign land, he still needed to reconcile with the brothers who had exiled him.

The CAPE Program Evaluation

The North Central Regional Educational Laboratory is conducting a longitudinal evaluation of the CAPE initiative, applying both qualitative and quantitative approaches. CAPE deliberately chose an education evaluator because the initiative hopes to demonstrate the impact of the arts on general school improvement. Evaluation methods include participant surveys, participant-conducted research, observation of key events, partnership portfolios, document review, in-depth case studies, interviews with key stakeholders, focus groups and participant logs. Areas to be measured are: student outcomes (learning in specific arts disciplines, reading skills, writing skills, math skills, critical thinking skills, shifts in attendance and in attitudes toward learning), changes in school climate for teachers, shifts in educational focus in arts organizations, arts inclusion in community organizations, shifts in school-community relations, and impact on arts education policy at the local, state and national level.

Beyond Babel: Conversations on the Bridge

The Tower of Babel was an attempt to use real estate to storm Heaven. It was no accident that its builders ended up speaking different languages. They were so focused on dominating the sky that they simply forgot how to talk to each other. They forgot that the heavens already exist on Earth—in our mutual sense of responsibility for each other, in shared discourse and in the arts. As the Tower begins to sway, brave souls build fragile bridges and, clasping the railings, reinvent the art of conversation.

CAPE is built on the belief that the integration of substantive arts programming across the curriculum is one of the primary pathways for catalyzing effective schoolwide change. The arts carve out space for new conversations in schools, enabling schools to reflect on their learning climate and creating an exotic terrain for exploring new possibilities.

For CAPE, partnerships are not about "bringing the arts to the schools." Partnerships are bridges for bringing falsely separated partners back into conversation. A successful partnership helps integrate the artist, the teacher and the parent in each one of us, so that all of our children can grow up in a world rich with possibilities, knowing that they are whole and ready to make choices we cannot even imagine today.

Arnold Aprill *is the Executive Director of the Chicago Arts Partnerships in Education (CAPE). He comes from a background in both professional theater and arts education. He has worked as an artist in residence for the Illinois Arts Council, the Delaware State Arts Council and Urban Gateways, and he directed an intensive arts-in-education program for the Chicago Teachers' Center at Northeastern Illinois University. He has taught directing, adapting, acting and performance aesthetics at the University of Chicago, Columbia College, and the School of the Art Institute of Chicago. His work as a theater director includes serving as Artistic Director at City Lit Theater Company and at the National Jewish Theater, and as guest director at Jump-Start Theater in San Antonio.*

Building Continuity and Systemic Change

A Primer on the New Arts Partnerships

by Richard Bell

In 1985 community leaders in Kansas City began to question how students were being educated in the arts, how the cultural resources of the community were being used for education, and how these activities were financed. Their answers provided a springboard for the design of a new arts partnership.

As we pass the midpoint of this decade's commitment to education reform, a new kind of arts partnership is emerging in communities across the country. Locally led and financed, these efforts jump-start the collaborative process to create district- or system-wide programs that use the cultural resources of the entire community. Whether these partnerships represent a sea change in the 45-year history of artists working in schools or are simply an important trend is still to be determined. In either case, the shift from federal to local leadership is becoming a reality, and we may soon achieve some of the goals viewed as unrealistic only a few years ago.

The ideas that follow are based on Young Audiences' experience with partnerships involving school systems and community cultural resources. This process began in Kansas City almost ten years ago and has spread to nearly a dozen other sites through 1995. Similar partnerships are currently being planned or carried out in such diverse communities as Rochester, Richmond, Baltimore, Portland, Charlotte-Mecklenberg and Minneapolis, to name a few. While the conclusions are rooted in the particulars of the organization's experience, much of what has been learned appears to apply to other systemic partnerships as well.

These partnerships are not offered as exemplars for the sequential reform of curriculum and instruction nor for schoolwide restructuring and change through the arts. While districtwide in scope, they are essentially field-tested models of the effective use of a community's arts and cultural resources in comprehensive programs that unite arts organizations, artists and schools for the improved education of all the children in the district.

The Old Partnerships

Historically, most arts partnerships have been designed from the perspective of individual arts organizations. For example, a symphony would form a partnership with several schools to bring students to the concert hall or a local arts-in-education program would join in partnership with a museum to create a visual arts residency.

In most cases, the partnerships have been defined by the following characteristics:

- The programs are designed by the arts organization(s);
- A high percentage of financing comes from the private sector;
- Project coordination and fiscal responsibility are assumed by the lead arts organization; and
- Project continuity is vested in key arts organization staff and major funders.

The problem with these partnerships has not been a matter of artistic quality or effectiveness in meeting the goals set out for them. Rather, the goals have not fully met the needs of students and schools. No matter how well designed and executed these programs may be, providing worthwhile arts experiences for the benefit of a few students has suddenly become passé because there is little opportunity or motivation to integrate these programs into the general curriculum and school budgets.

The New Partnerships

Much the same way an earlier generation of "one-shot" exposure programs gave way to workshops and residencies that were more participatory and of greater educational value, the old partnerships are now being supplanted by collaborations that involve the entire arts community and whose impact is systemwide.

Arts Partners is a sequential arts-in-education plan that allows each student to come into contact with most of a city's cultural resources during his or her journey from kindergarten through high school. Besides participating in the arts throughout their time in school, students' experiences with the arts are linked to specific areas of the curriculum. Arts Partners encompasses instruction in the arts, the use of the arts in teaching other subjects, and the planned use of community resources. In these new arts partnerships and their various manifestations, we have found eight common principles that define a process for building continuity and achieving systemic change.

The Eight Principles that Define the New Partnerships

1. Build Consensus for Continuity and Change

Kansas City was fortunate to have a farsighted community foundation (The Kansas City Community Foundation) that served as both a convener (bringing school districts, arts organizations and private funders together) and a major funder from the early stages of development in 1986 until the present. The essential quality of the convener is the ability to build consensus and celebrate success.

Every systemic partnership needs a convener, a highly respected organization in the community with the resources to mentor and support the partnership through its initial stages of development. As the name implies, the convener brings the partners to the table, makes the case for partnership, and "walks the walk" by publicly committing its financial resources and good offices to the project. As the partnership takes on a life of its own, the convener relinquishes control, influence and responsibility to the other members.

Consensus building lies at the heart of every successful partnership. It is also the most compelling characteristic of systemic change in schools and cultural organizations. A "top-down/bottom-up" approach is an abiding characteristic of nearly all school systems. District decisions and attitudes have a powerful impact on individual schools, and feedback from individual schools strongly affects decisions at the district level.

The convening organization ideally should be a funder, not a provider of services. It is almost impossible to assume the role of convener and also provide services through the partnership. In such cases, organizations are typically asked to suspend their disbelief that funds won't be siphoned from their ongoing programs by the partnership. The idea that the partnership can "create a larger funding pie," thereby increasing the size of each organization's slice, appears abstract—and to some irrational—until the full weight of the partnership takes hold in the community.

It is also important that the convener be able to underwrite a substantial portion of the partnership's work during the first three years. Without this leverage, the convening organization may not be able to help make the project part of each organization's institutional life. From a program perspective, the presence of a knowledgeable, objective funder helps to maintain the partnership's focus.

2. Use Community Champions

The importance of identifying local "champions" to provide leadership and rally community support to accomplish the changes necessary to make the partnership work cannot be overemphasized. In Kansas City, two prominent citizens, Adele Hall and Clifford Jones, carried out this role. They helped create a long-term commitment to implementing a comprehensive arts and education plan. The current arts partnership in Kansas City represents a decade of work.

—Janice Kreamer, President, Greater Kansas City Community Foundation

Even strong partnerships need the support of one or a few community champions. These are individuals who have the stature and record of achievement that allows them to intercede periodically on behalf of the partnership to help address important issues. The champion can also open doors to those whose good offices and support might otherwise be unavailable to the project: the symphony president, a leading corporation's CEO or a school superintendent. Often they exert their greatest influence in the private sector, but with the emergence of public/private sector partnerships, they increasingly can be helpful in the public sector as well. Most important, the champion provides access to the larger community outside the arts and education. As the public becomes more aware of the challenges facing today's educators, the role of the champion will become even more vital to the success of the partnership.

3. Involve All Students in the District

Arts Partners is a powerful community development model. It allows private funders to support the arts and arts education without contributing to redundant administrative systems. It also helps arts organizations meet the needs of students and teachers without compromising their primary missions. By redefining the role of the arts in education, the partnership provides equal access to community cultural resources for every student. It helps make Kansas City a special place to live.

—Janice Kreamer, President, Greater Kansas City Community Foundation

When asked to name the qualities that make partnerships successful enough to warrant line-item support in school budgets, superintendents talk about equity. The importance of reaching every student cannot be overestimated. Superintendents know that parents and school board members find this quality, perhaps above all others, compelling at budget time. From their inception, the new partnerships plan for implementation "at scale," reaching every child in the district, however brief some of these exposures may be.

The arts-in-education field has a long history of approaching partnerships through model projects. The rationale behind this approach is that a project must prove itself in one or a few schools before taking on the program and funding challenges of an entire district. Unfortunately, the advantage of model projects—intensive work in one or a few schools—also makes them unlikely candidates for districtwide replication unless larger political and funding considerations are built into the model. Partnership planners now attempt to maintain an effective balance between project breadth and depth to avoid the tendency of model projects to define their early development in ways that preclude implementation at scale.

More always needs to be accomplished at each school site: creating better support materials; enhancing the professional development of teachers and artists; improving instructional programs. The labor intensive nature of these activities requires ever-greater time and expense. As progress is made, the task of extending the results from project to nonproject schools becomes more elusive. While districtwide planning may appear more difficult to accomplish at the inception of a project, experience shows that a highly focused partnership can accomplish this goal more effectively early in the process than it can after a project is established.

Partnerships often face a dilemma in attempting to balance the school's desire to include as many students as possible with project goals that call for intensive learning experiences. Ironically, although these goals are not mutually exclusive, many worthwhile partnerships falter because project leaders discount the possibility of districtwide involvement at the partnership's inception.

In recent years, arts education advocates have been making the case that the arts should be a basic area of the curriculum—on a par with math, English, science and history—and that all students benefit from studying the arts, not just those who are talented. However, this argument is undercut by the prevailing view among many educators and most parents, who believe that serious study of the arts should only be undertaken by gifted students. This idea is associated with an even more deeply held belief that the primary role of school is to prepare students for work.

Making the case that the arts are as basic as the core academic subjects cannot be accomplished incrementally. Much of the arts' effectiveness in fostering creativity, building communication skills, or inculcating social values can only be appreciated if they are taught in all grade levels and schools. Just as space on the grocery shelf is reserved for brand-name products, academic subjects have a set place in the school day. Off-brands like the arts are marginalized, not because they are of lesser quality or have less intrinsic value, but because most of the shelf space is already filled.

If we are to break the repetitive cycle of time and value that has haunted arts education since the American experiment with universal education began, we must design projects that involve every child, even if that means some students will only engage the arts briefly. Over time, the distinction between academic subjects and the arts may disappear as the power of the arts to transform children and schools occurs across disciplines for all students.

4. Integrate the Arts with Other Subjects and School Priorities

I see a change in what we are doing with community resources...from five or six one-shot assemblies to a group of artists who are going to be in our school. They'll cover a range of performing and visual arts, and the classroom teachers will work with these artists to provide extended learning experiences for the kids. As we do that, I think we begin to have a very powerful curriculum vehicle for helping kids make sense of their world.

—*Mary Beth Van Cleve, Principal*

The debate between those who believe the arts must be taught for their own sake and those who would use the arts as a tool in helping students learn other subjects fails to address the central impediments to achieving more and better arts education for all students. It makes little difference which side of this issue prevails because the exclusion of either perspective would greatly diminish the outcome for students and the place of the arts in schools. In any case, it is unlikely the arts could be used to address social issues or the social studies curriculum, to cite one example, unless a quality arts instruction program was also in place.

Of far greater concern is the place of the arts in American schools. Little progress has been made in changing public awareness about the importance of a quality arts education, and many school budgets are stagnant. There is universal agreement in the arts field about the importance of increasing resources for arts education. Many believe that alternative approaches must be explored even if this means using the arts to address areas outside the traditional purview of arts education. After all, not so many years ago, art became an established school subject so that students would be better prepared to enter the New England cottage industries—the manufacture of hats and shoes. A few years before that, music entered the schools to prepare young men to sing better in church choirs.

More time is needed for the arts in schools, and using the arts to build communication skills, develop creativity and help students understand their emotions may provide powerful rationales for increasing support. The new partnerships embrace this challenge as an artist or scientist would—with curiosity and creativity—in the certainty that the process will be worthwhile whether or not the outcome is successful.

5. Offer Staff and Curriculum Development for Both Artists and Teachers

Fine arts consultant Tom Dole has always had a strong personal bias that arts teachers should also be involved professionally in their art form This has influenced the kind of person hired for the 85 certified fine and performing arts instructional positions in the district.

In-service training is an established concept both among educators and artists, but that is where the similarity ends. The formal, credit-bearing courses and seminars that make up most teachers' in-service activities are seldom found in the arts community. Instead, artists engage in a series of informal activities that include viewing and discussing one another's work, and researching all manner of topics and historical periods.

Every partnership obviously requires ongoing training for its participants. However, the new partnerships offer special challenges that make this training critically important. Most teachers and artists traditionally have concerns about one another's work. Teachers still often think of artists as outside experts whose experience and expertise lie beyond their grasp. Artists, on the other hand, can easily fail to comprehend in-school projects from the teacher's perspective, sometimes substituting their own sensibilities for those of the student. The new partnerships require participants to understand the creative process of the artist and the professional skills of the practicing teacher. The shared planning responsibilities also require artists and teachers to adopt one another's role.

Artists must learn how to modify their work to meet the requirements of the curricular framework. Teachers should explore working in at least one art form, and administrators must be conversant with instructional programs and arts organization services.

Generally, the people working in the partnership should design and carry out training, calling on outside experts as needed. In all training forums, participants should maintain their primary relationship as colleagues and professionals rather than alternating roles as experts and learners. With few exceptions, the group will know more about what needs to be learned and experienced than any person outside the group can advise.

6. Reflect a Community's Cultural Resources

Many of us connected with the larger arts institutions came into the early partnership process with healthy skepticism. The reality for us, while not without its challenges, has been such a positive one that it has left us permanently less territorial, more open to new ideas and more able to make beneficial changes in the way we achieve success for the Symphony.

—*Susan M. Franano, General Manager, Kansas City Symphony*

The new partnerships involve a broad group of arts organizations representing the full spectrum of art forms, ethnic groups and arts-in-education services. Not only does this insure broad community representation, it also relieves individual organizations of the responsibility to meet school needs that lie beyond their capacities. Initially, the partners present the best of what they have already developed in their ongoing education programs, and then as members are exposed over time to a wide range of arts-in-education services, they initiate new programs that the partnership has influenced.

The participation of a broad coalition of arts organizations also engenders greater participation from the private sector, stimulating business, foundation, civic, and patron support. What begins as an arts education project is eventually perceived as enhancing the community's overall quality of life.

Of course, the dream would be to engender a regular and creative interaction among cultural resources so that all would eventually be influenced in their primary artistic output. Only then would each organization's educational program move to the center of its institutional life.

7. Create Systemic Change in Both Cultural Organizations and Schools

Arts organizations and schools should approach partnerships primarily as a matter of enlightened self-interest. Unless each partner can identify a tangible benefit that is essential to its well-being and that cannot be accomplished outside the project, the partnership will likely falter. One litmus test for determining a partnership's strength is the question: *Would you allocate unrestricted funds from your organization to accomplish the partnership's goals?* If the answer is "no" for a majority of organizations in the partnership, the alliance should reexamine its reason for being.

Even the most cursory examination of arts organizations and schools reveals important contrasts in their infrastructure, funding and governance. The checklist in Figure 4.2 illustrates these differences and provides a useful tool for building partnerships that combine the best characteristics of each institution.

> *Figure 4.2: The Characteristics of School Systems and the Arts Community*

Schools Systems	**Arts Community**
• Public sector	• Private nonprofit
• Tax-based revenues	• Earned and contributed income
• Child-centered	• Arts-centered
• Market-driven	• Product-driven
• Hierarchical decision making	• Informal, nontraditional decision-making
• Governed by a board of community representatives	• Governed by a board of influential patrons
• Arts education has a significant, but limited place	• Arts education has a low priority

Building awareness of these differences is the first step in learning how to cause institutional change within organizations and systemic change in schools. Initially, partner institutions assume that change will only have to occur in *other* organizations. On the contrary, both schools and arts organizations change significantly in the new partnerships. The partners must recognize that each group functions through a complex infrastructure whose language, personnel and corporate culture do not translate easily from one group to the other. Consequently, they must devise a new governance process that emphasizes consensus building rather than traditional forms of decision-making. By involving both the central administration of school systems and the trustees and funders of major arts institutions, the partnership gains instant credibility that also enhances long-term stability. Without this broad-based, systemic support from schools and the arts community, the partnership will not become part of each organization's institutional life.

8. Harness the Engine of Earned Income

My district was already spending around $8 million of a $60 million total budget on the arts (in personnel, physical facilities, equipment and materials). The $80,000 we spend toward the purchase of community arts services through Arts Partners, phased in over three years, combines with an additional $30,000 from the private funding community and totally changes the way the arts happen in our schools.... Every child in our district has access to the cultural wealth of our community. I think that is a pretty good deal because it adds a great deal of value to existing programs at very little extra expense...it's like adding the sauce to the stew.

—*Dr. Robert Henley, former Superintendent, Independence Public Schools, Missouri*

As the partnership matures, usually over three or four years, the balance of financing should shift from private sector funding to the schools. Unless a substantial portion of project costs are paid by school sources (ideally 50-75 percent), the partnership is never likely to become an integral part of school life, much less self-sustaining. Working toward this goal is mostly a matter of building school system priorities into partnership activities—something that cannot be accomplished working up from a few schools to the entire district. From the partnership's inception, regular contact and participation must occur with the central administration.

The budget for the first year of Arts Partners was approximately $250,000, with the schools contributing 20 percent and the private sector providing the rest. This year, line-item budget allocations from the five greater Kansas City school systems amounted to 70 percent of total project costs of $875,000.

To summarize, then, in Young Audiences' experience, the new arts partnerships attempt to build continuity in the relationship between the arts organizations and the schools, and systemic change in the way these partnerships are defined, structured and financed. These programs generally begin by identifying leadership and by building consensus within the community by using local leaders who become champions of the change process. These programs involve all students in a district, attempt to integrate the arts with other subjects and school priorities, and offer staff and curriculum development as a support for both artists and teachers. These collaborations reflect a broad range of a community's cultural resources and manage to include a sizeable amount of earned income for sustained financial support. When all these principles are applied, partnerships and programs appear to survive and thrive.

If We Could See Beyond the Present Horizon...

A Family Arts Night was the culminating experience of the year's activities. The large number of students, parents and friends who came enjoyed participating in hands-on projects led by artists and students, an exhibition of student art work, the performance of a student puppet show, and creative movement workshops led by artists. Some families talked about using their Arts Card (a plastic card given to each child in the program that provides discounted tickets and free transportation on the local public transportation system) to see artists who came to the school perform and exhibit their work in other venues. Two large student murals, inspired by work with artists, reflected the spirit of the effort visually and through their titles.

—Tree of Knowledge and Tree of Learning.

As we look to the future, the signs are both unsettling and encouraging for the arts in education. At the federal level, the National Endowment for the Arts, the government's most effective catalyst for change and perhaps the only consistent champion of the arts in education during the last ten years, faces an uncertain future. Moreover, the Department of Education, whose historic decision to include the arts as part of education reform may be the most significant event of the last decade, cannot rely upon consistent political support of its current mission.

With the prospect of a diminished federal role, the leadership baton will pass to the states and communities that can muster the vision and resources to bring about systemic change in schools and harness the available cultural resources for all students. The next breakthroughs in the field may not occur in our large urban school systems, but perhaps in medium-sized cities and even smaller communities. There, the experience of working in partnerships, which make the most of limited resources, is already part of the ongoing fabric of community life.

What kinds of breakthroughs might occur in these communities? Perhaps baseline criteria will be established for evaluating the performance of arts organizations, schools and students. Longitudinal studies will measure students' knowledge and abilities—in the arts and in the relationship of the arts to other subjects and to success in later life. Models for certifying artists to work in schools will be created and field-tested. Arts specialists, though still highly skilled in one discipline, will be conversant enough with other art forms to coordinate the use of cultural resources in schools and in the community. Arts organizations will develop educational software that allows students to augment live artistic experiences with simulated interactions in a variety of formats. Funding sources not only will support projects that offer innovative approaches to intractable problems, but also will look with equal favor on proposals that complement and build upon what has already been accomplished. University arts and education departments will inaugurate training programs leading to a joint degree and certification.

In these communities, the sun will set at the end of each glorious, perfect day with the sense of satisfaction and finality that accompanies a job well done. It is a new horizon worth dreaming about—populated with trees of knowledge and learning.

Richard Bell is National Executive Director of Young Audiences, the national performing arts education organization which last year presented more than 60,000 programs to 6.5 million young people throughout the United States. He also currently serves as Vice Chairman of the National Coalition for Education in the Arts. He has written extensively on the role of the arts in education, including articles in Educational Leadership *and* Design for Arts in Education *and essays in* Toward a New Era in Arts Education: The Interlochen Symposium *and the Getty Center's* Roundtable Series. *Prior to his work with Young Audiences, he taught theater at the State University of New York at New Paltz, Hamilton College, and Columbia University School of the Arts.*

Teaching Kids to Listen

A Conversation with Mark Schubart

Mark Schubart and I worked together from 1967 to 1972, when he was director of education at Lincoln Center and I was an assistant director in charge of New York City school programs and the artists-in-schools component then known as the RP Program, short for Resource Personnel, an ungainly name we inherited from the federal legislation that originally supported it. Begun in 1967, the RP Program was one of the first in the nation to recruit and train gifted young professional musicians, dancers, actors and filmmakers to work in the classroom with students and teachers in activities relating to the themes of the Student Program performances in the schools and at Lincoln Center. "At first, the...RP's...dealt largely with preparation and follow-up for specific performances, but with each successive year, the range of their activities broadened to include participatory experiences in the arts, which began to help young people to get at the fundamentals of the artistic experience—involvement in the truest sense of the word. The RP program proved to be highly successful from every point of view...it opened up a significant new direction for the Program."[9]

In 1970, with support from Lincoln Center and funding from the Carnegie Corporation, Mark undertook a year-long study of the education program, which resulted in the report, *The Hunting of the Squiggle*, a widely read document that is as relevant today as when it was published in 1972. The report chronicles the development of Lincoln Center's education program, beginning in the early sixties in the context of what were then, on reflection, the halcyon days of support for the arts from the federal government and the New York State Department of Education. It examines in considerable detail the growth and development of the Lincoln Center Student Program and the central educational, philosophical and practical questions it faced. The study came to the conclusion that most arts institutions, Lincoln Center included, were not hospitable to young people and not necessarily well-equipped or financially able to devote the time, attention and resources needed to educate them in and about the arts. The result was a recommendation for a new kind of youth-oriented institution that would focus on the artist as educator, teaching aesthetic perception and literacy to young people in their formative years. Among the chief strategies for achieving this purpose, in addition to in-school work with artists, would be artist and teacher training and the identification, commissioning, presentation and analysis of art works deemed appropriate for youth.

The Lincoln Center Institute was begun officially in 1975 and relatively soon thereafter spawned a number of other institutes around the country; they now number 17. The Getty Center for Education in the Arts and the Bernstein Center for Education Through the Arts have missions somewhat similar to that of the Lincoln Center Institute; what distinguishes each of them is their philosophy of arts education and instructional approach.

In preparation for this interview, I gave Mark the following questions which provided a framework for our conversation:

- What can the field learn from your experience with the Lincoln Center Institute as partner with Teachers College, Columbia University and with the other centers in New York and around the country? What are some of the obstacles, the lessons learned?

- In retrospect, what would you have done differently along the way, if anything? And what advice do you have for other folks who might be thinking about designing their own dedicated arts-in-education organization (regardless of philosophy—aesthetic education, the Getty's Discipline-Based Arts Education, comprehensive arts in education and so forth)?

Jane Remer: I have talked with Scott Noppe-Brandon about the problems and promises of partnerships with schools, teachers and artists. I think that exploring some partnership issues with you from an institutional perspective would be instructive for the field. Can you speak about the origin of your partnership with Teachers College of Columbia University?

Mark Schubart: Our partnership with Teachers College of Columbia University, which is largely a partnership with Maxine Greene, is an interesting collaboration. The reason the partnership started was not because of Columbia but because of Maxine. I thought it was important to involve a philosopher and an educator early in this enterprise, since I am basically a flute player. The philosophical perspective of the person was more important than the institution to which she was connected. The need that I felt for the Institute was not for a university affiliation but for the professional skills of somebody in that particular field.

JR: How did you identify Maxine?

MS: I read some things that she wrote. It seemed to me that we were on the same wavelength. We were both concerned with the transaction between the person and the work of art—rather than the history, the traditions and the technical nature of the art form—as a place to begin.

More recently, we have become associated with other universities, notably the City University of New York (CUNY) in pre-service education. But that is a different kind of relationship; it is not a philosophical one.

JR: Tell me about this relationship.

MS: As you know, previously we focused our teacher-education activities exclusively on teachers who are involved in the program—in other words, teacher in-service training. Recently we have become interested in the notion of teacher pre-service, particularly in New York City. Obviously the greatest purveyor of teachers for the city is CUNY, and through a relationship with Chancellor Ann Reynolds, a member of our board, we have established some pilot projects.

The idea is to work with teachers before they go into service so that they can do their practice teaching in schools where we are already involved. So far, we have run workshops for the faculty at Brooklyn College and more recently workshops for students. Next year these students presumably will be in the schools. We thought that just putting aesthetic education courses in the colleges would not do the job. If our program works for teachers in service, why shouldn't it work for teachers before they go into service? We hope it will add new teachers to the roster who are pre-trained or who have had some experience with aesthetic education.

JR: How long will this pilot continue?

MS: We don't know. It will certainly go on next year and probably beyond.

JR: Tell me about the other institutes around the country.

MS: I am astonished by the variety of forms that this concept has taken in the various communities around the country. They all involve artist-teacher partnerships and teacher education in one form or another, but I think only Nashville is dealing with teacher pre-service. The trick is to link the pre-service with what happens in the school; otherwise it becomes just another abstract course. That is why I think that the follow-through with those teachers in the classroom is such an important part of their training. As you know and well remember, the idea of a partnership between teacher and artist has been fundamental to the Institute from the start.

When the Institute started, we never thought of it as a national program, and it isn't. We are not a national organization; we are an agglomeration of local associations. I have resisted the idea of replication from one place to another, because I don't think it works—the communities are too different. There are different people, different communities, different needs and different perspectives, and I think that is good.

I have believed from the beginning that for multiplication to take place, we would help with certain basic things with which we are all supposed to agree, like the philosophy and the basic three-step process. The other institutes are all following that basic model, but an enormous amount of variety exists within that framework. For example, not everyone has a summer session, and some are short, some are longer. The notions about art are very different—what is art and what is not art, which is fascinating.

From the start, we thought that if this kind of education is important, then it needs to have an institutional base, just as any other kind of education. The schools, the colleges and the arts institutions are not going to provide that, so you have to create new animals. That is essentially what we did here in New York. Some of the other institutes around the country are totally independent, separate and autonomous; some are connected with arts councils (in Tulsa, for example); some have university affiliations such as Albany, which has a facilitated-assistance relationship with Albany/SUNY.

JR: What do you mean when you referred to things with which you all basically agree, such as the philosophy, teacher education, and the three-step process?

MS: We have a description of the essential components with which everyone has to agree before becoming a member of this association. It is in very broad brushstrokes, but it spells out what distinguishes us from other arts educational organizations. It refers to the philosophy of aesthetic education and to the nature of the partnerships. It also outlines the program's three-step process involving intensive teacher-education programs, planning units of study for the school year and implementation in the classroom. We find it helpful and clear (See Figure 4.3).

The most important ingredient is the philosophy. That is what makes it what it is. Unless the purpose is clear, it becomes another amorphous project. Many of the other institutes are weak; not all of them are strong. They have financial problems, clarity problems...

JR: How did you add other institutes?

MS: I will tell you how the first one started. One summer, Michael Charry, a Juilliard graduate, conducted a performance of one of our works under study and became very interested and excited about the Institute. When he was appointed conductor of the Nashville Symphony, he called me and said he wanted to start an institute there, and that one began.

Then, through participation in the Nashville Institute program, a professor at Peabody College in Nashville was made head of the music department at the University of Delaware, and he started an institute there. Other people would hear or read about the Institute, or come to New York to observe it, and say they needed something like this in their communities. I would usually give them materials about our program, and then they would call to ask, "What do we do next?" I would say, "Get a bunch of movers and shakers together, and we'll talk." But we have never really tried to promote the replication of the idea. One or two of the other institutes have fallen by the wayside, largely for financial reasons. It always requires a combination of fundraising ability, leadership, conceptual clarity.

JR: Would you call yourselves partners with the other institutes?

MS: I would certainly say associates. We are not partners in the sense of depending on each other. We meet twice a year, usually once in New York and once at one of the other institutes. The subjects of great interest are repertory—the kinds of pieces we present; politics/advocacy; fundraising. We are still unclear about how people get into the association or how they get "fired" out of it. We have thought about having a formal process, but right now it is very collegial, with a lot of phoning and faxing back and forth. Another emerging area is the touring or sharing of productions. We have had pieces that tour other places, and we have borrowed pieces from other institutes.

JR: By the way, do you have any problem with connecting the notion of education of teachers and children and the development of future audiences?

MS: A successful education program is likely to develop new audiences in a way that is far more meaningful than audience development programs because it creates people who really care. We are talking here about a kind of literacy, and that is what interests me. To educate kids in order to fill seats is insane. You don't teach kids to read in order to sell books.

This is a very strong issue, and it is one reason that the Institute is very different from the education programs of the other Lincoln Center constituents. We all continue to meet, but we agree that we all have our own, quite different missions. The Philharmonic's job is to get kids to like symphonic music, and we are trying to teach kids to listen. It is the same thing, but the purpose is different.

JR: Back to partnerships. It sounds to me as if you have proceeded mostly independently in a very focused way.

MS: That is the strength *and* the weakness. The weakness is that there are many clients we cannot serve. Ours is a rather narrowly focused institution, specifically aimed at kids who are not gifted musically or artistically. We hope that, because of what we do, kids will want to go on and study music or painting or go to concerts. Nevertheless, that is not what we are about. That specificity allows us to keep the focus on what we are doing. I think the factors that made this possible are unique: we are Lincoln Center; we were able to raise a lot of money; and we were able to achieve a certain degree of independence.

JR: Were those conditions that you set for yourself?

MS: Yes, I think so. One thing that came out of the *Hunting of the Squiggle* study was that you really had to have the support to do it. We were not a partner with Teachers College. I mean, if Teachers College went out of business, it would not affect what we did, and if we went out of business, it would not affect what they did. So, in that sense, there was never a real partnership.

Are we in partnership with the schools? We have a very close relationship with the schools, the teachers, but we are not partners. We are the providers and they are the purchasers, which is not exactly a partnership.

The schools did not come to us and say, "We need you to do this, so let's do this together." We created it, and they bought into it.

JR: True, but think of partnership on a developmental continuum. In the first stage of the partnership, the provider goes to a prospective purchaser and says, "I've got this idea, these products and these processes, are you interested?" "Yes, sure." But then, the nature of the services changes because a dialogue has been created between the provider and the purchaser (the teachers, principals, superintendents, supervisors) about the process to create the product. You start to create mutual expectations. The conversation becomes "the artists need to do this" or "the teachers may need to do that" and vice versa. It seems to me that you have begun to develop these kinds of partnerships with your schools.

MS: Oh, yes, there is no question about that.

JR: Last questions. In retrospect, what would you have done differently, and what advice would you have for other folks running their own dedicated arts-in-education organization?

MS: What would I have done differently? Fundamentally, nothing. We should have taken fewer byroads, and we should have raised more money. Still, the basic direction is right, and I think the proof is that it is surviving and thriving.

The advice I would give to other folks is that the number one priority is philosophy—the concept, the focus. It helps to shape everything you do and to raise money. One of the greatest problems that I see with the arts in education today is that people still don't understand that education in the arts is not one thing. It is many things. People seem incapable of sorting that out; it astonishes me. You don't teach language. You teach spelling, grammar, literature, composition. Yet people talk about the arts as though they were one thing. Any organization has to pick out its task and do that one thing rather than try to do everything and shift constantly with the winds. It takes many kinds of arts organizations to do it.

Mark Schubart, Chairman of the Lincoln Center Institute, began his writing career in 1936 as Associate Editor for the magazine Young America. *In 1940, he joined the newspaper* PM *as Assistant Music Editor, and in 1944 he was appointed Music Editor of the* New York Times. *He entered the field of education in 1946 when he was appointed Director of Public Activities for The Juilliard School of Music. In 1949, he was appointed Dean and subsequently Vice President at Juilliard, a post in which he served until 1963 when he joined the Lincoln Center administration as Director of Education and, in 1974 when it was founded, Director of the Lincoln Center Institute. He is also a member of the Lincoln Center Council.*

☞ *Figure 4.3: Essential Components of Aesthetic Education Institutes*

In 1975 Lincoln Center founded the Lincoln Center Institute for the Arts in Education to foster the study of aesthetic education in elementary and secondary schools. In the ensuing years, institutes modeled after Lincoln Center's have developed in a number of communities across the nation. Each of these institutes is entirely autonomous financially, organizationally and programmatically. Although they vary in some respects in accordance with the particular educational needs and artistic resources in each community, it is agreed among them that there are certain basic components common to all and considered by all to be essential. These are:

I. Educational Purpose

Perceiving and understanding the aesthetic dimension in art and in life is as basic to enlightened citizenship as understanding the workings of numbers, of words, of man's history and social traditions, and should be a part of the learning experiences of all young people. Institutes promote the exploration of this aesthetic dimension by focusing on intensive examinations of works of art with the objective of heightening perception and developing the ability to make critical choices.

II. Program Structure

The program is designed for a broad spectrum of elementary and secondary school students and their teachers. It is offered to all teachers in a given participating school—not arts teachers alone—and involves these teachers and their students in a process of carefully planned observation and analysis of works of art and active participation in exercises and other experiences designed to illuminate the relationship between artistic choice and aesthetic response. Toward this end, a working partnership is formed between schools and each institute and among artists, teachers and students working in classrooms.

The partnership is an ongoing one that requires long-term commitments from the participating school districts which provide administrative and financial support, as well as time in the school day for curricular units of study in aesthetic education. The institutes, in turn, commit to working closely with these schools on a continuing basis to help them in this effort, and to serve as artistic resource.

The program is organized as a three-step process involving intensive teacher education programs, planning units of study for the school year, and implementation in the classroom. Teacher workshops are led by teaching artists—professionals in various disciplines—who also plan with the participating teachers and serve as demonstrators in the classrooms.

Essential elements are performing and visual arts resources of high quality to provide a repertory for study by teachers and students, and sufficient numbers of skilled professional artists able and willing to serve as teaching artists in the program.

III. Institutional Structure

To support and carry out the work of an institute there are needed:

- A clearly defined institutional identity either as a freestanding, independent corporation, or as a distinct component of an arts center, an arts council, an educational institution or some combination thereof;

- Active interest and support of representative community leaders with interests in education and the arts, with a number of these sufficiently committed to the institute concept to form a board of directors or trustees to oversee the organization;

- Sufficient financial resources or reasonable prospects of obtaining such resources to support the organization over a multi-year period in order to provide requisite continuity;
- Commitment to the idea of aesthetic education among educators in key school districts in the area, and a willingness on their part to work in partnership with the institute to develop a program for their schools;
- An administrator committed to the idea of aesthetic education and capable of leading the effort.

What Makes an Effective Partnership?

Lessons Learned from the National Endowment for the Arts' Arts Plus[10] Experience

by Mindy Richman Garfinkel

Inner-city students work with members of a professional opera company to create an opera—written, directed, scored and produced by teenagers.

Student teachers learn to incorporate theater education into their study plans before they ever step into their own classrooms.

A five-year-old girl tells her teacher that a key element of a story she is writing is "Dialogue, of course."

These examples hint at how the arts can play a role in the education of children through Arts Plus, an Arts in Education Program initiative at the National Endowment for the Arts. The program was phased out when, with the onset of diminished resources, the Endowment restructured its programs and operation in 1996. Begun formerly as a pilot in 1991, the staff originally saw the program as a way to support partnerships between arts organizations and schools that would enable them to bring together their best talents and resources to achieve common goals. Schoolteachers and artists would work together to complement each other's expertise, creating a richer learning environment in the classroom.

The partnership opportunity has "enabled arts organizations and artists to improve their level of artistry, so that they in turn can have a stronger impact on what is done in the schools," notes Louise K. Stevens in her 1993 Arts Plus evaluation report to the National Endowment for the Arts.[11]

> "[This program] changed my whole approach to choreography," explains choreographer and dancer Loretta Livingston. "I realized that the subjects and the movement I had been using really didn't connect, didn't speak to people. I began experimenting. I developed entirely new works for my own company, which we are performing now with great success. It has been a wonderful progression for me."[12]

Arts Plus partnerships are designed to increase the classroom teacher's familiarity and comfort with the arts. Throughout the multi-year process, most participating teachers learn to understand how they can use the arts in their teaching. Teachers from Cesar Chavez and Gardenhill Elementary Schools commented that[13]:

> "Our dance residencies with Loretta Livingston have been like taking a college course on how to use movement and dance as an instructional tool. Dance and movement are now a regular part of my curriculum."

> "The residency with Madeline Soglin of Loretta Livingston and Dancers has made my curriculum stronger, my students better people, and school a nicer place to work. "

> "Through the residency with LynnAnne Hanson, I have grown professionally—tremendously. I am a *risk* taker now. I think that the process, and not necessarily the final project, is really the most important."

Characteristics of Effective Arts Plus Partnerships

Between its inception and 1994, Arts Plus supported 21 partnerships nationwide, involving more than 150 arts organizations and artists and roughly 375 schools. The Arts Endowment supports three years of partnership work for each project selected. Although it is very early in the evaluation process, the following presents an informal look at what happened in selected Arts Plus community partnerships and some of the lessons that were learned by the Arts Plus participants and by the staff at the Arts Endowment.

During the first three years of the program, staff observed that partnerships of effective Arts Plus projects exhibit the following attributes.

The pursuit of artistic excellence and a demonstrated history and commitment to young people is critical to an Arts Plus partnership.
The artistic quality of a given arts group by itself does not guarantee the educational quality of an Arts Plus project. Conversely, an educationally vigorous project that does not appropriately involve quality artists and art works does not guarantee success, either.

Strong Arts Plus partnerships have project mission statements that are compatible with each partner organization's goals.
Ideally, potential Arts Plus schools and arts organizations approach a partnership after considering their long-term organizational goals and realizing that a team approach would be vital to their achievement. Prospective partners must clarify why they would commit their valuable resources (people, money, space, time) and outline the benefits to their organizations. Once the partners understand their individual goals, they can collectively work to reach an agreement on a project mission statement, a process that is usually very labor-intensive. The partnership joint mission statement becomes a road map that outlines who will benefit from the venture.

The key players in the project from the school and the arts organization must be involved in and committed to the partnership.
To maximize resources and help a partnership reach its goals, the key players at every level of the project need to be given an opportunity to contribute to the partnership design so that everyone can own the choices that are made and feel responsible for implementing them.

It is especially important to involve key leaders. "The involvement of the principals at the sites was critical," stated Christopher Forehan, principal of the Cesar Chavez Elementary School in Norwalk, CA, in his address to the National Council on the Arts in May 1994. "It was very apparent that the success of the program included the fact that the principals were right there with the staff every step of the way. Whether coordinating space for assemblies, guest workshops or residencies, organizing release time for quality planning, or participating in the residency workshops, the principal clearly had to be the education leader."

Commitment from the arts organization's leadership is equally important. During their final year of Arts Plus support, Carol North Evans, producing director of Metro Theater Company (MTC) in St. Louis, reflected on her company's experience and what it has meant to her company.

> [Our Integrating the Arts Program] has deepened the commitment of MTC members and staff, who have seen a change in individual teachers and know that they are a vital part of facilitating that change. It has strengthened a community bond with schools, with local districts, with superintendents and with agencies such as the Missouri Alliance for Arts Education. It has been a part of a growing bond with other arts organizations in a city that has not historically fostered that sort of thinking.... It has helped increase MTC's local visibility at a grassroots level. Teachers and their families are increasingly a part of our audience for local performances and events that are unrelated to this project. The program has helped MTC enhance a profile of organizational integrity with area leaders. For many years, MTC was known as a daring arts organization that developed unusual theater pieces. Now, the full measure of our mission is a part of our community identity.[14]

Partners need to communicate, clarify and understand each other's needs, priorities, roles and functions in the partnership.
Arts organizations that attend to the needs of the school partner and focus their organizational missions on education are more likely to be effective in a partnership than those who do not. Learning the language and schedule of the partners—such as discovering what is involved in developing an integrated curriculum or understanding the role of an opera company's supernumeraries—is a critical hurdle. Every Arts Plus site reported that the partners had to develop a careful schedule to work around the schools (avoiding test periods, concerts, proms, plays, big games or the janitorial schedule) and the arts organizations (avoiding production periods, auditions, fundraising events). Understanding the fundamental nature of each partner organization's "business" is critical to developing mutual respect.

In successful partnerships, key individuals—such as the project director, teachers, artists and principals—have good communication skills and learn to identify what concerns affect their own members as well as those of their partner organizations. They work hard to accommodate their partners.

There is no magic formula. While the partnership planning process provides a framework, the experience of working together is the most useful tool in making adjustments that allow the program to run smoothly.
Many thriving Arts Plus projects created partnerships geared to help schools deal with education reform. For example, Stage One: The Louisville Children's Theatre worked with three schools in different parts of Kentucky after the state's supreme court scrapped the entire school system through the landmark Kentucky Education Reform Act (KERA) of 1990. In KERA, schools were suddenly responsible for teaching a brand-new set of learner outcomes. "Literally dozens of the 75 outcomes defined in the KERA can be beneficially impacted by a comprehensive arts education program," wrote the partners in their original proposal for Arts Endowment support.

Successful partnerships depend upon each partner's ability to be flexible enough to adapt to unexpected needs and changing circumstances. "We thought we were running one pilot project, but what we really have is a separate pilot in each one of the classrooms we are working in," stated Yolande Spears, director of education for the Bushnell Memorial Hall.

Partners also found that they had to tinker with their original Arts Plus plans along the way. In some instances, teachers wanted more time to study and feel comfortable teaching a certain art form. Leadership changed at some school buildings and district levels, resulting in a drastic loss of support for the Arts Plus project. One school district unexpectedly reconfigured the population of its schools during the course of the three-year Arts Plus period, so that buildings formerly teaching grades K-8 shifted to K-5, and new junior high schools were created for grades 6-8.

In every case, key partners revisited their goals and objectives and reformulated their strategies to ensure that the fundamental aspects of the overall program would not be lost. Time lines were adjusted to accommodate a longer learning curve. In the situations where the new school leaders would not make Arts Plus a priority, alternative partners were found. Even in the reconfigured school district, partners found ways in which they could provide in-service training and mentoring to teachers who would be new to the partner schools.

Shared responsibility for planning and extended professional development are critical to effective partnerships.

Several Arts Plus sites reported that to make a partnership work, artists and teachers must learn how to plan and teach together. In the schools, Arts Plus evaluator Louise Stevens noted that in successful Arts Plus partnerships: "The emphasis on teacher training...must be supported by a philosophical approach to...professional development that offers opportunities for significant growth."[15]

The best of these sessions encouraged teachers to take an active role in their own professional development. In St. Louis, for example, teachers raved about their experience with the Metro Theatre Company because the artists do "not teach new strategies, rather they convey a new paradigm for thinking and processing educational objectives that allows for new and creative strategies to be found."[16] Nearly all Arts Plus sites have created semester- or year-long training programs. "Participants saw a dramatic difference when teachers made commitments to their own professional development that stretched for months and years,"[17] stated Stevens.

Shared responsibility is key to any partnership activity and is especially crucial for Arts Plus Programs.

Opera Memphis General/Artistic Director Michael Ching summarized how his company worked with Booker T. Washington High, an inner-city school, to share programmatic responsibility and at the same time create ownership of the partnership process. In this example, a student-created production called *Limits to Life* was developed. It featured a young character named Rachel Lyon, who searched her past and the past of many African Americans through times of slavery, the Harlem Renaissance, the civil rights era and the present day.

> The production was the culmination of many months of collaborative effort. Several English classes learned about possible ways to create a script. Each class then submitted a possible scenario for the script to a student committee that selected the historical scenario, which was then turned over to a special script committee of student writers who met regularly to flesh out the outline. Further modifications were made daily in teacher Marion Crooks' drama class. A professional choreographer, Marton Gales, was brought in to choreograph part of the show. Opera Memphis Music Administrator John Derby worked with student composers to develop the musical numbers. These were turned over for refinement and arrangements by music teacher Deborah Davis.

> Principal Elsie Lewis Bailey knew how to maximize the strengths available at her school. Since elaborate costumes and scenery would have overwhelmed the small and new drama department, some costumes were based on printed t-shirts produced in teacher Cecil Moore's visual art classes. The silhouette of a slave breaking his chain was designed by student Edward Sanford for the program cover illustration and commemorative t-shirt.[18]

Successful partnerships develop plans to ensure financial and institutional continuity.

Since the pilot Arts Plus sites have just completed or are just completing their funding period, it is too early to tell whether the programs will be continued. Most of the Arts Plus sites state that they are prepared to continue their projects, and some schools have committed thousands of dollars to the project in the year following the end of federal funding. Despite this good news, everyone faces a sharp challenge to raise funds. Still, there are indications that some partnerships will be sustained long after federal funding is gone.

In Montana, Helena Presents Executive Director Arnie Malina and local school district leaders have developed a partnership that uses different community committees. Each committee has members from various organizations (including artists and teachers) to encourage personal responsibility for the partnership's goals. Active committees (including curriculum, teacher training, advocacy, visiting artists, evaluation and documentation) plan and implement partnership programming. To ensure financial support beyond the Arts Plus period, Helena Presents and school district leaders have started a formal foundation for endowing the Arts Plus project. More than $100,000 was raised from individuals and foundations by Spring 1995.

Other partnerships considered expanding staff as the Arts Plus program grew. "The (Integrating the Arts Program) has become an institutionalized part of Metro Theater Company's mission. As the demand for expansion of the program continues, we are making plans to train other artists in program implementation and may add an education director to our permanent staff in the future," wrote Carol North Evans, producing director of the Metro Theater Company.[19] Stevens found that training a core of teachers who could then mentor others within a school was the most likely way to ensure that Arts Plus goals would be continued. With the trend toward site-based management, some participants found that by concentrating on a core group of five or six teachers within a school, the project was more likely to gain support in key site-based committees. The process is time-consuming, but partners found that the team approach—the combination of arts teacher, classroom teacher and teaching artist develops a shared passion for learning.

Successful partnerships broaden the base of funding.

Arts Plus is one way the NEA invests in communities by serving as a catalyst for growth and development. Most Arts Plus projects have now attracted both state and corporate support. In California, Chavez and Gardenhill Elementary Schools were awarded the state's prestigious Golden Bell education award in 1994 for work done through Arts Plus. The Dell'Arte/BLUES project was named the rural model site for arts education programming by the California Arts Council in 1994. The Multicultural Initiative, a project of Fairfax, VA county schools and Wolf Trap, secured an unprecedented $200,000 grant from TRW shortly after being named an Arts Plus site. In Utah, Enoch Elementary School's work in the Arts Plus project helped to get them designated as a model site arts school by the state office of education. Enoch teachers have since gotten their entire district enthused and involved in arts education.

Documentation is key to a partnership's ability to tell its story and to evaluate the effectiveness of its program.

Documentation is an absolutely critical function when approaching potential funders or new partners. It also serves as the raw data from which to sort out successes from failures to evaluate the partnership's effectiveness. However, the words "documentation" and "evaluation" struck fear or loathing into the hearts of Arts Plus participants. While the idea of program evaluation was not a new concept to most of the partners, several sites did not understand what documentation meant and how they should do it.

During the Arts Plus pilot phase, consistent baseline data were not collected among the 21 pilot sites. Data-gathering was made more complex because goals and objectives varied widely from site to site to allow maximum flexibility in achieving the broad Arts Plus goals. Sites had varying degrees of comfort and sophistication regarding evaluation. The Arts Endowment's staff has realized that Arts Plus participants need more direction in this arena, and all future projects will work with standard, baseline evaluation questions that have been developed by an Arts Endowment staff member with evaluation and research expertise.

Still, some participants learned to like the documentation and evaluation process. "We have come to rely on outside, objective evaluation of our various programs and, even after the expiration of the grant, have elected to continue this most worthwhile aspect," stated Charles MacKay, general director of Opera Theatre of St. Louis, and Robert Nordman, supervisor of music, St. Louis Public Schools, reflecting on the evaluation effort required by Arts Plus.

Learning to Unleash the Power of Partnerships

"There's a tremendous power in this work," exclaimed Dell'Arte's Project Director Peter Buckley. "We are learning to unleash it, use it, and we plan to master it and spread it as the years go on. These partnerships are absolutely vital to the future of arts organizations, educational institutions and the children themselves."[20]

Such interdependence in the arts and education is crucial to the ability to survive and thrive. The Arts Plus initiative encourages these relationships and gives people the opportunity to develop their own tools to move forward together.

Mindy Richman Garfinkel currently serves as the Congressional Liaison Specialist at the National Endowment for the Arts. Previously, she was the Arts Endowment's Senior Program Specialist in the Arts in Education Program. Prior to joining the Arts Endowment in 1988, she was a Grant Specialist at the U.S. Department of Education and a graphic artist. She holds a master's degree in organizational development from Johns Hopkins University and a bachelor's degree in art education from Ohio State University.

Notes

1. *The American Heritage Dictionary*, third edition, version 3.6a. Copyright © 1994, Softkey International, Inc.

2. Craig Dreeszen, *Intersections: Community Arts and Education Collaborations* (The Arts Extension Service: Amherst, MA, 1992), p. 11. In this report, Dreeszen has examined, analyzed and synthesized the concept and operation of partnerships in two projects in which over 250 professionals participated. Surveys were used to collect partnership cases that in turn were used to extract principles and success factors. Co-sponsors included the National Endowment for the Arts' Arts in Education Program, the National Assembly of Local Arts Agencies, the Arts Extension Service and the Kennedy Center Alliance for Arts Education.

3. Reprinted by permission of the author. The chart is updated to reflect the design Dreeszen currently uses, which emphasizes the evaluation component by putting it in a separate row of its own in the matrix.

4. Dreeszen, ibid, p. 17.

5. For a discussion and an analysis of networking and collaboration among schools and school systems, with the arts community as a resource to the process, refer to my book *Changing Schools Through the Arts: How to Build on the Power of an Idea* (New York: McGraw-Hill, 1982; ACA Books, 1990).

6. Dreeszen, ibid, p. 29.

7. Mary Joyce, *First Steps in Teaching Creative Dance to Children* (Palo Alto, CA: Mayfield Publishing, 1973, 1980).

8. This group of funders included: The Chicago Community Trust, Continental Bank, the Arie and Ida Crown Memorial, the Richard H. Driehaus Foundation, the Fel-Pro/Mecklenburger Foundation, Kraft General Foods, Inc., the Reva and David Logan Foundation, the John D. and Catherine T. MacArthur Foundation, Marshall Field's, the Polk Bros. Foundation, Prince Charitable Trusts, the Sara Lee Foundation, and the WPWR-TV Channel 50 Foundation. Additional support has been provided by Ameritech, the Chicago Tribune Foundation, the Gaylord & Dorothy Donnelley Charitable Trust, the Lloyd A. Fry Foundation, the GE Fund, the Harris Foundation, the Joyce Foundation, the Alexander Julian Foundation for Aesthetic Education and Understanding, the Louis R. Lurie Foundation, the Mayer and Morris Kaplan Family Foundation, the Northern Trust Company, the Woods Fund of Chicago, and the Illinois Arts Council.

9. *The Hunting of the Squiggle* (New York: Lincoln Center for the Performing Arts, Inc., 1972), p. 16.

10. As a result of the reorganization of the NEA effective in January 1996, the Arts Plus program no longer exists as a separate initiative. Many of its principles have been integrated into the guidelines for one of the four new main theme categories: Education and Access.

11. Louise K. Stevens, *Arts Plus Initiative, Findings and Outcomes: A Formative Evaluation* (a report prepared for the Arts in Education Program, National Endowment for the Arts, 1993), p. 7.

12. Ibid, p. 7.

13. The Music Center, final report, April 24, 1995. Artist in Residence and Teacher Partnerships Evaluation Comments, 1993-1994 Cesar Chavez and Gardenhill Elementary Schools, p. 3.

14. Metro Theater Company interim report, February 24, 1994.

15. Stevens, ibid. pp. 5-6.

16. Metro Theatre Company interim report, letter to Carol Commerford, Executive Director, Missouri Alliance for Arts Education, January 26, 1994.

17. Stevens, ibid. p. 11.

18. Opera Memphis interim report, October 12, 1994, p. 1.

19. Metro Theater Company final report, Project Director's overview, p. 5. (Evans, a paid professional director, spent at least 50 percent of her time on education activities, thus satisfying the Arts Plus eligibility requirement).

20. Dell'Arte final report, August, 1994, p. 4.

PART II
IS A PARTNERSHIP FOR YOU?

Questioning the Educational Imperative [1]
A Partnership Guide for Arts Organizations [2]

Is Arts Education for You?

Not every arts organization, museum, neighborhood arts group or community arts center wants or needs to get involved in education. In addition, education does not necessarily fit comfortably into the artistic mission, public personality or economic capability of each of these groups. Indeed, some people insist that, in schools and colleges at least, artists should not teach the arts, professional educators should. I think there is plenty of room for everyone, provided the work is top quality, pedagogically sound and appropriate for the age, background, abilities and needs of the learner.

I address this section of the book primarily to the directors, managers and board members who have thought about working as partners in and with the schools. It is for those hardy souls who are considering venturing beyond traditional outreach activities into the development of a more comprehensive, interactive education program, but who are not yet convinced of the wisdom, the necessity or the feasibility of the idea. As you are by now aware, an arts partnership is not a decision to be made lightly, for once taken, the commitment and resources required to succeed are considerable.

While reduced-price or free tickets to regular performances or exhibitions, open dress rehearsals, abridged touring productions, traveling exhibits accompanied by teachers' guides and the like are time-honored and vital services to the general and educational community, they do not, in and of themselves, constitute a partnership, and they require relatively little collaborative design effort with the recipients of these services. My job here is to provide you with a framework for weighing the pros and cons of partnerships in the context of your particular situation.

Arts Education Along a Continuum: Some Definitions

As I discussed in the first section of this chapter, I define arts-in-education programs as a range of engaging, interactive and informative events that exist along a continuum. They may consist of a series of related activities, extending from simple exposure to an arts event or exhibit to a comprehensive instructional program. These programs may incorporate performances in and outside the school, lecture-demonstrations, curtain talks, museum visits, classroom visits by artists, workshops and/or a short or long residency. As you move along the continuum from simple introductory or exposure programs to more complex arrangements, increased amounts of time and attention are spent on the professional development of teachers and artists, the collaborative design and development of curriculum and instructional materials, program documentation and evaluation, student assessment, and the dissemination of information about the program to a wide audience.

An education program may contain a combination of these elements. Activities may vary in number, length and intensity. They may be introductory, intermediate, or advanced and sophisticated. They may require active participation or more passive involvement. The defining characteristic that makes the effort "educational" is its instructional purpose, method of delivery and result (what learners will know and be able to do). What the arts organization plans to teach will have been identified as a need by the "audience," who will learn something specific—skills, knowledge, information or the ability to appreciate, perceive or do something differently, new or better than they could before.

Please note that in describing a program, I refer to activities, events and components in multiples or as an interrelated series. Individual performances or arts experiences, known in the vernacular as "one-shot, hit-and-run gigs," are usually by themselves not educational according to my definition. However, when taken together with other events and surrounded with instructional and educative activities, they can become so.

By the arts in education, I mean:

- attendance at performances, lecture-demonstrations and recitals; visits to museums and galleries, folk and traditional venues, and community cultural centers;
- instruction in all aspects of all the arts (using an inclusive definition of the classical and popular arts, styles, genres, philosophies and aesthetics);
- relating individual art forms to other arts disciplines (interarts);
- integrating the arts with other subject areas equally (interdisciplinary and multicultural);
- using the arts to illuminate other subjects or areas of interest (dance as a teaching tool, for example);
- employing other disciplines to interpret or explicate an art form; and
- studying the history, aesthetics, criticism and language of the arts and the related design, production, theatrical and commercial aspects of the industry.

Instructional activities for students, teachers and other participants can take place in any formal or informal environment conducive to teaching and learning the arts: secondary and elementary schools; colleges and universities; and arts, cultural and other hospitable community facilities.

Needs and Issues in the Field: What Can Your Organization Do to Help?

Despite making headway in the arts in education over the last 30 years, certain needs persist. They tend to gravitate around issues of considerable political and social sensitivity, and their economic implications are often profound. I would advise any arts organization contemplating an education program, especially one that will entail partnerships and collaborative enterprise, to consider these issues at some length.

Governing Questions

The governing questions when discussing these issues are:

- What can my organization do to help meet these needs or address these issues, and are we prepared to make this commitment?
- Do we have the leadership and the resources to carry out our good intentions?
- Do we have the institutional stamina to sustain the effort?

The Needs and Issues to Be Considered

The classical and contemporary arts are generally not accessible to the American public. They intimidate many people. A large segment of the population has no idea (and little motivation for learning) how to build a bridge from their lives to the formal presentation of dance, opera, theater, symphony and chamber music, museum and gallery exhibitions, and the like. In other words, because they have not been taught, most people are not "arts literate"; they do not know how to "read" the languages, symbols or metaphors of the arts. If we are to build our audiences, socialize and integrate our communities, and pass on our rich and varied cultural heritage, then the challenge is to find ways to introduce, engage and make articulate supporters, participants and advocates of many more of our citizens.

Many classical and contemporary arts providers, both in the schools and in the community, do not appear to address the issue of ethnic and racial diversity. They seem unconcerned about balance in their program content or in their choices of performers and teaching artists. This tends to reinforce negative and reverse cultural stereotypes and discourages children and adults who might otherwise respond positively to people of color or other minorities on the stage and in the classroom.

Many of the classical and contemporary performing arts are unaffordable for large numbers of people. The economics of the industry discourages both single and multiple ticket-buying. Since appreciation and understanding of an art form depends largely on repeated exposure and participation, high prices perpetuate and exacerbate the problems of developing an interested and knowledgeable audience.

Access to the arts is often denied, especially for those who are not within easy geographic reach or considered prime potential ticket buyers by marketing and audience development professionals. The "underserved" populations—code language for minorities, the poor, the disabled, the elderly—are frequently overlooked, except in social service programs for dropouts, pregnancy-prevention, drug abuse and the like. This situation, along with high prices, reinforces the elitist label attached to the arts and helps to defeat efforts at widespread acceptance and support.

Equity in the distribution and allocation of arts services to the public schools is almost nonexistent. Some schools have arts specialists; others do not. When they do exist, they are usually teachers of music and the visual arts who meet students once a week for 30 or 40 minutes. Some schools get many artist workshops, residencies and performances. Others get a few or none. Factors in this imbalance are geographic convenience, school population, school and community financing, and community attitudes toward the value of the arts in schools and in the larger society.

Cultural diversity/pluralism is much in demand but hard to define and attain. At stake is a complex struggle for parity in American culture. Too often, the debate becomes rhetorical or political, pitting one culture against another or emphasizing the differences rather than the underlying similarities, further polarizing an already fractured society.

Arts organizations frequently confuse their wants with school and learner needs. Some arts providers decide to design programs and services based upon what they want the schools to need or what they believe the schools ought to have. They do not consult the schools, let alone plan with them, to determine collectively what these needs are and how they can best meet them. This conduct, born either of ignorance or of arrogance, is based on the insulting assumption that the artist knows best and the schools know little or nothing about the arts and how to teach them. It is compounded by complete indifference to general curriculum.

Many arts organizations are more interested in filling empty seats for existing repertory or in delivering prepackaged products than in offering specially designed services that connect with young lives and contemporary interests. The programs and the products selected may not be appropriate to the age, background and sensibility of the intended audience. In many instances, the captive and unprepared audience ends up hostile to—rather than enthusiastic about—the arts that have been foisted upon them.

The notion that the goals of audience development and arts education are incompatible, if not antagonistic, is a widespread misconception. The truth is that they are highly complementary and synergistic. Education is a long-term goal; audience development is short-term. A good arts-in-education program for young people teaches, among many things, appreciation of and interest in the arts; it can develop candidates for future audiences who may currently lack the economic power or discretion over finances to buy tickets. A good audience development program educates audiences about the value of the product and the virtue of buying tickets—today. The main variables are time and money.

In today's highly complex and competitive world, effective arts-in-education programs cannot survive without partnerships and collaboration: public/private, federal, state and local. There is simply not enough money to sustain them otherwise. These partnerships are difficult to form and maintain because of the collaborators' different agendas and modes of operation. They require time, energy and constant dialogue among the participants to ensure that the results are far greater and more cost-effective than the efforts of an organization acting alone.

The Advantages and Disadvantages of an Arts Organization's Involvement in Education

Clearly, major policy and institutional change is required to improve the current predicament of the arts and of the arts in education. It would be reasonable to wonder what any individual organization could possibly do to improve the situation. It would also be reasonable to ask, "Why bother, when the deck seems stacked against us?"

I operate on the assumption that all politics are local and that effective and lasting change in our schools and communities will never happen all at once, by fiat or presidential proclamation. It will occur—because it always has—one school at a time, one neighborhood at a time and one arts organization at a time. With this as a working premise, let us look at some pros and cons for an arts organization to consider when deciding whether to get involved in education.

What are the Advantages?

Fundraising and Community Development. Arts education is attractive to funders, both public and private, federal, state and local. Arts education is valued as an end in itself and as a means to other ends, among them the preparation of students and adults for careers on and off the stage. It also helps to cultivate the individual traits that business and industry now need and prize: teamwork; independent, imaginative thinking; creative problem-solving; the ability to focus and concentrate; persistence; perception. Furthermore, arts education attracts the attention and support of those who see arts organizations as instrumental to community building and local cultural development; they are willing to support efforts that establish closer ties between an organization and its community.

Marketing and Public Relations. An education program gives the organization a greater presence and visibility, other venues to play, other markets to cultivate—in both the schools and the community. It is important to an organization's image that it be perceived as "giving back" to its local community.

Audience Development and Ticket Sales. An education program helps to build audiences who value and appreciate the arts (adults in the short run, children and youth in the longer run). It is an established fact that those who participate in arts education at an early age become the audiences of the future. Moreover, those who do participate are often convinced that the arts are useful for an examined and more fulfilling life.

Political. An arts education program that appeals to local decision makers and champions of change creates articulate advocates for the arts in positions of power and influence.

What are the Disadvantages?

Often an artistic director, an executive director, the board of directors, the staff or the artists will say they are not interested in, not trained, have no time for, or are afraid of working with schools or community centers. They see no immediate benefit in doing so. Here are some of the perceived disadvantages they mention most frequently.

A Distraction from Primary Purpose. Education will distract from the primary purpose of the institution—making, exhibiting, producing or presenting art.

Scarcity of Resources. The institution has insufficient money, staff, time, energy and space to design and carry out an education program.

Lack of Know-How. No one on staff knows schools or has the education experience or expertise to design effective programs for community audiences.

The Need for Instant and Tangible Results. It takes too long to design and develop a program that may, or may not, produce significant increases in community awareness of the organization and attendance at events, especially in a touring situation.

Conflicting Company Priorities for Money. Spending staff time raising funds for an education program diverts the focus from raising funds to support the organization's primary artistic activities.

Belief System. The arts must maintain their mystery, illusion and distance. They belong in the studio, the museum, the concert hall, the theater. The organization might risk losing control of its performers and of its artistic freedom in its choice of repertory.

Quality Control. The arts in the schools and community will jeopardize the quality of the performance because facilities, lighting and space are often inadequate and even dangerous.

Lack of Public Appreciation. The uninitiated, untutored audience will not appreciate our work and may give us a hostile reception.

A Planning Framework for an Organization's Arts in Education Program

Let us assume that you are a director of an arts organization and that you have asked your staff and your board of directors to read this chapter of the book. Further, assume that you have met with each group, separately or together, that you have discussed the pros and cons I have listed above, and that there is an expressed, if tentative, interest in looking into the idea. Where do you go from here? How do you begin?

Do some basic research. Your next steps might include taking a formal inventory of your existing resources, such as the capabilities and interests of your staff and board, and making a survey of untapped funding opportunities. You need to research the school community, gathering information about existing arts-in-education programs, the district and the schools and collecting and studying their instructional plans or curriculum frameworks. You then need to ask some hard questions and, if appropriate, start designing your program. The following suggestions may help you move from ideas into action. They are very basic and, for some, even simplistic. Nevertheless, they may prove useful as guidelines, even for the more sophisticated.

Start with the hard questions. Here are two important ones:

What can your organization, your staff, your arts resources do for the general curriculum, the schools, the community and the education of the people in them?

In what ways can you address the issue of arts literacy? How can you help your current and potential audiences to "see, hear, feel and respond" on a kinesthetic, emotional, aesthetic and intellectual level to the arts?

Review the Needs and Issues section of this article and start to set priorities for the concerns that you believe apply to your circumstances and community. Discuss these topics with your staff and board, then with appropriate representatives from the schools, the arts and the general community. Tailor these needs and issues to your own organization, the schools and the community. Later, when you have chosen an education partner, you will have a chance to make these needs program- and site-specific.

Consider choosing another arts partner(s). Many arts organizations form consortia to provide education programs and services. Consider a local sponsor; another arts group; a civic organization concerned with the welfare of children; the state or local arts agency; a foundation, corporation or business; or perhaps the Junior League or another volunteer organization with a history of community service. Meet to discuss missions, philosophy, education aims, available resources, communication systems, finances. Carefully define the educational and community-building purpose of the partnership; delineate the turf; spell out the roles and responsibilities; and put it in writing. Determine, if you collaborate, whether you will provide better services for the same or only a little more money and whether you will enhance your own and your arts partner's institutional capability and visibility.

List the resources you have and the services you think you can probably offer. Refer to the kinds of activities I mentioned earlier under the definition of education. Bring a draft list of your own choices to representatives of the population you have decided to serve (from the schools and/or the community) and ask them whether the activities do, in fact, interest them and respond to their needs. Refine the services and make them site-specific.

Decide whom you want to serve and choose your "education" partner. Start small: one school, or one grade or class in a few schools. For organizations that do most of their community service on tour, work with your sponsor, your booking agent and/or the local arts agency *well before* the engagement to determine who the most likely partners might be. Ask them to put you in touch with a key person in the local school district (the arts coordinator, the administrator in charge of curriculum and instruction) or the arts champion in the community.

Design your collaborative program. Working with your arts partner(s), if any, and your education partner(s), specify goals, objectives, activities, strategies for delivery of instruction and support services (professional development for artists and teachers, curriculum and resource material design), administrative staff and artistic personnel, direct program costs, anticipated outcomes (in terms of the needs of the learners!), evaluation and budget. When identifying resources, try, to the extent possible, to use or reallocate existing money, people, facilities, space and the like.

The following four characteristics of an effective educational program or service can help to guide you in your design efforts:

Artistic excellence. The performance, service or instruction represents the highest professional standards of the organization.

Aesthetic authenticity or integrity. The arts, whether taught formally or as a tool for learning other subjects or concepts, retain an identifiable, authentic aesthetic dimension. They are not bent out of unrecognizable shape nor put into inappropriate service for other ends where they serve neither the cause of the art form nor other authentic curricular objectives.

Artistic and educational scope and balance. The arts and educational goals and activities have parity, no matter which discipline is used as a strategy for illuminating the other.

Educational effectiveness. The program has a clarity of purpose, an appropriate methodology, a flowing sequence of imaginative activities and an observable, definable result that corresponds to your original intentions. Participatory activities are engaging, creative and suitable for the performing or learning environment. Program content is appropriate for the age, background and cultural sensibility of your audience or participants.

Begin. Proceed carefully, slowly and with patience. Keep your expectations modest and do not be discouraged by temporary setbacks.

Keep up a steady stream of communication between your "client" population, your partners and your organization. If you do not have an education director, designate one person as the education program liaison and administrator until you are sure you are in the field for keeps; then designate or hire a full-time education person as quickly as possible.

Monitor the program regularly to assess your work and make timely modifications where necessary. At the end of the trial or pilot period, meet with your clients and your partners to decide whether and how to proceed together.

Document the process and the product. Share this information with your entire organization, the board, donors, sponsors, partners and others in the arts community.

I hope this framework helps you to decide whether education is an appropriate activity for your organization. If you are already involved, I hope it has given you a new slant or perspective. David O'Fallon, Joan Boyett and Bennett Tarleton offer more guidelines, warnings and assurances from their rich experience.

The Arts Organization and Public Education

A Guide to Conducting a Self-Audit

by David O'Fallon

Today we know far more about the stunningly complex processes of learning and teaching than we did 90 years ago, but the template of American secondary education that was struck then is very much in place. Indeed we seem almost afraid to ask fresh questions about learning and teaching, perhaps because of what we might find.

—Theodore Sizer

According to the National Center for Educational Statistics, there are 45 million students in 85,000 K-12 public schools in America, 15,000 school boards and 56 governmental agencies that legislate state, district and territorial education. For the first time in the nation's history, voluntary national goals have been established as part of an unprecedented national movement to reform education. Yet schools are not monolithic entities. Instead, the American education system is a complex and varied web of institutions. Somewhere among the 15,000 school districts you will find one of almost every form and type of education, from the most creative to the most traditional, from the most progressive to the most authoritarian, from the most equitable and compassionate to the cynical and prejudiced. Most people agree that schools and education need to do better; few agree on what "better" means.

The ferment of education reform has created an opportunity for the arts. As an instrument of education reform and as legitimate subjects for study, the arts have a chance to move closer to the core of education. This is true in part because the broad direction of reform favors the kinds of thinking and ways of working used in the arts. These broad directions include:

- Learning as the active construction of knowledge rather than the passive reception of information, with students taking responsibility for their own learning rather than waiting for the teacher to dispense it;
- Teachers as guides to learning and managers of resources rather than knowledge experts;
- Curriculum that emphasizes the integration of knowledge and the relationships and connections among domains rather than each discipline (and teacher) operating in near isolation from the other;
- Assessment of learning that is as varied, imaginative and complex as the learning itself, and that uses performance and portfolios to show changes in

learning over time rather than standardized paper and pencil tests or simple and often misleading "snapshots"; and

- Increased awareness that significant education happens beyond the walls of the school, and that the resources of the community are needed to help all students achieve at high levels.

Arts organizations involved in education—or those contemplating the move—enter a field that is rapidly changing. To make the most of the opportunities presented requires an institutional clarity of purpose and direction. Without it, organizations that plunge headlong into education run the risk of being sidetracked and disrupted by competing interests. The following questions will guide you and your organization through a self-audit that will help you to construct a clearer picture of where you currently stand with education and whether it fits comfortably into your core mission.

1. Does your organization have a philosophy of education?

Developing and sustaining an education program of high quality is impossible without first comprehending what education is. Arts organizations are often criticized for not understanding education and for offering programs that briefly expose learners to an art form that might stir curiosity and stimulate awareness but that do not create real opportunities for sustained learning. If your organization is perceived as being in the flashy entertainment and exposure business, it will be difficult for you to be taken seriously as an educator.

To do well in the arts-in-education business, you must ground your organization's efforts in a clear understanding of education and of what you hope to accomplish. You must be able to articulate an education mission, strategy and program to avoid the criticism that your education program is just a marketing scheme to put bottoms in seats. To compete for funds to support education programs, you must excel in education, not just in the arts.

- Does your organization discuss the meaning of education?

Education is about people. What Americans want from schools and what they think the value of an education is, are wide open for debate. In my view, the heart of the debate is about what kind of person—what essential habits of mind and heart and spirit—we want to encourage and call forth. Education for some is the mastery of a body of knowledge and the attainment of a set of skills. Its purpose is to prepare for a productive life, to acquire and apply skills needed for employment. For others, education is more comprehensive and humanistic, with the goal of helping each person to attain his or her individual gifts and talents fully. Still others think that education is essentially the preparation and enculturation of young people into society. For them, the purpose is learning to respect authority, to work in groups and teams and to learn the approved answers to complex questions. Some turn to the root of the word, the Latin *educare*, which means to draw out. For them, education is about the task of becoming human, the ongoing exploration, creation and construction of meaning, both personal and social.

Participate in the debate about the meaning of education. Carry the discussion on with board and staff and go to the public tables where it is on the agenda. The education mission is inevitably a public one and unavoidably political. Your arts organization will be defined somewhere along the political spectrum, even if you do not declare yourself. Even to stand for independent thought is to take a position to which some would object.

- Does your organization understand why the arts are now part of the national goals and considered to be unique forms of knowledge and ways of learning?

To have credibility in education, an arts organization must be able to articulate the unique ways in which the arts change teaching and learning and their distinctiveness as forms of knowledge. Know where your organization stands on these issues. Without this self-knowledge, you risk being pulled into educational practices and espousing goals with which you do not agree. You also risk not being able to deliver on promises, real or implied, for which you do not have the resources.

2. What are the core values of the organization and how are these related to education and the education programs?

The core values of an organization are expressed in its mission and should shape the education program. Arts organizations should build from their strengths—know what they do best, know the central purpose for their existence—and act upon them.

For example, if a performing arts center's core mission is to produce new works of excellence, then this should shape and guide its education program. If it is dedicated to standard or more traditional repertory, then its education program should reflect this and use it as a point of departure. If the organization places a high value on building better communications with a more diverse population, then education efforts will be directed toward programs different from those best suited to discovering talent.

It is important to distinguish between education designed primarily to be about the artwork or event and education designed primarily for the person experiencing the work. These are not mutually exclusive, but an emphasis upon one will affect the other and not always for the better. For example, if the educational task is defined as "helping people know more about Shakespeare," then a great deal of information is likely to be provided about the playwright, the various versions of the play, performance history, particular choices made by this director and cast for this performance, and so on. If the task is defined as "helping the participants understand themselves better through Shakespeare," then more emphasis is placed upon the questions and the occasions beyond the performance itself in which the participants are invited, and excited by, challenges to connect the plays to their life experiences.

Education implies a *relationship* with the participants. Artwork exists in a context of production and reflection, of action and response, of intent and interpretation. The creative tension that exists between creator and performer, between performer and presenter—among all of these and audience and participants—is the territory in which education lives. As you shape and define your own views on education, these relationships are likely to change.

3. Is education part of the core mission—or is it viewed as something separate from the core mission? How is that relationship articulated?

Just as schools often place the arts on the edge of the day, some arts organizations try to append education activities onto their core programs. Although key personnel may assign high personal value to education, the operations and support to carry out the program may not be in place. Ask yourself the following questions:

- Are artistic decisions—the selection of a season, the choice of an artist— made with some discussion of the implications for the education mission?
- Is education discussed at staff and board meetings, including philosophy and mission, administration, operations and budgets?
- Will a board member be able to describe the organization's education programs and state their purposes?
- What is the education director's status within the staff? Is he or she given the same status as the administrative director, the marketing director, the development officer and artistic director? Are the communication systems for artistic and educational decision-making open and fluid?
- Do those charged with developing and administering the education programs value education?
- Is there support for the staff's professional development?

4. What are the goals and intended outcomes of the education program?

Education suggests change. If participants in an education program are the same at the end of the program as when they began, then something has not worked. Changes—learner outcomes, in education terms—are often subtle, not immediately or easily observed, and frequently complex.

- What are the goals of your education program?

As a designer and provider of education programs, you must know what outcomes you intend for each different group that your education program serves. Your goals will—and should—be affected by the expressed needs of the participants and the different communities they represent. What can be accomplished in a short period of time differs from what can be achieved in a longer period. Two or three workshops can achieve more modest results as compared to artist residencies or partnerships lasting months. The ages of the participants and their developmental characteristics are both important factors in setting program goals.

Many arts programs have goals for the number of participants, number of events or sessions, income to be earned and the like. Numbers may reflect quantity and scope of impact, but they do not indicate quality. For education programs, do you have clear goals for what is to be taught and what is to be learned? Are your education partners comfortable with these intentions, or better yet, have they helped you to define them?

- How do your intended outcomes meet the needs and expectations of your audiences, partners and community?

For example, if you primarily want to open young people to the unexpected and the unpredictable as part of artistic creation, and the school is interested in gaining control over adolescents, then negotiation obviously must take place. Teachers face increasing accountability for student achievement on tests mandated by district and state agencies. In some cases, salaries and tenure can be affected by test performance. How is your work perceived by the teacher and by a school facing such accountability? How does your program help the school to teach its curriculum?

5. Is there an education plan?

Education program plans should be part of the organization's overall plans. A sound plan should set specific education goals for different audiences and participants, link the education mission to the artistic mission, and set objectives commensurate with available resources (staff, budget, artistic resources, etc.).

An education plan should support the organization's core values and purposes and take the long-term view on how to develop them. A good education plan, taken from the perspective of several years at a time, should be concerned with staff development for teachers and supervisors and with evolving opportunities for curriculum design by the participants. Ask yourself:

- Do you repeat the same workshops, rely on the same resource people, use the same activities, and discuss the same issues over and over again? Or,
- Does the education plan encourage individual growth, both of your staff, volunteers and working colleagues, and of your clients and participants?

6. Have you considered the developmental stages and different needs of your participants?

The developmental stages of children must be considered. The methods through which children understand and make sense of the world differ substantially as they grow into teenagers and then adults. While we broadly acknowledge this, we increasingly have to consider it more specifically. Ask these questions:

- Do you consider the different developmental stages and ages of children?
- Are people who are knowledgeable about age differences involved in the planning and implementation of your educational programs?

One staff cannot have expertise in every area of human development and education. Know whom you can call upon to help you design education programs that draw upon the best understanding of how people learn. Early childhood specialists, guidance counselors and teachers of all grade levels and subject areas can help you.

Different cultures view education differently, including what is important to teach and what is not, how to learn, and how to assess and evaluate learning.

- Do you involve people from cultures other than your own in the planning, design and evaluation of education programs?

Ours is an increasingly technological society that is daunting in its complexity but full of promise for access to information hitherto unavailable so quickly and on such a mass scale.

- If schools are to train people so they can work in a knowledge society, what are the skills needed to cope with the new technology and in what ways will the arts be involved in producing them?

7. Are you familiar with the voluntary National Standards for the Arts and with state and district documents that identify essential areas and levels of knowledge for all students to attain?

Know about the National Standards for the Arts and what you think of them. The National Standards for the Arts are intended to describe, "What every young American should know and be able to do in the arts," including dance, music, theater and the visual arts. Described as voluntary, the national standards represent the broadest conversation in 30 years on arts education. They give levels of achievement in the four discipline areas for students completing fourth, eighth and twelfth grade. You should be familiar with this document because some state and local education plans are being written with the national standards as the reference. You may be asked to explain how your education program helps students build the content (what students should know) and the performance skills to demonstrate appropriate levels of achievement (what students should be able to do) suggested in the national standards.

Every state has some documentation—a state plan for reform or a curriculum framework, for example—that spells out "core" or "essential" learning. These are usually set out by grade or age. Increasingly, these are not organized by the old discipline or course of study titles, such as English or chemistry or social studies, but by broad learning goals. For example, here is a learning goal from one state's curriculum framework: "Students shall develop their abilities to apply core concepts and principles from mathematics, the sciences, the arts, the humanities, social studies, practical living studies, and vocational studies to what they will encounter throughout their lives."[3] Being familiar with these documents will enhance your ability to understand what challenges educators face and will indicate opportunities, or points of entry, for you to be a truly effective resource and partner.

8. How do you evaluate your education offerings?

Your staff cannot be experts in everything. They can and should track and monitor program development and effectiveness informally, but to be taken seriously as a resource to education, professional-level program evaluations must be conducted at regular intervals. Good evaluations do not reduce complex learning to meaningless and misleading numbers or gushing anecdotes about the smiles on children's faces. They deal with process as well as product, reveal strengths and help the staff and other stakeholders to address weaknesses.

- Is the evaluation suited to the education goals and purposes?
- What result or outcome did you seek to attain with the participants in your education program and how well did they achieve it?
- What evidence is there to support the findings?
- What are the recommendations for improvement?

Evaluation is not simply asking participants whether they liked or disliked an experience. It is attempting to determine how well the purposes of the education program have been met and how to improve performance in the future.

9. Do you communicate the message that education is an important part of the organization?

Many organizations that are active in education forget to publicize this fact in their advertising, marketing and general communications to the public.

- Do the playbills, programs, fundraising materials, PSAs, ads and other communications signal the importance of education? Is education communicated to every key stakeholder or to only a selected few?

Check the actual communications against the mission statements and plans. Sometimes passionate statements about education in the organization's internal documents find little echo in exterior communications.

10. Are your resources sufficient and appropriate to the mission?
Without the allocation of appropriate resources, organizations are hampered in producing education programs of quality. Ask these questions:

- Does the staff responsible have the knowledge, administrative support, board and director support, time and funds needed to carry out the mission?
- If resources are not limitless, are the priorities clear and the choices and compromises made with a sense of purpose?

Because education poses such large questions and is difficult to define, the risk is great that too few people, too little time and too little expertise will chase a large purpose, such as "all the arts for all the children." Without a clear definition, your journey into education will be boundless and formless, leaving you uncertain about what impact you are having and whether you have done well. Pulled and pushed by funding agencies—whose own priorities may change abruptly or not be clear—and by the needs in the surrounding communities, you may easily promise and attempt too much.

11. Is there a common understanding among board, administration, artistic leadership, staff, volunteers and artists of the education mission and goals and the plans and programs in place to carry them out?
Do not assume that your organization's stakeholders agree about education or about education goals and strategies. Just because the board has approved a mission statement that includes education does not mean that everyone knows about it, much less that they share an understanding of what it means and of the implications of doing it. It is important to take time at board meetings, to arrange time for board and staff together, and to continue the conversation throughout all circles of the organization. These conversations can, at the least, help to build a common vocabulary. Opinions may run from "everything we do, every show we put on is education" to "nothing we do is education until we have defined it, talked about it, learned from our participants and evaluated the results."

To make the most of the current opportunity in education, arts organizations need to understand the changing education world and the political, economic and social forces that are shaping it—the same forces that are affecting their own futures. This brief audit will help your arts organization to assess the depth and extent to which it wants to become a significant player in education—at any level. What level of participation, if any, do you seek in education? Do you aspire to becoming a full-fledged education partner—planning and committing to long-term education programs, doing teacher and artist training, designing curriculum, thinking through assessments—or simply an occasional service provider? What kinds of partnerships would you like to build with the schools and/or with other arts groups and education organizations in the community?

One thing is certain. If arts organizations are to have a significant, long-term role in education, they must move from being simple providers of prepackaged services to creators and shapers of sound educational programs. Take the questions here and throughout the book and make them part of a continuing conversation within your organization. Only through this kind of careful self-assessment can you truly clarify whether education should be at the core of your organization's mission.

Dr. David O'Fallon *is the Executive Director at the Minnesota Center for Arts Education, a state agency whose mission is to make the arts a fundamental part of an excellent education for all of Minnesota's students preK-12. Prior to this appointment, he was the Consulting Director for the Leonard Bernstein Center for Education Through the Arts, and from 1992-94 he was the consultant for the John F. Kennedy Center for the Performing Arts. Dr. O'Fallon served as Director for the Arts in Education Program for the National Endowment for the Arts from 1989-92, where he directed a $7.9 million Arts in Education program that worked with arts and educational organizations in all 50 states and territories.*

Beyond Audience Development
Why Work with Schools?
by Joan Boyett

Beyond Audience Development

For artists, arts organizations and presenters, the importance of developing arts education programs in partnership with schools goes far beyond short-term audience development. If this is the sole motivation, the individual's or organization's efforts will be deemed a failure. Evidence of a correlation between current expenditure on arts education programming and ticket sales is unlikely to be seen during the tenure of current board members, or even during the careers of the artists or existing administrative staff. Many informal studies have revealed that early experiences in the arts may be the most common denominator of current arts audiences. Yet the "greying" of audiences is a growing concern. To quote one arts administrator pundit, "Our audiences are being decimated by God."

The field of arts education is certainly not limited to the schools. Symphony orchestras, theaters, dance companies and presenters are discovering a great interest in lifelong learning in the arts. Adult audiences enjoy becoming informed listeners or viewers and will provide full houses for colloquiums or previews. This will undoubtedly create more loyal, even generous, supporters. But does it broaden the number and base of ticket purchasers? To ensure that this happens, an organization needs to influence the young.

Thus, for the long term, it is vital for all arts organizations to offer arts education. The most compelling reason is the very salvation of the arts, both in terms of preserving a specific art discipline or cultural point of view, and in building a populace that is knowledgeable and appreciative of a broad range of art mediums, styles and cultural heritages.

Common Misconceptions

For more than 30 years, America has been bemoaning a decline in educational standards. The Russian launch of Sputnik spurred an emphasis on math and science that translated into the "back to basics" movement in the schools. This occurred simultaneously with major societal changes: a growth surge in urban schools; a wider disparity in the population's socio-economic levels; and in many metropolitan cities, a vast influx of people from other countries bringing diverse languages, cultural traditions and expectations for education. The layering of federal mandates and state regulations on local schools, along with society's anticipation that the schools not only teach but also feed, nurse, counsel and babysit children, placed teachers and administrators under siege. Further, educators were to assume all these roles at the same time that the money schools received on a per-child basis steadily declined. In consequence, many school programs were eliminated, including the arts.

For years the arts community has blamed the lack of arts education on the schools. This is not only unproductive, it is also untrue. The arts have not been the only subject eliminated nor are they always the first to go. The Los Angeles Unified School District (the country's second-largest system) cut $1.3 billion from its budget over four years; it shortened the list of school electives and the number of periods in the day; even sacrosanct school sports programs have been curtailed. Yet it did not eliminate its music program, supervisor or music specialists.

Many in the arts field have also blamed the schools for the unfilled seats in their theaters, when in reality, the field of the arts has expanded exponentially. Statistics compiled by the National Endowment for the Arts provide vivid testimony to the growth in the number of arts organizations and in the size of audiences served. Since the NEA was established in 1965, the number of professional, nonprofit theaters has grown from 56 to more than 400; the number of orchestras with budgets more than $250,000 has doubled; chamber music and jazz ensembles have proliferated; professional dance companies have increased from 37 to more than 250 (and their annual audience has grown from one million to more than 16 million); and professional opera companies have had a four-fold increase from 27 to more than 100. In only 15 years, the NEA has also witnessed the evolution of the presenting field: in 1980, the Inter-Arts Program funded 27 organizations as compared to the 300 which received grants in fiscal year 1994 from its successor Presenting Program.

This is not to ignore that many arts organizations are struggling financially, but to acknowledge that our expectations of a public willing—and financially able—to support the arts has increased dramatically. Collaborations between the schools and arts organizations can provide a new source of revenue and be effective in meeting long-term expectations for expanded audiences.

Other misconceptions are common: the schools are not interested in partnerships, and they have no money. However, times have changed. Artists and arts organizations will find that the majority of their local school decision makers—whether a board member, superintendent or principal—will support the arts. Further, they will welcome a collaboration. School leaders understand and appreciate the benefits of a partnership with professionals who will share their expertise and passion with students.

Establishing a Partnership

So where does an arts organization or presenter begin to establish a partnership? First, research successful models. With the development of ARTSEDGE, the national arts education information network at the John F. Kennedy Center for the Performing Arts, this should be easier to accomplish. Arm yourself with information about what is being done. There is a whole spectrum of ways to work with schools from a series of introductory performances to comprehensive residencies. Don't be surprised to discover that programs vastly different in mission, content and scope are equally successful.

Second, identify the capabilities of your own arts organization. Obviously, a number of factors will influence this: availability of staff, union contracts, lengths of seasons, financial resources, interest and experience of personnel, commitment of board, etc. Identify the short- and/or long-range goals of the organization and see where they intersect with arts education.

Third, set up meetings with school personnel. Be aware that at least six constituencies play a role in bringing arts programming into the schools: board of education members or school trustees, top-level administrators, arts educators, local principals, parents, and school-site councils.

Though time-consuming, it is wise to meet with representatives of all these decision makers. Better yet, form an advisory council that represents the diverse perspectives in education and the arts. Artists and arts organizations will need the support of all factions to create the collaboration, make it successful, and, most importantly, maintain its continuance.

However, one of these constituencies is likely to have more influence than the others on a specific type of program. For example, if an organization plans to offer exposure-type performances in individual schools, the vast majority of funds to underwrite these programs come from parent-teacher associations. PTAs should be given enormous credit for maintaining and supporting the arts in education. The arts field will discover that parents want quality cultural experiences for their children and are willing to pay for them.

Decisions to subsidize artists-in-residence programs are generally made by local principals, increasingly with the concurrence of school-site management councils. Residencies are most often paid for out of a local school's categorical funds, including Title I and Title II, Migrant Education and GATE funds, to cite a few common sources. In addition, schools have special state grants which will support incorporating the arts into the curriculum or providing staff development for teachers. The passage of Goals 2000: Educate America Act legislation encourages collaborations between professional organizations and schools toward education reform and should be another source of funding.

If an organization or presenter intends to bring students in sizeable numbers to its institution, then the superintendent's backing is mandatory to approve and finance bus transportation. If the arts organization plans to charge admission during school time, it may require a resolution by the board of education to allow schools to collect ticket fees. Artists and organizations should check with school systems to see whether their activities can be funded by a master contract with the district, which will facilitate both the schools' involvement and the organization's payment.

Arts educators are key to any collaboration. They should be the presenter's or arts administrator's best ally and guide. For far too long, arts organizations have created programs in a vacuum and then tried to force them on the schools without the latter's input. Developing projects and programming that build on the schools' needs and the arts organization's capabilities lead to successful partnerships.

Funding Arts Education Programs

Do not assume that the schools have no money. Everyone will tell you this, but it is not true. The schools will not have enough money to fund the total cost of the arts education program, but make it a cardinal rule never to provide a complete giveaway. Artists and arts organizations have fallen into this trap for years. Once your subsidy goes away, so does the school's interest. In contrast, the more money a school contributes to a program, the more likely the program will continue.

It is not necessary to finance school transportation to bring students to your events. Dollars for the arts are in short enough supply that they should not be spent for gasoline. In the long term, it is better to be satisfied with fewer students in your seats than to underwrite buses.

How do arts organizations finance educational programs? A combination of funding sources, over the long haul, is far superior to a single source (unless the organization is fortunate enough to create a permanent endowment). This combination can include corporations, foundations, individuals, government agencies and revenue from the schools. Education is a priority with many corporations and foundations. Expect the program officers of the larger corporations and foundations to be knowledgeable about educational issues. Get a copy of the Department of Labor's *Secretary's Commission on Achieving Necessary Skills* (commonly known as the SCANS report) to make a case for the importance of arts education in preparing employees for the work force. Asking corporations or foundations to support arts education because it is a "good" thing to do no longer works.

It is also possible (even easy) to get individuals or a group of individuals to support arts education programs. The Music Center of Los Angeles County produces two programs annually—each with a budget in excess of $100,000— that are funded by the Blue Ribbon and Fraternity of Friends volunteer groups. Their contributions are in addition to the fundraising these groups do to support the Music Center's annual campaign.

For nearly a decade, government agencies have encouraged arts organizations to sponsor outreach or educational programs; some agencies actually mandate them for grant recipients. Unfortunately, a key source of leadership and support was lost when the National Endowment for the Arts adopted a new organizational structure in late 1995 that eliminated the Arts in Education Program and its promising Arts Plus grants. Nevertheless, government agencies at all levels will continue to play an important role in the development and support of arts-in-education programs.

Programs and Fees

What schools will pay toward an arts education program varies according to the nature of the project. Schools support student admission fees ranging from one to perhaps nine dollars, although in isolated instances a few schools may purchase full-price tickets to a blockbuster Broadway show. An educated guess is that four dollars may be the median ticket price.

A typical single, in-school performance will sell for $200 to $450, with the market supporting higher fees in the larger urban areas. Arts organizations should start in this range unless the schools in their area have a history of supporting cultural enrichment programs. In southern California, it is not uncommon for an individual school to spend more than $3,500 per year on school-site assemblies, but it would be a rarity to spend this amount on a single event.

Based on the experience of some of the larger arts education organizations, including Chicago's Urban Gateways and the Music Center Education Division, schools are moving beyond the single performance to a combination of assemblies and classroom workshops with professional artists. Urban Gateways has been very successful in packaging arts programs around a theme such as multiculturalism. Fees for the Music Center's Individually Designed Arts Packages, which are also theme-specific or curricular-based, begin at about $3,000, with the average costing in excess of $5,000.

Moving along the continuum, the most intensive arts education partnership programs are generally artist residencies. In this context, placing members of a touring company on a school campus for one day does not constitute a residency, valid as that experience may be. In arts education terms, a residency must involve a minimum of 12 sessions by the same artist with the same students. Initially, this program appears expensive to a school, since it is difficult for an artist to work with more than four classes of 30 students per day, making the per-capita cost seem high. Fees for residencies vary depending on union scales, length of term, number of sessions per class, and whether the residency will include schoolwide assemblies, curriculum materials, community site visits and/or staff development for school faculty. Residencies can range from $3,000 to $30,000 or more. As schools see the gains made in student outcomes—improved academic grades, critical thinking abilities, self-confidence and self-esteem, communication skills, and cooperativeness—they want more young people to participate. Residencies are the fastest growing program for many arts education organizations.

Staff development programs are also on the rise. Schools have a variety of funding sources to pay for teacher training. Since these projects also contribute to professional growth, teachers may receive credits toward salary increases. School districts' interest, nay demand, for involvement in the Getty Center for Education in the Arts' or Lincoln Center's institutes is testimony to the value and success of this type of education in the arts.

The Final Measure of Success

Artists and arts organizations have much to offer the schools and a collaboration is the key to success. It is not necessary to emulate another organization's project. What may work in one community is no guarantee for effectiveness in another. Success depends on tailoring what the artist, organization or presenter can offer to what the schools want. Because their needs are diverse, professionals in the field have wide latitude in establishing a partnership. Effective programs depend much more on personal leadership and consequential content than financial resources.

In many ways, arts education performances must have more expansive and rigorous standards for quality than those applied to a typical public arts event. In addition to artistic integrity, school arts programming must be educational in content and provide verbal rapport between the artists and audience. Years of experience have taught us that young people respond to a diversity of arts disciplines, repertoire and cultural heritages. The classical arts of symphonic and chamber music, Shakespearean drama and opera have an easier time of determining repertory. Most schools have music and literary texts to reinforce the arts experience. Further, arts educators are very willing to work with artists and organizations to select specific repertoire. Contemporary dance and the traditional arts have a greater challenge. Without advance instructional materials, teachers may be unable to prepare their students for the experience. Sending out intelligent, brief program notes is no guarantee that all the students will be informed listeners and viewers, but it is almost mandatory to develop these materials in consultation with teachers and school arts supervisors.

Students can relish arts performances totally foreign to their own experience and cultural awareness. There is an emotional thrill in watching an all-Hispanic audience mesmerized by taiko drumming or a predominately Korean student body captivated by the physicality of East Indian dance. Artists are role models for young people. Go on any school campus with a residency program and you can see students literally hanging on to the artists. If the artist happens to represent the child's own ethnicity, you will see children swelling with pride.

Even if other organizations offer educational programs in your community, do not be hesitant to establish your own or to explore the possibility of collaborating with others. More begets more. Some of this country's largest arts education organizations are located in the same southern California market: Getty Center for Education in the Arts, Orange County Performing Arts Centre, Performing Tree, Los Angeles Unified's Intergroup Cultural Awareness Program (ICAP) and the Music Center Education Division. In addition, the Los Angeles Philharmonic, L.A. Opera, Center Theatre Group, Los Angeles Master Chorale, UCLA's Design for Sharing, Young Audiences, Lewitzky Dance Company, Aman Folk Ensemble—to name only a few organizations in the same region—collectively spend millions of dollars on arts education each year. There has been more interest from the schools than any of these organizations can handle individually.

Moments of frustration may well occur in developing an effective arts education program in partnership with the schools. Yet not to invest in the future is to limit it. Arts education programs add to the health of the organization and attract funds to support its operations. Reread Charles Fowler's concluding paragraphs in *Can We Rescue the Arts for America's Children?*[4] to be inspired by the challenge. Fowler expresses the importance of the cause with sheer eloquence. The artist's, organization's or presenter's commitment to arts education is akin to a corporation's investment in research and development. Without this commitment there may be no future.

Joan Boyett has worked with children in Southern California for 25 years, producing programs in virtually all 82 school districts in Los Angeles County and for many districts in the surrounding regions. She is the Founder and Executive Director of the Music Center Education Division and the Vice President for Education of the Music Center of Los Angeles County. Nearly one million students and teachers from area schools annually participate in programs produced by the Education Division, which last year totaled more than 11,000 events in 18 languages.

The ABCDs of Arts Partnerships

by Bennett Tarleton

A. All partners must have complementary organizational missions and simpatico personalities in charge. (It takes two or more to tango.)
Sometimes the missions may not, at first glance, appear complementary. For example, what might the Salvation Army and a community theater have in common? Not much, probably. What about *beneath* their stated missions? Both are interested in giving people opportunities to develop their full human potential. So, what about a joint summertime theater arts project that serves inner-city youth? A mutually beneficial goal emerged for Theatre Memphis, which offered a series of theater arts workshops in conflict resolution specially designed for at-risk kids, and the Memphis Salvation Army, which had the young people and the vans for transportation to the theater. By joining forces, each partner met one of its implicit goals through the medium of the arts.

Likewise, the best artist-in-residence projects evolve from an understanding of what a school wants for its students (comprehensive arts education, we hope) and what a state arts agency can offer (an artist who can complement the school's commitment to comprehensive arts education). If the comprehensive arts education scenario is not available, and the school simply wants a project to enrich its ongoing visual arts curriculum, then adjustments have to be made to get purposes in sync. Where do these purposes intersect to create the basis for partnership? In this case, the school wants to increase its students' knowledge, information and skills by incorporating the work of an accomplished professional visual artist who works in a style and genre quite different from the school's specialists. The state arts agency's goal, which is not just to get work for artists in schools, but also to achieve greater literacy and competency in the arts, can feel comfortable that the visual artist will contribute a valuable dimension as a practicing professional and a career role model for the students in the school.

In my experience, the simpatico personalities are either there or not. It may take some time, some patience and someone to help you translate your different languages and make sense of your different styles. But if after a reasonable time you find yourself spinning your wheels, then walk away if you have that option. I have found that unless communication can flow freely among arts and education administrators and educators, unless there is mutual respect and a certain "chemistry" indicating that teamwork, or at least peaceful coexistence, is possible, it is wiser not to try to force a relationship.

B. All partners must bring something to the table—the more tangible the better—but sometimes energy and commitment are enough. (You have to ante up if you want to play the hand.)

In the Theatre Memphis-Salvation Army partnership, the theater brought to the table its ability to create a valuable theater arts experience for kids, and the Salvation Army brought its kids, who needed opportunities to learn conflict resolution through theater games, and its vans. (Don't underestimate the importance of those vans!) Tangibles: expertise and vans. Intangibles: Matched needs, wants and opportunities, and the willingness to make it happen. Beneficiaries: Theatre Memphis, with a successful summer project for its clients, and the Salvation Army, whose children grew in and through the arts. With the artist residencies, the state arts agency and the artist bring talent and an ability to work with young people, and the school brings its commitment to a more complete arts education program and the resources that will provide a high-quality artistic and academic experience.

C. All partners must leave the table with something they did not have before, especially the school children who are probably not at the table in the first place. (The sum must be greater than the parts.)
The key is to keep in mind what the children will get. The point of the partnership is not the partnership, but the educational result. What did the children leave with? If nothing is different at the end of the experience, then it probably wasn't worth the considerable time, effort and money usually invested. What did the children learn or at least have the opportunity to learn? How did they benefit educationally? These questions focus on using partnerships for the benefit of children—*not* on whether the partnership fulfills a 501(c)(3) obligation or a civic responsibility, creates a positive public image or gives us something to brag about. These questions must dominate discussions among potential partners—artists, schools, community arts resources, businesses. Where are the lesson plans? What will be taught? What will the children know that they did not know before? How will we know that changes have taken place —who's doing the evaluation? Artist residencies are not about providing work for artists, planning time for overburdened teachers or just fun for the kids. These partnerships are about students learning in, through and about an art discipline with a professional artist and a professional teacher.

D. All partners must clearly define, understand and agree on their responsibilities and communicate these understandings within their own organizations and to each other. (Building bridges for two-way traffic.)
When the answers to the questions, "Who is supposed to do what, when and with what results, and then what next?" are vague or confused, the partnership will probably disintegrate quickly. Disappointment and resentment breed rapidly under these circumstances, trust evaporates and the "we/they" schism opens or widens. This is a process that takes work by the individual partners, alone and in collaboration. It requires the ability to listen and hear everyone's concerns and the willingness to come to a consensus. It also requires a decision-making and power-sharing process characterized by civility, respect, patience, flexibility, insight and sensitivity.

I cannot think of a single successful arts-in-education project or program, whether artists' residencies offered by state arts agencies or field trips to museums, in which these "rules" were not operative.

Bennett Tarleton *has been the Executive Director of the Tennessee Arts Commission since 1984. He has served as a board member and officer of the National Assembly of State Arts Agencies and the Southern Arts Federation. He is a member of the national certification team of Young Audiences, Inc., and is a board member of the Association of Performing Arts Presenters. Previous positions include Executive Director of Dance St. Louis, Director of National Alliance for Arts Education and Coordinator of the National Aesthetic Education Learning Center at the John F. Kennedy Center for the Performing Arts in Washington, DC, and Curriculum Developer and Coordinator for the Aesthetic Program at CEMREL, Inc., St. Louis. Tarleton holds a B.A. in English Honors from the University of Missouri-Columbia and a M.A. in Teaching from Harvard University.*

Notes

1. This section is based on an article I wrote for the Spring 1994 issue of the *Dance/USA Journal*. It came hard on the heels of the deliberations of the Dance/USA National Task Force on Dance Education on whose steering committee I had served. The final report, *Widening the Circle: Towards a New Vision for Dance Education*, Mindy N. Levine, (1994) is a comprehensive and useful summary of the state of arts education in the dance field.

2. I use the term "arts organization" here to include agencies, companies, institutions and the entire array of visual, performing, folk, media, etc. groups of every imaginable size, focus and description.

3. Goal 2, from *Transformations: The Kentucky Curriculum Framework—Learning Goals and Academic Expectations*.

4. Charles Fowler, *Can We Rescue the Arts for America's Children? Coming to Our Senses—10 Years Later* (New York: ACA Books, 1988).

PART III
MAKING CONNECTIONS IN THE SCHOOL AND ITS COMMUNITY

Building Bridges
Whose Culture, Whose Arts, Whose Education?

Good Teachers Make Connections

Good teachers know that one of the keys to learning is building bridges from the known to the unknown. Before plunging into foreign waters, such as King Lear, they carefully prepare the way. They might ask questions such as, "Do you know anyone who has three children, prefers one above the others, spites the favorite who won't stoop to flattery, and ends up badly?" After some animated discussion based on the students' own experiences, and perhaps some research in the school library or the local newspapers, these good teachers might say that a man named William Shakespeare wrote a play about just such a topic hundreds of years ago. They might then ask, "What do you know about Shakespeare? What would you like to know about him? How do you think we can best go about learning those things?" And much, much later, they might ask: "Well, what did you learn about Shakespeare and his portrayal of King Lear?"

For most people, unfamiliar, complex artworks are not readily accessible without the keys to the kingdom of strange theatrical or aesthetic conventions and the code words to a foreign and mystifying language. Most of us also respond better to a potentially daunting new experience if we can begin comfortably with something we already know and understand. In the arts-in-education world of the late sixties and seventies, the issue of whose culture, whose arts and whose education we were dealing with was cloaked in the concept of "relevance." Today we use the words "multicultural" and "authentic." The problem is the same and, if anything, more perplexing: do we teach a dominant (Western) culture in a country that is no longer a melting pot but now a truly amazing conglomeration of people from nearly every land in the world? With so much to choose from, whose culture do we teach? And how do we arrive at a balance that respects all cultures?

Arts Organizations and the Question of Relevance

Ballet companies, repertory theater companies, museums with traditional and contemporary collections, symphony or chamber orchestras, opera companies and arts centers across the country struggle with the issue of relevance, not only for subscribers and paying customers but also for their school audiences. I am frequently asked: Can the *Ring* Cycle appeal to ll-year-old inner-city school children? Will *Swan Lake* be a winner for fourth graders of largely Asian heritage? Can sophomores with learning disabilities deal with *Macbeth*? Will Latino junior high kids dig Beethoven's last quartets or Stravinsky's *Rite of Spring*? Or are we better off sticking to tried and true children's fare, such as *Cinderella*, *The Three Little Pigs*, *Grimm's Fairy Tales*, or the popular and contemporary rock, rap, salsa, hip-hop and the like.

These questions are being debated energetically across the country, and no one has all the answers to the explicit and implicit questions embedded in them. By explicit, I mean: Can kids of a certain age and background relate to and understand a certain work of art that may make demands on them that are outside the realm of their lived experience and culture? Implicitly, if these kids are unlikely to relate to these experiences, should we give them what we think we know they might like? Should we ignore our organizational mission and abandon our repertoire and what we do best? (My response to this last rhetorical question is generally "no," but you must build bridges for understanding.)

As you are aware by now, one of my mottos is, "all the arts (of all cultures) for all the children and youth (of all cultures)." That motto, however, must be interpreted sensibly. The following factors provide a framework, based on experience and common sense, in which members of arts organizations might like to consider these questions:

- The age, background and sensibilities of the children. Common sense—or experience, if you have children or spend time with them—suggests that certain subject matter and levels of complexity and abstraction are appropriate for children and youth of a certain developmental age. If you want more information about this subject, many educational psychology and arts education books on the subject are available. Or better yet, meet with focus groups of teachers and supervisors who represent a cross-section of the populations you are serving.

- The language of the artwork. If the artwork is in German, Italian or Chinese, and the audience speaks none of these languages and cannot read the surtitles or wear earphones for simultaneous translation, you may have a communication problem. If the museum exhibit is abstract expressionism and the children have only seen representational art, then you could have a perceptual problem. If the music is completely atonal and your kids are used to folk, country, zydeco, salsa and reggae, then you could have a fidgeting problem. If the dance is ballet in form-revealing white tights and tutus, on point, and your teenage kids know hip-hop in baggy clothing, then I guarantee you will have a whistling problem.

- The subject matter and the values of the school community. If the theme of the artwork or the classroom workshop is about rape, murder, terrorism, interracial marriage, gay liberation, religious bigotry, political freedom or slave rebellions (to name a few themes that are common fodder for the arts), or if there is nudity, violence and coarse language, then the values of the school community may prevent your presentation of these "inflammatory" topics from being accepted or even tolerated. On the other hand, every one of these issues is in the headlines, in the movies or on TV these days, and discussing them in the context of an "artificial" arts experience is often healing, cathartic or profoundly transforming.

- The racial or ethnic make-up of the performers or the workshop artists. If the cast (or the workshop artists) are all Caucasian and your students are largely African American, Latino or Asian, then the students may think that the artworks do not speak to their concerns since they cannot see themselves reflected on the stage or in the classroom. You would undoubtedly get the same reaction if you put a group of Scots dressed in kilts performing traditional folk songs and dance into a rural southern school (all-white) or a suburban school (mostly white).

- The quality of the performers, the teaching artists, and the performances or exhibits. Without question, the single most important factor of an education program is the artistic quality and integrity of its performers, teaching artists, and performances or exhibits. Second best or make-do is never good enough for the students, especially in this age of megahits, MTV, blockbuster road shows, Disney extravaganzas and multimedia displays that take your breath away. Size is not the issue because you cannot compete with it—quality is. Kids know quality, and so do teachers and parents. If you offer second-rate work (I do not equate second-rate with second or junior companies of young professionals), you may be greeted with stony or embarrassed silence, resentment—or worse, hoots and catcalls of derision.

Notice that I have said "may have a problem" in most of the examples. With the exception of quality, many of these potential problems can be addressed by building bridges from the children's known worlds and personal experiences to the unknown world of the arts through direct instruction and through artist and teacher preparation that provides the knowledge, skills and tools for constructing these two-way thoroughfares.

An Example: Don Giovanni and the Babylonian Epic of Gilgamesh

It is a Friday afternoon at the end of September, last period, and I walk into an urban high school classroom of freshmen of mixed racial and ethnic heritage. The chairs have been pushed back against the walls, and the class is seated as an audience in three-quarter round. Seeing no vacant chairs, I sneak behind the piano and accompanist at the "stage" end of the room and sit unobtrusively in the corner on the edge of a table, facing the "audience."

Two professional opera singers are in the middle of a workshop at the Fiorello H. LaGuardia High School of the Arts. The workshop is part of New York City Opera's extended residency program that includes backstage tours, attendance at several operas and related visits to community sites. Today's workshop is one of a series in preparation for the upcoming performance of Mozart's *Don Giovanni*. On the blackboard, Michael Lofton (one of the artists) has written historical dates and facts about the time in which the opera was composed: 1776, the American Revolution; 1787, *Don Giovanni*; 1789, the French Revolution; 1793, Toussaint L'Ouverture and the Slave Revolt in Haiti; 1788, establishment of Australia as a penal colony; 1788, Sierra Leone established as a haven for freed slaves. Michael, playing the Don, is black; Michele McBride, as Zerlina, is white. The theme is actual or psychological slavery and the use and abuse of power and its explosive consequences. The artists and the teacher, who sits among the kids, have planned for all this in advance.

After an introductory discussion, the Don sings the aria "La ci darem la mano," in which he uses his Lord of the Manor power and natural charms to verbally seduce Zerlina, the young village maid about to be married to Masetto. The Don's voice is splendid and bounces off the walls. I watch the kids' reactions: some are fidgeting, some are slightly embarrassed, but most are attentive to the drama unfolding no more than ten feet away from them. Some of them have pulled out the librettos their teacher had distributed and are following the side-by-side English and Italian translations.

Zerlina succumbs and the aria ends. After hearty applause, there are questions, answers and speculations about the reasons for, and the extent of, Zerlina's capitulation: "She's seduced by the elixir of power." "Does she sleep with him?" "No, Donna Elvira rescues her." They turn to the Don's moral character and to the historical events surrounding the opera. Then Zerlina takes her turn.

She asks for volunteers and manages to cajole a young black student to be her jealous and suspicious husband-to-be Masetto, promising him that all he needs to do is sit on the piano bench while she sings. She explains the setting, her motivation and aspects of her character, then launches into a gorgeous rendition of the "Batti, batti" aria. The interracial picture has been satisfyingly reversed.

As Zerlina coaxes her Masetto to forgive her and, if necessary, "beat" her so that they may get on with their marriage, I notice an amazing transformation. The audience has become rapt, smiling, leaning forward in their seats. Zerlina coos at Masetto and delicately touches his cheek, and as he gets into the mood he slowly swivels so that his back is to the audience, but I can see his face plainly. His eyes are closed, his head is tilted toward Zerlina's shoulder, and he is transported. The look of bliss and serenity on his face is so angelic that I find my throat catching. By the end, Zerlina has completely won him over as student and actor, and they leave the stage, hand in hand, to wild applause. I am later told that the boy who played Masetto is a gifted, but angry, young man, and that this is a lovely breakthrough. Mozart's magic has triumphed once again.

There is more probing from the artists and from Norma Rosenblum, a 30-year veteran history teacher in the city's high schools. Norma asks the students what parallels they see between *Don Giovanni* and the *Gilgamesh*, a Sumerian myth and epic (ca. 2650 B.C.) that they have been reading from Babylonian times. (I have never heard of it; its themes are universal.) They talk about the arrogance of men who are vain and who seek eternal life and power—men who believe they are outside the law, but who are brutally punished when they defy the gods. They then discuss rape, seduction, manipulation and the abuse of power, all in the context of the opera but brought to earth with resonance from the students' personal experiences. No titters, no giggles, nothing salacious; the context is all.

The bell rings, and in a flash everyone is gone for the warm, fall weekend.

When I was a child, I sat in my family's living room with my father, listening to *Don Giovanni* at top volume, both of us reading the libretto in English and Italian, with me trying to learn a little of the second language as we went along. My dad, a lawyer, was a firm believer in preparing thoroughly for the opera, or Shakespeare or anything complex in the arts. I later saw memorable productions of *Don Giovanni* at the old and new Metropolitan Opera houses.

In some ways, I began to see and think about its meaning and significance for the first time at this in-school workshop. I was usually so taken with the music that I had never given much thought to all the messages in DaPonte's wonderful libretto. My own childhood experience has convinced me that the power of great music is transforming and irresistible, especially when it surrounds young listeners and gets into their pores. Add to this the opportunity to discuss themes, character, motivation and ancient and contemporary parallels with peers, professional artists and a scholarly teacher, and you get splendid arts education; more important, you get excellent general education.

Norma Rosenblum agrees. Here is what she has to say about the arts, education and the relevance to today's students:

> I am a history teacher and an opera buff. As a history teacher, I notice that all the great historians seem to revert to the arts—poetry, literature, music—when they can no longer find language adequate to explain mystifying historical events, trends and motivations. I believe that the arts provide places where it is both safe and easy to confront some of these powerful, ambiguous and elusive issues of life, death, passion, love and sorrow. And for me, opera cuts through all the bewildering complexities and lets you focus on the elemental drama in all human history. All the feelings that kids have today about power, powerlessness, anger, frustration, loneliness and longing are made vivid in the arts.
>
> Take the Greek tragedies and comedies, the Baroque operas, Mozart's *Clemenza di Tito*, Strauss' *Ariadne auf Naxos*, Shakespeare's *Othello*, the *Koran*, the ancient Chinese literature. The themes are eternal; they are powerfully expressed. You don't have to search for relevance; the parallels are *there*. You can put these works in modern dress or ask the kids to update them, and they may have even greater impact. The human condition hasn't changed, although technology has.

I play music for them—overtures, arias—and ask them to listen and tell me what they hear: What is going on? What is the drama? What are the emotions? We then take these ideas and relate them to whatever we are studying. It doesn't really matter, I can always make the connections. The music and the drama makes it come to life, makes it real for them. They can then describe these things in their own words, drawing their own parallels from their own emotions and lives. That is what relevance is: you set things up so the kids can make their own connections, but the connections go both ways, from history to contemporary life—which will one day be history—and back.

I played them the Catalogue aria (the song Don Giovanni's servant Leporello sings recounting his master's thousands of sexual conquests in many lands) the other day, and one of the students jumped up spontaneously and acted it out, lip-synching the Italian as he moved around the room flirting shamelessly with all the girls. In our discussion after this impromptu demonstration, the students brought it all up to date as they identified friends and contemporary figures who behave in the same odious manner. We talked about the ethics of this kind of behavior and the kind of person who feels he (or she) can flout common decency, defy the law and challenge the gods. They were fascinated.

History is a study of power and politics and human behavior. *Don Giovanni* is a classic study of the abuse of power in the Western world. I try to give my students a broad view and every means of access to this complicated and potentially boring or tedious subject. Most of our textbooks no longer deal with great literature, music and theater, let alone art history. I try to make up for the loss. When the kids or the parents ask me why I do this, I usually reply with a question: "How come so many of the commercials we hear these days use Puccini, or Wagner, or Vivaldi or Rossini or Richard Strauss, or Delibes? What is it that is so powerful about these pieces that Madison Avenue believes it can help persuade people to buy a product?"

By the way, I don't think the so-called classical arts or those of ancient history and long tradition from any hemisphere are necessarily better than the popular or folk arts. They are usually more complex and, with some notable exceptions, less repetitious and boring. As such, they can give kids a new perspective on sights, sounds, movements and interrelationships that they've never had before. Isn't that what education is all about?

Relevance, then, is not an absolute; it is a relative term. For anything to be relevant, you must create the atmosphere and ask the right questions to motivate the learner to pay attention and, given the proper tools, skills and information, to make the connections to his or her own life. As Norma Rosenblum has explained, these connections are limitless, and the arts can open the pores of the imagination so that the intellect embedded in those higher-order thinking skills that we all cherish can make contact with our emotions and perceptions and flourish in a full-bodied analysis, synthesis and evaluation of experiences that reflect the deep complexity of the human condition. Ultimately, though, in the presence of sublime artistry and craft, and in the heat of a transporting moment, intellect and thought really have nothing to do with it; the aesthetic experience is over-powering and all-consuming.

Making Connections: School Culture, the Artists' World and the Lives of Children

Building bridges between the arts, the schools and the community is a phenomenon that can occur because one dedicated, persistent person such as Norma has a vision and a mission. Yet building bridges between the arts and the schools is a much larger enterprise than simply being relevant, which as we have seen is not a simple task.

Building bridges is a dynamic and ongoing social process, one that requires the acquisition of knowledge, skills and understanding of what is known in education as the culture, climate and environment of the work-place. In this context, building bridges means constant communication among people in order to build trust and a shared understanding of the enterprise's purpose and of who is responsible for doing what—when, where, how and with what results. In the arts and education, that trans-lates into the need for making connections among school administrators, teachers, artists, children and the school community, which of course in-cludes parents and families.

Building bridges is about artists and teachers finding and using time to plan and design activities that promote transfer of the learning process from one domain to another. Building bridges also means an artist or a teacher taking time to meet groups of students and their families in their own neighborhoods and accompany them to arts and cultural events so that they can negotiate public transportation, feel comfortable in the often intimidating cultural arenas and learn the rules of acceptable con-duct and behavior in these unfamiliar environments.

Simply put, if arts organizations and artists do not have a basic grasp of a school's culture, of the classrooms in which they work, and of the children they are expected to "instruct," then the likelihood that they can identify appropriate subject matter or design sound curriculum units and lesson plans is very slim indeed. Understanding school culture and how it is often at odds with an artistic environment and world view is an essential prerequisite and context for relevant program design.

I can hear you sigh: "It sounds as if I have to go to school before I can work effectively with the schools." Well, yes and no. I hope this book helps to make you aware of some of these factors; you can choose to pursue them in greater depth as the need arises. But it must be understood that when we are talking about educational impact and program effectiveness, these phenomena cannot and do not exist in a vacuum.

The Landscape

An enormous amount has been written over the years about school culture,[1] the nature of the educative experience, the relevance of the arts and aesthetics in education, the conditions of extreme isolation and the difficulty of collaboration within most American schools, and the relative effectiveness of artists-in-residence programs. Research studies, evaluations, documentary projects and entire books have been devoted to the subject. Teacher preparation institutions and colleges of education offer numerous courses on these topics. It is fascinating and often dense information that some of you may find worthwhile to plow through. For the rest of you, I will try to sketch the landscape to help guide you in your work and as you proceed through the rest of the book.

In the present context, the word "culture" means a social environment in which people with similar belief systems, codes of behaviors, values, rules of conduct and definitions of power, authority and governance have tacitly or explicitly agreed to coexist, often for a common or shared purpose. The culture of the school, however, is not monolithic. It consists of different "sub-cultures," or separate parts related to the whole, that are not necessarily in harmony. There is the school culture of the administration and its expectations of the school as a whole. There is the culture of the individual teacher's classroom which, when the door is closed, may diverge radically from the norms of the school. Then there is the students' culture, and in this day and age in America, where we no longer speak of a melting pot but of diversity and multiculturalism, we have a cornucopia of racial, ethnic, age, gender and other special interest mini-societies that proliferate in every community across the land. Finally, there is the culture of the local community, which may at times be at odds or even at war with what goes on in schools under the name of education.

School, as a social metaphor, however, has a tangible, largely authoritarian, bureaucratic culture that is characterized by rules, regulations, traffic flow, time clocks, input, output and the like. When an arts organization or an artist enters this culture for a short or extended time, shock waves can roll across the school threshold or under the classroom door unless the organization and the artists have taken the time to understand the basic differences in these cultures. Time must be spent studying how they operate—figuring out what the rules are, what the expectations are, and most importantly, what is unacceptable as conduct and behavior and what is prized and valued.

Arts organizations and artists who wish to move along the continuum toward partnerships must recognize from the outset that, as outsiders to this culture, it is your job, your responsibility, to fit into the rhythm, the bloodstream and sinew of the tough muscular structure of the school culture. You must learn the rules, understand the priorities and then set about trying to devise and provide the most seductive, engaging and persuasive service you can that will help the school enhance and strengthen its culture for the benefit of the teachers and the students.

The Challenge and the Reward

Carving a niche for the arts in the school culture takes time and more time, talk and more talk. It takes negotiation and consensus. It takes sensitivity, respect, thoughtful language, persistence and a profound belief that the school culture gradually will absorb and learn to cherish, through firsthand experience, the power of the arts to extend, expand and transform the traditional rote and textbook approach to learning for its students and teachers. Through gentle persuasion and compelling demonstration, the objective is for the school culture to accept that it really is okay for children to color outside as well as inside the lines.

It is an uphill battle, especially since you are the other, the outsider. This makes it all the more imperative for the arts experiences you offer to become "relevant" to the students and their teachers by engaging them in the design process. It makes it all the more critical that workshops are cooperatively planned and carried out by artists and teachers together, that the curriculum you co-construct is intellectually challenging and rigorous and at the same time affecting, humanizing and full of aesthetic qualities.

How to Begin Building the Bridge: Some Practical Suggestions for Arts Administrators and Artists

Whether you are working within an existing arts program or are in the process of setting one up, the best way to determine how to build bridges with teachers and kids is to ask them for their help. First, however, you need to do some research and some homework. Learn the history and philosophy of the school. Get a copy of its mission statement or philosophy of learning, its policies, the staff profile, and the information it distributes to parents and the community. Get copies of curriculum guides, text-books and other instructional materials. Get permission from the principal and the individual teachers to observe classes, especially those with whom you are expected to work. Discuss with the teachers how you plan to conduct your observations and ask their permission to take notes.

When observing, look for the instructional style of the teacher, the rituals, the organization of the desks in the room, the way the walls are decorated, and what's on the blackboard and the bookshelves. Notice the code words or signals used, the acceptable and unacceptable behavior, the respect and courtesy (or lack of it) and the tolerance among different racial, ethnic and gender groups. Be aware of the volume of noise that is tolerated, its ebb and flow and the language (body and verbal). Consider how the teacher uses power and authority, how discipline is maintained and the way that disruption is handled.

Notice especially how the teacher organizes and presents material, paces instruction and allocates time. Observe the different techniques employed to reach all the children (the shy, the rowdy, the very bright, the slow). Keep track of the number of questions asked and how information is transmitted or sought out. In particular, be aware of whether students work in teams, small groups or other unusual arrangements and how much initiative they are encouraged to take.

Ask the principal and other administrators what their goals are. Ask the teachers about their personal and professional philosophies and what they most want for their kids. Depending on the age range and what may be considered rude, insensitive or off-limits, ask the kids what they most enjoy, their attitudes about current events and their needs and concerns. Ask them about their interests and experiences in the arts—*all the arts, including those that are most valued in their homes.* Ask them to bring in examples of their music, myths, folktales, handicrafts, culinary arts, dances, rituals and the like. This can and probably should be done in the context of the theme or topic you will be developing. You can also use polls, surveys, brainstorming sessions, poetry assignments, class journals and logs, conversations with the teachers, chat sessions in the lunchrooms, coffee after school with students and teachers, telephone conversations in the evening and so forth to gather your information. Keep a careful log of your work for reference.

Armed with this rich data, and I hope with a good training and supervisory support program and some books on curriculum design, child development and abstracts of the latest approaches in inquiry-based, authentic teaching and learning, you can begin to co-construct activities that are consequential, engaging, interactive and developmental in their scope and sequence. If you are fortunate to have the time and opportunity, you will do this with curriculum specialists, teachers and other artists. If not, you will have to learn to build the critical bridges yourself, a little more slowly.

It can be done. It *must* be done if we are to increase the number of arts-in-education practitioners and enthusiasts within the schools and in the community. Whenever my own energy flags or I begin to lose faith, I need only to remember the look of transported bliss and angelic serenity on young Masetto's face. Find your own indelible image, your own talisman. It will galvanize you, too.

The Continuing Search for Connections

In the three essays that follow, Barbara Carlisle, Derek Gordon and Simon Richey address the challenge of finding effective ways to connect the process of teaching and the content of the curriculum to the needs, interests and backgrounds of the learner. They do so in the context of the arts in education and of the artists' struggles to make sense and meaning of their art to themselves and to the students and teachers with whom they spend what often amounts to stolen time in classrooms and other learning spaces. The issues they are dealing with go to the very heart of the education question: what are schools for, whom are they for, and if artists and arts organizations—outsiders to the formal process—are to fit in and make a contribution, what must they know about schools, their culture, the politics of power, and the overt and covert value and belief systems that govern their structure and operation. In short, what blocks are necessary for building bridges?

Speaking a Language We All Can Understand

by Barbara Carlisle

I am a theater person with a peculiarly eclectic personal history: violin and piano lessons, because my father is a professional musician; dancing lessons since I was five; and a career as a choreographer and director. I studied theater at Ohio State University; I have worked in community, university and professional theater; and I have worked in the arts in education for 20 years in some fashion. That work has been complemented by painting and drawing classes, college teaching in the humanities and a Ph. D. in art history.

In the late seventies, I served the Michigan Department of Education as the fine arts specialist, overseeing dance, art, music and drama, and on a national level, connecting with the John D. Rockefeller 3rd Fund's Coalition of States and the whole idea of comprehensive arts education—"all the arts for all the children." All of us in state agencies tried hard, and with the help of Title III experimental programs, a host of innovative ideas—including the Very Special Arts Festivals, arts in compensatory education, magnet schools created by desegregation, arts in bilingual education, arts in career education, arts in vocational education—and a lot of federal program money, we started a movement. But in the late eighties much of it died. The federal government withdrew from education issues, and many of our efforts faded with the dollars. "Could it be just the money?" I began to ask. "Where did we go wrong?"

For five years, I served on the Rockefeller Brothers' Fund team that gave awards to outstanding arts programs in schools across the country. Subsequently this led me to spend three months in China looking at a totally different cultural perspective on education in the arts. Since then, alongside a career managing a professional theater company, working as an associate dean at Miami University's School of Fine Arts, and now as a theater department faculty member at Virginia Tech, I have continued to work with local and state agencies to find the key to making the arts a central part of education for children.

Looking at it all today, I find that something has happened to me. My own thinking has been exploded. I am now much less clear ideologically and much more critical of myself and my fellow artists and arts educators in our attempts to achieve our arts and education goals.

In 20 years the rhetoric from the arts education profession has not changed. Think of being in a foreign country where you don't speak the language. What do you do? You speak English louder, more slowly and repeat yourself. It doesn't work! We are doing the same thing in arts education—we are speaking the wrong language. We probably always were, but the extra money of the seventies allowed us to blind ourselves for a while. Now that fiscal austerity is upon us, now that as a society we have squandered resources on every front, we cannot hide any longer the possibility that we are proposing an argument that cannot be understood because we have utterly failed to learn the language and culture of the world in which we live.

Defining a New Vocabulary

In fall 1993, I was invited to be the opening speaker at the Tennessee Arts Commission's annual conference. The conference theme was "Tomorrow's Audiences Today," and my role was to connect the role of arts education with the conference theme. Rudely, I attacked the basic notion. Here are some arguments I gave.

1. I am not convinced that the school's job is to provide audiences for arts institutions, now or in the future, any more than the school's job is to provide customers for Oldsmobile. Would we invite Oldsmobile to do a lecture-demo on how they build a car, so that people would be exposed to Oldsmobiles at a young age and develop a taste for them? You could make a case! Demonstrate the nature of manufacturing in America, discuss relationships of design and utility, describe American free enterprise, show the kinds of jobs people could have after school in the auto industry—all the arguments we make for the arts. If it is good for the arts, why isn't it good for General Motors?

- Tomorrow's society needs much more from the arts than new audience members.

2. If the arts are important for every child, then they are important because they contribute to the child's education. We know the arguments—develop thinking, discover expressive modes, become acquainted with cultures of many kinds, make connections between ideas and expressions of those ideas, develop all kinds of mental and motor skills. Yet unless arts organizations want to contribute to that learning, I am not sure they deserve time in the school's already crowded agenda. Everybody wants a piece of school—environmental education, consumer education, education for peace and freedom, science education, vocational education, agricultural education, math education, foreign language education, multicultural education, global education, physical education, earth day, black history month, social studies, whole language. If we have a problem, we ask schools to cure it!

- So, the first question has to be: How can the arts really help with the school agenda, not just crowd it more?

3. If what we have been trying to do in the past 20 or 30 years is so great, why hasn't anyone bought it but us? Where they have bought it, why hasn't it turned out thousands of citizens dying for the arts? My claim is that *as we are doing it*, we do not intend arts education for everybody. Communication has broken down. Elementary kids don't get it. Other teachers don't get it. Principals don't get it. School boards don't get it. I don't think saying to ourselves, "If only we could convince parents, teachers, administrators, legislators, school board

members, principals, superintendents, corporations"—or whomever one feels is today's power broker—furthers the cause.

- When you are speaking in a foreign tongue, saying it louder, more often or more slowly doesn't help.

4. Why don't people get it? We don't match our rhetoric with our actions. We claim the arts are for everyone. Yet in spite of our inclusive rhetoric, we protect the arts. We insist on our own rituals, our own union rules, our own unique expertise, our own definition of what art is, our own taste. We show that you have to be specially educated with specific skills, specific language and specific repertoires of experience before you can appreciate the arts, let alone participate in them. We relegate arts educators who deal with the whole school population to the lowest status in our profession, making it obvious that we don't really believe in arts education. We make it abundantly clear that until you have lived our lives and seen the world through our eyes, you can do little but be a generous patron or a cheerleader. We will tell you how and when. Your job is to provide us the space, time, materials and status so we can bring you to this nirvana.

Do we mean to say this? Perhaps not, but we do by default. We are prisoners of our history. The arts we are *really* talking about result from aristocratic patronage—produced for an educated populace, dependent upon a subsidy of one kind or another, requiring an initiation of some sort. Even when we include traditional arts or folk arts, they get into the sacred enclave only when we true artists have sanctioned them. We say repeatedly that by dance we do not mean "ballet," but our brochures, our publicity pictures, our logos depict trained dancers in balletic poses. We say by music we mean all music, but the arts section of the paper shows the symphony in tuxedos, and our literature tells about the amazing young violinist who won a competition at Interlochen.

- For most of our population, the arts are a foreign language they have no need to learn.

5. Many school arts activities have little to do with either the arts or life. School arts projects, school plays and school bands are great for the arts teachers and sometimes for the kids, but after a brief sojourn on the refrigerator door or polite applause at the spring concert, they are gone. They don't connect either to art in the future or to life outside themselves. Should we be surprised that no one takes them seriously? Science projects teach us how the natural world works. Social studies show us what we must be when we grow up. Math helps us count things and figure out solutions to problems. History is confusing, but at least all these names and places still exist. But who can explain why we make large butterflies or recite "ta ta ti ti ta" when people hold up cards? If the arts teachers know, they aren't telling anybody. Many class activities are ones they learned at conferences as "neat and fun things to do." What good are they?

It doesn't have to be this way. My years traveling around the country for the Rockefeller Brothers Fund Awards program—and more recently in Tennessee, where I have been helping to identify outstanding school arts programs—showed me amazing projects that reach into the heart of the school and the community. However, both awards programs eventually ran out of schools to honor.

I came to understand that for every wonderful arts teacher who interacts with the rest of the school—who teaches and learns from fellow teachers in a way that lets all carry the work of the school forward, who builds on connections between the student's daily learning life and the life of arts learning—there are a dozen who build walls—who do projects that may have meaning in themselves, but that are isolated, repetitive and carry no meaning for the students.

- If arts organizations come into schools and support that isolation, they don't help the cause.

6. Our professional standards and goals do not lend themselves to change because they support a picture that perpetuates the privilege of an educated few. Take, for example, the best suburban high school with what everyone would agree are great arts teachers and great programs. Let us say they have 2,000 kids and two art teachers, two music teachers, even a dance teacher and a drama teacher. Each teacher has five classes a day in his or her specialty. If *no* students overlapped classes and each class had 25 kids (large for a studio class), then they would reach 750 students—only 37 percent. We could draw a truer profile of these students: half would be in at least one other arts class, and 50 percent would take their arts classes throughout their school years, so the true percentage is closer to 25. Ninety-five percent of these students are going to college or arts academies. More significantly, 80 percent have been taken to an arts event before high school by their parents.

The rest of the school—teachers included—doesn't mess with the arts stuff. They don't need them, and they don't want them. The fact that they attend the students' "show" doesn't amount to anything more than social schmoozing. Even fellow students who go to college will take no arts classes and attend no arts events once they get there.

- Our professional standards and goals perpetuate the status quo of a tiny, educated, elite artist world.

7. I live in a beautiful hollow in western Virginia, where people have cared for family farms for four generations, where they notice sunsets, protect forests and plant gardens, cherish antiques, make wood crafts and sew and knit and care for each other. They read books, run a local agricultural fair, and have an association to protect the environment and a local historical society to keep records of the cultural heritage. Yet if you asked whether they do much in the arts, they would all say no. They live rich and full lives, but they don't connect any of what they do to the arts. They don't go to galleries or concerts or plays, although they are 20 minutes away from all these.

They feel no absence. They don't imagine they are missing something. I say we taught them that. We taught them that playing country music at the Eagles Hall is not the arts. That making handmade birdhouses is not the arts. That belonging to the square-dance club is not the arts. That caring for gardens is not the arts. That making the best blackberry jam in the county or singing in the church choir doesn't measure up.

- Most people have no use for the "arts" in their lives. They are not hostile; they are happily indifferent.

8. If we want to protect the integrity of the arts as we know them—put conditions around certain forms and call them "folk" arts, for example—then we must accept the current statistics that about 15 percent of the American population attends, supports and uses the "real" arts. Our educational system maintains that very well—better in some places than others, of course. Less than one percent of our people call themselves artists. We have plenty of places for such people to go to school for one kind of training or another. In the public, private and nonprofit sectors, we have artists taking on apprentices of all kinds in all kinds of constructs. We have performing companies, colleges, art schools, dance schools, community colleges, Saturday classes and private teachers. They are not evenly distributed, but we have lots of them and they are all looking for students.

- Training a complement of artists for the future is not the problem, and it never has been.

9. Do we really want the arts to play an important role in the education of all children, whether or not they become our audiences of the future? Are we willing to say that our role as artists in education is to help individuals find the artistic impulses in themselves and make connections to the things that are important to them? That might not include training everyone in a specific cultural heritage so they can appreciate works in a museum. But it might include helping individuals—teachers and students—to see how the arts work, to see how even people with minimal skills can manipulate their visual, aural, kinesthetic and verbal environments and make artful statements. It may mean giving away some of our secrets so teaching professionals can understand basic artistic principles and apply them when we are not around. It may mean letting go of our insistence that everyone needs to be able to keep a steady beat in order to create musical forms, or that everyone has to recognize a Van Gogh to mess around with contrasts of light and dark. It may mean letting go of some of the baggage of our disciplines to reach their life blood, the tools that let people be creative and artful.

Do we really want 100 percent of the children in schools to learn to interpret the world they live in and express it to other people, whether or not it leads them to buy tickets to our dance company some day in the future? Even if it includes line dancing with MTV, playing with computer graphics or making a video of the auto body shop? Do we really mean it?

We can have an impact. We are already having an impact. All those subtle messages come through loud and clear. This is the arts; this is not. We decide. The arts are nice for those who are involved, but not vital. Children get that. School boards get that. Other teachers get that.

If in hard times a question of resources and what is essential arises, those who need and want the arts can obviously work that out for themselves. Providing the arts is not the school community's problem any more than providing classes in bartending or Japanese.

If we want something different—deeper penetration of the arts in the lives of all the citizens—we, the artists, the arts world, the arts educators, are the people who have to change the message. We have to examine our roles. We have to examine how and why we do what we do. We have to reexamine what we want and expect.

- Do we really want all the arts for all the children? What do we mean when we say that?

10. Arts partnerships will be marginal unless they can stir the souls of serious educators. Do artists believe that teachers are adult professionals who know what they are doing and care about the future of their students? I know we have amazing teachers, good teachers, average teachers and poor teachers. I also know we have good doctors and bad doctors, excellent and average bricklayers, good truck drivers and bad ones, and extraordinary and mediocre artists. We cannot afford to give up on any of them. If we assume that teachers and principals understand their jobs and want what will be good for their students, then we have to join in the educational work with a genuine desire to share a body of thought that might be put to use for the long-term benefit of the whole effort. We have to talk with educators as fellow professionals and listen to what they know.

- Good teachers are hungry for things that will help all children learn. What are we offering them?

11. When I have seen artist-school partnerships work, the artists have brought something unique to the long-term learning of students. The arts can do things for human beings that other human enterprises do less well. Life comes to us chaotically and without meaning. The arts put frames around things and help make sense out of them. They help us organize, select, reflect on and modify experience—even in simple ways for very young children. Spontaneous thinking, lateral thinking, structuring, illustrating, embellishing, elaborating, abstracting, detailing, personalizing, celebrating, ventilating—people use the arts to do many things. All teachers and all students can use them, if they know what they are doing. In a world increasingly complex and fast-paced, the arts may be a person's most valuable tool for coping with change.

If arts experiences consist only of doing what someone else has done or following directions according to a specified formula, then how does the teacher or student know what to do next when the artist is gone? The arts will never be incorporated into the vocabulary of life if the artist and student do not make a mutual connection about learning.

What if the arts become one more mysterious drudgery, like learning the multiplication tables without understanding what multiplying does or drilling a symbol language that does not relate to anything a student understands? What if the arts are only about appreciating what has gone before or is done by others?

- Good artist-educators, like any good educators, connect tradition and practice with continuing meaningful exploration.

12. Do we understand how our own disciplines work clearly enough to give their basic techniques to others—not just to those who understand them instinctively? We are used to assuming that what we do is uniquely valuable and that the value is apparent. We are used to our claims, and when others don't "get it," it is their ignorance that needs repairing. We repeat the claims. We ask for more facilities, more time, more attention and more respect to do our work better. We seem to believe that if we hold bigger conferences, do more clever workshops,

speak at more board meetings and design more brochures, then we will enlighten the rest of the world.

I wonder if we are the ones who need enlightening. How much do we understand about our own arts learning? Can we make real connections between arts work and student learning? Can we articulate the ways our own disciplines function so that those who would never choose to spend their lives in the arts can take from our processes elements that make sense to them?

- Do we honestly want to learn to speak more than one language?

13. Hard social/economic/political questions surround the arts. Are we secure enough in our reasons for entering the education arena to deal with them? In the past ten years, I have engaged with many people on many issues that have to be opened and discussed. We have to dispel these fundamental suspicions.

How willing are we to examine the class-based hierarchies of what we call art: Who says your art is real and mine is not? Who says entertainment is not art? Who says some art is good for you and some is not? Who says what is "minority" and what is "majority"?

How comfortable are we with questions about where terms like "classical, crafts, popular arts, folk arts, child art" came from and what they mean? How willing are we to deconstruct questions about who and what has determined what becomes "great" art? What is a masterpiece? Who can be a master?

Are we willing to explore the romantic view of the artist as outsider or anarchist? What is the history of this? Is it valid today? Do you have to be an outsider to be an artist? Can we evenly question who can and should support the arts, including the role of government?

How do we take these questions on and find ease and comfort with them? My experience teaches me that these questions divide the larger public (including teachers and school boards) from artists and from the arts and make them wary. Artists often want to deflect these questions and blame someone for their existence.

- We must participate with ease and comfort in the discussion.

A Finale

In discussing these topics, I have posed many more questions than answers. Artists and arts educators need help in answering the questions, but first we must be willing to ask them. It will do no good to go into partnerships with mixed messages, confused agendas, mismatched behavior and rhetoric, distrust of each other's professions, hostility about political, economic and cultural realities, insistence upon unproductive rituals, failure to understand the depths of our own disciplines, and determination to maintain the status quo of a privileged few while pretending to speak to the many. The conversation will be superficial and unproductive or based on false assumptions.

I am not convinced that, as artists and arts educators, we can be real partners in education unless we engage in serious self-examination. Unless we reassess our motives, deconstruct our histories and analyze what we have to teach that has lasting value, the arts will be just another burden to education—a need everyone would like to do something about, but a noisome buzz that detracts from rather than contributes to the work that must be done. Nevertheless, if we open these issues, a deep arts partnership in education could be a powerful force to help a troubled society confront the complexities of the 21st century.

Until then, no one can make us face these questions but ourselves. We must listen with ears open for our own biases, our own limitations and our own failures to communicate. Then we may begin to speak in a language we all can understand.

Dr. Barbara Carlisle is Associate Professor of Theatre Arts at Virginia Tech University, where she teaches playwriting, acting and arts management. Concurrently, she works with several projects that focus on centering the arts in the heart of teaching and learning, one with the Education Enhancement Partnership of Stark County, Ohio, another through the Tennessee Arts Commission, and, most recently, the Learning Communities Network, an initiative of the Rockefeller Foundation whose focus is strengthening professional development and adult learning in urban school districts. She writes for the theater and directs and produces work regularly. She received a Ph.D. in art history from the University of Michigan and a B.A. from the Ohio State University. She is author of The Making of a Grass Blade, *a study that describes successful arts partnerships in Michigan, and of a new book with Don Drapeau,* Hi-Concept/Lo-Tech, *which is a handbook for reinventing the art of theater from an understanding of its foundations.*

Making a Difference in the Community
Reflections on What Makes Good Partnerships
by Derek E. Gordon

I am always more than a little surprised when I hear people ask why a cultural institution should partner with schools. Perhaps this disbelief stems from my background in the community arts council movement and the conviction that the cultural institution is responsible for nurturing the community through educational opportunities and quality arts experiences. On the other hand, maybe I take too seriously the responsibility of 501(c)3 nonprofit agencies to live up to the mandate for educational programming that allows them to enjoy their tax-exempt status. Many institutions seem content to believe that their existence is enough to meet the educational requirement. This "if you build it, they will come" mentality may be valid in some communities, but in urban settings with diverse populations, cultural institutions that are not making the effort to reach into the community and into its schools are destined to become white elephants.

The graying of the United States' arts audiences has been much discussed, particularly as it applies to the symphony music world. Our aging audiences are diminishing from death, immobility or fear, leaving no one to fill the seats in the concert hall or at the board table. Institutions must cultivate new audiences that reflect their community's cultural diversity and its needs and priorities. Without a doubt, the most effective way to connect to a community's heart is to provide meaningful opportunities for its young people.

When talking to national and local funders, I have found that they are looking for long-term impact on a community's growth and development and, in particular, its young people. Funders are looking for measurable evidence that programs are making a difference. Today, they are more concerned with efforts that affect the overall quality of education and less disposed to support the perpetuation of an institution disconnected from its community. As we seek support from municipal governments, county agencies and the like, they want to know how much public service cultural institutions are providing. If we are to compete for the same dollars that support various social service agencies committed to the physical well-being of the community, cultural institutions will have to demonstrate their delivery of vital services to the community and its children.

Plain Talk: Finding a Reason to Believe

Cultural institutions need to perceive themselves as part of the solution to their communities' challenges and accept the responsibility for developing partnerships that will effect positive change. These efforts cannot exist in isolation, and diverse segments of the community need a reason to support them.

A case in point was a visit I made to the Nannie Lee Recreation Center in Alexandria, Virginia. We had met with representatives of the Alexandria Arts Council (a department of the parks and recreation department) and had been advised that we needed to speak with Jerome Ford to discuss any collaboration or support for community participation in the Kennedy Center's programs. Mr. Ford is a distinguished-looking African American who obviously had worked hard and against the odds to achieve his level of authority in the parks and recreation department. After a few moments of polite conversation, I explained our interest in becoming more involved with the Alexandria community and in having the community more involved in the Kennedy Center. A man of few words, Mr. Ford looked me squarely in the eye and said, "I've never set foot in the Kennedy Center, and until the Kennedy Center can do something for me and my community, I can't think of anything that would get me there."

While a little stunned by his directness, I was intrigued by his clear belief that a cultural institution like the Kennedy Center had a responsibility to make itself relevant to his community. I quickly replied, "I am here today to begin that dialogue and to explore the types of resources we could apply to developing such a partnership." In particular, Mr. Ford said he wanted us to bring programs like the Dance Theatre of Harlem and the National Symphony Orchestra into their community. Then he could consider using his resources to bring people to the

Kennedy Center. This was no small request, considering the size and stature of these institutions and the limitations of his facilities. After further conversation, I suggested that, while their recreation center could not hold the full company, perhaps we could develop a program featuring members of the Dance Theatre of Harlem and even provide professional dance instruction for young people in the community.

The center was interested in further developing their dance offerings, and the idea seemed to strike a chord with Mr. Ford. He was very proud that the recreation center had created a formal dance studio with mirrors, barres and a sprung floor. In the back of my mind, I was thinking of a project that had been percolating at the Kennedy Center for about three years, but had never gotten off the ground. Mr. Ford's challenge gave me new ideas about bringing the Dance Theatre of Harlem Residency out of the Kennedy Center and into the community. I also told him that we have open orchestra rehearsals for senior citizens, and that we would be delighted to coordinate seating for the center's seniors.

As the Dance Theatre of Harlem Residency began to take shape, the Nannie Lee Recreation Center became the model site in the program. Local cable community access stations did special editions on the project, and the Dance Theatre of Harlem school ensemble did three performances in T. C. Williams High School auditorium, an affiliate of the parks department in Alexandria. We invited Mr. Ford to be a special guest at the inaugural program of "Billy Taylor's Jazz at the Kennedy Center," and we invited him to the Dance Theatre of Harlem program at the Kennedy Center, which featured our residency students in a performance with the professional company.

Since then, Mr. Ford has brought a group of more than 50 seniors to a regularly scheduled National Symphony Orchestra matinee performance, for which they paid for the tickets and a special lunch at the Center. He also bought more than 75 tickets to a matinee performance of the Dance Theatre of Harlem. While these accomplishments are modest in number, the satisfaction I experienced at lunch with Mr. Ford—when I said, "Well, I guess we finally got you here," and I saw his beaming smile—was worth ten times the effort.

Fortunately, the Kennedy Center had been examining the need to provide programmatic opportunities to encourage diverse audiences to frequent the center. This community/school-based effort allowed us to accomplish a program we had long sought to establish and to make connections with various events that would introduce these communities to the Kennedy Center's regular series offerings. It also heightened our awareness of the need for ongoing opportunities to engage diverse communities through appropriate quality programming.

Arts Education Collaborations: Ten Critical Factors

With all this talk about effective partnerships, perhaps we should focus on some of the elements. In *Intersections: Community Arts and Education Collaborations*,[2] a report based on research collected by the Kennedy Center Alliance for Arts Education Network and the National Assembly of Local Arts Agencies, and supported by the National Endowment for the Arts, ten factors were identified as critical to successful arts education collaborations:

1. Coordination/coordinating entity
2. Leadership and vision
3. Effective planning
4. Broad-based community representation
5. Teacher participation
6. Artist participation
7. Public awareness and communication
8. Awareness of program catalyst
9. Site-specific program design
10. Ongoing assessment of the partnership

A principal finding of the report was the need for an adequate support system at the community level. Whether it is an individual, agency, institution or organization, the support system is the keystone of the partnership and is vested in the collaboration's success. Another consistent finding was the need for a good leader who facilitates common understanding among all partners and recognition of each partner's individual and collective needs. Both the philosophical and the pragmatic aspects of each partner must be considered to forge a vision of the collaboration that all members can support.

In addition to the critical factors, the report identified four guiding principles for successful collaborations:

1. Assure equitable access to cultural experiences;
2. Value all cultures—assure cultural diversity of programs and participants;
3. Value artistic quality in education; and
4. Ensure that the arts are indispensably a part of education.

To apply these guiding principles, artists and arts institutions must understand the current environment of local school control and the opportunities that restructuring provides for interactive problem-solving and planning with schools and other community resources. Success will depend upon shared goals and long-term commitments to transform the teaching and learning environment.

Shared Experience: Tips on How to Make Partnerships Work

Through our work at the Kennedy Center and at other community cultural organizations across the country, Kathi Levin, the center's senior program director for national programs, and I have developed our own list of tips for partnerships that work. These are basic management principles that apply to long- or short-term collaborations and that we believe make good sense:

1. Identify the goals to be accomplished. While people and organizations may be interested in working together, establishing a clear focus of what the project or partnership is designed to accomplish is important. With a clear sense of purpose and direction, meeting agendas, time lines and project activities can be carried out that productively use the time and resources each party brings to the partnership. This helps collaborators to value the partnership and realize the tangible benefits of working together.

2. Understand the roles each partner plays. In collaborating with other organizations, each partner gains an insider's point of view of the partners' organizations. Sharing information, gaining an understanding of each other's operating procedures, and learning more about each other's role within their community or industry is part of building good working relationships and trust among partners. While mutual agreement and consensus decision-making should guide the work of the partnership, it often helps to break down tasks and assignments among the parties. This helps each partner to contribute to the partnership's tangible success and can streamline the cumbersome operational systems developed just to involve everyone in every aspect of implementation.

3. Understand the resources each partner brings. In planning a project or long-term partnership, each party brings a range of material, financial and in-kind resources to the joint effort. Being clear about what each party has to offer, encouraging a sense of proportion and balance to what each party contributes, and mutually recognizing the value of these resources builds joint ownership of collaborative efforts.

4. Understand your partners' key priorities and parameters in the effort and make them integral to the project's goals. Knowing how the project or activity addresses each partner's specific goals and priorities will help the partners to understand each other's minimum/maximum expectations and to set appropriate limitations for the partnership's scope within each organization's overall mission. Understanding your partners' point of view will go a long way toward building a strong partnership.

5. Set attainable benchmarks for success in building the partnerships. Individuals and organizations like to realize success and recognize the value of their work. Setting achievable goals and deadlines enables everyone involved with the collaboration to keep focused and motivated toward the successful implementation of ideas. At the same time, combining different work styles and priorities can make initial efforts at joint implementation difficult. Honest and open discussion of what is and is not working in a collaborative effort will help to move the project forward, reinforce everyone's understanding of the collaboration's value and maintain goodwill among the parties over time.

6. Build upon your success and try new ventures. Initially, partnerships and collaborations can undergo a trial run to see how well the partners' priorities, work styles, and viewpoints match. Achieving success with a specific project or initiative within a reasonable time can lay a solid foundation for future efforts. An honest appraisal of the value of working together upon completion of your efforts can lead to a discussion of new areas to explore.

7. Promote your collaboration. Do not forget to publicize that a project or initiative is a joint effort among partners. Sometimes, the fact that certain individuals and organizations have developed a common agenda to be addressed by a jointly planned and implemented project is as newsworthy to your industry or community as the actual initiative.

Advice, no matter how good, can only be a guideline. The unique circumstances in any given community will probably require some refinement of these ideas. The important thing is to realize that whether it is support for education reform or for the survival of the arts, partnerships are an essential element of all successful initiatives. Nonprofit organizations cannot live in isolation, and through such partnerships their relevance and value to the community increases as does the community's sense of ownership and appreciation for those institutions.

Derek E. Gordon is Associate Managing Director for Education at the John F. Kennedy Center for the Performing Arts in Washington, D.C. He is responsible for overall planning, management and supervision of the programs and operations of the Kennedy Center's Education Department. He has been the Executive Director of the Pennsylvania State Arts Council, the Louisiana Division of the Arts, and the Arts and Humanities Council of Greater Baton Rouge and he has been a Program Associate for the Texas Council on the Arts. He holds Bachelor of Music and Master of Music degrees from Louisiana State University.

Bridge Over Troubled Waters

by Simon Richey

A dance company I know recently performed in a secondary school in a deprived part of east London and met with bewilderment and smouldering hostility. One of the women dancers later said of the experience, "I almost felt abused."

Plunging Into the Cultural Divide

The teacher had underestimated, it would appear, the sheer distance that separated the young people from the event they were witnessing. They weren't unfamiliar with dance. Far from it. No young person could have been in the audience who didn't go to discos or dance to music at parties. What was strange was the nature of the dance—it was an experimental piece—and the situation itself: the spectacle of dancers performing in front of them while the pupils were expected to sit quietly and watch. They had not watched dance in this way before—still less, experimental dance—any more than they had visited theaters to watch plays or opera houses to watch opera. In cultural terms, they had been dropped in at the deep end and expected to swim. Instead, they had been engulfed by the creeping sense of inferiority that afflicts people when confronted with a cultural event they don't understand followed by a resentment at being put in this position. They had witnessed the dark side of culture: its capacity to alienate rather than to unite.

If the term "culture" is used in its conventional sense, then the young people watching the performance were, of course, "uncultured." However, this fails to take account of the young people's involvement in their *own* culture and the vibrant part it plays in their lives. I am referring to such things as going to the cinema, watching TV, listening to pop music, attending gigs and playing in bands. Indeed, if a rock band had replaced the dancers performing in front of them, the young people would have constituted what might be called an "educated" audience. But this kind of culture, or popular culture, is often regarded warily by those who stand at the gates of young people's more formal cultural experiences. At best it is perceived as trivial, at worst as worthless. Many young people are indifferent to this. Indeed, insofar as it widens the gulf between their own cultures and the culture of adults, this perception may even be welcome. The problem with this standoff between the two cultures is that popular culture could provide a useful bridge into established culture that, in the manner of bridges, allows those crossing it to approach the country on the other side step by step.

Building Bridges from the Known to the New

If young people are to be introduced to new cultural experiences, in schools as elsewhere, then the initial experience might stay close to that with which they are familiar. The teacher who organized the ill-fated visit by the dance company might have more sensibly begun by using the young people's own dance styles as a starting point. She could have put on some music of their choice, for example, and watched them dance to it as they normally would. Better still, she could have accompanied them to a disco or a party and seen it firsthand. Slowly and sensitively, she could have then suggested ways in which they could experiment and take more risks with their dancing. Finally, she might have brought in a dance company whose style of dancing might have partially reflected the young people's own styles. In this way, their own culture would have served as a bridge into something more ambitious.

We further illustrate this principle when we consider teaching Shakespeare in schools. To sit young people in front of a Shakespeare play in the theater can be a bewildering and alienating experience, as many adults will testify. To show Shakespeare on film, however, whether in the shape of Polanski's *Macbeth* or Branagh's *Much Ado About Nothing*, is to use a medium with which young people are thoroughly familiar. Furthermore, because filmed Shakespeare usually attaches greater importance to realism than the theater, and because young people expect and understand realism in the cinema, a sympathetic connection is established from the outset. When, in *Macbeth*, Burnham Wood comes to Dunsinane, the theatrical way of treating this phenomenon invariably is doomed to clumsiness: a handful of actors shuffles across the stage bearing branches. In the cinema, a whole hillside of tree-bearing soldiers moves menacingly toward the enemy, and the effect is electric. Cinema is now so sophisticated that young people would expect nothing less.

Such an approach to one of Shakespeare's more ambitious stage directions also demonstrates how film can do greater justice to the original idea. Branagh's magnificent staging of the battles in *Henry V* further illustrates the point. Whether we should always regard Shakespeare on film as a precursor to Shakespeare on the stage or as an end in itself is a moot point. I have never seen *Much Ado About Nothing* on the stage, but I have seen the film and now feel as if I know the play. If young people can watch a Shakespeare play on film before seeing it in the theater, then they will have the chance to understand the plot and acclimate themselves to the language. Since in the theater both plot and language can prove a source of bewilderment, a film can usefully iron out any areas of confusion in advance and allow for a greater enjoyment of the theatrical experience.

Young people are increasingly familiar with what might be called the hardware of popular culture: video cameras, cassette recorders, computers and the rest. They use these things frequently to record what is going on around them, to tape music off the radio or to improvise computer graphics. Because they are media-literate, they understand the conventions of film and television—different ways of editing, of telling a story and so on. If these different kinds of media are the tools by which young people express themselves, as articulately in their own way as words, then they have the potential to be harnessed in the classroom. To some degree this already happens, but we could greatly extend its use. How about shooting an essay on Shakespeare from time to time, for example, or making a mock radio program on Lenny Bernstein's music?

Interactive video is a medium that can serve as a crucible for the meeting of cultures. On the cutting edge of technological development, interactive video nonetheless has the capacity to explore established culture with thoroughness and sensitivity. Like a Russian doll, it can reveal onion layers of information about a painting or a theatrical production or a dance as well as show the product itself. This capacity to lead viewers behind the scenes—to give insight into Van Gogh's motives for painting sunflowers or to enable reflection on the story line of *Tosca*—gradually leads them to an understanding of what the finished product was "getting at." Its potential in the classroom is immense, particularly its capacity to introduce young people to new cultural experiences sympathetically.

Making Young Guests Feel at Home

If schools have something to learn from popular culture, so too do those cultural institutions to which young people, at times, are taken: opera houses, theaters, galleries and the rest. However well-prepared a young person might be for such a visit, these places can intimidate and frighten. Since informality is the hallmark of the cultural venues that young people routinely frequent, established cultural institutions could take a leaf from their book and consider the extent to which they put young people at ease. How welcoming are these facilities? How sympathetic to young people is the front of house staff or the curators? How attractive is the product?

Galleries, I suspect, still have some distance to travel in this regard. Theaters, opera houses and dance venues, at least in the United Kingdom, have tried in recent years to cater to the needs of young people and to make them feel at home. With few exceptions, galleries have not. The reasons for this discrepancy are not immediately clear, but it remains the case that very few galleries cater specifically to young people, not even to the extent of setting aside a particular gallery space for their use. Exhibitions are often unimaginatively designed and poorly captioned. A "take it or leave it" attitude prevails, and we should not be surprised if many young people choose to leave it.

Yet the potential for change and innovation is huge. Interactive video has a role to play here, and a limited number of galleries have begun to use it. Film, graphics, music and theater could all be deployed to shed light on paintings and artifacts and on the artists who created them. A suggestive overlap between conventional exhibitions, shop window displays and billboards, for example, points to any number of interesting developments.

In recent years, the Gulbenkian Foundation has funded projects designed to put some of these ideas into practice. It has supported an initiative that considered the potential of the cultural media in schools—the "cultural hardware" referred to earlier—and different ways of promoting their use. The project ran a number of experimental initiatives in schools that tested different ways in which young people could use the cultural media as tools for investigation and expression. Seminars and conferences were then organized so that the teachers in the schools could meet and share their experiences. The foundation has funded the development of an interactive video program that introduced young people to aspects of contemporary dance and taught them the rudiments of dance notation. Specifically, the program helped 15- and 16-year-old pupils, who were studying dance at examination level, to consider dance on film. It exploited the capacity of interactive video to freeze the frame, observe the same image from different angles, and slow down and speed up the film. Another grant from the foundation enabled a major gallery to set up a young people's council to advise the gallery on ways in which it might be more responsive to the needs of the young. The gallery believed that young people could best convey those needs and arranged a system by which their voices would be continually heard.

Established culture needs to be more attentive to those voices. Nor would it do established culture much harm to rough it a little.

Simon Richey is Education Director of the UK Branch of the Gulbenkian Foundation. He joined the foundation in 1984 and oversees both educational projects and arts projects by young people. Born in London in 1946, he has taught in inner-city schools in London and worked as an arts advisor to a national youth organization.

Notes

1. Contributors Sharon Ryan and Sam Shreyar deal with this subject in the next chapter. Their writing and thinking have prompted me to clarify my own thoughts about the difficulties artists have in working in a public school environment.

2. Craig Dreeszen, *Intersections: Community Arts and Education Collaborations* (The Arts Extension Service, University of Massachusetts, Amherst, 1992).

CHAPTER 5

Arts Partnerships in the Classroom

PART I
CREATING A CLIMATE FOR THE ARTS IN THE SCHOOL COMMUNITY

Behind the Classroom Door
Artist/Teacher Partnerships as a Strategy for Instructional Change

Building Professional Capacity and a Constituency for the Arts: Some Fundamental Questions

Most classroom and subject area teachers tell me they like the arts, appreciate or are in awe of professional artists, and think their kids definitely benefit from exposure to both. Yet very few of these teachers say they use the arts regularly, if at all, in the classroom; they still consider them "soft" subjects and are not really convinced of their hard-core instructional value. They tell me their repertoire is limited to running a filmstrip or a video, playing the phonograph or a tape machine, making Thanksgiving turkeys or paper snowflake cutouts (at the elementary level), or teaching a Haiku poem. There are, of course, many exceptions, but unless teachers have studied the arts or pursued them as secondary or parallel careers, their pre-service training has not equipped them to deal with these disciplines.

If we expect to establish a firm and enduring presence for the arts behind the classroom door, then we need to start building understanding and acceptance of the value of the arts and developing the professional capacity of teachers to use them competently, confidently and routinely. The current wave of enthusiasm for reform, instructional standards and assessment of all the disciplines, including the arts, is in our favor. But we have learned that these national and state efforts are unreliable and by themselves will not provide the continuity needed to create positive and enduring change behind the classroom door. After 30-odd years, I am convinced more than ever that such change can be accomplished only if those of us at the local level work together to create a climate for change within the school and to foster energetic support for it within the community.

So how do you go about doing it? How *do* you create an atmosphere conducive to change? How *do* you build capacity in classroom and subject area teachers? How *do* you build bridges between the arts, other subjects and the lives of children? How *do* you build a constituency for the arts, artists and arts specialists behind the classroom door and in the school community? And, perhaps most important, how do you make sure that new efforts build on and do not displace effective programs, adding to the breadth and depth of their firm community foundations? I have addressed these questions in some detail from the school perspective in my book, *Changing Schools Through the Arts: How to Build on the Power of an Idea*. I now want to look at some of them from the perspective of the outside arts organization, agency and artist.

Since I consider partnerships to be a key strategy, the central questions for this chapter become: What is the incentive for teachers to form these time-consuming relationships? What do teachers need and what value is added to curriculum and instruction by the arts, the artists and classroom arts partnerships? How can we build, sustain and evaluate partnerships in which artists serve as resources to classroom and subject matter teachers as well as arts specialists? What is the nature of these partnerships, and what do they look like in the classroom? What resources and support systems— such as training and professional development of all the partners—do we need to give them shape, continuity and substance?

The Art of Partnerships: Creating a Climate for Artist/Teacher Collaboration

Too many partnerships that feature artists in the schools falter or break down behind the classroom door. In partnerships that I observe, I am often assured that there is organizational commitment, a decent program structure and a sound design. Yet I find myself searching in vain for specific information about program content and the instructional objectives of the workshop, the curriculum unit or the course of study. I want to know about anticipated "learner outcomes"—what students, teachers and other participants are expected to know and be able to do as a result of the instructional program. What changes will the program have generated?

By what standards and criteria will success—for both the program and the learners—be measured and by whom? More often than not, I am amazed by the claims made for many artist/teacher partnerships because the amount of instructional time—contact hours—is simply not sufficient to realize even half of the promised outcomes.

I am always concerned with quality, and so I want to know how much time will be spent on artist training and professional development of teachers and on bringing artists and teachers together in common instructional pursuit. More often than not, scant attention—and even less money—is paid to providing opportunities to build the artist/teacher connection, the most important dynamic of the partnership if any significant and enduring learning is to take place.

I look for information about what will be done to:

- create and sustain a trusting relationship between the artist and the teacher, including professional development opportunities for artists and teachers, separately and together, and supervised monitoring of the working artist in the classroom by both artists and experienced educators;

- develop an understanding of and agreement about the nature and source of the curriculum that will be taught and learned by the teaching partners (there is no guarantee that what is taught is actually learned and then applied with skill, imagination and a judicious intelligence);

- determine the juncture at which the teacher's curriculum and the artist's activities are fused, for what purpose, using what strategies, how results will be assessed, and by whom;[1] and

- identify and pay for the considerable preparation and planning time that both the artist and teacher need, alone and together, to establish a cooperative, collaborative team-teaching approach.

Artists who work in schools quickly discover that most teachers think and behave very differently from most artists. To generalize, teachers live in a very rules-oriented, time-dominated artificial society that is largely based on the factory model of efficient production within rigid and regulated time frames. In most of the nation's schools, there is little or no discretionary time, teachers work in isolation from their peers in separate classrooms, and, unless site-based management or other alternative approaches to education have been adopted, they have little access to decision-making power in matters of school climate, governance, curriculum, instructional materials, texts and the allocation of funds.

Teachers, much like the rest of us, are products of their training and professional milieu, which traditionally places high value on uniformity, correct answers, convergent thinking, discipline and order, and proper conduct and behavior. As a rule, they are pressured to look for efficient ways to generate product rather than indulge in the luxury of time-consuming, open-ended processes. Because of age- and grade-level expectations, teachers are obliged to transmit as much knowledge, information and skills as possible within arbitrary, inflexible time frames so they can move their product (the students) on to the next station (grade) within the factory metaphor. Success in education has traditionally been measured in numbers—by the number of hours clocked in seats, courses taken, and by the number of students who demonstrate they can read, write and compute at or better than the national norm on standardized tests. These days it is also measured by the number of kids who show up and stay in school, move smoothly from grade to grade, and graduate.

Unless they are artists or culture enthusiasts, teachers—like most Americans—know little about the so-called "fine" arts. They have lives that may be rich with the arts, artifacts, culture and traditions of their ethnic background or racial heritage, but for the most part, until very recently, that has not counted for much either in our society or in the schools. The colleges and universities that prepare teachers for work in education pay little attention to the arts—fine, folk or popular. Few licenses for generalists or subject matter specialists require more than a cursory knowledge of the arts, usually visual arts or music. Not surprisingly, most of our educators and our educational leaders—like the rest of American society—are not arts literate or arts devotees.

To most artists starting out in schools, all this comes as quite a shock. Unfortunately, a few of them become defensive: they believe they are special and resent the lack of respect. Others develop an antagonistic, holier-than-thou, you-just-don't-get-it attitude that permeates their behavior with teachers and principals and poisons the atmosphere, making any kind of cooperative relationship impossible. These artists will make a grand entrance into a school, proceed to behave like the stereotypical prima donna, do "their thing" theatrically, and bolt out the door, usually to the loud applause of the kids and the general dismay or outright annoyance of the teachers and the administration. This is no way to help build a constituency for the arts in the schools.

Luckily, the overwhelming number of artists who work in schools do not fit this description. Most are dedicated perfectionists who want to share what they know with students and teachers. Unfortunately, however, most artists are given very little help in building these professional and instructional bridges.

While at first glance, teachers and artists appear to have little if anything in common, they do share certain characteristics. Both teachers and artists (performing and visual) are (or can be):

- Performers who use the classroom as a stage and believe in theatrics and a technical bag of tricks for calculated instructional and other effects;

- Proud masters of their "performance" skills, their knowledge, their experience and training, and the special niche they have carved out in their professional lives;

- Specialists in the art of improvisation and thinking on their feet when, inevitably, things don't go as planned;

- Disciplined, diligent workers who know the value of time and how to focus and stay on task; and

- Perfectionists who will try and try again to get the teaching or artistic process "just right" so that it produces a desired or at least unexpectedly delightful result.

There are undoubtedly many more differences and commonalities between artists and teachers. A good way of building the artist/teacher connection would be to discuss the list of commonalities with your teacher-partner and think of items to add to it. I would also examine the differences I have mentioned and make a list of those, adding your own to them in the process. In this way, you start a dialogue based on your own experiences that can lead to greater understanding of both stylistic as well as "cultural" similarities and dissimilarities between you and your partner. This approach should prove immensely helpful as you continue to search for, discover and try out ways of working together more effectively.

From Theory to Practice: Two Classroom Scenarios

To help develop a better understanding about the nature of classroom partnerships, I have constructed the following two imaginary scenarios involving artists in the classroom. Although I deliberately made them starkly different for contrast and comparison, they are by no means far-fetched. I have witnessed scenes just like these and, I would venture, so have you. Nor are they intended as archetypes of the worst or best: we have worse situations and much, much better ones.

Scenario One: "How Can We Know the Dancer from the Dance?"[2]

Betty, a modern dancer, arrives late and out of breath at a fourth-grade classroom door. She bursts in without knocking. The teacher, Ms. Corey, who is drilling her students for the upcoming reading test, is startled and has forgotten that Betty is coming. Suddenly remembering, she hastily and with some annoyance tells the students to put their workbooks away. The artist instructs everyone to help move the desks against the wall, take off their shoes and sit on the floor in staggered rows. The room is filled with much giggling, a lot of chair screeches and several refusals to remove shoes. The teacher offers no encouragement and retires to the back of the room, out of the picture. Most of the kids sit in tangled clusters of friends, others have decided not to participate and are sitting at their desks.

Betty launches into the workshop, introducing the session by offering only her name, the name of the sponsoring organization, and the statement, "We're going to learn about movement, and you're going to have lots of fun making your own dances today." The workshop is free-form and improvisatory, with no discernable beginning, middle or end. Its unstated purpose and sequence of activities are a mystery to Ms. Corey and her students. It has succeeded, however, in getting the children excited and overheated. More often than not, they are out of control, causing Betty to do a lot of yelling, threatening, cajoling and pleading. Ms. Corey occasionally attempts half-heartedly to intervene and restore order and discipline, to little avail. No one pays any attention to the kids who sit dully on the sidelines. Betty talks non-stop, asks no questions, and jumps from one activity to another, sometimes frantically trying to keep everyone's interest and attention. The harder she tries, the more control eludes her.

At the end of the period, Betty apologizes for not keeping her promise about making dance. She says she will return the following week, gathers her belongings, nods quickly at Ms. Corey and leaves without another word. The noise behind her is deafening. The principal, Mr. DeLorenzo, who has come upstairs to see what the disturbance is all about, passes her in the hall without recognition or acknowledgment. Reassured that no major mayhem has occurred after peeking behind the door and asking if everything is okay, he returns to his office muttering, "Artists! I love 'em, but most of them just don't get it. I'm going to have to rethink this residency. We just can't have chaos like that around here."

The Teacher Ms. Corey's Reflection: How embarrassing, so much noise that Mr. D. heard it all the way downstairs. Heaven knows how I'm going to get these children to settle down again in their seats so we can get back to business. I completely forgot that Mr. D. told me the artist was coming today! Why is she here? What am I expected to be doing? Why can't she control the children? I don't like my classroom disrupted or rearranged. I can't stand this wildness and noise and lack of order. I suppose I should do something to help out. After all, it's the arts and a nice enrichment, but I don't know anything about modern dance, and I really don't see any point in this. What does this kind of dance have to do with my kids or my curriculum? What good will it do them to learn this stuff?

What a shame that Betty doesn't have a clue about the kind of structure, attention and discipline that children this age need or about how kids behave when they don't have any idea what they are doing or why. And her so-called lesson! It had no rhyme or reason, no logic that I can see. She has no plan, no motivation; she doesn't make any connection to my students' lives and experiences. I really find her dance outfit offensive. It's too revealing. Today, Ernesto slipped in his socks—if he should fall and get hurt, I'll be blamed. I wish I could say or do something, but I don't feel comfortable talking to Mr. D., and I don't know who else I could discuss this with. Oh well, fortunately it will soon be over. Still, I'm really worried that we're taking so much time from the drill for the reading test coming up next month.

The Artist Betty's Reflection: Here we go again! The teacher not only forgot the date, but she also doesn't have a clue why I'm here! What is it with this school? And this teacher! She shows no interest, disappears to the back of the room, doesn't pitch in, doesn't participate and won't discipline the kids. Am I always expected to do everything? Teachers just don't give a damn about artists. Why do these kids hate to take their shoes and even their jackets off? Why do they act out so unpredictably? What's the matter with them? Why aren't they into what I'm doing? Dancing is for everybody!

Next time maybe I'll speed things up and get them moving faster; that should help. I wonder whether they even like me or understand what I'm trying to do for them. I have to keep more control. Today, I ran out of time and never got them to choreograph a phrase. I must tell Cindy (the program coordinator) that I get no cooperation and support. If these kids keep going wild and the teacher remains uncooperative, I'll ask to get switched to another class or another school. What's with the principal? Either he didn't remember me or he just snubbed me. Oops, I'd better make tracks or I'll be late for my company dance rehearsal. Oh well, another day in the schools. I suppose it's a living.

Scenario Two: "I Taught My Dog To Sing"

Musician/composer Pete arrives at the sixth-grade classroom door, which is decorated with student-made posters bearing his name and profession, a cutout of his instrument (the clarinet), the name of his sponsoring organization, and a profusion of Polaroid photographs that the teacher and several students have been taking during the course of the residency. When he enters, he notices that the students' compositions in invented notation systems are posted all around the room. He is greeted warmly by the teacher, Mr. Jack Jeffrey, and his students, and greets everyone in turn by name. The students have already put the half-completed instruments they are making on their desks and readied the "found" materials and tools. They stand clustered around the teacher's desk, momentarily interrupted in their intense discussion about the concert they plan to put on for the other classes in their grade.

Pete joins the discussion briefly and then suggests that they make planning for their concert a part of the day's agenda. As he does each visit, he goes to the chalkboard and writes his name, the name of the sponsoring arts organization, the aim of the day's lessons, some key points that will be covered, the main activities, and the homework assignment. Mr. Jeffrey suggests that the students take out their project journals and copy down the aim, the key points and the homework.

The artist and teacher have agreed during one of their weekly planning sessions that a good way to start today's workshop would be to have the students write their ideas about the proposed concert in their journals, break into small groups to share these thoughts and then report to the whole group. Pete and Mr. Jeffrey have also discussed and agreed on the purpose of these workshops, their structure and sequence, the role and responsibility of each instructor and the ways in which they, as a team, will evaluate the effectiveness of each workshop and of the residency as a whole. They have also discussed these issues with the students and have collectively determined the standards for individual and overall residency success.

The rest of the double-period, 80-minute workshop runs pretty much as planned. The students write in their journals and discuss plans for the concert. Pete makes sure to play each of the musical compositions and to discuss them with the class. For contrast and comparison, he plays some Mozart, Weber, Benny Goodman and Klezmer. Progress is made on the homemade instruments. Mr. Jeffrey encourages the kids to share the information they have researched about the history of the clarinet and its use in contemporary, classical and popular music.

Both artist and teacher think on their feet when called for—they improvise and interact. They exhibit pride and pleasure in their teamwork and offer praise for student effort. They take turns writing vocabulary and other information on the chalkboard. The pace is varied, and the activities come chock-a-block one after the other. There is individual work, large and small group work, question and answer time and reflection time. The students are fully engaged, energetic and focused, with no need for artificial motivation.

The usual cutups occasionally disrupt the class, but their peers or the artist or the teacher generally bring them back into the flow with a humorous quip, a challenging question or a particularly intriguing problem to solve. At one point, Mrs. Johnson, the principal, drops by, joins the activity, exchanges a few words with the students, the artist and the teacher, and then bows out gracefully, publicly inviting the artist to stop by for a chat before he goes home. Finally, Pete, Mr. Jeffrey and the students have concocted an addition to the homework assignment that a student volunteers to write on the chalkboard. The artist leaves to a chorus of student voices saying, "Ooh, so soon? Is it really time yet?" Pete assures Mr. Jeffrey that he will call him at home this evening as previously arranged, since their next scheduled planning session is a week away, and the next workshop is in two days.

Evening phone call:

Pete, the Composer/Musician: Well, Jack, how do you think it went? Did I get the flow better this time? Was I clearer in my instructions on how to use the tools? Did I talk too much or too fast again? How can we help the kids shape this concert that they're dreaming up? It's unwieldy the way they've got it now.

Jack Jeffrey, the Teacher: Whoa, Pete, slow down. Take it easy. Can we take it one by one?

They begin to discuss Pete's questions, and the dialogue is open and supportive. The tables turn:

Teacher: Pete, listen. I really tried to get into the instrument-making myself, but I'm all thumbs. I feel awkward, and I don't want to look like a fool in front of these kids. They all seem to do it so much better than I do. Can you help me with this?

They discuss ways to solve this problem and come up with a few ideas that they agree to try out. Then:

Artist: Jack, we've got to get Susan (the school's vocal music teacher), Charlie (the school's band teacher) and the other sixth-grade teachers in on this aspect of the project now. I know we've talked about this and they've agreed, but time's slipping away and it's critical. We need their help, especially if we want to take this show on the road for parents and the community. How should we proceed? What will work best in terms of schedule and the "politics" of the situation?

They discuss and agree on strategies, reminding each other not to short-change the process in the excitement of getting to the performance/product. Next:

Teacher: Pete, I'm particularly pleased about the way you've got Ernie responding to instructions. He's not nearly as hyper as he was a few weeks ago. I think we've got him motivated, but you know he can always go off, and when he does, he just sets the whole place off. Any thoughts or ideas on this?

They discuss this persistent problem, don't come up with an ideal solution, but agree to keep thinking about it. The conversation concludes on a humorous note:

Teacher: Did I tell you the one about the woman who taught her dog to sing?

Artist: No.

Teacher: Well, the woman's husband is an opera singer, and one night he comes home and she tells him she taught the dog to sing the tenor aria, "La Donna è Mobile" from Verdi's *Rigoletto*. Her husband looks at her, then the dog, who is cheerfully wagging his tail and barking away. He turns to her and says, "So, how come he's still barking?" She replies, "I said I taught him. I didn't say he learned it!"[3]

Artist: That's a good one.

Teacher: Yeah, it kinda sums up the work we're trying to do together. In fact, it sums up the challenge every teacher faces day in and day out. Maybe I can't sing or compose or even make those damned instruments, but I'm learning a lot about music, Pete. Thanks.

Artist: It's great working with you, too. I had a good talk with Mrs. Johnson (the principal) this afternoon, and she's going to get the parents to find us more trash materials. She'll also make the arrangements for the concerts once the kids have figured out what we're going to do. She's great. Quite a leader. I've learned tons about how your school works and something about what it takes to make a good teacher. I'm in awe and in your debt. Thank *you!* Bye, Jack.

These scenarios and others like them can be analyzed in several ways. You can compare and contrast them from the point of view of the artists, the teachers, the principals and the sponsoring organization. Although I have provided the action, the dialogue and the reflective subtext, you can give the characters your own names and characteristics, situate them in your own locale, choose whatever age group and demographics you wish, and otherwise elaborate on or embroider the scenarios so they become locally recognizable and familiar. You can then analyze these situations in terms of the guidelines and criteria in this section and the rest of the book to identify the problems and propose various solutions.

Here are a few of the specific issues I would tackle:

- In the first scenario, what does the dancer need to know and be able to do (or not do) in order to improve (a) her classroom workshop, (b) her relationship with the teacher, and (c) her communication with the principal?
- In what ways can both artists become more effective resources to the teachers, the specialists and the schools in which they are working?
- What are the differences and similarities in attitudes and behavior between the artists, teachers, principals and, by implication, the sponsoring organizations in both scenarios?
- Can you draw any conclusions about the amount of time allocated to each residency and the likelihood of instructional impact on the students?
- What might be inferred as the climate and culture of each school and the attitude toward the arts in the curriculum?
- What ways might be employed in both situations to increase teacher confidence and capacity in the arts, to relate the arts to the teacher's curriculum and to build a wider constituency for the arts in these particular schools and their communities?

I urge you to complete this exercise and to try the technique in your work with other artists and teachers. I have found that these and similar mini-dramas stimulate thoughtful, provocative and productive discussion for those who plan programs and artist and teacher workshops.

Anatomy of a Classroom Partnership: Some Guidelines for Team Building

Rest assured that the process for building an effective classroom arts partnership follows no single blueprint. Nevertheless, the following section can help to guide you in your own inquiry and to generate your own responses. The key is to work through these issues with your prospective teaching partner, which I suggest that you do in the context of these criteria:

How will the proposed answer or solution offer approaches that are most likely to be effective with students in the classroom; *and* build the teacher's confidence and capacity in the arts; *and* build an arts-supportive constituency in the school community?

A Compact for Arts Learning

At a New York City Opera Artist Training Retreat, the issue of school and classroom partnerships threaded throughout the proceedings. Toward the end of the second day, Robert Cooper, a high school assistant principal and the workshop facilitator, and I acted out a scene in which he played an arms-folded-on-chest, recalcitrant teacher. I was the eager opera artist trying to establish rapport and a framework for a partnership during our first planning session.

As the "teacher," Bob was difficult. He warned me, as "artist," that the plans I had for the kids and the way that I wanted to proceed in the classroom were not going to work—period. I was having a very hard time convincing him that we should at least give it a try: if it didn't work, I reasoned, he could bail me out. But he wouldn't budge until I repeated to him that he was in charge as the knowledgeable and licensed pedagogue, and that I was simply a knowledgeable artistic resource. Desperate, I suggested that we talk to the supportive supervisor, who might help us figure out some solutions to the problems he persistently and stubbornly raised. (This easily could have backfired on me, but fortunately it didn't.) Bob finally relented a bit and agreed to at least try some of my ideas, and the scene was over. I commented that a teacher with that attitude would probably never have volunteered for this program, and that, fortunately, most teachers I have known over the years wouldn't have remained that hostile for that long!

The exercise vividly brought to life many of the issues about partnerships that we had been discussing during the retreat and raised a critical new one: the need for the teaching artist and the teacher to spend quality time developing what I call a "compact for arts learning." This is an agreement that spells out the purpose of the project, the goals of the instructional relationship, the terms and conditions under which the partners agree to operate, and the rules of the game.

The compact for arts learning idea proceeds on two very important assumptions. First, regardless of the partnership's power structure, the classroom is the teacher's domain, the kids are his or her legal responsibility and the artist is a visitor in that environment. A guest shows the host courteous deference and respect, learns the house rules and behaves accordingly. Second, teachers are well-trained, licensed professionals who take great pride in their work, have a wealth of experience, understand their students and, for the most part, know how to deal with them. Artists must keep this information in the forefront of their thinking and planning and convey this attitude at all times or there will be no hope of cooperation, much less partnership.

Whether the compact for arts learning is formally written or simply discussed by the artist/teacher team before, during and after the workshops or residency is a matter of individual preference and time. However, these issues should be dealt with regardless of the length of the artist's visit in the schools because partnerships should be concerned with more than simply the delivery of instruction to students. In my view, the ultimate goal of these partnerships should be to build professional capacity and support among both artists and teachers for teaching the arts in entire schools.

In the artist training that I do, I urge everyone to establish their own compact for arts learning. As you begin, your first discussions should revolve around a set of questions that relate to the climate and environment of the school. These contextual questions should help both artist and teacher begin to build an institutional and community constituency for the arts:

The Culture and Environment of the School and the Classroom

1. What is the school's philosophy and mission? Where do the arts fit in?
2. What are the distinguishing characteristics or the personality of this school's organizational, social, political and community life? What style of leadership is exerted? Where is the locus of control, and what is the power structure? Is there parental and community involvement? What pressures and demands are made by these and other groups, and on whom? Who, within this mix, are a likely core of supporters of the arts in the general education of all students? How should the artist perform his or her ambassadorial roles in this complex environment?
3. What is the culture of the school, i.e., who comprises the school, what are their core values, how do they interact and behave toward each other? What is acceptable and unacceptable conduct, speech, dress? What is considered acceptable behavior and dress by the artist? How is order, discipline and respect maintained? What are the school's disciplinary policies and procedures? What are the systems of reward and recognition?
4. What are the teacher's classroom rituals, the organizational and methodological preferences? What are the special signs and signals used for beginning and ending tasks? How does the teacher prefer to start and end classes? Who will be responsible for what areas of classroom control, management and discipline?
5. Do the students have special needs, gifts or potential? How are these identified, and how will they be addressed and handled, and by whom? Is there information about individual students that might be helpful? What special resources can the artist bring to or share with the teacher to meet these needs?

6. What are the artist's classroom strategies, rituals, organizational and pedagogical preferences? What instructional approaches does the artist favor, and do any of these particularly please or disturb the teacher? Are there any activities or subjects that the teacher wishes to emphasize or avoid, or discuss first before introducing the artist and the lesson?

Now that you have sketched out some details about the culture and environment of the school and the classroom—the way things appear to work, the way people behave and their expectations—you need to address a second set of issues to establish your compact for arts learning. These are questions that deal with the content, form and methods of teaching and learning.

The Framework for Curriculum and Instruction

1. Define what constitutes an effective artist/teacher partnership for you in this situation. Team- or co-teaching is difficult to develop and sustain. Like any relationship, a partnership requires time for planning and feedback, ample opportunity to build trust and confidence, a meshing of individual styles and personalities, honesty, respect, a sense of humor and dedication—and chemistry. Will you have the motivation, time and opportunity to team-teach? If so, what are the optimum circumstances and conditions for this to occur and are the resources available? How will you communicate and make time for ongoing formal and informal interaction? (For further discussion of this topic, read what teachers and artists have to say in section two of this chapter.)

2. Determine goals, objectives, content and teaching strategies for the partnership. What will be taught and learned? What is your collaborative agenda? What main strategies will you use? What will drive instruction in the partnership? Is the curriculum:

a. *artist-driven*, i.e., dependent on the art form, expertise, invention, imaginative resources (and possibly the ego) of an individual artist?

b. *event-driven*, i.e., does the observation, encounter and interaction with an artifact, an object or a performance largely dictate what is to be studied, learned and engaged in?

c. *theme or concept driven*, i.e., is a topic such as "war," "relationships," "families" or "the environment" going to determine what will be taught and learned?

d. *creativity- or creation-driven*, i.e., hands-on participation in making an opera, a play, a dance, a museum exhibit or a mural?

e. *curriculum-driven*, i.e., the forces for revolution in 18th-Century France, the African Diaspora, the theme of sin and redemption in

Hawthorne, the concept of gravity and motion, or the relationship of fractions to time in musical notation?

f.   *a course of study, a unit, a workshop, a series of lessons?*

g.   *concept and process oriented? fact and product oriented?*

3. Define the power structure of your arts partnerships. What is the division of labor, the role and function of each team member? Will you pass through developmental stages or will your roles and responsibilities vary according to specific needs and expertise? The following might be considered modes or stages of an artist/teacher partnership that you need to discuss and particularize for your own situation.

Mode I: Artist-dominant. The artist knows all, asks or tells all, does all and is in control of instruction. The teacher is an observer or learner and may or may not enter into the action as a disciplinarian, motivator, authority figure and reinforcer.

- How will this mode ultimately build teacher capability and an arts-avid constituency in the school community? How will it encourage the cooperation of the school arts specialists?

Mode II: Artist/teacher parity. This is often referred to as co-teaching. The artist and teacher share power, responsibility, time and accountability for results.

- What kind of training, professional development and planning time do you need and have available to build this kind of relationship? How does it affect capacity and constituency-building in your school community?

Mode III: Teacher-dominant. The teacher controls the design and methodology of instruction. The artist serves as resource, demonstrator, illuminator, commentator and translator.

- Are there sufficient resources (time, money, materials) for the classroom or subject teacher to develop the skills, knowledge and mastery of artistic material and processes for this situation to develop?

Mode IV: A combination of the above. Modes I - III are employed at various times throughout the project or program depending upon situational needs, opportunity and available expertise.

- Is there sufficient time and motivation to design a combination of modalities? This can be an interesting but extremely intricate endeavor that takes both time and good timing to bring off.

4. Decide what kind of teaching modalities will predominate in this partnership. Are most of the activities basically a transmission of information, skills or processes that students learn by rote, repetition and workbook activities? Or is learning transactive, that is, a dynamic inter-change between the teaching partners and among the partners and the students? Or is the instructional experience transformative, that is, does it go beyond what anyone involved in the process planned for or even dreamed might happen—a world full of eye-popping epiphanies? A little bit of all of the above?

5. Decide how instruction will be monitored and evaluated. What roles will the artist and the teacher play in the ongoing assessment process? What performance and content standards will be used? How will we know "it" when we see it, that is, what characteristics and criteria are we using to define achievement, what are the indicators for successful performance, and how will we record them? If the district has a curriculum framework, will it provide the context for evaluation? What attention should be paid to the voluntary national arts standards and to state arts education guidelines and frameworks?

Evaluation Criteria: Characteristics of Effective Artist/Teacher Partnerships

Once you have launched your partnership, you will want to monitor its progress and make mid-course corrections. I have developed a simple set of easy-to-remember guidelines that provide a handy framework for evaluating a broad range of phenomena from classroom workshops to the design and implementation of large-scale programmatic efforts. Feel free to use them, adapt them or add to them as you wish.

Effective instruction or educative activities in arts partnerships are generally characterized by:

- *Artistic excellence.* The quality of the arts encountered, presented or developed is first rate. There is no compromise allowed in this area.

- *Aesthetic integrity.* The art forms retain their identity. They are not bastardized or bowdlerized as a convenient, showy or manipulative means to an end. (I did not use the word "purity," for which every-one has a different definition.)

- *Artistic and educational scope and balance.* The arts and educational goals and activities have parity regardless of which discipline is used as a strategy for illuminating or extending the other.

- *Educational effectiveness and impact.* The program or workshop gives clear evidence that what is taught is being learned and applied by those identified as the learners. Outcomes are described in both mea-surable and analytical terms by those experts, peers and practitioners who are competent to make sound critical judgments.[4]

Tools for Self-Appraisal: Keeping Journals, Logs and Diaries

I always recommend to the artists and teachers (and administrators) with whom I work to keep journals, logs or diaries of their in-school workshops, residencies and other experiences. These devices serve several purposes.

First, they function as a documentary record of thoughts, feelings, problems, solutions and precious anecdotes that, unless written down daily, vanish into the collective unconscious forever. These ruminations and notes often form the basis for project reports, articles for school or organizational newspapers, or even for books and other publications. (The poets Kenneth Koch and Philip Lopate are good examples of the latter.)

Second, when reviewed over time, these reflections serve as very important teaching and learning assessment tools. They become "process journals" or "developmental portfolios" or "scrapbooks" that are invaluable for your own enlightenment, for discussion with your instructional partner, or for review with the project supervisors.

Finally, they are a good disciplined strategy to help you keep track of your original goals and to determine whether you are on the path you originally set out for yourself. If not, you either need to find substantiating reasons (with your partner) to choose the branch you may have taken, or quickly veer back on course. We all improvise; we all digress. This is a good tool for self-correction.

Who Shall Teach the Arts, Revisited: Artists as Resources to Teachers

In *Changing Schools Through the Arts: How to Build on the Power of an Idea*, I devoted a chapter to exploring the question, "Who shall teach the arts?" My response then was, and still is, classroom teachers, arts specialists, artists and others who have the capacity to do so—in collaboration. I presented that discussion largely from the point of view of the school, and I now want to revisit this issue from a different perspective—that of the arts organization, the arts agency and the teaching artist. It is a closer examination of complex issues such as school culture, values and attitudes toward teamwork and joint action. It is a discussion that is long overdue, and one that I have been looking forward to for some time.

The context for this examination began in Chapter Four where we looked at the need to build bridges between the cultures of the arts world and the school, the teachers and the artists, the artists and the students.

Then, in the first section of this chapter, we explored the landscape of artist/teacher partnerships in the classroom and the roles that artists can play in building effective collaborations. We also examined ways in which artists and teachers can create a climate for collaboration by engaging in activities that build their own professional capacity.

In this section, I have asked several artists and teachers to speak from their own considerable and diverse experiences; the artists represent different arts disciplines, and the teachers are generalists and specialists. They talk about the kinds of work they have done, the partnerships they have developed in the classroom and the lessons they have learned from these collaborations.

What they tell us confirms what we already know. Collaboration and partnership are hard to come by for many reasons, including lack of time, lack of mutual understanding, lack of trust and lack of confidence. Despite these formidable barriers, we *do* have successes and some clear indications of paths to follow that will help to build a constituency for the arts in the schools, with artists acting as ambassadors.

Artists in the Classroom: What is the Value Added?

Why even have artists in the classroom? After all, artists, as outsiders, cannot change schools, schooling or teachers. They *can*, however, act as effective catalysts for and resources to the school development process if a comprehensive plan is in place. Or, in the absence of such a plan, they can be professionally stimulating instructional partners in the classroom to teachers and arts specialists. I believe, and in this chapter I am attempting to demonstrate, that artist/teacher partnerships can be one of the most effective strategies for achieving enduring instructional change behind the classroom door—not just in the arts, but in all academic subjects.

But why are artists important as resources in the classroom (as distinct from in the studio or on the stage)? How can they help teachers to build instructional capacity and literacy in the arts? How can they help build a constituency of teachers, principals, supervisors, students and parents for the arts in every classroom in the school and perhaps in the community? And how does their work in the arts extend to and affect the general education of all students?

Consider the following ways in which artists can add an instructional dimension and value for students and teachers in the schools:

- They teach skills in and information about their art form, which they demonstrate as a process and a product, and they explain how and why they do what they do and manage to make a living at it (or at least survive);

- They go beyond skills, process and product, creativity and practice to include history, cultural context, aesthetics, criticism, research and inquiry in their efforts—firmly anchoring their work in the reality of the general curriculum and the values of the local community;
- They connect their real-life careers, skills, information and arts processes to the learning process and to other subjects using core concepts or themes as linkages;
- They devise arts activities that make use of what Howard Gardner calls our multiple intelligences—our different ways of learning and knowing the world—to stimulate and develop critical thinking, problem solving and higher order cognitive processes in arts and other academic disciplines;
- They learn how to share instructional power in the classroom to help make learning in and through the arts a motivating, satisfying and significant experience for as many children as possible by designing projects that deliberately bring arts specialists and classroom teachers together;
- They serve as ambassadors, interpreters, translators and connectors of the arts, arts resources and other artists to parents and other community members; and
- They act as liaisons who identify and secure resources within the local cultural community, establishing linkages with arts organizations and community agencies.

So what *is* the artist's relationship to the classroom teacher, the arts specialists (where they exist), the students, the principal, the parents and the larger community? What is the teacher's role? What is or should be the artist's connection, if any, to the standard curriculum? How are all these bridges to be built? And what is the impact on teaching and learning of these relationships and connections?

Figure 5.1: Mask Making—An Illustration of How an Artist Can Add Instructional Value and Help Build a Constituency for the Arts Within a School

The following is a concrete but fanciful example of a unit that an artist might design in collaboration with a classroom teacher and the school's arts and music specialists. It is inspired by an idea that is included in the Kentucky Arts Council handbook, *Education Reform Opportunities for Artists and Craftspeople*.[5]

The original example links various activities within the project description with the specific goals and "academic expectations" (learner outcomes) contained in the Kentucky Curriculum Framework [See Chapter Three]. With the approval of the authors, I have elaborated on Judy Sizemore's published example and added some ideas of my own.

Mask Making[6]

A mask-making project should go beyond the production of a mask. It should be rooted in some aspect of the curriculum currently being taught and learned (perhaps language arts or social studies). Students should be able to connect their existing knowledge of masks, occasions for using them and their significance from their own experience...(e.g., Halloween, West Indian Carnivals, the Lone Ranger, Batman). Building on this information and personal experience, include an interactive discussion of the role of masks in a particular culture or in different cultures.

Slide sets can be borrowed from the National Gallery of Art at no charge...or ask the art teacher and the librarian to help your students find or make such slides. Use these to show the masks of African, Alaskan or Native American culture and help students make observations about the masks. Compare and contrast these masks with those from the students' experiences.

Introduce appropriate terminology, like symmetry or radial balance, and both you and the teacher write the words on the board, asking the students to look them up in the dictionary for homework as you help students analyze and compare the masks they are viewing and the masks they make.

Integrate the mask-making project into a study of folktales. Ask the music teacher to work with you and the classroom teacher on finding appropriate folk songs to learn with the folktales. Help children work in groups to write skits based on these folktales and their masks. Work with the music teacher, who will help students to make up some of their own songs related to the skits. Invite someone from the local community with a dance or movement background (the physical education teacher, a parent volunteer) to add dance or movement to the skits. Encourage them to perform the skits, the songs and the dances for other classes and perhaps their parents and others at a community open house.

Have students develop written reflections on the performance experience of the skits or the mask-making process from the beginning to the end of the project.... Encourage math entries based on the project, such as the measuring and other skills required to build the masks or an invented notation system for the folk songs, that are appropriate for inclusion in their portfolios.

...Design your project so that students must use critical thinking and creative problem solving to complete the activity...for example, include activities that have them analyze, prioritize, categorize, evaluate and compare the process of making the masks, their meaning and how they might authentically use them in their own lives (at a party, a masked "ball," even to "hold up a bank").

Work with the arts specialists and the classroom teachers to design activities in which you can facilitate and reinforce the transfer of learning of various arts and thinking processes from one domain to another.

Building Capacity and a Constituency for the Arts, Redux

As we move on to the balance of this section and the rest of this chapter, artists, teachers, professors, arts administrators and evaluators from around the country grapple with these thorny issues. They will discuss their experiences and the lessons they have learned about classroom partnerships. They will consider how artists have tried to become effective resources to teachers and how teachers have struggled to adapt themselves to working collaboratively with artists. These discussions will help to further define the challenging question of how best to make allies of artists, classroom or subject matter teachers and arts specialists so that they are all prepared and eager to work together behind the classroom door, in the galleries and museum halls, or anywhere else that productive learning can transpire.

By way of transition, I will use an excerpt from elementary school teacher Norma Moran's essay "Reflections of a Classroom Teacher on Working with Artists in the Classroom" to take us straight to the heart of the matter:

> To be effective, an artist needs to present to the teacher a detailed outline of how the art form can be used in the classroom and to discuss in advance how the artist can connect with the teacher's classroom agenda. The artist and the teacher should discuss how the teacher can help and reach an agreement about how they will work together. Absent this kind of advance discussion, the teacher is left without a collaborative agenda and may feel relegated solely to the role of classroom manager...

> ...teachers provide a critical link between artists and the classroom. Teachers know the basic curriculum requirements; they know developmental issues for their specific grades; they know the children; and they understand the organization of the school and the school system. Experienced teachers can also make better curriculum connections across grade levels and subject areas. They have had more experience with finding entry points and with making applications in and across the curriculum. Teachers can also help artists to understand the abilities of the students and the unique personality of the class with which they will be working.

Indeed!

Knowing the Place for the First Time

A Learning Journey

by Carol Ponder
with Susan Standbrook and Karen Catignani

I am a professional actor, singer and musician, and I was privileged to be part of something truly extraordinary during the 1994-95 academic year—a collaborative partnership with two gifted and dedicated sixth-grade teachers in an inner-city Nashville public school. Together we explored the possibilities for creating and teaching curricula that address mandated public school subjects through the artistic and creative processes inherent in the creation and production of works of art.

My collaboration with these fine teachers was part of the first full year of the pilot model school program of the Leonard Bernstein Center for Education Through the Arts. Staff, teachers and artists associated with the Bernstein Center have been working to extend the principles of aesthetic education, pioneered by the Lincoln Center Institute in New York City during the 1970s, and integrate them into the general public school curriculum.

In the Lincoln Center Institute approach to aesthetic education, professional artists (called teaching artists, or TAs) have worked with classroom teachers in partnerships for more than 20 years to prepare students for deeply experiencing works of art, most often in the disciplines of theater, music, dance and (more recently) visual arts. Through a series of activities, students participate in aspects of the work of art and solve some of the challenges inherent in its creation and production. Frequently the activities are designed to parallel the processes that went into creating the particular work of art under study. These institute partnerships between artist and teacher have been short term and aimed at one particular work of art.

Within these partnerships, the TA's role has been to explore the work of art under investigation and to discover windows into that work, elements of resonance that serve as entry points for the activities that will open up the work of art being introduced to teachers and students. In a summer session workshop (usually one to two weeks long), the teachers have an opportunity to explore the works of art for themselves in seminars led by TAs. Then, during the following school year, the teacher and the TA together plan the several-weeks-long investigation of the work of art in which they will lead the students, starting from their shared experience of the work of art from the previous summer session. At this point, the teacher's knowledge of his or her class, of general developmental issues and of individual children, becomes a very important part of the planning. Ideally, the TA and the teacher individually lead different classroom sessions.

Although the effects and outcomes of this approach to aesthetic education are difficult to quantify, overwhelming anecdotal evidence indicates that it has a profound effect on the participants—students, teachers and TAs alike. Students who may not excel in regular class work may shine in creative dance, theater or music explorations, surprising their teachers and classmates—and themselves—with their aptitude and expertise. Students of all kinds become excited about and involved with the arts and with new kinds of knowledge and self-discovery. During summer session, teachers often have powerful experiences with the works of art that resonate on a very personal level, and during the school year they often find themselves relating to their students in a new way as they explore the work of art together. Artists can also partake in the process of deep self-discovery and frequently perceive new, valuable ways of relating to their art form and their audience. Aesthetic education of this type encourages the breaking down of teacher/student definitions as all become co-learners in the process.

The idea central to the Bernstein Center is: Why not try to recreate within the general education curriculum the joy, personal involvement, and active, creative learning that is inherent in The Lincoln Center Institute's aesthetic education practices? The Bernstein Center project was designed to investigate what "learning through the arts" as a basic model of knowing and learning entailed and to explore the possibility of this concept as a key to systemic school transformation.[7] The essential part of the design expands the short-term, single-focus partnership between artist and teacher common to the Nashville and other institute approaches to aesthetic education. The project specifies that the artist, called an *artistic design consultant* (ADC), and the teacher collaborate for an entire school year and investigate several works of art. They work together to encourage students to be active and creative learners by designing a series of projects in which students can explore curriculum topics through study of the works of art and the arts disciplines.[8]

The Bernstein Center solicited proposals from interested schools in the Nashville area in fall 1993. By the beginning of 1994, ten schools had been selected by a committee of 15 community leaders and had begun preliminary program planning and design. The Nashville Institute for the Arts (NIA) provided artistic design consultants, and each school was encouraged to select a focus classroom teacher and to put together a design team. The *focus classroom teacher* would be the one with whom the artistic design consultant works most closely and would serve as the school's liaison for the project. The *design team* (composed of teachers, a parent or two, the focus classroom teacher and the artistic design consultant) would monitor the progress of the project and devise ways to spread the work being developed in the focus classroom throughout the school.

The first Bernstein Center Summer Session was held in June 1994. During the summer session, focus classroom teachers, design teams and artistic design consultants worked together to investigate works of art, to begin identifying and designing connections to the school curriculum, and to work out logistics and communications for the coming school year. The project's first academic year began in fall 1994. Each school chose two or more works of art to investigate.

I was invited to be the artistic design consultant at Head Middle School, which had enjoyed a long history of aesthetic education with the NIA. Susan Standbrook had been designated as the focus classroom teacher, and another teacher, Karen Catignani, had served for years as the school's liaison to the NIA.

The three of us would be the principal partners in the Bernstein Center collaboration at Head Middle School. Susan and Karen had already begun working together the previous year to link works of art to curricular topics in their classrooms. By the end of the year, I was working in Karen's classroom almost as much as Susan's officially designated *focus classroom*.

Susan had been a teacher for the Metropolitan Nashville school system for seven years, where she had taught both fifth and sixth grades. Her undergraduate degree was in psychology, and before returning to school to become a teacher, she had worked for five years as a social worker and counselor for teenagers. Public school field trips to performances of the Nashville Symphony and Nashville Academy Theater afforded Susan her first classroom link to the arts, and her interest in the arts expanded over time to include dance and visual arts.

Karen had taught for Metro Nashville for 21 years, almost entirely at the sixth-grade level. Her undergraduate degree was in elementary education, and she had also completed a M.Ed. in middle school curriculum. Her interest in the arts had intensified in high school, where an English teacher inspired her to think about and appreciate the written word—an appreciation that carried over into other art forms.

As a stage actor and singer, I had worked throughout the Southeast in more than 100 plays and musical revues and had recently begun working in film and television as well. I also had worked extensively as a vocal coach, taught acting workshops and private guitar lessons, and had worked for three years as a teaching artist in the NIA core program and for seven years as an artist collaborating with Head Start teachers in the Wolf Trap Early Learning Through the Arts program, administered in Nashville by the NIA. Through my work with the NIA and Bernstein Center, I had developed a keen interest in systematic reflection and portfolio use and had led workshops exploring these topics for the two organizations.

The Task of Connecting the Arts and the Curriculum

The task for Susan, Karen and me during our school year together was to find ways to connect sixth-grade curriculum topics through the processes and practices of aesthetic education. We based our work (as did the partners in the other nine pilot schools) on linking specific works of art with topics from the general curriculum and studying them together, using the tools from the artistic discipline. In every case, we started from our personal experience and knowledge of the particular work of art by identifying strong points of interest, or entry points, and then searching for connections in the curriculum.

The following description of activities in two units of study is indicative of our work. One study unit was rooted in Igor Stravinsky's *The Rite of Spring*. This music for symphony orchestra, organized in a series of musical tableaux depicting folk rituals of the ancient Russian people, is heard today as a hallmark of modern composition. The music is characterized by an extreme use of harmony and dissonance to color mood, abrupt changes in musical character and complicated use of meter and accent.[9] We agreed on three entry points that would help the students understand *The Rite of Spring* and offer many curricular opportunities: (1) Stravinsky's use of the tone colors of various instruments to paint effective and strikingly different musical pictures; (2) his use of harmony and dissonance to create great tension and texture; and (3) his exciting use of rhythm, accent and meter.

The curriculum connections to tone color and to rhythm were the most fully realized. The students first listened to sections of *The Rite of Spring* and wrote their initial responses in journals. To begin the rhythm investigation, we experimented with creating musical notation that captured the specific rhythmic aspects of the music. Then the students painted watercolors that incorporated the notation they had created and the perceptions they had gained during the investigation of tone color. (Tone color refers to the darker or brighter sounds made by various orchestral instruments, and to darker or brighter colors in the visual spectrum.)

In science, the students had been investigating various biomes, or ecosystems (a community of plants and animals within a particular environment). The students selected a section from *The Rite of Spring* that suggested a particular biome and created a series of visual representations of the biome that combined elements of music, visual arts and science. As they worked, the children wrote their observations in the journals, enabling each child to create a personal context for the information they were learning in these areas.

The rest of the sixth-grade classes joined Susan's and Karen's classes for our investigation of *Macbeth*, Shakespeare's exploration of ambition, duty, love and fear set in medieval Scotland. We decided that it would be a great idea to kick off the study unit by asking the drama club from a local high school (many of the students had gone to Head Middle School and were known to our students) to perform some scenes from their production of the play for us. This proved to be even more successful in exciting and inspiring our students than we had imagined.

The professional production in which we were grounding the study unit, and which we attended about halfway through our investigations, was performed by the Haworth Shakespeare Festival and Committed Artists of Great Britain (which toured their production of *Macbeth* in the United States during 1994-95). Stephen Rayne, who conceived and directed the production, had decided to focus on the tribal aspects of *Macbeth* and the inherent conflict between Christianity and earth-based spirituality in the play and had chosen to set this production in contemporary South Africa, where he perceived direct parallels to medieval Scotland.

The teachers and I agreed that language is the most common barrier to an understanding and a rich experience of Shakespeare's plays for Americans of all ages. Consequently, we decided to make understanding and appreciating the language our first entry point. The second entry point consisted of examining the challenges that contemporary actors and designers face in creating a successful and satisfying performance from Shakespeare's scripts.

We chose six scenes from the play to study and to connect to the curriculum. I led sessions with the students that directly explored the play, enabling them to experience some of the challenges in preparing a Shakespearean play for performance. Then the students formed small groups to "translate" one of the six scenes into contemporary language, and we gave each group the freedom to choose a connection to the curriculum. To parallel the director's decision to set the play in an alternative setting, and the process he went through to achieve this, we asked the students to create their scenes in another setting—a time and place of their own selection—and designed the production components based on their choices. We encouraged students to look at any of their academic subjects (social studies, language arts, science, math) for possibilities. The groups had to research their chosen settings in order to design and execute them or to describe them in writing and with drawings and models where full execution was not feasible. The students chose settings from various areas of the curriculum, such as the rain forest from science (biomes) and Ancient Greece from social studies (ancient civilizations).

The teachers also took the investigation into the language arts. They used *Macbeth* as the text for the reading skills curriculum throughout the study unit and, as part of the English curriculum, they had each student imagine and write a description of a possible setting.

All research into alternate settings, design and construction of sets, costumes and props, and all rehearsals took place during regular class time, with the teachers, for the most part, as facilitators. At the end of the process, the groups performed their scenes for their classmates.

In planning and executing these two projects, and others throughout the year, the main tool we brought to the task was conversation—literally hours and hours of transactional talk. Our planning and reflection before, during and after a project all happened in conversations. As Susan put it toward the end of the year, "We just all talk at the same time until something good comes out—everybody knows when we hear it." Our whole partnership can be seen as a conversation between the essential elements of art and education.

Common Experience, Trust, and Playing to Strengths

Our conversations were so lively and fruitful because we each brought very different elements to the table. Susan and Karen had the big school picture. They knew the basic curriculum requirements. They knew the developmental issues for sixth graders, and they knew the individual children. They understood the organization of the school and school system in which they worked and the resources that were available. As experienced classroom teachers, they understood how to lead young minds into greater knowledge of their world. I had a working knowledge of theater and music, both as performer and theoretician, and I had practice in creating powerful aesthetic education experiences for young people. I also had experience in working with portfolios, and I knew how to create methods for reflection on our work that drew on the language of several arts disciplines and that would produce documentation.

We began our collaboration with some common experiences. We had already built a relationship based on mutual trust and respect during the previous years that I had worked at Head Middle School as a teaching artist. Since all three of us had been involved with the NIA, we had a common vocabulary and experience in aesthetic education, and we had a similar understanding of what "learning through the arts" could mean. Still, throughout the course of the year, we discovered that we produced our best work when we stayed grounded in our own strengths, even as we learned from each other. For instance, I led a fruitful investigation of created notation for *The Rite of Spring* activities, and the teachers knew how to take this technique and use it to learn about biomes. For *Macbeth*, I facilitated text and emotional analysis and character development, and I helped the students to understand the different production elements. The teachers helped the students to locate interesting settings within their other subjects and led them in new research techniques as they designed their productions.

As the year progressed, we became more familiar with each other's territory, and this often helped us to be more efficient and creative in our planning—as long as we were careful not to forget what we knew best. We did forget, of course. During *The Rite of Spring* work, I struggled for several days trying to figure out exactly how the biome projects could be approached, and I wasn't having much luck because I barely knew what a biome was. Finally, I realized that I didn't have to know—the teachers knew that. (I knew much more by the end of the unit!) Similarly, Susan and Karen had tried without much success to picture how created notation could be useful in our investigations. Yet once I had led the students in an initial investigation of the concepts and practical challenges of personally created musical notation, the possible curriculum applications became much clearer for us all.

Susan, Karen and I developed a deeply affectionate relationship over the course of the year. We all agreed that a good collaboration takes time to develop and that it is much easier to work with someone you like. At the beginning of the year, before *The Rite of Spring*, we did a unit of study built around *Seyavash*, a newly created ballet and orchestral score. Susan and Karen had done most of the planning for the unit during the previous summer session, working with another artistic design consultant, and I focused largely on helping carry out those plans and on learning more about my teacher and student collaborators.

We didn't always connect: we frequently felt lost in the conversation, and we had to learn to trust that we could figure out the current conundrum together. By wandering around and bumping into each other conversationally, we were able to identify our common experiences and values more clearly. By the year's end, we all agreed that our mutual respect and trust, and our willingness to listen to each other, were the biggest things we had going for us.

Partner Roles and Functions in the Teacher/Artist Collaboration

Even though we started with some common vocabulary and a mutual trust that we had the same general goals, we still had to create a collaborative rhythm that worked for us. As classroom teachers, Karen's and Susan's schedules were overflowing, and their work load increased by joining the Bernstein Center model school project. Although they had previously experimented with aesthetic education activities in their classrooms, they now were formally committed to throwing out old lesson plans, changing the student/teacher relationship, introducing a completely new partner into the mix, and documenting the process as much as possible. We all quickly realized after we had begun to work together that, as the new partner, I would have to assume some roles in the collaboration that were not directly related to my identity as an artist.

When we began the year, I thought that well-organized weekly or bi-weekly meetings with comprehensive agendas would be the best way to plan together. I was wrong. While Susan and Karen kept track of the school agenda, I tried to make sure that we stayed on course with our projects, so that our goals for each unit of study didn't get lost in the daily exigencies of school life. In looking back on the year, I realize that I wasn't always successful, but I did discover some methods that worked.

Susan and Karen were always strongly grounded in their teaching: they had clear goals and strong through-lines in their processes. Nevertheless, they worked day to day in a highly improvisational and flexible manner. In addition, my schedule as a freelance performer was constantly changing. We found that trying to find time for long meetings and to prepare a meeting agenda in advance irritated us, and it was also rather unproductive. We soon realized that several short meetings a week were more productive. Although we might set a time for one meeting a week, most of our face-to-face conversations happened in drop-in meetings, dialogues before and after planned activities, or in 15-minute sessions planned the day before around a specific topic. We also made great use of the telephone, both at night and on weekends, and of an in-house e-mail system, which the Bernstein Center provided. E-mail turned out to be an excellent medium for sending messages that needed thoughtful preparation and responses. Through e-mail, we exchanged detailed lesson plans, carefully considered observations and responses to questions, and also notes of personal encouragement or affection.

I tried to complement Susan's and Karen's improvisatory planning style by listening hard and participating in our conversations, then taking time later to consolidate our ideas and solidify our designs. Even in our more formal meetings, we were most productive when talk was unstructured. Everyone took notes, but it largely became my job to catch the good ideas and to be sure they got some attention. I also learned how to listen to more than one conversation at a time (teachers take it for granted that they can successfully do five things at once) and to pull together ideas from several different conversational fragments. I frequently wrote up the results of my work and either dropped them off at the school or sent them via e-mail for Susan and Karen to peruse when they had a chance.

As is frequently the case, the school had very limited support resources. Susan and Karen were able to do some of the clerical work (scheduling, typing, photocopying), but any support work that I could do was unbelievably helpful in facilitating our collaboration. I took notes at larger faculty meetings, wrote them up and returned them to the participants. When it was time to complete a reflection sheet or questionnaire at the beginning or end of a unit of study, I usually wrote the final draft and made copies for the students. There were all kinds of one-time support needs. For example, when the local high school drama club came to Head Middle School to perform scenes from their production of

Macbeth, I handled the communication and logistics. I occasionally picked up supplies and generally tried to be as helpful as possible within the confines of my part-time schedule.

Susan and Karen also changed their expectations of the partnership once we got started, and they had to make adjustments as well. Susan had expected me to function primarily as a teaching artist off whom she could bounce some ideas. She had no idea that I would be so involved in planning and executing our activities, and that our conversations together would be so intense. To accomplish our complex projects and to accommodate our planning time, she grew comfortable with holding meetings while her students were engaged in other projects and with communicating in fits and starts, adapting to whatever time we could find within the crowded school day. She also found that she gave other teacher tasks less attention, as our work, in many ways, was heaped upon her existing work load. Things like grading papers and other paperwork were constantly being shuffled to one side, but eventually did get finished.

Karen also was initially surprised by the differences in our work from the kind of arts-related work that she had done before. As a result, she had to think through and rework every part of the curriculum touched by our collaboration. She constantly felt that things such as preparing the students for my visits and following up on our activities could be done better, but recognized that she had to settle for what time and energy would allow. All three of us made a concerted effort to keep our lines of communication open so that we could maximize our available time, energy and resources.

The Importance of Reflection, Documentation and Communication

Encouraging systematic documentation of and reflection on our work was part of my job for the Bernstein Center, but we soon discovered that this was also central to an ongoing, long-term collaboration, and I tried to use these tools to keep us on track. Each week, I was only in the school for several hours of planning and support work and for strategically placed classroom sessions, and Susan and Karen conducted most of the curriculum connections work during regular classes. They frequently took the work far beyond our original plans, following up student enthusiasm by discovering new and interesting directions for investigation with the students.

Somehow we needed to capture and report this work for each other. Susan and Karen said that just seeing me around the school would sometimes remind them to take time to reflect on what was happening in the classroom when I was not there and to write it down or record it on audiotape. Three times during the year, we scheduled sessions for me to sit with each of them and reflect on what we had done, what we were doing and what we wanted to do. I taped and transcribed these conversations and returned copies of the transcriptions to Susan and Karen. These became touchstones for our progress throughout the year and helped us each time to take the best next steps in our work.

Our efforts at reflection and documentation also enabled us to communicate with the people and groups outside the context of our three-person, two-classroom collaboration who were participating with us in the project. One of the main groups was the NIA, which provided all of the works of art for our units of study and supplied teaching artists for *Seyavash* and *The Wonderful O*, the first and last works studied during the year. The teaching artists were very generous in working closely with us to coordinate their efforts with ours.

In the school, five additional teachers, one parent and the three of us comprised the design team. At first, we were all unclear as to how the design team might function to spread the work being done in the focus classroom throughout the school. As the different units of study and projects developed and became more than plans on paper, the design team's focus became clearer. By January, encouraged by the participation of the school's principal, the design team had begun regular bi-weekly meetings. We discussed emerging issues for the project and ways to implement a "learning through the arts" approach throughout Head Middle School. We began to identify ways in which we could provide information and resources to interested teachers and to plan future courses of action. We also began to realize that expecting the participation of all faculty at Head Middle School might be unrealistic. While no one opposed the project, many faculty members were limited in their participation by time, family and other outside commitments. Still, we continued to think about ways to invite teacher participation at any level possible.

Individual resource teachers in the school worked directly with us in our efforts. The music specialist led her classes in the *NIA Guidebook* investigations of tone color and rhythm in *The Rite of Spring*. She planned with us throughout the year, coordinating her efforts with all four works of art that we studied. The physical education teacher, a design team member, led sessions during his classes in basic dance and movement vocabulary for *Seyavash* and in stage combat and movement for *Macbeth*. By facilitating more in-depth investigations of the tools of the artistic disciplines with the students, these two teachers made it possible for Susan, Karen and me to dig deeper and find more complex solutions to the challenges within our investigations.

We also communicated regularly with the Bernstein Center throughout the year. Part of my job was to deliver written reports of our daily activities, and although I sometimes chafed under the burden of paperwork, I was always glad to have the documented resources to look back on. Five other artistic design consultants were also working in similar partnerships in nine other schools, and they were keeping similar records. The six of us held weekly meetings, and these sessions turned out to be one of our most important resources. We discussed the work in our schools, shared ideas and inspirations, and helped each other over rough spots with highly productive brainstorming. A Metropolitan School Board liaison and the Bernstein Center's director of schools center and manager of research also frequently attended these meetings, and they shared valuable insights from their unique perspectives.

The Model Project's Challenges, Problems and Barriers

Although the larger school environment in which Susan, Karen and I were working provided us with many resources, it also created challenges, problems and barriers for our collaboration.

The school structure made lesson continuity difficult. The sixth-grade classes at Head Middle School were organized into self-contained teams of three teachers, who taught all required subjects to roughly 90 students, 30 per home-room class. Each teacher taught reading to her homeroom class and then taught two or three other subjects to all three classes as the students moved from room to room throughout the day. This made it difficult to achieve continuity when we tried to connect works of art with different curriculum topics. Because the schedule of changing classes limited the blocks of time available for working on individual projects, Susan and Karen had to do much (although not all) of our arts-connected work with their homeroom/reading classes. Our three-way collaboration was further complicated because Susan and Karen were on separate teams. This meant that anything we planned together had to be conducted throughout the whole team, to some degree, by one teacher.

A teacher transfer caused the loss of key support. Well after the school year began, several teachers were transferred from Head Middle School because of unexpected enrollment patterns throughout the school system. Judy Paxman, a teacher on Susan's team who in past years had organized and facilitated aesthetic education and related projects between Karen's and Susan's teams, was transferred. Judy had a talent for taking an idea from planning conversations among the NIA teachers and then coming back the next day with concrete plans for making the idea happen. She was especially good at coordinating and encouraging activities between teams and among teachers on her own team. In some ways, we never quite recovered from losing her. Although I could do some of the planning and facilitating she had undertaken, I did not have her knowledge of the school's organization, personnel or resources.

Even more significant, Susan lost important support within her team. Although the other members of the team were sympathetic toward her endeavors as the Bernstein Center focus classroom teacher, they were not interested in experimenting with arts-based curriculum in the same way. Without Judy's encouragement and extra work, some activities that would have been most effectively undertaken as a team didn't happen or were not as fully realized as they might have been. For example, student portfolios are an important tool for creating continuity and connections for students in this kind of work. Susan ended up with more than 90 portfolios in her room, and she only had time to work with them in-depth during her homeroom/reading class. If Judy had remained a part of the team, then at least they could have split the portfolios between two classrooms (and teachers' energies), and at best the two of them might have been able to persuade the other teachers to take a more active role.

The differing personalities among the classes required plans to be modified. The mix of students and the resulting chemistry in a classroom is certainly beyond the teacher's control, but it makes a huge difference in the kinds of activities that can be done. This yearly change provides great opportunity for in-novations and fresh starts, but also presents problems. In the year before the Bernstein Center project, the students in Susan's class had been avid, self-moti-vated journal writers, and she had planned to make journal writing an important through-line in our year together. Unfortunately, the students in her new classes did not take to journal writing in the same way, and the activity consumed our attention and energy instead of providing an easy thread for connecting different pieces of class work. Figuring out how the students in a class are going to function as a group is part of the work at the beginning of any school year. Sometimes ideas on which a great deal of time has been spent have to be seriously modified or dropped altogether. (Of course, teachers hope that newly inspired and wonderful ideas will take their place.)

The greatest barrier to collaboration is the lack of time. Even though Karen, Susan and the rest of the school were supported in their innovation and experimenta-tion in learning through the arts by the Metropolitan School Board, they were still held accountable to the existing standards and measures of the public school system. Certain subjects had to be covered, and certain goals in standardized testing had to be attained. Because we were attempting to cover the necessary academic ground through new methods that we were developing as we went, in many ways Susan and Karen were doing twice as much work in the same amount of class time as before.

Public school teachers never have enough time to accomplish the ever-in-creasing basic work load for which they are responsible, and successfully introduc-ing any new ideas, programs or methods of working is almost an act of heroism. The lack of time, as much as personal preference, dictated how and when our planning occurred. Simply finding a time when three (and sometimes more) people could hold a conversation in the same room was a challenge. Constantly working under the pressure of too little time was enervating.

Learning through the arts is a huge idea, and this kind of collaborative plan-ning takes a phenomenal amount of energy. Sometimes the planning time we had together was less fruitful, because everyone was simply too tired to think creatively. We learned to accept this and push on anyhow, but so much more could have been done. We had far less time for reflection, individually and together, than we needed. If there had been more time to review videotapes of activities or to go back over notes, our planning throughout the year could have been more tightly woven, every activity more clearly thought out, and every impulse more intentional.

Many good ideas and planned activities never happened because of a lack of time. In *The Rite of Spring* unit, we were excited by the possibility of small groups of students working together to create multi-media presentations of individual biomes that would include elements of visual arts, dance, poetry, music and guided reflection. We did not have enough time. In another idea that fell by the wayside, we were going to use created rhythmic notation as a starting point for analyzing poems. If the concept of tone color was extended to include emotional responses (light or dark), then poems could be mapped or otherwise visually rep-resented with created notation. Susan, in fact, saw potential in created notation for the analysis and reflection of many subjects, but we never had time to develop the idea. Similar plans and designs connected with the works of art all had to be abandoned along the way for a lack of time.

At year's end, we still did not have many suggestions for solving this problem. Within the school's improvement plan, many of the teachers wanted to request a half-day without students every two weeks just for planning. Making this happen is more difficult than it might sound: the whole school must request the half-day; the school board must approve the plan; and the parents and the school must work together to make sure that students are properly cared for during that time.

Whether or not these teachers get their half-day of planning, time will always be a problem in school, especially for highly motivated and innovative teachers. So many things in the world are interesting and worthy of investigation! Through this collaboration, I tried to learn what every school teacher knows: accept this reality and deal with it, if possible, without too much rancor.

Lessons Learned

Listen to each other and keep the conversation going. Try to learn each other's enthusiasms, reservations, talents and points of view. At the same time, stick to what you know best so that you can bring the richest possible personal and professional resources to the conversation.

It takes time to develop the trust and common understanding through which a fruitful collaboration can exist. Discover what you like and admire in your colleagues, and don't be afraid to look beyond job descriptions to find and communicate with the person who performs the function. Mutual respect and trust can be your greatest assets as a team—and it's just more fun to work with a friend!

Be sensitive to each other's agendas, but take responsibility for your part of the collaborative big picture. Artists often feel they have to think, talk and act like teachers, and teachers often think they ought to be able to learn enough, somehow, to suddenly become artists. Instead of following these impulses, try to learn more about each other's areas of expertise while graciously celebrating who you are, and work to weave together your diverse talents and skills.

Take the time to learn how your partners are held accountable in the world beyond your collaboration, recognize the risks they are taking, and support each other in taking those risks. Recognize that a larger outside world dictates the amount of available time and resources and the context within which you will work. Try not to waste energy bemoaning the facts. Instead, seek to identify specific barriers to your work and find ways to overcome them. Also, uncover existing resources and take advantage of them. For example, figure out how to use as many communication options as possible—notes to each other, telephone, e-mail, audiotape and videotape—to facilitate the constant conversation needed for collaboration.

Keep good records of what you are doing, how it feels and how well it works. Find time to reflect on your records, individually and together, and include this reflection in your documentation. In this way you can build, step by step, on the work you have done together and take advantage of sudden inspirations.

Encourage each partner to go a little further, but recognize the limits of energy and focus and don't push each other past productivity. Find the balance between pushing the boundaries of what you can accomplish and wearing each other out. Try always to be aware of that dynamic balance.

Knowing the Place for the First Time: The Arts and Professional Growth

Susan, Karen and I began to see changes in attitudes and practices throughout the school, in varying degrees, by the end of the year. For the three of us, the changes were profound. Karen looked differently at how her students worked and saw in a new way how important it was for them to find a balance between working with each other to find solutions to challenges and being able to solve problems individually. Her experiences from this year expanded her interest in learning styles, and she searched for a good workshop on the theory and practicalities of the concept. During the second half of the year, she began to create arts-process activities that were unrelated to our work together. For instance, she had her students write rap songs about *Treasure Island*, an activity that allowed the students to create a work of their own that demonstrated their mastery of the book.

Susan also began creating her own activities beyond our planning together. She saw her students in a new way as she observed them tackling challenges different from those found in a more traditional curriculum format. Through the varied arts-based activities in the different units of study, she saw them creating their own learning, solving different, more complex problems and making complicated connections between curriculum topics and works of art. As a result, she came to expect students to be risk takers more than she ever had before. For herself, Susan stretched her expectations for her students beyond the curriculum boundaries and became most inquisitive about how each child learns. Susan also found great validation in our work of her natural teaching style—active, creative, versatile, opportunistic, flexible. At the same time, she found that our work together made her more aware of just how valuable collaboration can be.

As for me, I came into this year with an intense respect for public school teachers and students, but that respect has deepened into something akin to awe. I can never thank Susan and Karen and their students enough for allowing me to be an integral part of the school-year's work. Being in constant collaboration with dedicated, exciting, creative, risk-taking, problem-solving people has made me approach my own artistic endeavors with more clarity and openness and with the creative pump well primed. Working constantly to try to make the creative aspects of my work available to others has helped me to demystify my own art forms for myself and to put the tools of my trade closer to hand. Although I am first and foremost a performing artist, I cannot imagine ever again not being involved with the arts in education.

Toward the end of the year, Susan and I received this e-mail message from Karen:

"...some time ago, I told you that I had come across a quotation that sort of summed up our journey this year. It's from *Little Gidding* by T. S. Eliot:

> We shall not cease from exploration
> And the end of all our exploring
> Will be to arrive where we started
> And know the place for the first time."

Carol Ponder is an actress, singer and musician who has performed on stage in more than 100 plays and cabarets throughout the Southeast. Since 1991, she has worked as a Teaching Artist in theater, music, dance and opera with the Nashville Institute for the Arts. She is currently a Process-Portfolio Consultant for the Leonard Bernstein Center for Education Through the Arts, and during the 1994-95 school year she worked as an Artistic Design Consultant at Head Middle School in Nashville. During 1993-94, she was one of three original Artistic Directors for the Eakin School Project, an experimental program which became the Leonard Bernstein Center for Education through the Arts. She has worked with the Wolf Trap Early Learning Through the Arts Head Start Program in Crossville and Nashville since 1988. She has also worked as a consultant in process-portfolio, systematic reflection in aesthetic education, and training teaching artists for the aesthetic education institutes in Utica, Syracuse and Rochester, New York.

The Connective Process

A Partnership Between Artists and Teachers

by John Bertles

The other day I discovered a treasure trove of my class work from elementary school in the sixties. Besides spelling tests and badly written stories, I also found a stack of artworks. There were paintings, sketches, silkscreens and even some crude clay sculptures. This finding unleashed all kinds of memories of my classes as a kid. But as I came out of my reverie, I began to realize just how innocent the general attitude toward the arts was compared with today. Back then, the arts seemed to float in a disconnected bubble, with no obvious connection to the real world. It was "art for art's sake." However, in today's budget-cutting, cost-slashing educational world, the arts have to become smaller, nimbler and especially, more relevant.

One way to make the arts more relevant is to bring out the inherent connections between classroom curricula, the arts and the world that surrounds the students—something that I call the "connective process." This essay examines the connective process and the respective roles of the teacher and the artist in putting together a successful curriculum-based arts residency.

Before we go further, however, I think we must ask ourselves: Why should we teach the arts in the classroom? To differing degrees, nearly everyone agrees that we should, but why? A thoughtful answer to this question may lead us to a better understanding of the role of the arts in our classrooms and in society— and conversely, why the arts are perpetually being slated for budget cuts.

The arts in our current national situation have to be likened to the early mammals of the Jurassic Age, speedily dodging the slavering jaws of the bigger dinosaurs. Today's dinosaurs have decided that the arts are superfluous, noncontributors to our society's money-oriented consciousness: if it does not add to our GNP, eliminate it!

This attitude ignores the pervasiveness of art in our society. I ask my students to imagine a world without the arts. There would be no movies, no plays, no sit-coms. No music, no dancing. No comic books, no fiction stories—only instruction manuals. Then I ask them what humans need to survive: food, clothing and shelter. Do the arts affect even those simple basics? Of course! Art enables us to have different kinds of food (culinary arts), rather than the same thing every meal. Art enables our clothes to have different cuts, designs and colors (fashion design), rather than monochromatic uniforms. Art enables our homes and apartments to have a certain style (architecture and interior decoration), rather than four bare walls. In short, art affects nearly every niche and corner of our society.

So, why do we need the arts in the classrooms? Just as we cannot examine a human without looking at emotion, we cannot understand a society without looking at its arts. The arts have been part of every culture in history, from the caves of Lascaux all the way to the Internet. The arts reflect the emotional core of humanity. Beyond their hard-to-pin-down aesthetic value, the arts are a powerful tool for teaching about the interdependency of human knowledge.

The Connective Process

Knowledge, as a generic term, is not a series of isolated subjects; it is a web of intricately interconnected ideas. Every snippet of knowledge has connections to every other bit of knowledge. These connections can be used to present a more balanced view of a subject.

Look at an orange on a table. From the front you see only an orange disk. Move to the side, and the disk becomes a sphere. The more ways you view that sphere, the more perspective you can gain, and the more you will know about that orange.

To teach the concept of fractions in math, comparing those fractions to currency might be useful, as in quarters and half-dollars, or to music, as in quarter and half notes. Each view gives a different perspective on the idea of fractions and has the added benefit of showing the real-world usage of fractions.

The connective process uses multiple real-world examples to illustrate a single concept and then explores the implications of that concept and its relation to other subjects. For example, over the last seven years, I have been teaching arts residencies using a subject with an extremely narrow focus—building musical instruments from recycled materials. Using the connective process, I can start from this tiny subject and relate it to practically the entire scope of human experience.

I am well aware that this is a grandiose claim, so let me validate it. Musical instruments make sound when something vibrates. The faster the frequency of the vibration, the higher the pitch of the sound. This is the process by which all forms of energy move from one place to another (except that light travels in tiny parcels of energy called photons and also in wave energy). What else, in a child's world, moves in waves? Water, radio, television, microwave ovens, light (the rainbow shows what happens when light waves are separated into specific frequencies), heat (what kid has not wondered about the wavy things above the classroom radiator on a cold day?), electricity, etc.

By using my trash instruments, I can open a window to the world around the students. Perhaps years later, when these kids encounter wave theory in their high school physics classes, something will click in their heads. Kids have an extraordinary ability to acquire information. The more data that they can accumulate, process and store, the easier it is to make connections as the tiny bits of information begin to snowball into an aggregate of knowledge.

Let me give you another example and perhaps show the process by which an arts subject can shed light upon a related, nonarts subject. There are limits to the kinds of musical instruments built around the world. A flute works the same way (a vibrating air column activated by blowing over a tube) all around the world. But different cultures build instruments from the materials they find around them. Cultures in tropical climates tend to build flutes from bamboo. Cultures in drier climates tend to build flutes from clay. This helps students to understand the diversity of global resources and how cultures exploit those resources.

Further examination of flutes in different cultures leads to other interesting conclusions. In the Andean mountains, South American Indians often use extraordinarily large pan-pipe flutes, sometimes exceeding four feet in length and several feet wide. These instruments show these cultures to be nonmigratory, whereas migratory societies in the North African Sahara build very compact clay flutes and make no instruments they cannot easily carry.

Such practical considerations lead directly to lively discussions and discoveries by the students. I never give the students rote information: "Societies in North Africa are migratory." Instead, I give them a piece of a puzzle: why are flutes smaller in North Africa than in the Andes? In resolving the puzzle, the students make discoveries for themselves.

We could easily take this example further: Why do cultures migrate? This leads to a discussion about the depletion of limited resources—the main reason (after war) why societies migrate. Once they have exhausted an area's resources, a group moves to the next area, leaving the original area to rejuvenate itself slowly. This can lead to an examination of the environmental devastation that colonial imperialism brought to Africa. The increased use of intensive agriculture led to more permanent towns and villages in areas where poor soil and little water were unable to support those dwellings. As surface water ran out, wells were dug deeper and deeper. Finally, as the wells depleted the subsurface aquifers, the land became more arid, allowing the wind to carry the preciously thin layer of topsoil away. This line of thinking leads us directly to one reason that the Sahara desert is gradually encroaching upon the arable land of Central Africa.

By using the connective process, we have taken a tiny arts-related subject and, through a process of exploration, progressed through a wealth of other fields that seem to have no connection. The crucial point of this process is the way in which the students form their own conclusions (based upon the skillful management of discussions). Students have incredible amounts of information thrust upon them—from school, parents, siblings, peers and especially from television. Unfortunately, they are handed most of that information on a silver platter, rather than in a form they must chew before digesting.

I think of kids as small versions of adults. Their capacity for logical, step-by-step reasoning is not lacking, merely underexercised or understimulated. I believe that children must be challenged early and often to develop these critical faculties. We cannot expect young children to absorb information as mere facts and dates. Young adults have even more difficulty in developing the ability to reason logically without having had constant practice throughout the elementary years.

It is also a good idea to introduce the notion that some knowledge is not absolute. I clearly remember "facts" that were taught to me as a kid, especially in astronomy, that turned out to be fallacies through misunderstandings or incomplete information.

I realize that instituting such a time-consuming process in the harried world of the classroom teacher—with syllabi, testing and statewide standards—may be unpopular or even impossible at first. Initially, leading children through the steps necessary for self-discovery is certainly slower, and the digestion of facts may be considerably delayed during this formative period. However, the investment of time in this method should lead inevitably to the students being better able to "process" and comprehend information more completely. Furthermore, as the students get older, the process will get easier. Thus they will not have to be taken by the hand and led to answers, but can find them for themselves. In fact, this process of questioning, and the resolution of those questions, is at the heart of the connective process. Students learn to reject simple explanations and look for the deeper implications. They begin to see the web of interrelations that underlie all knowledge.

I have no illusions that my students will go on to a career building musical instruments from trash. What the students learn about musical instruments will not help them to get a job, write a resume or raise a family. However, I *do* hope to teach them a process of thinking that can lead to deeper understanding.

The connective process should not be confined to arts residencies; it should be used in many ways for many subjects. The arts can be an excellent starting point for making those connections. After all, the arts exist in every society and culture and use a nearly universal language that transcends cultural differences.

The Artist and the Teacher: How to Form a Working Partnership

We have questioned the interrelationship of the artist and the teacher in recent years. From my own experience, nothing is more frustrating than watching a classroom teacher correcting homework while I work with his or her kids. On the other hand, from observations of other artists and self-analysis, I know that the classroom teacher must feel underutilized—even frustrated and bored. Clearly, many artists are missing an invaluable ally—the classroom teacher.

So, let me play devil's advocate and ask: Why not let the artist teach a class alone and let the teacher have another prep period? Why not let art be like gym or library or Star Lab, or any of the other pullouts? Because unless artists are certified teachers, state laws prohibit them from being in a classroom without a licensed teacher or responsible school person.

So, if the artist and the teacher find themselves in the classroom together, then why shouldn't they try to work together? I sat down one evening and tried to list the advantages and disadvantages. However, I only ended up with positives. I could not find a single reason why teachers and artists shouldn't work together. Here are some of the advantages.

The teaching artist, by the nature of the profession, is something of a gypsy—in one school one week, another school the next. The classroom teacher might be able to take some units, or portions of units, taught by the artist and use them year after year.

Conversely, the teacher has skills and techniques that would clearly benefit the artist. Many teaching artists have not had professional training and often teach by the seat of their pants. Sometimes the teacher can distill an artist's jumbled explanation into a concise statement. Furthermore, many teaching artists are unaware of the organizational and disciplinary techniques that many teachers use to prevent their classes from dissolving into noisy chaos.

This brings up another subject. Language, as we all know, is an inexact science. Interpretations of language can differ drastically from person to person and from class to class. The teacher has spent an enormous amount of time and energy building a vocabulary of codewords that he or she trains the kids to recognize and use. The artist can save precious time if he or she can tap into those codewords or have the teacher "translate" them.

Another way the classroom teacher can help the artist is with social dynamics and discipline. Teachers know their kids; they spend every day with them. They know that Rasheed cannot work with Lisa, and that, with tools, Geoffrey has to be watched like a hawk. The teacher is aware of classroom politics and dynamics that the artist cannot know. The teacher's active participation can save the artist from many difficult situations.

The final advantage of the artist and teacher working together is probably the most compelling (yet it has a catch, which I will discuss). The arts can be discussed in a group and shown to a group, but eventually, when the students begin to create art, they need individual attention. An artist who wanted to give individual attention to 30 students in 40 minutes would have about 70 seconds with each kid. With a teacher and an artist, the two instructors can give more individual attention, or one can give individual attention while the other maintains order, structure and flow.

Teaching the arts is a difficult task, one that not everyone is suited to do. You have to be careful what you say about an individual student's creation. That is why I am very picky about whom I trust to give "artistic advice." Unlike math or science, where there are only right and wrong answers with no maybes, the arts exist in a gray zone where right and wrong do not exist. This does not mean that students can do whatever they want and be praised indiscriminately, but it does mean that you must be extremely careful about what to say and when to say it. Terms like "more or less effective" are useful.

I am not saying that only an artist can teach the arts. Nevertheless, I believe that a true teaching partnership between an artist and a teacher is hard to achieve. I would like to list my criteria for creating a true teaching partnership to show why it is so difficult.

First, we must have the time for many long planning sessions. Good teacher/artist partnerships don't spring full-grown from one or two planning sessions; they are born and nurtured from many such meetings. Second, we must have worked together long enough to know how the other works. Third, the teacher should have a deep sensitivity toward critiquing student works, so that he or she would not inadvertently make a destructive comment to a budding artist. Finally, the teacher and I must have great respect for each other and some electricity between us, a spark that feeds off the other's enthusiasm. This last is an extremely subjective phenomenon.

I am not sure that a true teaching partnership, where the teacher and artist take equal roles, can really exist. At least, I have never been in a situation where these criteria were met. I have worked with teachers with whom I could definitely have formed wonderful, exciting partnerships, but for the most part, the time and funding were not available for any extensive planning meetings. I am, however, deeply committed to a variation that I call a revolving, or alternating, teaching partnership.

The revolving teaching partnership acknowledges that teachers and artists have strengths and weaknesses that may not overlap. For example, an artist may be able to critique a student's work with great sensitivity and yet not be able to prevent a breakdown in discipline. A teacher may be great at teaching the curriculum subjects but have only a basic idea of how the arts work. That does not mean they cannot create a great curriculum-related arts residency together. The revolving teaching partnership relies on using the teacher's strengths to offset the artist's shortcomings and vice versa. By combining those strengths and weaknesses, the teacher and artist can create a workshop that is greater than what they teach individually. This is what makes the revolving teaching partnership such a useful concept. It is extremely practical in terms of how the two instructors cooperate to create a unified residency that will excite and energize the students and each other.

To succeed, you must first have planning, planning, planning! The artist and the teacher must meet to hammer out a sequential series of workshop classes. The teacher and the artist also need to talk after each class, even briefly, so that either may upgrade or change the next lesson without surprising the other. The artist must be aware of how the teacher is going to relate other lessons to the workshop in the period before the next cooperative class. Finally, the teacher and the artist must be trusting enough so that either can jump in on the other's lessons without egos being bruised.

The ideal chronology of a revolving partnership (assuming weekly visits by the artist) should move something like this. First are the planning sessions and teacher preparation with the kids. Then the artist comes in for a first session with the students. The classroom teacher must be a constant presence during that first workshop, interrupting, interpreting and adding information. By the teacher showing his or her commitment to participate in the workshop, the students will inevitably commit themselves more deeply to join in as well. At the end of that first workshop session, the artist and the teacher should have made the connection between the art and the curriculum subjects clear, without the artist actually trying to teach the curriculum subject.

During the next week the classroom teacher should return frequently to the connections the artist made, extending the activities and building a body of proof of how the connection works. The teacher does not need to spend endless amounts of time trying to make those links; keeping them on the students' minds so that they are constantly seeing new connections and searching for their own is usually sufficient.

When the artist returns for the next workshop, the students are ready for the rhythm of the process. They are aware of what their two instructors are trying to do and prepared to take advantage of it. As more connections are made during the following weeks, a snowball effect begins to take place. The students can now take the initiative in the connective process and apply it to other subjects, with a result that the accumulation of knowledge is no longer linear, but exponential.

As a specific example, let me explain how the revolving partnership could work in my field of building musical instruments. In an early planning session, I would ask the teacher what the students will be studying in their regular curriculum during the residency. Let us say that the teacher tells me they will be studying a country in Africa—a typical third-grade social studies subject. I would then suggest that the students build an African musical instrument to complement their studies—say, the African finger piano.

Many teachers would be happy to have only that incidental connection between the two subjects. Yet that is only the beginning of the connective process in a revolving teaching partnership. During my first workshop with the kids, I would mention that the African finger piano also has other names—kalimba and m'bira to mention two. Using the connective process, we can contrast why the Americas have only two or three languages while Africa has more than two hundred. This sets up the classroom teacher to talk in greater depth at a later date about how Africa consists mainly of tribal-based ethnic and cultural groups and about the effects of colonization and artificial border-drawing by the European powers. Current events can be used to illuminate these ideas further—recent tribal upheavals in Rwanda, for example.

In that first workshop, I might also tell the kids that gourds are used as resonators in nearly all African instruments to make them louder—kind of like the body of a guitar. That might inspire the classroom teacher to go over in greater detail the resources an African culture might use.

I might also touch upon the idea that most western instruments have a series of clear single tones, while the majority of African instruments incorporate buzzing or rattling sounds along with the tones. I would explain that much African music is not meant for sedentary listening, but as an accompaniment to dancing or singing. This might inspire the classroom teacher to explore how an African community functions and the role of dancing and singing in the social structure of that community—something that is vital to many African cultures. The teacher might then introduce some simple African dance movements and related songs.

The above examples are hypothetical, although I have used some of them before. To give you one more example of how I use the connective process in a revolving partnership, let me tell you about a residency I did for Carnegie Hall at a school in Queens, New York.

Carnegie Hall wanted to teach kids in grades 4-6 the concept of melody as used by the composer Igor Stravinsky. While the teachers in the school were happy to get any arts enrichment at all, my responsibility was to work with those teachers to make connections between my subject and their classroom curricula. At the initial planning sessions, the teachers gave me an idea of what they would be working on during my residency, and I managed to devise some links.

Melody has two components—time (duration of notes, also known as rhythm) and pitch (high and low notes). During the planning sessions, I found that all the classes would be using bar graphs in their science projects. Armed with this information, I showed melodies as bar graphs and then had the kids write their own melodies in that format. Not only could the students understand music better, they also saw an alternative application for bar graphs.

Furthermore, I found it useful to draw a correlation between melody and language. Sentences, like melodies, have a rhythm and pitch content, and the students had a great time playing with the differences in expressiveness between saying a sentence in a normal tone and a robotic monotone. At the same time, they were learning more about how both melody and language work.

Carnegie Hall had given me a time line of Stravinsky's life, which I used very briefly in one workshop. When I returned the next time, some teachers had asked the kids to create a time line for their own lives. In some instances, the students' creations were monumental, incorporating photographs and other memorabilia pasted onto a display board. This is a perfect example of how the revolving partnership can help illuminate not only the arts subject but also the classroom subject. The students gained an intimate knowledge of a brand-new process, one they could draw on in future studies. The teacher acquired a new use of a familiar pedagogical device to use with future classes without needing to rely on an artist. Given the paucity of regular arts classes, only by increasing a teacher's professional repetoire can the arts have a long-term effect in the schools.

A Final Word

Knowledge and its organization have become much more complex since I took my art classes in the sixties. Increasingly, links are found between subjects that seemed once to have no correlation. Chaos theory, fractals and complexity theory have become the new vogue in viewing the connections between many disparate subjects and are used increasingly to explain everyday puzzles such as the weather. As students enter as young adults into this complex web of interrelated information, they need to be prepared for the challenge of making sense of it all.

The educational concepts and systems of my childhood do not reflect these complexities and consequently are becoming gravely outmoded. Yet I see those old concepts still being used in the modern classroom as though time has stood still. We cannot educate students in writing, reading, math, science and social studies as if those subjects stand by themselves. Since the arts have developed from all these subjects, I think that they can be used to reflect a deeper understanding of them. I know of no other medium that can be so relevant to so many different concepts. Students react to the arts in such a positive way because so much of childhood is based on a startling explosion of creativity.

We need to show children the vibrant network of knowledge that binds all subjects together if we expect them to join our ever-more-complex world as contributing participants. Teachers and artists must combine their talents to prepare them for it.

John Bertles is an educator, composer and builder of musical instruments from recycled materials. He is the founder of Bash the Trash, which offers educational performances, workshops and staff development programs throughout the Northeast. He is Lead Teaching Artist for Carnegie Hall and has created curriculum-based arts-in-education programs for the John F. Kennedy Center for the Performing Arts, the Guggenheim Museum, the New York Philharmonic and Fordham University, among others.

Movement Thinking

by Bella Lewitzky

I care passionately and deeply about the arts in education, and I have been dancing since I was seven years old. With rare good fortune, I was accepted as a protégé of Lester Horton, who created 15 works for me and fashioned a technique on my body. Later, I became the founder and artistic director of the Lewitzky Dance

Company, which is celebrating its 30th year as an international/national touring company. I have devoted much of my life to this field, and I would like to share some of my experiences with you.

I grew up in a valley surrounded by mountains. This country childhood gave me the space and light in which to grow. My father was an excellent "Sunday painter." I stood by him at his easel in our living room, and he taught me form, shape, color and the purpose of art. When I decided that I wanted to be a dancer, my family embraced the idea. Art was a natural part of our family life.

Some years later, my daughter one day exhibited a reluctance to attend kindergarten, and I decided to go to school with her to find out why. I asked the teacher what she expected of her students. She replied, "They must know their names, phone numbers and how to line up!" Although I support public education, in this case I thought it best to explore alternatives. I discovered Dr. Lola Hanson, a remarkable teacher trained in the educational philosophy of John Goodlad. She had founded Council Grove, an elementary school of ten boys and ten girls based on Goodlad's principles and on Dr. Hanson's own belief that art was essential to education. Dr. Hanson and Council Grove became my "university" in child education, with the arts taking on a central role.

In the seventies, my company and I had the good fortune to be among the pioneers, I as a teacher and the company as dance artists, in two programs that dealt with artists in the schools. The first was Project IMPACT (Interdisciplinary Model Programs in the Arts for Children and Teachers, 1970-72) aimed at developing an arts-centered curriculum.[10] The second was the National Endowment for the Arts' Artists in Schools Dance Program, which flourished from the seventies to the late eighties and was coordinated by Charles Reinhart. My company and I spent five busy years in these ground-breaking programs that engaged distinguished modern dancers who helped to introduce, and in some cases, establish dance in hundreds of the country's classrooms, cities and towns. In tandem with the NEA's Dance Touring Program, also coordinated by Reinhart, I am sure these residencies were responsible for the wider acceptance of modern dance in the United States and abroad.

My company and I were recently involved in the Lila Wallace-Reader's Digest Foundation's Arts Partners program. Three partners were involved: a sponsor, Occidental College; an arts organization, Lewitzky Dance Company; and the community. We spent the first part of our residency attempting to find the "community," which we achieved with the aid of several remarkable school principals and community leaders. The program had three objectives: (1) to break down the barriers between the college and the community; (2) to introduce dance (here, modern dance); and (3) to help create an audience for the campus theaters.

We went through much trial and error. We taught what I call "six-to-sixty-years-old movement classes" wherever the community would ask us to go. Our approach was to keep the movement possible for all the participants so that everyone could be successful. We followed this format: a warmup; "problem solving" on four or five different motion topics, from which three or four movements on each topic were selected; and then a small dance phrase made by combining them. Four dance company members served as leaders-teachers, and the rest of the company spread throughout the class as helpers.

Although this was relatively successful, the art was not visible in the dance, and that troubled me. I changed our class to include an ending section that demonstrated the same motion topics performed by the dance company. I had selected sections of our dance repertory to make this clear. For example, if a class problem had been to invent as many turns as possible, then the dancers performed sections of our repertory that used turning movement. We then would end with a question-and-answer period. This change was vital to our purpose and supplied what I felt had been lacking. As nearly as can be ascertained, we came quite close to achieving our established goals.

More recently, we were involved in an outreach program for the California Center for the Arts in Escondido. I prefer to teach the third and fourth grades in elementary school, where I find the window of learning opportunity to be highest. The center wisely permitted us to concentrate our efforts in one place for four days. It was wonderful to see the comprehension and growth made by the students in this time. As I addressed them on the final day, I advised them to tell their parents that they weren't simply running around, they were "movement-thinking." One child who clearly understood this was able to answer an interviewer, who asked, "How do you invent those shapes and movements?" The child responded, "I think them in my head, and then I do them." He added, "I used to copy Michael Jackson, but not now!"

I recognize that, as a nation, Americans do not value the arts. It frustrates me to know that most people do not understand the capability of the arts to communicate profound and intelligent thought. In all of my work in schools and other institutions, I have found the arts to be a priceless route to experiential learning and invention (creativity and problem solving). And so I will continue to share, wherever I go, the joyous understanding that the arts can impart—lessons that I first learned at my father's easel.

Bella Lewitzky *is the Founder and Artistic Director of the Lewitzky Dance Company, which was formed in 1966. Under her artistic guidance, the company has become one of the leading international modern dance companies, performing to critical acclaim in 43 states and 20 countries on five continents. In 1946, she founded with Lester Horton the Dance Theater of Los Angeles, one of the few institutions in the United States to house both a dance school and theater under the same roof. She is an internationally recognized choreographer, dancer, lecturer and teacher. She has been the recipient of numerous national, state and city awards and grants as well as five honorary doctoral degrees.*

CAPE Theater Artists Speak

The Voices of Reginald Lawrence, William S. Carroll and Ralph Flores

I asked Arnold Aprill, Director of the Chicago Arts Partnerships in Education (see Chapter Four), to identify three theater artists currently working in the CAPE program and to put me in touch with them. Here is a collection of their thoughts about the collaboration of artists and teachers in the classroom.

Use What Works!
by Reginald Lawrence and William S. Carroll

We have found no uniform approach to the collaborative process that works every time. Every person, every school, every classroom we have entered have all been different, each with unique challenges. No quick fixes, no diagrams or lesson plans will matter in the final evaluation more than a commitment to your students, regardless of ability, and a willingness to use what works.

1. Use What Works! Neither party has all the answers. If one party did, would partnerships be necessary? You are both breaking new ground, sharing your successes and failures. Learn to trust each other. Use only what is effective. If either party holds onto ineffective tactics, the students will suffer.

2. Recognize the interdependence of the collaboration. The best partnerships in which we have worked all have one thing in common: both the teacher and the artist recognize the need for each to do his or her job.

For example, the artist should adjust to whatever works for the teacher. The teacher has established what is acceptable classroom behavior long before the artist arrives. There is no bigger waste of classroom time and energy than an artist attempting to discipline a class with a set of rules nobody knows. Agree ahead of time to use the teacher's preexisting system. Recognize that the artist needs the teacher's system of discipline to be effective. Without it, rapport between the artist and student will likely be undermined.

3. Raise your expectations and challenge your students to exceed their perceived limitations. You can never think too big. Stretch. Both art and education are the business of cultivating dreams. If you limit your scope, your students will limit theirs, too. This is especially true for those of us who work with the "at risk" population. You may be pleasantly surprised at how these youth, so often written off as "unteachable" or "undisciplined," can "problem solve" with imagination. The arts are great equalizers.

4. Students are also initiators and collaborators; start where the kids are and make the classroom a safe place for their ideas. Genuinely encourage students' honest responses and emotions. Allow them to explore material without forcing a bias on them. Art and good teaching often involve piercing the protective shells that students have often spent a considerable time constructing. This may be frightening and thrilling at the same time. Insights given in such an environment may challenge both teacher and artist to see things in new ways.

For instance, when collaborating with a freshman English teacher's class at Chicago's Lincoln Park High School, MPAACT artists were struggling to make Richard Wright's *Black Boy* alive for a class of students with profound literacy problems. A student from that class eventually provided a workable solution. He spontaneously composed lyrics to a hip-hop version of *Black Boy*, with musical accompaniment from a classmate. Suddenly a light went on! We had been approaching the material all wrong. We needed to use the preexisting skills and interests of the student to bridge the literacy gap. Once revamped, the unit was quite successful, and it continues to be used in the school today.

Reginald Lawrence and *William S. Carroll* *are founding members of MPAACT (Ma'at Production Association of Afrikan Centered Theatre), a Chicago based performing ensemble established in 1989. At present, they are working to integrate theater into the English curriculum at Lincoln Park High School as part of the Chicago Arts Partnerships in Education program.*

The Importance of Knowing and Understanding Language
by Ralph Flores

Most youth I work with want an opportunity to speak about what they are experiencing. This usually happens through rap sessions. However, I have found it more effective to assign specific topics and then allow students to write about it in whatever format they wish—poems, songs, letters, essays or scenes of a play. I allow them some anonymity, which gives them the freedom to open up and be more candid than they otherwise might be. Last summer I worked with a group of teens to produce a theater project entitled *Voces Ansiosas/Anxious Voices* at a local Equity theater, where the students performed for two weekends to a very receptive audience.

The exercise that has proved most successful has been cold readings from a script. I have had both the students and the instructors participate. First we discuss the scenes they are about to see, and then we analyze them and put them into a contemporary context. Then I call a couple of students in the audience to read (I like to call on students who either look uninterested or act up). They immediately figure out the importance of knowing and understanding the language so that you can infuse it with emotional impact. I tried this with a couple of the bilingual teachers, who were real sports. The students were intrigued that their instructors, whom they had perceived as all-knowing and unshakable, were vulnerable, nervous and human. It gave them an insight they had not seen before in their teachers. For a brief time, there was a shared experience in which the roles were equal.

I have to maintain a delicate balance when I am in the classroom, constantly reminding myself that I am a guest at this institution and that there is a certain protocol for class management. Although my approach is somewhat looser than that of a regular instructor, I still need to maintain discipline and make sure that I have discussed the do's and don'ts of the classroom with the instructor. I always remind myself that I am there for only four weeks and that this teacher will be there for ten months.

Conflicts between differing teaching methods and disciplinary tactics have been the biggest obstacles I have found. Some instructors find it uncomfortable and possibly threatening to have an outsider motivate or challenge the students that they work with on a daily basis. I find that the best way to coordinate these collaborations is to bring the artist and the teacher together before the program starts to develop and design the curricula for the residency. In this way, both the instructor and the artist will understand what each expects from the other, and any conflicts in philosophy or methodology can be discussed and resolved. Above all, the focus in this whole collaborative effort should always be the students, whose lives can be motivated, inspired, challenged and illuminated.

Ralph Flores is Arts Programming Director at Association House of Chicago, a social service agency in northwest Chicago. He is an actor, director and producer and serves as the Artistic Director of Theatre By Design, a company he co-founded four years ago.

Making Music Connect

A Conversation with Phyllis Free

Jane Remer: With the Kentucky Center for the Arts' Creative Connections program as a context, can you tell me how you were able to integrate music into the Watson Lane School curriculum? I would also like to know the degree to which you have been able to establish partnerships with teachers in the school.

Phyllis Free: My approach to this project has been two-fold. I was part of the Watson Lane Creative Connections school committee that selected the books we would use. We were given a bunch of books—children's stories—that they were using in their curriculum, and our task was to come up with ideas about how we could relate our arts discipline to the books. We each chose to work with four books and wrote our ideas. My approach was to write curriculum suggestions for relating music activities to these particular books. I wrote activities that I thought teachers could do without having to be a trained music person. When it came time for my residency, rather than going in as a musician, my objective was to model ways that the teachers could incorporate the music into the curriculum within the context of each story.

Much of this has to do with making interdisciplinary connections. For example, we had a book called *Ben's Trumpet*, so some activities I did had to do with how sound is made and produced in the trumpet. We demonstrated that with long tubes and a lot of pantomime for playing. I used many different styles of recorded music, so they would get used to the sound of the instrument. I would point out different styles or let kids tell me what they knew about styles of music, so that I was reinforcing what they already knew.

We talked about the history of jazz—that jazz is an American form with its roots in the African experience—and about some of the concepts used in jazz, such as call and response and syncopation. We did some activities involving call and response and some rhythm activities contrasting the straight, martial beat and syncopation. I also made it into a geography lesson: I played several selections—about ten seconds each—and gave them information on where the artists were from, what part of the country, and asked them to show me where these places were on the map.

We did a lot of pantomime in conducting, and I thought that was very useful for students to develop auditory discrimination—to distinguish among the brass family the difference between the trumpets and trombones, for example. We had everyone doing just the trumpet parts as they came in, then divided into two different groups. Then, where there were clear entrances for trumpets and trombones, we had the kids enter appropriately.

JR: Did the kids conduct or did you? How did they know when to enter?

PF: In this story, I started as the conductor. Then I invited kids to help conduct. At first I said, "Listen hard to the music." When the trumpets came in, I gave them a verbal cue and said, "There it is." Next, I played the music again and had them show me they recognized the trumpet sound by raising their hands when they heard it. I could see more and more of them beginning to get it as we moved along.

Actually, I used the conducting more in another story about a child who doesn't like going to the concert hall. We actually role-played this one since many of these students had never been to a concert or a hall. We pretended we were all in our orchestra seats, and I told them it's okay to talk to your neighbor when the lights are on. Then I flicked them off and explained that this was their cue to be quiet—to watch and listen. The actual story was about a concert in the park. We talked about 3/4 and 4/4 time, different styles of music, how recordings are done by layering different instruments, and how the producer in the studio plays the same role as the conductor—literally cuing entrances. I had them pantomime playing electric guitars, acoustic guitars and synthesizers while listening to a recording; that gave me a chance to talk about technology and music. Once they had learned to identify the string sounds, listening to Vivaldi, I played popular music that has string sounds and talked about how those are produced with the synthesizer. I let them choose whether they wanted to pantomime playing the string parts on a violin or a keyboard synthesizer.

In this experience, we had lots of kids conducting, and they could rotate and choose which instruments they wanted to play or decide to be the producer.

JR: Let's talk about partnerships now.

PF: The way we set this program up didn't give us an opportunity to develop any ongoing partnerships or collaborative relationships with teachers. I was, however, very insistent on the teachers participating in the activities, and most of them did so enthusiastically. There were music specialists right across the hall from where I was doing my Creative Connections work. The music teacher and I would say "Hi" to each other and "Gee, wish we could work together," but the way we set up our program didn't accommodate that. The music specialists usually cover three schools, which makes scheduling even more difficult. Still, we need to make connections with whatever specialists there are. We have to forge partnerships, not just with the classroom teachers, but also with the arts specialists.

Along with the classroom teachers, arts specialists should be directly involved in curriculum planning and arts strategies workshops conducted by artist consultants. The role of the artist, then, should be not only to demonstrate strategies for the classroom teacher but also to serve, on a consulting basis, as a link between the arts specialists and classroom teachers. In this way, the artist can facilitate communication and help to implement coherent strategies for arts integration across the curriculum. However, if classroom teachers and arts specialists are to work more closely together on an ongoing basis, then I believe it will be essential for school principals and site-based committees to address the barriers caused by scheduling.

Phyllis Free is an interdisciplinary artist who specializes in drums and percussion, rhythm and improvisation. As a music instructor, she serves on the faculty of the Kentucky Arts in Education Institute at Eastern Kentucky University and conducts workshops for the Kentucky Center for the Arts' Artsreach and Creative Connections programs. She teaches private lessons at Mom's Musicians General Store and conducts professional development training workshops in Different Ways of Knowing for elementary school teachers as an arts consultant with The Collaborative for Elementary Learning—The Galef Institute. A performer and recording artist, she is the drummer for the Louisville-based band Yer Girlfriend and is a general partner in Esther Records.

Reflections of a Classroom Teacher on Working with Artists in the Classroom

by Norma Moran

When my colleague Jane Remer asked me to write an essay for this book, I was both surprised and flattered. She told me that she specifically wanted me to write about what happens in artist/teacher partnerships behind the classroom door. She explained that she had several essays written from the artist's point of view, and she wanted my perspective as a classroom teacher. She asked me to read the artists' essays that appear in this section and to respond to them. I readily agreed and dug into my assignment, relishing the opportunity to reflect on the work I had done with artists over the years in my classes. Here, then, are some of my thoughts.

My first experience as a classroom teacher working with an artist was as a participant in the Guggenheim Museum's Learning Through the Arts Program. Eager to expand my knowledge, I was blessed with the opportunity of working with artist/sculptor Nadine De Lawrence, an incredible talent. She taught us about color, space, form, style and presentation; she taught us how to use black and white, make collages and sculpt with clay. When I applied my own knowledge of child development, I was able to grow in the field of children's art and understand its particular stages of artistic development.

The students and I inherited a boundless store of knowledge from this artistic collaboration and I continue to draw from it each year and incorporate it into my theme studies. Although this first experience with the Guggenheim program was just the beginning of many experiences working with artists, it left a lasting impression on me.

We must foster these kinds of partnerships between artists and teachers so that we all can benefit. In many communities, they provide the children's only link to art and culture, other than television and movies. I would like to share some of the lessons I have learned about creating an effective teacher/artist collaboration.

The Unique Role of the Artist in the Classroom

In John Bertles' essay, "The Connective Process," he comments that he is "...not sure a true teaching partnership where the teacher and artist take equal roles can really exist." This somewhat parallels my experience, because I believe the gift of performance and presentation is the sole domain of the artist and cannot be replicated by the teacher. Nevertheless, when a teacher and an artist teach components of an art form together in the classroom, it can be a collaborative, shared experience.

The artist's presence in the classroom serves two important purposes: (1) the artist can give the children an aesthetic and cultural learning experience by performing his or her art form; and (2) the artist can encourage an appreciation of the arts by bringing out the artist in each child. The arts invite students to be active participants in, rather than mere observers of, their world. This is every teacher's ultimate dream: to teach in a way that will inspire and impart the knowledge that will bring forth talent. Although an artist's performance does not necessitate the child's or the teacher's participation, bringing out the artist in each child requires active participation and a collaborative agenda from day one.

The Elements of Successful Teacher/Artist Collaborations

The essence of a successful teacher/artist collaboration, in Bertles' words, is in "...creating a workshop that is greater than what the teacher and artist could teach individually." I believe that successful collaborations include:

- schools with clearly defined purposes for undertaking the project;

- artists who have detailed outlines of what their work can entail and how it can connect with a teacher's curriculum agenda;
- teachers who are enthusiastic and eager to participate and who have curriculum agendas that fit in with the artist's field of experience; and
- sufficient time for the collaborators to plan and meld their styles.

When care is taken to ensure that all of these factors are in place, then chances are excellent that a good partnership will be created. Let me explain.

The Need for a Clear Purpose

All too often, school administrators select artists to visit the school without benefit of any preplanning with the teachers to define the connection between the curriculum and what the artist has to offer. Consequently, artists come into the schools with prepackaged programs that do not meet school or classroom needs.

For example, when a mime is brought into the school, is it because a teacher requested one as a resource for a clown or body theme instructional unit or because money was available and the administration thought it would be nice to do? The latter reason is frequently the case, and curriculum content takes a back seat to performance. When that happens, the potential benefit from the artist coming into the school is rarely fully realized.

Effective Artists Know How to Connect with Curriculum

To be effective, an artist needs to present to the teacher a detailed outline of how the art form can be used in the classroom and to discuss in advance how the artist can connect with the teacher's classroom agenda. The artist and the teacher should discuss how the teacher can help and reach an agreement about how they will work together. Absent this kind of advance discussion, the teacher is left without a collaborative agenda and may feel relegated solely to the role of classroom manager. When teachers are excluded from any kind of meaningful involvement, they can resort to all sorts of unusual activities: bathroom trips, grading papers, sitting uninvolved, circulating to see who's attentive, closet cleaning, etc.

I remember a time when a cooperating teacher and I were given an opportunity to work with a musician. She arrived each day with her repertoire of songs and instruments. As quickly as she would breeze in, she would breeze out. Both of us tried to adjust her focus, but we were only partially successful. She was excellent— and we both resisted any temptation to clean closets—but we agreed that it would have been better if the artist had known in advance that we were teaching units on communities and measurement and made some effort to connect with us.

Enthusiastic Teachers Can Connect Artists to the Classroom

Teachers who collaborate with artists in the classroom should be enthusiastic and eager to participate. Unfortunately, not all teachers are prepared to divert valuable time and energy from traditional teaching to collaborating on art experiences that may be fun but not relevant to today's classroom needs.

Nevertheless, teachers provide a critical link between artists and the classroom. Teachers know the basic curriculum requirements; they know developmental issues for their specific grades; they know the children; and they understand the organization of the school and the school system. Experienced teachers can also make better curriculum connections across grade levels and subject areas. They have had more experience with finding entry points and with making applications in and across the curriculum. Teachers can also help artists to understand the abilities of the students and the unique personality of the class with which they will be working.

Preparing the Children and Managing the Classroom

The teacher should prepare the students and the artist, outlining any classroom rules that may affect the collaborative experience. In my experience, the presence of an extra adult in a classroom is always unsettling to students at first. An important task for the teacher is to find a way to ease the artist into the classroom and create a comfortable place for him or her. Artists need to know that this phenomenon occurs with children. I have always prepared my classes for the advent of a new person (except in classes where they have been thrust upon me). It helps to explain everyone's roles to the students before the artist arrives, what days the artist will be in the room and what he or she hopes to accomplish. A written schedule on the board helps to remind the children. This kind of pre-planning is especially important for early childhood classes. These children have short attention spans that have to be lengthened gradually. Adding 15 minutes to a visit for introductions and explanations is a recipe for disaster.

I am always surprised by artists who do not recognize that class discipline is the teacher's domain. No artist can possibly hope to know the discipline code of a school or an individual teacher. Today, many schools in certain demographic areas are struggling to maintain discipline. Discipline—and the reasons for lack of discipline—is being discussed and reassessed in urban educational centers throughout the United States. I think teachers understand this much: our cities have changed; our nuclear family has changed; our educational system has changed; and therefore our children have changed. Our efforts to understand this social change have not even scratched the surface. Some classes tend to be well-behaved; in other classes, a poor mixture of children leads to unpredictable behavior, and the class takes on a personality of its own and is often difficult to control. Artists who work in education must understand that each class is different, and teachers can help them to prepare properly before entering the classroom.

Remember, the artist is walking into an unknown situation and all the class-room nuances may not be readily understood. The teacher has a unique ability to help the artist to understand what needs to be done to put a smile on every-one's face and engender a warm spirit among all the participants.

Misjudging Students' Abilities: Some Lessons I Have Learned

Activities that reach beyond children's abilities inhibit their effectiveness and affect classroom behavior. I remember a workshop in which a visual artist had planned for the students to make individual albums which would include their year's work. It was an excellent idea for a top kindergarten class: it was within cognitive curriculum guidelines in terms of developing sequencing, memoriza-tion, dexterity, and phonic skills.

The artist wanted the cover page to include a layout of letters, cut from newspapers and magazines, that spelled out the child's name in the title. The task sounded like it was within the scope of kindergarten learning, and the children started well. However, we did not realize that the children were unable to read different types of print—large, small, boldface, italics.

What happened next was almost laughable. Three adults scrambled to locate letters for the children to cut—letters the children would have recognized without the added element of different print attributes. We didn't have enough magazines; too many children were asking and waiting for help; and time was running short. Finally, we agreed to abort the idea and have the children write the title on their covers instead.

In retrospect, I still think that the activity was very good and involved the students in cognitive learning. Yet I learned a valuable lesson from that one small mistake, and it still makes me smile.

On another occasion, during an artist's residency, a dancer wanted to begin each session of her program with my third-grade class by doing body movement routines. She would start with the hands and work her way into using the entire body. This was a year when I had some very difficult children, and they had their own ideas about how to move their bodies. This constant preparation before the start of each session made the whole class difficult to control. After several visits and several attempts to gain their interest, I was forced to remove several children from the circle of activity.

When the dancer began to do improvisations, the children showed more interest and controlled themselves long enough to watch or participate. I noticed the children begin to grow. Instead of performing their ten-minute body rou-tines, they began to focus on their improvisations. In the final performance, all but two children made the transition from nonparticipant to participant. This artist was very understanding. Her response to the behavior was "This is what we have to work with." She was not frustrated, and she allowed comfort zones to be established for both teacher and artist. We did not alienate any child, but established the control that was necessary for cognitive learning.

One year I worked with a singer/guitarist who taught my five-year-olds some very wonderful songs. But I couldn't understand all the children's complaining and resistance when it came time for them to go to her classroom. Do you have any idea how difficult it is to convince 23 five-year-olds to go somewhere? My teacher instincts were alerted right away. Why should a group of five-year-olds—developmentally at the age when children like to sing—not want to sing?

I realized that the artist had chosen songs with too many choruses. She would teach one chorus by repetition and, when that one was learned, move to the next chorus until it too was learned. These children were not feeling the sense of task completion that is so urgent at their age, and the stopping and starting was driving them nuts. It was comical to hear the brighter ones comment "It's about time" or "Is it lunchtime, yet?" when they completed a song. Unfortunately, this was a year when I had three student teachers in my room, plus a community helper. The artist would leave our building and race to another school, so there was little time for collaboration. The children sang these and other songs at a parent sing-along, and we shortened the songs for the parents' benefit. Still, if I could have taken more time to work with the artist, I could have helped her to adjust the program to better suit the learning needs of the children.

Time to Plan and Collaborate: The Critical Element

The importance of creating time for teachers to plan and to meld their styles with artists cannot be overstated. I was thoroughly impressed by the time and commitment described by Carol Ponder, Susan Standbrook and Karen Catignani in their article "A Learning Journey." What really comes across in their discussion is their use of time, especially stolen time, to plan, discuss and implement. It almost guarantees success.

I have always been slightly amused by the way visiting artists juggle several teachers' schedules, work around preps and make adjustments when unexpected changes occur. They set up schedules just as well as administrators do. How frustrating it must be for them not to have all this scheduling prearranged. I am amused not by their frustration, but by how quickly artists adapt to school agendas.

One experience I had with a dancer was particularly interesting. After juggling three teachers' schedules, unexpected schedule changes, test date considerations and trip dates, this artist still managed to collaborate with us on three shadow puppet theater performances. All three classes performed at separate times. We invited parents, friends, relatives and other classes to attend. Of course, I took extra time to work with the children in areas such as completing puppets, assigning parts, rehearsing lines and developing classroom management routines for rehearsals. In turn, she took time to buy supplies, bring story books into class, build a shadow puppet screen, type a script and do other behind-the-scenes jobs. It was worth the extra effort to see the entire process of collaboration culminate in a successful show.

Scheduling time before and after each collaborative session for discussion, review and evaluation seems to be the best plan. This time helps teachers to focus on the artist's agenda, to prepare for the next session and to change or adjust that which did not work well. With all this to do, 45 minutes per visit hardly seems adequate. It brings to mind memories of walking a class down the hall, artist in tow, as we attempted to bring closure to our session. A 90-minute session works well—an hour of collaboration and 15 minutes, before and after, for discussion.

Reading through all the artists' essays has given me an opportunity to reflect on the importance of the collaborations I have formed over the years with various artists in my own classroom. It has also reminded me that artists are not the only ones who miscalculate or misjudge, as evidenced in some of the lessons I have learned—and believe me, I have learned many lessons. But I am your everyday, ordinary teacher. I respond to difficulties and stresses as do most other teachers. Yet I am consistent: like other teachers, I try very hard and I keep the children in mind at all times. People underestimate the amount of work that teachers do, with or without collaborations. I believe that the essence of teaching is the exploration of knowledge, and when we make miscalculations and figure out what went wrong, we are strengthened in our work.

Bringing an artist into the classroom can be refreshing and invigorating for all involved, but, unfortunately, many teachers never have such an experience. I was lucky because at the heart of my collaborations was a principal who believed in art and culture in the schools. He welcomed any opportunity to sponsor a teacher/artist collaboration.

So let's accept all the challenges that the artist/teacher collaboration entails—a clearly defined purpose; artists (and teachers) who know how to connect with the curriculum; enthusiastic teachers who want to collaborate with artists and who will be turnkeys in the classroom; and sufficient time to plan. You'll find that it is well worth the effort.

Norma Moran has been teaching both in and outside of the New York City school system for nearly 20 years. She taught in District 4 in Manhattan for almost ten years and now teaches near her home in District 11 in the Bronx. She holds a master's degree in early childhood and elementary education from Hunter College School of Education.

Learning, Life and the Arts— Like Lunch

by Deborah Brzoska

"All the arts, for every child." Starting as a public school arts educator in the early seventies, I took these words to heart. "*Every* child"—not just the talented few. "*All* the arts." As a dancer myself, this was particularly meaningful. "The arts" were in lowercase, small "a" arts, part of each person's everyday life, no big deal, like lunch.

To provide this type of broad-based arts education requires the restructuring of schools. It requires tenacity and clarity of purpose. It requires rethinking turf issues, teacher licensing, class scheduling and school finance. It requires teachers to open their doors and welcome arts partners into their classrooms. It requires artists to believe that teaching is an art, worthy of their time, focus and energy.

I supervised a dance educator last year who was beginning a full-time teaching position in our K-12 dance program after many successful years as an artist in residence. The first shock to this dancer came during the third week of school: two weeks were up and he was still there. By the end of the first semester, he remarked to me, "This is very hard. The kids treat me differently here. I'm used to being a guest artist." Hard or not, this particular dance educator was doing a remarkable job. I assured him that he was successful, that his life had meaning and that he was still an artist. He was just no longer a "guest."

If the arts are ever to become "like lunch" in our country's public schools, we must begin to think of artists not as guests, not as pampered visitors or quirky outsiders, but as part of the regular public education family. We must blur the lines between teacher and artist, get rid of labels like "artist-teacher" or "resident artist" and recognize that a good teacher can be anyone who touches the lives of kids.

We have to jettison the notions that "those who can't, teach" or that teaching is for those whose performance career has ended. We have to help all teachers gain the dignity and rewards necessary to sustain them through life's most difficult but important work.

One of the finest teachers I have ever known is a brilliant dancer, a woman whose creative energy lights up a room. Kids flock to her classes. She teaches, coaches, encourages, models and shares herself with them; she changes their lives. Over more than a decade, I have hired her many times in several public school settings. I have to keep hiring her because she keeps leaving. She keeps leaving not because she isn't successful, not because she doesn't love what she does, but because teaching doesn't lend itself to the positive self-image that adults need just as badly as kids. She keeps leaving because the system doesn't afford the flexibility necessary for artists to teach and do their art simultaneously.

The good news is that I think she will be back. We are in the process of creating an exciting new school in the Vancouver, Washington school district where the arts are indeed like lunch. A team of teachers, artists, parents, students and community leaders have come together to design a secondary school where math and dance, science and art have equal value. The word "equal" is critical. The arts will remain outside basic public education if we think they are less—or greater—than every other academic pursuit.

From the beginning, the planning process for this school has included many arts organizations in the Vancouver, Washington and Portland, Oregon metropolitan area. We have received an overwhelming response from artists and arts agencies who wish to join with our school in partnership—a word that cannot be taken lightly. For too long, schools have failed to reach out to the community as equal partners. Instead, they have held out a hand, palm up, expecting others to give freely while giving nothing in return. Schools must give up this welfare mentality, which can drain the life from potential partners. Instead, schools must ask what they can do in return.

One of the most significant things that our school will do is to give brick and mortar to the arts. Few artists in our community have the luxury of studio, rehearsal or performance space. Our town's symphony performs in a church. Although the local horizon holds little hope for funding for arts facilities, our rapidly growing district has a great deal of new school construction underway. The school district is providing more than $6 million in bonds to completely renovate an historic school into our new magnet school for arts and academics. We have invited artists to help us design studio, exhibition and performance facilities. We have received a $750,000 grant from the state to share our school as a community arts center.

When the school opens, we will blur the line between teacher and artist. Nontraditional hiring and scheduling practices will allow artists to teach full-time or part-time. Some will have the use of performance or studio facilities in exchange for working with students. Some artists will practice their art alongside students in the classic apprenticeship manner. A variety of creative approaches will allow some artists to meet state teacher licensing regulations. The opportunity to work in this kind of school should draw back those gifted artists who are teachers in their hearts. A variety of school doors must be open to artists, allowing them to fit themselves in on a continuum, ranging from one-time workshops to ongoing, long-term work with students.

The first thing we must do to open the door for artists is to end our love affair with the traditional school day. School schedules were invented to coincide more with sports practices than with artists' lives. With professional artists working with us on the design of our school day, we are building in flexible time frames, part-time teaching slots and "interim" learning experiences that support artists' touring or performance schedules. It is amazingly easy to be creative with school scheduling and still comply with state statutes. If the arts and the artists are to thrive in schools, this must be the first order of work.

With its interdisciplinary, student-centered learning focus, we have structured the school for maximum flexibility. Learning will take place in two- to three-hour blocks, allowing teachers and students to break into smaller groups for various activities, reconvene, and reconfigure as student learning needs require. Local artists will collaborate with teachers to design and deliver interdisciplinary learning and will offer in-depth, participatory arts learning experiences. During these arts experiences, teachers may shift to learner roles, participating alongside students in music, art, theater, film, dance, creative writing and the visual arts, and help students to connect artistic learning with other subjects. Students at the school will have an extended school day, allowing time for meaningful project-centered learning, student performance opportunities and apprenticeships with community artists.

Staff and students will collectively plan and operate the school—student and parent participation in the process is critical. A daily program called "Advocacy" is built into the heart of the school. Here, a teacher advocate serves as the "significant adult" for 12 to 14 students and remains their advocate for as long as seven years. The advocate monitors students' learning plans; knows and communicates with families; advises students in performances, portfolios and projects; assists in locating mentors; and guides students' artistic growth and academic achievement over time.

The second thing we must do to open public school doors to artists is to change the climate in schools. Few public school teachers have received professional training in arts education, and most teachers have had little or no arts in their lives. It is no wonder that in traditional American schools, the arts remain on the periphery.

Anxious for school reform, many arts advocates strive vainly to change the climate in existing schools. They run head-on into teachers, good ones, who have had successful careers and have ignored the arts. These teachers have no incentive to change. Having similarly banged my own head against the brick walls of more than one traditional school, it is apparent to me that a more successful approach will be to *open* a school, to take advantage of new legislation for school choice, and to *establish* a school climate conducive to the arts.

Our school district is now beginning to encourage "focus" schools, in which all students will choose to attend based upon their sincere desire to focus on a subject area—in this case, on the arts. Teachers, too, will not be randomly transferred from within the district or assigned to the school, but will apply to work at the school based upon their own desire to work in an arts-immersed setting.

Everyone who works at the school will be willing collaborators with colleagues and students, be learners themselves, be flexible, be advocates for the needs of students and agree that the arts are essential to self-fulfillment. Our interview and hiring process for teachers and artists will look for these attributes. We have been consistent and honest in articulating our school's guiding principles, and we actively seek individuals in both the education and arts communities who value lifelong learning.

The following statements from teachers and artists who plan to work at the school illustrate the character and vigor of these fine educators:

> "I have a strong desire to work with educators who understand and support the value of the arts in learning and an even stronger desire to work in an arts-immersed environment with a broad range of students."

"My passion is to work where learning is not offered up to students in subject area isolation, but where deep learning can occur more meaningfully for kids because it is active and connected to the world they live in."

"It is impossible to separate the arts from life so it makes no sense to separate the arts from education."

"Our society may well be remembered as one without merit: the society that created a better microwave oven but squeezed the life out of the human spirit. I want to be a part of this school to contribute to a future where exploration, vision and expression of the human spirit provide the fuel for forging a capable, compassionate and creative citizenry."

Kids need and deserve all that the arts have to offer. We owe it to students to change old schedules or to open new schools if this is what it takes. Students need to have eye-popping contact with the arts, to experience the excitement and the drudgery of practicing the arts. They need to find new ways to express themselves and to link the arts to culture and to history and to science. At our school, we give students an education that presents learning—and life—as a rich, interwoven whole, where the arts are an equal piece, neither ignored nor glorified, but simply and always present. Like lunch.

Deborah Brzoska is Fine Arts Coordinator in the Vancouver, Washington Public Schools, where she currently leads the development of the district's magnet school for arts and academics. Ms. Brzoska is known for her work in arts curriculum, dance education and interdisciplinary arts. She has served as group leader for the National Assessment of Educational Progress in the Arts and is a frequent presenter on arts education for such organizations as the Getty Center for Education in the Arts, the Kennedy Center for the Performing Arts and the American Council for the Arts.

Notes

1. I have borrowed and embellished this useful phrase from Norma Moran, whose essay appears in this chapter.

2. "Among School Children," William Butler Yeats, *The Collected Poems of W. B. Yeats* (New York: Macmillan, 1953), pp. 212 ff.

3. I heard this joke, on which I have elaborated to suit the scenario, from Robert Cooper, the assistant principal at Martin Luther King, Jr. High School in New York City. Bob and I have collaborated in several teaching situations, including the New York City Opera High School Education Program.

4. Elliot Eisner has long maintained the value of the experienced, insightful and articulate critic as evaluator and the need to balance numbers with interpretive assessment.

5. Judy Sizemore, *Education Reform Opportunities for Artists and Craftspeople* (Frankfort, KY: Kentucky Arts Council, 1995).

6. Ibid, p. 9.

7. Scott Massey, *Leonard Bernstein Center Schools Mission Statement*, Leonard Bernstein Center for Education Through the Arts: Nashville, August, 1994, p. 7.

8. Ibid, p. 8.

9. Mark Putnam, *A Teacher's Guidebook for the Nashville Symphony Orchestra's Production of* The Rite of Spring *by Igor Stravinsky* (The Nashville Institute for the Arts: August, 1994), p. 2.

10. Project IMPACT operated in five public school systems: Columbus, Ohio; Eugene, Oregon; Glendale, California; Philadelphia, Pennsylvania; and Troy, Alabama. It was funded by the U. S. Office of Education and the National Endowment for the Arts with coordinating services provided by the JDR 3rd Fund and additional support from the professional arts education associations.

Part II
Creating an Instructional Support System

Professional Training and Development

Building the Infrastructure: Professional Training and Development for Artists, Arts Specialists and Classroom Teachers

If most institutional arts partnerships falter or break down behind the classroom door, as I maintain, then what can be done to build an organizational support system that helps to create a receptive climate for collaboration? Put differently, what do artists, arts specialists and classroom teachers need to know about each other's culture, professional domain and the common ground they share, and where do they go to get this information? What do they need to do, separately and together, to navigate these crosscurrents so that they can communicate effectively and learn to work in concert? What sort of preparation does each group need to maximize the effectiveness of its individual contribution and to integrate the arts into the curriculum? What role can artists and arts organizations play in both pre-service and in-service training for classroom, and perhaps specialist teachers?

Teachers, arts specialists and artists must have opportunities to participate as colleagues in pre-service and in-service courses, workshops and seminars, and they must be given officially sanctioned and remunerated time to plan for these collaborations. Without this infrastructure, there will be virtually no hope of building a team that reflects or balances the expertise of the classroom teacher as arts integrator, the specialist as developer of sequential skills, knowledge, history and aesthetics, and the artist as the creator, interpreter and producer. Consequently, there will be little chance of developing an arts-infused curriculum.

The infrastructure can be built in many ways, and school districts, teachers unions, and arts and higher education institutions have important roles to play in the process. We have already encountered examples of work in this area by national, state and local arts centers, institutes and organizations—the Kentucky Center for the Arts' statewide professional development efforts, ArtsConnection's Performing Arts Institute for Teachers, the Lincoln Center Institute and its affiliates, the Leonard Bernstein Center, and the Kennedy Center's local and national efforts.

State and local arts agencies are also important sources of training and support. According to *The Education Commitment: An Overview of State Arts Agencies' Arts Education Activities*, artist residencies can help teachers as well as students. "Through time spent together in the classroom and through formal in-service instruction, artists provide teachers with new resources and help them to expand their repertoire of skills, lesson plans, materials and ideas for application throughout their careers."[1] In the example cited, a residency program in Washington state focused on artist/teacher cooperation and featured a 40-hour or more in-service curriculum. Teachers specialized in one particular artistic discipline and worked with an artist to build hands-on production experience, develop lesson plans and undertake supervised arts instruction.

Arts alliances, arts institutions, arts centers and museums offer training and professional development workshops and programs for artists. A few dedicated arts-in-education organizations also provide such opportunities. These programs are offered either to artists on the organization's roster or to the general artist population. They vary in length from a few days to year-round and focus on a wide spectrum of topics, such as career and networking opportunities, tips on how to become an effective artist in the schools, and how to develop performances and workshops in, through and about the arts.

Most arts-in-education professional development opportunities, however, focus on teacher training, using artists as the instructors. Generally, no attempt is made to bring artists and teachers together as teaching and learning equals in the enterprise. The arts institutions assume that teachers, not artists, need the training. This assumption, of course, is false. Here is a revised version of my thoughts on the matter based on what I wrote some years ago:

> Many artists-in-the-schools programs founder on the rock of inadequate preparation of artists, who usually have no pedagogical training or lesson planning skills, are new to the culture of schools, know little of classroom management techniques, and are unfamiliar with the various stages of child and teenage

development. Some artists are born teachers; most are not and life in the schools bears little or no resemblance to life on stage, in the studio or the garret.

There is no longer any excuse for artists to allow themselves to be sent into unfamiliar settings to "sink or swim" at the expense of the kids and with no respect for or attention to the teachers. Orientation, training and supervision are essential, and experienced artists and educators should be responsible for formal training sessions, mentoring and hands-on staff development workshops that provide instructional methodology, practical information on schools and schooling, tips on the do's and don'ts, and a regular forum for the exchange of ideas that have failed and of those that appear to work.

A support system for monitoring and supervision should be in place, and self-assessment and formal evaluation should be an integral part of the process to maintain artistic excellence and authenticity, instructional integrity and a reasonable balance between artistic and educational outcomes. It is unthinkable that teachers would be allowed to work in schools without adequate preparation and supervision; the same holds true for artists.[2]

To illustrate both the virtue and the necessity of artist training, we will take a quick look at the work of three arts organizations: New York City Opera's Artist Training Workshop, the Kentucky Arts Council's technical assistance workshop for local artists, and the Kennedy Center for the Performing Arts' workshops for teachers and their exemplary handbook, *Artists as Educators*. We will then move on to the other practitioners represented in this section whose varied and rich experience supports the need for the pre-service and in-service professional development of all potential allies—the artist, the specialist and the classroom teacher—that enables both collaborative planning and the construction of an arts-integrated curriculum.

What Artists Need: The New York City Opera Education Program's Artist Training Retreat

New York City Opera (NYCO) has offered an elementary program to area schools since the inception of its education department in 1966. Recently, the department launched a high school initiative to integrate the study of opera into the core curriculum, particularly language arts, social studies and music. To develop and implement the program, the department formed a three-way partnership with the Manhattan High Schools Superintendent's Office and two schools adjacent to the Lincoln Center campus where NYCO resides. The schools are the arts-focused, special admission LaGuardia High School of the Arts and the open-enrollment, comprehensive Martin Luther King, Jr. High School.

With help from a small New York State Council on the Arts planning grant and modest professional development funds from the Manhattan superintendent's office, NYCO education and artistic personnel spent a full year working through the program's goals, objectives, design and learner outcomes with representatives from the schools. As a planning, design and evaluation consultant to NYCO, I was included in this process. In the second year, we continued to plan and to try out different approaches for the in-school and at-Lincoln Center aspects of the program. The artists spent periods of concentrated time in the schools with teachers and their students and visited the State Theater to attend performances, go on backstage tours and participate in special workshops with NYCO's education and artistic staff.

Most of the artists engaged for this program were City Opera professionals; a few were from opera companies and colleges of music in the city. Some had in-school performing and teaching experience; others did not. While NYCO held several orientation and training sessions with the artists throughout the early phases of the program, a more comprehensive and focused approach to professional development had been planned from the beginning. Everyone wanted more information about schools (their purpose, culture and organization); urban teenagers and their current concerns; curriculum, instruction and age-appropriate practice; the elements of a good lesson and tried and true teaching strategies; how best to form classroom partnerships and build in teacher/artist collaboration; and how to relate the art form of opera to the school curriculum.

In late spring 1995, we made plans to hold a two-day summer retreat in the New York State Theater rehearsal rooms. Participants included NYCO's education staff, the high school program artists, experienced guest artists, and teachers from Martin Luther King, Jr. Robert Cooper, an assistant principal for language arts at King who had been involved in the project from the beginning, served as the workshop facilitator. I was his sidekick.

Bob and I had brainstormed the workshop's design one day during a lunch meeting with Education Director Jo Hodak Weiss (see Appendix G). Bob then revised it several times with input from the staff, the teaching artists and me. The following account describes the program's maiden voyage, which will continue periodically throughout the school year. I thought that it was a success for a number of reasons:

Planning, Facilitation and Leadership

As a workshop leader, Bob was inspired and inspiring. He prepared a detailed agenda, a script actually, that traced the sequence and content of events from the opening moment to the last. He spoke from authentic classroom and administrative experience as well as from his familiarity with the NYCO program, the staff and the artists who had worked at King. He was a classic example of a good trainer and teacher: he "modeled the model" (enacted the process he was describing); he commented on everything he did, explained every exercise and new term of art and used the chalkboard as he went along.

Bob was crystal clear in his directions, responsive to the group's moods, reactions and ideas, and moved in and out of the "center stage" spotlight to encourage discussion among the participants. He showed us the old reliable "chalk and talk" approach of frontal teaching and then moved into his mode of preference: the Socratic method of questioning and encouraging metacognition—that is, reflecting on the process, analyzing the knowledge being shared and synthesizing the information being exchanged.

He varied the pace, had rich and challenging activities flowing cheek by jowl, and quickly made everyone feel comfortable and eager participants. His arsenal of teaching techniques, bag of fail-safe tricks and the theoretical foundations to back it all up were impressive. His sense of humor, energy and general classroom demeanor gave new meaning to the notion of teacher as performer. Everyone, myself included, learned a great deal about pedagogy and methodology simply by being in the presence of this master teacher.

Pacing and Variety of Activities

The rest of us were alternately students and teachers. We wrote in our journals; we brainstormed in large groups using different formats; and we broke into small groups in different configurations and then regrouped to share our findings and observations. We role-played several scenes with often hilarious (but profoundly true) results. After each activity we reflected on what had just happened, why, and then how the experience might be integrated into our own classroom repertoire.

Content

Having a group of professional opera artists with considerable onstage experience think about the purpose of schools and schooling and then transform the question "what are schools for" into a consideration of "what is music" and "what is music for" created an enthralling and powerful experience. To move from that to yet another metaphysical abstraction, the mission of schools and the school culture, was daunting but soon it, too, became concrete by example.

A discussion of the distribution of power within the school hierarchy came as a complete surprise to most of the artists. They had no idea how large high schools in an urban center manage to direct traffic, let alone cope with the business of teaching and learning for thousands of students in a sprawling, largely bureaucratic environment.

A review of teenage problems and adolescent behavior was illuminating, as were the ideas about how to deal with difficult situations and students. After listing teenage issues on the board, one participant observed drily that we had enough material for four operas right in front of us.

We delved into lesson plans and created some of our own together, examined the various strategies for cooperative learning, and then wrestled with the various modes of assessment, including process portfolios. These activities gave us all a taste of how much breadth, depth and stamina it takes to make a thorough professional educator.

Evaluation

The two-day retreat was pronounced a success by the participants. They named as the most helpful aspects and topics: lesson plans, methods (brainstorming, breaking into groups, role-playing), education terminology, classroom management and organization, and guest artists. On the downside, the participants universally cited the almost unrelieved intensity of the workshops and the exhaustion caused by the amount of material covered. Recommendations for improvement included a greater focus on the artist's work, more time for the development and application of ideas, more small group sessions, and the addition of a third day. We have already made notes and plans for future revision based on feedback from the pilot.

What Teachers Need: Harnessing the Artists' Power and Process

Several days after the retreat, Bob and I were discussing ways to improve the event in its next developmental incarnation. Bob was concerned that teaching artists about schools and schooling was only half of the picture. He also wished that he and his subject area teachers could be trained in the arts—with and by the artists. I heartily concurred. Here are excerpts from our conversation about the needs of teachers and arts specialists:

RC: Most of us teachers are stuck in our traditional ways of looking at our subjects, whether it's language arts, social studies or math. We tend to rely on speaking and writing as *the* means of communication, and we don't include other ways of expression—we really don't know much about them. We need to learn how kids can express themselves in the arts and through the arts.

JR: I have seen many teachers learn this from the artist by watching the process, by discussing it and breaking it down, and then doing it, either alone or with the artist as a partner in the classroom.

RC: Yes, but ultimately that teacher must be able to harness the artist's power to use it in his or her daily teaching. Teachers have to learn how to create learning opportunities that stretch the ABCs and go beyond.

JR: That means they have to learn how to think and process information as artists do...

RC: ...and talk the same language. Teachers—and supervisors—need a more expansive view of how to create these learning opportunities. I think we need to set up training sessions for teachers and artists together where we push the *process* of artistic expression. But we have killer roadblocks to all this, don't we?

JR: Things like time, opportunity and resources...

RC: True, but there is something even more difficult to deal with: the unspoken but strong perception by our "academic" teachers that, when the going gets rough, the arts and arts specialists are among the first things to be cut. This leads most teachers to think that the arts are expendable, not valued, not basic for children. Then there is our way of separating the curriculum into neat and convenient blocks or subject areas, with very little integration, let alone interdisciplinary study. Most teachers are isolated and do not know how to teach in teams, integrate learning or make connections with other subject areas—certainly not in the arts, since very few have had any formal training. The one or two methods courses in college don't help much.

JR: We have to work on finding ways to help your teachers value and use artistic principles in the classroom, to build on the overarching themes, core concepts or processes that cross the curriculum. We also have to remember to include the arts specialists from both schools in our planning sessions, training and our schoolwide plans. Ultimately, we need to bring the artists, the teachers, the specialists, the NYCO staff—everybody—into the training process together around issues of mutual concern. It will take some doing, but the instructional cross-fertilization will be well worth it, don't you think? This way, we can start to build that constituency of supporters for the arts within the school that you and I have talked about.

RC: Yes, indeed, but it's going to take some persuasion to get our arts specialists to work directly with the subject area teachers. They are not used to that.

What Arts Specialists Need: Respect and Inclusion

What do arts specialists need from artists? First and foremost, they need respect and reassurance that artists are interested in team building and not in competing for time, attention, space and other scarce resources. Depending on their own areas of expertise, arts specialists might want professional demonstrations and workshops in their own art or related forms that supplement, expand on and deepen experiences for children. They might welcome opportunities to team with another creative person who has a slightly different slant to bring some of their own more ambitious lessons to life. They would probably welcome professional camaraderie and reinforcement, since so many arts specialists that I have worked with are delighted to be the facilitators and coordinators of schoolwide projects as well as resources to classroom teachers.

Over the years, I have been in countless schools with artists-in-residence programs that either bypass or ignore the arts specialists. Often, as we learned from Phyllis Free in the previous section, the artist and the specialists work in adjacent classrooms without knowing it, or worse, knowing it and feeling frustrated that they have no time to connect and work together. True, some specialists seem to prefer their self-containment and independence and are reluctant to get involved with artists or other teachers. In addition, some prefer to work only with those designated as gifted and talented. In the long run, as Judy Burton will point out in her essay, this attitude only deepens their isolation from the rest of the school and prevents any recognition of the contribution they can make to schooling and general education. It is important for arts specialists to understand that continued isolation jeopardizes their visibility in and importance to the school community and sabotages any effort toward building that all-important local constituency for the arts.

If arts specialists are not included in the schools' way of doing business or don't seek the artists out, then arts organizations and artists must make a serious and concerted effort to connect with them. Insist on including arts specialists in the planning and design process, try to enlist their help in leadership positions, ask them what their needs are, and take time to discover the intersections and the common ground. I am convinced that ignoring or bypassing arts specialists is ultimately selfish and shortsighted, since without them it is highly unlikely that a high-quality, sequential curriculum in all the arts will ever be available to all children in all our schools.

The Kentucky Arts Council's Technical Assistance Workshop for Artists and Arts and Cultural Organizations

Artists as Resources to Integrated Learning in the Classroom[3]

Arts education has been a top priority of the Kentucky Arts Council (KAC) for many years, and its board and staff recently adopted the idea that the council must take a leadership role in arts education reform as it applies to the Kentucky Education Reform Act (KERA). The KAC has historically been committed to the potential that artists and arts organizations have as resources to the classroom. The council's Artist-in-Residence Program has long been respected nationally for the early ground it broke in getting artists, students and teachers to plan and work together. Through its past experience with the National Endowment for the Arts' Arts in Schools Basic Education Grant and its current Basic Arts Program model schools, the council has learned a tremendous amount about what motivates districts, schools and teachers to improve and incorporate comprehensive, integrated arts education into general instruction. Many of the KAC's current efforts are in the area of technical assistance for artists and organizations working in schools. Their professional development workshop for artists, to my knowledge, is the first of its kind in the nation.

In July 1995, the KAC and cosponsor Kentucky Alliance for Arts Education conducted a technical assistance workshop aimed at providing artists and arts and cultural organizations with information about Kentucky's education reform effort. The session was held at the Kentucky Center for the Arts, and approximately 180 people attended on a first-come, first-served basis.

The workshop was funded by the Goals 2000 Arts Education Leadership Fund, an initiative established by a partnership of the National Endowment for the Arts, the National Assembly of State Arts Agencies and the Emily Hall Tremaine Foundation. Ashland, Incorporated, the John F. Kennedy Center for the Performing Arts and the Kentucky Arts Council provided additional funding.

The Kentucky Education Reform Act and the Department of Education's Curriculum Framework call for the appropriate use of community resources as a way of providing real-life learning opportunities for students. Although many Kentucky artists have been "doing KERA" for years, the KAC was responding to their need to improve their work to fit better into the new KERA classroom.

The workshop offered a short, intensive "laboratory" to help participants learn and develop new personal and professional plans and educational materials. The synergy of a self-selected group of people working together with facilitators and local- and state-level advisors produced results tailored by and for each individual. Participants were able to increase their understanding of the applicable concepts and components in education reform, discover new potential for partnerships and resource sharing, and develop their capacities to work more effectively in a school setting.

The laboratory focused on the key components of reform, including curriculum design and an exploration and demonstration of best practices using different classroom learning models. These included: the Galef Institute's Different Ways of Knowing (DWOK); Foxfire; Howard Gardner's applied theory of multiple intelligences (which underlies parts of the KERA legislation), and thematic, integrated instruction and the incorporation of traditional and folk arts into the curriculum. In addition, sessions were offered on building bridges through multicultural projects and on looking in-depth at the state's approach to arts assessment. Artist handbooks, excerpts from the state assessment guidelines, the curriculum framework and other resource materials were distributed.

Facilitation and support were provided by staff members of the KAC, the Kentucky Alliance for Arts Education, the Kentucky Center for the Arts, Stage One: The Louisville Children's Theatre, Kentucky Educational Television, Advanced Systems in Measurement and Evaluation, the Kentucky Department of Education, the Collaborative for Elementary Learning and many others. Classroom teachers were also present to counsel and advise throughout the workshop.

Participants were able to hear insightful comments, constructive criticism and ideas about how their educational materials, school programs or projects could be improved and made more attractive and useful for teachers and students. Groups of approximately 25 people were organized to move through various sessions together. Each participant's own materials were passed out for group critique, discussion and idea generation.

Useful Distinctions Between Artists and Arts Specialists

An abundance of material was prepared and distributed at the workshop, including Judy Sizemore's handbook *Education Reform Opportunities for Artists and Craftspeople,*[4] in which a section is devoted to "Professional Artists and Crafts People in the Classroom." This helpful reference draws an important distinction between artists and specialists and mentions some of the things artists can do to become more useful as resources to all teachers:

> The arts are an integral part of education in Kentucky's transformed schools. Art and music teachers are recognized for the critical role they play in helping students reach their full potential as learners. There is also an important role to be played by professional, practicing artists and craftspeople, but that role is quite distinct from the role of art and music teachers.

> Naturally, there is the distinction of media. Schools do not generally have dance specialists, storytellers, writers, theater artists or folklorists on staff, so your contribution in those fields will be welcome. Even if your field is visual arts or music, your particular speciality within those broad fields can supplement the existing art and music programs.

> There is also an extremely important legal distinction between your status and the status of arts specialist teachers. Art and music teachers are certified employees of the school district. You are not. You should never be placed alone in charge of students. You should always work in collaboration with a teacher....

> ...you can provide...a fresh approach and new ideas that the teacher can build on. That's why you must design the project so that it reflects your uniqueness as a practicing professional in your field and demonstrates your understanding of educational reform.

> There are several ways you can make your proposed workshop or project appealing to teachers, whether you propose to work with classroom teachers or with arts specialists [The following is a summary of points that she makes, with a few additions of my own]:

> • Try to put teachers at ease

> • Make a connection between your art and the ongoing work of the teacher

> • Make a connection between your project and your professional work

- Make a connection between your project and your life experiences [and the lives of your students]

- Design your project with education reform in mind, particularly the appropriate academic expectations [readers can substitute local curriculum frameworks and learner outcomes]

- Design your project so that students must use critical thinking and creative problem solving to complete the activity

- Be sure that your project is appropriate for the age and development level of the students

- Be certain that it can be accomplished in the amount of time that you and the teacher have allotted for the activity

- Have a typed lesson plan for your project that you can leave with the teacher

The Workshop's Evaluation

According to Kentucky Arts Council Executive Director Lou DeLuca and Assistant Director Dennis Horn, and to an analysis of the evaluation forms turned in by participants, the workshop met its goals. At my request, Dennis sent me a representative sample of ten of the completed Participant Evaluation Forms. They asked the following questions on a scale of 1 (low) to 5 (high):

- How helpful did you find the following (a listing of conference activities);
- Overall, I feel the workshop...(a series of questions about provision of information and insights; understanding schools, teachers and students, and meeting participant expectations).

The responses were largely positive, clustering in the 3-5 area. Some verbatim excerpts of the answers to open-ended questions are shown in Figure 5.2. The participants included a number of recommendations in their evaluations. One idea is to develop a committee of experts to review and critique artists' and organizations' educational materials. Another is to hold a follow-up workshop aimed more directly at getting teachers and artists/organizations talking together about needs and appropriate responses in the classroom. A third is to decentralize the technical assistance workshops and hold them more frequently at different locations around the state. KAC plans to follow up by working on ways to integrate many of the useful suggestions, especially those dealing with cultural diversity and the inclusion of more teachers in the process.

I have often wondered why more state (and local) arts agencies do not organize and engage in professional development initiatives, regardless of whether a reform plan is in place. It is an activity that state agencies are uniquely suited to perform, and I hope this example will inspire other agencies to investigate the possibility. It is an important service to the arts and education community and will help build the infrastructure and support needed behind the classroom door.

Figure 5.2: Selected Comments by Participants in the Kentucky Arts Council's Technical Assistance Workshop

The following is a sampling of responses to open-ended evaluation requests for additional comments on the workshop; suggestions on activities, events or services for follow-up; and opinions about the value of a periodic review of education program information by a state-level committee of experts:

"Enjoyed sessions incorporating children and teachers. We need a teacher/artist workshop (statewide)...having the opportunity for critique and criticism by experts is always welcome...."

"Multiple Intelligences session was excellent! I would like to have had the option to attend all four Best Practices sessions.... I'm a little concerned that there isn't more diversity among panelists, facilitators, and attendees—race, class, etc...regional and local meetings that take into account the traditional culture of that region or community would be the most effective. We don't want to lose touch with our native art or to overlook the art in our everyday life in favor of THEATER, DANCE, ART, CULTURE."

"I listened to several presenter/facilitators talk about teaching students about other cultures, but what about the students' own cultures? Never once did I hear about the importance of the student learning about his or her own culture and heritage, and how this would enrich the student's self-worth...regional meetings would allow participation in all workshops...more in-depth workshops."

"Promote these sessions for professional development so that other teachers can be involved...."

"More information on methods to incorporate the arts into the high school curriculum; gatherings which include artists, arts groups *and* teachers...."

"I am fascinated by the Arts Resource Directory. Perhaps it would be helpful to the resource people to have from the schools and others a listing of their needs, wants, etc., together with indications of when, why, where...."

"As an independent artist, I'm regularly in the schools. I've trained in DWOK and Multiple Intelligences, and I'm a former educator. I found the study guide discussion helpful.... I would love a long session on portfolios...it would help me to know how to tie what I'm doing to the students' writing. What do the teachers need? Literary arts is one area we didn't cover."

"I thought the conference overall was an outstanding success. My only "wish" is that there could have been a better balance between artists and educators...the cry I heard across the board was the difficulty of opening and maintaining a dialogue between artist and teacher...maybe offer more workshops led by a classroom teacher and workshops specifically for teachers led by artists...congratulations on an invaluable two days."

Artists as Staff Developers: The John F. Kennedy Center's Workshops for Teachers

Professional artists and arts educators can perform a great service for classroom and subject area teachers by offering training and professional development in the various arts disciplines. The John F. Kennedy Center for the Performing Arts provides many such occasions locally and nationally in its Professional Development Opportunities for Teachers Program. For example, their two-day seminar "Artists as Educators: Planning Effective Workshops for Teachers" is designed to introduce artists and arts educators to the process of planning, presenting and evaluating participatory workshops for teachers. It is conducted at the Kennedy Center by individuals experienced in designing effective workshops for teachers. The seminar explores all the possible connections between the artist's and arts educator's own artistic expertise and the needs and interest of teachers. Participation is limited to artists and/or arts educators who have extensive experience working with or performing for young people. Each participant receives a binder of resource materials that supplements the content of the seminar.

The excellent handbook, *Artists as Educators: Becoming Effective Workshop Leaders for Teachers*, written by John C. Carr and Lynne Silverstein in 1994, contains a summary section that I think complements the Kentucky handbook nicely. Titled "In a Nutshell: What Teachers Want and Need from Participatory Workshops," it lists the chief things that teachers want, which include:

- knowledge and inspiration provided by a credible workshop leader who has worked successfully with young people
- activities that help them recognize connections between the arts and what they are teaching and that help them recognize the benefits to students of connecting the arts to other curriculum
- activities that help them increase their creativity, knowledge and appreciation of the arts and that are transferable to the classroom
- opportunities to: try out ideas through active participation; tap into their own creativity; build confidence in teaching about and through the arts
- clear, focused, well-organized sessions that offer practical suggestions that are both specific and in-depth; for activities manageable within classroom time constraints; that are targeted to appropriate grade levels; for which there is a written outline and teaching materials; for appropriate references/supplementary materials; for materials/supplies available on a limited school budget and information about source(s) for ordering materials/supplies

- respect from a workshop presenter who is enthusiastic and acknowledges teachers' maturity and experience
- camaraderie that allows them to work collaboratively and share experiences with colleagues in a stimulating professional environment

The examples from the New York City Opera, the Kentucky Arts Council and the Kennedy Center address the expressed needs of artists and teachers who want to form instructional partnerships. They have at least three very important themes in common: respect for distinctive roles and responsibilities, a focus on authentic practice (that is based on sound pedagogical theory), and professional capacity building. In translation, these themes acknowledge that artists and teachers who want to work together must recognize that they have separate contributions to make, that they need to learn how to make them through practical experience, and that collaboration builds the power of each to increase the combined instructional impact on the learner. When done well, this impact goes far beyond superficial and sporadic enrichment; it goes to the heart of the learning process in an environment that encourages sustained thought, imagination, daring and reflection. The question, of course, is: How do you create and support this environment—for teachers, and for all the children?

Beyond Enrichment: A Closer Look at Training and Development Issues

The preceding illustrations describe different kinds of professional development opportunities for artists and teachers. Taken together, they start to make the point that for artists, arts specialists and classroom teachers to learn to work together, we need to build an appropriate infrastructure. Actually, we need to do much more than that.

In my opening paragraph, I included the following questions: What sort of preparation does each group need to maximize the effectiveness of its individual contribution and to integrate the arts into the curriculum? What role can artists and arts organizations play in both pre-service and in-service training for classroom, and perhaps specialist teachers? I might have added, What is the role of the artist and the arts organization in curriculum development practices using the arts?

These are extraordinarily tough issues that Judy Burton addresses in her trilogy. To my knowledge, few in the field are tackling some or all of these questions head on, with the exceptions of the Getty Center for Education in the Arts, the Leonard Bernstein Center for Education

Through the Arts, and the Lincoln Center Institute in its pilot program with Brooklyn College of the City University of New York.

Pre-service training in the arts for classroom teachers has been an area of concern for more than 30 years. It is a subject that has concerned the International Council of Fine Arts Deans, the Holmes Group[5], and college and university schools of education across the country. It has also been a frequent topic in *Arts Education Policy Review*, a bimonthly publication of Heldreff Publications, and its predecessor *Design for Arts in Education*.

In 1967, when John D. Rockefeller 3rd and Kathryn Bloom were discussing the mission of the JDR 3rd Fund's new Arts in Education Program, the focus on teacher education was rejected largely because Mr. Rockefeller felt that the terrain was too vast and would require more energy and resources than he was prepared to spend at the time. In the seventies, Junius Eddy[6], then at the Rockefeller Foundation, prepared an internal report for Arts Program Director Howard Klein, titled "Perspectives on the Arts and General Education." In this paper, he recommended the Foundation focus its attention on, among other areas, teacher education, declaring:

> The one element in the whole arts-in-general-education equation that seems to me crucial but has never, really, been given concerted attention up to now is the question of the preparation of teachers—at the undergraduate pre-service level and at the graduate level involving experienced teachers. It would relate, furthermore, to the preparation of more arts-aware classroom teachers for the elementary grades, of teachers in other subject matter areas at the middle school and secondary level, and of more rounded specialist teachers of the arts at all levels.

> I have been led to this emphasis partly because it has seemed to me that, **as a training device, the in-service teacher workshop— whether conducted over a six- or eight-week period in the summertime, over several weekends during the school year, or as a one-shot supplement to a performance visit by professional arts organizations—is simply not adequate to the task if we are serious about effecting genuine long-range change in this field.** [emphasis added] Ultimately, I suspect it will take a series of interlocking efforts in which pre-service training, based in a number of differently styled colleges and universities, is augmented both by graduate-level work (in part to prepare the needed teachers of teachers) and by all the requisite institutes, workshops and seminars utilized in retraining endeavors. [January 1974, pages 34 and 35]

As a consequence of Junius' recommendation, the Rockefeller Foundation undertook a number of pilot projects which yielded promising results but which were discontinued as the Foundation turned its attention away from arts education. His comments are as, if not more, pertinent today as they were in 1974.

I spoke recently about the role of artists and arts organizations in pre-service education with Dr. Jerrold Ross, who is dean of the School of Education and Human Services at St. John's University. During his tenure at New York University, Dr. Ross was director of one of the two (now-closed) National Arts Education Research Centers that were funded by the National Endowment for the Arts and based at NYU and the University of Illinois. Jerry has long been an advocate of a tripartite curriculum,[7] which he described to me as follows:

> ...one in which liberal arts content—half of the curriculum in history, literature, the social sciences, the humanities, the physical sciences—are combined with courses in how children grow and develop, coupled with numerous field experiences that ought to be sprinkled throughout the pre-service curriculum, from the time the students are sophomores, even before their student teaching. They also need an integrating course, whether they are undergraduate or graduates, to pull together the liberal arts content, educational psychology, the history and philosophy of education, and pedagogy in a way that helps teachers understand what the relationship is among all these disciplines. To my knowledge, this doesn't exist anywhere, and as a result, pre-service teachers come out with a fragmented grasp of what education for young people ought to be.

> In my view artists and arts organizations should bring to the public schools the highest standards of performance and production to which young people should either aspire, if they are thinking of becoming professionals, or which they should recognize as they develop into critically thinking audiences.

> Using the services of artists and arts organizations for teachers and students in higher education would be an interesting innovation that I believe should extend to schools of the arts which train our talented young artists. As of now, there is little connection or cooperation, and I would like to see the practice that exists in schools of elementary and secondary education transferred to higher education.

We can now profit by taking a closer look at several of the professional and curriculum development issues I have merely touched on. If you accept Judy Burton's premise, as I do, that teachers, arts specialists and artists are natural allies—three vital parts to the instructional equation—then additional fundamental questions arise: What role can the artists and others play in this conceptual triumvirate and what do they need to know and be able to do to be effective? Burton addresses these questions and more in her trilogy: How can artists work collaboratively with classroom teachers and arts specialists to design an arts-integrated curriculum? What kind of instructional methodology works best for teaching about the arts (history, criticism and aesthetics), through the arts (arts integration) and in the arts (the developmental and sequential knowledge, techniques and skills needed for creation and performance)? Where and how does the artist fit most comfortably as an instructor in the school culture?

Scott Noppe-Brandon explores the issues of professional and curriculum development filtered through the lens of his aesthetic education experience as practiced by the Lincoln Center Institute and its national affiliates. Carol Fineberg provides us with insights as she defines and discusses the nature of the arts-integrated curriculum and then compares and contrasts it with the phenomenon of transfer of learning from an arts discipline to another academic discipline. Sharon Ryan and Sam Shreyar wrestle with the cultural considerations involved in attempting to design programs and develop curriculum that intersect the interests, backgrounds and needs of artists, teachers and children.

This chapter only skims the surface of the issues involved in building partnerships behind the classroom door, and this book includes only a relative handful of essays and treatments of the topic. There are many more programs, resources and knowledgeable people busy at work around the country. The arrival of the Internet has made contact with many of them possible. The World Wide Web and the field's increasing electronic sophistication should make identifying, collecting and sharing this kind of information a matter of easy, daily routine.[8]

Putting it into effect, however, is another matter entirely, as you have seen from my recounting of events that date back almost 30 years.

Natural Allies: A Trilogy

Judith Burton has written three pieces for this chapter: a case study, an essay, and a set of guidelines and criteria for designing and developing classroom instructional collaborations. The pieces were not written in the order they are presented. The first, the case study "Natural Allies: A Tale from the Classroom," is an imaginary scenario. It was written last and grew organically out of a series of editorial discussions between us and my need to see what "Nirvana" looked like in someone's fertile imagination (laced with experience), since I have yet to find it here on earth. I had originally asked Judy to write an essay, the second piece, about the training and professional development needed by artists, teachers and arts specialists to work together successfully in a functional in-school triumvirate. "Natural Allies: Children, Teachers and Artists" was the result. That piece prompted me to ask her for a set of guidelines and criteria that would be useful to the reader as a summary of all the rich points made in the essay. The guidelines complete the trilogy. We are all the beneficiaries of this process.

In the case study, the arts project grew out of a race riot and the decision by a principal to discover whether and how the arts and artists could help the school deal with the volatile issues of race, ethnicity and culture. The initial motivation, therefore, was not learning in the arts for their own sake, but learning about and through the arts as instruments for other social objectives. As the project developed, however, learning in the arts (music, dance, visual arts and the like) began to achieve parity and a healthy balance was struck. While based on an imaginary series of events, the process by which this was achieved is profoundly instructive.

In her essay, Judy discusses the elements of an effective partnership, identifies the problems and needs, examines the roles of the artist, the specialist and the classroom teacher, and then proposes suggestions for meeting those needs through training and supervision. Her "Natural Allies: School Planning Guidelines for Visiting Artist Curriculum Initiatives" summarizes her main points. These three pieces, taken together with Scott Noppe-Brandon's discussion of similar issues and with the other contributions to this chapter, begin to define the magnitude of the question, "Who shall teach the arts?"

As always, some answers are provided, but inevitably these answers provoke more questions. These questions must not be avoided, ducked or dismissed. They are essential to the ultimate success of finding and keeping a place for arts behind the classroom door. Judy's work here sheds more light on the central issues and fundamental problems. Her thoughts will enrich the continuing dialogue.

Natural Allies

Part 1: A Tale from the Classroom

by Judith M. Burton

Slurs and Fisticuffs

A small town was turned upside down by a riot involving groups of Native American, African American, Chicano and Irish American youngsters. Cultural slurs and fisticuffs flew in all directions, and some of the youngsters ended up in the hospital. The principal of the local elementary school decided to confront matters by inviting artists and performers from each of these communities to speak to the youngsters through their art. "By expanding youngsters' contacts with the world beyond school," the principal explained, " I had hoped that we could show them ways of expressing ideas that cross different cultures and are nonviolent."

The principal set aside several school assemblies and challenged each artist to show not only how art forms communicate in special ways but also how they can open the youngsters to caring about the ideas and values of others. Many teachers in the school suddenly found the event to be rich in artistic possibilities and potentially useful for the deeper exploration of human values and behavior. One teacher said, "I immediately thought, wow, what a great idea for working through some heavy duty feelings."

Defining Needs

As teachers met to sort out their own feelings and fears, they continued to explore the event's possibilities for learning. The discussion brought the full-time visual arts and part-time music specialists into leadership roles for the first time. "I realized," said the visual arts teacher, "that the other teachers were actually taking me seriously for the first time—after all these years of arguing for the arts!"

From these discussions, the fifth- and sixth-grade classroom teachers, along with the arts specialists, decided that they would inspire their classes to become "discoverers" of the roles played by the arts in culture and to become "interpreters" of their meaning. The teachers reasoned that, developmentally, the youngsters were passionately interested in the workings of society—the rules, hierarchies, structures and details that make cultures distinctive. They also knew that youngsters at this age are highly curious, have great and focused skills of inquiry and, while they are essentially concrete thinkers, with help they can make imaginative leaps into the unknown.

As the discussion proceeded, the teachers invited the assembly artists to become active participants on the planning team. "I liked this idea," said the dance artist. "I wasn't just being invited to do a one-shot event, I was being engaged in thinking things through from the beginning. I knew that my work would be part of something bigger, that it would be continued and built upon by the teachers and the other artists."

Sharing Expertise

Having identified some developmental needs and abilities, the teachers set goals for the project: to explore how art forms communicate in their special ways and to learn how they offer knowledge, wisdom and insight about people and values. Then the team turned their efforts to becoming more informed about each other and about the project. The classroom and specialist teachers knew they needed to get to know each other and also the artists and their ways of working. They knew the artists needed to know about the children and about classroom routines and expectations. The classroom teachers, specialists and artists were of different nationalities and divergent expertise, and as the planning sessions proceeded, they quickly recognized that they all harbored ill-formed assumptions about each other. So the team decided to become collaborative learners. One classroom teacher said, "This was scary stuff—I had never been this exposed before. I had always avoided the arts and tiptoed carefully around other cultures." "I worried that the teachers would be threatened by way-out ideas," mused the artist-musician, "particularly the music specialist, who seemed a bit conventional."

The team decided to meet after school twice a week for the month preceding the project's start. The team began its collaborative learning on safe ground by developing a bank of project resources to which everyone would contribute: books on the arts, culture, history and geography of the groups in the local community; newspaper clippings from the local press and library; old photographs and personal diaries; and examples of art and videos of performances, both contemporary and ancient. The teachers and the artists pooled resources, each learning from the discoveries of the others and from the discussion about the likely responses of the youngsters to the same materials. After an in-depth examination of the information on hand, the team decided to explore new ways of presenting ideas and information. The team members expressed a common sentiment about the experience: "Sharing ideas with others was a mind-blowing event. We all learned so much. We learned to do and think about so many new things—most of all how to collaborate. After all, that was what we wanted to teach the kids!"

As the team shared expertise, taught each other and discussed possible outcomes, the time came for them to focus their efforts more directly on the specifics of the project and on what they hoped the youngsters would learn. "First, we discussed our own collaborative learning," explained one teacher, "and then we considered how our learning could be translated into forms that would motivate and support the fifth and sixth graders." The team responded to the task by designing a sequence of activities that raised a series of questions: How are ideas about life and human value formed artistically? How are such ideas transported across cultures? How do such ideas shape the evolution of cultures? What effect does this have on the way different peoples come to live together and form shared values? In essence, they hoped that their students would learn much about the different cultures represented by their classmates and, from this rich knowledge, learn how to build a shared culture within which human caring would help counter prejudice. "Our final objectives and expected outcomes for learning interwove concerns for artistry, the culture and caring," said the teacher.

With the school principal's help, the team began to confront practical problems of time and space. They used some imaginative thinking to devise a timetable that permitted art and music, usually taught separately, to be folded into the school day. The physical education teacher, who had expressed interest in becoming the "dance specialist," was also welcomed to the project. The classroom teachers, who previously had taught subjects in separate blocks, began organizing their teaching to flow more organically in response to the anticipated flow of learning. With the help of the specialist teachers, the classroom spaces were redesigned to become "centers," which could accommodate different kinds of activities, and the school hall and gymnasium were commandeered for extended periods each week. Letters were sent home informing parents of the project and inviting their interest. Parents were also asked for permission to allow their youngsters to work after school, and arrangements were made for their safe return home.

Regularly scheduled faculty meetings kept the other teachers in the school apprised of the project. "Frankly," said a third-grade teacher, "I thought it all sounded like a mess. I thought they would really lose their grip on the kids, and we'd have our own mini-riot here in the school." Notwithstanding the mixed reception from their colleagues, and the team members' own fears, the classroom teachers, specialists and artists were ready to begin.

Understanding Across the Arts

The fifth- and sixth-grade classes were divided into four teams of 15, and each team included youngsters from different cultural backgrounds. Each team was assigned to an artist-shaman, and the classroom teachers and specialist teachers acted as elders or wisepersons. For periods of time each week, groups of classroom and specialist teachers and artists would work together in the classrooms. The adults participated directly in the lessons and, during classroom time, they would confer with each other and with the children equally. "We really wanted to model cooperation and to increase our own learning alongside the kids," pointed out a fifth-grade teacher. "We also wanted to be flexible enough to redirect or extend activities as the need arose."

Since the four participating artists represented different cultural heritages and were skilled in different art forms, the first phase in the sequence of learning was to "initiate" each group into the secrets of the art form. "We wanted to combine participation with critical awareness," explained a sixth-grade teacher, "so the kids could use their own creative imaginations to open doors to adult cultural forms and explore their meanings." The artists engaged youngsters in creating textiles and prints, writing poems and plays, composing music for percussion and choreographing dances to drum music.

As the youngsters created their own imaginative works in each art form, the specialist arts teachers also challenged them to learn about that art form as it existed across different cultures, from its earliest manifestation to its most contemporary practices. They collected and read histories, criticism, newspapers, programs and magazines, and they visited local museums, theaters and performance centers to see works in action and to talk with other artists. "As the visual arts specialist pointed out, "We were exploring the kids' abilities to see common threads between their lives and artistic efforts and those of folk from other cultures."

From the Arts to the Culture

Intersecting with the work of the artists, the classroom teachers invited the youngsters to "sleuth" their local communities and collect information about their symbols—dress, religious practices, lifestyles and histories of the different peoples who composed their daily environments. This involved scouring newspapers and magazines; taking pictures and making drawings; listening to conversations on the street and in the shops; and talking about the arts, languages and legacies of the different cultural groups. Parents and local community activists were invited into the classroom for talks, discussions and demonstrations, and many returned for more participation as the project evolved. Drawn into this enterprise was the local West African postman: "I was shocked when the kids invited me to talk about where I came from and my experience here. I left school without graduating. 'What am I doing in a classroom?' I thought. 'They'll know more than me.'" His visit was such a success that he habitually dropped by to check on progress after his daily mail delivery to the school. As the project unfolded, the classroom teachers, specialists and artists continued to meet after school to check on progress, to share new materials and to redirect their objectives in the face of unexpected and exciting occurrences.

Art, Culture and Personal Integrations

As they were completed, the youngsters' drawings, poems and photographs were pinned to the classroom wall, where they jostled for attention with the efforts of the "shaman artists" and "wisepersons," and of the parents, the postman and other representatives of the cultural groups they were studying. This joint display of work stimulated much discussion about the arts of different cultures and peoples and about the relationship between the children's artworks and those of mature artists. It also helped the children to sharpen listening abilities and to practice sharing ideas and learning from each other. Most of all, as knowledge and experience grew, the youngsters began to discuss their conflicting values and practices and to articulate their fears and prejudices.

In the words of one teacher: "I was amazed at the kids' capacity to learn and share and not get into fights. They really worked responsibly together. There was a kind of free flow of experience among them. It seems their imaginations were captured from the word go." Observed the visual arts specialist: "I was not prepared to have my own sense of artistry and value challenged. I learned alongside the kids, and I was amazed by the spectrum of different ideas they explored and by the different ways they articulated their ideas in the art forms." "It was exciting to see how the kids learned to use dramatic and poetic language," recounted the theater artist on the team, "how they used all the stuff they were learning during the week about their cultures and community, and how they opened up to things through art and music and dance. It all carried over into stunning and rich imagery that gave background to the script they developed." Reflecting on her experiences in the project, one fifth-grade girl offered: "What I learned most of all was that people are the same and different, all at the same time, and that art, like we have been studying, helps you to understand that."

This sequence of learning culminated with intense discussion, research, writing and drawing about how ideas of life and human value are transported across cultural boundaries, how they coalesce to shape the evolution of new cultures, and the various effects this has on the way people live and on what they value. Through their discussions, the children learned that the arts, in all their forms, express the thoughts, responses, hopes, desires and anticipations of human beings the world over. They learned that while styles of art change from culture to culture, epoch to epoch, they nonetheless always act as vehicles for human voices to be in conversations that transcend geographical boundaries and historical time. Moreover, they learned that their own voices were important contributors to this dialogue and that their voices needed to be nurtured and exercised with care. As one sixth-grade teacher pointed out: "I was a bit skeptical in the beginning. I thought everything might descend into play, you know. But I think it was the quality of the kids' responses that really amazed me in the end. I know now that we underestimate them quite a bit."

As an integral part of the program, the youngsters made project books into which they put their writings, poems, sketches, photographs, drawings and invented notations for musical compositions and for choreography. They also put into the project books information from books and newspapers they had read, impressions from visits to museums and performances, and descriptions of interviews with people from different cultures. Finally, each book was personalized as a "prized object": every youngster created a special cover, included end papers with careful lettering and decorated borders, and constructed some foldout and pop-up pages. The books became not only in-depth records of study and learning, but in their fabrication also expressed the pride of their owners in this accomplishment. The books were displayed in the local library and, thanks to the imaginative wisdom of the librarian, were set within a small exhibition of rare books and manuscripts, where the dialogue with the past could take yet another interesting turn.

Challenging Attitudes and Values

Of course this kind of interdisciplinary teaching and learning must be planned and must be able to accommodate all sorts of twists and turns. Flexible blocks of time are necessary to accomplish this, for real learning in the classroom, as in life, does not occur in 35-minute blocks or within the singular confines of units of study. Moreover, these kinds of collaborations between and among teachers and artists take confidence and a willingness to break new ground and to negotiate possible outcomes. They also may require an adjustment from long-cherished forms of understanding and practice. In this example, teachers had to transgress the traditional boundaries of their "disciplines," collapse their attitudes about curriculum as discreet subjects, pool expertise and fulfill a range of different roles as specialists, generalists, leaders, followers and collaborators as they seized opportunities to encourage learning.

Taking ample time for prior planning was also important to the success of the project: it enabled the team members to get to know and respect each other, to collect and discuss resources, to inventory the needs of the children, and to begin the process of defining roles and learning together. The two classroom teachers assumed responsibility for coordination from the beginning: they arranged meetings and visits, and they communicated with outside institutions, parents and the community. In fact, the local community and the parents became so enmeshed in the project that they set up a mini-museum of cultural artifacts in the youngsters' classroom. This set in motion a new branch of the project in which the children learned to act as "docents," guiding younger children in the school around their classroom museum. Indeed, the outcomes of the project became public in various ways, with poetry readings, plays, art exhibitions, music and dance performances.

Assessment and Attainment

From the inception of the project, the team grappled with how to assess and evaluate attainment. The school teachers were enmeshed in conventional grading, while the artists saw little necessity to grade at all. Unsure of what to do, yet knowing they would be held accountable, the team invited a school-reform specialist from the local college to help them develop a plan. Through discussion, they realized that they could "formalize" some of their more informal assessment procedures. Both teachers and artists recognized the need to diagnose the children's progress and difficulties continuously and to redirect efforts. Consequently, they developed a form of pupil profiling in which they wrote descriptions of their students' progress, recording over time such things as growth in skills and technical expertise; growth in the complexity of their concepts and ideas, and their ability to carry through and complete their work; growth in their ability to express ideas and support them with evidence; and growth in their independence and cooperative abilities.

In addition, the team worked together to assess attainment by taking evidence from the books, the plays, the musical and dance performances and also from the behavior outside school in the many locations where the children became audiences for art. Here, comments were sought from the parents who attended public displays and from the community resource people. The students were also invited to design their own self-assessment criteria, in effect drawing them in as partners to the recording and appraisal of their own learning. No grades were ever given during the project, and no final assessment interviews were carried out. Rather, the teachers, specialists and artists all gave descriptive feedback to each youngster at appropriate moments, reinforcing, redirecting, praising and helping according to individual needs and within the flow of learning that characterized the school day. The children were quite clear about their accomplishments and about where they needed extra effort and attention. As one fifth-grader said succinctly, "Yeah, it was good. You got lots of good attention. I never did know what those letter grades meant."

A Final Word

Within this kind of learning, the arts became personal symbol systems *and* bodies of cultural knowledge. They evoked curiosity and inquiry and made possible imaginative response. They became integrators of information from divergent sources—complex webs of wisdom and insight. Along the way, as a consequence of these rich experiences, youngsters learned to care about themselves, each other and the ideas and cultures they shared. In summing up the experience, the school principal commented: "This project brought the whole school to life. The cross-curricula dimension has offered us a model to explore further with other grades. It certainly helped our classroom teachers and specialists to work together more effectively. I think working with the artists in this way opened us all to new possibilities for integrating our own learning and knowledge as teachers—in addition to being amazed at what the kids accomplished."

Natural Allies

Part 2: Children, Teachers and Artists[9]

by Judith M. Burton

Introduction: Schools and Culture

While some regard the art world and the school world as remote from one another, each having its own concerns and practices, educators increasingly acknowledge that schools need to look outward. They must harness cultural institutions in the service of education and attempt to dissolve the real and imagined boundaries between the schools and the world of professional artists.[10]

Artist-in-school programs have burgeoned during the second half of the twentieth century. Children have come to experience how artists work and have often been able to carry out joint projects with them. This kind of cross-fertilization and collaboration has many benefits for students, teachers, and artists and performers. Students can enhance their skills and knowledge in the arts, deepen their understanding of cultural diversity and develop a more positive attitude toward the arts. Teachers benefit by acquiring new approaches and ways of working, broadening professional horizons and developing new competencies. For artists and performers, the opportunities to expose artistry to the insights and questions of young people not only augment their incomes and challenge the clarity with which they express ideas, but also allow them to nurture new audiences.[11]

Developing Artist/Teacher Partnerships in the Classroom

The potential benefits of professionally active artists and specialists and classroom teachers working together for the education of children are enormous and critically so these days. This kind of collaborative effort, which calls upon each partner to draw on his or her individual strengths, insights, knowledge and skills, nurtures not only the artistic development of students but also their aesthetic and general education. However, *none of the benefits that potentially accrue from this liaison are automatically guaranteed.* In practice, many problems and frustrations have been uncovered during the conduct of residencies and visits that point to the need for more thoughtful, formative training of artists and teachers and more focused and ongoing professional development opportunities.

The Role of Artists in the Classroom

The professional artist brings into the classroom the aura of the cultural context in which young people live their daily lives. Artists represent living traditions and can raise significant questions both about the past—the roots and traditions from which they spring—and about future practices and concerns. Artists can also raise questions about the relationship between the producers of art and the divergent movements, styles and social institutions that have accommodated them. Our children will shape the future, and no proper understanding of the contemporary world—and of the human culture—seems possible without having some knowledge of the roots and traditions from which various artistic inheritances have grown.

Artists not only bring culture into the classrooms and studios in many, sometimes subtle ways, they also confront traditional notions of excellence by presenting the arts as contemporary, dynamic modes of creation. Through the presentation of their own work or that of others, artists can contest the nature of knowledge and challenge notions of fixed, absolutistic criteria of judgment. Being confronted by artists' practices and works helps young people to understand that forms in art, music, dance and poetry are not only ways to express and communicate ideas but also ways *to have* ideas. The arts are a means for using the imagination to shape thoughts, perceptions and feelings through the human body, sound, paint, stone, clay and words. Moreover, as forms of thought and action, the arts exemplify a range of values that have shaped and added richness to the quality of many lives. Culture is both experiential and intellectual knowledge without which children are not fully educated, sentient and feeling human beings.

The presence of artists in schools can achieve other goals, too. Artists mostly enjoy the opportunity to work together and in collaboration with teachers of various disciplines.[12] Working with other artists often results in the creation of works that transcend the usual boundaries of singular art forms. In addition, within the schools, artists are often given the chance to explore radically new ideas and stretch their ways of thinking and working to meet challenges from science, mathematics and language.

We sometimes forget that the sciences and mathematics are not always about the empirical, quantifiable and analytical; they frequently engage subjective, intuitive and creative insights. Similarly, the arts do not always rely upon the subjective and affective; they also engage analytical and disciplined habits of mind. Because the arts engage human experiences of vast import and divergence, they can stretch toward other arenas of knowledge without transcending them. Because of their capacity to layer and synthesize meanings within unified wholes—"artworks"—they bring hitherto disparate phenomena together and make connections. Because they encourage the work of the imagination, the arts mobilize the mind to curiosity and promote flexibility in thought.[13] Put simply, engaging in artistry, at its best, brings with it the enrichment of knowledge and habits of mind we should surely prize in education.

Artists and performers form bridges to the larger culture, raise important questions about excellence and value and, through their work, challenge the way things are known and conventionally interpreted. Through the arts, they can help students to reflect on ideas, issues and events that are of concern to themselves and to society and to be insightful about the myriad forms through which ideas find expression in the visual, musical, literary and dance arts. Artists and performers can also share with youngsters their personal working habits, their need for discipline and hard work and their sense of enjoyment in accomplishment. They can share how they get their works into the public domain: included in exhibitions, published in books or performed in concert halls. They can also share what it is like to receive appraisals of their work and how they deal with critical reviews. More important, perhaps, the personal contact with artists in schools helps young people to learn that the arts are not isolated and elitist activities resulting in artifacts enshrined in museums and concert halls or entombed in books.

Naturally, many teachers are very wary of the notion that children can work alongside artists and that "apprenticing" can stimulate and nourish a child's ideas and forms of expression. Specialist teachers often worry that if children work alongside artists in fashioning a work, be it mural, dance, musical performance or writing a story, then the youngsters' own creative instincts will be engulfed, and their personal forms will be diverted into those of the artist.[14] Classroom teachers are often similarly concerned that their youngsters will be caught up in what has been termed "undifferentiated mush," in which learning is more fun than purposeful. However, if participating artists are guided in how to offer activities that relate to the general needs and interests of students, and they are sensitive in listening and responding respectfully to youngsters' own concerns, then they can endow a child's creative acts with a validity that extends into the world beyond the classroom.

In a positive sense, by working alongside artists and performers, youngsters can learn much about new art forms, extend their existing skills, learn how to critique their own efforts without feeling unduly frustrated and find out how to present themselves and their work with a serious, professional air. Working alongside artists can reinforce the need for practice, warm up and drill and an openness to exploration and experimentation; it can help youngsters understand more about the need to rework ideas and take them on journeys from inception to completion. Most of all, youngsters learn invaluable lessons about cooperative and active learning. While the teacher may have set much of this in motion, the imprimatur of the outside professional supports not only the teacher's action but also the students' artistic endeavors. In short, with the right kind of preparation and in-school collaboration, the professional artist or performer can become a significant role model for practice and for reinforcement of the significance of making art to the individual child.

Artist Training

Many professional artists who accept residencies or visits go into schools "cold"—without the guidance or support of the school or arts agency that hired them. Without good training opportunities, these artists usually learn on the job through trial and error.[15] Other artists or arts groups do receive special training from agencies or foundations, typically given by other artists who have been in the field or by specialists in curriculum design or child development. Yet such training is often sporadic and limited in scope and depth, inhibited by limited funds for training and by the urgency of getting the artists into the schools.

In the schools, classroom teachers are often too overburdened to offer on-site training, nurturing and critical response, or they may be unsure how to help artists apply the insights they have gained through the training. Thus, since schools make minimal amounts of time available for preparing artists for thoughtful integration into the classroom, it is no wonder that so many feel their work has little long-term impact.

Agencies and foundations need to offer thoughtful training to their artists before sending them into the schools. Although artists who work in schools can teach each other much that is important, their insights are often specific to their experiences, and they can also reinforce bad practice if they lack adequate prior training. Thus, professional artists need the guidance and insights of professional educators to help them prepare for work in schools.

Artist training should not take the form of a "mini" art teacher training course; had artists wanted to become teachers they would have done so! Instead, the role and practices of professional artists in the schools need to be clearly conceptualized, and colleges, schools of education and professional development centers might be solicited to develop courses specifically tailored to professional artists who undertake school residencies. More than anything else, a glaring and present need exists for pilot projects to lead the way in this kind of training.

What would be provided in such training? First, professional artists would benefit enormously from insights about children—how they develop artistically and learn within the various domains. They would profit from the challenge to reflect sensitively on their own artistry—to examine the nature and complexity of their knowledge and skills. Acquiring the skills of dialogue and questioning would not only allow artists to make their insights and knowledge available to youngsters at an appropriate level, but also help children to construct expressive forms. For instance, artists and performers need to pose questions that stimulate curiosity, inquiry and imagination and not "tell" or offer technical recipes to the students. They would benefit from knowing how to activate and reassure teachers and students in domains, such as drawing, painting, dancing and musical performance, that traditionally are threatening to the uninitiated.

In addition, as part of their training, artists and arts groups need insights about how to deal with schools as institutions—their rules, regulations and ways of doing things. They need guidance in how to interact thoughtfully and collaboratively with both specialists and classroom teachers and in understanding the conditions under which teachers must work in their schools—timetables, bells and grade expectations! This helps artists to be clear about their own role and not to confuse it with that of the teacher. It also helps them know how to establish ground rules with the teacher about the nature of their participation: as observer, participant or collaborator. Artists need to know, in principle at least, how they fit within the curricular scheme of things and be sufficiently comfortable with their place in the flow of learning to grapple with the daily details of planning their in-school participation.[16]

Lastly, professional artists in schools need ongoing help and guidance for their efforts. Artists in schools generally welcome visits by other professionals who can observe a lesson and give them a critical opinion. They welcome relationships with teachers in which mutual feedback is ongoing and integral to the development and flow of ideas for the classroom. After their residencies, artists also need feedback from the schools about how well their contributions fit into the curriculum and what long-term effect they had on learning.[17] Agencies, foundations or colleges could provide a valuable service by offering periodic discussion forums with educational profession-als in which artists could ask questions and predicaments could be addressed.

The Role of the Arts Specialist

If professional artists are to be adequately prepared for their work with teachers and students, then teachers too must be prepared. This preparation requires some education or reeducation of arts specialists to help them embrace their dis-tinctive role in the collaboration and not feel resentful or resistant to working alongside a fellow professional. Arts specialists are trained in a combination of arts and education courses at the bachelor's level (B.A.), or they acquire under-graduate training in their artistic discipline (B.F.A.) and add the theory and practice of education at the post-baccalaureate level (M.A.). Thus, specialist teachers in the schools are frequently practicing artists themselves and often tailor their curriculums to their own interests and skills.

While the notion of specialist teachers working with professional artists has been questioned in recent years, such collaborations can potentially be of equally great value to the students and to the artist and specialist.[18] First, by inviting other artists to contribute to their curriculum, specialist teachers can extend the possibilities of their own knowledge and teaching. They can challenge them-selves to explore and reflect on new ideas, even testing new artistic materials and forms that would be difficult or impossible to attempt when teaching in isola-tion. Teachers and artists working together can invite young people to debate significant questions relating to the culture, artistic practice or skills, or to values and judgments. The public meeting of different minds in professional dialogue offers youngsters a practical demonstration of how different vantage points can be thoughtfully discussed.[19] Indeed, a well-done collaboration would establish the specialist teacher with a bona fide role in the wider artistic community, linking the artist's life and out-of-school concerns with those of their students in school. Such a collaboration would help to reduce the profound sense of isolation experienced by specialist teachers and help to build those bridges between the school and the culture that are so necessary for good education.

However, arts specialists must not lose sight of their distinctive contribu-tions in these collaborations. The specialist teacher needs to manage the class, carry through on preparation and follow-up and create the overall context for the professional artist's contribution. After all, the presence and participation of the teacher as an effective partner ensures that rich and long-term learning will take place, both for the teacher and for the students.

Arts Specialist Pre-Service Training

The "art of pedagogy" should be the focus of pre-service teacher training courses for artists. To be effective in the classroom, artists need to be sensitive in learning the art of fitting method and content, pacing it to the needs of students, and showing respect for the capacities and personality of the teacher. Specialist teacher education at its best challenges young artists to rethink the nature of their artistic knowledge—to know it differently, within the context of students at different ages and developmental levels—and to design pedagogical challenges that respect the integrity of their artistic disciplines. The levels of knowledge, insight, imagination and skill that young artists bring to pre-service teacher education programs matter a great deal—the richer and deeper their insights, the more the artists will inform and be informed by the study of developmental, curricular, cultural, historical, contemporary and methodological issues.

Just as the specialist's formative training in the arts should be grounded in an informed understanding of the culture, so too should be their teacher education. Course work should raise, for study, questions about how the specialist discipline relates to the other disciplines on the school timetable, for all subjects offer young people both knowledge and different perspectives on themselves and the world and culture in which they live. Indeed, we are at a stage when expanding knowledge can hardly be constrained within conventional, formal constructs and must be reorganized within new configurations. Thus, only through the full panoply of the school curriculum can youngsters' minds be nurtured in full flexibility, range and depth; only through opportunities to stretch knowledge across disciplines can they be said to be educated.[20] While the art, music, dance and drama teachers should certainly be concerned with transmitting the particular skills, insight and integrity of their own art forms, they should also be able to relate those skills to general learning and to conceive of their work as part of a greater network of enterprises. Schools are institutions of the culture, and the arts form special bridges to that culture—but they are not the only conduits.

Consequently, specialist teachers in training need to learn how to integrate their work with that of other teachers across the curriculum and to understand that the boundaries of distinct disciplines are only social constructs and that the human mind has great need to make connections on a wider scale. Specialist teachers need to know how to use museums and other cultural institutions as part of their work and how to collaborate with other artists in the classroom. This kind of learning should be embedded in courses that help the specialist teachers in training know how to stretch their personal boundaries to work imaginatively with others without feeling engulfed or threatened. Ideally, young people in training would hear about the experiences of professional artists who already work in schools, and they would visit schools with exemplary models in which practitioners discuss their procedures and the pros and cons of collaboration.

Rethinking Formative Training in the Arts for Specialists

Regardless of whether they plan to teach or to be professional artists, young people in specialist training need to be able to envision themselves as active and indigenous contributors to a rapidly changing cultural environment. Today's arts audiences are found not only in traditional venues, such as galleries, theaters and concert halls, but also in community institutions such as schools.

To meet the future needs of artists and society, art schools, colleges and universities need to rethink some of their current practices in formative education programs to make them more responsive to the contemporary environment for both artists and arts specialists. Today's young artists and arts specialists should be encouraged to think of themselves as "humanizers of the environment"— workers in an everyday world who interpret and give narrative meaning to shared experiences, even when they are being subversive! Consequently, the kind of education offered to these young people must increasingly take account of environmental influences usually seen as incidental and left out of the reckoning.

Young artists and performers as well as arts specialists need to be taught how to reflect thoughtfully on their own evolving insights, not simply as a means of enriching the depth of their own practice, but also as a means of communication. It is no coincidence that so many great artists and performers speak so wonderfully about their own work and frequently seek interactions with other artists, often from other disciplines.[21] In short, we need specialists in the arts who have rich artistic and aesthetic insights; minds that are open, curious, insightful and imaginative; and knowledge about their culture in all its diversity. Those who educate young artists during their formative years must themselves possess critical, reflective insights and be able to affirm the influential force of artistic learning in contemporary culture.

The Role of the Classroom Teacher

For classroom teachers, working with professional artists and performers in schools may be something of a mixed blessing. Many teachers have no arts background beyond sixth grade. They see themselves as nonartists and lack confidence in motivating their students in artistic experiences.[22] Other teachers have had such traumatic experiences with the arts, often in their own education, that they fear introducing them into their own classes.

Nevertheless, working alongside artists and performers, especially if in-service training is available to ease the way, can do much to overcome fear and impart new knowledge and skills. To serve classroom teachers well, this kind of learning needs to be carefully paced and long term. Teachers who are helped to acquire confidence at their own pace will grow in their appreciation of the arts and in their abilities to contribute to the collaboration. They will also be able to conceive ways to integrate the arts within the flow of their own classroom concerns and to structure arts experiences within the curriculum. This connection to the classroom and the curriculum draws upon teachers' distinctive pedagogical skills, their knowledge of curriculum development and the design of sequences that lead to good learning. To accommodate the visiting professional, the classroom teacher must not only make time available to the visiting artist or performer but also carry through on the support work, both before and after, that makes such experiences educationally successful.

Within this kind of collaboration, the professional artist may provide the specialist expertise, and the classroom teacher may help to construct the networks or connections to other subject areas. To succeed in this role, classroom teachers need to be imaginative and insightful about possible cross-disciplinary learning, and they need to know about the *multiple layers and depths* at which the integration of concepts and ideas can take place. They need to be insightful about "distinct forms of knowledge" and know how to work toward new interrelationships and synthesis. Above all, classroom teachers need to be skilled in what the philosopher Karl Popper called the "logic of the situation"—opening new perspectives on problems and issues in such a way that isolated bits and pieces of knowledge find wider contexts in new and useful unities for the children they teach.[23] If classroom teachers are to be effective, they need to be full-fledged collaborative partners, guiding the work of the visiting artist or performer into the flow of curriculum and learning concerns. Successful collaborations do not happen automatically. They are the products of careful planning, commitment and ongoing practice and reflection.

Classroom Teachers: Training for Work with Artists

The training of the general classroom teacher, at whatever level, should also be framed by an understanding of the cultural context within which they will practice. Unhappily, even casual travelers to Europe these days remark upon the knowledge of language and culture they find among young people that is missing in their American peers. Critics claim that the kind of rote skill learning offered to children in many American schools is less demanding than the type of education offered in other countries.[24] Perhaps the lesson is that, as in many European countries, all classroom teachers should be knowledgeable about their culture and its rich diversities, and they should be trained in the arts, the bridges to culture.

This does not mean rigorous, professional training, but training that offers sensitive and thoughtful insights about the arts and their contribution to what has been called the "thinking curriculum." Such training should not be acquired through reading alone, but through reflection, discussion and visits to museums, concerts, etc. In addition, training should also include opportunities to work with artists' materials to develop an understanding of how they can be transformed into visual, musical, movement and dramatic ideas. Teachers in training should also have opportunities to meet with professional artists and performers (in fact, all professionals, i.e., scientists and mathematicians) to learn about their work habits and professional lives.

While classroom teachers need not become great artists, they do need to be given opportunities to try their wings, to acquire confidence and to appreciate the power of artistic ideas and the potential of aesthetic experiences to link other disciplines. Ideally, all teachers should be imaginative in putting their talents to work beyond conventional subject matter. Engaging in what Jackson calls "transformative teaching" helps youngsters to "transform knowledge" into their own constructs of thought and action.[25]

If teachers are to be adequately trained to accommodate visiting professionals within their classes, then artists, specialists and classroom teachers should be brought together from time to time during their formative education—to reflect, to try out ideas and to learn how to plan together. From each of their distinctive perspectives, they might discuss where ideas come from and the skills involved in sequencing them. For instance, they might explore ideas about rhythm as it relates first to human biology and anatomy and then to the symbol systems of music, language, drawing and dance. They might experiment with how the materials of the musician, visual artist, poet and dancer can shape ideas about rhythm and its artistic functions. They might learn how to move flexibly from visual to verbal to musical and movement ideas and learn how each is distinctive yet thematically connected. Finally, they might reflect on how best to make insights about rhythm available to youngsters through appropriately paced use of language and dialogue. This kind of interchange and mutual learning is possible if the colleges and universities commit themselves to this kind of work and foster such collaborative training in pre-service education.

In-service Training

Interdisciplinary learning that involves the arts and professional artists is much easier to promote, of course, if teachers have been exposed to the concepts in their formative training. For the most part, unhappily, this is not the case, and teachers need considerable in-service or professional training on the job. At present, such training is often combined with sessions to plan visits and residencies and is usually carried out by nonexpert personnel hired by agencies or foundations or by the professional artists. Curiously, many arts organizations, agencies and foundations mistakenly believe that teachers need training in the arts more than artists need training in pedagogy. Such beliefs often lead to conflict and confusion, creating resistance and closure to the possibility of collaboration.

Ideally, in-service training should be a *collaboration* between practicing classroom teachers and practicing artists. It should consist of artists teaching teachers and teachers teaching artists, each offering their professional insights and skills, fashioning joint and separate responsibilities and charting the learning to be accomplished during a residency or visit. For example, classroom or specialist teachers have much to teach the artist about the children in their classes: their developmental capacities, prior experiences in various art forms and individual student idiosyncrasies. The teacher will have much to say about how the classroom or studio might be set up for activities, how learning might be paced and sequenced and the kind of language to which the children will respond best. The teacher might also engage the artist in a discussion about his or her art or about aesthetic ideas for stretching toward other subject disciplines. In response, the artist could question how far particular groups of youngsters might be expected to pursue their ideas and suggest activity models for teachers to contemplate. Artists might also engage the teachers in prior explorations of activities so that together they can discover pitfalls and possible extensions. Artists might also invite teachers to read certain texts, visit museums or carry out supportive activities in the classroom as companion learners or presenters. Together, artists and teachers should decide on their in-classroom relationship and expectations for discipline and learning, and they should chart lines of authority so that youngsters understand clearly and feel supported by the different contributions of both. Additionally, teachers and artists together should examine their goals and expectations and plot how they will know whether they have achieved them.

Of course, all this takes time, and a residency will only fulfill its goals and expectations if it arises from proper planning. Indeed, the residency will profit enormously if the school principal and some of the parents also participate in its planning. In the end, the school principal is responsible for making possible this kind of planning time in the service of the students' rich education.

Natural Allies

If we fail to educate all children in and through the arts, we risk the collapse of our finest inheritance—our culture, separate and shared.[26] Today's education cannot simply be a denial or handing on of the past; past and present must be re-linked, active, positive and thought of as multifaceted. The new enterprises of education must have an all-round partnership between classroom teachers, artists and specialists. The kind of personal involvement by teachers, professional artists and performers—committing and sharing their thinking and actions to educate young people in schools—would go a long way toward making classrooms dynamic and humane places. Such partnerships need to be formed within new perspectives and educational practices, new insights about children and how they learn and new thinking about artistic content, methodology and its relationship to teaching. Such partnerships also need to be forged and strengthened by constructive feedback and assessment that promote ongoing individual learning and active collaboration. All of this, of course, will affect the way in which artists and teachers are educated and the ongoing professional development and support they receive throughout their careers.

As the new voluntary National Standards are incorporated into curriculum structures, we must be careful that they do not lead back to the rote habits and isolationist practices of the past. We must also work to ensure that the movement to rework assessment and evaluation in education does not take what Jackson calls the "engineering point of view," for the arts are among those arenas of knowledge and practice that are not amenable to precise fragmentation and objective certainty.[27] The search for evaluative precision, which relies on quantitative and empirical data, often backfires by promoting the kind of learning that is remote from the personal contexts of perception, thought and action that it is to inform.

As Dewey has pointed out, to teach well we need to be conscientious students of our own practice. We should have learned from recent history that the role of schools today has changed: they are asking that we do more and different things, for more and different people, for longer than ever before. This means that we must honor diversity in schools as well as outside and acknowledge that teachers, artists and performers, working in collaboration, can design the kind of imaginative curriculum for learning in which youngsters can be linked to their culture. If it is well done, then youngsters will acquire skills in the symbol systems that enable them to make sense of themselves, others and the world in which they live. They will be able to say about that world what is in their hearts to say. In this endeavor, teachers and artists are natural allies.

Natural Allies

Part 3: School Planning Guidelines for Visiting Artist Curriculum Initiatives

Commitment

- Is the school *committed* to a curriculum endeavor involving visiting artist(s)?
- Is the artist's participation envisioned as *integral* to the general curriculum of learning?
- How will the artists be chosen? Do they have a *clear conception* of their roles and how they will fit within the routines of the school?

Preparation

- Have clear goals been set for the residency experience?
- Has sufficient time been allocated for detailed *planning*, preparation, follow-through, feedback and assessment?
- Have clear roles been defined for participation and *collaboration* of all participants in the residency?

- Are adequate *facilities* and materials available for the work of the residency?
- Have the artists met students in advance of working with them?
- Is the anticipated learning calibrated to the *developmental needs* of students?
- Have activities been planned that span practical (studio/performance), theoretical (appreciative, i.e., aesthetic and critical) and integrated (across the arts or/and other subject matter disciplines) learning?
- Have activities been planned that involve parents or community members?
- Are assessment and evaluation planned as ongoing features of the residency?

Communication

- Do all participants in the residency feel comfortable with each other's role and expertise?
- Are plans made for ongoing *conversation and dialogue* among all participants with a view to keeping goals aligned, learning on track and assessment focused?
- Are *parents involved as learners* and in supportive roles?
- Are there plans to publish a *narrative account* of the residency, or mount a final show/exhibition so that the school community can appreciate accomplishments?
- Are new residency initiatives planned to *grow out of, build on and compliment* prior initiatives?

Training

- Are *in-service opportunities available* for teachers who wish to become involved in residencies—short- or long-term?
- Is the training sequential and detailed, and does it involve both artists and teachers working *actively and collaboratively*?
- Are there opportunities for artists to *reflect* on their artistic-aesthetic knowledge and practices and to learn how to extend their insights to young people from different cultures, ages and developmental stages?
- Are there opportunities for specialist arts teachers to learn how to use the complementary insights and practices of visiting artists to *extend the horizons* of their own specializations?
- Are there opportunities for classroom teachers to learn how to use the arts as catalysts for rethinking the boundaries of subject matter, for exploring new *interdisciplinary possibilities* and for promoting richer learning?
- Is *ongoing support and education* available to classroom teachers, specialist arts teachers and artists following their formative or pre-service training?

Dr. Judith M. Burton *is an internationally recognized scholar, lecturer, author, and a highly respected "developmentalist" known for her research on the artistic-aesthetic responses of children and adolescents. Her widely acclaimed series "Developing Minds," published in* School Arts, *has become essential reading for art education students and teachers across the country. She has taught in public schools and universities in Great Britain, France, Portugal, Canada, Brazil and the United States. Currently, she is Professor and Chairman, Arts and Humanities at Teachers College, Columbia University, where she has co-founded the Center for Arts Education Research. Previously, she chaired the Department of Art Education at Boston University. Dr. Burton was raised and educated in London, England, where she studied painting at Hornsey College of Art and Education at the London University Institute of Education and at Manchester University. After coming to the United States, she earned a doctorate degree from Harvard University Graduate School of Education.*

The Role of the Arts and Aesthetic Education in the Classroom— Asking Questions, Seeking Answers

A Conversation with Scott Noppe-Brandon

The Lincoln Center Institute for the Arts in Education (LCI) is in the final phase of a multi-year research and development project for evaluation and curriculum development funded by the Lila Wallace-Reader's Digest Fund. The project has been conducted by LCI in association with Harvard Project Zero and Teachers College, Columbia University. The research has taken place in LCI and in four of the 17 affiliated aesthetic education institutes in Utica, New York; Bowling Green, Ohio; San Diego, California; and Nashville, Tennessee. Two progress reports (September 1993 and August 1995) about the project have been widely distributed, and a four-day conference in March 1996 will consider the results of an effort that is "committed to advancing the knowledge of aesthetic education and its practice [by LCI and its affiliates] in elementary and secondary schools."[28]

According to the August report, the research sought to answer questions such as: Where do aesthetic education programs fit on the map of school and life experiences? What do children derive from the programs that inform their views of art? What is the impact of these aesthetic education programs on teachers and classroom pedagogy? What is the nature and degree of the programs' schoolwide impact?

On April 3, 1995, I met with Scott Noppe-Brandon, executive director of the Lincoln Center Institute in New York City. I had given Scott four generic questions to address regarding artist-teacher partnerships in the classroom from his vantage point and through the filter of the LCI aesthetic education philosophy. They were:

- What are the factors that contribute to a successful partnership?
- What do you see as the greatest obstacles?
- What solutions have you found that worked?
- Do you have a working definition of an ideal artist/teacher partnership (chemistry, time, scheduling, activities, etc.)?

Scott and I have both been dancers and educators, and like many of our dancer/educator colleagues, we share a tendency toward philosophical rumination and the habit of answering questions with more questions. If you are looking for a neat sequential line of pat answers, you will not find them. Instead, you will find a series of responses and further questions that frame the complexity of the issues. Given the many different approaches to the arts and education behind the classroom door, I doubt there ever will be definitive answers. That is part of the excitement of this continuing research and development journey that some of us have chosen to take.

Jane Remer: What factors are you finding that contribute to a successful partnership in the classroom?

Scott Noppe-Brandon: As you know, the Lincoln Center Institute has always been based on having teachers as collaborators with artists. Our premise has been that by providing teachers with training in aesthetic education, we could equip them with what they need to enter into an ongoing partnership with teaching artists. But it's not that easy to create a relationship where there is shared authority and the high level of communication that is important to a relationship's success.

I want to know about the conditions for building better partnerships, and the Institute is examining that from two perspectives: How can we improve our process for training teachers? And how can we, as an institution, build better partnerships with schools?

Part of our work with the Lila Wallace-Reader's Digest Research Project includes an examination of partnerships and collaborative efforts. At the Nashville Institute, as part of the project, we have been examining the relationship between the school, the arts specialist, the teaching artist and the Institute. We are asking a number of questions: How do we explain ourselves to one another? How do we grapple with different philosophies of education and arts in education? How do we see the arts fitting into the school day? How can the arts specialist and the teaching artist complement one another in the classroom?

We are finding that one of the strengths of the partnerships we build at the Institute is that teachers begin the program as students. They come into the program at summer session, and they take classes. By allowing them to be in that situation for a few weeks, they are encouraged to drop their "teacher/I-am-already-a-professional" hat and just learn. We put them into an environment that immerses them in the arts and activities related to specific performances, and that allows them to have a visceral and intellectual relationship to the arts—one that they might not have had if they had come into the program thinking "How am I going to connect this back to the curriculum? What am I going to do with my students?"

The downside of this structure is that the teaching artist, from the beginning, starts to take on the status of "I know" and "I have information; you're the novice." Part of the problem is that this relationship, which works during the summer session, doesn't transfer well to the school year. Yet once the teaching artist goes into the school, that model has been established, and everybody expects the teaching artist to resume that role. We have to make sure that when the teaching artists go into the classroom, they don't behave as if they have the answers and teachers and students should be the obedient learners. That doesn't give the teacher or the students the tools they need to trust their perceptions and integrate what they've learned.

JR: In your artist training component, are you dealing with instructional design and partnership development issues directly?

SNB: In our training of teaching artists, we are studying ways to include an understanding of educational approaches being used in the schools. That knowledge is important, because even the best teaching artists will go into a classroom and forget that teachers have their own, equally important ideas.

We've involved teachers in training teaching artists. We are providing much more information—on child development, classroom management, questioning techniques, methods of inquiry, and reflective practice—as part of the teaching artists' training. They cannot use the "I'm going to stand in front of you and deliver information" model; they need to have a two-way interaction with the students, and they cannot *control* the interaction if they are going to do it well. Fortunately, the teaching artists are accepting this and we've learned a lot from them as they've started to use it.

On the other side, to help strengthen the teachers' authority in the partnership, we are starting to build into their training the idea of "co-learning." We are trying to find out what happens when the teachers and artists are really co-learners in the summer session. Yet an inherent conflict exists in that approach because the teacher does not teach during the summer session, the teaching artist does. So, we are looking at ways to make the structure more conducive to full partnerships.

JR: ArtsConnection [in New York City] has begun to address this issue in its summer and year-round institute for teachers. They are finding that it is possible and desirable to immerse the teachers in an arts discipline and, at the same time, give them the opportunity to design and lead classroom activities in that discipline as well as relate it to other areas of study. They are conducting research to determine whether the teachers, now armed with these "field-tested and critiqued" practices and activities, can return to the classroom and implement them successfully. ArtsConnection has also instituted follow-up supervisory visits by master artist teachers and educators for feedback and support.

SNB: We are discovering that part of the problem with these partnerhips is informational; part of it is attitudinal. If the teachers who come into the program immediately adopt the "I don't know, you do know" position, then it is much more difficult for the partnership to be established. We're not going to rid ourselves of that situation completely, because it contains a certain degree of truth. The teachers *don't* know as much as the teaching artists do about the arts. Since the program's premise is that you learn to respond to a work of art by learning to understand and believe in your own perspective, the teaching artist should be modeling ways for the teachers to do that. But we want them to be able to do that without projecting the attitude, "I am the expert; listen to what I tell you."

We are finding that reflection and inquiry are as important in building the teachers' understanding and confidence as experiencing the work of art. I would even go so far as to say it should be a 50-50 balance between the two. Inquiry and reflection stimulate questions and dialogue; they deepen the experience with the work of art. The more time you spend deepening the experience, the more it seems that people shed their "you know, I don't know" coats and you start to get more equal participation. You see, then the relationship is no longer expert and novice, it's really explorers. I think this approach is starting to change the process.

JR: Tell me about some of the obstacles you encounter.

SNB: So much depends on the level of commitment of the teachers and the schools. And that, we've found, correlates strongly with their understanding of how the program might work with their own educational strategies and philosophy. Both the school and the Institute need to give these teachers the time it takes to build the understanding that is necessary for a collaborative environment. Very few schools are able to give that kind of time, although many have the interest and desire.

In many schools, the second-grade teacher doesn't know what the third-grade teacher is doing. Yet I don't think discussion about collaboration is productive unless there is an overarching, driving philosophical notion for people to argue about. If the participants don't first come to grips with the underlying implications of the concept of collaboration, the arts—or any central theme or idea—may be treated simply as a license to add or subtract from the subjects being taught, rather than as an opportunity to engage in a process that is potentially transforming.

JR: There *are* schools which have identified the arts as central to the curriculum, even a driving force for school improvement. Many of these schools have developed effective organizational partnerships with the arts and cultural communities, and instructional partnerships in the classroom. How does this fit into your experience with partnerships?

SNB: I guess that if you looked at those environments, you would find a solid block of teachers and the administrator in that school willing to talk about issues beyond how many students are in the classroom. I know that's true for the schools in which our program is most successful. They are trying to figure out why they are bringing the Institute program into the school, how it affects learning, how it affects teaching and what impact it has on the kids and the school.

I think the cultural organization needs to discuss these issues with the school. We can merely define our interactions in structural terms—are we going to meet six times—and that's it, or we can say, we are going to meet to discuss: Why are we doing this? What is its origin and philosophical purpose? What are we trying to accomplish? What are we trying to learn from one another? Why is it valid?

JR: I agree with this philosophical approach, but then I wonder about the time and opportunity for significant instructional impact. If I understood you correctly, the summer session lasts three weeks, then the artist returns to the classroom for...

SNB: Sixteen days is probably the norm for a school. The average school has two units, and each unit averages four days of teaching for the artist and four for the teacher—eight days per unit. So in a school doing two units, there would be 16 days of teaching, plus two planning meetings and two performances—one for each unit. The premise of our collaborative effort is that a teacher and a teaching artist should jointly plan the instructional activities for the kids. So if the teaching artist teaches four sessions, then the teacher also teaches four sessions on his or her own.

JR: Nevertheless, do you think it is realistic to expect that a classroom partnership of any instructional depth, scope and durability will emerge from such a short period of time, especially when none of the experiences are co-taught?

SNB: Again, we have to ask, what levels of involvement do the teacher and the organization want? My intention with this program was to set a minimum standard for commitment: you must participate "x" number of days per year or you cannot participate in the program. Right now every participating teacher must complete the three-week experience and conduct at least two units of study in the classroom, with each unit having a performance and a minimum of six instructional sessions built around that performance (three by the artist, three by the teacher). Many schools are happy with that program. Yet what they get out of that experience does not utilize the full potential of the program.

Our current structure works well: it has the right educational concepts; it is based upon partnerships; and it has a good rationale and a sound aesthetic philosophy. Yet what does it ultimately achieve in terms of making aesthetic education not just a service to schools but an integral part of education?

Through our support from Lila Wallace-Reader's Digest Fund and other funds, we have established focus schools in which we are doing research. We are examining whether and how the impact of our program, which is normally classroom-centered, could be magnified if it were linked to the rest of the curriculum, if it permeated the school and extended into the community as well. The Institute is trying to create program intensification models by working in a deeper, richer way with schools that want more from us. We have been fortunate to be able to conduct this work as part of a research project, which means that the models we create don't necessarily have to succeed. This project is about documenting the process, learning from it, and using that information to continually improve the program in the future.

We are investigating questions such as: Why do educators want this educational concept in a school? How can they own it? How can we help them to own it? What does it mean for a school to adopt aesthetic education beliefs? I believe that we all have to try to build good schools, but I don't think the arts need to be at the center of the curriculum any more than other subjects. For myself and for arts organizations, the Lincoln Center Institute included, I think the critical questions are: When and how does an outside organization help teachers start to bridge the gap between being a student learning in and about the arts and being a teacher concerned with curriculum, classroom sequential units and a curriculum framework? What can we do to help facilitate that process and to understand that process better?

JR: Who do you find more reluctant to engage in this reflective, potentially subversive change process, the artists or teacher?

SNB: Often it is difficult for both. Many wonderful people work in this program who are fine artists and educators. But the teaching artists often try to accomplish things that have nothing to do with the basics of the program, which involves a true partnership and engagement with the needs and structures of particular schools. Some artists want to be missionaries and bring a kind of freedom to the students, but tightly structured schools aren't necessarily bad learning environments. The artists also have to remember that they are not teaching from a formalist base. Our program is not about teaching the fundamentals of an art form. They are not training dancers, so they don't have to teach them to do a perfect plié—for instance.

With the teachers, I think it is more an issue of getting them to trust their own knowledge and perceptions. Several years ago, we thought there was a problem with the music part of our program. We brought teachers together with teaching artists to talk about what they saw and heard. They spoke well and at length, but at a point when the teachers thought they didn't have the right words, they shut down. Many of them feel that as the teacher, they are supposed to be the expert; otherwise, they can't teach it. The Institute doesn't expect them to be experts, but we do want them to develop the habit of mind to start asking all kinds of questions and having a curiosity about music. It is about developing the inquiry process.

JR: Do teachers stumble over the term "aesthetic education?"

SNB: Sure. What is it? Our new working definition is: Aesthetic Education is the cultivation of a discriminating appreciation and understanding of the many forms of art and experience. It involves direct encounters with selected works of art, experienced under optimal conditions. Over time such experiences contribute to the development of aesthetic literacy. This is the capacity to perceive and respond imaginatively to works of art; an openness to aesthetic experiences; knowledge of the forms of aesthetic expression; and the ability to draw personal meaning from works of art.

JR: If you could define the ideal—the nirvana—instructional partnership, how would it look? What would teachers be doing, what would the artists be doing?

SNB: Teachers who participate in the program assume a variety of roles in the classroom. After they participate, some teachers immediately want to connect to other subject areas in which they are most comfortable; these teachers are the *curricular contextualists.* They try to surround a work of art with its social context, especially if they see this approach as influencing the way they teach other subjects. Other teachers want to be *teaching artist helpers,* since they could never do what the teaching artist does. They try to do follow-up based on what the teaching artist did, rather than rely on their own thinking or their own discovery. Finally, there are *co-teachers,* who think that they understand the context and concept well enough to look at the work of art and work with the teaching artist to come up with activities for the kids.

JR: What about the role of artists as facilitators and resources, rather than as direct providers of the service? Educators frequently ask this question, especially when the issue of institutionalization comes up. They want to know at what point it is reasonable to expect that the teachers (specialists, classroom teachers) will have learned enough to carry most of the burden, the responsibility and the leadership themselves, using the artists as resources. It is the whole issue of dependency. On the other hand, what happens to "the creative use of community resources," the imperative in which I believe. It is a dilemma—institutionalization (self-sufficiency) versus partnership, which values sustained cooperation with community resources, but which, in the extreme, can lead to dependency.

SNB: I have had administrators ask me, "When do teachers graduate?" We have had teachers who have been back every summer for 19 years, and they clearly don't feel they are ready to graduate. They *still* want the teaching artist in the classroom. In these situations, I guess that the teaching artist's role is very different from the one with a first-summer teacher. We probably should reconsider the relationship with teachers who return regularly, because there may be some codependency. Yet, I also believe that schools *should* work with their communities' resources, and so you have to strike a balance.

JR: Have you thought about the possibility of restructuring the concept of the artist/teacher collaboration into three phases: an initial period of artist dominance during which basic skills and concepts are taught; then a middle period of equal, shared responsibility, or co-teaching; and a third (and in my view, ideal) period in which the curricular and instructional leadership shifts to the teacher, with the artist serving as a living example and an instructional resource to larger curricular objectives?

SNB: We have started to talk about that as a model. In the focus schools, we are also studying the effect on the nature of the relationship when the faculty takes on more responsibility in the beginning. We are trying to see if we can create some models that work for us.

JR: As I mentioned before, ArtsConnection has begun working in this direction. You might want to compare notes. This is such an important discussion for the field to have because it addresses the pressing issue of developing a paradigm for curriculum design and instruction—teacher as authority and student as receiver of wisdom, teacher and student as colearners, and teacher as coach, facilitator and resource with the student responsible for charting the instructional journey. These are three very different operational models of contemporary education, representing three very different political and social belief systems.

But, back to practice, I still wonder whether a three-week summer period plus the amount of time the artist spends in the schools is sufficient to build the kind of collaborative relationship that we are talking about, much less the teacher-as-leader/artist-as-resource model.

SNB: Education has many, very complex problems. To assume that we are going to come into a school with short-term arts experiences and turn that institution around is probably unwise. So we have to define and accept what we *can* do and congratulate ourselves for the good work that we are doing. I think the Institute is in a very interesting period: we want to do more work and be more involved in the schools, but we also need to spend time exploring what kind of program can tap into the substantive educational issues. These issues have no easy answers. The best we can do is get our program into the schools, ask good questions, rework the structure when it is needed and be honest with ourselves.

JR: One final question: Where do you position the Institute and its work in the context of Goals 2000, the national research agenda, the voluntary standards, and the like?

SNB: If you view Goals 2000 as a public policy document, I am glad the arts are in it. I am thrilled that we can say we, at least on paper, are equal with the other subject areas, and that people are spending time thinking about the arts in the schools.

Yet, I have some concerns about the standards themselves. When I first read the standards, looking at grades 4, 8 and 12 and what was expected at each level, especially in the arts, the expectations seemed to be unachievable. For example, students are expected to compose in three different languages. I don't know whether any Juilliard students would be that sophisticated.

I also think the balance between making and responding was skewed way too far toward making. I believe—and that's why I am with the Lincoln Center Institute— that responding to art is an equally important activity.

For me, the question is, what do you need to create a good school? In that sense, the standards become somewhat meaningless because they don't give the answers. The answers are much more complex and individual. I am reminded of a conversation I had with a supervisor several years ago. I asked whether the standard of teaching had gone up as a result of the work by organizations that are helping people in how to teach the arts. She replied that she used to see a lot of students tracing their hands to make turkeys for Thanksgiving, but she doesn't see that as much any more. Now she sees teachers talking about the life of Picasso or getting kids to understand Impressionism. It may not be taught well, but at least they are not tracing turkeys.

So I think the standards will raise the ante a bit. Public policy in the arts, and learning in general, is a tough terrain.

JR: Any last thoughts on Nirvana?

SNB: I think we will know more as the research on the local schools comes in, but each Nirvana will look different. Most important, you have to keep questioning yourself and the process you are going through. If you think you have the answers, then you are shutting out the solutions under the misguided notion that you are already creating something excellent, whether it is or not. If it were easy to do, a lot of smart people would have figured it out a long time ago. We have to continue to be curious and honest.

In the Lincoln Center Institute's August 1995 progress report (on page 9), a quote from an introductory note sets the tone of the curricular framework that has been designed by a team from Teachers College. It is an eloquent and an elegant statement by Dr. Frances Schoonmaker about children and the value of the arts to their lives, and worth citing here:

> Those who work with children and youth in our schools have the ethical responsibility to treat them as human beings who have...capacities that need to be developed and expressed. Students long to be in a relationship, to belong, to be loved and cared for. They struggle with the drive for independence and the desire to be taken care of. They experience the fear, loneliness and terror of pain, separation, abandonment and death. They search for order, form and pattern in their lives. They try to make sense out of experience and find appropriate forms for expression of a range of deep emotion.

Those who work with and care for them need to help them have faith and hope in a world that is complex, sometimes harsh and infinitely interesting. Through art, human beings have struggled to give expression to their own experiences in interpreting their multi-faceted world. And through aesthetic engagement with art, we can equip children and youth to imaginatively engage with life as they encounter it.

Amen.

Scott Noppe-Brandon *is the Executive Director of the Lincoln Center Institute in New York City where he coordinates all aspects of the Institute's development. In addition he serves as the project director for several long-term research efforts: among them a five-year Evaluation and Curriculum Development Project in aesthetic education, underwritten by the Lila Wallace-Reader's Digest Fund, in association with Harvard Project Zero and Teachers College of Columbia University. Prior to 1987, he was a consultant to such agencies as the Ohio Arts Council, developing arts-in-education programs with special emphasis in program philosophy and structure, curriculum and criticism. He received a B.A. in Arts Education from Ohio State University and has completed course work for a Ph.D.*

The Challenge and Promise of Integrated Curriculum and Transfer of Learning

by Carol Fineberg

High school students study four novels, write scenes based on those from the novels under the guidance of a seasoned playwright, see their scenes performed in staged readings, and in the process develop a deep understanding of the novels, the authors' techniques, the issues of changing an original work from one art form to another, and so on.[29]

Third-graders and their teacher devote Tuesday and Friday afternoons to a series of ten-week arts-in-education residencies: they compose original music about their lives in New York, create original art that describes their neighborhood, learn ethnic and folk dance, and practice storytelling with a professional actor.[30]

Students practice counting through dance and music, recreate their ABCs with painting and body movement, and try to understand Colonial America better by portraying the people and events of that era.[31]

Elementary and middle school teachers spend a week during the summer planning extended arts activities with artists; when they return to school in the fall, they introduce puppet making, mural making, dramatic improvisation and playwriting to their students along with social studies, science and math units.[32]

Teachers learn in workshops how to make art a tool for learning other subjects. They learn to make art accessible to students, and they use the arts to teach language arts, social studies, science and math.[33]

The above vignettes only hint at ways in which teachers and students reckon with the challenge of developing an arts-integrated curriculum. They illustrate how the arts and other parts of the curriculum interact. They also remind us that teacher preparation and the time set aside to plan collaboratively and discover connections are as important as the time artists or arts teachers spend with students.

What do we mean by an arts-integrated curriculum (referred to hereafter as an integrated curriculum)? Educators, evaluators, funders, artists, arts organization heads, parents and advocates of arts education all encounter the language, if not the practice, of integration when they talk about the benefits of arts in education. Part of the barrier to understanding integration is found in the terminology usually associated with it. Recently the Southern Arts Federation, in an attempt to develop a common language for integration advocates, included integration in its definition of arts in education as "the process of incorporating the arts into the general curriculum."[34] The Galef Institute in Kentucky recently described the process of integrating the arts and the general curriculum: "Teachers use the arts as a vehicle for teaching academic subjects beginning with social studies, history, literature and leading ultimately to a fully integrated day, including science and math."[35] Some programs, like New Rochelle's Thinking Through the Arts or New York City's Arts Partners, promise cognitive consequences when teachers and artists collaborate to integrate the arts into classroom activities. They suggest that when arts integration is given an opportunity to work systematically over time, the result is a documentable transfer of learning, from making or composing in the arts to critical thinking or problem solving in one or more of the other academic domains.

An integrated curriculum contains intended teaching and learning in one or more academic domains laced with activities related to the arts. Frequently an integrated curriculum is *thematic* and requires team teaching, including arts specialists and/or the use of community artists. Teachers and artists have developed integrated units of instruction on the theme of the Italian Renaissance, the Harlem Renaissance, the scientific phenomenon of metamorphosis, and math units on shapes and forms using geometric terminology and algebraic equations. In each unit the arts are called upon to illustrate values, events and personalities or to emulate creative processes used by visual, literary or performing artists. Advocates of integrated curriculum presume that students will acquire and internalize knowledge, skills and attitudes better when the arts are included in the process of learning. To offer a successfully integrated curriculum, however, teachers need *at least* the following supports:

Organizational support. Schools must provide teachers and their collaborators with time to plan, time to execute, and time to reflect on and evaluate the outcomes of their teaching. Schools must have a coordinator, someone on the school staff responsible for seeing that these conditions are met. Teachers may need to be exempted from state testing requirements (so they can substitute one assessment process for another). Frequently, teachers and artists need to be remunerated for the extra time that integration takes, and they need appropriate space and time to carry out their work.

Expertise. Teachers and artists need to rely on each other's expertise in content and process. They need to be able to call upon other resources to fill in knowledge, skill or process vacuums.

High standards. Students need to meet rigorous academic *and* aesthetic standards. They need to acquire and apply aesthetic skills, just as they need to acquire and internalize subject area content and processes. Producing 25 identical Kachina dolls from a pattern or slopping paint thoughtlessly on brown kraft paper to represent ancient cave drawings does not exemplify high aesthetic standards. Moreover, dancing in geometric patterns will not substitute for learning how to calculate area, perimeter and volume. Spending a lot of time working on colonial artifacts is only going to be worthwhile if students also understand their meaning and know how these objects symbolize the cultural history and values of a particular time and place. Teachers and artists need to be mindful of the national and state publications that articulate performance and content standards in the various curriculum areas, including each of the arts disciplines.

Characteristics of Integrated Curriculum

An integrated curriculum requires a planning process resulting in learning activities that combine arts making and reflecting with other subject matter traditionally taught in schools (math, science, social studies, foreign language, literature, writing, thinking and reasoning).

Integrated lesson plans may call for students and/or teachers to:

1) include slides of paintings and sculpture to illustrate an idea, a place or a time frame;
2) build architectural structures or choreograph sequences of dance shapes that use some of the mathematical language learned in geometry;
3) compose an original song to illustrate an abstract idea such as patriotism or an historical event such as the drive of Cherokees from Florida to Oklahoma;
4) write a play that includes such literary conventions as exposition, development, climax and resolution;
5) compose a dance to express an historic event such as a battle or an abstract idea such as family values; or

6) improvise a dramatic scene that depicts conflict between warring princes during the Middle Ages in Europe or between South Africans of different groups on the eve of the end of apartheid.

Integration advocates optimistically predict that, as a result of an integrated curriculum, children will understand and use problem-solving processes intrinsic to the arts when solving problems in other domains. While the hope is sincere, the conditions for fulfilling it are both complicated and difficult and depend upon our understanding of transfer of learning.

Transfer of Learning

Basically, transfer of learning requires the learner to apply what he or she has learned in one domain to another. The more remote the domain, the more likely the transfer process will need help. For an illustration of simple transfer, we need to look no further than sports.

A youngster learns to hit a softball. She internalizes the hand-eye coordination. She learns that if she keeps her eye on the ball and tries to connect with it while the ball is still in front of her, then she is likely to hit it smartly. The same youngster is invited to learn how to play tennis. She surprises her instructor by connecting with the tennis ball time after time, once taught the proper stance to address the ball. She simply used what she learned about keeping your eye on the ball at the tennis—a transfer of learning.

Here is a more complex example: A young fellow who knows how to drive a stick-shift car attempts to drive a U-Haul double-clutch truck. The enterprising youth knows enough about hand-foot coordination to apply this skill to driving the U-Haul. After a few rough starts, the truck is on its way.

Arts education advocates are often tempted to describe the arts as a means by which students learn to excel in "academic" domains such as reading, math, problem solving or critical thinking by virtue of their participation in arts programs. In fact, some of the earliest and ongoing arts-in-education programs combined art-making with reading (Learning To Read Through the Arts (LTRTA)[36] or mathematics (Architecture in Math)).[37] Thinking Through the Arts[38] linked a strong art, music, dance and drama curriculum with critical and creative thinking as evidenced by a rigorous testing program. The recent Morrison Institute publication *Schools, Communities, and the Arts: A Research Compendium* includes summaries of studies that point to successful transfer of learning, such as Sherry DuPont's Creative Drama Program in which students improved their reading skills.

Both common sense and good research tell us that in order to transfer skills and knowledge from the arts to other parts of the curriculum, certain conditions have to be in place, and these conditions are not easy to create. They are:

- Clarity of objectives—what skill or knowledge is supposed to transfer?
- Clarity of destination—to what domain are the arts objectives transferred?
- A "pitcher"—a person who will be responsible for teaching the stated skills, knowledge or attitude

- A "catcher"—a person who will be responsible for aiding the transfer process in the new domain
- Time to construct bridges—an opportunity for both the pitcher and the catcher to plan activities to promote the transfer process

When these conditions are present, students (the batters, to keep to the sports analogy) more than likely will be able to hit home runs.

While much transfer takes place outside of formal schooling, transfer of learning in school, especially the *transfer of thinking processes*, can be fostered through the arts. To facilitate transfer, the school must have people prepared to make the connections between domains and to help students reflect upon their own thinking processes. As Perkins points out, research shows that transfer takes place:

> ...when learners are shown how problems resemble each other; learners are familiar with the problem areas; examples are accompanied with rules, particularly when the latter are formulated by the learners themselves; and, perhaps most important, learning takes place in a social context that encourages learners to spell out principles, explanations, and justifications.[39]

Schools that wish to use the arts as a means of facilitating transfer of learning need to engage process facilitators—pitchers and catchers. Pitchers are often teachers or teaching artists who have an objective that they would like students to achieve; they offer the catcher an opportunity to collaborate in a project to fulfill the objective. Catchers are also teachers or teaching artists, but their areas of expertise usually differ from the pitchers. A pitcher might be a social studies teacher; a catcher might be an artist in residence or the school's art or music teacher. A familiar pitcher-catcher transaction might revolve around developing a coordinated unit in the social studies curriculum that requires specific skills and understanding to be acquired. (If this also sounds like the makings of an arts-integrated curriculum, it is!) The pitcher might throw to the catcher a challenge to reinforce map-reading skills or to interpret cartoons. The art teacher— the catcher—might then develop a unit on mapmaking or cartoons and help students develop visual symbols for ideas and events stemming from the social studies unit. Thus the students are given an opportunity to transfer what they have learned in social studies to the art room, where they apply their knowledge in a new and different symbolic language. For example, when a team of students studied the effects of environmental protection policies on a city or town, their teacher helped them to discover that simple solutions are not always appropriate. With this understanding they decided to create a photomontage in the art room that showed the many consequences of a deceptively simple solution to water pollution. The art teacher encouraged them to search for the visual language that best conveyed their message.

Transfer of learning is more complex than the baseball analogy suggests. The batter needs the support of both pitcher and catcher to hit a cognitive "home run." Nonetheless, we might say that teaching for transfer is a lot like batting practice.

Table 5.1: Facilitating the Process of Transfer to and from the Arts Domain

	Domain—subject, content, process and objectives	Pitcher—teacher or teaching artist
Site	The visual arts classroom	Art teacher—leads class through an exercise where they analyze the historical and aesthetic elements of three paintings that they have worked on to illustrate life on the prairie during the mid to late 19th century.
Subject	Critical thinking including the process of analysis	
Objectives	Analysis of the various elements of three genre paintings transferred to analysis of historical material	
Site	7th grade math class:	Math teacher teaching that all measurements are approximations to a specific degree of accuracy.
Subject	Measurement	
Objectives	Acquisition of measuring skills using ruler, compass, straight edges transferred to creation of scale models	
Site	HS Music studio	Musician in residence (composer) teaching intervals in 12-tone scale in comparison to other 8-tone scales. Musician points out that the process of inventing a new scale is a consequence of divergent thinking and can lead to a major innovation.
Subject	Musical composition	
Objectives	Exploration of the 12-tone scale as an example of divergent thinking	

© Carol Fineberg

Bridge—the means by which the transfer is assisted; may involve development of a common language, specific activities to promote transfer	Catcher—teacher or teaching artist	Domain—new subject, content or process Nature of intended transfer of learning Learning outcome
Common planning time—the art teacher or artist sits down with the social studies teacher and together they explore the process of critical analysis of a painting and analysis of a passage from a primary source (diaries, journals, newspaper articles) coming from prairie states and territories.	Social Studies teacher—develops lessons that require reading and analysis of primary sources that shed light on life on the prairie in the 19th century.	Social Studies—Students analyze historical material in an authentic assessment process; teacher gives students an excerpt from a primary source to analyze using the skills practiced in both the arts and social studies classes. Students analyze the historical data embedded in selected diaries and journals; they describe the process of analysis and its kinship to aesthetic analysis as practiced in the art classroom.
	Architect in residence: develops model making activities with heavy dose of measuring, guessing measurements, checking measurements, etc.	
Common planning time with history teacher who is teaching unit on 20th-century innovations.	History teacher—develops lessons on 20th-century iconoclasts including musicians who develop different conventions for composition.	Students write essays in history class on other kinds of divergent thinking and are required to format their essays in non-traditional ways (they write about, engage in and reflect on the process of innovation).

In addition to promoting the idea of teachers and their artist/art teacher partners as pitchers and catchers, the school needs to provide time for team meetings so that the process of transfer can be activated in a timely, rational sequence of events. Pitcher and catcher—artist and teacher—must meet (preferably on school turf) to plan common and complementary learning strategies. Together they must devise pathways to enable students to transfer what they have learned in one class to another.

School leadership as well as artists and teachers need to buy in to the promise of transfer by enabling the teaching adults to confer, to practice and to reflect upon their works in progress. School administrators can provide this time to construct bridges between domains, another essential ingredient for transfer. The members of the teaching team must be willing to explore new territory together and be equally responsible for student outcomes.

Table 5.1 demonstrates how this works in real arts-in-education situations. In the first column, "site" refers to the place where the learning for transfer takes place; "subject" is the academic subject taught (i.e., art, music, social studies, math, etc.); and "objective" is the specific skill, understanding or knowledge that students are expected to learn and transfer to another domain. The second column refers to the domain in which the knowledge, skill or understanding is lodged, and in the cell adjacent to "objectives," it contains a description of the intended transfer. The third column identifies the person who prepares students for the transfer process, the pitcher. The fourth column contains descriptions of processes that help to bridge or link the domains for transfer, and the fifth column describes the facilitator, or catcher, who will help to ensure that students apply knowledge, skills or understanding from one domain to the next. Finally, the sixth column—Domain: new subject, content, or process and learning outcome—describes the nature of the intended transfer of learning and the expected student behavior. This matrix should be a helpful planning template for those who wish to design activities for transfer of learning. Teachers and artists can fill in the cells according to their own specialities and expertise.

Regardless of whether transfer is initiated by artists or teachers, the purpose is to enable students to increase their knowledge, skills and understanding of multiple domains by applying what they learn in one domain to another. This self-conscious process of transfer adds to their intellectual power and their capacity to think imaginatively.

Detecting and Documenting Transfer of Learning

How do we know when intentional transfer of learning has occurred? If we ask students the content of their decision-making process, we frequently find clues that suggest transfer has taken place. In addition, we must look for specific, predicted instances where and when the transfer has occurred. This means that we must use either traditional kinds of tests (whether constructed by teachers or professional test designers) or observe how students perform certain identified tasks. We must reflect on the test or performance results and consider whether the performance was a result of planned transfer or serendipity. Only then will it be evident that the arts give learners an opportunity to apply what they have learned in visual, musical, theatrical or literary frames to science, mathematics and the humanities.

We need more research that explores the ways in which the arts facilitate transfer of thinking skills as well as knowledge about and in certain domains. We need situational set-ups where the conditions exist for planning and executing transfer. We need the comparative instruments and procedures to establish that a cause and effect relationship indeed exists. Finally, we need to disseminate the results of this research to a crosssection of educational decision makers: teachers, parents, administrators, and, yes, students. A predicted consequence of this research and dissemination process: the arts will have a stronger foothold in school curricula, and both the arts and nonarts subjects will be better taught and learned.

Conclusion

A curriculum in which the arts are entwined with other academic subjects offers benefits to both learners and teachers, not the least of which is the opportunity to widen and deepen knowledge and skills in more than one domain. While an integrated curriculum does not *guarantee* transfer, with careful and intentional planning, teachers and artists can *plan for transfer*, heeding the need for a transfer support system. It is hoped that as teachers and artists work and plan together for integration, they will ask themselves what they expect students to learn and in what domains. They also need to ask themselves who needs to assist in the transfer process so that students are more likely to demonstrate the transfer in appropriate settings. As the conditions for transfer are established and maintained, teachers will see the power of the arts as an instructional enabler as well as a valuable body of knowledge and skill in itself.

Dr. Carol Fineberg has been involved with the arts-in-education movement since the early 1970s when she served as Project Manager for the New York City Arts in General Education (AGE) program. She established C. F. Associates, a consultant firm specializing in the development of curriculum and instruction, evaluation and assessment, and proposal writing, in order to spread the power of the arts to educate children well. Dr. Fineberg has trained scores of artists to invent and implement integrated curriculum units. She has concentrated most recently on research and evaluation assignments that investigate a causal effect between arts education and cognitive development. A précis of her 1992 study on the arts and cognition may be found in Schools, Communities, and the Arts, *sponsored by the National Endowment for the Arts and the Morrison Institute of Arizona State. A graduate of Smith College, Dr. Fineberg earned her doctorate at New York University's School of Education.*

Arts Partnerships in the Classroom
Some Cultural Considerations
by Sharon Ryan and Sam Shreyar

The word partnership implies a pair of individuals working collaboratively on some joint project, so when one thinks of arts partnerships in classrooms, the image of an artist and teacher co-teaching a group of children often comes to mind. To be sure, teachers and artists play a central role in any arts program being enacted in a classroom but such collaborations do not occur in a vacuum. They operate within a much broader social context, constituted by the school community or culture, its purposes, the ways in which it functions and consequently the actions encouraged and expected of its members.

In other words, an arts partnership in the classroom involves a number of cultures—the culture of the school, the culture of the teacher, the culture of the artist and the cultures of the students—that operate and interact with each other. At the classroom level therefore, arts partnerships are complex and dynamic multicultural interactions occurring within a particular organizational social context.

Our task in this essay is to explore this notion of arts partnerships as the coming together of many cultures in a school and how such an understanding might enhance the way we enact arts programs in schools. Such a task requires that we begin with an examination of what is meant by the term culture and to suggest how it is possible to employ a conceptual model of curriculum approaches to conceive of a school both as a particular culture and at the same time as a multicultural site, within which a number of other cultures operate and interact simultaneously. We then offer some insights from our own experiences in schools working with artists and teachers before turning to how conceptualizing arts partnerships in classrooms as multicultural projects may not only explain some of the barriers inherent in such endeavors but also some of the possible pathways toward meeting such challenges.

Cultures and Curriculum

A culture is an integrated system of meanings, values, standards of conduct and artifacts that shapes and informs the ways people in a society live.[40] Cultures might best be understood as systems with three interrelated levels. At the deep level are value systems and philosophical assumptions. Value systems are akin to theories, they are used to inform individual's choices, priorities and views of the good life; philosophical assumptions are meanings that we attribute to our views of the world, or to our views of ourselves and of knowledge. On the middle level are norms of behavior or patterns of interaction and action. The way individuals in a community behave is informed by the value systems and philosophical assumptions that they hold to be true and valid. On the surface level are the artifacts of a culture or the products resulting from the ways that individuals belonging to a community act in their world. They are expressions that embody the culture's values and norms. Taken together, these three levels inform the processes by which people form communities and live and work together with shared understandings. At the same time, the world is not made up of one culture. Rather, many cultures operate simultaneously in the same space. Each culture is distinguished not by physical boundaries but by its system of values, norms and artifacts.

By thinking about schools as cultures it might be possible to reframe the way we analyze, enact and think about arts partnerships in the classroom. One possible lens through which to conduct this analysis might be an examination of the approaches to curriculum design and enactment used by schools, teachers, and artists. Implicit in any curriculum design are particular values as to the purposes of schools and philosophical assumptions as to what knowledge is of most worth. These purposes and decisions about knowledge are then translated into the goals and means of instruction, the norms of teaching. Similarly, values and philosophical assumptions underpin the perceived role of the students and the nature of the teacher-student relationship. This frames how students and teachers act in the school culture and consequently what knowledge is learned. At the school culture's surface level are the artifacts produced by the culture's members which include things like test scores, grades, portfolios of student's work, texts, performances, works of art and the like. These products or artifacts are dependent on a particular school culture's purpose and the knowledge it seeks to develop in its students. In short, school cultures adopt curriculum designs that best fit their value systems and philosophical assumptions.

Curriculum Conceptualizations: A Continuum

Over the past 30 years, curriculum theorists have developed a conceptual framework that can be used as a guide to make sense of the wide variety of curricula enacted in schools.[41] They have devised three generalized views of curriculum, teaching and learning generally known as transmission, transaction and transformation. Each has its own values and philosophical assumptions that underpin the ways teachers and students act and the artifacts they produce as members of the school culture.

Transmission. The transmission orientation is underpinned by the values of social efficiency. The purpose of the schools is "to create a coolly efficient, smoothly running society,"[42] by preparing students for a particular existing role in that society. The knowledge considered to be of most worth is the antecedent information and skills which will enable children to be more in tune with the adult roles that they will occupy as future citizens. Thus, emphasis is on the accruing of information and the refinement of particular skills determined externally by educators who sift, sort and place students into particular tracks that are related to student's later functions in life. The criteria of efficiency is translated into particular norms of the teaching and learning process. In this orientation teachers are the authority, transmitting the predetermined knowledge and skills to students as efficiently as possible through direct instruction, drill and recitation. The child is expected to be a passive unknower. In part, this vision of the passive, unknowing child can be traced to Locke's views on psychology and education, in which the child is seen as a tabula rasa or a blank slate to be filled with information. In his words, "Let us then suppose the mind to be, as we say, white paper, void of all characters, without any ideas."[43] Just like a computer, the teacher downloads the information, into the quiescent children. The outcomes are judged by whether the children's products are neat and exact representations of the information given. Hence, most schools operating within a transmission model focus on standardized test scores, the external measurement of their efficiency of teaching the information.

Transaction. The transaction orientation to curriculum believes that the purpose of education is to prepare students to participate in the reconstruction of themselves and their society. The knowledge of most worth is that which enables children to reconstruct experiences, to be able to solve problems, so that they might be able to apply their critical thinking skills to the problems within democratic society. Knowledge is not considered as information external to a person's experiences but the process of acting intelligently in experience. John Dewey, a leading proponent of this approach to education, placed knowledge within an interaction between a capable and developing child and that child's material and social environment.[44] Constructivist thinkers like Piaget and Vygotsky also believe that children learn by acting on their environment. That is, children invent or construct their understanding and knowledge of the world by actively exploring ideas, objects and the world of people. In practice, transactional orientations to curriculum engage the child as an active participant in the educational process. Children's interests and developmental needs guide their inquiries and explorations and provide a base for the teacher's educational planning. The teacher's role is that of facilitator, to set up the environment to find points of connection between the child's interests and the curriculum subject matter, the intent being to enhance children's understanding at higher levels of meaning. As such, the teacher and child co-construct the curriculum together in their transactions. Because emphasis is placed on children acquiring deeper understandings of their world, evaluations seek to eliminate static products and focus more on the process of children's thinking skills. Therefore, descriptive assessment practices are used such as portfolios, project work and teacher observations of student's growth and development.

Transformation. Transformational orientations to curriculum view the purposes of education in schools as the transformation of the social and political status quo and aim to address the inequities that reside within the world. Here the knowledge of most worth is that which enables children to see these inequalities and empowers them to change these structures and transform the world into a better one. Therefore, the question of what knowledge is of most worth is expanded to include the more critical questions of whose knowledge is it, whom does it benefit, and why that knowledge? Knowledge is viewed as more than just a process of making meaning, it is a process of critically thinking about the way knowledge is constructed, by whom and why, and implies that individuals take some action in terms of this knowledge. It is education for social action, encouraging students and teachers to understand and challenge the inequalities implicit and explicit in their world. Freire argues that education for critical consciousness refers to "learning to perceive social, political, economic contradictions and to take action against the oppressive elements of reality."[45] Critique, empowerment and agency are the criteria on which educational experiences are created. In practice, the aim is to encourage students to critically question their own implicit theories, the values that determine their actions and facilitate their understanding of the external power structures and of how both of these knowledge sources impact on each other to maintain the way things are. By educating students to be critically aware of the dynamic interplay between their own understandings and actions and other's constructions of the world, the students and teacher then work to create alternatives. The child is an active thinker and also an activist in the classroom and beyond. Assessment of student's development is a negotiated process whereby the teacher and student look for evidence of contribution to action and an ability to respond to the socio-political context within their school and the larger world.

Taken together, these three curriculum orientations can be conceived of as a continuum of the possible worlds in which artists and teachers come together to collaborate on an arts education project. While not every school culture nor every artist-in-residence culture may fit neatly into one of these categorizations of curriculum, this framework serves as a guide for thinking about the relationship between a school culture and the culture of visiting arts programs and the collaborations of artists and teachers in the classroom. What we are suggesting is that no arts partnership in a classroom occurs in isolation. Rather, every teacher, artist, student, school and arts organization has a particular cultural orientation to curriculum, art, teaching, and learning. It therefore follows that not everyone involved in an arts education collaborative program will hold similar cultural beliefs. In fact, in our research with artists, teachers and children we have found that cultural differences tend to pervade arts education partnerships in the classroom.

Many Cultures

In 1994-95 we spent a year working with an artist-in-residence program serving the New York City public schools. In each of the three residencies, we found varying degrees of cultural difference. Often we witnessed clashes between the culture of the schools, the cultures of the artists and the cultures of the children participating in the arts education program. Each of these cultures operated alongside the other with a limited understanding of the differences that separated them. Rarely did we observe members of one culture acknowledging the differences of another culture, and rarely did we observe any attempts to build bridges of understanding between these differences.

The school environments we observed subscribed to a transmission orientation to curriculum. Teachers were expected to teach to the test and to transmit basic skills of reading, writing and mathematics to the students through drill and recitation in order to raise the student's test scores. In these schools the arts were not valued as a basic skill. Aside from children's illustrations displayed on classroom walls, art was not present in the curriculum. These values were so pervasive in the schools we visited that even if teachers believed in transactional or transformational approaches to curriculum or in the importance of art, their practice on the whole reflected the transmission and efficiency values of the school culture. As one of the teachers we worked with commented, "I really wanted to implement a whole language curriculum, but with the need to increase student test scores, I have to focus on traditional approaches to teaching the basic skills as they are best suited to the tests my children will face."

On the other hand, the artists entered these transmission-oriented school cultures with the intent of collaborating with teachers to implement a participatory, transactional approach to the teaching of art. The artists sought to engage children in the constructive processes of creating art, to free them to make meaning from art. As the artists were weekly visitors to the school culture, they had more freedom to implement their beliefs and approaches to education and the arts. Unlike the teachers, they were less constricted by the overriding values of the school culture and so enacted learning experiences that were very different than those experienced by children and teachers in the classroom.

The dominance of the transmission culture of the schools not only constricted teachers in the kinds of curricula and pedagogy they enacted with their students but at the same time was in direct opposition to the aims, intentions and actions of the artists. Consequently, at the micro level of the classroom partnership, artists and teachers were operating from very different points of the curriculum orientation continuum. These cultural differences in approaches to curriculum between artists and teachers were further complicated by the fact that neither of them took into account the cultures of the children.

All of the children who participated in this arts education program came to the school with their own set of understandings, ways of acting and being in the world, that they had learned within the realms of their home cultures. Yet their culturally determined ways of knowing were often ignored, even marginalized in the dominant school culture that focused on transmission and efficiency. For the most part, the curriculum was predetermined, offering little opportunity for children to infuse their own experiences into its enactment. Rarely did we observe teachers using students' ideas or interests as the core from which to design their curriculum. As a consequence, students were expected to be passive recipients of a fixed world of knowledge determined for them by others.

To a lesser extent, the children's home cultures were also overlooked within the artist residencies. While these artists aspired to implement transactional and inclusive arts experiences for their students, for the most part they were only partially successful in this aim. That is, the artists enacted curricula that actively engaged students but as these curricula were derived from the artists' interests and experiences, little attention was paid to the experiences of the children who were participating in the program. For example, one artist attempted to implement a multicultural curriculum by using the dances of North American aboriginal peoples while the children she was teaching were much more interested in the dances of their own hip-hop culture. Instead of including the children's perspective, the artist continued to expect the children to conform to her ideas about the curriculum. Thus, while the children loved the opportunity to move and dance, they were less motivated to participate in the arts curriculum because their interests were ignored. Similarly, a visual artist we observed had children build houses when every one of these children were in fact living in urban apartment buildings. As a result, many of the students had difficulty completing the task, unable to understand what was expected of them as it was outside their lived experience.

The differences between the culture of the schools, and the culture of the artist residencies and the fact that neither paid much attention to the cultures and interests of the students, required the students to make difficult leaps between three cultures. Not only did they have to alter their behavior and ways of understanding of their home culture to survive in the dominant transmission culture of the classroom, but they had to change again when entering and participating in the more transactional culture of the arts programs.

The cultural differences we observed in these particular artists residencies made collaborations between teachers and artists difficult and complex and forced children to undertake sometimes quite difficult transitions. Hence, the aim of implementing meaningful arts experiences for children within the context of their schools and classrooms was undermined. No matter how well meaning an arts program is, the inherent power of the arts in education cannot be fully released without all participants attempting to acknowledge and address these issues of cultural difference and their manifestations in the schools.

Considering Cultures and Building Bridges

Arts partnerships in classrooms are extremely complex multicultural educational endeavors. Successful arts partnerships require that participants recognize and acknowledge that approaches to education and curriculum, including their own, are culturally constructed and therefore not universally shared. But just because there will be inevitable differences does not mean they need to become areas of conflict within an arts partnership in the classroom. Acknowledging that such differences will exist and finding ways to make them visible and understandable to all those involved is a first step to addressing them and thus enhancing the experiences offered to students. We would like to assert that central to any efforts to build bridges of understanding between different cultures in an educational context are knowledge of, and dialogue about, how and why one conceptualizes and enacts approaches to education. As such, the curriculum conceptualizations outlined in this essay offer one framework for dialogue and the construction of a deeper understanding of our work in arts partnerships.

Used as an analytic tool, the curriculum conceptualizations might enable teachers and artists to examine and reflect on their own practice as well as guide their observations and analysis of each other's practice. That is, teachers and artists can think about the values and assumptions they hold about curriculum, teaching and learning and how these values play out in their interactions with students. In the same way, they can observe each other, employing the curriculum conceptualizations to make sense of what they see in the classroom setting. Moreover, artists and teachers collaborating together can use the curriculum conceptualizations as a framework for discussing their respective views about the challenges they face in the enactment of the arts program in the classroom and which conceptualizations might be best suited to include the interests and experiences of the children they serve. In short, observation and dialogue framed by the curriculum conceptualizations is one pathway for teachers and artists to understand their own practice, each other's perspective on education, the context in which they are working and how best to enact a collaborative arts curriculum inclusive of the student's voices.

In this essay, we have only just begun to unravel the cultural and curricular dimensions of arts partnerships in the classroom. However, we believe that examining arts partnerships as multicultural projects offers new insights and illuminates important variables that lead to the success of such collaborations. As such, we believe that more research into this area is required, particularly the recording of teachers', artists' and students' voices about their enactment and participation in successful arts partnerships. In the meantime, we would like to suggest that all of us involved in the world of arts education take time to think about our work as a cultural endeavor. We might also consider what such a perspective offers us in terms of reconceptualizing arts partnerships in the classroom so that every child has access to high quality, meaningful arts education.

Sharon Ryan has over a decade of experience as an early childhood teacher, adviser and consultant in Australia. Receiving the Lillian de Lissa scholarship in 1994 brought her to New York where she is currently a doctoral candidate and adjunct instructor in early childhood education in the Department of Curriculum and Teaching, Teachers College, Columbia University. Her interests include the arts and education, early childhood education, teachers' theory making and reconceptualizing teacher education. She and Sam Shreyar work together as consultants specializing in arts education projects.

Sam Shreyar has an M.A in early childhood special education and an M.Ed. in early childhood education from Teachers College, Columbia University. He is currently working on his doctorate in early childhood education and is an adjunct instructor at Teachers College. His interests include early childhood education, curriculum design and the arts and education. This past year he was awarded the Harry Passow Fellowship. Sam also has many years of experience as a classroom teacher in urban and rural settings in New York State. He and Sharon Ryan work together as educational consultants specializing in arts education projects.

Notes

1. *The Education Commitment* (Washington, D.C.: National Assembly of State Arts Agencies, 1995), p. 13. This booklet provides an overview of the impressive breadth and depth of state arts agencies' work in education, gives many specific examples, provides statistics and is a useful reference tool. Examples include how the SAAs prioritize arts education grant-making, how arts education contributes to education reform, how artist residencies support comprehensive school curricula and how creative partnerships help states achieve their education goals.

2. *Changing Schools Through the Arts: How to Build on the Power of an Idea* (New York: McGraw-Hill, 1982; ACA Books, 1990), pp. 142-143.

3. The description of the Kentucky Arts Council and its technical assistance workshop is based on language and information graciously provided by the council's assistant director, Dennis Horn.

4. Judy Sizemore, *Education Reform Opportunities for Artists and Craftspeople: A Handbook* (Frankfort, KY: Kentucky Arts Council, 1995).

5. The Holmes Group is a consortium of approximately 100 research universities that is investigating issues of teacher education and in-service training in the arts. It is named after a dean at Harvard University. In the view of several arts educators, the Holmes Group represents an opportunity for arts professionals to enter into useful dialogue and perhaps affect national policy and practice. (Based on my 1986 entry in the Chronology from *Changing Schools Through the Arts*.)

6. Junius Eddy has worked in the arts and education field since the sixties. His illustrious career includes stints as Arts Education Specialist in the Arts and Humanities Program of the Office of Education, Department of Health, Education and Welfare; a program advisor and officer at the Ford and Rockefeller Foundations, and as a consultant to the JDR 3rd Fund's Arts in Education Program. Junius is a prolific writer whose many reports, essays, articles and books have chronicled and influenced the development of the field. One of his most influential pieces was "The Upsidedown Curriculum," written for *Cultural Affairs*, a publication of the Ford Foundation, in 1970. In this short piece, Junius reflects on what he and others perceived then as new opportunities for the arts in education. Junius also helped me assemble some precious historical material for the Chronology in *Changing Schools Through the Arts*. See the bibliography for further references.

7. Dr. Jerrold Ross has written extensively about the need for collaboration among generalist, specialist, and the visiting artist. One of his most persuasive essays, "Who Shall Teach the Arts," may be found in the July/August 1986 issue of the journal formerly known as *Design for Arts in Education* and now the *Arts Education Policy Review*. In this piece, Dr. Ross proposes "one *non-governmental* body facilitating the interaction among the three constituencies so often isolated from one another at the most critical time in the development of successful arts experiences for the schools—the beginning." (p. 11). He says, among other things, "Until all three [parties] collaborate, there can be no solution to the regrettable recurrent problem of *who* shall teach rather than *how* shall we teach the arts." (p. 9). He adds, "Just as teachers need artists to create or identify works of art, so artists need to be shown ways in which to work in the schools." (p. 10). He concludes with:

> I am...urging even a loose federation of arts and arts education agencies...Over the many years of public and private funding, what has been lost to our young people through neglect or disappearance of the few successful efforts in arts education must be legion! A public/private initiative must be undertaken. The time for such action has always been now, and perhaps now is the best time of all. What a pleasure would then result...never to have to read, or write, another article on "Who Shall Teach the Arts?" (p.11).

(Contact Heldreff Publications, a division of the Helen Dwight Reid Educational Foundation, 1319 Eighteenth Street, NW, Washington, DC 20036; 202-296-6267).

8. By way of introduction, I would encourage you to look into the Internet services provided by:

- American Council for the Arts' ArtsUSA (http://www.artsusa.org/)
- John F. Kennedy Center for the Performing Arts' Arts Edge (http://artsedge.kennedy-center.org/artsedge.html)
- The Getty Center for Education in the Arts' ArtsEdNet (http://www.artsednet.getty.edu)
- New York Foundation for the Arts' Arts Wire (http://www.tmn.com/artswire/www/awfront.html)
- The National Endowment for the Arts' arts.community (http://arts.endow.gov)

9. Thanks are due to Lisa Jo Sagolla, Shellen Lubin, Jill Schultz and Steve Schiff for their assistance in the preparation of this paper.

10. The term "artist and performer" is used rather generally in this chapter to refer to individual artists, groups or companies working in or across the visual or media arts, music, drama and dance. Also, the word "training" is used to mean a special kind of education, namely, helping to develop skills and proficiency through specialized instruction and practice.

11. See *The Arts in Schools: Principles, Practice and Provision* (London: The Gulbenkian Foundation, 1982, revised 1989).

12. D. Morely, *Under the Rainbow* (Newcastle, England: Bloodaxe, 1989). Report of a conference held at Darlington Art Centre, England, where artists and educators shared views on the philosophy and practice of collaborative projects.

13. For interesting and challenging reflections on the nature of "subject matter" and knowledge see Israel Scheffler, *In Praise of the Cognitive Emotions* (New York: Routledge, 1991).

14. This perception has been reinforced over the past 50 years by the work of Victor Lowenfeld for whom copying, or the emulation of adult art, was a denial of children's own creative possibilities.

15. Personal communication with many artists who stress this as a persistent concern.

16. Ibid.

17. Ibid.

18. The experience of recent years has lead many arts educators to believe that visiting artists programs have burgeoned at the expense of the specialist teacher; indeed, statistics for large urban centers such as Boston, Chicago and New York reveal a dismal demise in full-time specialist art teachers at all levels of schooling.

19. The work of John Dewey, Philip Jackson and Maxine Greene reflects fully and wonderfully on the importance of cross-disciplinary, integrated and transformational learning.

20. See the works of Scheffler, Dewey, Jackson and Greene.

21. Read the writings of, among others, John Cage, Leonard Bernstein, Jean Cocteau, Robert Henri, Wassily Kandinsky and Hans Hoffman.

22. Personal communication with pre-service classroom teachers.

23. Sir Karl Raimund Popper, *Of Clouds and Clocks: An Approach to the Problem of Rationality and the Freedom of Man*, Arthur Holly Compton Memorial Lecture Series, 1965 (St. Louis: Washington University, 1966).

24. This is far from a new notion; such observations have been made over the years by scholars of comparative education such as Edmund King, George Bereday, Brian Holmes and Joseph Lauwerys. Unhappily, such sentiments find their contemporary echo in books such as Hirsh's *Cultural Literacy* and Bloom's *The Closing of the American Mind*, in addition to the recent plethora of journal articles and newspaper commentaries on the academic status of American students in comparison with their European counterparts.

25. P. Jackson, *The Practice of Teaching* (New York: Teachers College Press, 1986).

26. J. M. Burton, "The Arts as Vehicles for Inclusion," Paper given at Sarah Lawrence College, New York, July 1994. In press.

27. P. Jackson, *Life in Classrooms* (New York: Teachers College Press, 1990).

28. Lincoln Center Institute, Progress Report II, August 1995.

29. Urban Writes, a program developed by the American Place Theatre in New York City and funded in part by the NEA.

30. Arts Spectrum, a program developed by Young Audiences/New York with funding from District 3 in Manhattan and the American Express Company.

31. Arts Infusion, a program developed by the Greater Augusta Arts Council in Augusta, Georgia.

32. Arts EXCEL, sponsored by the Westchester Arts Council in New York and funded in part by the NEA and participating school districts.

33. "Different Ways of Knowing," The Galef Institute, *Teacher-to-Teacher*, Vol. 3, No. 2, 1995, p. 11.

34. "Alphabet Soup: A Glossary of Arts Education Terms and Acronyms," *Southern Arts Education Connections*, Vol. 3, No. 1, Summer 1995.

35. "MagneTek Support Intended To Help Children At Risk." News release, MagneTek, Inc. (no date).

36. Developed in concert with the Guggenheim Museum, described in *Schools, Communities, and the Arts*, Morrison Institute for Public Policy, Arizona State University and the National Endowment for the Arts, 1995, p. 21.

37. Validated by the New York State Department of Education, this White Plains, New York program has been replicated in a number of sites throughout New York State.

38. Validated by the New York State Department of Education, this New Rochelle, New York program promises increases in higher level thinking skills as a direct consequence of institutionalizing a comprehensive arts-in-education program. The program has been replicated in five sites in New York State.

39. David Perkins, *Outsmarting IQ: The Emerging Science of Learnable Intelligence* (New York: Free Press, 1995), p. 225.

40. R. F. Murphy, *Cultural and Social Anthropology: An Overture* (Prentice Hall: Englewood Cliffs, NJ: Third Edition, 1989).

41. S. Jungck and J. D. Marshall, "Curricular perspectives on one great debate." In S. Kessler & B. B. Swadener (Eds.), *Reconceptualizing the Early Childhood Curriculum: Beginning the Dialogue* (New York: Teachers College Press, 1992), pp. 93-102.

42. H. Kliebard, *The Struggle for the American Curriculum* (New York: Routledge, 1987).

43. B. Russell, *A History of Western Philosophy* (New York: Simon and Schuster, 1945), p. 610.

44. J. Dewey, *Experience and Education* (New York: Macmillan, 1938).

45. P. Freire, *Pedagogy of the Oppressed* (New York: Continuum, 1994) p. 17.

CHAPTER 6

Determining Program and Instructional Effectiveness: Research, Evaluation, Assessment and Standards

Backing Up the Claims
What Will Students Know and Be Able to Do, and How Will We Know It When We See It?

Prove It!: Beyond Faith, Motherhood and Apple Pie

Many claims have been made about the value of the arts in general education. In the area of curriculum and instruction, these claims range from asserting the intrinsic worth of the arts as expressive products of the human imagination to declaring the arts as intelligences with distinct, inherent powers. The arts are also said to contribute to the development of higher-order thinking and reasoning skills and to serve as effective instruments for learning other subjects, skills and processes. Still others maintain that the arts have the power to increase self-respect and stimulate a healthier self-concept, to foster cooperative learning and to promote tolerance for and understanding of people from many backgrounds, races and cultures. Finally, many people say that the arts can make a significant difference in the quality of community life and help to build a better society: they improve the climate and environment of the schools, raise attendance, lower the dropout rate, reduce crime and violence, combat the drug problem, promote racial harmony and integration, and counter the damaging effects of poverty. As Dr. Eva L. Baker has written,[1] about the only claim for the arts we haven't heard (yet) is their ability to reduce cholesterol.

Thirty or more years ago, for the most part we could—and did—get away with our flamboyant rhetoric without having to offer incontrovertible evidence to back it up. In the era of the Great Society and relative federal abundance, the arts were considered (when they were thought of at all) like motherhood, apple pie and the American flag: no one was against them and very few people saw them as a subversive threat to community values. My own belief in the power of the arts is based on faith and on many years of personal and objective empirical evidence. But that is not good enough anymore (if it ever was) because the arts are not everyone's crusade or religion.

The paradox is that as the arts have gained attention, stature and credence as subjects of study that belong in the basic curriculum of American schools, the glare of the spotlight—coupled with shrinking resources and competing needs—has prompted many people, especially those in charge of school budgets and the hard-pressed funding community to say: "Prove it." Some parents, teachers and principals also want hard evidence because they think that schooling should be "grim"—they assume children are not learning unless there is silence, order and an atmosphere of deadly seriousness. The bursts of joy, the explosive energy and dynamic sense of fun that often accompany an arts-related experience immediately make the arts suspect as either trivial pursuits or distracting entertainment.

Today, "prove it" can rarely be satisfied by smiles on children's faces, smudged and charmingly misspelled letters of appreciation, and attitudinal questionnaires hastily completed by teachers. "Prove it," now that the arts are finally at the curriculum and instruction table with the rest of the "academics," means that they too must undergo rigorous scrutiny in terms of their benefits to children and youth. Furthermore, arts specialists, classroom teachers and artists are now to be held accountable for the quality of instruction and the achievement of significant results, never mind whether they have the preparation and training to do so with confidence and competence.

Capturing the comparative impact and effect of the arts on large groups of students without having to resort to mechanized and standardized measurements of simple tasks has always been difficult. The quest has been to develop valid and reliable instruments and techniques that are sensitive, responsive indicators of individual success or achievement—instruments capable of measuring more than relatively easy-to-observe skills and performance in the individual art forms and rote learning of facts such as names, dates and places. Researchers and evaluators have found it extremely difficult to construct, much less agree on, the most valid and reliable means by which one either measures the impact or describes the nature and degree to which the arts process may be instrumental in effecting and affecting learning in other domains. The typical experimental design of target and control group often cannot adequately account for the many variables present in a complex classroom situation. Many researchers and evaluators today have come to rely increasingly on case studies, critical observations by experts, interviews and a whole new battery of psycho- and sociometric indicators in the attempt to capture elusive information. Examples of current practice can be found in the Morrison Institute for Public Policy report, *Schools, Communities and the Arts*, which was based in part on an earlier study by Dr. John McLaughlin,

Building a Case for Arts Education: An Annotated Bibliography of Major Research, and in Dr. Robert Stake's book, *Evaluating the Arts in Education: A Responsive Approach*, which preceded both studies.

There are of course those who still think the arts need no defense for their place in schooling; they insist that they are by definition educative. Others complain that the arts are too mercurial, too elusive; they have no one right answer and to try to capture or quantify their impact is not only impossible, but dangerous. These people insist that research and evaluation in the arts disciplines only succeeds when qualitative (descriptive or "soft" in research parlance) not quantitative (hard) data are used as indicators. Many artists are positively defiant about evaluation, fearful that it will crash through and destroy the delicate web of romance and mystery that surrounds their work and the seductive mystique of their profession. Dr. Elliot W. Eisner, professor of art at Stanford University, offers these people a measure of comfort and assurance: he has long insisted that evaluation need not always be thought of in terms of cold, quantifiable evidence and that careful, honest, critical observation by experienced evaluators can accurately portray growth, development and progress, or the lack of it. Dr. Robert E. Stake is equally insistent that accurate portrayals of the complexities of the programs, the art forms and the transactions and dynamics between and among teachers and learners are reliable indicators of value and worth. His excellent book, *The Art of Case Study Research*,[2] is an eminently readable guide to his thorough and responsive approach; I refer to it regularly in my work.

Like it or not, however, research and evaluation will continue to be an important factor in developing the respect, recognition and support the arts-in-education field must gain in order to be taken seriously. Thus, arts organizations, agencies and artists need to understand that research and evaluation, far from being threatening and punitive, are ultimately powerful allies in the quest to build professional capacity, a school constituency and community support for the arts in general education.

In my view, there are four primary challenges to overcome to develop effective research and evaluation tools: (1) getting enough money up front to buy the time, talent and experience to do it right; (2) identifying good, solid research questions that reflect the realities of schooling (not simply the wish list of the arts provider or educator); (3) constructing the right research or evaluation design, including appropriate methodologies for investigating authentic questions in authentic situations that are likely to produce valid and reliable results; and (4) identifying a researcher or evaluator whose philosophy, style and methodology is compatible with the intentions and purposes of your programs and services.

Current Issues

The Arts are Hard to Measure; There is No Panacea for Large-Scale Efforts
Quality, originality, creativity and imagination—all elusive and subjective characteristics of the arts—*are* stubbornly hard to measure, especially on a large scale. At the moment, there are no standardized tests for large populations of students that are fair and that don't cost a fortune to design and administer.

Several promising alternative, research and evaluation techniques are being developed and explored at the moment, prominent among them the "portfolio" approach that has long been used by artists to document the growth, development and success of their process and resulting products. Because educational research and evaluation of any kind is incredibly difficult (we are dealing, after all, with human behavior and a multitude of unpredictable, intervening variables), the education community and, recently, the arts community, tends to jump on the latest methodology bandwagon, whether or not it is appropriate for the task. In our eagerness to find justification for the arts, we seem to grab at any new approach and try to apply it indiscriminately. A word, therefore, of caution.

Portfolios, for example, however promising, are not a panacea for the arts because they present their own set of problems, as Dr. Eva L. Baker and Robert L. Linn warn us. They "are intended to provide qualitative information on a rich, diverse, unpredictable and, most importantly, individual set of performances...they allow the collection of a cumulative record of a student's growth. Let's not lose [sight of] these key goals by converting portfolios mindlessly to inappropriate sources of quantitative information—at least without monitoring the effects of those actions on teaching and learning. Some things are only good for one (or a few purposes)."[3]

Standards and Assessment
The standards and the National Assessment of Educational Progress (NAEP)[4] arts assessment (scheduled to occur in 1997, the first since the early seventies) represent significant breakthroughs for the arts in education. This is especially true when viewed in the context of the Goals 2000: Educate America Act (in which the arts appear as one of the nine core subjects in the National Education Goals) and the Improving America's Schools Act (the reauthorization of the Elementary and Secondary Education Act).

The extended, careful and inclusive consensus process by which the standards and the NAEP were put together have been exemplary because they became national, not just federal, collaborative efforts. Many states and localities refer to these standards when constructing their own curriculum frameworks and their own sets of program evaluations and student assessments. Dr. John J. Mahlmann, executive director of the Music Educators National Conference (MENC), discusses the issues of quality and accountability in his essay on who shall teach the arts. He makes a compelling case for the application of the arts standards regardless of who provides the instruction.[5]

The scope of the NAEP assessment of the arts (only at the eighth-grade level in a selected number of schools and districts) has been severely cut back because of funding. An increasing concern is that since the results of the NAEP assessment are predictable—because we already know the arts are not being taught sequentially, if at all, in most American schools—the assessment is likely to bring more dreary news. In American education, confirming evidence of failure in an area whose value is already questionable can backfire and lead to abandonment rather than a call to arms for drastic, systemic and nationwide support for improvement. Consequently, it is critical to begin planning a campaign now to put the inevitable bad news in a proper historical, economic and political perspective.

Standards raise some other important questions that deserve our attention. The debate in the education and research communities revolves around the concentration or distribution of power, the issue of fairness and the politics of a democracy. At issue is the definition of the term standards: Are they quantifiable measures of established excellence, goals to be reached, or a set of attributes to be held in common by students across the land? Whatever the definition, since more than measurement is being sought, who determines what is "good enough" or of value in these standards? Who defines the criteria by which the content and performance of these standards are judged and by what geographic and socioeconomic indicators? Finally, who are the judges who chose them, and by what standards were *they* selected?

Not surprisingly, many politicians, business people and parent groups are in favor of "world class standards" for all American youngsters, on the premise that higher standards and their attainment will earn the children and the country a competitive edge. Others are concerned about the implications of the word "national" and the danger that the consensus process will lead to standardization, uniformity and conformity. Included in this group are many of the nation's governors, school superintendents and educators such as Theodore R. Sizer, chairman of the Coalition of Essential Schools, a national network dedicated to local school reform, and Elliot Eisner, whose views are presented later in this chapter. Sizer and his colleagues' concerns will be examined briefly here.

Standards and School Reform

Some people believe that standards and assessment will drive systemic reform and school restructuring. Others believe that national standards and assessments by themselves will not necessarily accomplish widespread school reform, which can take place only at the local level. They believe that standards and assessments can serve as a guide and a catalyst, but not as the agent of change in our system of local jurisdiction and control.

In an article "Standards and School Reform: Asking the Essential Questions" that appeared in the *Stanford Law and Policy Review* (Winter 1992-93), Joseph P. McDonald, Bethany Rogers and Theodore R. Sizer—all connected with the Coalition of Essential Schools—raise some thoughtful issues. Among them are who shall set the standards and by what right, because whoever sets them (and by extension measures whether they are met) is exercising a great deal of power over American education.

The authors point out that a standard answers the question, "What is good enough here?" Standards always involve criteria, and the criteria of "good enough" will vary depending upon who sets them and how they are established. In the authors' ideal world,[6] "the individual school takes the initiative in setting standards, and the process is powerfully affected by parents, by those who critique student work on a national basis, and by state officials. Each group's rights are represented directly and not, as is often the case now, through token representation on centrally controlled committees. Our vision of this public forum is full of tension as these constituencies play out their rights, but we believe such tension is the only protection for democracy itself."

In brief, the authors echo Judith Burton's concerns expressed in the previous chapter. They fear that "racheting up standards in order to improve the educational outcomes of all kids" might end up stifling the very diversity, creativity and inventiveness that so many of us say we are trying to encourage. While they support raising standards for all students' work, the issue for them lies in *how* that is done and *whose* standards are used. They believe that the individual school should be the one to take the initiative and bear the ultimate responsibility for setting standards which would grow out of the work of students and their teachers.[7] Further, they believe that we need to develop this capability among teachers since "one cannot teach to a standard one is incapable of imagining." The most profound question they ask is, "Who is capable of setting and maintaining standards if school people are not?"[8]

That is a good question, worthy of wide debate, and I encourage you to engage in it. I would add that, if school people are not capable now, part of the task and opportunity for arts organizations, agencies and artists is to pitch in and help build that local capacity.

Persistent Needs of the Field

The arts and education field has persistent needs, which include the processes by which we conduct research and evaluation, the content of these studies, and adequate funds to pay for the time and expertise required. For example, we still need to learn how to develop research and evaluation designs that have an organic connection to the work that takes place in real schools and arts venues under everyday conditions. This means that the practicing professionals in the research and evaluation and in the arts and education communities must sit down and talk together to construct authentic questions that resonate with all the stakeholders and correspond to their perception of reality. To do this, we will have to develop a better system of communication than the one we now have. Research and evaluation jargon can be impenetrable and therefore daunting; we must find a way to translate the terminology so that the language is accessible and more user-friendly.

We still need much more research and evaluation of the hard questions, most of which continue to beg for answers grounded in the authentic realities of human development and cognition. We have growing information about the validity of the claims we make for arts education's programmatic value, but we do not yet know by what means—cognitive, affective or social—the arts actually make the difference individually profound. It is a major challenge to which we must rise because we need to be more accountable for the nature, quality and impact of the work we do.

One promising effort that will respond to this need is Champions of Change: The Impact of the Arts on Education initiative of the GE Fund and the John D. and Catherine T. MacArthur Foundation, in cooperation with the President's Committee on the Arts and the Humanities. The goal of this research program is to study the effect of the arts on general education and to determine whether and under what circumstances they have the power to encourage transfer of learning and improve educational outcomes. The initiative will support a set of research projects around the country that may help to clarify the nature and degree of impact of learning in, through and about the arts on students, teachers and artists. Results should start to become available by 1997.

Evaluating Arts Partnerships: What Do I Need to Know, and What Can I Do on Monday?

For those of you new to this aspect of the field, I will offer some suggestions about what you can do if, on Monday morning, you realize that you need to start providing colleagues, funders, potential clients, your board and others with some evidence of the value of your own work. You can refer to Appendix I for some sources to investigate if you want to learn more about the topics in this chapter.

First, an anecdote for perspective:

It was late 1965, and I remember calling the U.S. Office of Education to ask them what the guidelines and criteria were for evaluating a large Title III federal grant that had just been awarded to Young Audiences, where I was working at the time. I think I must have talked to about a dozen people before I was finally hooked up with the Arts and Humanities Research and Development Program. The gentleman I spoke to said there *were* no guidelines for evaluating our kind of program, that I should use my common sense and, in effect, make it up as I went along. I was surprised since the requirement for evaluation was written into the contract for the award. When some of my colleagues from other organizations and I asked the same question at the Office of Funded Programs at the New York City Board of Education, we were given a few pamphlets on behavioral objectives (the "in" thing in those days) and a vague offer of technical assistance.

As far as I could discern, there was no precedent for ascertaining the educational impact of outside arts organizations' services on student learning in schools. Numbers and descriptions were used as evidence of effectiveness because all most people knew how to do was to quantify how many students and teachers attended so many performances, workshops and the like. Impact was a given; it was assumed our services were, *sui generis*, beneficial. Looking for clues to an alternative paradigm, I studied the Board's resource materials, reviewed evaluations of other academic programs, did some research in the library, and ended by creating my own design, complete with pre- and post-tests, on-site observations, group and individual interviews and elaborate questionnaires. Either it sufficed or no one paid any attention to it because we were refunded for the following cycle.

Since then, I have learned a great deal about research and evaluation from people such as Elliot W. Eisner, John I. Goodlad, Jack Morrison, David Perkins and Robert E. Stake. I have conducted a number of comprehensive studies employing a wide variety of techniques and methodologies. I have never been able to develop a template because I find that programs, especially arts-in-education programs, are like people: no two are alike, and each one deserves individual and specialized attention. Here are some of the more basic lessons about the process that I have learned along the way:

- Do not confuse a research study with an evaluation. Research examines hypotheses, gathers data and presents conclusions or trends based on the data. Evaluation takes the process a few steps further; it analyzes and interprets the data and generally makes recommendations for improvement or solving a problem or, in some cases, whether or not to abandon the program entirely.

- Evaluation can be as simple or as complicated as you want to make it. Usually the more complex the program, the more detailed the evaluation needs to be. If funds and time are limited, however, draw boundaries on the scope of your inquiry and set priorities for which areas to study. You can examine the effectiveness of the partnership (institutional issues of purpose, organization, structure and operation) and/or of the program (instructional issues of teaching and learning, curriculum and staff development and the like). These areas are, of course, interrelated but require different approaches, methodologies and instruments.

- Your organization's staff and your partner's staff can conduct the evaluation informally, or you can hire an outside consultant who will give you a more objective and generally more expensive report. Often a combination approach is a good idea. If you decide to work informally, be aware that the process is phenomenally demanding and time-consuming. The burden on school people is often unwelcome and overwhelming.

- The critical factor in any evaluation is the process of framing the questions you want to answer, the problems you want to solve and the issues you want to address. The very process of framing these questions by all the key players in the partnership (and the outside evaluator) is at least as important as the investigation itself. Very often people discover that the questions they need answered have little or nothing to do with the goals and objectives they originally set for the program. Program goals and objectives should always grow out of needs to be served, questions to be answered and problems to be solved, and these issues are best determined by the partners working and planning together. Be sure to include the concerns of all the stakeholders (artists, teachers, parents, students) as you frame these guiding questions, not just those of the funders, the school district— or the evaluator. Finally, be sure that you establish standards, guidelines and criteria for effectiveness or achievement that are authentic and site-specific and that recognize national, state and local arts frameworks.

- Take advantage of difficult and demanding proposals that you are required to prepare for challenge grants, arts council funding and the like. These can be remarkable opportunities for you to evaluate your program "on the run"—to examine all your assumptions and question all of your sacred truths. Use these occasions to work with your key staff (and your education partners, if that is appropriate) to clarify language, goals and objectives, strategies, and the roles and functions of everyone in the organization or partnership. Often an outside program advisor or evaluator can facilitate this process.

- Professional researchers and evaluators can be identified through your local school district, arts council, local colleges and universities, state arts education alliances and national data banks (including those of the National Assembly of State Arts Agencies and the National Assembly of Local Arts Agencies), your colleagues at home or across the country, or your local library.

- Do some research on current practice in the field; surf the Internet for information and sample reports; visit the local schools and the district's assessment offices to get their help and guidance; ask your colleagues around town for assistance and to share their experience, if they are willing; state and local arts agencies and alliances are also good sources of technical assistance, information and guidance.

Refer to Appendix I, which contains some very useful sources of information that will start you out in the right direction on Monday morning.

Narrowing the Focus

The potential territory of the topics covered in this chapter is vast; our discussion will be limited. The contributors will address research, evaluation, assessment and standards and provide their own definitions for you along the way. Do not expect uniformity of approach or consensus of opinion; there is great diversity and some conflicting points of view. Do not look for single, simple definitions of all the terminology either; I have discovered that no matter what reference you use or whom you ask about, say, metacognition, self-regulation, formative and summative evaluation and the like, you get definitions that vary. We have done our best to help you at least gain a basic understanding of the ecology of the field and the premises underlying the various viewpoints.

John McLaughlin provides a very useful overview of the field and then discusses the promising model for research he believes is embedded in the Basic Arts Program, now (1996) in its fourth and final year in Kentucky. Terry Baker discusses restructuring schools through a constructivist approach to arts education and describes the principles upon which arts education might be built, citing some examples to bring his theories to life. I have talked with Robert Stake about the current issues in educational evaluation in the arts from his seasoned perspective and asked him to give some indications of where we are and in which directions we should be going. Since the Music Educators National Conference (MENC), led by Executive Director John Mahlmann, was instrumental in developing and carrying out the national consensus effort to design a set of voluntary standards in music, dance, theater and the visual arts, I asked John to share his thoughts about the issue of standards as they relate to arts instruction by professional arts educators, classroom teachers and artists. Elliot Eisner's essay discusses the issue of standards and criteria as the linchpin of educational reform.

Read on, learn what you can from our contributors, and then chart your own next steps. Remember, there is no one right way to do research or evaluation in the arts in education. The process can be daunting, agonizing, exciting; it is always rewarding because you invariably learn something valuable, especially from your mistakes. Remember: Each effort should be shaped by and responsive to the program's purposes, the needs of various participants, your potential audiences, and the problems that you and your partners determine you want to solve together.

Paraphrasing Freud, defining the question is half of the answer—for those of you who like to measure things.

Assessment, Evaluation, and Research

Building Blocks for the Future in Arts Education

by John McLaughlin

The publication in 1983 of *A Nation at Risk: The Imperative of Educational Reform*[9] prompted an unparalleled number of reform efforts affecting every state in the country. Within months, states had produced new guidelines for curriculum and new statewide tests, and extra federal and state dollars were allocated for compensatory education, most of which were pull-out programs similar to those that had already been labeled ineffective.

Individuals and organizations working on behalf of the arts and arts education saw both an opportunity and a threat in this new push for education reform. Although arts education was prominently featured in the texts of other reform-related reports published in the period from 1982-85,[10] the most influential report, *A Nation at Risk*, did not include the arts in its description of core subjects. In fact, many of the new reform efforts appeared to be more of the same, with the rallying cry of "back to the basics," which most reformers maintained we'd never left. Compounding the problem was the fact that in most states, the arts were simply not part of the basic curriculum.

By the mid 1980s, arts organizations began to mobilize nationally in an effort to attain a more central role for the arts in the school curriculum. Led by the National Endowment for the Arts, Music Educators National Conference, and the American Council for the Arts, among others, these groups convened meetings and formed coalitions to develop common goals for the arts in education and to formulate strategies for achieving them. Many of these efforts focused on developing ways to measure the educational worth of the arts in the school experience. Consider some of the statements issued from these formal and informal coalitions and meetings of the late 1980s:

> "As in other subjects, students should be tested in the arts and their work evaluated in order to determine what they have learned, and arts education programs should be evaluated to determine their effectiveness."[11]

> "...ways must be found at the local level to meet or exceed the goals and standards established by professional arts education associations and accreditation authorities. These should include criteria for school programs, certification of personnel, the participation of arts organizations, and artist and teacher preparation programs."[12]

> "...successful education in the arts disciplines involves the continuous solutions to problems well beyond the capabilities of advocacy. These include curriculum and teaching, support systems, and policy issues such as testing, research, and technology."[13]

"We recommend that strategies be developed for evaluation that address the nature of the individual art forms and their respective instructional strategies."[14]

These statements and others clearly indicated the belief that, to be taken seriously in the schools, the arts would have to be willing to be a part of a state's assessment (testing) plans. All students would have to be assessed in the skills and knowledge they had gained through arts instruction. Arts education programs would have to be seriously evaluated using some credible criteria of excellence and quality. Moreover, research would be needed to understand how the arts contribute to broad educational goals. Assessment, evaluation and research would all have to become familiar topics of discussion for the arts and arts education organizations involved in this movement.

This point of view was not universally embraced. Although a master artist or arts teacher working with an artistically talented student has a highly refined critical ability to assess that student's progress, the idea of assessing *all* students in the arts seemed completely abhorrent to many arts professionals. One fear—a reality in many states—was that the testing would amount to a series of multiple choice humanities items on statewide tests, and the concept of creation in the arts would fade out of school arts programs. In addition, the arts organizations that were in the business of providing artists and arts programs to schools had, at best, a tenuous understanding of the educational jargon. Further, state arts agencies had entered the business of stimulating arts curricula development through the National Endowment for the Arts' Art in Schools Basic Education Grants (AISBEG), and they became increasingly confused over some of these issues. Yet this did not stop the states from requiring grantees to submit evaluation/assessment plans that incorporated concepts and terminology of which they had little knowledge or understanding.

The educational landscape changed again in 1990, when President George Bush launched a new wave of education reform dubbed "America 2000." Initially, the arts were again omitted from the goals, but this time the arts coalitions fought for, and won, a place for the arts in the revised Goals 2000: Educate America Act formulated at the beginning of the Clinton presidency. Subsequently, with unprecedented consensus, the arts became the first curriculum area to complete its voluntary national standards, which were released with great ceremony by Secretary of Education Richard W. Riley in March 1994. These *National Standards for Arts Education*[15] now provide a framework for state governments and local school districts to include the arts in the basic curriculum at every level of schooling.

By the late 1990s, the arts will be included in the National Assessment of Educational Progress (NAEP) for the first time in almost two decades. This NAEP will measure progress according to the new standards in the arts, and guidelines[16] have been set to encourage an innovative assessment that matches how the arts are taught, instead of using the multiple-choice, humanities-based model. Some states were already very advanced in the way they were assessing the arts and have been able to take full advantage of the recommendations set in the guidelines. The work of Harvard Project Zero (in collaboration with

Educational Testing Service) in Pittsburgh's Arts PROPEL Project has provided an innovative model for long-term, student self-assessment in the arts.

Finally, research has taken a more central role in the discussions of arts education. *Building a Case for Arts Education: An Annotated Bibliography of Major Research*[17] helped to identify research that demonstrates how the arts address broader goals of education such as: communication skills, problem-solving ability, creative thinking, human development, special needs, career choice and self-esteem. The National Endowment for the Arts has built upon that 1990 compendium with research done in the intervening five years in a report produced by the Morrison Institute in Arizona. A 1994 initiative by the Arts Endowment sought to build a consensus among professionals in the field on future research needs. Its report, *Arts Education Research Agenda for the Future*,[18] sets four goals for arts education research:

- to focus the attention of arts educators, researchers and the broader community on basic issues in arts education that can improve teaching and learning in the arts;
- to identify what arts educators view as priorities, given limited resources;
- to provide a conceptual framework and overall philosophy for inquiry in the field of arts education as other disciplines are doing with their respective research agendas; and
- to connect theory and practice, to make research an agent of improvement in teaching and learning.

As arts organizations seek to gain a firm footing in the schools during the current wave of education reform, they must understand the concepts and applications of these three key building blocks in education—assessment, evaluation and research. To succeed long term, arts education initiatives will need to be informed by a rich and varied base of ongoing research, and new and innovative assessment and program evaluation techniques.

Assessment, Evaluation and Research: Understanding Current Practice

Education reform has stimulated an extraordinary level of activity in recent years. Theorists and researchers are seeking to create and test new theories and methods of assessment and evaluation, and many new areas for investigation in education and the arts are being researched. The following presents a brief overview of current practice.

Assessment. Assessment is best described as a snapshot in time. (Old-timers would call it testing.) Assessment measures what a student can achieve at a given moment. The old style of multiple-choice testing would test the student on a series of criteria set by the testing companies. These criteria frequently drove school curriculum and were unrelated to a full education. Moreover, these standardized tests often addressed only the lowest-level thinking skills (based on Bloom's *Taxonomy of Educational Objectives*[19]), and high-level thinking skills, such as analysis and synthesis, were left out. Yet it is widely acknowledged by business, industry and the U.S. Department of Labor in its SCANS[20] report that these higher-level skills are among those that students will need in an increasingly technologically based, information-age workforce.

Assessment has undergone some revolutionary changes as educational researchers have sought more effective methods of measurement. As Howard Gardner[21] and other major educational reformers, theorists and researchers point out, the only real knowledge is that which can be applied to real life situations. As a result, current assessment trends are focused on what is called *authentic assessment*, in which students apply knowledge and skills to situations they might encounter in their own lives. Students no longer study for the test by cramming facts, of which 75-90 percent will be forgotten within six months. Instead of multiple-choice questions, *performance events* and *open-ended questions* are used. This form of assessment requires students to demonstrate their knowledge by manipulating materials to create a product or by giving an answer in which they are judged on their problem-solving and thinking processes and on the sources of information used to back up their response.

In an attempt to move away from the snapshot mode of assessment, *portfolio assessment* is gaining increasing credibility. In portfolio assessment, students are informed of the assessment criteria at the beginning, and they assemble samples of their work over time. They can see the progression of their work, and they are often involved in reflecting on and discussing their progress. A similar approach is used for *project assessment*, in which students work on projects over time, either alone or in collaboration (as in real life), and they, too, use the metacognitive approach[22] to discuss their own process and the learning/thought processes associated with completion of long-term work.

Finally, as more schools move toward *nongraded continuous progress*—students learn at their own rate and are assessed by where they begin and where they end based upon certain criteria—more districts and states are developing learning descriptors of sequential skills and knowledge to help teachers identify students' progress along a continuum.

All of these innovative methods of assessment help the arts. They enable students to show the skills and knowledge they have gained over time and to apply them to real life situations. More importantly, students can be assessed in the way they have learned, for example, by applying color theory to do a water-color using only primary colors. This is the only real way to assess creation in the arts. As Isadora Duncan said, "If I could tell you what I mean, there would be no need for dancing."

Evaluation. Evaluation measures a program change (positive or negative) or the lack of it over time. It shows the beginning, the middle and the end. The data collected, therefore, can be both formative (the process) and summative (the product or impact) in nature.

For too long, most education projects have been evaluated solely on what students actually learn, ignoring the degree to which program goals and objectives have been achieved. Current program evaluation practice calls for long-range collaborative planning in which all cooperating parties set the specific goals, objectives and strategies of the project. By clearly establishing desired outcomes that are measurable at the beginning, it is much easier to determine the ultimate effectiveness of a program's process and its instructional and operational impact.

To construct successful mechanisms for program evaluation, arts organizations should set goals, objectives and strategies that:

- can be measured over a period of time sufficient to allow change to occur;
- are achievable—not broad or an attempt to reset the course of human events and history;
- involve all key partners in their setting and programming;
- are based on current and past successful practice and theory;
- ensure that all partners are qualified to work within their part of the program;
- include assessment of students, attitudinal information from key partners, and any other data and documentation that could be useful (no one ever suffered from too much data); and
- use evaluation data to help shape further program growth.

Research. Finally, research has become increasingly important to proponents of arts education across the country. Sound research on successful arts education models and practices is crucial to effective policy formation. Research, including assessment and evaluation, often focuses on new and innovative programs that are attempting to answer questions about the effect of teaching and learning in the arts.

Qualitative research—which includes more than just numbers, such as interviews and case studies—has gained increased acceptance in the educational research community. Teacher-directed action research[23] has become increasingly credible, especially when the teacher, or team of teachers, works in concert with higher education personnel and other partners to ensure quality program design and data collection analysis.

Arts research with clear-cut goals and objectives, conducted over time (longitudinal), can yield some important lessons. However, not all research will yield overwhelming or broadly applicable results. Just as in the natural sciences, much research is done that shows nothing of great value. Whatever lessons are learned, the results of research should be used wisely. The best that educational research can do is suggest trends, and proponents of a study should never get into the habit of claiming that this or that point has been "proved."

A Current Model for Research

The Basic Arts Program (BAP), a four-year program being conducted in three primary schools in Kentucky, is nearing the end of its third year (1995). The major goal of the program was to implement the mandates of the Kentucky Educational Reform Act (KERA) by fusing the arts with Howard Gardner's theory of multiple intelligences[24] as the core of the school program. The three schools participating were chosen for their willingness to meet the program's criteria and to serve as research sites during the four years of the program.

All three schools have site-based management and, with technical assistance from the Kentucky Arts Council and the researcher, each has created, in varying degrees, a school-based arts and multiple intelligences focus to their school programs. This is a key BAP feature, since the research is concerned with the program design and implementation process as well as the end results. Because these schools were not designated as magnet schools or schools of choice, the BAP gives researchers a unique opportunity to track the intensive use of the arts with an intact school population.

Each school was required to:

- teach at least four art forms;
- plan yearly for the arts as core to the primary program (K-3);
- use professional development in the arts and in multiple intelligences;
- develop integrated curriculum and assessment;
- use supporting cultural resources in the program;
- match the $25,000 funding given each year; and
- develop a plan for institutionalization of the program and for extension of the program to the fourth and fifth grades.

Funded by the National Endowment for the Arts and the Kentucky Department of Education, the research design is a modification of the four universes—students, faculty, administration (principal and site-based council as well as district administration), and parents/community—used by John Goodlad in his matrix for the *Study of Schooling in the United States*. The research seeks to determine the effect of the BAP on these four universes plus a fifth—the artists and cultural groups that work with the schools.

Data collection has included attitudinal surveys and innovative performance events that match KIRIS (the Kentucky Instructional Results Information System, a system for scoring schools that includes high stakes assessment at grades 4, 8 and 12 and other measures). It also includes student-discussion instruments; yearly teacher interviews; a 30-page, individualized professional development instrument; videotaped lessons and student products; parental surveys and the collection of critical incident anecdotal records of student change. There is also provision for the documentation and evaluation of school events, professional development, and the use of cultural resources. Documentation and evaluation has included yearly retreats, which has proved helpful to the schools in their attempts to digest and make use of the lessons they are learning throughout the process.

Now at the end of the third year, the research has begun to show some results. Some of the statistical results may add to the growing body of literature that builds a case for the many uses of the arts in educating children. Other results speak directly to the structural changes and attitude adjustments needed for school reform to occur. A third set of data documents the change in confidence on the part of students and teachers and the resulting recognition the schools receive.

A preliminary study of the statistical results allows for some generalizations:

- KIRIS scores *improved* in all three schools (one school was in the cash rewards category, a program of financial incentives for successful schools that is built into KERA);

- daily attendance *increased;* one school achieved its projected attendance for the first time;
- writing portfolio scores *increased;*
- disciplinary referrals *decreased;*
- referrals for special education testing *decreased;* and
- the students' ability to discuss the arts *increased.*

In terms of the structural changes, the research will provide:

- suggested mechanisms for joint faculty planning for collaborative projects;
- innovative ways to deliver professional development;
- ways to integrate the arts and multiple intelligences into the full curriculum;
- a way to screen potential faculty for their strengths and to use those strengths and weaknesses to develop an individualized professional development plan; and
- a supervisory tool to rate classroom structure, teaching, and materials in terms of the arts integration and classroom instructional collaboration present.

Lastly, based upon the third set of data, the changes seen over the first three years were:

- increased parental and community involvement in the schools (in one school, a parent finished a GED[25] as a result of involvement in the program and has gone on to enter college for his teaching credential; in another school, student-created music has become such a huge "hit" with the entire town that they have had to move the performances to the high school);
- increased creativity in student performances at each of the schools; for example, in one school, the children created and produced their own original opera (as a result of two teachers participating in the national Metropolitan Opera Guild Project), with all of the students taking active roles in all aspects of its production over the course of a semester;
- a shift in emphasis from product-based arts teaching to an emphasis on process, and a move away from 40-minute arts experiences to experiences that can take weeks to accomplish;
- an increase in the teachers' abilities to collaborate with artists and cultural institutions to design meaningful arts experiences for students that reflect the state curriculum guidelines and assessments; and
- an increase in teachers' knowledge of the arts and in their abilities to work with them in their classrooms; most importantly, teachers know that when they do not have all the necessary skills, they can collaborate with artists and cultural institutions to accomplish their classroom objectives.

The full results of the four-year project are expected to be released in summer 1996. These early findings have created a substantial amount of excitement about the potential of the final results.

Conclusion

Assessment, evaluation and research are strong building blocks that, if properly understood, can be used to build a solid foundation for arts education at the core of each child's education. Effective research and evaluation can furnish convincing evidence to policy makers and those in the position of power. As Harold Williams, president and chief executive officer of the J. Paul Getty Trust, said in a speech at Ohio State University: "Any attempt to shape public policy and arts education cannot avoid taking into account this enormous, loose-jointed, non-hierarchical system that reaches from individual arts teachers in the classroom to the arts agencies, including the NEA, at the federal level."[26]

Williams accurately sees the dilemma of arts education—of education in general—in this country. Research is traditionally conducted through the university by masters- and doctoral-level students. This research rarely informs teaching practice, so while our body of educational research grows larger and larger, classroom practice tends to stagnate. Ultimately, neither research nor practice informs policy setting, and education becomes hostage to the political process, often preventing true reform in the classroom.

Some current trends, however, provide a note of hope. The increasing credibility of teacher-directed research and the involvement of the larger school community in site-based decision-making in school policy are starting to show possibilities for true reform based upon strong practice and relevant research.

The most powerful lessons of the Basic Arts Program are those about teachers in the process of change, breaking down the mindsets and outmoded paradigms that no longer apply. They are lessons about teachers literally breaking down walls between classrooms in order to work together. They are lessons about trying new methods of instruction and assessment. And they are lessons about believing in and valuing children with different forms of intelligence, not just the top reader and the strong math student.

After only four years, the Basic Arts Program already shows considerable promise. Two of the schools were able to effect a change at the district level: Following the fourth and last year of the program, one school will become a magnet school for the arts and multiple intelligences. This school will be an open-enrollment school; parents will choose the school rather than children being selected through auditions. In the other school's district, the superintendent has committed to spend the next three years moving the basic arts concept to the remaining schools in the district—an elementary, middle and high school.

These programs need to be studied, especially over time, because the process of change is slow, and we need to uncover the key factors that cause and sustain positive change. This has not been possible within the limited span of four years, especially since school personnel has changed. More research is needed to understand precisely what it takes to institutionalize a program so that it can withstand the predictable swings in economic and political fortunes to which the schools constantly are subjected.

A window of opportunity now exists to achieve progress for the arts in the schools. Recent research such as the Basic Arts Program increasingly demonstrates that placing the arts at the core of the school curriculum can begin to transform schools, especially in relationship to the teaching/learning process. These kinds of strong research studies should continue to build a solid case for including the arts as part of a basic education, and more innovative assessment, evaluation and research can help to assure that the arts will never again be questioned as a core subject in the school curriculum.

Dr. John McLaughlin has been an independent consultant in arts education for the last six years. He has written books and articles on arts education, including Building a Case for Arts Education: An Annotated Bibliography of Major Research *and* Toward a New Era in Arts Education: The Interlochen Symposium. *He works with schools, districts, universities, state and local arts councils, and cultural institutions in evaluation, assessment and research. Dr. McLaughlin has done extensive professional development in the area of the arts and multiple intelligences and school transformation. He is a former Director of Arts Education for the American Council for the Arts.*

New Currency for the Arts in Education
From Change Theory into Promising Practice
by Terry L. Baker

Changing Times for Arts Education

In city after city, school systems have eliminated central office arts supervisors and administrators, obliterated budgets for supplies, equipment and materials, and instituted policies that encourage schools to look elsewhere for educational experiences in the arts. In most cases, these decisions have been based upon financial considerations. While the arts have never enjoyed support from a rich base of research and documentation such as other disciplines have marshalled, most policy decisions about the arts have not been informed by research data on pedagogy, child development, or student achievement and performance. Nor have such decisions been based upon an understanding of the nature of the arts or of the consequences of their absence from society. Policy makers have been unimaginative in their failure to project beyond the immediate situation.

School policy is often set by individuals who have little direct experience with children or classrooms. Standards are set against highly abstract and remote notions of what each discipline represents, and assessment is so far removed from actual lived experiences that a relationship between the test and the learning can hardly be imagined. Efforts to change these realities have led to a rebirth of "experiential learning" and "authentic assessment." The characteristics of these approaches have much in common with work in the arts, but the arts have not had a major role to play in current school reform efforts. This essay rests on the belief that good education includes education in the arts. Conversely, education that does not include the arts cannot be considered good for our children. It encourages a reconsideration of the possibilities suggested by these questions and of possible roles arts education programs can play as the nation struggles to realize new educational practice.

Change Spawns New Opportunities

Arts education has changed dramatically several times over the years, often because of social, economic or political shifts in the nation. The arts first came into the schools driven by workforce needs—music because the nation needed a supply of church choir directors and the visual arts because industry needed designers.[27] Even business is now calling for ways to link "mind" and "feeling" in employees and leaders.[28]

We are in a time of great change and uncertainty. Changing times affect all aspects of our lives, and educators are not exempt. Although arts educators are fond of claiming that they are often relegated to the periphery, they, too, are affected as they continue their quest to find a place for the arts. Mims and Lankford[29] have reviewed elementary arts education programs across the country to determine how teachers are allotted time and money to provide arts education under new mandates for arts curriculum that is "outcome-based," "discipline-based," or "multicultural." Their conclusion: "Time and money, which we contend are two of the most crucial variables affecting the way art is taught in American schools, are shrinking at the same time as art education's recommended content is growing." Arts educators have both realistic and justifiable complaints, but must admit, in fairness, that time and money are not available for any of the other disciplines to implement the dramatic changes in curriculum, pedagogy or organizational structure being recommended by reformers or dictated by policy makers.

There will never be more than 24 hours in a day, and only so many of those hours can be devoted to any single discipline. To argue for more time will simply prolong or intensify the "turf wars" that characterize much of our curriculum discussion. Moreover, although money is a more flexible commodity than time, it seems to be shrinking in value and becoming more scarce these days. Arguing for more money is always an unavoidable task, but it is one that will be largely fruitless and disheartening for some time to come.

Thus, perhaps it is time to consider some alternatives. Are there other ways to use the time and the funds that we have available for schooling to achieve our primary aims? Can we abandon old battles to take up new ones on new battlegrounds? Should we? Since arts educators have spent decades refining their ways of helping children to learn art concepts and processes and to develop attitudes and opinions about arts and aesthetics that enrich their lives, is it advisable to move away from present practice toward different configurations, different alliances and different constructs? If arts educators and the arts are to continue to contribute to the expansion of human capacity, then they cannot function in isolation or as separate domains. Other human capacities—the ethical, moral, productive—can be joined through the imagination to reintroduce the arts to schools, especially in schools where they have been lost, cut or abandoned. And this can be done within our existing—even shrinking—resources.

Times of change spawn new opportunities for the creative and imaginative. These days arts educators may find dramatic opportunities to move from the borderlands to the heartland of education. The range of choices is wide. Many are choosing to define change as amplification—simply put, the same as before, just more of it. They argue that arts education will be better if its offerings are increased in the schools. Their goal is to embed the arts in the mainstream of educational practice, often nostalgically seen as it was in "olden days." They rush to make the arts appear like other subject matter disciplines, to create national standards before others create theirs and to build the case for the arts using research strategies that have proved reliable for other disciplines.

Others choose to directly assault tradition. They do not take their arguments from the past or try to repeat history. Instead, they assert that, through the power of imagination, we can create new visions of the possible and produce expanding realms of lived experience. These arts educators are stretching our notions of consciousness and the cognitive experience of art by including the full range of physical and emotional sensations. As a result, they are finding new value in the creative, participatory and performance aspects of arts experience.

Standards

The "whole arts" experience for these teachers, artists and critics parallels the "whole language" experience in verbal literacy: it is grounded in the direct sensory experiences of the student and artist and builds on their active construction of new knowledge, understanding, and presentations or products. In this world, there are new roles to be played. Students become the makers and shapers of new arts experiences. Teachers become co-constructors, mentors, coaches and direct participants in activities and projects. Artists become teaching artists working alongside both students and school teachers. In this expanding world, new standards of excellence can evolve.

No matter which route to change is chosen, very practical considerations remain. Who will pay for these expanded efforts to teach the arts? What value do the arts have in education, and how is that worth determined? How do artists and teachers move from their familiar roles as keepers and transmitters of information and skills to more active participation in the learning lives of their students? How can they continue to deliver needed information, vocabulary, and technique while they also support, encourage, listen to, and learn with their students? How are standards determined and by whom? Do standards set within the educator's traditional "scope and sequence" paradigm function as intellectual or emotional stimuli, or do they set limits that inhibit? Should the students, the teachers or the community bear the responsibility for meeting standards? Are national standards inherently "better" than locally set standards? What happens in schools or classrooms when limits are removed and students work beyond the boundaries of predetermined standards and measures?

Engagement, Imagination

Information clearly is the blue-ribbon stock for our new times. The many varieties of information pile up in our electronic, service-agency, corporate and educational warehouses—including information about and conveyed by the arts. Yet, for information to have value, its meaning must be understood, and it must be put to use. In the everyday world, meaning is determined by some relationship with people, organizations, social systems or other kinds of information. For most of these relationships to be created, human beings must find a way to connect with the information, to engage it directly, and to shape its use.

In examining this complex web of engagement, relationships and under-standing, some arts educators, cognitive and social scientists, and policy makers are finding value for the arts in education. They maintain that by using the arts to describe, analyze and attach value to the elements of this web, we can establish their general worth and hold arts educators accountable.

Art does not exist and cannot be perceived without imagination. Imagination is the currency in this domain, for only imagination allows the potential of productive information to be realized, new relationships to be dreamed, and new meaning to be established. Imagination moves the mind beyond narrow boundaries into the realm of the possible. Imagination, in its inimitable unlimited way, defines a path toward excellence and standards beyond our current scope. Imagination, then, becomes a central building block for school arts programs and policy.

The Arts and Their Quest for the Mainstream of Education

One change initiative after another has swept through American education during the past 30 years. As these efforts gathered force, arts educators have rushed—along with educators in other disciplines—to claim their place. "Aesthetic Education," "Arts in General Education," "Interdisciplinary Arts Education," "Discipline-Based Arts Education," "Art for Art's Sake," "Reading, Math, et al., Through the Arts"—the proponents of these approaches and more have sought their places in the mainstream of educational practice. As the nation geared up to define and enforce national educational standards, arts educators were among the first with their lists of "standards." In each case, however, the arguments made for the arts—and the places sought for the arts—were fragments of the whole. The effort has always been to find a winning argument, to define a slot or place in the curriculum, to find allies among the "others."

To the political and intellectual give and take that has shaped educational policy and practice, arts educators brought enthusiasm, integrity, powerful exemplars and a rich experience base to the table. They had almost no base in research, a participant constituency with little clout, few powerful friends in government, and an undercultivated relationship with the driving force in America—business. No one had calculated the immense wealth of arts-related industries in this country, and those industries, for some reason, had paid little attention to the sources of talent vital to their success. In the sixties and seventies, few in business, politics or education denied that the arts were "good" things for kids and the country, but their support for the arts was mostly motivated by charity or self-serving public relations.

Advocates for arts education found ears and minds closed to arguments about the primacy of the arts, the need for the arts to be central in the curriculum, and the contributions the arts make to the growth and development of children. The arguments were weak—often arguments of faith rather than data-rich illustrations, such as those used by other disciplines. At the tables of educational power, arts educators had little currency, and they usually had to settle for the scraps.

Beginning with almost nothing, arts educators, sympathetic researchers, artists, arts organizations, and some colleges and universities have slowly built a basis for exchange and support over the past 30 years. We can now say with certainty that the lessons learned in the arts translate to the workplace, to family and community life, and to other intellectual pursuits. We have documented the relationship between study of the arts and higher SAT scores and between the study of music and performance in math.[30]

We have now documented the financial connections between the arts and business that are vital to the economic health of the nation.[31] Quality of life issues determine where many businesses locate, including access to art and culture and to quality schools that include the arts in their curriculum. Entertainment and arts-related products are now America's number one export. Across the country, tourism and entertainment, communication, architecture, public relations, advertising and the arts themselves—theater, music, visual arts, folk arts—account for 2.5 percent of the GDP.[32] New economic factors—"human capital," defined in terms familiar to the arts, such as imagination, creativity, productivity—are now included in more traditional economic calculations. "Cultural goods" and "cultural consumption" have become economic touchstones for cultural economists, but they continue to struggle with the spontaneity and unpredictability of art, and with issues such as "taste," the fluctuations that characterize the careers of many artists, and the fact that one artist cannot simply be substituted for another in the labor market.

The changes in our society—most visibly reflected by stressful reductions in available capital, pressure to change all businesses' administrative structures, and cutbacks in social benefits and support—have another side. These changes breed new opportunities that they either force or encourage many to seek. The federally funded School to Work initiative, for example, has led to the creation of several new schools across the nation that feature the arts. One such effort is being undertaken in Pittsburgh, where the Manchester Craftsman's Guild is starting a new school in partnership with the Pittsburgh public schools that will integrate the arts, work and social skills with academic instruction. The Annenberg Challenge Grants, in many cities, are also linking arts resources and arts education with thorough school change efforts, resulting in hundreds of new schools. Change creates opportunities for arts education, many of them derived directly from change efforts themselves.

Arts Education and the Real World

The usual school experience in the arts is far removed from the lived world of the artist and from the daily experience of the arts "consumer." Business people and most educators would agree that in-school and out-of-school experiences with information differ, but not all would agree that students would benefit from greater verisimilitude. Perkins assumes that all would agree with some "deceptively simple" goals of education: "...the *retention, understanding* and *active use* of knowledge and skills."[33]

For some educators, the most valued education is the one most removed from the world, cloistered within the academy. They are not swayed by marketplace justifications for educational practice, which argue that students need to be prepared in ways that relate more directly to the jobs they will have in the "real world." The priorities of business are not their currency. In noisy times such as ours, much is to be said for distance, clarity and secure knowledge. However, we see mountains of evidence that what we think we know is not so certain and that the very nature and circumstances of our inquiry changes the "truth" that we seek. We are increasingly assured that students prepared in the objectivist environment of most of our schools do not fare well in the complex and messy world we now inhabit.

Educators who try to find ways to make sure that the skills, information and problem-solving abilities they stress in their classes prepare students for work and life in the real world increasingly seek ways to teach that more accurately mirror that world. As we find new change efforts in schools benefiting from curriculums that build on connections with the world outside the classroom, it is time to reconsider the ways in which such connections can benefit arts education.

In the world outside the classroom, information changes rapidly, flows in growing amounts and at very rapid speeds, and is available to almost everyone. The world outside the classroom is complex—topics overlap, multiple perspectives predominate, and the tools of various disciplines are used simultaneously and collaboratively. Inquiry in the real world is "...inherently interdisciplinary, and interdisciplinary problems are inherently broad and open ended. Such problems rarely have one, easily accessible right answer."[34]

Elliot Eisner points to the ways that our understanding of the role of aesthetic dimensions would change if we were to have a greater understanding of how we make meaning and construct our knowledge of the world. "To make knowledge is to cast the scientist in the role of the artist or a craftsperson, someone who shapes materials and ideas...." In such circumstances, "...aesthetic considerations and criteria must operate to some extent."[35] Not only would the knowledge bases, ways of knowing, and techniques used by subject matter specialists be used in complex and interrelated ways, but individuals would also perform in interdisciplinary ways.

The rote drills and practices in traditional classrooms are seen as preparing students to approach life's established set of meanings. They are not intended to prepare students for a life spent responding to and manipulating information. Increasingly, we are discovering that these skills do not transfer well to the real world. It is not that the skills are unimportant. Some insist that the complexities of experiential learning lead teachers to focus on entry-level skills and understanding, since no one is expected to recreate anew the whole of human understanding.[36] At the same time, however, these teachers work to embed skills development in a context of developing meaning for the student and to make the process of assimilating knowledge one of "acting on" rather than simply "taking in."

Restructuring Schools to Achieve Greater Understanding Through Arts Education

School change efforts that build on curricular revision or conceptions of student learning are frequently defined in terms of "raising standards," "increasing the amount of information delivered to students," or "rearranging the school schedule to allow more instruction." In a school arts program thus conceived, the goals would be to have "more art," "extra hours for the arts in the school day," and "a set of national standards for student achievement in the arts."

Less frequently, but more profoundly, school change efforts view student development as the achievement of "higher-order understanding" gained by controlling and manipulating raw information, data and "authentic" experiences. As Richard Elmore[37] points out, education of this sort "...requires a transformation not only of educational practice but also of knowledge about teaching and learning that underlies practice." Interestingly, however, for such a shift to occur, it would have to be deeply seated within the essential ways of knowing that form the heart of subject matter disciplines.

Yet few school restructurers approach their work by advocating greater knowledge or understanding of the disciplines. Instead, they concentrate on more easily deliverable resources such as money, time, space, supplies, political clout and, of course, standards—resources without which greater knowledge and understanding could not be achieved, but which are wholly inadequate in and of themselves to produce the insight and comprehension we require.

Proponents of school change geared to produce greater understanding and higher-order skills are showing renewed interest in the arts. These educators are finding that the long-neglected arts and the work of artists embody habits of mind and ways of working that fit a model of teaching in which knowledge is shaped and created from direct experience and raw information. Conceptions of arts education have changed and grown, moving away from narrow views of the arts as simply recreation, enrichment or enhancement, or as specialized work for the gifted or talented child. Widespread recognition of the "mindfulness" of artwork and study supports its integration into the school curriculum and broadens notions of acceptable arts instruction to include, along with studio work, the study of aesthetics, philosophies of art, criticism, and the history of arts disciplines.

Objectivist or Constructivist Education and the Arts

Across the nation, two separate sets of beliefs about how we learn and know prevail among school-improvement advocates, though school practitioners are seldom purely aligned with one or the other. The first group of educators sees learning as a mastery of facts, teaching as basically technical work, and curriculum as a narrow canon of material. Their ideas derive from "objectivist" philosophies. The second group sees learning as the gradual construction of meaning through an increasing number of perceptual experiences. Experience and meaning are inextricably intertwined, and meaning for each individual is shaped and formed by their idiosyncratic perceptions. For these "constructivists," teaching and learning are seen as intellectual work, and the curriculum is viewed as a diverse and changing course through varied materials.[38] Darling-Hammond sees these two approaches as being on a "collision course."

Her colleagues, Lieberman, Wood and Falk,[39] argue against the "one best way" approaches taken by so many of the more doctrinaire reformists. Following Dewey, who warned his own followers against "either/or thinking," these researchers advocate that local school communities should articulate their own educational goals and tailor curricula and instructional approaches to their own contexts and students.[40] Lieberman and associates argue for "learner-centered" schools that foster problem-solving and critical inquiry, but they admit more traditional features as they are deemed appropriate for local contexts.

As we recognize that there are different ways of knowing, we must think differently about how we teach, particularly how we teach the separate subject matter disciplines that embody our understanding of ways of knowing. We must ask which of the different ways of knowing are caught in the different disciplines, and we must ask which ways of knowing teachers should attempt to present in class.[41] While research centers such as Project Zero, Stanford University and the Pennsylvania State University continue to detail the ways of knowing associated with each of the arts, teachers across the nation are defining and refining curriculum practices. For example, multiple intelligences theory is being applied, with great local variation, in Gloucester, MA, the Key School in Indianapolis, and Provincetown, MA, among many others. Aesthetic imagination is being explored in the curriculums developed at the Lincoln Center Institute and the Touchstone Center. Discipline-specific instruction is refined and applied in the several discipline-based arts education programs sponsored by the Getty Center for Education in the Arts. In all these cases, the curriculum planners are working to create instructional programs that reflect our growing understanding of the ways we know in the world.

The arts have had and will continue to have roles in the school change efforts of both objectivists and constructivists, but the roles they play in each will be quite different. From the objectivists' perspective, basic information can be learned about each of the arts, and sets of skills allow students to perform or create in the arts. Yet the performance and creative aspects of work in the arts also guarantee that students who are fully educated will move into constructive modes. In these modes, the learner, rather than the subject matter, inevitably becomes the center of the experience. Even when students are asked to replicate and copy, or to appreciate and interpret existing artwork, they bring their own perceptions, skills and interpretations to the task. When they are set on the task of creating their own expressive works, they are working at the extreme edge of constructivism. When they participate as members of an audience or when they simply receive information about art, the constructive learner is building a personal interpretation of experience. Such learning is open to change, seeks relationships and linkages, and forms and shapes the bases for new experience. The learning is active, calls for imaginative exploration of possibilities, and prepares students for projections into uncharted territory.

Maxine Greene sees the imaginative life that flows from aesthetic experiences as "Journeys to Possibility."[42] For her, the arts open the "what if" world of action and productivity, the opposite of which is narrowing, channeling and automatizing, which she compares to W. H. Auden's Kingdom of Numbers—all boundaries—where things are tracked, categorized and predicted inside the boundaries.[43] In Greene's universe, the arts cannot be bounded; they are neither good nor bad, beautiful nor ugly. They are freeing, inspiring, opening. The paths they provide cross boundaries. The many doors they pass are always open. For her, the arts cannot be justified on the basis of narrow categories or confining characteristics. Their presence in the school curriculum rests on the belief that they are the best vehicles for choice. The best arts education is that which gives students the tools they need to make creative, imaginative and productive choices—choices for engagement in life through heightened sensibilities, strong and refined perceptual skills, and control of powerful tools of communication.

Building Arts Education from Current Theory and Research

Much recent education and arts education theory is derived from cognitive research that investigates the ways that we consciously know and understand in the arts and the ways we communicate our knowledge to others. Researchers, theorists, and those educators planning and shaping new school programs and practices want to know how students learn and how they make meaning from their experiences. These frameworks depart from the more traditional conceptions that were derived from the curriculum content and skills acquisition issues commonly used to justify schooling in other subject areas. The full development of human knowledge and understanding requires complex instructional support that includes, but is not limited to, the scientific, particularistic and fragmented kinds of instruction found in most schools.

Much of what we typically call arts education in the schools, as Dennie Wolf points out, is for survival's sake, borrowed from the structures of other disciplines and mimicking their practices.[44] However, if students are to realize their greatest growth, all forms of human thinking and intelligence need to be cultivated in their most complex and demanding forms. Painstaking investigations support the belief that artistic thinking and aesthetic awareness are complex and challenging mental states and that they are important aspects of cognitive activity, with special importance for child development.[45]

Research completed during the past 25 years—at Harvard, Stanford, New York University, the University of Illinois, Pennsylvania State University, Teachers College and elsewhere—expands our understanding of the role of the arts in child development. We can now distinguish artistic thinking from other forms of thinking with some specificity and, at the same time, see previously unrecognized similarities between artistic and scientific thinking. Educators have documented important processes both for encouraging artistic thinking skills and for recognizing the kinds of understanding embedded in the making of artistic products.

General cognitive theory has moved to more complex notions of intelligence—the development and cultivation of knowledge and understanding. Much remains to be learned, but cognitive theory has defined a broad thoroughfare from which to conduct both practice and investigation. That thoroughfare passes through schools, cultural organizations and homes—the whole expansive landscape of the lived world. The maps for this journey are still sketchy, but we know which directions to take, and we know that, if we are to move very far, we must be accompanied by discipline specialists, teachers, school administrators, parents and students—all those whose everyday practice will test theory.

Project Zero, originally a "think tank" and source of ideas and theory, is conducting "teaching experiments" and working with public schools to test new ideas in the context of "active school environments."[46] Project Zero's recent discussions of its work have emphasized its movement into implementation and organizational work, and it has encouraged practitioners to develop their own versions of such highly visible Project Zero concepts as "multiple intelligences." Other research centers, most notably Stanford University, New York University and the University of Illinois, have substantially contributed to an understanding of the ways that the arts aid learning. However, since schools usually do not work in step with researchers, most school arts programs are at different stages of development.

What Imaginative, Expressive, Arts Learning Would Look Like in Schools

Some common principles should undergird a late twentieth-century school arts program. Though they are not the only guiding principles for arts programs, they seem crucial for all education in our times and for arts education that follows a constructivist path. They demand inter- or related-discipline thinking and practice. They call for collaboration, shared resources, and total-school planning, and for outcomes that demonstrate the students' abilities to apply their knowledge and skills in new ways and new domains. These principles, all grounded in a set of expanded "relationships," support student outcomes that are easily endorsed by most educators:

1. The arts are best employed in the school curriculum when they are fully integrated, when they actively expand the range of students' ways of knowing, when they engage students' imaginations in productive ways, and when they contribute to the construction of broader understanding of complex thought and behavior.

Students who engage in this sort of school curriculum will:

- develop observation and analytical skills by using primary data and manipulating materials;
- be prepared to analyze relationships between different categories of experience;
- have visual, kinetic and auditory skills to apply to various kinds of inquiry;
- use discussion, argument and debate skills as socially acceptable ways to examine differing constructions of meaning;
- be able to tackle ill-defined, real-world problems and make sense of them;
- be able to understand and use information from several art forms in attempting to solve complex real-world problems;
- be able to think through themes, issues and problems that are linked and to understand the relationships between them;
- compare the results of inquiry based on different perspectives;
- develop and pursue their own questions and learn to develop theories;
- integrate reflection and assessment into their learning processes and use production and presentation skills to exhibit their learning;
- develop interpersonal communication skills as required for inquiry; and
- develop information processing skills through investigation of large or whole concepts.

2. Teachers—arts educators, other subject matter specialists, and classroom teachers—are central to the design and implementation of the total arts program and require extensive professional development and support.

Primary responsibility for both the design and the implementation of the new arts education program rests with the teachers. Few are adequately prepared for such responsibility. Professional development, very broadly imagined, is the surest route to building the intellectual capacity needed to create new curriculum and to use new teaching strategies effectively.

In partnership programs, each side must share knowledge and skills rather than one partner transferring skills to another. Teaching artists have much to learn from teachers and should spend time observing classroom teachers working with their students. Similarly, teachers will need to have a realistic amount of time to learn all the skills and information that the artists bring, since the schools benefit from the valuable resources they can provide.

Realistic professional development focuses on the strengths of collaborative programming and on enhancing the ways that teachers can build on the artist's work and transfer the skills and techniques to other classroom work. The intention should be to share and grow rather than to make teachers into artists or vice versa. For some teachers, personal development in the arts and culture is more important than professional development. They see deeper understanding of the arts disciplines as the key to expanding their roles as teachers who use the arts and to expanding the use of the arts in their classrooms.

While artists will function in new and more extensive ways in the schools as a part of the program, teachers must set the educational goals and standards. Teachers who meet these responsibilities will:

- participate in summer institutes and ongoing mentoring relationships to help each other and to learn from specialists;
- learn to incorporate a design process into their daily work;
- extend themselves beyond the normal professional boundaries to work with teachers from other disciplines, artists and others from the arts community; and
- develop their "art's side" through personal growth experiences in the arts and work with artists to help them develop their "education sides."

3. The arts program, perhaps more than programs in other school disciplines, needs to consider local and regional resources carefully and make conceptual compromises that enable the resources to be used fully.

Rural and suburban areas do not always have immediate access to dance companies, visual arts galleries, professional theaters or the artists who work in them. School libraries are often poorly stocked with arts-related materials, books or videos. The program design in these schools should find ways to compensate for the scarcity of resources by using film, broadcast television or distance-learning arrangements. One-shot field trips, performances and exhibitions are not sufficient for a program that works to integrate the resources fully into the general education of all students. When students are given access to the books, instructional materials and other resources found in museums, libraries, public broadcasting systems and other community institutions, instruction and student learning are strengthened, resulting in:

- broader and deeper understanding of the place of the arts in the world;
- encounters with the highest standards of excellence in the arts;
- an understanding of the nature of the work that artists do; and
- control of information about the arts to which they previously had lacked access.

4. The school arts program needs to cultivate relationships with local colleges or universities.

The work needed to implement this kind of arts program requires the teaching staff to acquire new skills and ways of thinking. Building a close working relationship between the college and university faculty in the region and the participating schools will result in:

- the identification and preparation of a well-prepared group of future teachers;
- a set of new professional development activities and providers for in-service teachers;
- new sites for performances and exhibitions; and
- access to useful repositories of art and music archives.

5. The school program needs to be shaped in ways that allow extended contact between students and working artists.

For a constructivist arts education program to be effective, students must observe and develop the work skills of professional artists. The student/artist relationship needs to go beyond the typical one-shot performance or short-term residency. Artists should be fully integrated into the life and culture of the school, and students should serve a kind of cognitive and productive apprenticeship with them. These artists may be teachers who also produce art as working professionals outside school, but contact with teaching artists, artists in residence, studio artists and performing groups is needed if students are to have a wide range of mentors and models. Students who have such extended contact will:

- have a more complete understanding of the place of artwork in the real world;
- develop skills needed to apply their expanding collection of perceptions to the problems and tasks that artists face;
- be able to make more informed decisions about their own professional or avocational ambitions;
- gain knowledge about the educational path required for the development of professional artistic skills; and
- see the contributions that artistic endeavors make to society.

6. School change in the arts builds new spaces and new time configurations that allow artists, teachers and students to work in studio settings.

Schools that undertake a constructivist approach will work to create what Maxine Greene calls "larger meeting places in schools...studios"[47] within which new social, professional and learning relationships are developed among teachers, students, artists, and the larger community. Existing space will be redesigned to create new spaces for collaboration that bring professional artists/instructors together with teachers and students in a studio setting and facilitate creative thinking, self-expression, and skills development that build on the artists' creative processes—to create an alternate model for learning and teaching. These studio-like settings are not limited to visual arts studios but also include theater, dance studios and concert halls. They are working/meeting places for artists.

The artist functions as a discipline specialist in these new spaces. In the arts, as in other subject matter disciplines, an appropriate understanding of professional practice in the field is required to achieve full comprehension. Artists provide access to that kind of understanding, and they work with classroom teachers, sharing their knowledge and building a more secure base for the expansion of visual arts skills throughout the curriculum. This powerful combination of discipline knowledge and instructional skill enables the children to add artistic thinking and working to their other ways of experiencing the world—building strong social relationships, communicating, and succeeding in school. In subtle and complex ways, the presence of the studio program in schools works, with the rest of the school community, to reshape the schools.

Times of change require that traditional boundaries be crossed, even obliterated. Among the most pernicious boundaries are those that have been created between and within academic disciplines. Scholars, educators and practitioners within single disciplines avidly and sometimes viciously defend their terrain. Those who cross the boundaries in the academic world may suffer castigation and exile from the domain. In the real world of work and commerce, however, these boundaries must be crossed regularly and to good effect. As schools move closer to the world outside the school walls, they need teachers who are skilled at crossing the boundaries—teachers who can both work in interdisciplinary ways and relate the subject matter to the work of the practitioner.

Artists and arts educators should be among the best prepared for these tasks. Most arts educators are also practicing artists, and in recent years, many artists have supplemented their incomes by instructing. Few would deny that arts educators need help to become better artists and that teaching artists need more education to become better teachers. Nevertheless, they are a group poised to cross boundaries in changed schools. We need to see our artists and our arts educators as "discipline specialists" who have unique skills and knowledge to bring into the classroom.

7. School change in the arts should build on three broad characteristics of effective education—engagement, relationships and understanding.

Engagement. Those who observe artists and students of the arts at work inevitably record the intense involvement that is a characteristic of such work. Csikszentmihalyi noticed in his early studies "...how totally involved the artists became with what was transpiring on canvas,"[48] and that inspired him to focus most of his adult research on that observation. Artists are not the only humans who are involved in their work, but to have "art" in the work of art, we must have the phenomenon of "engagement." What Csikszentmihalyi calls "flow" is the mental state that happens "...when we are actively involved in a difficult enterprise, in a task that stretches our physical or mental abilities...when challenges are high and personal skills are used to the utmost...." He sees the engaged person narrowing his or her attention and becoming, "...involved, concentrated, absorbed."[49] Dennie Wolf describes another form of artists' engagement in which they become aware of the work of other artists and begin paying attention to the techniques, styles and composition used by others. She calls this stage of development "becoming alert."[50] Maxine Greene, in her more extensive discussions of the arts, characterizes such experiences as "aware engagements"[51] and describes them as provoking attentiveness. Greene builds her argument for the integration of arts and aesthetic education on this nexus of engaging experiences and heightened attention.

Relationships. The investigation of the ways that students build, use, participate in and explore a variety of relationships is central to the study of both cognitive and social growth. "Relational knowing," according to Perkins, is essential for the existence of sapient beings.[52] These relationships begin with interpersonal interaction. Contrary to widespread notions, artists do not separate themselves from society and work, lonely, in garret rooms. As in any other intellectual activity, the artist knows about other people—especially other artists, draws from their experiences, uses their information and skills, and presents in the same public domain. Their work is social in the same way that the work of others is social. It is shaped by perception derived from vast social networks and the sharing of values. It embodies and conveys information. It is available for interpretation by others. At this level, the artist and the student of art engage in establishing relationships with other artists. Wolf identifies this "...increased alertness to the works and minds of others" as a new and previously unrecognized dimension of artistic learning.[53]

Understanding. The domain of understanding has to do with both teacher and student outcomes, and it relates to the construction of shared "meaning" as a result of collaborative discourse that is dynamic, complex and inquiry-oriented rather than that aimed at the delivery and receipt of information, facts and skills. Perkins and his group at Project Zero have settled on five characteristics of understanding: (1) relations—where the subject sits in relation to others; (2) coherence—how well the web of relations hangs together; (3) standards of coherence—consistency from context to context; (4) generativity—show understanding through productive use; and (5) open-ended—always more understanding to be gained.[54] The measure of understanding is performance—a complex manipulation of the information, concepts or skills related to the topic—but the open-ended characteristic of understanding means that the performance is never completed, the circle never completely closed.

Call It Good Education

The fundamental argument presented here is that the arts provide ways to prepare students to live securely in the world because they have gained the tools necessary to think, feel and relate to the physical, social, intellectual, emotional and aesthetic components of their lives. They know how to be productive. They understand complex relationships, and they know how to broaden and deepen their understanding. We do not call such education "arts education," "mathematics education," "science education," or "reading education." We call it good education. It is education that strengthens students' capabilities to engage and make meaning from many cultural and artistic forms and to use better the experiences they have with cultural organizations. As Elliot Eisner tells us,

> We need a more generous conception of what it means to know and a wider conception of the sources of human understanding. The poet, the painter, the composer, the playwright, as well as the physicist, the chemist, the botanist, the astronomer have something to teach us. Paying adequate attention to such forms of understanding in schools is the best way to make them a meaningful part of our students' intellectual lives.[55]

While much school restructuring activity is generic, the unique characteristics of different subject matter disciplines introduce both new challenges and new possibilities to the process. The arts require special skills, materials, some new school policy and programming support, and informed leadership. Nevertheless, the arts add opportunities for enhancing active and collaborative learning, providing new and engaging ways for students to explore the physical and social dimensions of their communities—peers, teachers and the larger school community—and of new professional and instructional relationships with professional artists. The arts also enable students to discover additional media and modes for presenting or displaying knowledge—channels for admitting sensory and emotional perceptions to the construction of meaning—and new ways of enhancing cognitive development using sensory and emotional channels largely ignored in other subject matter disciplines.

This recommended approach to education is "constructivist" in the deepest, most systematic sense. Students and teachers in these schools are not simply set free to do whatever they want in whatever way they choose. They are set free to plan together, to make and produce together, and to hold their work up to internal and external review against exacting criteria and standards. The arts, far from being the "easy," "trivial" or "fun" subjects of rumor and myth, are immensely challenging, complex, and call for highly developed and refined skills. Artists, as Jacques D'Amboise insists, work with intense "passion" and a demand for "excellence,"[56] even in these times when we realize that "excellence" must be variously defined and must accommodate diverse standards. Whatever the standards, the quality of excellence must represent the highest, and for there to be "art" in the arts, there must be excellence.

No One Best Way

No one best example exists of a school that grows from the principles described here. In fact, the eclectic character of the schools that have been designed using these principles is indicative of the power of these principles when they become part of school change efforts. Several growing schools and school change initiatives in the nation demonstrate the principles at work. The Galef Institute's Different Ways of Knowing project, New York City's New Visions Schools, several Annenberg Institute for School Reform efforts in such places as Chicago, Los Angeles and New York City, and the College Board/Getty Center for Education in the Arts' Interdisciplinary Arts Education Project all support schools that have incorporated or demonstrate many of these principles. Simple descriptions of these schools mask the underlying principles.

Two schools in the same city, the New York Museum School and the Arts-Related Industries School, look and feel very different. Their students would describe very different motives for choosing these schools. The daily schedules are different, and their curriculums seem different in focus. Nevertheless, both schools begin with student/parent/society interest in the topics, activities and content of the school curriculum. Both meet city and state requirements and standards for all subject areas. Both engage students in the creation of knowledge through dialogue with "persons-in-conversation"—teachers, artists, working adults, other students.

Both schools recognize specialized knowledge and skills and, at the same time, blur the social and work role distinctions between teachers, students and artists. Both develop collaborative partnerships with outside organizations—business and industry in one case and diverse museums in the other. Both schools have Board of Education waivers in hiring staff, allowing them to employ professional artists or museum educators as full-time educators and to have certified teachers from all disciplines work in field sites away from the home school to provide education. Both schools have blurred traditional distinctions between junior high school and high school, creating a grades 7-12 structure in one case and a 7-14 structure in the other. Both schools make direct experience with professionals in the field—their objects, artifacts, personnel, organizations and practices—the initial point of contact and the constant referent for learning. Students in both schools build their curriculum together with teachers and arts professionals, business personnel, arts administrators, support staff, technicians and parents.

Most important, the arts are everywhere in both schools, and the students develop full knowledge and understanding of at least one art form, along with an ability to see relationships among the arts and with the processes of other disciplines. Traditional classroom teachers, arts educators, teaching artists, parents and professionals from outside the schools and from deep inside industry, all work in integrated ways to support the learning efforts of the students.

At the Museum School, seventh-grade students spend large portions of the school year working with museum educators, curators and Board of Education-certified teachers in museums such as the Jewish Museum, the Brooklyn Museum, the Museum of Natural History, the New York Historical Society and the Manhattan Children's Museum. The students study in an object-based curriculum and complete their lessons in history, social studies, English, earth science, biology, mathematics, art and music. They return to the home school for classes that cannot be conducted in the museums, such as physical education. The curriculum is demanding and engaging. It calls for the students to use the skills of museum curators to gain understanding. They work to apply special knowledge in chemistry, biology, history, technology, math and communications to presentations of that knowledge in museum exhibits. They demonstrate their knowledge in the ways used by museum personnel, and they hold their exhibitions of knowledge to the standards of museums and museum professionals.

A student enrolled in the Arts-Related Industry School, a new school based on practice at the Young Adult Learning Academy, may be studying geometry and working as an intern with an architectural firm. That student's geometry class will incorporate the work experience and call for the student to demonstrate understanding of basic geometry concepts and skills through the creation of an architectural product or exhibition that meets the approval of the work-site mentor and of the math instructor. The same student will be working as a peer mentor with a seventh- or eighth-grade student to introduce the younger student to the world of work in architecture and to the process of constructive learning.

In the same school, another group of students might be interns at a television network—ABC—or with a production crew from HBO. These students will be working on American history and will be investigating and collecting information for a new series on the American revolution. They will investigate actual sites in New York City and the Hudson Valley and will produce their own videotape products as classroom exhibitions of their work, but they will also be working alongside professional video artists, editors, set designers and sound technicians.

Arguably, programs such as this could only exist in a city with rich museum or arts industry resources. However, the same type of program can be shaped in schools with much-reduced resources. At P.S. 92 in Central Harlem, for example, an IBM researcher, Don Nix, is demonstrating that a school in a blighted neighborhood, with a long history of underperforming by staff and students—and with little direct access to outside resources—can use what Nix calls "Expressive Learning."

Nix deliberately choose this school as an extreme case to demonstrate his points. The school has consistently ranked at the bottom of New York City schools in reading and is undergoing state review. The staff is very young—experienced teachers opt for more luxurious assignments. In fact, two years ago, when the city temporarily decided to remove a wrinkle in its hiring policy by terminating "per diem" teachers (uncertified temporary hires), the school was left with only four teachers to begin the term. Nix works an hour-and-a-half a day with two classes of nonreading third-graders. He has shown how available computer and video equipment and processes can engage these students, build their communication skills, add to their knowledge, teach where and how to gather knowledge, give them the means to apply their new knowledge and skills in imaginative ways to the creation of video documents, and allow them to demonstrate to parents, teachers and staff that they can command artistic tools. Coincidentally, the students' reading comprehension scores have risen significantly, and Nix has prepared the regular teaching staff of the school to take up his classes.

Conclusion: Getting Back to First Principles

The changes required for learning such as this to occur do not involve any change in our understanding of what content of skills are to be taught. They do not require that arts educators step aside and let someone else take their places. They do require new thinking and planning, and a willingness to try new structures, new working strategies and new collaborations that put the learner, rather than the teacher or the subject, at the center of instructional life. In these schools, policy will be based on new sets of basic principles; standards will be set in accordance with the curriculum, experience and practice of each school; and assessment will be based on demonstrations of skill and knowledge in the world beyond the classroom.

For education of any sort to exist in our society, powerful aggregations of resources, personnel, political clout—turf—apparently need to be created. So we apply labels to the various educational domains. Perhaps a democratic society demands such arrangements, but in this vision, the various educational domains work peacefully together and in harmony. Music educators do not worry about whether their art is diminished by being "used" to teach math. Art educators do not worry about whether teaching artists are taking their jobs away from them. Drama specialists do not worry about the ways that the grammarians ignore the literary arts. In this world, art educators help students make art, design integrated curriculums with mathematicians, explore the archives of museums, and work along with specialists in other subject matter disciplines to help students choose the appropriate disciplinary tools for specific problems and tasks. They do not close the door to possibilities.

Charles Fowler, to whom this book is dedicated, exhorted arts educators,

> ...to see ourselves first as educators. We are teaching basic human understanding of life in all its dimensions, what writer William Gass called "a treasure of human consciousness." If our intent is to establish the arts as basic education, then everything we do in schools must illuminate the necessity of the arts and their educational value for all people. We need to get back to first principles.[57]

Dr. Terry L. Baker is Senior Research Scientist at the Education Development Center. He is the former Director of the Four Seasons Project at the National Center for Restructuring Education, Schools and Teaching at Teachers College, Columbia University. He has served as Dean of the Research Division and Senior Research Scientist at Bank Street College of Education and as Associate Dean of the School of Education at Hofstra University. He was Senior Assistant to the Chancellor of the New York City Public Schools, the Co-director of the Hunter College Teacher Corps Arts and Humanities Project and Director of the Pittsburgh Arts Education Project. Dr. Baker worked for several years in the schools of East Harlem developing alternative educational programs and schools, special curriculum projects and research activities. He is a former high school and college English teacher.

Current Issues in Research and Evaluation of the Arts in Education

A Conversation with Robert E. Stake

Dr. Robert E. Stake is professor of education and director of the Center for Instructional Resources and Curriculum Evaluation (CIRCE) at the University of Illinois at Urbana-Champaign. CIRCE is widely recognized in educational research circles as a site for innovation in program evaluation design. Bob and I first met in the early seventies at a JDR 3rd Fund-sponsored American Education Research Association preconference on research and evaluation in the arts in New Orleans when I was still working at the Learning Cooperative of the New York City Public Schools. We met again soon after when I was at the JDR 3rd Fund's Arts in Education Program and he was putting together the Fund-sponsored publication of his book, *Evaluating the Arts in Education: A Responsive Approach*. We also had the opportunity to work together with the network of principals and other administrators in the New York City Arts in General Education (AGE) program. His books and other writings have made an indelible impression on me, and I have been able to adapt many of the principles of his "responsive" approach to my own system of evaluation. His recent book, *The Art of Case Study Research*, is a gem and recommended reading (see bibliography).

We had occasion to meet again in Chicago at a spring 1995 meeting, hosted by the MacArthur Foundation and the GE Fund, in which a small group of us helped to shape a request for proposal for a new arts-in-education research initiative. Bob agreed to contribute to this book, and what follows are his answers to my questions and our ensuing dialogue. The exchange is included almost verbatim. It will give you an idea of the density and complexity of the issues and the continuing difficulty of communicating across the educational research language barrier.

Robert Stake: Jane, you have raised four questions that deserve long and careful deliberation. I do not intend to provide that "on the one hand, on the other hand" deliberation, but I *will* give you my views succinctly. As you know, I am neither artist nor arts educator, yet as a devoted supporter of arts education, I have developed some pretty strong views. More generally, my views about education more or less follow the ideas of specialists in curriculum study. As you also know, my views about the evaluation of education are at odds with a number of specialists in that field. I hope these words may be of some use.

You ask: What are the issues and current trends and practices in assessment and evaluation in educational programs? I have four.

The first key issue is "achievement testing": Will arts educators and advocates of arts education overemphasize standardized student achievement tests as the conceptualization of additional learning and the criteria for improvement in teaching the arts? There is a fundamental misperception that innovative teaching will result in additional learning that can be discerned with student achievement tests, attitude scales, or other brief and objective procedures. Fundamental learning occurs in the absence of teaching; much long-term learning can be attributed to years of instruction by parents, teachers, peers, the media and self-arrangement of experience. Education does occur and teaching makes important contributions, but what shows up as gain on standardized tests is almost entirely simple maturation of intellect. A few months of good teaching will not show up on most of our standardized assessments. Measurable gains in insight, knowledge and attitude require extended engagement.

Jane Remer: Bob, can you please explain what you mean by "the conceptualization of additional learning," and can you unpack your key issue a little more?

RS: For conceptualization you may substitute "index" or "evidence," and for simplification you can omit "additional." The question would then read: Will arts educators and advocates of arts education overemphasize standardized student achievement tests as the index or evidence of learning and the criteria for improvement in teaching the arts? I include it to keep in mind that a special program or innovative teaching is only an add-on to what the larger world is teaching the children.

A second key issue is "performance assessment": Will arts educators stick to (and protect and improve) traditional sensitivities to the progress of individual arts students? Even in the arts, where performance and product review have been standard bases for evaluation, some current trends in assessment of student performance move us toward systemic use of portfolios, problem solving and analysis, and the composition of communications as evidence of achievement in the arts. These "authentic assessment" procedures have wide acceptance as part of an instructional repertoire but are increasingly criticized by experts in measurement for their unreliability—for their imprecision in discriminating between good and poor performance. The purpose of discriminating high achievers from low achievers and the purpose of coming to understand a young artist's achievement are significantly different tasks.

JR: Can you simplify your statement so that it is clearer: What do you mean by "stick to (and protect and improve) traditional sensitivities to the progress of individual arts students?"

RS: In other words, "Will arts educators hold the line, insisting on measuring arts achievement in traditional ways?" The point is not so much to stick to older assessment methods as to stick to traditional criteria and standards.

A third issue is "children's creativity": Will the community of arts educators acknowledge the changes in epistemological philosophy elsewhere in education and reflect upon the value of a constructivist position in arts education? As I see it, the arts education community has lagged behind other curricular fields in embracing a constructivist epistemology. Educational leaders in language, science, mathematics and other fields have changed greatly in the last decade, diminishing the emphasis on specific knowledge and increasing the emphasis on learners constructing their own knowledge—even when that knowledge is not favored by experts. Furthermore, these educators have moved toward acceptance of the idea that the discipline's knowledge base is unavoidably changed by what novices, merely by their thinking and talking, contribute to reshaping the definition of the discipline. For the most part, as I see it, arts educators remain protectors of classic views of the disciplines and critics of popular and juvenile expressions.

JR: Can you explain what you mean by "a constructivist epistemology?" I know what the words mean, but they need a contextual translation. Your third issue also needs translation. If you want the arts community to move, you need to help them understand where to.

RS: In truth, I cannot explain it in simple, and certainly not graceful, language. You could substitute "approach to knowledge" for epistemology. I provided a paraphrase of constructivism earlier. In this book, of course, it is your job, not mine, to teach the arts community things they need to know. I think the implications for evaluation are considerable if you examine the arts as defined by both experts and nonexperts.

My final issue is "the quality of evaluation": Will promoters of arts education recognize that it is in their best long-range interests to require a certain toughness, authenticity and validity to their evaluators' work? Educational evaluation has come to be seen by its sponsors and by its practitioners as more a promotional activity than an inquiry activity. Almost all hiring of internal evaluators and contracting of external teams is undertaken to authenticate, protect or expand the activity, not to understand its quality. This is not surprising for "advocates," but it has become the dominant expectation even of the evaluators. Before or during a study, most evaluators embrace the advocacy. They work to protect sponsors and developers, minimizing embarrassing questions and even suppressing troublesome indications of poor quality. Efforts to validate the findings are absent or half-hearted, and no professional review is likely.

JR: Crystal clear. How, if at all, have these issues and the field's ability to address them changed since you wrote *Evaluating the Arts in Education* in 1975?

RS: The fundamental things about quality in arts education and how you go about finding it are pretty much unchanged. But the politics and economic context of doing evaluation has changed a great deal. We probably had a more generous, open-minded and less cynical education profession 20 years ago, but as a sub-profession [arts education], we have been badly treated, regularly considered to have little of consequence to say or to contribute to good public education. We continue to have a coterie of admirers and friends who appreciate us and promote our collective works. A few of our supporters are attached to foundations, and we are encouraged to think of unique ways to integrate the arts with general studies, but the public that needs to be persuaded to invest in a sound education for all is well outside our call. Program evaluation has not changed much, but if anything, it is looked to less for important judgments of what is good.

JR: What impetus, if any, do you believe the current reform movement (Goals 2000, voluntary national standards, national research agenda, NAEP arts assessment and the like) will have on local research and evaluation efforts?

RS: I do not consider the current reform rhetoric to have even a small, genuine movement behind it. I do not expect these stirrings to invigorate local research and evaluation efforts.

JR: Bob, two sentences is tantalizing. Please expand a bit.

RS: Okay. Goals 2000, national standards, a national research agenda, and the NAEP arts assessment were for the most part intended to address a real weakness in our national system of education. As they stand, they are more a political movement than educational movement. They are an expression of political wishfulness, an effort to arouse a profession in which many politicians and many citizens have diminishing faith. They are partly an effort to indicate that politicians are alert and trying to do something—to find words that raise aspirations and consolidate purposes. The commitment at neither state nor federal level is strong enough to underwrite action. The efforts are an opportunity for diverse advocates to indicate their aspirations for education, but the current reform process is one of standardization, consensus and diminishing the importance of the uniqueness of community, school and individual.

The nation is strongly and wisely committed to a certain autonomy for the teacher. Few teachers abuse it, and most stick pretty close to the convention. It is a wise policy even though many teachers are less than minimally competent. Simply imposing standards on incompetent teachers does little more than deny them opportunity to include some teaching that they are good at. The nation may not be able to afford it, but it should continue to aspire to providing in each classroom a teacher who decides when, how and how much the components of a syllabus should be taught to these particular children. There are many able teachers who could help the less able teachers if the conditions to provide such help were created. That would be a far more effective reform strategy, although much more expensive, than providing information about and censure for deficiency in teaching and learning (which are the mechanisms of most state reform efforts).

For the most part, good teachers and poor teachers alike are not aware of and are not in intuitive harmony with, nor supportive of, national reform of arts education. The current reform rhetoric does not have a popular, professional or political movement behind it. There is no genuine reform movement. I do not expect these stirrings to create any invigoration of local research and evaluation efforts.

JR: What kinds of questions should arts organizations be asking about program effectiveness and the impact of teaching and learning in the arts on students and other learners?

RS: Many questions about program effectiveness are based upon unrealistic expectations as to what kind of difference a modified teaching and learning might make. Such questions must be raised by those who share in the provision of arts programs, and answers must be looked for mostly in traditional, intuitive review. Raising those questions to measure impact in a formal and objective fashion is an invitation to disappointment and a deterrent to making opportunities for aesthetic experience. Even while believing in the vital place the arts can play in general education, everyone should resist representing the quality of arts projects in terms of what can be produced for educational change. The impact questions should be of the sort: "Have we made this a place where arts experiences may thrive? Is this a way to share with children the good life for which we work?" For persons not intending careers in the arts, the evaluative measure should be in the quality of opportunity for reflective knowing, not in the quality of what can be done with that knowing. The sophistication of measuring effectiveness and impact lies far below the sophistication of young people to put their artistic senses to work. It is better simply to reflect upon what is happening and to talk about it than to seek or require impersonal indices of effect and impact.

JR: A lovely point and beautifully stated. It is, as far as I can recall, consistent with your philosophy of more than 20 years. What troubles me is that it seems so absolute. You seem to be saying that since we are not yet sophisticated enough to measure effectiveness and impact, we shouldn't bother trying. What troubles me is, (1) I believe that we *can* determine impact and effect if we are clear about it in cognitive and behavioral terms, even if we don't quantify it mathematically, and (2) educational decision makers and others who make policy do not readily accept reflection and description as sufficient evidence of value. We have tried this approach for years and failed miserably to convince others beyond those already favorably inclined or converted. The challenge, I believe, is to find a combination of approaches of integrity that will, when taken together, tell a persuasive story—the truth, whatever it may be—about what one can learn in, through and about the arts.

You see, we may not want or be able to standardize arts instruction—I, too, am wary of standards without criteria that are set too far from the schoolhouse—but I believe we must come up with an eclectic approach to determining impact and effect, or I guarantee we will lose whatever momentum the current reform climate affords us and again find ourselves out on the stoop. Part of our job, of course, is to educate the American public that quantitative measurement is not the only way to evaluate knowledge, intelligence, creativity, sensitivity, intuition, imagination, talent and the like.

RS: Our quantitative efforts are sometimes suggestive and often helpful, but they are never valid indications of effective education. We are nowhere near the threshold of a valid quantitative assessment scheme for arts education. But I do not say don't bother trying; I say don't make promises that cannot be kept.

We can arrive at indications of achievement, effect and even efficiency, but we have no better ways than arts educators did 30 years ago. Paying close attention is the key. Whether we call it qualitative or not is unimportant. Being knowledgeable and attentive as teachers, reviewers, supervisors, critics and evaluators is the best we can do.

Our professional judgments have not been our failings. Our history is not one of failing to describe to the public what good arts education is. We could be much better than we are, but we have not failed miserably.

The vast majority of the public *does* accept personal judgment, reflection, subjective interpretation and storytelling. It is their preferred method of evaluating. They are quite supportive of our interpretive works when we make sense, when we are sensitive to their values, when we bring *them* into the reasoning process, and when we elevate the consideration to complexities to which they had not been attentive. True, they will scream "subjectivity" and "bias" when their ox is being gored. True, we do not have econometric ways of aggregating judgments across large political entities. But those are the realities with which we work. We will never be far from bias and misrepresentation. I see these as challenges, not as perfidies.

All evaluation work, Lee Cronbach once told me, is case study. We evaluators have to keep the quality dimensions prominent, but not let them dominate the perception. Understanding quality is understanding performance, not understanding criteria.

There is so much nonsense to dispel. Mischief as well. I hope this will be useful.

Dr. Robert Stake is Professor of Education and Director of the Center for Instructional Research and Curriculum Evaluation at the University of Illinois. Since 1963, he has been a specialist in the evaluation of educational programs. Among the evaluative studies directed were: works in science and mathematics in elementary and secondary schools, model programs and conventional teaching of the arts in schools, and development of teaching with sensitivity to gender equity; education of teachers for the deaf and for youth in transition from school to work settings, environmental education and special programs for gifted students, and the reform of urban education. He has authored Quieting Reform, *a book on Charles Murray's evaluation of Cities-in-Schools; two books on methodology,* Evaluating the Arts in Education *and* The Art of Case Study Research; *and* Custom and Cherishing, *a book with Liora Bresler and Linda Mabry on teaching the arts in ordinary elementary school classrooms in America. Recently, he contributed a case study of a school to NCREL's evaluation of the first year of Chicago School Reform.*

The Arts: Who Shall Teach?

by John J. Mahlmann

Many years ago, the celebrated cartoonist of "Peanuts," Charles Schulz, contributed occasional material to Sunday school curriculum publishers. One of his cartoons has stuck with me. The scene is a church youth-group meeting. A nerdy-looking teenage boy is holding up an outlandishly ornamented, grimacing, tribal mask. A girl is introducing him: "And now, Norbert will lead our evening discussion on the topic: 'It doesn't really matter what you believe as long as you're sincere.'" In the context of this article that tag line might be rendered as, "It doesn't really matter who teaches the arts as long as that person 'knows something about art,' and has a heart in the right place."

In fact, that line already has a home in many discussions in today's schools because the status of arts education, always precarious, forces many local-level policy makers and education leaders to try and put the best possible face on a difficult situation. Let us be candid. The stark truth is that in too many school districts, the arts remain the runt of the curricular litter.[58] In spite of state mandates and declared policies to the contrary, the arts are still among the first to go under the budget knife when the "fat-trimming" starts among the financially challenged. Those forced to do the trimming all too often try to justify themselves by building loose arguments that try to equate any form of student self-expression with arts education. Of course, no such equation can be drawn. The canons and criteria of individual arts disciplines simply go by the board. The justifications, in turn, are all too often paralleled by a confusion between "activities" in the arts or "exposure" to them and substantive teaching and learning.

Concerns about the kind of creative activity that legitimately can be called "doing art" and about what an education in an arts discipline really is converge in the question, "Who shall teach the arts?" It is the teacher who incarnates the response to both concerns. Arts educators, speaking both individually and through their professional associations, have long maintained that the question "Who shall teach the arts?" has a simple answer: "Qualified people." That answer, however, simply moves the question to another level. How do we determine who is qualified?

Three Answers

Answers to that question arise from three main sources: (1) the ends and therefore the nature of education that we as a society have defined; (2) the credentialing process, i.e., the professional and legal consensus about what "qualified" means; and (3) the problems created by the inevitable dissatisfactions that can emerge from pursuing (1) and (2). Each of these is considered below.

1. Determining who is qualified from the ends and nature of education. Here the answer to "Who shall teach the arts?" takes shape from the broad societal purposes that we expect education—and arts education—to meet. Throughout the history of our civilization, people have insisted that a central task of each generation is to transmit its achievements, values, meanings and heritage to the next. In modern times, Americans have bestowed that responsibility, for better or worse, largely on the education system. Moreover, we expect the schools to play a major role in creating full human beings from the raw material of our children.

An education in the arts is central to that effort because, as the *National Standards for Arts Education* points out: "If our civilization is to continue to be both dynamic and nurturing, its success will ultimately depend on how well we develop the capacities of our children, not only to earn a living in a vastly complex world, but to live a life rich in meaning."[59]

These aims of education help us to determine whom we should trust with—in effect—our civilization. If, for example, a chief aim of education is to teach our children how to live a life rich in meaning, then some of the teachers who nourish that process should be qualified to teach the arts. This is only common sense, since many characterize the arts as the apotheosis of humankind's attempt to create meaning. When you want to unlock a door, you go to someone who has already found a key. But beyond that, the fundamental ends of education require, by their very nature, not just someone who can pass out ready-made keys, but someone who is qualified to teach children how to make their own. "Qualified" in this context means people who know the arts from the inside— from their own engagement with ideas, from their own struggle to bend recalcitrant materials to new purposes, and from their own search for meaning.

2. Determining who is qualified from the credentialing process, i.e., the professional and legal consensus about what "qualified" means. The insistence on qualified instructors in the arts has already produced a broad consensus among arts educators. Professional arts educators in dance, music, theater and the visual arts have all published standards, as have practitioners in other areas of arts education. This professional activity is consonant with what it means to be a "professional" in this country; namely, it means being a member of a group who has undergone a specific course of training and education, leading others in the profession to recognition that the person is competent to "profess," i.e., "to make an open declaration of" a body of knowledge and skills in his or her own right.

In arts education, this recognition is often exercised through degrees granted by institutions of higher education, including arts institutes and schools of teacher preparation. Another source is the public's recognition of quality in artistic production. These forms of recognition are overlapped by a formal credentialing apparatus (by licensing or certification, or both) in the 50 states and the other U.S. territories. All provide credentials to public school teachers in some way. Some states depend on the credentialing processes developed by professional education associations. Not all states insist on credentials for teachers in all the arts disciplines. Nevertheless, wherever they may be in force, credentialing processes make a statement that "this person is qualified to teach an arts discipline as we define the subject."

Currently, the National Board of Professional Teaching Standards (NBPTS) is planning to draw up a new set of standards for teachers in all subjects and at several levels of competence. An NBPTS credential will, in the near future, become the teaching profession's complement to state-level licenses and certificates, a "national" answer to the question "Who is qualified?" In this context, "qualified" will imply a much greater—and much needed—uniformity among the individuals who are pronounced qualified by their peers and by public authorities. Indications of quality in professional practice, now minimal, will become more reliable when the certification procedures of the NBPTS become fully operational. Beyond entry level, a large part of moving up the credentialing ladder in any area of teaching will be strongly tied to on-the-job demonstrations of teaching competence and the mastery of specific teaching skills.

3. Determining who is qualified in the face of problems created by dissatisfactions with (1) and (2). Here, making a determination about "Who is qualified?" becomes more complicated. Sometimes people who would make superb teachers have no formed educational philosophy or have no training as teachers. Often such people are excluded from making a contribution in the classroom because they have not jumped through the required credentialing hoops.

To their credit, some states have devised alternative or temporary credentials to take advantage of the skills and contributions of these "outsiders." However, both educators and artists can testify that the success of artists-in-the-schools programs comes primarily from the contribution the visiting artist makes to the *education* of children, not from the individual artist's level of competence in a particular arts discipline. The point of creating the credentialing alternative is thus not to transform visiting artists into teachers overnight, but to create a way for educators and artists to work together to create an educational result that neither could create alone—to link a special competency to learning.

How do we know what "qualified" means here? Critics of the bureaucratic weaknesses to which education—like all institutions—is prone inevitably complain about restricting the use of artists in the classroom who lack a teaching credential. "Why not let them come in," the critics ask, "especially when many are so talented personally and so eager to work with children? Arts programs are so short of teachers anyway, and they would add so much."

The argument has merit. But there is another side. Personal competency in music or watercolor painting is not the same as the competency to teach someone else an art form, especially a child. A terrific local dancer may—or may not—understand "scope and sequence" in an arts curriculum and may not have a clue about how her expertise can enhance either one effectively. Nor does being a good actor carry with it the ability to teach others about dramatic structures or to motivate them to give their best performance in a school play.

Getting to Criteria

Uncertainty in answering such questions underscores the necessity for criteria that will identify core competencies. Often master teachers or evaluators can make determinations about "Who is qualified?" by observing teachers in action.

Many who lack official credentials are excellent teachers; many who have credentials are poor teachers despite their attainments. How does the would-be teacher organize and present material? How well does he or she lead children to their own insights? How effectively does he or she use time? Does the prospective teacher have techniques to reach difficult students, to challenge those who find things easy, and to encourage those who do not?

Many credentialing bodies may need to open up their procedures and carefully examine them in response to these questions. Professional teacher associations, unions, and other credentialing groups will doubtless retain their role and function as gatekeepers. But if the boundaries of "Who is qualified?" are to become permeable membranes between schools and the arts community, much more flexibility and common sense are required than we see now.

Similar criteria should apply in distinguishing the qualifications of classroom teachers from arts specialists. For example, can the would-be teacher teach sight-reading and notation in music or help a student to make the appropriate choice of media in a visual art? Can he or she give guidance on a more effective interpretation of a character in the school play or change choreography to achieve a specific artistic objective? Some in both groups will be able to; some will not.

Artists in the Schools. Budget-constrained school districts often attempt to overcome the arts specialist vs. classroom teacher dilemma by turning to an artists-in-the-schools program or to programs mounted by community arts agencies and local arts groups. Rather than support teaching positions, the schools hire freelancers to save on salaries and benefits, or they find *pro bono* services. These become, regrettably, the default arts education program.

In the end, this solution is destructive because it undermines sound education policy on four grounds. First, it allows budget questions to drive decision-making about education, using economic criteria to shape what happens between teacher and child. The available means thus determine education's ends rather than ends informing means. Second, this solution pulls the feet of school board members and school administrators comfortably away from the fire. By shifting from educational to economic grounds, school boards, like Procrustes of old, are free to shape their victims (in this case children) to the budgetary bed they have already constructed—with the added benefit of being able to portray themselves as hard-headed about finances! Third, and worse, this solution prolongs the protracted battle between arts educators and their colleagues in other disciplines over resources. Finally, and perhaps worst of all, the default solution gives children an experience of the arts that can often deprive them of more carefully crafted opportunities to learn about and create art, to develop valuable skills and abilities at a level deep enough to shape their lives.

But let us be clear. Artist-in-the-schools programs, in and of themselves, do not present problems. These programs are powerful and valuable components of arts education that can provide opportunities, experiences, insight and learning that are available in no other way. The problem arises when they are substituted for a balanced, sequential, curriculum of arts education taught by *qualified* teachers.

Redefining the Issue: The Standards

In the context of the national education reform movement, the question 'Who shall teach the arts?" increasingly will be answered in terms provided by the *National Standards for Arts Education*. Whether making decisions about the competency of those who are already "in the pipeline" or building bridges between the nonteacher artists and the credentialing apparatus, the question "Who is qualified?" boils down to criteria about teaching competency. In that context, the standards now point to: (1) those who can themselves demonstrate the skills and knowledge called for by the arts disciplines; and (2) those who can demonstrate the ability to help young people develop the competencies the standards call for, including, for example, selecting instructional materials and strategies, diagnosing problems, evaluating learning, and the like.

In arts education, the *Standards* ask students to know and be able to do the following by the time they have completed secondary school:

- **They should be able to communicate at a basic level in the four arts disciplines—dance, music, theater and the visual arts.** This includes knowledge and skills in the use of the basic vocabularies, materials, tools, techniques and intellectual methods of each arts discipline.

- **They should be able to communicate proficiently in at least one art form,** including the ability to define and solve artistic problems with insight, reason and technical proficiency.

- **They should be able to develop and present basic analyses of works of art** from structural, historical, and cultural perspectives and from combinations of those perspectives. This includes the ability to understand and evaluate work in the various arts disciplines.

- **They should have an informed acquaintance with exemplary works of art from a variety of cultures and historical periods** and a basic understanding of historical development in the arts disciplines, across the arts as a whole, and within cultures.

- **They should be able to relate various types of arts knowledge and skills within and across the arts disciplines.** This includes mixing and matching competencies and understandings in art-making, history and culture, and analysis in any arts-related project.[60]

Ending on a Presupposition

In essence, "Who shall teach the arts?" is a question undergoing redefinition. Within the context of the *Standards*, the answer will become "someone who is able to bring children to the knowledge and ability to do what the standards call for." Regardless of what new credentialing processes may require, "qualified" increasingly will mean someone who:

- can guide children through a balanced, sequential process of learning that achieves clearly stated outcomes;

- can instill in children an appreciation for the various art forms and the products of the arts disciplines in all their diversity;
- can bring children to clearly stated levels of performance in a given arts discipline; and
- can help children arrive at a knowledge of the cultural and historical context of the arts disciplines.

All this presupposes something that has not yet happened: teachers in the arts disciplines must find an intellectual and pedagogical home in the *Standards*. They must see in the *Standards* what is only now becoming visible: the best opportunity they will see in their lifetimes for bringing the arts not only to the core of the curriculum, but also to the mind and spirit of every child. Having perceived the urgency of that reality, they must act on it by working to implement the *Standards* in every state and school district.

Dr. John J. Mahlmann is Executive Director of the Music Educators National Conference, the largest arts education organization in the world. He studied at the Pennsylvania State University and Boston University and served on the faculty of those institutions, as well as Texas Tech. He also taught courses at Columbia University Teachers College, Northern Virginia Community College, and George Washington University. Dr. Mahlmann was formerly Executive Director of the National Art Education Association.

Standards for American Schools: Help or Hindrance?

By Elliot W. Eisner

The following has been abridged with the author's permission from an article that appeared in the June 1995 Phi Delta Kappan journal, pp. 758 - 764. It is reprinted with permission of the Phi Delta Kappan.

Efforts to reform American schools are not exactly a novel enterprise. In the 1970s "accountability" became the central concept around which our education reform efforts turned. If only we could identify the expected outcomes of instruction and invent means to describe their presence, school administrators and teachers could be held accountable for the quality of their work. In April 1983 *A Nation at Risk* was published, by the late 1980s [its effects] seemed to have faded, and its passing set the stage for America 2000—the reform agenda of the Bush Administration, now signed on to by the Clinton Administration. America 2000 was intended to do what the curriculum reform movement of the

1960s, the accountability movement of the 1970s, and *A Nation at Risk* and the "excellence movement" of the 1980s has been unable to accomplish.

We now have in Goals 2000 (the Clinton version of America 2000) an approach to education reform that uses standards as the linchpin of its efforts. Standards are being formulated for the certification of teachers, for the content of curricula, and for the outcomes of teaching. Virtually every subject-matter field in education has formulated or is in the process of formulating or revising national standards that describe what students should know and be able to do. If anyone detects a slight echo of the past in today's reform efforts, let me assure you that you are not alone. We seem to latch on to the approaches to reform that are replays of past efforts that themselves failed to come to grips with what it is that makes school practices so robust and resistant to change.

Consider, for example, the concept of standards. The term is attractive—standards imply high expectations, rigor, things of substance. To be without standards is not to know what to expect or how to determine if expectations have been realized—or so it seems. Yet once we get past the illusions that the concept invites—once we think hard about the meaning of the term—the picture becomes more complex. To begin with, the meaning of the term is not as self-evident as many seem to believe. A standard meal we would agree is nothing to rave about; a standard can represent a value that people have cared enough about to die for; standards can also refer to units of measure. The National Bureau of Standards employs standards to measure the quality of manufactured products. Electrical appliances, for example, must achieve a certain standard to get the UL seal of approval. Which conception of standards do we embrace in the reform movement? Surely we do not mean by standards a typical level of performance, since that is what we already have without an iota of intervention. As for standards that represent beliefs or values, we already have mission statements and position papers in abundance, but they do not have the level of specificity that reformers believe is needed for standards to be useful.

The third conception of standards—as units of measure that make it possible to quantify the performance of students, teachers, and schools—seems closer to what we have in mind. The idea of measurement provides us with a procedure that is closely associated with such values. Measurement makes it possible to describe quantity in ways that allow as little space as possible for subjectivity.[61] For example, the objectivity of an objective test is not a function of the way in which the test items were selected, but of the way in which the test is scored. Objective tests can be scored by a machine, with no need for judgment. Standards in education, as we now idealize them, are to have such features. They are to be objective and, whenever possible, measurable.

Those who have been working in education for 20 or so years or who know the history of American education will also know that the vision I have just described is a recapitulation of older ideals. I refer to the curriculum reform movement of the 1960s. It was an important event in the history of American education, but it was not the only significant movement of that period. You will also remember that it was in the late 1960s that American educators became infatuated with "behavioral objectives." The idea then, like the notion of standards today, was to define our educational goals operationally in terms that were sufficiently specific to determine without ambiguity whether or not the student had achieved them.

The specifics of the procedures, given prominence by Robert Mager's 1962 book, *Preparing Instructional Objectives*, required that student behavior be identified, that the conditions in which it was to be displayed be described, and that a criterion be specified that made it possible to measure the student's behavior in relation to the criterion.[62] It all seemed very neat. What people discovered as they tried to implement the idea was that to have behaviorally defined instructional objectives that met the criteria Mager specified required the construction of *hundreds* of specific objectives. The quest for certainty, which high-level specificity and precision implied, was soon recognized as counterproductive.

Those who know the history of American education will also know that the desire to specify expected outcomes and to prescribe the most efficient means for achieving them was itself the dominant strain of what has come to be called the "efficiency movement" in education. The efficiency movement, which began in 1913 and lasted until the early 1930s, was designed to apply the principles of scientific management to schools. School administrators caught up in the efficiency movement gradually learned that the basic conception and the expectations that flowed from it—namely, that one could mechanize and routinize teaching and learning—did not work. Even if it were possible to give teachers scripts for their performance, it was not possible to give students scripts. There was no "one best method," and there was no way to "teacher proof" instruction.

My point thus far is that what we are seeing in American education today is a well-intentioned but conceptually shallow effort to improve our schools. My point thus far is to make it plain that the current effort in which we are enmeshed is no novelty; we have been here before. My point thus far is to suggest that successful efforts at school reform will entail a substantially deeper analysis of schools and their relationships to communities and teachers than has thus far been undertaken.

To try to do justice to the aspirations of the national education reform movement, I will try to make a sympathetic presentation of its arguments. I start with the acknowledgment that there is a sense of sweet reason to the arguments that the reformers have made. After all, with standards we will know where we are headed. We can return rigor to schooling; we can inform students, parents, and teachers of what we expect; we can have a common basis for appraising student performance; and we can, at last, employ a potent lever for education reform. Without standards, we are condemned to an unbroken journey to an abyss of mediocrity; we will remain a nation at risk.

By establishing national goals for each subject that schools teach, we will be able to achieve professional consensus that will give us a unified and educationally solid view of what students are expected to learn. By trying to define standards for each field, a single vision of a subject will be created, teachers will have an opportunity to profit from the goals and standards formulated by their peers, and ambiguity will be diminished because teachers will know not only the directions their efforts are to take, but also the specific destination toward which their students are headed, and have something of a timetable to help determine not only whether, but when, they have arrived. As if they had just taken a cold shower, a population of sometimes lethargic and burned-out teachers will be reawakened and become alert. Our nation will, at last, have a national educational agenda, something that it has never possessed. Ultimately, such resources and the approach to education that these resources reflect will help us regain our competitive edge in a global economy. Parents will be satisfied, students will know what is expected of them, and the business community will have the employees it needs for America to become number one by the year 2000, not only in science and in math but in other fields as well. Our students and our schools will go for and get the gold at the educational Olympics in which we are competing. Our schools will become "world class."

An attractive vision? It seems so, yet a number of questions arise. You will recall that the standards about which reformers speak are national standards. The organizations—and there are dozens—that are engaged in formulating standards are doing so for the nation as a whole, not for some specific locality. Put another way, in a nation in which 45 million students in 50 states go to approximately 108,000 schools overseen by some 15,000 school boards and in which 2.5 million teachers teach, there is the presumption that it makes good educational sense for there to be uniform expectations with respect to goals, content, and levels of student achievement. I regard this assumption as questionable on at least two counts.

First, the educational uses of subjects are not singular. The social studies can be used to help students understand history, to help create a socially active citizenry, or to help students recognize the connection between culture and ideas. Biology can be used to help students learn to think like biologists, to understand the balance of nature, to appreciate the limits of science in establishing social policy, or to gain an appreciation of life. The language arts can be used to develop poetic forms of thought, to learn to appreciate great works of literary art, to acquire the mechanics of written and spoken language, to learn to appreciate forms of life that require literary rather than literal understanding. Mathematics can be taught to help students learn to compute, to understand the structure of mathematics, to solve mathematical problems and to help students appreciate the beauty of structures in space. Where is it written that every subject has to be taught for the same reasons to 45 million students? Despite the effort to achieve professional consensus about the educational agendas of specific subjects, the virtue of uniformity is, to my mind, questionable.

Uniformity in curriculum content is a virtue *if* one's claim is to be able to compare students in one part of the country with students in others. Uniformity is a virtue when the aspiration is to compare the performance of American students with students in Korea, Japan, and Germany. But why should we wish to make such comparisons? To give up the idea that there needs to be one standard for all students in each field of study is not to give up the aspiration to seek high levels of educational quality in both pedagogical and educational outcomes. Together, the desire to compare and the recognition of individuality create one of the dilemmas of a social meritocracy; the richness of a culture rests not only on the prospect of cultivating a set of common commitments, but also on the prospect of cultivating those individual talents through which the culture at large is enriched.

A second problematic feature of the aspiration to adopt a common set of standards for all is a failure to recognize differences among students with whom we work. I am well aware of the fact that deleterious self-fulfilling prophecies can be generated when the judgments educators make about individuals are based on a limited appreciation of the potentialities of the students. This is a danger that requires our constant vigilance. However, the reality of differences— in region, in aptitude, in interests, and in goals—suggests that it is reasonable that there be differences in programs.

You will remember that I referred to standards as units of measure that make possible the "objective" description of quantitative relationships. But there are qualitative standards as well. To have a *qualitative* standard you must create or select an icon, prototype, or what is sometimes called a benchmark against which the performance or products of students are matched. To have a *quantitative* standard you must specify the number or percentage of correct answers needed to pass a test or the number of allowable errors in a performance or product and to use that specification as the standard. In each case, there is a fixed and relatively unambiguous unit of measurement. In the qualitative case, the task for both judge and performer is one of matching a performance with a model. This kind of matching is precisely what occurs in the Olympics. Olympic judges know what a particular dive should look like, and they compare a diver's performance to the model. The diver, too, knows what the model looks like and does his or her best to replicate the model.

With respect to the quantitative case, the application of a standard occurs in two different ways. The first has to do with determining the correctness of any individual response. An item response is judged correct if the appropriate bubble is filled in, or if the appropriate selection is made, or if some other indication is given that the student has hit a prespecified mark. The prespecified correct response serves as a standard for each item. Once these item responses are summed, a determination is made as to whether the total number of correct responses meets a second standard, the standards specified as a passing grade by the test-maker or by some policy-making body. Notice that in both cases innovation in response is not called for. The test-maker determines whether a student's score is acceptable, not by exercising judgment, but by counting which bubbles have been filled in and comparing the number of correct responses to a fixed predetermined standard.

There are, we must acknowledge, a number of important tasks that students must learn in school in which innovation is not useful. There are many important tasks and skills that students need to learn—i.e., conventions such as spelling, and arithmetic—that are necessary for doing more important work and that educational programs should help them learn. The more important work that I speak of is the work that makes it possible for students to think imaginatively about problems that matter to them, tasks that give them the opportunity to affix their own personal signature to their work, occasions to explore ideas and questions that have no correct answers, and projects where they can reason and express their own ideas.

Paradoxically, many of the groups that have been working diligently to formulate standards are not really formulating standards at all. They are formulating goals. Consider the following, all of which purport to be standards.

> "Accomplished teachers work with families to achieve common goals for the education of their children" (Board for Professional Teaching Standards, 1994).

> "How Progressives and Others Addressed Problems of Industrial Capitalism, Urbanization, and Political Corruption" (United States History: Exploring the American Experience, 1994).

> "Construct Personal Meaning from Nontraditional Dramatic Performances" (National Standards for Arts Education, 1994).

Such broad, general statements are aspirations that can function as criteria with which to interrogate the work students produce. But criteria are not the same as standards. John Dewey described the difference in *Art as Experience*, one of his most important books, which is largely unread by educators. In a telling chapter on the relationship of art criticism to perception, written when he was 75 years old, Dewey said that, in assessing works of art, standards are inappropriate; criteria are needed. Standards fix expectations; criteria are guidelines that enable one to search more efficiently for the qualities that might matter in any individual work. Describing the features of a standard, Dewey wrote:

> There are three characteristics of a standard. It is a particular physical thing existing under specified physical conditions; it is *not* a value. The yard is a yardstick, and the meter is a bar deposited in Paris. In the second place, standards are measures of definite things, of lengths, weights, capacities. The things measured are not values, although it is of great social value to be able to measure them, since the properties of things in the way of size, volume, weight, are important for commercial exchange. Finally, as standards of measure, standards define things with respect to quantity...

> Yet is does not follow because of absence of an uniform and publicly determined external object [a standard], that objective criticism of art is impossible. What follows is that criticism is judgment; that like every judgment it involves a venture, a hypothetical element; that it is directed to qualities which are nevertheless qualities of an *object*; and that it is concerned with an individual object, not with making comparisons by means of an external preestablished rule between different things.[63]

To say that by the end of a course students will be able to write a convincing essay on the competing interests of environmentalists and industrialists that marshals good arguments supported by relevant facts is to identify criteria that can be used to appraise the essay; it is not to provide a standard for measuring it. Regarding the meaning of criteria, Dewey wrote:

If there are no standards for works of art and hence none for criticism (in the sense in which there are standards of measurement), there are nevertheless criteria in judgment.... But such criteria are not rules or prescriptions. They are the result of an endeavor to find out what a work of art is as an experience, the kind of experience which constitutes it.[64]

One might wonder whether it is appropriate to think about the appraisal of work produced by students at the elementary and secondary school level as being comparable to the assessment of works of art. Criteria may be appropriate for paintings and poetry, but schoolwork requires the application of standards. As plausible as this might seem at first glance, things are not so simple. The creation of conditions that allow students to display their creative and reasoning abilities in ways that are unique to their temperaments, their experience, and their aims is of fundamental importance in any educational enterprise—in contrast to one concerned with training. And because such features are important, it is criteria that must be salient in our assessment.

Standards are appropriate for some kinds of tasks, but, as I argued above, those tasks are instrumental to larger and more important educational aims. We really don't need to erect a complex school system to teach the young how to read utility bills, how to do simple computation, or how to spell; they will learn those skills on their own. What we do need to teach is how to engage in higher-order thinking, how to pose telling questions, how to solve complex problems that have more than one answer. When the concept of standards becomes salient in our discourse about educational expectations, it colors our view of what education can be and dilutes our conception of education's potential. Language matters, and the language of standards is by and large a limiting rather than a liberating language.

The qualities that define inventive work of any kind are qualities that by definition have both unique and useful features. The particular form those features take and what it is that makes them useful are not necessarily predictable, but sensitive critics—and sensitive teachers—are able to discover such properties in the work. Teachers who know the students they teach recognize the unique qualities in students' comments, in their paintings, in the essays they write, in the ways in which they relate to their peers. The challenge in teaching is to provide the conditions that will foster the growth of those personal characteristics that are socially important and, at the same time, personally satisfying to the student. The aim of education is not to train an army that marches to the same drummer, at the same pace, toward the same destination. Such an aim may be appropriate for totalitarian societies, but it is incompatible with democratic ideals.

If one used only philosophical grounds to raise questions about the appropriateness of uniform national standards for students in American schools, there would still be questions enough to give one pause. But there are developmental grounds as well. The graded American public school system was built on an organizational theory that has little to do with the developmental characteristics of growing children. Each grade was to be related to a specific age. If you examine the patterns of human development for children from age five to age 18, you will find that, as children grow older, their rate of development is increasingly variable. Thus the range of variation among children of the same age increases with time.

What this means is that children develop at their own distinctive pace. The tidy structure that was invented in the 19th century to rationalize school organization may look wonderful on paper, but it belies what we know about the course of human development. Because we still operate with a developmentally insensitive organizational structure in our schools, the appeal of uniform standards by grade level or by outcome seems reasonable. It is not. Variability, not uniformity, is the hallmark of the human condition.

I do not want to overstate the idea. To be sure, humans are like all other humans, humans are like some other humans, and humans are like no other humans. All these claims are true. But we have become so preoccupied with remedying the perceived weaknesses of American schools that we have underestimated the diversity and hence the complexity that exists. The verities of unappreciated complexity are large. Let me suggest only a few. When evaluating students in the context of the classroom, the teacher takes into consideration much more than the specific features of a student's particular product. The age, grade, and developmental level of the student; the amount of progress a student has made; the degree of effort that the student has expended are all educationally relevant considerations that professionally competent teachers take into account in making judgments about a student's progress. Experienced teachers know in their bones that the student's work constitutes only one item in an array of educational values and that these values sometimes compete.

Beyond the details of the classroom, there are more general questions having to do with the bases on which educational standards are formulated. Should educational standards be derived from the average level of performance of students in a school, in a school district, in a state, in a nation, *in the world*? How much talk have we heard of "world class" standards?

If national policy dictates that there will be uniform national standards for student performance, will there also be uniform national standards for the resources available to schools? To teachers? To administrators? Will the differences in performance between students living in well-heeled, upper-class suburbs and those living on the cusp of poverty in the nation's inner cities demonstrate the existing inequities in American education? Will they not merely confirm what we already know? The socioeconomic level of the students and the resources available to them and their teachers in a school or school district do make a difference. If those urging standards on us believe that the use of standards will demonstrate inequities—and hence serve to alleviate them—why haven't these already painfully vivid inequities been effective in creating more equitable schools?

And, one might wonder, what would happen to standards in education if by some magic all students achieved them? Surely the standards would be considered too low. At first blush this doesn't sound like a bad thing. Shouldn't the bar always be higher than we can reach? Sounds reasonable. Yet such a view of the function of standards will ineluctably create groups of winners and losers. Can our education system flourish without losers? Is it possible for us to frame conceptions of education and society that rest on more generous assumptions? And consider the opposite. What will we do with those students who fail to meet the standards? Then what?

Perhaps one of the most important consequences of the preoccupation with national standards in education is that it distracts us from the deeper, seemingly intractable problems that beset our schools. It distracts us from paying attention to the importance of building a culture of schooling that is genuinely intellectual in character, that values questions and ideas at least as much as getting right answers. It distracts us from trying to understand how we can provide teachers the kind of professional opportunities to continue to grow through a lifetime of work. It distracts us from attending to the inevitable array of interactions between teaching, curriculum, evaluation, school organization, and the often deleterious expectations and pressures from universities.

How should these matters be addressed? Can schools and teachers and administrators afford the kind of risk-taking and exploratory activity that genuine inquiry in education requires? Vitality within any organization is more likely when there are opportunities to pursue fresh possibilities, to exercise imagination, to try things out, and to relinquish the quest for certainty in either pedagogical method or educational outcome. Indeed, one of the most important aims of education is to free the mind from the confines of certainty. Satisfaction, our children must learn, can come from the uncertainty of the journey, not just from the clarity of the destination.

I am not sure that American society is willing at this time to embrace so soft a set of values as I have described. We believe that we can solve the problems of crime by reopening the doors to the gas chamber and by building more prisons. But it's never been that simple. Nor is solving the problems of schooling as simple as having national standards. And so I believe that we must invite our communities to join us in a conversation that deepens our understanding of the educational process and advances our appreciation of its possibilities. Genuine education reform is not about shallow efforts that inevitably fade into oblivion. It is about vision, conversation, and action designed to create a genuine and evolving educational culture. I hope we can resist the lure of slogans and the glitter of bandwagons and begin to talk seriously about education. That is one conversation in which we must play a leading role.

Dr. Elliot W. Eisner is Professor of Education and Art at Stanford University. He was trained as a painter at The Art Institute of Chicago and later studied design at Illinois Institute of Technology's Institute of Design, a school that reflected the principles and aims of the German Bauhaus which was closed by the Nazis in 1932. His work at these institutions, and his doctoral studies at the University of Chicago, provided the major conceptual resources for his scholarship in three fields: Art Education, Curriculum, and Educational Evaluation. Professor Eisner's published work includes 15 books. His latest book, The Enlightened Eye: Qualitative Inquiry and the Enhancement of Educational Practice, *explores the uses of critical methods from the arts for studying and describing schools, classrooms, and teaching practices.*

Notes

1. Eva L. Baker and Robert L. Linn, "What Works in Performance Assessment," National Center for Research on Evaluation, Standards and Student Testing (NCRESST) conference, 1992.

2. Robert Stake, *The Art of Case Study Research* (Thousand Oaks, CA: Sage Publications, 1995).

3. Eva L. Baker and Robert L. Linn, "Portfolios and Accountability," ibid.

4. The National Assessment of Educational Progress is the only nationally representative and continuing assessment of what America's students know and can do in various subject areas. Since 1969, assessments have been conducted to provide comprehensive information on student knowledge and skills at ages 9, 13 and 17, and more recently for students in grades 4, 8, and 12. By making the information on student performance and related factors available to policymakers, parents, practitioners, and the general public, NAEP is an integral part of our nation's evaluation of the condition and progress of student achievement. NAEP is a project of the National Center for Education Statistics, U.S. Department of Education and has been governed since 1988 by the National Assessment Governing Board (NAGB) which determines subject areas to be assessed, assessment objectives and specifications through a national consensus process. Known as the nation's report card, NAEP gathers information from a nationally representative sample of students to provide results for the nation.

The NAEP arts assessment framework and the process to develop the test itself was begun in December 1992 under the direction of the Governing Board, the Council of Chief State School Officers (CCSSO), the Council for Basic Education and the College Board. The task was to produce a paper on issues in arts education; hold hearings nationwide to gather input from all concerned with arts education; develop a draft assessment framework and distribute it widely for comments and suggestions before revision, and develop a test for measurement of NAEP results. (This information is based on a June 1993 brochure distributed by the Council of Chief State School Officers, project coordinator for the NAEP Arts Education Consensus Project.)

5. John Mahlmann amplifies his case in the introduction to the publication, *National Standards for Arts Education.* MENC is a national professional association and service organization that played an important leadership role in the development of the national arts standards. The Arts Standards were developed by the Consortium of National Arts Education Associations under the guidance of the National Committee for Standards in the Arts through a grant administered by the MENC. The grant was awarded by the U.S. Department of Education, the National Endowment for the Arts, and the National Endowment for the Humanities. The publication *National Standards for Arts Education* is available from the Music Educators National Conference, 1806 Robert Fulton Drive, Reston, VA 22091.

6. Theodore R. Sizer, *Horace's School* (Boston: Houghton Mifflin, 1992), Chapter 8. I highly recommend this book to those of you who are looking for a compelling study of the questions related to local school reform. While the arts are barely mentioned, the discussion can generalize to all disciplines and prove extremely useful to those who wish to learn more about the culture of schools and the problems facing American education, particularly at the secondary level.

7. Ms. Bethany Rogers, who works with Ted Sizer as an associate at the Annenberg Institute for School Reform, has added the following for clarification:

> We are concerned with equity and access.... We hope for standards to grow out of the work of kids and teachers in schools. However, we also recognize the important influences of other sources of authority—parents, communities, disciplinary experts, the state. The article walks a careful line. On the one hand, we maintain that good standards amount to a collection of "images of excellence" (images and

qualities that spring from real instances of student work rather than the imagination of a central committee). Such images serve to generate conversation within and across schools, communities and professional organizations about "what is good enough" and might lead to what we called "benchmark comparisons" among schools. (To some degree, the national standards have served as a provocation for this dialogue, as school people and others begin to form broad, shared ideas about how student work might actually embody those standards.) On the other hand, we understand the need for standards to "remain tentative, lively and open to all manner of possibility." Good standards should create conversation, and often, dispute. The down and dirty talk—"No, really, is that good enough? Has this student demonstrated deep understanding? Habits of critical thinking? What does that look like here?"—among teachers about their students is at the heart of the matter.

8. "Standards and School Reform: Asking the Essential Questions," *Stanford Law and Policy Review* (Winter 1992-3), Joseph P. McDonald, Bethany Rogers and Theodore R. Sizer (Coalition of Essential Schools).

9. The National Commission on Excellence in Education, *A Nation at Risk: The Imperative for Education Reform* (Washington, D.C.: U.S. Department of Education, 1983).

10. Mortimer Adler, ed., on behalf of the Paideia Group, *The Paideia Proposal: An Educational Manifesto* (New York: Macmillan, 1982). Ernest Boyer, *High School: A Report on Secondary Education in America* (New York: Harper & Row, 1983). The College Board, *Academic Preparation for College: What Students Need to Know and Be Able to Do* (New York: The College Board, 1983). John Goodlad, *A Place Called School: Prospects for the Future* (New York: McGraw-Hill, 1984). The Council of Chief State School Officers, *Arts Education and the States: A Survey of Education Policies* (Washington, D.C.: Council of Chief State School Officers, 1985). William J. Bennett, *First Lessons: A Report on Elementary Education in America* (Washington, D.C.: U.S. Department of Education, 1988).

11. *Toward Civilization: A Report on Arts Education* (Washington, D.C.: National Endowment for the Arts, 1988).

12. National Coalition for Education in the Arts, "Concepts for Strengthening Arts Education in Schools," 1987.

13. Music Educators National Conference et al., *K-12 Arts Education in the United States: Present Context, Future Needs* (Reston, VA: Music Educators National Conference, 1988).

14. John McLaughlin, ed., *Toward a New Era in Arts Education: The Interlochen Symposium* (New York: ACA Books, 1988).

15. Consortium of National Arts Education Associations, *National Standards for Arts Education: What Every Young American Should Know and Be Able to Do in the Arts* (Reston, VA: Music Educators National Conference, 1994).

16. The National Assessment Governing Board, *Arts Education Assessment Framework* (Washington, D.C.: The National Assessment Governing Board, 1995).

17. John McLaughlin, *Building a Case for Arts Education: An Annotated Bibliography of Major Research* (Lexington, KY: Kentucky Alliance for Arts Education, 1990).

18. National Endowment for the Arts and the U.S. Department of Education, *Arts Education Research Agenda for the Future* (Washington, D.C.: National Endowment for the Arts and U.S. Department of Education, 1994).

19. Benjamin Bloom, *Taxonomy of Educational Objectives, Book I: Cognitive Domain* (New York: Longman, 1956).

20. U.S. Department of Labor, *What Work Requires of Schools: A SCANS Report for America 2000* (Washington, D.C.: The SCANS, 1991). In the Bush administration, the Secretary (of Labor's) Commission on Achieving Necessary Skills was established in 1990 by then Secretary Elizabeth Dole. It defined workplace skills that high school graduates needed to master which were called foundation skills and competencies. The foundation skills included basic and thinking skills and personal qualities such as responsibility, self-esteem, sociability, self-management, integrity and honesty. The competencies included resources (identifying, organizing, planning and allocating time, money, materials and workers); interpersonal, information, system and technology utilization skills. Arts education advocates assert that the arts can play a significant role in developing these workplace skills and competencies thereby reinforcing the claim for their (the arts) value in general education.

21. Howard Gardner, *The Unschooled Mind: How Children Think and How Schools Should Teach* (New York: Basic Books, 1991).

22. Cognition refers to knowing. Metacognition refers to knowing what you know and how you came to know it, and is usually arrived at by stepping back from an activity and reflecting on the steps taken, the approaches used and the paths followed to acquire knowledge.

23. Teacher-directed action research refers to classroom-based inquiry in which teachers postulate hypotheses, formulate research designs and carry out investigations under controlled circumstances.

24. Gardner's theory of Multiple Intelligences is described in his book, *Frames of Mind: The Theory of Multiple Intelligences* (New York: Basic Books, 1983).

25. General Educational Development Test—a high school equivalency certification awarded to those who complete the courses required for high school graduation outside of a formal school setting.

26. Harold Williams, "Public Policy and Arts Education," a speech given at Ohio State University, May 22, 1993. Available from Getty Center for Education in the Arts.

27. Elliot W. Eisner, *Educating Artistic Vision* (New York: Macmillan, 1972), pp. 29-63.

28. Bruce O. Boston, *Arts Education for the 21st Century American Economy* (New York: American Council for the Arts, 1994), p. 15.

29. Sandra Kay Mims and E. Louis Lankford, "Time, Money, and the New Art Education: A Nationwide Investigation," Studies in Art Education, 1995, 36 (2), pp. 84-85.

30. The College Board, *Profile of SAT and Achievement Test Takers for 1990, 1991, 1992, 1993* (New York: The College Entrance Examination Board, 1994).

31. The Port Authority of New York and New Jersey and the New York City Partnership recently published a study, *The Arts as an Industry: Their Economic Importance to the New York-New Jersey Metropolitan Region*, in which they documented 77,000 people in the city employed in arts-related businesses. Their jobs ranged from semi-skilled to high-tech, from self-employed professional artists to back-office support staff.

32. David Throsby, "The Production and Consumption of the Arts: A View of Cultural Economics," *Journal of Economic Literature*, Vol. XXXII (March 1994), p. 1.

33. David N. Perkins, "Technology Meets Constructivism: Do They Make a Marriage?" in Duffy, Thomas M. and Jonassen, David H. Ed., *Constructivism and the Technology of Instruction* (Hillsdale, New Jersey: Lawrence Erlbaum Associates, Publishers, 1992), p. 44.

34. Ibid.

35. Elliot W. Eisner, "Aesthetic Modes of Knowing," in Elliot Eisner, Ed. *Learning and Teaching, The Ways of Knowing* (Chicago: The University of Chicago Press, 1985), pp. 23-36.

36. Catherine Fosnot, "Constructing Constructivism," in Duffy, Thomas M. and Jonassen, David H. Ed., *Constructivism and the Technology of Instruction* (Hillsdale, New Jersey: Lawrence Erlbaum Associates, Publishers, 1992), p. 171.

37. Richard E. Elmore and Associates, *Restructuring Schools: The Next Generation of Educational Reform* (San Francisco: Jossey-Bass Publishers, 1991), p. 9.

38. Linda Darling-Hammond, "Retraining the School Reform Agenda: Developing Capacity for School Transformation," *Phi Delta Kappan*, 74 (10): 1992, pp. 753-61 (New York: NCREST Reprint Series, 1994), pp. 1-18.

39. Ann Lieberman, Diane Wood, and Beverly Falk, "Toward Democratic Practice in Schools: Key Understanding about Educational Change," in *Quality 2000: Advancing Early Care in Education* (New York: NCREST Reprint Series, 1994), pp. 19-46.

40. Ibid, p. 27.

41. This statement paraphrases Elizabeth Vallance's comments about ways of knowing and their relationship to mathematics, but her comments could be applied equally to any other discipline including the arts. Elizabeth Vallance, "Ways of Knowing and Curricular Conceptions: Implications for Program Planning," in Elliot W. Eisner, Ed. *Learning and Teaching, The Ways of Knowing* (Chicago: The University of Chicago Press, 1985), pp. 199-217.

42. Maxine Greene, "Journeys to Possibility," paper presented at the Western Region Assessment Fair, Puyallup, Washington, October 14, 1994.

43. Ibid, p. 1.

44. Dennie Wolf, "Artistic Learning: What and Where Is It?" in Gardner, Howard & Perkins, David. *Art, Mind & Education* (Urbana, IL.: The University of Illinois Press, 1989), p. 154.

45. Elliot W. Eisner, (1992) "The Misunderstood Role of Arts in Human Development," *Phi Delta Kappan*, April, pp. 591-595. Hanna, J.L. (1992) "Connections: Arts, Academics, and Productive Citizens," *Phi Delta Kappan*, April, pp. 601-607. Gardner, H., *Frames of Mind: The Theory of Multiple Intelligences* (New York: Basic Books, 1980). Arnheim, R., "A Plea for Visual Thinking," *Critical Inquiry*, 6 (April 1980), pp. 489-497. Winner, E., *Invented Worlds: The Psychology of the Arts* (Cambridge, MA: Harvard University Press, 1982).

46. Howard Gardner, "Toward More Effective Arts Education," in Gardner, Howard & Perkins, David, *Art, Mind & Education* (Urbana, IL: The University of Illinois Press, 1989), p. 166.

47. Maxine Greene, "Texts and Margins," *Harvard Educational Review*, Vol. 61, No. 1, February 1991, p. 38.

48. Mihalyi Csikszentmihalyi, *The Evolving Self* (New York: Harper Perennial, 1993), pp. xi-xii.

49. Ibid, p. xiii.

50. Wolf, 1989, p. 150

51. Greene, 1991, p. 28.

52. D. N. Perkins, "Art as Understanding," in Gardner, Howard & Perkins, David. *Art, Mind & Education* (Urbana, IL: The University of Illinois Press, 1989), p. 117.

53. Wolf, 1989, p. 150.

54. Perkins, 1989, pp. 111-131.

55. Elliot W. Eisner, "What Really Counts in School," *Educational Leadership*, Vol. 48, February 1991, pp. 10-16.

56. Jacques D'Amboise's comments as panelist cited in Baker, Terry L. "A Passion for Excellence: A Report from the Chancellor's Work Group" (New York: Chancellor's Office, New York City Public Schools, 1990), p. 8.

57. Charles Fowler, "The Arts: Complementary Partners in General Education," Presentation at the Getty Center for Education in the Arts' Conference: "Beyond the Three Rs: Transforming Education with the Arts," Washington, D.C., January 14, 1995, p. 5.

58. The tide may have turned on this issue. The national education goals undergirding the *Goals 2000: Educate America Act of 1994* now include the arts as one of the areas of "challenging subject matter" in which all children should be expected to achieve competence at the end of grades 4, 8, and 12. The *National Standards for Arts Education* (Reston, VA: Music Educators National Conference, 1994) detail what children should know and be able to do in drama, music, theater and the visual arts at these grade levels. Whether national recognition of the arts as part of "basic" education and a new tool for benchmarking student progress will spur similar recognition in school budgets around the nation is still uncertain.

59. *National Standards for Arts Education* (Reston, VA: Music Educators National Conference, 1994), p. 5.

60. Ibid, pp. 18-19.

61. The presence of subjectivity in scientific work has long been regarded as a source of bias. Most measurement procedures aspire to what is called "procedural objectivity," which represents a process in which the exercise of judgment is minimized. A competent ten-year-old can do as well as a Nobel Prize winner in measuring a room. Tasks that can be accomplished without appealing to human judgment can also be done by a machine. Optical scanners can score multiple test forms more quickly and more accurately than humans. Some idealizations of science aspire to a pristine quantitative descriptive state that does not depend on human judgment or interpretation at all. For an extended discussion of the concept of "procedural objectivity," see Elliot W. Eisner, *The Enlightened Eye: Qualitative Inquiry and the Enhancement of Educational Practice* (New York: Macmillan, 1991).

62. Robert Mager, *Preparing Instructional Objectives* (Palo Alto, CA: Fearon Publishers, 1962).

63. John Dewey, *Art as Experience* (New York: Minton, Balch & Co., 1934), p. 307.

64. Ibid, p. 308.

CHAPTER 7

Catalysts for Community Activism and Commitment: Arts Agencies, Foundations and International Associations

Catalysts for Change in Schools and Their Communities

Taking a Few Steps Back

In this chapter, we take a few steps back from our close-ups of the people and dynamics of local arts partnerships to zoom out to a long shot of the bigger picture. The voices we will hear are those of arts and foundation administrators who are usually at several removes from the dramatic action of the classroom and the daily struggle to build strong partnerships among schools and local arts organizations. While they all talk about an uphill battle, our contributors should be justifiably proud of their efforts to provide impetus and support for important work in the field. They undoubtedly know they can help construct the stage or the platform, supply the rigging, the lights and the sound system, to continue Doug Herbert's theatrical metaphor, but they are keenly aware that without the folks at the local level "working together to script, produce, perform and direct the play," that stage remains an empty space. Many of them also know that their own institutional, financial (and frequently political) base of support is fragile or subject to pressures, social forces or acts of God over which they have little or no control. Some of them may even dread what might happen, should catastrophe strike, to dash the high hopes and expectations they have carefully cultivated and nurtured. It would be much like the troupe showing up to find the theater is closed until further notice, or worse: burned down.

There is a delicate synergy between institutions that are effective catalysts for community action and the relationships they develop with local players. It is an association that can be fraught with danger because it tends to veer somewhere between (fickle) patronage and (committed) partnerships. In the former, the catalyst may terminate support at any time, suddenly and without warning, leaving the good faith and sometimes overly dependent beneficiaries of its largesse stranded mid-program. In the latter, if the terms and conditions of the partnership and support are clear from the outset, there should be no surprises. Still, even in the best of circumstances, programs fold quickly and unceremoniously, as you will see in a moment in my example from the JDR 3rd Fund. However, if the local folks understand from the beginning that nothing is certain and that swift change is not unusual, they will be better prepared to build safeguards into their programs from the start. That is why throughout this book I keep harping on the evolutionary notion of change—one school, one arts organization at a time, and on the critical need for orchestrated capacity- and constituency-building and community support in each joint venture.

Effective catalysts in the arts in education field make a verbal and tangible commitment to their vision of the arts in education. They provide articulate leadership and support in the form of money, resources, technical assistance, and community volunteers. They can also provide a comprehensive and, occasionally, coherent view of the often messy or chaotic arts-in-education landscape. They function as matchmakers, partners, advocates and activists and, for the most part, they appear to be in business for the long haul. These institutions are not what is conventionally known as change agents—they do not design and manage the change process. They are outside agencies that frequently act as burrs under the saddle, cheerleaders and affirmation-providers to help those with local power and responsibility in the arts organizations, the schools, the districts and so forth—to define and determine their own local destinies.

Acting as a catalyst is hard and often frustrating work. By way of introduction, we will take a look at my experience at the JDR 3rd Fund and some lessons I have learned that should prove instructive to those who seek to become catalysts in their communities or those who plan to work with them.

Reflections on the JDR 3rd Fund Experience: A Cautionary Tale for Those Who Would Be Catalysts (or Work with Them)

The Lessons and the Legacy

I spent from 1972 to 1980 at the Arts in Education Program of the John D. Rockefeller 3rd Fund, where I had the good fortune to work with its director, Kathryn Bloom, her gifted staff and an army of arts and education professionals from across the country. My experience at the Fund is chronicled in my book, *Changing Schools Through the Arts: How to Build on the Power of an Idea*, which serves as a building block and frame of reference for this book and most of the work I do.

The JDR 3rd Fund was an operating foundation supported exclusively by John D. Rockefeller 3rd. One of its main initiatives was the Arts in Education Program (1967-1979), which had as its mission "all the arts for all the children in entire schools and school districts." During the 12 years of its operation, the Fund was a major force for advocacy that vividly illustrated the idea of the arts in education in local practice at various sites around the country. The Fund's experience is relevant here for several reasons, perhaps least of all for the successes, of which there were many.[1] The successes included Mr. Rockefeller's idea of all the arts for all the children as it became manifested in pilot projects and comprehensive demonstration programs around the country; two national networks of states and cities dedicated to translating the idea into local reality; publications and reference materials; and a wealth of conceptual language that has become commonplace in the arts-in-education lexicon. The Fund pioneered a number of the promising pathways for the arts in education at the national, state and local levels, and the lessons learned from its history can be compelling as well as instructive.

In the mid-seventies, the Fund, an operating foundation, formed and coordinated two national networks: The Coalition of (nine) States (education departments) for the Arts in Education, and the League of (six) Cities for the Arts in Education. The Coalition's purpose was to build statewide, comprehensive arts-in-education plans and support for local districts. The League's purpose was to design and carry out comprehensive arts-in-general-education plans that focused on school development (read "reform") through the arts. The main strategies we used were institutional partnerships between the Fund and the school districts, interschool and intercity networking and leadership training, and broad-based community arts resource collaborations with the schools.

The League sites and the Fund shared a common philosophy about the arts as basic education. Letters of agreement spelling out the arrangement and the commitments, roles and functions of the partners were signed by Fund Director Bloom and each city's school superintendent. While League members agreed on a common mission and a program framework for the content of teaching and learning, the specifics of the curriculum and the methods of instruction were left to the discretion of the individual districts. My favorite musical metaphor for the League's program was six variations on a theme.

The content framework included instruction in the individual arts disciplines (in the arts); instruction relating the arts to each other (inter-arts, among the arts); interdisciplinary teaching and learning (through the arts, relating the arts to other subjects, with the arts serving as vehicles to illuminate other areas or vice versa); and effective use of the community's arts and cultural resources in and out of school. No specific strand was dedicated to teaching about the arts—aesthetics, criticism, history—though a few districts included some of these domains in their programs.

Within the League, we had numerous discussions about support systems for these programs—adequate time for planning at all levels of the program and within the school, staff development for teachers, artist training, curriculum development—and concern about program evaluation and documentation, but very little mention of student assessment. As sparse as the evaluation and assessment landscape may seem today, it was even more barren then, although some efforts were under way at the federal level at the National Institute for Education, in the regional educational laboratories, notably CEMREL,[2] and in several of the Fund's pilot projects.[3]

The individual programs were launched in each of the cities, and partnerships with the Fund were established between 1973 and 1975; the League of Cities network followed, forming in 1976. League representatives met regularly in central locations and during site visits to each city to discuss common concerns and solve urgent problems. Then Mr. Rockefeller, the Fund's only benefactor, was killed in an automobile accident in 1978; since the JDR 3rd Fund was unendowed, the Arts in Education Program closed down in 1979.

Attempts were made by the Coalition and the League to continue as independent networks, but they ultimately proved futile. The reasons were both simple and profound: networks cannot survive without a coordinating and convening hub, and neither of the two groups had the time, resources or energy to undertake the job, even on a rotating basis. No other foundation or educational institution was interested. (We tried them all.) The networks died, and ultimately, one by one, their programs died with them. The local champions lost interest or moved away; the district and school leaders changed jobs, moved on or retired; the local arts councils and the arts community, the Junior Leagues, and the other civic groups that had been staunch supporters lost heart and turned their attention and their resources elsewhere.

During its lifetime, the Fund produced a prodigious amount of descriptive and documentary program material that it disseminated widely. I wrote hundreds of pages about the League's origin in the New York City Arts in General Education (AGE) program and the transplantation and transformation process to other sites. I also managed to assemble and codify many of the guidelines and criteria we devised and used along the way. This story ultimately became the basis for *Changing Schools Through the Arts*, appearing first in 1982 and again in an expanded version in 1990. These and other informal and published materials by Fund-sponsored project directors, evaluators and historians, probably more than the programs they documented, have been responsible for the infusion and proliferation of the language, ideas, concepts and practices of the Fund's relatively short 12 years of work. *Changing Schools* was certainly responsible for the birth of the ArtsConnection program in New Orleans in the eighties that is still alive today, and it is also at the heart of the Creative Connections program under way in Louisville, Kentucky. From what I have observed and am told by colleagues, the Fund's principles and strategies are embedded in whole or in part in many other efforts around the country.

The Fund left a legacy of practice, print and language, but it was the Fund's and our colleagues' failure to think about and plan for building longevity into the structure of the national networks and into the fabric of the members' individual programs that led to their dismantling. I am now convinced, with the benefit of hindsight that, networks aside, our neglect of the critical issues of curriculum, instruction, staff and professional development, evaluation and assessment—the content and the infrastructure of educational programs—was the ultimate undoing of the individual programs. In other words, we did not succeed in building professional capacity or a constituency for the arts within the schools, districts and state education departments, and though efforts were launched to develop local community support from the movers and shakers, the political and educational leadership sands kept shifting too quickly and a beachhead was never firmly established.

When asked to explain what happened to the networks and their individual programs, I used to say we couldn't have foreseen the early and untimely death of Mr. Rockefeller, who I later learned was in the process of endowing the foundation. Or I would suggest that we weren't in business long enough; we didn't have the time to devote ourselves to those issues; networks cannot survive without a coordinating hub; money and resources were scarce. Or I would simply reply that all our champions had retired, moved on or been voted out of office. These are all reasonable responses, but they beg the question.

I now realize that we should have addressed each of those issues from the very beginning. They should have been part of our long-range institutional and strategic planning. We should have prepared for the worst and the unimaginable, and we should have developed guidelines and criteria for all the instructional and support areas, just as we did for so many others.

What I am also suggesting is that the disappearance of the League network activities and the individual partnerships between the school districts and the Fund did not necessarily have to mean the death of the individual arts-in-education programs in each of these sites. If the Fund, as the catalyst for change, had encouraged each site to pay attention to building a capacity, a constituency, and local community advocacy and support for the arts in education, and if we had discovered a way to help the individual districts to focus on their own needs in curriculum, instruction, professional development, evaluation and assessment, then these programs might have had a greater chance of surviving. I may be wrong, and we will never know, because we cannot go back to the future. But I share these thoughts about the roles and responsibilities of the catalysts for change at this juncture because I continue to see the same perils on the horizon for the country as a whole—particularly at the national level—and I fear that the fragile roots we have again put down may be quickly torn out and destroyed unless we pay attention to some of the lessons from our collective past.

Keep this cautionary tale in mind as you read through the following essays. Ask yourself the hard questions about your role as a goad, supporter and motivator or partner. How and in what ways are you encouraging your partners, constituents, grantees, panelists, board members, and advisory committees to examine whether their own activities or programs are building the infrastructure for support and the capacity, constituency and community attitudes so essential to the change process and the prognosis for its future? How can you help them build the bedrock foundations so essential to long-term effectiveness? And how can you impress upon them the urgency of the task?

Building Longevity into the Definition of a Catalyst

For the purposes of this book, and perhaps for the future of this field, if there is to be one, I think we have to redefine our notion of the word catalyst. Unless we want to perpetuate the pattern of abandonment or disintegration of so many of our promising programs and practices after an arbitrary time period (a grant cycle, a term of leadership, the need to move on and "share and spread the wealth"), catalysts must take responsibility beyond stirring up the dust and getting things started. This issue is closely related to the one embedded in the subtitle of the next and concluding chapter: "The Oxymoronic Quest for Durable Change." I will examine the conditions for sustaining programs and partnerships in more detail in that chapter, but for now, the central question is:

What can a catalyst do to contribute to the durability of programs that feature education in, through and about the arts?

Then, there are two more questions to guide your consideration of this complex issue:

1) When and how does (or should) a catalyst relinquish control to become a supporter and sustainer of—even a partner in—an enterprise?

2) If this role is not feasible politically, economically or from the standpoint of social or institutional policy, what can the catalyst do to help create the conditions necessary for longevity in the initiatives it spawns?

The specific answers to these questions will vary for each organization, and I urge those of you for whom this inquiry is appropriate to pursue it by asking yourself:

- What resources, in addition to money, can we provide over the long haul to this initiative that are within our mission and our means, that are desperately needed, and that no one else can provide?

- What can our organization do to help identify the forces for change, innovation and support for this initiative within our community on a continuing basis?

- What can we do to facilitate the building of a permanent network of communications of the leadership and the key players in the initiative?

- What is our long-term role in this initiative: facilitator, convener, technical assistant, mentor, buyer of time for planning and training, research and evaluation? Should we consider becoming an operational partner?

- If our commitment is to be limited in time, who will be identified and equipped to take our place and how are we helping to build the interest, motivation and capacity for this replacement?

- Have we discussed all of these questions with our current beneficiaries, and what say have they had in the deliberations? Have we asked them what we can do together that will help them prepare for the short and long-term roles we have defined together?

In sum, I am arguing for catalysts to shoulder a greater share of the responsibility for the grants they award, the initiatives they launch, the marriages they make. This reconsideration of role and function should ideally become part of the conceptual base and practical arrangements for any new program, grant or collaboration. I think it will go a long way toward building a more secure future for the arts in education because it will help to develop local capacity, industry and commitment.

Voices from the Field

In the essays, interviews and case studies that follow, respected leaders from national, state and local arts agencies, foundations and an international association will explore the question: What constitutes an effective catalyst for local community activism and the arts in the education of all children? They will share their frustrations, their successes and many of the lessons learned along the way. Doug Herbert will provide an overview and discuss the history of the National Endowment for the Arts and its role as a catalyst in recent national policy efforts. Lani Duke will share some of her attempts to develop partnerships at the Getty Center for Education in the Arts, emphasizing the need to stay the course and be persistent in seeking out and sustaining partnerships at all levels. Jane Polin will give us the guidelines the GE Fund uses to determine the overall effectiveness of arts partnerships. Jonathan Katz will share his thoughts about the future from the vantage of the National Assembly for State Arts Agencies. We will have a chance to hear from Bob Lynch and Nancy Langan, and take a look at three partnership profiles culled from monographs published by the National Assembly of Local Arts Agencies. Hollis Headrick will tell us about his experiences at the New York State Council on the Arts and the hard-earned lessons he has learned about building and evaluating partnerships at the state and local levels. Bill Aguado and Shirley Trusty-Corey will talk about their roles as tireless advocates and technical assistants at the city and borough arts council levels. Finally, Jennifer Williams will provide an international perspective on arts partnerships and the issues of common concern we share with people from other countries.

Forces at Play in the Big Picture

There is always a danger in a book such as this in getting caught up in the seductive mechanics of partnerships for their own sake, thereby losing sight of the reason for these arrangements in the first place: the improvement of general education through quality arts instruction for all our kids. I, for one, must always be on guard that the medium doesn't get to be the motive or the message, and that in my enthusiasm for guidelines, criteria and bullet lists, I don't wander off too far from the students, the teachers, the principals, the artists, and the parents.

There are times, however, and this is one of them, when it is both imperative and fruitful to step back a while to study the federal, national, state and other forces at play so we may learn about their stake in the local action. By so doing, we will be better equipped to approach them, take advantage of their work and to integrate the lessons they have learned into our own endeavors.

It is in this spirit of inquiry and fact-finding that I send you out, again, on the next to last lap of our learning journey. I have only one request: As you move through the pages, keep track of the various ideas and strategies discussed that appear to move the arts deeper into the curriculum, build professional capacity in teachers, create a climate of acceptance, and develop a larger constituency for the arts in the local community. I suspect you will end up with a number of ideas you can start using first thing Monday morning.

The National Policy Window for Arts Education

by Doug Herbert

In his 1989 Nancy Hanks Lecture, Leonard Garment observed that "major public policy initiatives usually go nowhere until historical events open a 'policy window.'" The passage in 1994 of the Goals 2000: Educate America Act, the most sweeping education reform legislation to be enacted in 30 years, opened such a policy window for the arts in America's elementary and secondary schools.

The groundwork for taking advantage of this policy window had been laid several years prior to this historical event, when a series of national developments—many a reflection of state and local activities—helped to prepare a national policy framework for the arts in education. What constitutes such a framework, and why is it important? What major developments have helped to create it? More importantly, what lessons can be learned from recent national-level actions and strategies that can be applied at the state and local levels? Finally, what must be done at all levels in the years ahead to get through the open window to a new tomorrow for the arts in the schools? These are questions I will address from the vantage point I have had since 1987 at the National Endowment for the Arts.

The Policy Framework: Its Definition and Importance

The United States, unlike other countries such as Japan and England, does not have a national curriculum. The federal government's relationship to its counterparts at the state and the local levels in American education is best characterized as bottom up: local control, state authority, and national support and encouragement. Thus, policy decisions about what is taught, when, how, and by whom are made at the local and state levels. However, in carrying out its role of support and encouragement, the federal government sets a policy framework in which it articulates what is considered to be in the national interest. This seems fitting, since the federal share of public education spending is only 7 percent of the nearly $250 billion it costs to educate our children in grades K-12 annually.

The passage of the Elementary and Secondary Education Act (ESEA) in 1965 ushered in a new era of federal-state-local relations in which the federal government established certain general principles and expectations for which it offered funding to the states and local school districts. For example, Title I (formerly Chapter I) funds within the ESEA have assisted states and local school districts with special services for disadvantaged students. The Eisenhower Professional Development Fund, which until recently provided dollars for teacher professional development only in math and science instruction, was a federal response to the national concern that the Soviets and other nations were outpacing us in technology and space exploration that can be traced to the launching of Sputnik. (It is no accident that the National Science Foundation's education budget, which supports state- and local-level improvements in math and science instruction, dwarfs that of its counterpart in the arts by nearly ten to one.)

Where have the arts been in that policy framework since 1965? For the most part, the arts have either been mentioned as a "good idea," or suffered from benign neglect by not being mentioned at all. Following its original enactment, sections of the ESEA offered support to the states and to local school districts for arts instruction, but often in ways that addressed various socioeconomic objectives ahead of those that dealt with students acquiring knowledge and skills in the arts. Additionally, when federal funding was used to implement arts programs, these programs too often were developed as discrete projects—perceived as "add-ons" that vanished from the education landscape when the typical two- or three-year cycle of federal support ended.

As Jane Remer observed in her excellently compiled and interpreted chronology in *Changing Schools Through the Arts* (1990), the arts programs that were developed between 1965 and 1975, when Washington backed educational initiatives with funding, lacked "a secure institutional base or policy commitment...the arts were regarded as supplemental, not basic, or to use the federal lingo, 'cultural enrichment.'"[4] A 1977 study confirmed this view and also concluded that "more money does not make a difference [because] it doesn't purchase the things that matter..., more committed teachers, more effective project directors and more concerned principals."[5] The lesson learned: federal funding should be used to build commitment among practitioners and policy makers to the allocation of local resources for ongoing arts programs and to institutionalizing these programs within local schools and school district budgets.

The situation deteriorated after the Department of Education's Office of Arts and Humanities was abolished in the early 1980s. Not only did funds earmarked for the arts within the ESEA diminish—and eventually become directed only to the Kennedy Center's education department and its affiliate, Very Special Arts, but the arts also lost a champion within the federal education agency, a role so effectively played by Kathryn Bloom in the sixties and early seventies, and later by Harold "Bud" Arberg.

The "Quiet Revolution" Pays Off

The impetus to formulate an arts education policy agenda and to secure a place for the arts in the national education policy framework began in the mid- to late-1980s. In particular, several discernable trends and a few national studies and reports about arts education are important to note. Among the national developments, the Getty Center for Education in the Arts launched an initiative to support a comprehensive approach to the teaching of visual art. Called Discipline-Based Art Education, or DBAE, the approach proposed a balanced curriculum of history, critical analysis, and aesthetics in addition to art production and creation. Another influence on arts education to emerge in the mid-1980s was the work of Howard Gardner and his colleagues at Harvard Project Zero. Gardner's theory of multiple intelligences, put into practice in schools through Arts PROPEL and other projects, fostered an increasing body of research and widespread discussion of the cognitive processes inherent in the creation of art.

In 1988, the National Endowment for the Arts concluded a two-year study mandated by Congress to determine the state of arts education and to make recommendations based on its findings. The report, *Toward Civilization*, found the arts in American schools to be in triple jeopardy: (1) They were not viewed as serious learning, but more as extracurricular matters or even forms of entertainment in schools; (2) where the arts did exist in schools, they most often were taught with a predominant or even exclusive emphasis on production and performance skills; and (3) the stakeholders in arts education—from the teachers to the artists to the principals, parents and school-board members—did not agree on what constituted an education in the arts.

Toward Civilization advanced several broad goals for teaching and learning in the arts: "Arts education should provide all students with a sense of the arts in civilization, of creativity in the artistic process, of the vocabularies of artistic communication, and of the critical elements necessary to making informed choices about the products of the arts."[6] With its concurrent call for state education departments and local school districts to make arts education a sequential part of the basic curriculum from kindergarten through high school, *Toward Civilization* focused federal policy attention on arts education as part of basic education—as an academic subject important in its own right.

The fact that this call for a comprehensive, sequential arts education for all students came from the federal arts agency rather than the education department no doubt diminished its impact on state and local education policy, but it was significant nonetheless. It marked a "true turning point," according to Harold Williams, president of the J. Paul Getty Trust. The report, according to Williams, "laid the cornerstone for any future policy on arts education."[7]

Toward Civilization also marked a significant change in policy direction for the National Endowment for the Arts' arts-in-education efforts. Prior to 1988, the Arts Endowment had been a longstanding supporter of the state arts agencies' artists-in-residence programs—a concept it had pioneered in the late 1960s. Under Frank Hodsoll's chairmanship in the 1980s, the Arts Endowment challenged state arts agencies to broaden their own arts education policies and programs and provided funding incentives to them to do two new things: (1) form partnerships for arts education by reaching out to their departments of education and others in the arts, education and private sectors; and (2) develop and implement, through partnerships, strategic plans to make the arts basic to education in each of the states.

The Not-So-Quiet Revolution

The passage of Goals 2000: Educate America Act in 1994 began a new era of federal-state-local relations in education that holds great promise for arts education. The beginnings of this new era, however, were not so auspicious. The genesis of Goals 2000 can be traced to late 1989, when then President George Bush and the 50 state governors devised the National Education Goals. For the first time in American history, we had articulated an overarching, national vision for education. Goal three of the National Education Goals called for all students to demonstrate competency in "challenging subject matter," for which the subjects of math, science, reading, writing and geography were specifically listed. This omission of the arts from the list of challenging subject matter in goal three shocked the arts education community into the realization that national policy was shifting and the arts were about to be left behind again.

Matters came to a head in 1991 when the National Education Goals Panel, charged with determining how best to achieve the new National Education Goals, held a series of regional hearings. The Arts Endowment's efforts to make state arts agencies more aware of the need to be involved in educational policy, combined with similar networking efforts by the Music Educators National Conference and other national professional associations, the Alliance for Arts Education, the American Council for the Arts, and others, mobilized arts education advocates to declare that the National Education Goals could not be adequately achieved without the arts.

The results were impressive: dozens of individuals testified at each of the hearings—most times outnumbering other special interests' representatives—clearly articulating a case for the arts as basic to education. Arts education advocates experienced a political "coming of age," though they would not reap the fruits of their efforts for another three years.

Partly in response to this advocacy and other calls to add the arts to the National Education Goals, in 1992 former Secretary of Education Lamar Alexander formed an America 2000 Arts Education Partnership with the National Endowment for the Arts to implement several of the recommendations in *Toward Civilization* and to further partnership efforts between the Department of Education and the Arts Endowment. He also encouraged the formation of an independent task force, known as the Arts Education Partnership Working Group, to recommend further actions that could be taken to make the arts a more visible and vital part of national education reform.

The Partnership Working Group, co-chaired by James D. Wolfensohn, former chairman of The Kennedy Center, and Harold M. Williams of the J. Paul Getty Trust, issued a report which declared that the arts had the power to help reshape elementary and secondary education. The report, *The Power of the Arts to Transform Education*, concluded that schools with strong arts programs evidence a range of benefits for students, teachers and the general learning environment:

- The arts are forms of understanding and ways of knowing that are fundamentally important to education;
- The arts are important to excellent education and to effective school reform;

- The most significant contribution of the arts to education reform is the transformation of teaching and learning;
- This transformation is best realized in the context of comprehensive, systemic education reform; and
- Art educators, artists, and arts organizations must be strongly encouraged to actively join in local, state and national reform efforts.[8]

The report was completed just as the Clinton administration took office. The new secretary of education, Richard Riley, embraced the findings and recommendations of the report, and he and President Clinton inserted the arts into the National Education Goals as a core subject in the new administration's proposed Goals 2000: Educate America legislation.[9] Moreover, the report's enunciation of the "transforming powers of the arts" was adopted, in some instances verbatim, in the Improving America's Schools Act (IASA),[10] the Clinton Administration's bill to reauthorize the Elementary and Secondary Education Act.

Arts education advocates unquestionably benefitted from Secretary Riley's longstanding commitment to the arts during his tenure as governor of South Carolina (for instance, legislation was enacted to require every school to have art specialists). Still, the secretary and other federal policy makers had clearly heard the message to the National Goals Panel, and they were taking action.

By mid-1994, a decade after the National Commission on Educational Excellence had declared our nation's schools "at risk,"[11] the arts were included in a new federal policy framework that promised to change elementary and secondary education for the benefit of future generations of Americans. To the credit of those who put aside their differences for the first time to influence the development of that framework, the arts were not only mentioned, but also considered basic and in the vanguard of a new vision for teaching and learning.

Developing Tools for Policy Action

By including the arts in both the Goals 2000: Educate America Act and the Improving America's Schools Act, President Bill Clinton, the Congress, and the U.S. Department of Education have taken a clear stand on where the arts belong in schools—not at the margins or on the periphery, but at the core, as both a basic subject and as a transforming power within the overall curriculum. However, this new policy framework can only be a springboard for getting the arts into the curriculum. State and local education reform efforts also need to be provided with the tools to make the arts a part of classroom practice. Through a variety of partnerships at the federal and national levels, a number of these tools are being developed. They include:

Voluntary national standards. A consortium of national professional associations in arts education, with the financial support of the Department of Education and both the Arts and Humanities Endowments, undertook a two-year effort to develop a national consensus definition of what all students should know and be able to do in the arts (dance, music, theater and the visual arts) by the end of grades 4, 8 and 12.[12] This effort paralleled those in science, history, geography and the other core subjects listed in the National Education Goals. Whether in the arts or the sciences, these standards are to guide the states in devising their own content standards—a key component of the Goals 2000 legislation. Although the states are not required to develop standards in any subject, the arts are more firmly positioned in the national education policy framework than at any time in the past.

National, state and local-level assessment efforts. An old adage in education is, "That which is tested gets taught." Yet arts education has not succumbed—nor should it—to the short-sighted notion that learning is measured effectively by exercises that put a premium on rote memory and lower-level thinking skills. Education reformers have recently declared the need to develop and use more "authentic" assessments, which would be based on new state and local standards in core subjects and more accurately determine students' and schools' achievements.

Ironically, for years the arts have pioneered methods of authentic or performance assessments that tap students' abilities to demonstrate their use of knowledge instead of merely determining their acquisition of facts. As Gordon Ambach, executive director of the Council of Chief State School Officers, has remarked, this situation is very much like "old hats suddenly in vogue."[13] Those who teach the nonarts subjects have much to learn from those who teach the arts—a turn of events on which the arts education community should not hesitate to capitalize.

At the national level, *Toward Civilization* recommended including the arts in the National Assessment of Educational Progress (NAEP), which most people know as "The Nation's Report Card." NAEP regularly assesses national samples of students to determine their proficiencies in basic subjects. The arts have not been included in the NAEP subject schedule since the 1970s. Many strongly believe that if the arts are again in the National Assessment, then state- and local-level policy actions to include the arts in schools would increase.

With Arts Endowment funding, supplemented by support from the Getty Center for Education in the Arts, the first phase of a planned 1997 NAEP arts assessment—the development of a consensus framework of outcomes and the means of measuring their achievement—was completed in 1994. In fact, the efforts to develop the content standards in the arts and the assessment framework occurred simultaneously—a fortuitous set of circumstances no one could have predicted. More importantly, the two efforts were complementary, creating a common vision for arts education.

Increasing evidence and documentation of the benefits of arts education. We all know them, those wonderful stories of how the arts have changed the education and lives of children, or of how the arts have opened new horizons for teachers, or of how they got parents involved in their children's educations for the first time. The problem until recently has been twofold: On the one hand, many of these stories are anecdotal, which is not to say they are unimportant, but they are not always convincing enough to change the attitudes and actions of policy makers. Second, the stories—and even the more systematic studies—have been reported in disparate places and ways, never as a "critical mass" of evidence that local advocates can readily use before school boards and with principals, teachers, parents and others.

The methods for collecting and disseminating evidence about the benefits of arts education have improved over the last decade. We have a growing body of research that affirms the cognitive learning and the important "habits of mind" that are intrinsic in the process of making art. Moreover, we now have discrete studies of schools where the arts are a strong curriculum component that document the arts' contribution to excellence in teaching and learning.

The National Endowment for the Arts has worked in partnership with the Department of Education and the arts and education fields to support arts education research and to develop a national research agenda. More recently, the Arts Endowment commissioned a compilation of research studies which support the often-made claims of the benefits of arts education. The report, *Schools, Communities and the Arts: A Research Compendium*, summarizes research studies that have been determined to be sound in their methodologies and presents them in a lay person's language. It is being made available in both print and electronic formats.[14] For the first time, arts education advocates can use this resource to help make their case by readily drawing on well-founded evidence of what the arts can do.

Lessons from the National Level

So, what have been the keys to the gains made during the struggles of the past decade to gain credibility for the arts as an essential part of education? Looking back, the success in getting the arts into the current national education policy framework can be attributed to two critical factors—leadership and partnership.

Leadership

At the federal level, former National Endowment for the Arts Chairman Frank Hodsoll committed himself to a new vision of arts education not only for the Arts Endowment, but also for the nation's schools and students. He believed firmly that the arts are at the center of civilization. Through his vision and leadership in producing *Toward Civilization*, Hodsoll helped the country to understand why the next generation of Americans will need arts education to meet the cultural, educational and economic demands of a new century.

His successors, Chairmen John Frohnmayer and Jane Alexander, have continued to provide national leadership by focusing attention on arts education and its role in education reform, by pursuing partnerships with the Department of Education and others at the federal and national levels, and by implementing many of the recommendations in *Toward Civilization*. Speaking to representatives of more than 100 arts, education, business and foundation leaders about the prospects for putting the arts into current education reform efforts, Alexander asked them to work with the Arts Endowment and the Department of Education to benefit future generations. "Let us harness our creativity into putting substance behind the (national voluntary) standards, and action behind the words," she said.

Despite the groundwork done by the Arts Endowment and many others, the arts might not have been included in the national education policy framework without the leadership of Secretary of Education Riley. The combination of his own beliefs and the increasing evidence that the arts are serious learning ensured a place for the arts in the federal policy framework. As he has often stated: "The process of studying and creating art in all its distinct forms defines, in many ways, those qualities that are at the heart of education reform in the 1990s—creativity, perseverance, a sense of standards and, above all, a striving for excellence." Secretary Riley has also used the bully pulpit of his office to speak about how the arts contribute to education reform, which has been a recent and welcomed addition to national advocacy efforts.

Outside the federal realm, a number of national organizations and their leaders have played important leadership roles. Among these are the Music Educators National Conference, which, on behalf of the Consortium of National Arts Education Associations, coordinated the development of the National Standards in Arts Education; the American Council for the Arts, for its longstanding arts education advocacy efforts, its publication of arts-in-education titles, and regular sponsorship of national conferences on arts education issues; the Getty Center for Education in the Arts, which has been instrumental in broadening the concept of visual arts education and focusing national attention on the role that all of the arts should play in education reform; the John F. Kennedy Center for the Performing Arts, in particular, its National Alliance for Arts Education Network, for its commitment to coalition building among the arts, education and business sectors; and both the National Assemblies of State and of Local Arts Agencies, for their leadership and technical assistance to their respective member organizations.

Several school and education associations also have been strong and consistent supporters of the arts as part of basic education. For the past half decade or more, the National Education Association and the National School Boards Association have included the need for comprehensive arts education in their statements of principles and beliefs. Likewise, the National Association for the Education of Young Children includes the arts in its "appropriate practices" for the education of three- to eight-year-olds. And on behalf of school administrators, both the American Association of School Administrators and the Council of Chief State School Officers have generously given their national-level executives' time and other organizational resources to promote greater understanding among their members of the value and the role of the arts in education. Others have made important contributions as well, but the point is: strong leadership has not been limited to a few organizations; it has been exercised by many organizations across the arts and arts education spectrums.

In many respects, from the time that *Toward Civilization* was released in 1988 until the passage of the Goals 2000 act in 1994, the National Endowment for the Arts "held down the fort" on matters of federal policy and, to some extent, financial support for arts education. The Arts Endowment's vigilance at the federal level—persistently focusing on the promise of the arts in education reform, seeking partnerships with the Department of Education to act on that promise, and exercising leadership in the state arts agencies' efforts to make both policy and program changes in arts education—contributed significantly to changes in attitudes and actions at all levels.

Partnership

Partnership means sharing a vision, commitment and resources among organizations that might otherwise "go it alone" without the same potential for success. Or as it has been described: "It is when two or more groups achieve a goal they never could have achieved individually." To succeed, partnerships require open communications, a striving for consensus, a willingness to compromise, and a high degree of tolerance for process.

The Goals 2000 Arts Education Partnership, which is composed of national organizations from the arts and education sectors, government agencies and representatives of the business and private sectors, is committed to ensuring that the arts become a visible and vital component of Goals 2000 reform plans at the state and local levels. To achieve this goal, the partners have developed an action plan that each organization is promoting to its own constituency. They are calling on their constituents to replicate the national partnership at the state and local level in an effort to make the case for including the arts in state and local education policy and to increase and improve the quality of arts education.

The National Endowment for the Arts and the Department of Education, as partners, have been the catalysts for this effort. At the invitation of Chairman Alexander and Secretary Riley, representatives from more than 100 national organizations met in fall 1994 to affirm their belief that the arts are important to achieving the National Education Goals. They agreed to work together to ensure that the state- and local-level panels that are developing reform plans under the Goals 2000: Educate America Act recognize and act on the potential of the arts to transform education. The partners have developed an action plan, *The Arts and Education: Partners in Achieving Our National Education Goals,* to influence the attitudes and actions of decision makers, parents and others to achieve two goals: (1) to make the arts part of state and local academic standards and curriculum development; and (2) to open in-service professional development opportunities in the arts for teachers.[15]

More recently, with the support of the Arts Endowment and the Department of Education, the partners have established the Goals 2000 Arts Education Partnership as a permanent organization to implement the action plan and to maintain communications and coordinate advocacy and actions at the national, state and local levels. The partnership is headquartered at the offices of the Council of Chief State School Officers and has a full-time director to manage the continued work of the member organizations.

Leadership and Partnership at the State and Local Levels

These national lessons must be the hallmarks of state and local efforts to improve arts education as well. What does that mean? First, someone must provide the leadership to gather others together to develop a shared vision and then goals and strategies for action. At the state level, this can be the state arts agency, the department of education, or the alliance for arts education. In fact, the state arts agencies have been encouraged to provide such leadership by applying to a special Goals 2000 Arts Education Leadership Fund, which was established in 1995 by the Arts Endowment and the National Assembly of State Arts Agencies with private-sector support. The Leadership Fund is intended to assist states in implementing plans for ensuring that the arts are in state and local Goals 2000 reform plans.

At the local level, local arts agencies increasingly are making arts education a priority. They are providing leadership by making arts education a critical component of community cultural planning, and they are committing staff and other resources to collaborative efforts with schools to increase and improve arts education. In Ohio, for example, the Hamilton-Fairfield Arts Association has created a pilot program in cooperation with the local schools and with Miami University of Ohio to demonstrate the positive effects of teaching the arts a minimum of one hour each day. The results thus far are impressive, and the evaluation findings are receiving national attention.

The process of building and sustaining partnerships, whether for policy change or for implementing comprehensive arts education programs, takes time and an understanding that mutual ends can be reached through patience, honesty about motivations and capabilities, and the willingness to compromise without foregoing your own principles and beliefs. The old adage, "You have to give a little to get a little," certainly applies to arts education partnerships.

Implications for the Future

As a country, we have determined that the American education system is inadequate for preparing our children for life in the new century. At the same time, we have affirmed that, in making changes in our education system, the federal role will remain one of advising, encouraging and assisting, leaving the decisions about what is taught, and how it is taught, to the state governments and local schools. The Goals 2000 legislation, passed with strong bipartisan support, continues to be embraced by the Congress. This legislation, coupled with the Improving America's Schools Act of 1994, will prove to be an historic change in education policy. For arts education, so long left out of the national education policy framework, these developments are the "policy window" Leonard Garment spoke about in 1989. For arts education advocates, it is a long-awaited and rare window of opportunity for the arts to take their rightful place in our country's elementary and secondary schools. It is a window that will probably remain open only a short time.

If we are to make the arts available to children and young adults in our schools in the substantive ways they both need and deserve, we must *lead, become partners* and, most important, *act* to ensure that we get through that window before it closes. We can consider the present situation through the metaphor of theater: Goals 2000, including the policy framework it provides and the state and local school actions that it encourages and supports, is like a new theater space. The stage is there, along with the rigging, the lights and the sound system. However, without the actions of the education policy makers and administrators, parents, teachers, artists and advocates at the state and local levels, working together to script, produce, perform and direct the play, it remains only an empty space, a framework, that fails to realize its promise and potential. Let's act now to raise the curtain on the future.

Doug Herbert *is the Director of Arts in Education in the Education and Access Division at the National Endowment for the Arts. He became Director of the National Endowment for the Arts' Arts in Education Program in 1992 after having served as the program's Assistant Director for more than four years. Prior to joining the Arts Endowment, he was the National Program Director for Very Special Arts, an educational affiliate of the John F. Kennedy Center for the Performing Arts. He began his arts career as the Managing Director of the Prince George's Publick Playhouse. He holds a master's degree in management from the Johns Hopkins University and a bachelor's degree in English from the University of Maryland.*

Staying the Course

A Conversation with Leilani Lattin Duke

The Getty Center for Education in the Arts was formed in 1982 to:

> ...focus on the issues and challenges confronting today's art educators and policy makers. It is based on the conviction that the ideas and values communicated through art are an essential part of every child's education.... The Center is one of the J. Paul Getty Trust's seven operating activities, which are addressing the critical needs related to the presentation, conservation and understanding of art, with the objective of making a significant contribution to the fine arts and related areas of the humanities.... In order to address the many complex problems related to art education in schools, museums and other education settings, the Center is envisioned as a locus for coordinating programs in other places and drawing widely on the expertise of consultants and experienced practitioners. It has undertaken a series of research and development projects in three major programmatic areas: providing education and training opportunities in visual art education for school personnel; experimenting with the application of television to education in the arts; and identifying and disseminating information about promising school art education programs.[16]

Lani Duke and I first met in New York in the early eighties during the year she spent conducting field research for the Getty Trust prior to the formation of the Center. The JDR 3rd Fund's Arts in Education Program had just closed down and Lani wanted to get my perspective about the Fund's experiences and some of the lessons we had learned that might be useful to the Getty in the design of its programs. I remember a long dinner, lots of passionate conversation, areas of strong agreement, bones of real contention. It was both stimulating and frustrating, because in those days I was a proselytizer, and in my evangelical fervor, I remember trying to convince Lani that the Center's philosophy and programs should emulate and continue from where the JDR 3rd Fund had left off; Lani and her colleagues had a very different perspective and an entirely different set of ideas. In those days I thought they were incompatible; since then I have learned differently.

Despite some of our philosophical differences, we have always shared many of the same views about institutional change, schooling and the need for policy, partnerships and collaboration to make the arts a valued part of American education. These principles were clearly articulated in a Rand Corporation report to the Getty and are included in *Beyond Creating*, the Center's landmark 1985 publication. The final section on "critical elements" necessary for change identifies the conditions and factors that must exist for substantive visual art education programs to be successful. They include positive changes in perspectives by members of the school community, the efforts of a politically skilled art advocate, strong district support, outside resources, support and involvement of teachers and principals and active involvement of art specialists, academic rigor, a conceptual base, a written curriculum, a sequential curriculum, well-specified instructional goals, in-service teacher training and program review and evaluation of instructional goals and substance.[17]

Most of these principles are as valid today as they were ten years ago, and that is one of the more important lessons to be learned from the history of our field. Certain tenets cross philosophical boundaries and pedagogical approaches: they apply to arts (plural) education and for that matter, educational change of any dimension or in any discipline.

The Getty continues to engage in important programmatic and policy work at the national, state and local level. It is associated with school reform efforts and sponsors or joins in research studies intended to advance the knowledge base and practice of the field. I asked Lani to share her extensive and valuable experience with us, which she most willingly has done.

☞ *Getty Center for Education in the Arts*

Mission Statement

The Getty Center for Education in the Arts is dedicated to improving the quality and status of arts education in the nation's public schools grades K-12.

The Center's programs are primarily concerned with the visual arts and are guided by three premises:

(1) The visual arts should be an essential part of every child's education because knowledge of the arts is a principal means of understanding human experiences and transmitting cultural values;

(2) If art education is to become a more substantive part of general education, its content must be broadened to include instruction based on the domains or disciplines that contribute to creating and understanding art: art production, art history, art criticism, and aesthetics—an approach known as discipline-based art education (DBAE);

(3) The most effective art education programs are based on working partnerships among teachers, school administrators, artists, museums, universities, parents, and others in a community who assume responsibility for supporting them.

Federal/National Partnerships

Jane Remer: What are some of the important lessons that you have learned about developing and sustaining arts and education partnerships at the national level?

Leilani Lattin Duke: I have tried to think of the lessons we learned that have been common to our different partnerships. The one thing we surely have learned is that you need to appeal to your partner's priorities and self-interest when advocating for arts education. If you approach a prospective partner without knowing what that organization is trying to accomplish and achieve, they are unlikely to become a partner or to advocate with you because arts education is not high on their agenda. For example, when we began to work with the National Conference of State Legislators (NCSL), we did a lot of homework—including focus groups interviews with their members—before we were ready to go to them and say: "Here's where we think we have natural intersections of interest."

We have also learned that a partnership is not a one-shot experience. You cannot just initiate a multi-year project with national partners and then expect them to sustain it. You have to constantly nurture their support and build their learning curve. With the NCSL, we have had some success because the staff person who worked with us became a convert to arts education. Now, she really champions arts education within the staff and within the committee structure. That has been very helpful.

With the National PTA, we tried another way to sustain and institutionalize arts education within that organization. Every year, we seemed to be working with a new staff person. Finally, we suggested that they create cultural affairs committees through their state networks. Each state now has a cultural affairs committee, and these committees have enabled us to keep the flame of arts education alive. The committees make suggestions to their local chapters, and they publish a newsletter about arts education and send it to state presidents and other committees three or four times a year.

With the National School Board Association, we have had to rely on our own staff and energy to sustain the initiative. We did some great work with them, but once the work was done, their staff had little commitment to keep it alive. If we didn't constantly remind them to send the "Be Smart and Include Art" kit to school board members, it would just get lost in all their other priorities.

I guess those have been our chief lessons about national partnerships.

School Partnerships

JR: What have you found to be the best collaborations or partnerships with schools and districts, and why?

LLD: We found that the top-down model, where the foundation just brings its program into a school, is not very effective. You need to invite school personnel and policy makers in leadership positions to work with you to help grapple with policy issues. No matter if it is a school board member, a parent, a superintendent or a principal; once they become vested with the value of arts education, they become much more effective than outsiders can be in working within the school environment.

JR: That is precisely what we experienced with the League of Cities program at the JDR 3rd Fund in the 1970s.

LLD: It never changes, does it? In preparing for this discussion, I reread the Rand report that we had commissioned in the early 1980s, which is always a good thing for me to do. Interestingly, the fundamental lessons that were learned by examining sites at seven different school districts from 1981-83—the ingredients for a successful districtwide arts education program common to all seven sites—have only been proven again to us as we have worked with school districts over the past ten years. These lessons aren't new. They are fundamental and generic in terms of what needs to be done. It's not rocket science.

JR: No, it just seems like it, at times. What do you see as the major obstacles to or pitfalls of these collaborations?

LLD: Personnel turnover is endemic to the profession, and it makes the task so difficult. Just when you get a superintendent or a school board really committed, the superintendent moves on or a new school board is elected.

I think our biggest problem with arts education has to do with values. A school doesn't stop teaching history or English or geography when a superintendent leaves a district. Yet we always seem to need a champion for the arts in a policy-making position because schools have not embraced—nor has our society—the value of the arts. That is the fundamental problem. That is why we spend so much time on advocacy. That is why it was so important to get the arts into Goals 2000, to get them into the National Assessment of Educational Progress (NAEP)—so the arts are treated as a core subject that superintendents cannot ignore. It is still a big challenge for us all.

The other obstacle we have seen is that arts teachers don't receive pre-service training in a way that enables them to take a leadership position within a school. You start from behind with the general classroom teacher, who feels so uncomfortable teaching the arts, and you have to try to attract them to programs with in-service staff development. We keep scratching our heads about how to leverage some change in the pre-service area, because hundreds of new teachers are being turned out each year.

JR: The Lincoln Center Institute has begun some exploratory work in the pre-service training area with faculty and students in the City University of New York system. It will be interesting to learn about their experience. What thoughts do you have to share with the arts community about working with schools? To the school community about working with the arts community?

LLD: I think you have to take the long view and look at schools as more than just venues for arts education. You have to look at schools as change agents, see where the arts fit within that larger context of curriculum, and understand the goals and reform that schools hope to achieve. In other words, it is just like working with organizations at the national level: try to figure out what the school wants to do—is it committed to reform? Sit down with the principal and ask him or her to articulate the vision for the school, and then try to figure out together how an arts education program would help them to achieve some of their goals.

That is very different from the mindset with which most arts organizations come to schools. They approach schools with a mindset that suggests: the arts are wonderful; you are missing something if you don't give your kids instruction in or exposure to them. That won't create a kind of lasting infrastructure for the arts. When we ask educators in our staff development programs to prepare a one-year plan and a five-year plan for arts education, we have learned that when they approach the task by knowing what is happening in the whole school, not just one subject area—particularly when we can get a team that has some teachers and a principal—it does make a difference.

JR: I'm so pleased to hear what you're saying because, as you know, these were fundamental principles that undergirded and guided the work we did at the JDR 3rd Fund. What I find even more interesting is that they remain fundamental principles, and that, alas, the values struggle remains the same, in spite of those lessons learned. You, in particular, have been working both vertically and horizontally in so many arenas. If the Getty hasn't come up with at least some kind of pathway or hope that there's light at the end of the tunnel—other than persistent, agonizing advocacy—perhaps we are talking about a kind of fundamental social change that people like you and I certainly can't accomplish alone.

LLD: If you believe that schools reflect the values of society—which we both do—the answer is pretty clear: until society places greater value and emphasis on the arts, it is not going to happen in the schools. Nevertheless, I can be optimistic when I think that more schools around the country now really understand and see the value of arts education than 15 or 20 years ago. When we examined the schools that have been part of our staff development institutes, we found that they do not go back to the way they were. Once art is in the school, it becomes a permanent part of the curriculum—they even hire arts teachers. Unfortunately, those schools are not the majority, but they are growing. It takes staying the course, and constantly advocating. We have more advocates for arts education than we did 20 years ago, and we have some leverage with Goals 2000. I just hope that, as the goals are implemented in the states, state and local arts agencies and arts education groups really work to make sure that the arts are part of their school reform plan.

JR: In Goodlad's change-theory terms, you are talking about progress school by school.

LLD: That's right. Site-based management is the school-by-school model.

JR: That can be a two-edged sword. Have you discovered that?

LLD: Yes. It's much more difficult school by school than it was district by district. At the district level, you had a superintendent and a board who could make it happen in all their schools, and now you have to go principal by principal. That is daunting.

The Arts and School Reform

JR: Now that the arts are receiving attention at the federal/national level, what are the implications for teaching and learning behind the classroom door? What can local arts organizations, agencies and schools do to ensure the place of the arts in the education of every student?

LLD: We don't think for a nanosecond that these actions at the national level will create and cause a chain reaction at the local level without an enormous amount of work. For example: Teachers look at nine or ten sets of national standards and say, "We can't possibly deal with all of these standards." It takes people at the grassroots level to make things happen, using what is happening at the national level to get their foot in the door. The national arts standards gives them some credibility that they may not have had before. Yet once that classroom door closes, teachers are going to teach the way they want to teach regardless of whether they are dealing with reform in math or reform in art. We see that time and time again.

JR: The Getty Center for Education in the Arts has spent a remarkable amount of time and money doing some important work at the national level. Do you feel a sense of frustration about the notion of trickle-down, or have you found ways to use it?

LLD: I think we have found ways to use it because most of our energies go into the staff development area, not into advocacy. In the staff development area, we reach thousands of teachers through summer institutes and through the follow-up. If the arts hadn't been in Goals 2000, it would have been a tougher sell. So these national initiatives do help the teachers that we reach, and they love teaching art because it opens up a whole new world for them. National initiatives help teachers to believe they are on the right track and provide them with arguments for parents, superintendents or principals who want to know why they are spending time teaching art when they should be teaching math, science or reading. And now they can answer, "Because it's in the national legislation."

JR: Let's talk about this in the context of NAEP. You and I probably know what will be revealed by the national assessment: precious little art is being taught or learned; what is being is taught is sporadic and of uneven quality. My fear is that people will say: "Very little is being done; what is being done isn't very good; it can't be that important anyway; this just reinforces my negative feelings about the arts; and anyway, who cares!"

LLD: I agree with you 100 percent, and I had this discussion a year ago at the National Endowment for the Arts. I told them that the answer to the "so what" question really needs to be thought through. The "so what" question is: "We know the arts aren't being taught well, kids aren't learning about the arts, so what?" We have to develop a strategy now to deal with that inevitable question, just as the National Geographic Society did when they commissioned a NAEP on geography and learned that kids did not know much about geography. National Geographic had a whole campaign that positioned the critical nature of geography and what kids were missing if they didn't study geography. They had the whole strategic plan ready to go as soon as the results came back from the NAEP. The arts people have got to do that, too.

I don't think that the NAEP is going to have a positive national impact, but I do think it is already having an impact on states that are using the NAEP model to design state assessments in the arts. The national NAEP may never happen because of the congressional budget cutbacks, but the work has already had an effect on about 19 or 20 states that have formed a consortium and have been working collectively to help develop items for the NAEP arts test and for their own state assessments. The consortium is being managed by the Council of Chief State School Officers. In fact, there are consortia in math and other subjects. The one for the arts has more states included in it than any of the other subjects, which really surprised us.

JR: Let me go back to the voluntary standards. I believe that just the fact that they now exist has prompted the same kind of activity at the state level. Attention is being given to arts frameworks and definitions of curriculum and instruction that I would like to think is a result of activity at the federal level. Do you agree?

LLD: I think the national activity has done a lot, but in fairness, many states were ahead of the federal activity. Through their visual and performing arts frameworks, a number of states had gone a lot further before the national standards efforts began. Those state frameworks served to inform the national effort, which resulted in the kind of synergy, compatibility and coherence that you see in other subject areas.

JR: Yes, that's true. I've seen a good example of that in Kentucky and their KERA legislation. Thank you, Lani, for your responses. It is good to have your perspective on past and current events and to know that the Getty Center for Education in the Arts will continue to provide leadership and be a catalyst for getting and keeping the arts in schools.

Leilani Lattin Duke *is Director of the Getty Center for Education in the Arts, an operating entity of the J. Paul Getty Trust. Prior to joining the Getty Trust in 1981, she served for three years as Executive Director of the California Confederation of the Arts. From 1971 to 1979, she worked for the National Endowment for the Arts, where her responsibilities included administering the Arts and Artifacts Indemnity Act for the Federal Council on the Arts and Humanities, managing the Federal Design Education Program and directing the Special Constituencies Program.*

Making Creative Connections Within A Business

Jane L. Polin Shares Some Lessons Learned

This year, as always, the GE Fund is focused on educating today for a better tomorrow...we believe that objective evaluation is as essential to success as careful planning and effective implementation. We evaluate also because our initiatives are funded solely by donations of competitively earned GE resources. It's our obligation to impose on ourselves a rigorous "return on investment" discipline for allocating these resources among competing alternatives. Finally, we must be certain that we are managing our programs so that our commitment to education produces not rhetoric but results.[18] *—Clifford V. Smith, Jr., President, the GE Fund*

On the front cover of its annual report is the statement of purpose of the GE Fund, a corporate philanthropy that makes grants in the United States and other countries. This statement reads:

We seek to educate—grade school through graduate school and beyond. Education develops resourceful leaders who grow the economy. It produces informed voters and consumers. It fosters understanding and respect for one another. The GE Fund is a catalyst, supporting programs that provide for the education and well-being of men, women and children around the world.

The GE Fund is guided by the vision of its President Clifford V. Smith, Jr. and the creative energy and imagination of its program manager, Jane Polin. The fund is organized into ten program areas, and most of the proposals it supports are submitted upon invitation. Grants advisory committees review and make recommendations on requests for assistance.

Beginning in 1994, the GE Fund took a leadership role with a major arts-in-education research initiative, Champions of Change: The Impact of the Arts on Education. This initiative is assessing the impact of the performing and visual arts on education by evaluating how several programs "change" students, teachers, artists and other participants. It is also collaborating with the John D. and Catherine T. MacArthur Foundation and the President's Committee for the Arts and the Humanities in this major research project to determine the nature and extent of the impact of the arts on learning.

The Arts & Culture Program supports many programs that make creative connections. These initiatives frequently involve partnerships that are about "making successful connections—schools with arts organizations, students with artists, parents and volunteers with schools, and teachers with external resources."[19]

Jane Polin and I have worked both separately and together on a number of projects and programs of mutual interest since the late eighties. I currently serve as a consultant and evaluator for the GE Fund, one of whose projects, Creative Connections, is featured in an earlier chapter. I believe that the GE Fund is doing some pioneering work behind the scenes as well as out front in the national scene today. As a result, I asked Jane to write an essay for *Beyond Enrichment*. Busy executive that she is, she gave me instead a copy of a speech she made to the Business Committee for the Arts in October 1993 and suggested that I update it and shape it to fit within the framework of the book. I agreed to this task, and following are the collaborative results.

Sailing The Seven C's for Creative Connections

How to Navigate the Waters for Effective Collaborations[20]

by Jane L. Polin

GE and other corporations are facing a growing shortage of highly skilled workers. We see a tremendous need for workers who are creative, analytical, disciplined and self-confident. To develop future leaders, we need to encourage the development of broad abilities beyond technical skills. At the GE Fund, we believe that hands-on participation in the arts is one of the best ways to develop these abilities in young people.

In grants made nationwide, the GE Fund has invited arts organizations, large and small, to forge partnerships with the public schools, and we recently invited a cooperative educational service center to form a partnership with local arts organizations and groups. In all instances, the direct participation in the arts by students, teachers, staff and parents has had a revitalizing, transforming impact on the schools and the arts organizations.

To make these partnerships work, we identified arts organizations that are truly committed to education as part of their mission, not just as an ancillary activity. Similarly, we chose to work with schools and educational centers that recognize the arts as an academic area held to the same expectations and standards for performance and evaluation as any other subject matter, not just as an extracurricular activity. In short, we chose to work with artists committed to education and educators committed to the arts.

Accomplishing this goal of transforming education through the arts within one school building, let alone an entire community, requires the talents and resources of many constituencies: teachers, parents, artists and others concerned with developing the abilities of all children through the arts.

In many cases, we have supported the outstanding arts-in-education work already in progress; in other cases we have funded arts organizations fully committed to the arts in education. In our most ambitious efforts, we have launched complex collaborations among partners who have never pursued a common goal together before, even though they may have worked in the same building or the same community.

Here are the lessons we have learned about developing successful collaborations from our experiences with these programs. They can be grouped into seven grant-making fundamentals that I have labeled with "c" words, for convenience.

Construction

The first "c" word is construction, which represents the planning process. The various parties need to be able to read from a common score, which, ideally, they will have created and notated together. Planning time is spent building relationships as well as expectations. Although often viewed as a luxury in our work, planning is essential to the construction of successful collaborations.

Communication

The next "c" word is communication. As collaborators, we all need to communicate often—to make decisions, to inform, to celebrate, to correct, to do all the things that communication enables us to do. And this communication cannot just be a beautifully prepared report to the funder. The communication involves meetings, conference calls, electronic mail, faxes and all those other devices designed to help us communicate more quickly and effectively. Communication is vital to collaboration.

Context

The third "c" word is context, which is shorthand for environment. Funds and fund-seekers alike must acknowledge the context of collaborations. Context is not just about place; it is also about time. Some states and localities are prepared to embrace the arts within the context of the reform movement; others are not yet ready.

Constraints

The fourth "c" word is constraints—the visible and less visible barriers to getting work done. There are constraints ranging from entrenched patterns of individual and group behavior to practical problems such as funding limitations. There are scheduling issues, labor contracts, missing advocates and, ultimately, fear of failure. By better acknowledging the constraints up front, collaborations can be strengthened.

Critique

The fifth "c" word is critique, or evaluation. As the funder, you are hard-pressed to find out what's really going on in a complex collaboration. Events are occurring that you would love to know about and probably some that you are glad that you didn't know about. Regardless, without an outside set of eyes and ears to provide some objective feedback, you will have little sense of whether or not your funds are investments generating terrific returns or simply a lost gambling bet. The GE Fund has engaged outside consultants to give us a critique, and their comments have led to actions that have improved these collaborations.

Commitment

The sixth "c" word is a big one: commitment. Commitment comes from involvement—local ownership by businesses as well as all the other partners. Commitment also requires sizable resources of time and money; we often make commitments over three or more years. The partners must know that you will be around for the long term, and we, the funders, need that same assurance.

Counselor

The final "c" stands for counselor. The initial GE Fund role in developing collaborations is often that of matchmaker, setting the parties out on a blind date and hoping that they find enough common interests to go on a second date with still no guarantee of commitment on either side. Eventually, these blind dates can lead to meaningful relationships. For better or worse, our role sometimes evolves into one of "marriage counselor." We try to help the partners learn about, understand and live with the immediate and long-range economic and other realities of their relationship. As a counselor, our role is to remind them of the fundamentals I have outlined in all of the preceding "c" words and to provide the necessary support so that partnerships can grow, mature and endure.

 The role of grant maker as counselor often extends beyond the grantee to other GE operations in the region and around the country. We can transfer best practices from grants made elsewhere. As corporate service providers to our business colleagues in the field, we can enable them to do their jobs as community leaders better and more easily. As a result, they can also identify positively with GE in a way that goes beyond the considerations of any single business and speaks to the values of all GE business leaders.

One More C: Catalysts

In the context of this book, foundations and their executive and program staffs are important catalysts for change. The GE Fund exemplifies the best tradition of those private and corporate philanthropies that take chances, lead the way and act as stalking horses where other more conservative organizations fear to tread. They have clear missions, they have clear policy guidelines, they reach out for expert advice and assistance, they seek out potential allies and advocates, and they do not shrink from controversy. In fact, they often create it. Another "c."

Foundation leaders such as Jane Polin and Lani Lattin Duke have originated, participated in, or stimulated unusual and productive collaborations, often among groups of unlikely bedfellows. They have been able to do so largely because of the commanding (another "c") presence and political weight of their institutional banner names and financial bases: cash. Yet another "c."

Catalysts for change usually have perceived or virtual power: money, political suasion, intellectual authority, scholarship, single-minded passion and vision. They almost always have a respected (or feared) institutional base or constituent "army" of power. These are more often than not identified as national or local champions, and as Richard Bell and others have already pointed out, they are critical for launching programs, leading the march for financial support and assembling the political support necessary to forge lasting community alliances for the arts in the schools.

Jane L. Polin has held the position of Program Manager and Comptroller at The GE Fund (formerly The GE Foundation) since 1988. Her responsibilities include program management for the GE Fund's arts & culture, public policy, United Way, and matching gift programs, and financial administration of GE's philanthropic support (1994: $46.3 million). In 1989, she introduced the nation's first program to match employee and retiree gifts electronically by phone, an innovation in corporate giving now being used by AT&T and others. She has also led the GE Fund's award-winning efforts to support the role of arts education. Ms. Polin served as a National Endowment for the Arts panelist for Arts-in-Education funding in 1989, 1990, 1994, and 1995. She earned a B.A. in music from Wesleyan University and holds an M.B.A. in marketing from Columbia University.

The National Assembly of State Arts Agencies

Stimulating School Reform at the Federal, State and Local Levels

by Jonathan Katz

History and Background

From their beginnings, the National Endowment for the Arts and the state arts agencies (whose creation the federal agency stimulated in the mid-1960s) invested almost immediately in funding artists and arts organizations in schools. Programs such as "poets in the schools" became popular in communities all over the country as a result of favorable newspaper coverage and films about prominent artists, such as poet Kenneth Koch.

The National Assembly of State Arts Agencies (NASAA) and the National Endowment for the Arts worked together through the 1970s and early 1980s to adapt federal guidelines to support the wide variety of school and community residencies initiated by state arts agency arts education coordinators. Since its inception, NASAA has played an active role in the arts in education as the vehicle through which the state arts agencies communicate with the Arts Endowment about the best ways to combine resources.

The rapid spread and growth of local arts agencies greatly enhanced the reach and impact of residencies by individual artists and companies. By the mid-1980s, federal-state-local partnerships had provided schools in cities as diverse as New York City, St. Paul, Minnesota, and Fredonia, Kansas, with visiting or resident artists as resources in the classroom and other community settings for more than a decade.

NASAA again became a forum for federal-state dialogue in the mid-1980s, when Arts Endowment Chairman Frank Hodsoll's landmark survey of arts education practice in the United States, *Toward Civilization*, persuaded him that his agency's arts education priority should be to achieve through planning processes the structural inclusion of the arts as basic to the school curriculum. His proposal to shift funding away from artists precipitated a discussion with the state arts agencies through NASAA that ultimately resulted in a strengthened federal-state partnership and one of the most cost-effective programs in U.S. government history.

During the ensuing five-year transitional period, the Arts Endowment supported state arts agency arts-in-education activities in two categories: One focused primarily on the programs that provided school systems with artists to help achieve learning objectives, and the second supported planning and implementation of collaborative efforts between state arts agencies and state departments of education to make the arts basic in each state in at least some schools. These Arts in Schools Basic Education Grants (AISBEG grants, as they were known) stimulated arts education plans and implementation activities in more than 40 states with a federal outlay of only $4.3 million.

A NASAA survey of state arts agencies, in consultation with the Arts Endowment, identified the guiding principles for awarding a single arts education grant to each state arts agency in support of a comprehensive strategy. The resulting partial-formula, partial competitive funding was meant to assure that each state would have the resources to make some progress to allow the good planning and management that comes with a measure of predictability and to reward effective strategies.

These principles have continued to undergird the federal-state arts partnership in the 1990s. This framework, which encourages leadership, high standards of achievement, and flexibility at all levels of government, has built an infrastructure that in 1993, according to NASAA's report, *The Education Commitment: An Overview of State Arts Agencies' Arts Education Activities*, supported more than 132,000 artists in 6,900 projects in 2,800 communities. Five million dollars awarded by the Arts Endowment's arts-in-education program to state arts agencies generated an additional $22 million from state legislatures and leveraged public and private resources totaling $500 million in program activity at the local level.[21]

As its work with the Arts Endowment has evolved over the years, NASAA's role as a catalyst for progress in arts education has expanded as the funding and the influence of state arts agencies has grown. I was once a poet in the schools for the Kansas Arts Commission; after I became NASAA's executive director in 1985, I coordinated a "think-tank" and report to the field on practical ways to evaluate arts-in-education programs. This was followed by NASAA's first book-length publication, *Arts Education Handbook: A Guide to Productive Collaborations,*[22] which focused on how to achieve successful partnerships among parents, educators, the arts community and others with a stake in effective education reform. More recently, with NASAA's assistance, state arts agency leaders played an important role in successfully advocating at regional hearings for the arts to be explicitly mentioned as a key curricular area in the third goal of the Clinton administration's Goals 2000: Educate America Act.

Stimulating School Reform at the Federal, State and Local Levels

The 1993 arrival in Washington, D.C. of Richard Riley as secretary of education, Terry Peterson as his special assistant, and Scott Sanders as deputy chairman for partnership at the Arts Endowment offered NASAA unique partnership opportunities. All three had come from South Carolina where, as governor, chief education planner and state arts agency executive director, respectively, they had fully integrated the arts in that state's exemplary educational reform. Two new collaborative initiatives with tremendous potential for improving arts education at the local level are especially noteworthy: the Goals 2000 Arts Education Partnership and the Goals 2000 Arts Education Leadership Fund.

The Goals 2000 Arts Education Partnership, convened jointly by the Arts Endowment and the U.S. Department of Education in 1994, brings together more than a hundred business, education, government, foundation and arts groups for the specific purpose of integrating the arts in state and local education improvement. In 1995, the two federal agencies awarded the Council of Chief State School Officers, which represents the heads of state departments of education, and NASAA a cooperative agreement to manage the partnership's activities. Committees will focus on federal, state and local efforts, while task forces aim to increase public awareness and advocacy, encourage high educational standards, and involve more groups. Overall, the strategy is to unite in local school districts the people affiliated with the groups participating nationally. The federal agencies have made a three-year commitment to the partnership.

The Goals 2000 Arts Education Leadership Fund is a collaboration between the Arts Endowment and NASAA. Its purpose is to fund activities in each state to make the arts part of education reform. Eligible applicants are state arts agencies or their designee, frequently a statewide alliance for arts education affiliated with the John F. Kennedy Center for the Performing Arts. An approval process coordinated by NASAA enlists a national panel to review each state's application to assure that proposed strategies have a good likelihood of success. An initial grant of $200,000 from the Emily Hall Tremaine Foundation requiring a three-to-one match of funds from non-governmental sources has stimulated multi-state funding from the Getty Center for Education in the Arts, the Dayton-Hudson corporation and its Marshall Field's department stores, the Kennedy Center, Hallmark and Coca-Cola, while funding for individual states has come from many more businesses and foundations. The total private funding has exceeded a million dollars. More than half the states have begun project activities, and more than 35 states are expected to participate.

Although raising a million dollars in a tough year is exciting, the real payoff is seeing the variety of creative approaches the states have put together to make a difference in the local school districts. Some of the strategies involve awareness campaigns, regional meetings, establishing information networks and databanks, workshops, arts education assessments and professional development for teachers. The leadership and coalition building within the states has been fantastic.

Lessons Learned

As these initiatives have developed and evolved, I have learned that partnerships depend first upon the strength of the leaders' vision and then upon the partners' ability to find the common purpose, to keep the goals in view, and to let them shape the working relationship. Trying to implement programs by virtue of authority alone works much less efficiently, whether from federal level to state, or from state to local level. What *has* worked is shared responsibility—for developing a partnership's vision, for creating its strategies and for making decisions. NASAA's role as a vehicle for partnership between the state arts agencies and federal agencies has been crucial.

The Future

Currently, the states, through NASAA, and the Arts Endowment are engaged in a most important conversation about how to combine resources to maintain the arts education support system that we have built up over almost 30 years. The impact on arts education of nearly a 40 percent cut in the Arts Endowment's appropriation in fiscal year 1996 from its 1995 level remains to be seen.

NASAA's commitment to managing the Partnership and overseeing the Leadership Fund is strongly supported by member state arts agencies. In my view, these national initiatives are crucial to local progress in improving arts education. Although the changing environment for public arts support could lead to a scaled-back effort in a worst-case scenario, ideally, the sustained support of our member agencies, coupled with some new funding partners, will enable us to achieve the Partnership's and the Fund's maximum potential for making a difference in many localities.

Two new publications, *Schools, Communities and the Arts: A Research Compendium* and its summary brochure *Eloquent Evidence: Arts at the Core of Learning*, document the growing evidence that the arts offer learners unique tools for problem-solving; help students achieve standard educational goals such as better SAT scores; enhance the learning of reading, writing and math skills; develop creativity; motivate enthusiasm for and persistence in learning; prepare students for jobs; enable students to understand themselves better; and that the arts are especially valuable in engaging the interest of at-risk youth. These valuable tools result from the combined efforts of the Arts Endowment, the Morrison Institute for Public Policy at Arizona State University, the President's Committee on the Arts and Humanities, NASAA and the GE Fund. Partnerships such as this, coupled with the current public interest in improving education, offer new opportunities for the including arts education in school curricula.

These fact-based messages are clear: In the next few years, thousands of individual school districts will either include the arts or limit the learning they offer. To those who are aware of the importance of including the arts in schools as basic student learning, the challenge is to share effectively, within state and local decision-making processes, what they have known from their own experiences to be true and can now begin to demonstrate.

Jonathan Katz is Executive Director of the National Assembly of State Arts Agencies (NASAA), which represents the government arts agencies of the states and six jurisdictions. NASAA serves these agencies as a vehicle for arts policy development, advocacy, leadership development, research, information and communication. During 1995, NASAA and the National Endowment for the Arts coordinated the Goals 2000 Arts Education Leadership Fund, which raised over a million dollars in private funds to integrate the arts in state education improvement agendas. Previously, Jonathan Katz was Professor of Public Policy and Administration at the University of Illinois at Springfield, where he directed the Community Arts Management Program, and he served as Executive Director of the Kansas Arts Commission. He has written and edited several books about arts policy, including Building Coalitions for a Creative America: A Practical Guide to Federal Resources for Cultural Activities.

State Arts Agency Partnerships: Beyond Enrichment?

by Hollis Headrick

In the last ten years, the term "partnership" has become a buzzword and cliché. Why has this form of relationship become so prevalent in the arts? What do we gain by working together? What issues must be faced when you peel back the glossy veneer of cooperation, photo opportunities and sense of satisfaction at the latest culminating event at the school? For example, what is the nature of learning? What is good teaching practice? What is our mission? I believe these and other questions are ultimately worked out in the process of establishing and developing successful partnerships.

I would like to share my experiences about partnerships at the state and local level from my perspective as the director of the Arts in Education Program at the New York State Council on the Arts (NYSCA). I began working at NYSCA in 1985 as one of two staff members assigned to manage the first funding cycle of its new Arts in Education Initiative. As a musician who had worked as an artist in residence, I had experienced firsthand the joys and frustrations of teaching in partnership with teachers, school administrators and other artists. My task was to transform my experience in the practice of.an arts education partnership into a statewide funding policy that would link cultural organizations and schools.

I learned that identifying the characteristics of good partnerships—and setting policies to support them—is easy. However, I also learned that creating and sustaining partnerships—and finding common ground among the partners— is a demanding process that should not be viewed as a cookbook recipe in which you simply have to follow the directions and combine the right ingredients.

There is very little difference *in practice* between state-level partnerships and the partnerships that take place in a community between cultural organizations and schools. Excellent partnerships share many of the same characteristics regardless of the participants or the specific mission of the partnership.

After ten years of concerted effort, we can now reflect on state arts agencies' steps, beginning in the mid-1980s, to form partnerships with state departments of education to create and institutionalize the "arts in education" field. These relationships influenced, and continue to influence, education in this country and force us to confront these tough questions about partnerships. Relationships between state arts agencies and state departments of education also illustrate common traits of local-level partnerships among arts organizations and schools.

The Beginning of State-Level Arts Education Partnerships

In 1969, the National Endowment for the Arts established the original artist residency program, which placed artists in schools to provide in-depth artist contact over a sustained period of time. These residencies, while generally recognized as valuable for schools and artist employment, often did not integrate with school curriculum and instruction. For many state arts agencies, the only money for arts education came from Arts Endowment funds for artist residencies, since most states concentrated their support on cultural organizations in the various arts disciplines. Responding to *Coming to Our Senses: The Significance of the Arts for American Education* (1977) and the 1983 report *A Nation At Risk* (the National Commission on Excellence in Education), reform-minded citizens representing the arts and education began a grassroots effort to address the dismal state of arts education. Consequently, in the early to mid-eighties many states passed legislation that added language to department of education mandates, declaring that art "should be basic to education," or words to that effect. Although state arts agencies applauded the move, few were equipped to deal with the ramifications of this renewed interest and advocacy for arts education.

The National Endowment for the Arts became the catalyst for changing the state arts agencies' approach to arts education. In 1986-87, the Arts Endowment began to emphasize "making the arts a basic" and expanded the types of funding and activities that it would permit state arts agencies to undertake within its State Arts Education Grant funding category. In addition to the typical artist residencies, states were now encouraged and expected to support collaborative programs among arts organizations and schools—model programs, professional development for teachers and artists and other efforts to improve arts education at the state level. The most profound and controversial aspect of "making arts a basic" was the requirement that state arts agencies begin to work collaboratively with their state departments of education. When this new focus was announced in 1986 by Arts Endowment Chairman Frank Hodsoll, state arts agency administrators raised their voices in protest. They feared the consequences of assuming new duties and responsibilities—previously the province of education—that they thought were being thrust upon them.

This mandated relationship with the department of education penetrated a central issue of collaborations—mission and institutional identity. Few state arts agencies had had any previous relationship with their departments of education. If a relationship did exist, for most it was tacit acknowledgment at best and antagonistic at worst. Although the state arts agencies have struggled with this mandate since 1986, in most cases they have successfully collaborated with their departments of education, occasionally with stunning success. In some states, department of education regulations were changed to require students, for the first time, to have credit for arts classes to graduate from high school. Other states began summer teacher institutes in collaboration with their departments of education and offered other types of professional development for teachers and artists. In others, state arts agencies collaborated with their state alliances for arts education and departments of education to become advocates and partners for school reform that includes the arts.

New York Launches a Collaborative Arts in Education Initiative

The New York State Council on the Arts (NYSCA) was one of the first state arts agencies to collaborate directly with its department of education. As a result of 18 months of field meetings with arts organizations, professional education associations, artists and teachers, a NYSCA/State Education Department (SED) interagency team created the Arts in Education Initiative in 1985. As stated in the 1985-86 NYSCA Funding Report: "The primary role of this Initiative is to develop sustained partnerships between the educational and cultural community for the benefit of children in pre-kindergarten through twelfth grade. In order to accomplish its goals, the Council worked closely with two offices of the New York State Education Department: The Office of Cultural Education and the Office of Elementary and Secondary Education."

Several problems were identified and had to be addressed in creating this initiative. The school arts practitioners, who were represented by powerful statewide professional organizations, were concerned that collaborative arts projects would substitute for or replace arts teachers. The team had to take steps to assure the arts teachers that this wasn't the program's intent. SED and NYSCA also were concerned about the funding mechanism. NYSCA's legislative rules stipulated that state education aid cannot be used directly to match NYSCA funds. This was solved by having NYSCA contract directly with cultural organizations. These organizations were then responsible for matching the funding one to one, with at least 15 percent of the matching funds coming from the schools.

NYSCA and SED both set out to create a model partnership for other arts organizations and schools. The two agencies began their official collaboration with a reservoir of goodwill, built upon the success of previous pilot arts projects that had been funded throughout the state. In addition, the statewide Artists in Residence Program, administered by the New York Foundation for the Arts, had established a good track record that helped to provide a beginning point for the discussions.

The resulting Arts in Education Initiative was innovative in a number of ways: (1) it anticipated the Arts Endowment's shift in emphasis from residencies to partnerships; (2) it required arts organizations to plan and implement collaborative, curriculum-based programs with schools; (3) it required the projects to be integrated into the school curriculum; (4) it supported projects that served a school's arts curriculum or another academic subject such as social studies, science or math; (5) it provided support for organizations and schools to plan or implement projects based upon their abilities; (6) it required the arts organization and the school to complete a comprehensive two-part grant application that clearly outlined goals, objectives, specific learner outcomes, relationship to the curriculum, project team, work plan and evaluation process; and (7) it offered multiyear support to sustain projects over a two- or three-year grant period.

Ten Years Later: A Look Back

After ten years and more than $25 million in grants to arts organizations for school programs, has the NYSCA/SED collaboration been successful? Using numbers as a measure of success, more than 200 programs are now funded each year in almost every county in the state, with local funds from schools and other sources matching the NYSCA funds at least three to one. Artists and arts organizations have established new relationships with their communities, and this outreach has fundamentally changed some arts organizations and schools. In some schools, the programs have become institutionalized, and the arts have changed the way teachers approach their curriculum. The value of the arts has been reinforced in some schools and introduced for the first time in others. Overall, the concept of partnership is now part of the consciousness of many of the educators and arts organizations in the state. While the NYSCA/SED Arts in Education Initiative—now called the Arts in Education Program—cannot claim all the credit for these accomplishments, it has played a catalytic role in bringing together the arts and education communities. The following are some of the lessons learned over the years that are instructive not only for partnerships at the state level, but also for the local level.

1. Choose your most experienced staff to begin the collaborative process and give them the autonomy to make decisions to move the process forward. Each agency carefully chose its interagency team members to ensure a productive working relationship. The collaborative team was supported from the top and, within certain constraints, team members from one agency were free to negotiate directly with members from the other. The initial success of the interagency team also resulted from carefully resolving the fundamental concerns of both the education and arts communities.

2. During the early part of the collaborative process, each partner has to do the hard work of determining how the new endeavor fits into its present or expanded mission. The early planning discussions allowed all parties to think about how this new collaboration would fit within each partner's perceived mission and turf. Since NYSCA was going to administer the project, the agency held considerable discussions to establish its role and to determine the new initiative's relationship to the agency's existing arts discipline programs. For SED, this aspect was relatively simple since the agency did not need to change its mission fundamentally to provide arts education for the state's students.

3. Once a program is initiated, it must be carefully nurtured by both partners, and each must bring something to the table to create equality and balance. The collaboration permitted the interagency team to develop professional relationships that supported each other's ongoing work. Once the staffs became more knowledgeable about the other agency's activities, we found more areas for cooperation beyond the grant-making mechanism. NYSCA was offered additional opportunities to inform school practitioners about the Arts in Education Program through the conferences sponsored by SED. SED, NYSCA and the New York Foundation for the Arts cosponsored an annual summer arts-in-education conference for several years. NYSCA also helped SED to distribute arts syllabi and curricula to artists and organizations so that programs would be integrated more appropriately with the SED documents. NYSCA staff served on the SED Curriculum and Assessment Committee for the Arts and Humanities that developed the new arts frameworks in 1995. A section of this document supports the value of collaborative programs, advocates the need for arts partnerships, and highlights the concomitant need for professional development for artists and teachers. Staff from the two agencies were also instrumental in shaping the long-range goals of the New York State Alliance for Arts Education to address the need for statewide arts education advocacy.

4. **To support a partnership over the long term, the organizations must "buy in" from top to bottom.** While supportive activities took place among the interagency staff, the institutional relationship between NYSCA and SED changed over the years, and the nature of these changes paralleled similar collaborative relationships among arts organizations and schools at the local level. The interagency team remained active and involved for the first two years of the Arts in Education Initiative, monitoring its progress formally through periodic staff meetings and through the SED staff's service as ex-officio members of the arts-in-education peer advisory panels at NYSCA. Program funding increased from $2 million to a high of $3.2 million by 1989-90. However, some structural weaknesses in the collaboration began to show. Both agencies had made equal contributions to the partnership's design and implementation in the first three years, but the collaboration began to be seen as one-sided. In this instance, NYSCA granted the funds, hired new program staff, provided catalytic funds to develop the field and had administrative support from NYSCA management and council members. The SED role was never expanded substantially beyond the initial collaboration. Funding streams were identified at SED, but the collaboration was never officially acknowledged and valued by senior management in the Office of Elementary, Middle and Secondary Education. The SED/NYSCA team became increasingly frustrated that they did not have the necessary authority or access to policy makers to improve and expand the collaboration.

5. **The Arts in Education Program is perceived by the state department of education and the schools to be a program and service from the outside.** A long-range plan was never developed as part of a formal evaluation process to examine whether the original goals of the state-level partnership were being met. A routine method to inform the commissioner of education or the state Board of Regents about the progress of the Arts in Education Program and its impact on the schools was not instituted. When all is said and done, regardless of the NYSCA/SED program's genesis in 1985 and its recognized accomplishments, the program is still viewed as driven primarily by arts organizations who want to serve young people and teachers, not by the needs of curriculum or school reform. This "outsider" status is mirrored in most of the relationships among arts organizations and schools and in society at large, where the arts are considered to be a minor dimension of our culture.

Some of the issues highlighted above are common to the relationships among state arts agencies and their department of education partners by virtue of their function and size. Some of the problems were due to financial constraints and staff cutbacks at both agencies that were beyond the control of the interagency staff. Reorganization and a balancing of internal priorities within each agency made it even more difficult to give the necessary time to evaluate the program's impact on the field and to plan for the future. These comments are not meant to be overly critical of the relationship, but are offered as instructive guidelines for the future. In the end, both agencies have benefitted from this collaboration.

Evaluating Local Arts Education Partnerships

The nature of partnerships can be further explored by considering the complexities of implementing arts projects in schools at the local level. By examining the partnership process on several levels, we can begin to approach the subject with more insight and recognize its prospects, problems and pitfalls.

NYSCA funds partnerships with arts organizations and schools through its Arts in Education Program. The program's notion of collaboration is rooted as much in "guerilla school reform" as it is in matching local cultural resources with the needs of schools. Reform doesn't always enter the school under an official banner or methodology from the state department of education or through the rhetoric of the latest education guru. It can be in the form of a writer, a painter, a dance company, an ensemble of musicians or museum education specialists. The collaborations and metamorphoses cut both ways. Artists and arts organizations can be changed as much as schools by the collaborative process and begin to look upon themselves and their identities in new ways.

At NYSCA, we try to determine the quality of partnerships and how they best serve students, schools and arts groups. The standards for judging partnerships are based on the evaluative criteria stated in the Arts in Education Program guidelines. Although the guidelines have been revised twice since 1985, when they were developed by the interagency staff with input from the field, the basic premise has not changed.

These guidelines have helped the development of collaborative projects by providing a framework and set of evaluative criteria for organizations to follow as they plan their programs. They are not prescriptive: they do not stipulate the amount of contact time that artists or organizations have with students, what areas of the curriculum must be addressed, grade levels that must be served, the amount of planning time that must be included, or the levels of fees or services that must be built into the budget, nor do the guidelines suggest types of program evaluation. These aspects of the individual programs are co-planned by the arts organization and the school. The program design must be justified in relation to the goals and objectives of the program. Since these criteria form the basis for judging the quality of the partnerships, a review of each one will bring us closer to understanding the nature of successful partnerships. Much of this review takes place through staff site visits to the field.

The quality, expertise and background of the artists and/or arts professionals is of paramount importance. The NYSCA staff looks at qualifications such as teaching experience, education, and a record of performances and/or exhibitions, including artists' work samples, videotapes and lesson plans. In a school setting, a chief indicator is the artist's grasp of his or her medium and how well that is communicated in a concise and engaging manner to students. Is the artist a good teacher who can also handle the demands of classroom management in cooperation with the teacher? These qualities are evident by the conduct of the artist, how he or she interacts with the students, the attentiveness of the students and their concentration on the task. In addition, the artist or arts professional's strengths and weaknesses are revealed by paying close attention to the age-appropriateness of the activities and to how well the artist has planned a lesson or unit.

The clarity and appropriateness of the proposed program goals, the specific activities and learner outcomes associated with each goal, and the quality and depth of the program demonstrate how well the project is integrated into the curriculum and the rigor of the program design. This is evidenced by the amount of contact time among artists or arts professionals and the core group of students and teachers. This criterion also reveals whether the program has been thoughtfully planned and whether the partners understand their roles and responsibilities. The partners should also be able to demonstrate a shared understanding of the program's rationale and of how it fits into the school curriculum. The most frequent mistake made by partners is overstating the outcomes attributed to the activities and goals of a project. This is where the depth of the partners' understanding of the teaching and learning process quickly becomes evident. Both schools and arts organizations often present a long list of outcomes and achievements that will be the results of their collaborations. When examined in more detail, program plans sometimes clearly show that the amount of contact time is insufficient to meet the goals and objectives since learning takes time to assimilate. Field observation can detect inappropriate activities for children—whether too advanced, too elemental or just plain boring. Full-fledged curriculum development by artists or arts organizations can only be successfully undertaken after activities or units have been field-tested and modified by artist and teacher feedback. Arts organizations need to understand that teachers can be helpful in understanding more than dynamics of classrooms. They can also be of great assistance in helping the organizations and their artists to learn the basics of creating a simple lesson plan and how to construct a more complex curriculum framework to guide the teaching process.

The commitment of the partners and the nature of the collaboration team is at the heart of all partnerships. It is evidenced by financial commitment and adequate planning time devoted to the collaborative process and to identifying the specific roles and responsibilities of the collaborative team. This criterion probes beyond the mechanics—what is being taught and how—to a more fundamental question of the motivation for the collaboration and the authenticity of the relationship. The question "Why enter a collaboration?" is important, particularly for arts organizations. Most do not view education and their relationship to local schools and community as a vital aspect of their missions. For example, in 1994 only 22 organizations of the more than 300 that applied to the Arts in Education Program defined their primary missions as serving children pre-K to 12 in school settings. The vast majority of organizations are not in business to serve children; they are in business to create, present, preserve and perpetuate various art forms.

Organizations respond to the availability of certain types of grants from funding sources (corporations, foundations, etc.) by creating programs to secure those funds. This was the case when the Arts in Education Program was established, and new money was available to support ventures into education. NYSCA and SED were seeking to stimulate activity, but many organizations entered the field without clearly understanding the demands of school-based programs and the requisite knowledge to make them successful. Many large institutions attempted to portray exposure programs as substantial educational experiences rather than one-shot introductions to their institutions.

We are past that stage now, but conversations with arts organizations—and less frequently with schools—reveal that some are not prepared for a collaborative relationship. Schools may enter the relationship because of the interest of one or more staff members who only have a rudimentary idea of what learning in and through the arts means. Like their arts partners, schools may also enter partnerships because they think that funding can be secured for a program, without contemplating the needs of students or how the project integrates with the curriculum.

Although the lack of commitment and a shared vision can be disguised by grantsmanship, its presence can clearly be detected by observing the program. A few questions and observations can determine the nature of the relationship. Is the school principal supportive and knowledgeable of the project? Is there sufficient planning time to establish a trusting relationship with the cultural organization and to plan the class activities? Is the project valued enough so that an evaluation process is in place? Can both the arts organization, the participating teachers and the school administration articulate the program's goals and objectives? Do they have a collegial relationship or one in which the artist is threatening to the teachers? Has the school made a cash contribution sufficient to demonstrate its commitment to the project or is the arts organization bearing most of the responsibility for raising funds for the project? These are a some of the questions that are examined during the evaluative process.

The project fits into the overall instructional plan of the school and strengthens existing arts curricula or improves other subject areas through the arts. Many schools and arts organizations undertake residencies or collaborative projects without determining how the projects will contribute to the students' learning over time. Some projects clearly integrate with state curricula at certain grade levels, but frequently the school and the organization don't have a clear rationale for why one teacher gets the program this year and another teacher gets a different program the next year. The school must take the lead in this aspect of the collaboration because the arts organizations do not have enough knowledge or experience to know where the program best fits within a school curriculum plan. This becomes even more critical in a multiyear partnership, with a sequential program that serves several grades.

The extent to which the scope of the program supports school reform or the efforts of school-based management teams can be an important lever for introducing a partnership project or solidifying an existing one. Arts programs have clearly demonstrated that they engage children in multiple ways of knowing, connect insights and understanding across areas of knowledge, create an overall climate of excellence and bring new techniques to school-based teachers. Taking advantage of arts programs can help school-based management teams develop thematic projects, allow for new professional development opportunities and connect the school to the wider community. School reform plans and discussions during site visits can provide evidence of the arts partnership's relationship to the school agenda and infrastructure.

The quality of the evaluation process is an integral part of planning, and refining the program helps to determine whether the partners value reflection and understand that the partnership is a dynamic rather than a static process or canned product. Evaluation is one of the least understood program components. Arts organizations are aware of the need for evaluation, but frequently they don't know how to create the necessary instruments or tools to guide the project. Schools are also weak in this area and are unsure how to evaluate the success of the partnerships in a systematic way. Teachers are more skilled at observation of student behavior and attitudes but usually know less about the art form. When NYSCA staff is in the field, they look for specific ongoing evaluation processes and ask the collaborators to describe their evaluation strategy and to produce evaluation instruments if they have them.

Some of the other benchmarks we use to determine the quality and potential strength of partnerships include: What is the history of the partnership? What changes in administration and/or staff have occurred during the life of the project? Are there similar resources in the area or is this the only project of its kind in this community? Can this project serve as a model? Are the resources of the cultural organization being used creatively?

The variations and permutations of the different kinds of arts education partnerships that can be formed are endless. Successful partnerships are unique endeavors that balance the qualities of partners and their abilities to work together, exhibit an understanding of students' needs and abilities, and effectively contribute to the students' learning in a way that neither partner could accomplish alone.

Toward a Whole Greater than the Parts

The unparalleled confluence of so many factors supporting the value of arts education has created a window of opportunity to advance the arts in education. The school reform movement has stimulated debate about the nature of teaching and learning and about the role the community should play in invigorating the school curriculum. Research about how children learn in and through the arts has become widely accepted, due to the work of Howard Gardner and others. Foundations, such as the Getty Center for Education in the Arts, have exerted enormous influence pedagogically through their support for discipline-based arts education and direct funding for larger projects. The National Endowment for the Arts, through its partnerships with state arts agencies and its advocacy role in Goals 2000 legislation and the National Standards for Arts Education, has fostered arts partnerships at the national and state level. National professional associations, such as the National Art Education Association and the

Music Educators National Conference, have extolled the arts as tools for learning and important elements in school reform. The state arts agencies have directed funding and support to artists, arts organizations and schools in almost every county in the United States. Arts organizations have responded to changes in funding priorities from state arts agencies, foundations and corporations by investing more resources in arts education and outreach. This investment was not dictated solely by the priorities of philanthropies, but also by the arts community's enlightened self-interest as it struggles to reach new audiences whose demographic composition is rapidly changing.

If all this information, research, advocacy and arts programming has influenced schools, arts practitioners, arts organizations and—more broadly—society at large, then what have been the results? In New York, like most other states, the state education department has an education reform plan for school improvement. This plan outlines a role for arts organizations and artists as contributors to an excellent education. The NYSCA Arts in Education Program is more than ten years old, and the New York Foundation for the Arts' statewide Artists in Residence Program has been serving artists, schools and students since 1974. Does it all add up to more than the sum of its parts? Does all this activity generate programs and partnerships that push the arts beyond enrichment and into the mainstream of education? Yes and no.

I say "Yes" because I have witnessed the results firsthand from visiting and observing collaborative arts projects in schools across the state. I have met with hundreds of arts organizations from multimillion-dollar institutions to small, idiosyncratic artist-run organizations. In my experience, teachers are now much more understanding of and open to collaborative arts programs, even if they have not participated in them directly. Many teachers see the inclusion of the arts in the curriculum as necessary, while others see it as nice, but unnecessary. I have seen schools changed because the energy and discipline of the arts has provided a focal point for reform. Arts organizations that previously dabbled in school lecture-demonstrations now have sequential arts curricula that include periodic staff development for artists and teachers. Principals have told me that artists and arts organizations are treated the "same as staff" during their workshops in the building. I have met students who have excelled because of the arts and astounded teachers who had been unable to reach them in any other way.

I also say, "No, not yet." Although great strides have been made in raising the consciousness of schools and the arts community, the struggle still continues—*district by district, school by school*. Arts partnerships have not made as much of an impact as intended for several reasons. First, the arts are not yet a valued part of our society. Since schools are microcosms of society and reflect its prevalent values, the arts' "outsider" status is replicated in many, if not most, schools. If chief and local school administrators think that arts are important, and they allocate time, money and staff for the arts, then partnerships will be encouraged and supported. If not, then efforts to create change will be up to the agitators on the inside—teachers or administrators—or those on the outside—parents or arts organizations.

Second, teachers need professional development opportunities in the arts. If teachers were educated in the arts *before* they began their teaching careers, then partnerships and an understanding of the arts would be an accepted dimension of all educational experiences. Fortunately, professional development opportunities are increasing in the arts, both for teachers and for artists.

Third, arts organizations must be interested and committed to arts education as they interpret their missions. Arts organizations need to learn much more about education practice and child development. Arts groups must understand that the effort they devote to education will be returned in direct proportion in the school setting. Those that claim they do not receive enough attention and planning time for a five-session "residency" do not understand the school environment. For these groups, their programs do not contribute sufficiently to be truly integrated into the curriculum or to become a priority for a school. The more serious education programs offered by arts organizations—those that include the evaluative criteria discussed above—will be treated as a legitimate part of a child's education and not an enrichment. A short residency or collaborative program by an arts organization will be enrichment, but it will never be a true partnership until it can demonstrate its intrinsic value to the complete education of children.

Finally, but almost always stated first, we don't have enough money. In a state as large as New York, with more than 700 school districts and more than one million students in New York City alone, NYSCA's high point of $3.2 million for arts in education could never institutionalize collaborative arts partnerships. The state education department would also have to play a dramatic role by supporting staff development and programming needs by systematically distributing financial resources. This is unlikely to happen in the present economic and political climate.

Have the arts gone beyond enrichment in the schools? While the answer is both yes and no, I hope that this overview has provided some new insight and will stimulate further investigation. Visit schools. Inquire about arts education programs provided by local arts organizations. Call the state arts agency and state education department. Most importantly, talk to young people and observe them while they are engaged in the arts. Their voice is seldom heard and they don't vote. Yet their welfare should be the motivating force for all of our actions.

Hollis Headrick *is Director of Arts in Education of the New York State Council on the Arts, a position he has held since 1990. He helped to initiate the Arts in Education Program at NYSCA in 1985. He serves on the state Curriculum and Assessment Committee for the Arts and Humanities, the New York City Arts Education Advisory Committee and the New York City Arts in Education Funders Group. He is a jazz drummer and has been an active performer and presenter of jazz and contemporary music for the past 20 years. He has also been a concert producer for the Jazz Coalition, Composers' Forum and Jacob's Pillow. He was an artist in residence in the Boston Public Schools and has taught at the Community Music Center of Boston and the Greenwich House Music School in New York City. He studied at the Berklee College of Music in Boston and the Creative Music Studios in Woodstock, New York.*

The National Assembly of Local Arts Agencies

Catalysts for Community Building Through Local Arts Partnerships

Jane Remer with Robert Lynch, Nancy Langan, Louise K. Stevens, Adrienne Hines, Vicki Poppen, and Bill Cleveland

Headquartered in Washington, D.C., the National Assembly of Local Arts Agencies (NALAA) represents the nation's 3,800 local arts agencies in developing an essential place for the arts in America's communities. NALAA assists its member agencies with leadership, professional development activities and research. It also provides information and publications, fosters public policy development and initiates public awareness campaigns. NALAA actively participates in developing national arts education policy by identifying funding sources, collaborating with other national arts service organizations and government entities, and advocating for the inclusion of the arts in the core curriculum.

In the last several years, under the leadership of President and CEO Robert Lynch, education has become a priority of the organization. Says Lynch:

> The role of local arts agencies is to develop an essential place for the arts in our nation's communities. Local arts agencies are vested with the responsibility to further local cultural and artistic interests and to ensure access to them. Many get involved with arts education services, services to other arts organizations, grant-making and cultural planning. A significant and ever-growing role for these agencies is the development of initiatives that respond to their communities' educational needs.

> Local decision-making plays a critical role in arts education. We all recognize that funds for arts education are scarce. Our challenge is to convince those who control the purse strings to spend their resources on arts education. Success in this has been achieved primarily when many voices have banded together in partnership. We should recognize that a great many decisions will ultimately be made locally. Therefore, all partnerships and advocacy,

whether federal, state, regional or local, must be directed toward the final outcome of affecting local decision-making.

Arts in Education Coordinator Nancy Langan describes NALAA's role in promoting the arts in education at the local level as follows:

NALAA works with local arts agencies, arts councils, city arts commissions, and mayors' offices of cultural affairs from across the United States. These organizations share the goal of serving all the arts, all the various art forms, and all the people in a particular community. A recent NALAA survey found that 84 percent of local arts agencies were involved in arts education in some way: 57 percent produce artists-in-the-schools programs; 42 percent are helping with curriculum design in partnership with school systems; and 71 percent are involved with advocacy and lobbying, trying to make the case for funding arts education with decision makers. The partnerships of artists, arts organizations and cultural institutions at the local level can be a tremendous resource for community arts programs and public school education.

We are particularly excited about our new Institute for Community Development and the Arts. The mission of the Institute is to promote additional government funding for the arts by educating state and local arts agencies, government officials, and funders about using the arts as community change-agents for solutions to economic, social and educational problems. Beginning in 1995, and during the next three years, we will research 1,000 arts and community development programs from across the country and measure the total local government support for the arts in 160 cities. Using this information, we will produce 21 publications that describe these innovative programs, how to adapt them locally, and the nontraditional methods being used to fund them. In addition, we will provide companion videos, annual symposia in Washington, D.C., sessions at our annual convention, reports to Congress and public access to institute databases.

Perhaps the most exciting aspect of the project is our Institute Partners. They include the National Conference of State Legislators, the U.S. Conference of Mayors, the International City/County Management Association and the National Association of Towns and Townships. All are part of our Peer Education Network, which is designed to encourage elected and appointed government officials to educate each other on a collegial level about the value of the arts in community development. For example, at the January 1995 meeting of the U.S. Conference of Mayors in

Washington, D.C., the opening plenary luncheon was dedicated to arts and youth-at-risk programs. Mayors from Chicago, Seattle and Fort Myers spoke about the arts programs in their communities to an enthusiastic audience of 550 mayors. Working with our partners, we will continue to develop these sessions and regularly publish articles about arts and community development innovations in our partners' publications.

Among her many responsibilities, Nancy has gathered and made available a great deal of pertinent information about the field. In addition to her regular column in the NALAA newsletter, she compiles and distributes policy, funding and other information on a regular basis. She has also organized several annual preconference sessions and dedicated three issues of NALAA's Monographs to the arts in education. When we discussed the nature of NALAA's contribution to this book, Nancy and Bob agreed that a selection of mini-case studies and other material from these publications would be appropriate in a section dedicated to catalysts for community activism.

Local arts agencies have become important leaders for community building through local arts partnerships. They have done so in a variety of clever and imaginative ways that should prove instructive to the field. The selections I have included are taken from three issues of Monographs—*Arts in Education: From National Policy to Local Community Action* (April 1994); and *Arts in Education Planning: Three Local Communities*, Volume I (January 1995) and Volume II (April 1995). I have chosen them because they represent different approaches, different communities and different solutions to common problems at the local level. To set the stage, I have provided an introduction, "Sound Advice," by Louise K. Stevens of ArtsMarket Consulting, Inc., that was published in the January 1995 issue.

Sound Advice[23]

By Louise K. Stevens, President, ArtsMarket Consulting Inc., Marion, Massachusetts
National Assembly of Local Arts Agencies-Monographs
Vol. 4, No. 1, January 1995, pp. 12-13
The approach [to planning] that I have found to be very effective is built on the concept of cultural planning, incorporating the same core sense of integrity into the process and dialogue. From the discussions you have had in your own communities, you all know very well how important it is to bring together constituencies that historically have not spoken to each other to build an entirely new understanding of needs, opportunities and skills that can be shared back and forth.

It is very important to be as inclusive as possible and to make sure that you are reaching out into all sectors. You can't forget the organizational and structural needs of the educational system. Those of you who have done cultural planning probably remember that intensely long period of pre-planning where you got to know the players and spent a lot of time building those relationships. The same kind of process is equally important in any kind of community arts-in-education planning.

In arts-in-education planning between the arts and the education communities, your goal is to build understanding and a sense of shared values. Having a shared sense of value of the role the arts play in education is an important starting premise. It is very hard to jump into strategies until you have had that kind of philosophical dialogue, and that may take quite a while. Allow yourselves enough time to do that.

Learning each other's language is also important. Finally, each must have a clear understanding of the other's priorities and realities. This may boil down to nuts and bolts items, such as scheduling, which we may think are simple but which are very complicated within the education system. Arts groups must be open to seeing the planning process from the educators' standpoint, as well as from the standpoint of unions, businesses, PTAs, administrators—everyone with whom you are dealing. Doing community-based, arts-in-education planning is no less comprehensive and intensive a process than doing any kind of cultural planning. The process is the same in terms of bringing diverse people together, finding a structure, giving them a sense of leadership and moving forward with them to do creative problem solving.

The process we used in Richmond began with the collection of some baseline data. It was almost more important for us to find out where things weren't connecting than where they were; we learned where the gaps were. From that information, we were able to begin to set a structure of themes that would become major goal areas.

We held a plenary meeting with several hundred people to give them a chance to hear all the different findings and major theme areas. We asked them to select a particular theme area in which they wanted to focus, and these became task forces. The task forces met repeatedly for six months and also did a great deal of work individually between meetings.

We spent a lot of time moving from philosophy into goals. We created a philosophical framework for the entire plan. We began to use education words rather than arts words. The four goals that evolved from the different themes were each supported by in-depth action plans.

We carefully built mutual ownership, shared respect and trust. An arts-in-education plan like this—no less than that of a cultural plan—not only takes a very long time to develop, *but also should take a very long time to implement*. This is a ten-year commitment. We all know how many collaborative initiatives between schools and the arts are done for a pilot of one year, two years, maybe three—after that we go on to something else. The realization that we were talking about a long-term relationship was absolutely critical to the eventual success and the collective buy-in of the plan. Take enough time to lay out those "10-year, 20-year" statements. I think it will pay off in the long run.

The other point I reinforce repeatedly is that you are focusing on the children. An arts-in-education plan is not and should not be about finding new employment for artists, about finding new dollars for arts organizations, or about finding new dollars for school systems. It is about connecting the arts to the children in the schools and to their lives.

Richmond, Virginia

The Arts Council of Richmond: Forging Partnerships that Assure Implementation
By Adrienne Hines, Executive Director, Arts Council of Richmond, Inc.
National Assembly of Local Arts Agencies-Monographs
Vol. 4, No. 1, January 1995, pp. 2-6

The Arts Council of Richmond, Inc. kicked off its three-year pilot arts-in-education program called Partners in the Arts with a $150,000 grant from the National Endowment for the Arts' Locals Program, the largest non-museum grant in Virginia's history. Partners will serve 120,000 students in Richmond's metropolitan school systems.

Partners has linked the schools and the broad community of artists, parents, community arts and cultural groups, and new funding sources in a way they had never partnered before. Our success in reaching this point is largely because we carefully built relationships with our education partners over seven years—meeting their needs and earning their trust and respect.

Forging Partnerships with Schools

Metropolitan Richmond, with a population of 750,000, includes the City of Richmond and the counties of Henrico, Hanover, Chesterfield, Goochland and Powhatan. The nucleus of this area is the City of Richmond, whose most recent demographics show 55.2 percent African American, 43.4 percent white and 1.4 percent other nationalities.

The Arts Council of Richmond is a 43-year-old, private nonprofit organization with an annual budget of $950,000. Five full-time and four part-time staff members work with a 45-member board to produce three large annual festivals, public art exhibitions, programs and services for schools, and advocacy and networking for arts and arts organizations.

Shortly after being hired by the arts council, I visited the superintendents of the four large area public school systems and asked them what services the arts council could deliver. They answered: "Be an advocate of good education and a watchdog for the arts in education." I made it my business to attend school board meetings and budget hearings. Our staff worked with me to build relationships in these schools with the art and music supervisors and with the librarians by providing programming they found valuable. As a result, the schools began to see us as a resource provider.

An Opportunity for Leadership

As worries heightened about tight budgets and a lack of growth in numbers of arts teachers, I formed an education committee to look at the state of the arts in the four systems and invited each of the four superintendents to assign a representative. Each appointed an assistant or deputy superintendent with oversight for curriculum. We coordinated meetings of "visiting dignitaries" from model programs around the country with the committee, which also included arts and music supervisors. These meetings stimulated a desire to design a model program that would be right for the 122,000 students in Richmond's four public school systems.

Research and Planning

We were determined to bring many voices and partners to the table in the planning process. My established relationships with school superintendents and educators assured good school participation. At the same time, my relationships with community leaders and funders brought in those partners. Our staff and others helped to bring in artists and arts organizations. The large number and intensity of the voices in the planning process ultimately led to the buy-in of the finished plan and to the willingness and determination to implement it.

The one-year planning process and research was made possible by a 1991 $30,000 National Endowment for the Arts planning grant matched with public funds from area school systems and private funds from corporations, individuals and foundations. Our school partners gave us guidance in selecting a consultant to facilitate the process. We wanted to have an actively involved consultant, so we immediately ruled out those who preferred to do research and make recommendations in isolation. We ended up choosing Louise Stevens of ArtsMarket Consulting as an ideal consultant for this kind of process.

The planning process brought together a broad-based community coalition of 125 committed individuals reflective of the metropolitan area's diverse ethnic and cultural mix: administrators, classroom teachers, curriculum specialists, artists, arts organizations, parents, students and community volunteers. Drawn from the six jurisdictions (City of Richmond, Chesterfield, Hanover, Henrico, Goochland and Powhaten Counties), each participant cared passionately about the arts in his/her community and in the schools.

The Challenge of Change

The research indicated that significant changes were needed. As we began planning, it was important to understand the differing levels of comfort with change. Still, we underestimated the discomfort some of our arts partners would experience with the comprehensive program that ultimately was recommended. The plan is much more far-reaching than any of us had envisioned.

Major issues included: Which agency would implement the plan? What sources of funds would be used? And what kind of management oversight would be involved? The school partners determined that the arts council was the appropriate agency to implement the plan. However, it still took compromise and negotiation to arrive at a management scheme that was agreeable to all. In the end, we adopted a management mechanism that is somewhat different from the one our planning document recommends: a governance committee that reports to the arts council board and is made up of 21 individuals who represent artists, arts organizations, community leaders, funders and public and private schools. The program is directed by a full-time professional program director, Dr. Stephanie Micas, and a part-time assistant. The arts council executive director and director of development manage the fundraising; other staff provide public relations/marketing, bookkeeping and other needs.

These negotiations delayed implementation by a full nine months, but resulted in a stronger partnership. When facing this fear of change, it is important to listen, to compromise and to keep talking until all partners can participate.

Partners in the Arts' Services and Programs

Over the three-year pilot program, the broad-based committees, co-chaired by educators and arts administrators, will help to deliver:

- Teacher training through workshops, seminars and conferences to educate non-art teachers on how to use the arts in their curriculum (cost: $70,000 annually).
- Grants for innovative curriculum-based arts programs developed by teachers and principals with artists and arts organizations, with funds for these programs awarded on a competitive basis by a knowledgeable panel (cost: $100,000 annually).

- A database and information about workshops, residencies, tickets, tours and more, available to all teachers and arts organizations (cost: $30,000 annually).
- An advocacy campaign to educate the general public about the importance of arts in education (cost: $20,000 annually).

New Funding for Partners in the Arts

An important magnet for our school partners was the promise of new funding to implement Partners in the Arts with a three-year budget of $900,000. Our $150,000 National Endowment for the Arts grant is being matched in part by our public school systems at $1.00 per student for three years (33¢ per student per year). We have exceeded our corporate goal of $100,000; we were close to our goal of $150,000 from individuals by June 1995, and we are just beginning to see results with our $300,000 goal from foundations.

We are succeeding with corporations, individuals and foundations partly because we included them in our research, planning and oversight process, giving each partner a stake in the implementation of our plan. The Arts Endowment's Locals Program funding is leveraging new public and private dollars in a way that no other funding can. Without exception, these new funds have not negatively affected pre-existing program funding.

The Big Vision

A project the size and scope of this one, which has taken most of my time for the last three years, has had implications for the entire arts council. We have had difficulty balancing the time and resources of our administrative staff and board members during these three years, to the extent that we provided other programs and services that our community wants and needs. In successfully managing the planning process, we have emerged as a recognized facilitator for good comprehensive planning, with an ability to bring diverse partners to the table.

Partners in the Arts is probably the biggest vision we could have developed for metropolitan Richmond. It makes a fundamental change in the way the arts are delivered to our students, and if we are successful at the end of our three-year pilot, we will have set the stage for a truly significant impact through the arts—an impact that our partners at all levels will want to institutionalize for the future.

Adrienne Hines has been Executive Director of the Arts Council of Richmond, Inc. for the past ten years. Partners in the Arts is the arts council's first metropolitan area collaborative planning effort.

Portland, Oregon

Cultural Planning Leads to Arts Education Initiative
By Vicki Poppen
National Assembly of Local Arts Agencies-Monographs
Vol. 4, No. 4, April 1994, pp. 7-10.

Consistently listed as one of the nation's most livable cities, Portland is located on the Columbia River, an hour's drive from the rugged beauty of the Oregon coast. The city's population is approximately 475,000; the four-county surrounding metropolitan area, 1,625,000.

History of the Initiative

The region's arts industry experienced a major expansion during the early eighties, but by the end of the decade, the growing arts community had outgrown the region's ability to finance it. Several arts organizations closed their doors, and many of the area's major institutions faced ongoing budget deficits. This crisis prompted a group of concerned citizens to launch ArtsPlan 2000+, a community-driven cultural planning process that was to become the basis for hundreds of initiatives designed to strengthen the region's support for individual artists, arts organizations and education. Over 18 months, community leaders and hundreds of citizens from the Portland metropolitan area participated in task forces and focus groups to develop a comprehensive plan for the region. One result of this collaborative process has been the development of a new arts education initiative called ArtsPlan Schools.

The Wolf Organization was hired to coordinate the planning process. A general public survey indicated strong support and appreciation for the arts, including a desire for increases in arts education for children. In response, an arts education task force of approximately 30 people was convened, representing arts teachers, school administration, artists, business, parents and arts organizations. The task force met for more than a year, developing a list of recommendations necessary for a high-quality arts education for all students in the region.

The first priority recommended by the arts education task force was to form a regional planning and coordinating body for arts education for information sharing, advocacy, planning and coordination of arts education programs, fundraising and other initiatives in arts education. This body, the Regional Arts Education Steering Committee, was officially organized in 1991 as a joint committee of Metropolitan Arts Commission and the Northwest Business Committee for the Arts.

One of the Steering Committee's first tasks was to develop the delivery model for meeting the regional arts education recommendations. The process for implementing ArtsPlan Schools sought to follow the lead of national Goals 2000 education reform efforts as well as those occurring within the state. Some of the primary similarities were:

- site-based arts education implementation;
- outcome-based educational goals;
- emphasis on teacher professional development; and
- parent involvement in the learning environment.

Rather than develop or adopt a model for districtwide implementation, the steering committee believed that site-specific interpretation and implementation would lead to long-term change in the individual institution. The broad-based ArtsPlan Schools program goals would form the basis of an incentive and technical assistance process.

Initially, one of ArtsPlan Schools' most unique characteristics was its focus on offering incentives and rewards to individual schools as they progressed in implementing arts education goals and strategies. As schools would develop activities and programs to help meet the goals, they would receive incentives such as posters, public recognition events, cash awards and artist services.

State Reform Affects Program Development

At this early stage of program development, implementation was focused on the incentive program. If funding had been readily available, then ArtsPlan Schools would have progressed with this focus. However, two events took place in Oregon's educational arena that made the Regional Arts Education Steering Committee reevaluate its program priorities.

First, Oregon passed a property tax limitation bill that, over the next five years, would drastically limit the amount of funding available for Oregon's public schools. Second, Oregon's 21st Century Schools Act was initiated and developed as a result of national and state research on workforce requirements for the 21st century. With the decline of the agriculture and timber industries, state policy makers sought to determine the skills students would need to have after high school to be successful, contributing members of society in an environment difficult to predict. As a result, Oregon education reform has become "outcome based," focusing on what children should know rather than on what subjects are taught.

This major change in Oregon's educational system created an immediate need for more teacher professional development and support from the community at large. Schools were being required to offer arts education as one of the core curriculum subjects but weren't able to hire arts specialists or train classroom teachers to teach the arts. The message from the schools was clear: they needed help in meeting the broad education outcomes through professional development, arts community resources and direct funding.

City Backs Plan with Money

The city was approached by the Portland Public School District for help to ease some of the programs that were being cut because of decreasing revenues caused by the property tax limitation bill. The three areas in which they requested assistance were: security, community schools program (after-school sports and some arts programs) and cultural arts programs. At the time, Portland was experiencing a one-time surplus due in part to the increase of Municipal Golf Course fees. The city allocated $300,000 to the public schools to support these three areas, including $100,000 for the arts. Portland Mayor Vera Katz (who authored the original education reform bill for Oregon when she was a state legislator) and the steering committee determined that ArtsPlan Schools would be the framework by which this support would be delivered. It was also decided that this initial funding should go toward those needs stated as most crucial to the schools—professional development for teachers and direct funding to implement programs. An additional $40,000 was committed from Multnomah County, and a combined support package, which included a staff support person and equipment from the Portland Public School District, provided the financial foundation for a one-year pilot program that would provide direct services to 12 pilot schools and fine-tune the delivery process.

ArtsPlan Schools—Research and Development Phase

We are now implementing the research and development phase of ArtsPlan Schools. The participating schools and artists/arts organizations will be developing broad-based approaches to achieve their arts education goals. Most important to this process is allowing the school community to take risks, to try new approaches and to find new solutions to educational requirements through the development of high-quality, arts-rich learning environments.

Planning and Funding for the Future

A framework for the next two years of ArtsPlan Schools' development includes additional site-specific, professional development opportunities for teachers. The Arts

Teams on Loan program will increase in numbers as we involve pilot school participants in providing assistance to new sites. ArtsPlan Schools will offer assistance from the arts community by collaborating with educators as they develop specific learning methods. ArtsPlan Schools will offer training opportunities for artists and arts organizations to keep them informed and involved in new developments in educational reform efforts.

The Metropolitan Arts Commission is currently undergoing a major transformation from a division of local government to a private, nonprofit agency. Part of the transition agreement secured with the region's local governments is for an increase in support for regional services and programs, which will include the ArtsPlan Schools initiative. Ongoing funding support from the regional government agencies, the business community (via the Northwest Business Committee for the Arts), and the participating schools will ensure that schools continue to benefit by creating partnerships with artists and arts organizations who are informed and involved in the education of our area's youth.

Crisis creates opportunity. In the Portland metropolitan area, we are still unsure how this story of education reform and the arts will unfold, but we have an opportunity to make the arts an integral part of the solution, rather than a peripheral activity waiting to be engaged. ArtsPlan Schools offers a different approach that echoes the movement in Oregon to allow individuals to create their own methods of meeting high standards for education by using the resources best suited to their individual needs. ArtsPlan Schools is giving the education and arts communities the permission to take risks and to try new strategies—the essence of the learning process itself.

Vicki Poppen has been Arts Education Program Director for the Metropolitan Arts Commission for ten years. She has served on many committees, boards and task forces in arts education and is a standing member of Oregon's Arts-in-Education State Advisory Committee. She has served as a member of the National Governance Committee and as Regional Vice-Chair for the Kennedy Center Alliance for Arts Education Network. Most recently she worked with the Oregon Department of Education on the development of state performance standards and assessment methods in arts education for Oregon's education reform initiative.

Kalamazoo County, Michigan

Breaking the Mold: The Kalamazoo Countywide Arts Enhancement Feasibility Study
By Bill Cleveland, Director, Center for the Study of Art and Community
National Assembly of Local Arts Agencies-Monographs
Vol. 4, No. 4, April 1995, pp. 11-14
In early 1993, the Kalamazoo Valley Intermediate School District's nine superintendents asked a broadly representative group of community leaders to study the feasibility of expanding arts education opportunities for area students. Supported with seed money from the Gilmore Foundation, the study was spurred by the superintendents' concern with the declining quality of county school arts offerings and evidence of the positive impact of the arts on student achievement in other communities.

The Process

In a region sensitive to "top down" mandates, the study's steering committee believed that the process should offer the widest possible opportunity for community input and also include broad exposure to successful programs from around the country. Working with the steering committee, Vicky Hardy and I, the study consultants, responded with a four-phase community engagement process designed to accomplish the Study's mission: (1) assess the current state of arts education; (2) convene forums and conduct interviews in the community; (3) examine local, state and national models; and (4) recommend a sensible design and implementation strategy for the community.

Models

More than 40 model programs from Michigan and nine other states provided a valuable compendium of programmatic do's and don'ts. Model sites were selected not only from recognized exemplary arts programs, but also from examples of projects that were changing larger education systems. The steering committee chair made it clear that the study teams needed to examine models that just about broke every barrier.

A visitation committee divided into two teams that traveled statewide and throughout the community and eventually ventured to other regions, such as San Francisco and Florida. In addition, individuals were brought in to talk about their models—and what they would do differently if they had the opportunity—with the committee.

Partnerships figured prominently in exemplary programs. Typically, the best arts programs were the products of both strong commitment and a strong leader. Collaboration among locally based artists, arts organizations and schools was key as well.

Environment

As the committee moved from vision to design, they began to focus on the complex and unpredictable environment. Given the significant differences among the nine districts, a mandated countywide program did not appear feasible. They also ruled out the magnet or art center option used by so many other communities. A continuing state impasse over educational funding necessitated a program that could be implemented and developed in a variety of economic scenarios. Most importantly, all nine districts would need to believe that it would be in the best interest of their students to join in a multi-district effort.

Standards

Faced with these complexities, the committee decided to establish minimum design standards to guide the program-building process. This obliged them to consider design options that diverged substantially from those of the models they had studied. Rather than recommend a comprehensive curriculum or central facility, the design focused on the student, teacher, parent and local school as the center of the program.

The Product: Education for the Arts

The committee's recommended design emphasized local initiative and leadership by parents, students, teachers and their principals as basic building blocks of the program. The immediate goal of the program, now called Education for the Arts (EFA), is to provide a countywide support system that can adapt to the wide variety of needs and conditions and stimulate the growth of arts education.

The long-term goal of EFA is to achieve the systematic infusion of the arts at all levels in all schools. To accomplish this the program will use its funding, training and information resources to support and provide incentives for schools to implement sequential multi-year arts instruction and to use the arts to teach other subjects in all grades.

The recommended two-part EFA program seeks to provide an enhanced arts education for all K-12 students and more intensive training for talented and motivated students. The first of EFA's two major elements, Arts Program Supports and Enhancements, is designed to strengthen arts programming for all classrooms by providing funding and program support directly to teachers and their schools.

The Bank

The study also recommended developing a funding system for these supports and enhancements, coordinated by an Arts Enhancement Bank. The bank will use its resources to encourage and reward long-term commitment to ongoing arts education for all students. Its support guidelines will provide incentives for the development of new partnerships and innovative curricular approaches. The loans/awards will be granted based on the degree to which the schools are perceived to be committed to long-term change.

Advanced Instruction

The second EFA element will provide talented and motivated students with advanced instruction by arts professionals working with arts teachers. The structure and funding follows the example of Kalamazoo's cross-district, countywide vocational Education or Employment (EVE) program. This will give middle and high school artists access to professional training and the county's finest arts facilities. The typical Education for the Arts student will travel to studios and theaters at other schools or community sites a few days a week, enabling participants to receive advanced training with a strong connection to their home school.

Lessons Learned

From the beginning, the committee recognized that they would need to build community support for the effort. The committee's top leaders were powerful and respected members of the community, and their presence signaled the significance of the effort. Their willingness to put their reputations on the line for the project made the difference in crucial situations.

The firsthand exposure to model programs dramatically broadened the community's understanding of the benefits of the arts in education and of the wide variety of programmatic approaches, and it contributed to their ownership of the design process and product. Despite their successes, many of the models studied were not supported by their local educational systems. This made a strong impression on the study design team and led to the development of an incentive-based program. The frank discussion about the lack of incentives by the representatives from model programs would not have been possible in a more impersonal review process.

The design team was kept relatively small. Team members, which included teachers, artists, administrators, representatives of higher education, parents and community members, were selected for their open-mindedness, expertise and the respect they enjoyed among their peers. Their reputations protected the process and gave credibility to the eventual product. The design team resisted the temptation to commit early to an existing model. Although the design process was ongoing, the final design sessions were purposefully not convened until very late in the study. This gave the team the perspective and flexibility it needed to turn the system on its head, focusing on incentives for students, teachers, artists and schools rather than trying to force the entire school system to move in one direction.

The emerging design elements were shared with the community for feedback early and often. This protected the study from a "design shock" reaction that could have undermined the process in the eleventh hour.

Keeping Faith

On April 13, 1994, the nine school boards that comprise the Kalamazoo Valley Intermediate School District voted unanimously to approve the Feasibility Study Steering Committee's recommendations and to begin implementation of the EFA Program. Shortly thereafter, the Kalamazoo-based Gilmore Foundation made a significant contribution to the Education for the Arts Program to help fund the initial three-year phase. In September, a 40-member EFA Advisory Council was appointed to oversee the program's development, and it is currently conducting a national search for EFA's first executive director. The advisory council will be housed within the Kalamazoo Valley Intermediate School District, but maintain its strong, broad-based community connections generated through the planning process.

Bill Cleveland *is Director of the Center for the Study of Art & Community. He consults with arts, educational and philanthropic organizations in the development of community arts programming. He has pioneered Artsreach Community Artists, California Arts-in-Corrections and California State Summer School for the Arts. Mr. Cleveland's book,* Arts in Other Places: Artists at Work in America's Community and Social Institutions, *was published recently by Praeger Press. He is also a musician.*

An Oasis in the Desert

A Conversation with Shirley Trusty-Corey

Shirley Trusty-Corey and I first met in New Orleans in the early seventies. She was then coordinating the arts-in-education program for the public schools and facing yet another budget crisis. Since then, Shirley has helped fight that and many other battles for the arts in New Orleans, the state and elsewhere around the country. When she finally retired from the school system, it was not long before she again picked up the cudgels at the local arts council. As its executive director, she has continued her distinguished career as an unflagging, persuasive champion of change for the arts and education. We have worked together periodically since those early days, and I caught up with her again for a telephone interview that I believe will give you the flavor of her unquenchable energy and determination.

Jane Remer: You are probably the only person I know who began as a theater artist, then worked for many years in the New Orleans schools system, and then became the director of the local arts council. That is a unique perspective, and I think your ruminations on that journey and the lessons learned along the way will be tremendously useful to people in the field today.

Shirley Trusty-Corey: Looking at the whole field from both perspectives—working within the school system and leading an arts agency at the community level—I am humbled by the fact that the work is never done. In my opinion, we have never sufficiently institutionalized arts education to make an impact, so the battle continues. Having arts education recognized and integrated into a school district in some significant way beyond the applause of model programs is enormously important.

Model Programs

Model programs serve as a bellwether. Yet once they are accepted, they are the best and the worst of news. The good side is that they are successful and usually seem to do so much good. On the downside, if we plant one tree or have one little oasis in the desert, it is sometimes perceived as larger than it is. People point to model programs and say, "Yes, things are bad, but what about the success of this program?" That tends to soothe everyone's conscience. We must use model programs—the recognition and accolades—as pressure points and push on even harder. It is the beginning of real progress, not the end.

Leadership

Since superintendents and school boards come and go, local arts agencies and other city, state or regional groups that are relatively more stable and care about arts education are significant in applying pressure for sustaining support. The target is to achieve and integrate arts education within educational systems. Local arts agencies and others who care must keep an ongoing vigil.

New Partners for the Arts

I am finding that people are becoming much more responsive to social service and educational issues. The same needs have been out there for decades—they haven't changed—but the world seems more receptive to dealing with them. The linkage between arts education and the missions of social service agencies is apparent. We recently had a seminar here at the arts council that is part of our ongoing program called "Collaborations for Youth: A Dialogue Between Social Service Agencies and Arts Agencies." People from more than 75 agencies attended. They were so eager to talk to one another; so many linkages were being forged. Increasing my level of awareness was important to me, too. I am still trying to institutionalize these things, to open some new funding patterns, and to establish some new ways of thinking. Only by doing that can we make a difference.

An Ecology for the Arts

Using whatever linkage you can to create an ecology in which arts education can flourish is so important. For example, we have a wonderful program in our own local school district. However, the Arts in Education Office still struggles so desperately not to lose its foothold. It has an incredible staff that burns out periodically. Yet as the budget comes and goes, and it wanes or increases, they are still there, supported by so many principals who care. They are having a big opening at our local contemporary arts center of the incredible visual arts work done by resident artists and teachers working in partnership. Wonderful artists working with committed principals and teachers have produced a consistently high quality of work at this annual event since day one. Yet it gets bigger every year because their packaging and marketing and their sense of using it in the community gets stronger. It is important to widen the circle of involvement.

As I sit today in a city notorious for its very high crime and murder rate, excessive even for urban centers, I hear these same discussions about the need for teaching values, the need for finding other engagements for young people and the community. I say part of that answer continues to be arts education, and yet, we are still having those same budget problems in our school system.

On the other hand, we have a new superintendent who has been fighting the budget fight for years. He recognizes the importance of the arts, and he is pushing it back up in the order of priorities. I am delighted, and he needs support and recognition for his actions.

Arts at the Core, Artists as Equalizers

The artists in the schools are part of the great equalizer; they help people to understand the arts on a personal and more human level. Still, as we deal with arts in the schools, we must not lose the arts! We need to train teachers to deal appropriately with the arts—to deal with all those things that scare people about the arts.

I was renewed by a stunning performance at Paul Taylor's first appearance in Louisiana last Saturday. Though I may be moved and touched by the children, the Taylor dancers renew me. You have to build and sustain that aesthetic sense. That is what we are trying to help them to be touched by, to learn to express, to understand. We must have that artistic core in whatever ways we can deliver it. If you don't keep that core, then you haven't gained much.

JR: How are you identifying money for education at the arts council?

STC: I struggle with that every day. I am trying to identify some funding pots and categories that are simply labeled "arts education." This could provide an avenue for collaborations of arts institutions and artists in schools to come together. It has been done many ways in other places, but we have not done it yet here. One solution we are pursuing is to work with the city's recreation department. Many people want to fund recreation programs, and I am trying to get them to think about integrating arts and cultural programming.

JR: Do you have anyone on staff who is dedicated to education?

STC: No, and that is driving me crazy. I struggle to keep my agency and arts education alive. I take on many projects I shouldn't because I care. Although we don't have a full-time person committed just to arts education, we have absorbed that in a number of ways throughout the agency.

JR: Thanks for all the material you sent to me about your current work. Can you tell me more about your job-training program?

STC: We have received funding through a federal job-training placement act that has given us a job-training program through the arts for the past three-and-a-half years. It used to be a summer program; now it has moved into the school year. It enables me to hire artists and to have them work with young people through a school- and work-training program. For example, we have hired artists to train high school students in music, theater, art and computer graphics, using four university sites and drawing on the best of the university faculty and community artists. It is a good model that I want to perpetuate. We were able to do that particular model for only one summer, but we have kept the program alive. The Department of Labor has responded most favorably to the visual arts component because they can touch, see and feel it. They would not fund leotards or tights for the dancers, and I kept saying, "But, you buy gloves for metal workers!" You are training them for a craft and they need tools or uniforms. I don't see the difference. Unfortunately, the analogy didn't seem to work.

JR: What's next on your busy agenda?

STC: I am preparing to sit on the Arts Endowment panel that reviews Arts Plus projects. I don't have time, but I keep doing it because I want to stay informed about what is happening in these collaborations between educational institutions and community organizations in the arts. I want to try to find ways of moving my city, state and region forward. I guess once this thing gets inside you, you can't get rid of it. It just won't go away.

JR: I'm glad you've still got the energy to be a champion, Shirley.

STC: I am certainly older, a little wiser, a little sadder. On the other hand, I am more committed than ever. Arts education matters.

Shirley Trusty-Corey has been the Executive Director of the Arts Council of New Orleans since 1991. During her tenure, Mrs. Corey has helped to establish programs at the Arts Council that have garnered national acclaim from arts agencies throughout the country. These programs include the Entergy Arts Business Center, which serves as a business incubator for arts organizations, and the Urban Arts Training Program, which mentors 100 inner-city youth annually and has received national attention for fostering arts education in the lives of urban teens. Previously an arts administrator in the New Orleans Public Schools for 30 years, Mrs. Corey left a legacy of policies and programs that continue to expand and develop. She received her B.S. degree from Loyola University and an M.A.T. in theater from Tulane University.

Sharing Power in the Bronx

A Collaborative Work in Progress

by William Aguado

Much has been written in recent years about the arts as an integral part of community development. Certainly, many models have demonstrated the value of the arts in downtown or "main street" redevelopment initiatives. Yet only recently have the arts been thought of as partners on the neighborhood level. Though considerably smaller in scale, the potential is nonetheless as dramatic.

One important institution is frequently omitted from the urban community development equation—the local school. In urban settings, the school is perceived as being physically located within a community, but representative of an institutional culture and value system inconsistent with those of the families and children being served. This institutional culture is shaped by the vested interests of the in-school community—unions and the politics of local education governance, school boards and the central boards of education—that demand and receive absolute loyalty from teachers, administrators and support personnel. These special interests and educational politics shape attitudes and behaviors while assuring adherence to the prevailing set of institutional values.

In the absence of any coordinated political influence, the students and their parents are left out of this equation. Similarly, any attempt to introduce new educational ventures and reforms is generally met with resistance since it is outside the purview of the institutional culture. Herein lies the difficulty for the introduction of meaningful and sustained arts education initiatives.

To meet the challenge of revitalizing communities and education by utilizing the arts, several issues need to be considered: Can the "arts" enhance the educability of today's urban student and assume a leadership role for the community's sustained well-being? How can a community cultural experience complement the school's educational goals? Can the arts play a role in building bridges between the schools and the community served?

The Bronx Council on the Arts (BCA) in New York City has long been concerned with the professional development of artists and arts organizations, and we recognize that the arts require a nurturing environment to flourish. Toward that end, our local revitalization and planning efforts—and our involvement in other community endeavors—helps to create an infrastructure that supports the arts and ensures their longevity.

When BCA first became involved with the arts in education several years ago, we focused on developing professional arts initiatives for the bilingual student. Though these initiatives were professionally conceived and implemented, we were nonetheless concerned about their lasting effect on the students and the school. Moreover, we soon realized that nearly 85 percent of the schools' arts budgets were being allocated to non-Bronx cultural resources.

Our challenge was to make the Bronx arts resources a priority in Bronx Schools. We firmly believed that Bronx cultural resources could become a bridge to and resource for the communities surrounding the schools and, at the same time, provide the arts organizations with a vital income stream. Similarly, the local artists and the traditional cultures of their families could also be valuable contributors to the local arts education development in the schools. To accomplish these goals, BCA committed itself to marketing Bronx arts organizations to Bronx school and district administrators and to providing training and resources to artists and arts organizations who were interested in collaborating with schools.

An initiative currently in its embryonic stages could have far-reaching implications for the students and the community. As a case study, it has all the ingredients necessary to become a prototype for an education/cultural/community model. However, it is a work-in-progress and one that will no doubt be redefined and reconfigured many times as it is adapted to the realities of the community and the local school experience.

This interesting opportunity began with a South Bronx elementary school principal at one of our recent planning sessions. The principal was concerned with developing an arts curriculum for her school, but she thought that it was equally important to join with others to develop complementary community cultural outlets, such as an arts center. The rationale was a simple one: a community cultural initiative would both enhance the existing and proposed arts curriculum in her school and provide additional cultural venues for the residents of her neighborhood. Arts education would not only take place in the school, but it would also be reinforced within the community. The principal has also discussed her idea with the principals of three other schools that are within walking distance of her school and serve essentially the same neighborhood but at different grade levels. Imagine the potential of four principals banding together to advocate for local cultural programming as a way of furthering their educational goals.

This community, like many others in the South Bronx, has been plagued with many of the social ills documented by the media—dilapidated housing, crime, substance abuse, few city services. The demographics of the Bronx help to explain and define the nature and scope of problems the borough faces with respect to the 1.2 million people who live here.

The borough is largely populated by both the very young and very old, groups that are traditionally most vulnerable and most in need of assistance. More than 42 percent of South Bronx residents are 19 years old or younger. Roughly one-third of all Bronx adults do not have a high school degree, and approximately 27 percent of adults over 20 years old cannot read at the fourth-grade level. Low levels of educational achievement are directly correlated to high unemployment and poverty rates.

However, like the rest of the South Bronx, this community has shown signs in recent years that it is experiencing a rebirth. The existing housing stock has been rehabilitated while new, subsidized one- and two-family homes are being built. The ethnic composition is still largely Latino, but a community of homeowners has evolved. These homeowners have the same aspirations for upward mobility as their counterparts in the suburbs, but with perhaps a little more determination.

The neighborhood comprises about 20 city blocks, and it is bounded by commercial strips and/or major thoroughfares on all four sides. These major access points are in the midst of major commercial revitalization efforts as well, spawning the beginning of an economic base that complements the ongoing housing development efforts.

A new family multiservice center is being built to address the community's substantive human services needs. This facility, situated in the geographic center of this neighborhood, will provide social and human services to the population whose children attend the four aforementioned schools. In an interesting twist, the proposed family multiservice center, at the insistence of the four principals and the local leaders, will be expanded to include arts programs and cultural services as an integral part of its mandate.

This development signifies the clear recognition that the community's cultural life is a vital adjunct to the social service and educational needs of the residents. In fact, many acknowledge that the arts can help define the community's identity by serving as an anchor for the residents' well-being. The principals view the family center's arts programs as critical to their educational mandate because they will reinforce the in-school arts and education experience. These programs will also provide much-needed, professionally designed, leisure and cultural activities for the local residents.

Because of BCA's experience in cultural planning, we were asked to facilitate an educational/community cultural planning process. Those involved thought that our participation in the planning process would insure its integrity, enabling the participants to address their goals within the context of the arts and their application in the schools and on a community level.

The planning process is being designed with two subgroups: one for the educational community and one for the community-at-large. The educational effort will include teachers, parents, students and artists as well as representatives from the community. The neighborhood planning process will solicit the participation of community and business leaders, artists, parents, educational leaders, and others. Together, the combined subgroups will serve as the planning committee.

The following broad-based planning process is designed to be flexible so that it can be modified and shaped as the process evolves. As the facilitator, BCA will be responsible for:

- forming the planning committee and the education and community subgroups by selecting representatives from the various school, neighborhood and cultural constituencies;
- helping the planning committee to identify its priorities and to set its goals and objectives;
- preparing an overview of the area's demographics with an emphasis on traditional cultural values;
- preparing an educational profile, including reading and math scores, ethnic/racial composition, economic levels, etc.;
- initiating a structural analysis of the community, i.e., an inventory of existing educational, social, recreational, cultural, business and housing profiles;

- initiating a needs assessment tailored to the planning subgroups, but consistent with the general planning goals, that focuses on local traditional cultural values as a critical component of any program design;

- initiating a real estate inventory to determine what facilities are currently being used and for what purposes, and identifying vacant storefronts and buildings that could be converted to cultural purposes, e.g., art centers, artists' studios, rehearsal spaces, galleries;

- completing the educational profile, structural analysis, needs assessments, demographic analysis and real estate inventory; preparing a general image of the community; identifying the community's strengths and weaknesses; and developing a list of educational, community and cultural priorities;

- helping each planning subgroup to fine-tune the priorities and to reconcile them into a master list for the planning committee;

- working with the planning committee to integrate the subplanning groups into an implementation plan for each of the component parts—i.e., each school would have its own arts education plan based on its respective needs and priorities, and the community would have a cultural plan;

- assisting the planning committee to create a budget and fundraising plan to accompany the implementation plan; and

- helping the planning committee to identify new representatives who are deemed to be crucial to the respective implementation and fundraising plans.

As the plan is being developed, BCA will introduce specialized training services to facilitate "building partnerships." This concept of partnership is centered on the belief that successful collaborations "share power." Sharing power will not only further the agenda of the planning committee, but it will also serve as a catalyst for change, a fulcrum for creative problem-solving, and a mechanism for building consensus. This effort will address the special needs that may arise and insure that the planning process remains on track and with a common vision.

The training sessions will focus on issues such as:

- increasing understanding and communications among the planning committee members;

- building a framework for developing cultural projects of mutual benefit;

- providing the participants with project planning skills and assistance; and

- developing strategic planning skills to nurture the design of long-term collaborative plans.

The ongoing commitment of the school principals is vital to the planning process; each principal must be comfortable with the arts and education plan. At the same time, the plan must represent the students' and the parents' values, priorities and cultures, which is critical to ensuring sustained student and parent participation. It will also help to breed mutual understanding and commonality of purpose—the ingredients necessary for a successful and sustained arts education experience.

As the community-at-large becomes vested in the planning process, they will have a better understanding of the tools and skills needed to design meaningful cultural programs. The insights they gain into the needs of the community and the schools will enable them to make more informed decisions about the key ingredients of a successful arts venture. The family multiservice center will be better equipped to design cultural programs that will have the desired impact on children and their families. Perhaps more important, the cultural services provided will be directly linked to the school's arts programs, thus reinforcing the schools educational goals.

As we begin the planning process, we realize that the road ahead is filled with many obstacles. The long-term process must remain focused and consistent with the priorities of the community and the schools. Every planning stage will have its ebb and flow, and we will have to allow for such dynamics. However, by realizing the importance of "sharing power" or building partnerships, the participants will be in a better position to address difficulties as they arise to reach a mutually accepted consensus. To be sure, planning is only a process, not one written in stone, but one constantly being shaped by the realities of the community and the schools.

As difficult as it appears to be, the process could have a profound impact on the educational achievement of the students and the livability of the community. That is not a bad agenda for development, especially since it is centered on the arts. Moreover, the emergence of a cultural infrastructure shared by the community and the schools enhances its long-term application. This infrastructure will sustain the community's long-term commitment to the arts and provide the appropriate skills for future cultural planning and programming.

Imagine! This initiative was instigated by one principal with a vision for her school and her community. She is a principal who not only is an educational leader, but also a community leader and arts facilitator. It is lesson for all of us to observe and watch closely.

Can this model be replicated in other communities? My answer is an emphatic yes! However, the planning process must be inclusive and representative of the communities involved to succeed. The successful implementation of this plan will ensure that lively arts programs will be a regular part of the curriculum and will have a cultural support mechanism in the community. Best of all, the arts, education and community constituents will be encouraged to speak with one voice—a voice that is truly representative of a community.

*Born and raised in New York City, **William Aguado** has been Executive Director of the Bronx Council on the Arts since 1981. A graduate of Hunter College, he received an M.A. from Fordham University. Mr. Aguado is currently a member of the Comptroller's Cultural Advisory Council, and the Metropolitan Transit Authority Arts Advisory Committee. His board affiliations include: the Eugenio Maria de Hostos Community College Advisory Board, Bronx Council, New York Foundation for the Arts, Phipps Development Corporation, Bronx Special Olympics, Pathways for Youth and the Alliance of New York State Arts Councils. Among his many awards, Mr. Aguado was the recipient of the Arts & Business Council's Encore Award, the Mayor's Art Commission Award for Design, the New York State Joint Legislative Proclamation, and the Bronx Borough President's Citation for Service.*

The International Arts and Education Initiative

by Jennifer Williams

In the United States, the United Kingdom and Canada in recent years, an education policy and program has become almost essential to a cultural institution's profile. To bring greater clarity internationally to the arts and education field, the British American Arts Association (BAAA), a London-based arts resource organization which develops projects to stimulate debate in arts policy, has launched the International Arts and Education Initiative. The Initiative, a long-term effort to highlight issues, increase understanding and help forge links between the fields of education and the arts, marked its first public event with a three-day seminar and conference in February 1995. These meetings were aimed at constructing a framework that could be used to assess almost any cultural institution's approach to education.

The three days of intensive discussion began with a one-day seminar, Cultural Institutions: Technique and Innovation in Education, held at the National Gallery in London. At the seminar, 80 participants scrutinized their personal definitions of education and discussed how these definitions translate into education programs. A majority of those who attended were education staff from cultural institutions, and many found that going back to fundamentals was extremely useful to their work.

The momentum carried over to the conference, "Responding to Contemporary Diversity: Cultural Institutions and Education," held over the next two days at the South Bank Centre and the National Film Theatre. More than 150 delegates and 28 speakers from nine different countries, representing a crosssection of art forms, disciplines, cultural institutions, funding groups, educational organizations and individual artists, attended. Participants came from as far away as South Africa, Venezuela, Canada and the United States, and Europeans attended from Finland, Austria, Eire and the Netherlands. Discussions were organized around topics such as where and how education fits into the organization's structure and operation; whether a program's objectives should be purely educational or aimed at audience development; and the content and length of programs. Other issues included the relationship of these programs to their community and the wisdom and feasibility of collaboration with other community institutions. Time was also devoted to the type and amount of training required for education staff, management and artists, emphasizing the need to be aware of social and political issues as well as educational techniques. Questions of financing centered on who should pay for these programs—the arts institutions or external public and private agencies—and the difficulty of raising money for education rather than the primary cultural purpose of the institution.

Partnerships with Schools

In England, where local management of schools is a relatively new development, the discussion about partnership revolved around the changing needs for the arts and for education in collaborations. Schools find themselves with new objectives concerned with marketing and image, value for money and ever-changing curriculum parameters. The basic challenge to partnerships was generally thought to be best met through negotiation and consensus.

In discussing what cultural institutions can do for teachers, students and the schools, several things were mentioned. First, cultural institutions can support and confirm what a teacher is already doing—teaching an arts subject can be a lonely business. Second, they can link teachers with people working on the cutting edge of the profession, keeping them in touch with new developments, putting them back in touch with their profession (treating them like the professionals they are). Third, students benefit by gaining access to real excellence in performing—noticing how a professional performer sits, how they frame their performance with stillness and silence, how they take risks. Vocationally, students also learn that there is such a thing as a career in the arts. Fourth, the schools benefit financially by collaborating with cultural institutions because such programs often come complete with funding from arts councils, local authorities, private trust money or commercial sponsorship.

The tougher questions remaining to be resolved are: How do you sustain access to the cultural institution for teachers, students, and parents after the education program has finished? How do you enable the work with schools to be a "two-way street" in which artistic practice is influenced by contact with young people from different musical backgrounds and interests? How do you work with school curricula and schedules? And how do you offer in-service training to educators that moves beyond straight skills training and design it within the context of the curriculum?

Recommendations for the Future

Most conference participants identified the lack of a significant body of research as a problem in cultural institutions' never-ending search for support for educational activities. A second clear recommendation centered on the need to establish various forms of exchange: exchange of programs, exchange of models of good practice, professional exchange globally, and exchange of information.

The immediate need for thoughtful analysis of the strengths and weaknesses of the relationship between education and a cultural institution's purpose and process was clearly highlighted by the conference. Most of the writing about cultural institutions' education programs focuses on techniques and resources or on the responsibilities of institutions attempting to respond to the changing demographics in society. Little of the literature currently available looks at the operational, managerial and professional questions raised by the now pervasive education programs. Nor is there a body of research about the effectiveness of such programs within cultural institutions. One recent exception is a report, entitled *Centrestruct*, written for the Arts Council of England's touring department on the work of touring companies and venues in the subject of education and audience development.

The field of arts and education is characterized largely by workers who believe deeply in the development of individual human potential and in the strengthening of our diverse communities through some combination of creativity and learning. By conducting its International Arts and Education Initiative, the British American Arts Association is working to mobilize this army of dedicated people to realize its potential as a catalyst in the transformation of institutions and people.[24]

Jennifer Williams is Founder and Director of the British American Arts Association. Prior to coming to Britain in 1976 from Seattle, she was coproducer and actor of her own professional touring puppet theater. A fellow of the Royal Society of Arts, she frequently speaks at conferences all around the world. She is author of Across the Street, Around the World, *a handbook on cultural exchange (published 1996) and an artist involved in making books, etchings, and other constructions.*

Notes

1. The work of the JDR 3rd Fund's Arts in Education Program is described in several books, chief among them: *An Arts in Education Source Book: A View from the JDR 3rd Fund,* edited by Charles Fowler, with Kathryn Bloom, Junius Eddy, Jane Remer, Nancy Shuker, and Fowler (New York: The JDR 3rd Fund, 1980), available at the American Council for the Arts and various libraries around the country, and Jane Remer, *Changing Schools Through the Arts: How to Build on the Power of an Idea* (New York: McGraw-Hill, 1982; ACA Books, 1990).

2. The Central Midwestern Regional Educational Laboratories (CEMREL) was one of 20 national educational labs established to bridge the gap between sound educational research and its actual practice in the schools. It existed from 1967 to 1975, during which time its Aesthetic Education Program made significant contributions to the field of curriculum and instruction. A few of the original regional labs are still in operation today in the Midwest, Southwest and Northwest.

3. A major contribution to the field of research and evaluation at the time was the book *Evaluating the Arts in Education: A Responsive Approach*, edited by Robert Stake, with assistance from the JDR 3rd Fund. Published by Charles E. Merrill, Columbus, Ohio, it is now out of print.

4. Jane Remer, *Changing Schools Through the Arts: How to Build on the Power of an Idea* (New York: McGraw-Hill, 1982; ACA Books, 1990), p. 219.

5. *Federal Programs Supporting Education Change*, vol. III as cited in *Education Laws 1978: A Guide to New Directions in Federal Aid* (National School Public Relations Association). Quoted in Jane Remer, *Changing Schools Through the Arts: How to Build on the Power of an Idea*, (New York: McGraw-Hill, 1982; ACA Books, 1990), pp. 219-220.

6. National Endowment for the Arts, *Toward Civilization: A Report on Arts Education* (Washington, D.C.: U.S. Government Printing Office, May 1988).

7. Harold M. Williams, "Public Policy and Arts Education." Remarks presented at Symposium on Public Policy and the Arts, Ohio State University, May 22, 1993. Published by J. Paul Getty Trust.

8. The Arts Education Partnership Working Group sponsored by the John F. Kennedy Center for the Performing Arts and The J. Paul Getty Trust, *The Power of the Arts to Transform Education* (Washington, D.C.: The Arts Education Partnership Working Group, January 1993).

9. Public Law #103-227, *Goals 2000: Educate America Act*, approved March 31, 1994.

10. Public Law #103-382, *Improving America's Schools Act of 1994*, approved October 20, 1994.

11. National Commission on Excellence in Education, *A Nation at Risk: The Imperative for Educational Reform* (Washington, D.C.: U.S. Government Printing Office, April 1983).

12. National Committee for Standards in the Arts, *National Standards for Arts Education* (Reston, VA: Music Educators National Conference, 1994).

13. Gordon M. Ambach, "Education Reform In and Through the Arts," keynote address at Getty Center for Education in the Arts Conference, 1993.

14. National Endowment for the Arts and Morrison Institute for Public Policy, *Schools, Communities and the Arts: A Research Compendium* (Washington, D.C.: National Endowment for the Arts, September 1994). Available in both print and electronic formats from Alliance for Arts Education Network, John F. Kennedy Center for the Performing Arts, Washington, D.C. 20566.

15. Goals 2000 Arts Education Partnership, *The Arts and Education: Partners in Achieving Our National Education Goals* (Washington, D.C.: National Endowment for the Arts, January 1995).

16. *Beyond Creating: The Place for Art in America's Schools, A Report by the Getty Center for Education in the Arts*, April 1995. The J. Paul Getty Trust. Excerpted from the Foreword by Harold M. Williams, President, The J. Paul Getty Trust.

17. Ibid, p. 54 ff.

18. The GE Fund 1994 Annual Report.

19. Ibid, p. 10.

20. Adapted from a speech made to the Business Committee for the Arts in October 1993.

21. *The Education Commitment: An Overview of State Arts Agencies' Arts Education Activities* (Washington, D.C.: National Assembly of State Arts Agencies, 1994).

22. Jonathan Katz, ed., *Arts Education Handbook: A Guide to Productive Collaborations* (Washington, D.C.: National Assembly of State Arts Agencies, 1988).

23. Adapted from the transcript of a presentation to the NALAA Arts Education preconference held in Fort Worth, Texas in June 1994. Reprinted with permission of NALAA.

24. BAAA will produce a publication late in 1996 that incorporates a conference report along with the findings of the Cultural Institutions and Education Research Project. *Interchanges*, the newsletter of the *International Arts and Education Initiative*, is also available. It aims to extend information to a network of people involved in arts and education all over the world. For more information, contact BAAA, 116 Commercial Street, London, El 6NF, UK; Phone: 01144 171 247 5385 Fax: 01144 171 247 5256.

CHAPTER 8

Conclusion

The Oxymoronic Quest for Durable Change

Nothing endures but change. —Heraclitus

The People, Yes: Where To? What Next?

In his influential and widely distributed piece, "The Upsidedown Curriculum" that appeared in the Ford Foundation's 1970 Summer issue of *Cultural Affairs*, then arts and humanities program advisor Junius Eddy opens with a somewhat optimistic quote from John Goodlad, and ends with some observations of his own that have an eerily familiar ring:

> Since the time available for non-remunerative pursuits is likely to increase, it is necessary that we examine immediately the imbalances in the curriculum. In spite of an assumed "culture explosion," we continue in the schools to neglect art, music, drama, dance, sculpture, and, in fact, almost everything that smacks of being nonutilitarian. Ironically, we may discover not long after 1980 that in the 1960s and 1970s we had an upside-down curriculum, with what was considered then to be of most worth proving to be of little value to the masses of people. Let us at least hedge our bets by assuring a reasonable balance among the several realms of human inquiry.
>
> *John I. Goodlad, The Educational Program*
> *[from ca. 1970] to 1980 and Beyond*

And Junius concludes:

> In some ways, the new wave of educational reform may well present the arts-in-education movement with a unique tactical opportunity. For once, the arts—by which I mean arts educators, artists, and their community-based resources—can join in a movement with nonarts educators and find themselves in the

company of sympathetic companions from many different camps, all moving in the same general direction over reasonably common ground. Toward what end? Well, that of course is the Ultimate Question... For the questions persist. *Is* it possible to define common goals? Agree on joint objectives? Create new options? Discover better alternatives? Develop unifying strategies? Settle on immediate tactics? Nice, big, global questions.

Interestingly enough, they turn out to be variants of the same question, because the concept of *change* is centrally at issue. Certainly, it is easier to think up such questions and ask them at random than it is to suggest answers. But this may be one of those times—following a period of intense and active involvement in new program development—when it's important once again for those concerned about the future of arts and humanities education in this country to try to come to grips with basic issues and principles. And therefore, I suppose, it follows that we must address ourselves to those difficult fundamental questions. As Carl Sandburg put it in *The People Yes:* Where to? What Next?

Opportunity Knocks, Again: Are We Ready?

Opportunity knocks—again. Are we prepared to take advantage of the current wave of reform before it inevitably rolls back out to sea? Are we ready to move from the rhetoric of national policy to local community action? What lessons have we learned for the long haul?

I have worked in this field throughout the country for more than 30 years. I work with arts organizations, school districts, national foundations and as a consultant for arts and education providers. I observe the view from the national scene, the state perspective, the local vantage and from behind the classroom door. I have lived through several cycles of good, bad and worse times, a spate of task forces, innumerable pieces of promising legislation (most of which no longer exist), and political, social and economic upheaval.

What I see clearly today is that while the arts have made significant advances and inroads, they are still struggling for a permanent and respected place behind the classroom door. Despite all the resources, energy and good intentions that have been spent on the cause in the last three decades, it sometimes seems that all we have to show for our efforts are isolated pockets of improvement, model projects, encouraging initiatives, and a few new pieces of legislation. There is progress of a sort, but it remains largely superficial, tangential and marginal. While we have grown much more sophisticated in our rationales and more comprehensive in our thinking about teaching and learning, there is no visible trend toward systemic change in state and local curricula and no broad-based acceptance and institutionalization of the arts in all our schools and districts. For most of our school children, the arts are still afterthoughts.

Opportunity knocks, but we have all heard the call before, and we have also seen the door slam tightly shut. We are now in a period that seems dangerously rich with fleeting promise: voluntary national goals that include the arts; voluntary national standards that include the arts; a national research agenda for the arts; legislation providing money for the arts to states and local school districts if they, in turn, elect to include them in their education plans; compensatory education funds for the arts—again; strong state and local arts agencies with articulate national leadership organizations; diminished but enduring arts and humanities endowments and an institute for museum services with arts education agendas; several corporate, public and private foundations acting as stalking-horses, taking risks for the field; coalitions, partnerships, alliances, networks—all organized around the arts and frequently including education as a priority. What's wrong with this seemingly opulent picture?

You know the answer. It could, and will, change dramatically—soon. Count on it. There is every indication that federal and public funding for the arts will be even more drastically reduced and that private philanthropic dollars will be unavailable to pick up the slack. We don't need to belabor the reasons; political, social and economic pressures are always behind these cycles. These may turn out to be the most difficult times we have faced in quite a while. In some ways, it reminds me of the fifties, before any of this activity was even a glint in the eye of the legislators, politicians, educators and arts visionaries who brought about the "great society" and the decade or so of unprecedented growth for public support of the arts and education in this country. What is to be done?

Making a Difference: Building Arts Partnerships that Last

As you are by now aware, I believe that all schools should teach the arts as individual disciplines and as tools for learning other subjects, providing that artistic integrity and balance is maintained when designing and carrying out interdisciplinary curriculum. I also believe that all schools should make effective use of their community's arts and cultural resources in and outside of the schoolhouse. This belief is predicated on the assumption, reinforced by experience, that arts organizations, agencies and artists can—under certain very important conditions—serve as resources to educational change and progress, not merely as embellishments or feeble stopgap measures to replace the loss of licensed specialists.

Chief among these conditions is the process of networking and collaboration, notably in the form of lasting partnerships. *Lasting* is the operative word here. Effective business partnerships usually involve serious long-term commitments. They are generally expected to endure as long as they continue to deliver the goods, not to dissolve arbitrarily according to artificial time limits, boredom or impatience. For the arts community to begin to have a more significant impact and to be more useful as a resource to the schools, it will be necessary for many organizations to rethink the nature and length of their commitments. I think they have a significant role to play as long-term instructional allies of classroom teachers and arts specialists as well as invested advocates for community awareness and support. For those roles to be credible, let alone effectively played, the arts community must consider long-term partnerships.

If the arts are expected to make a difference in schooling, then they have to be taught steadily and sequentially throughout the grades. Because they (and other subjects such as history, math and science) are a complex subject area, they benefit from being taught by several different kinds of instructors who have different experiences, styles and perspectives to share. In this case, I am referring to classroom teachers, arts specialists and professional practicing artists. If partnerships—*ongoing* partnerships—among these three groups of professionals can be formed, nurtured and sustained, then significant teaching and learning, in the arts *and* other subjects, have a good chance to take place. These partnerships can also help create and sustain many of the other conditions necessary for longevity.

Are we ready this time? What have we learned to help us work together to get the job done?

Critical Lessons Learned: Building the Local Infrastructure for More Durable Change

I hope this book has made a contribution to your store of information, to the dialogues you will have with your colleagues, to the debates you will undoubtedly have with your political, social and artistic conscience. Let me sum up in large strokes where we have been and some of the main ideas or themes that have emerged:

- Unless we create the climate for and commitment to change locally, federal and national initiatives will not take root and prosper behind the classroom door, **and the changes now under way will not endure.**

- Unless we build administrative and instructional capacity on the part of superintendents, principals, classroom teachers, specialists and parents; develop a constituency within the schools; and marshal broad-based community support, **the changes now under way will not endure**.

- No matter the shape or name of reform, now or in the future, unless the arts build a political and professional constituency—at the national, state and local level, and especially behind the classroom door—the current momentum has little chance to take root and hold. **The changes now under way will not endure.**

- Unless we build a vivid awareness at all levels of the national, state and local community of the instructional, social and emotional value of the arts for all children **the changes now under way will not endure.**

- Unless we accept inclusive definitions for all the arts (the classical, the popular, the ethnic, the traditional, the folk and so on), unless we accept all teaching and learning philosophies (discipline-based art education, aesthetic education, interdisciplinary teaching and learning, arts education, education in, about and through the arts), unless we accept all styles of teaching and learning (different ways of knowing, multiple intelligences, constructivism, Piaget, Dewey, etc.), **the changes now under way will not endure.**

Avoiding the Godot Syndrome: A Framework for Immediate Action

In an article published in the July/August 1995 *Arts Education Policy Review*, Doug Herbert, whose title then was NEA Arts in Education Program Director, wrote:[1]

> ...In the future, our ability to make sense of the arts education landscape—to make connections across disciplines, to bridge ideological and sometimes political (with a small p) boundaries, and to develop and sustain partnerships between the arts and education communities—will determine our success or failure in the long struggle to make the arts essential to elementary and secondary education. I am not advocating a "melting pot" of all arts education approaches. Like most things in life, part of arts education's strength today is in its diversity. That's as it should be. Similarly, while we have entered a radically new era in education

reform with the establishment of national education goals and national voluntary standards for what students should know and be able to do in core subjects, the decisions about exactly what is taught and how it is taught remain in the hands of state- and local-level decision makers. Accordingly, a diversity of curriculum approaches and methods of delivering arts learning should accompany that state and local autonomy.

I have been reflecting recently on the challenge implicit in the title I gave this final chapter: How *do* we go about ensuring that the current gains of the field increase and survive beyond the millennium? How do we reconcile the oxymoronic need for stabilizing constant change which then ironically becomes the "desirable" status quo? I am not a philosopher and have no handy metaphysical answer for this dilemma. Unfortunately, the arts and education fields are usually so absorbed in fending off the latest wolf from the door or struggling with the latest round of budget-cutting that collective brainstorming or long-range planning is deferred to more luxurious times that, like Godot, never arrive.

While I don't pretend to have a global answer, I think I do have some pieces of the puzzle. One piece is John Goodlad's notion of the two tiers of "reform," one at the national level and the other grassroots. He puts his faith in the grassroots movement. While I see enormous value in the leadership, policy directions and financial incentives that have come from the federal government, national foundations and coalitions of national organizations, I basically agree with him. Another piece of the puzzle lies in the philosophy of educational change through the arts, which moves forward one person at a time, one classroom at a time, one schoolhouse at a time, one district at a time, one arts organization at a time, and so forth, until we have built a critical mass of pioneers, practitioners and advocates who believe in and practice the arts for learning. A third piece consists of the four interrelated themes that echo throughout the book: creating the climate and then building instructional capacity, a professional constituency and a receptive, supportive community for the arts in education at the local level. I think they are fundamental conditions to strive for if we are ever to complete the puzzle. I also believe they offer a useful framework for immediate action.

Creating the climate for change is difficult; most people are fearful of the unknown and resist dislocation. It is a slow and painstaking process of inclusion where people can convene to discuss the new ideas, come to consensus, make decisions about them, take actions, evaluate the results, modify their decisions, and repeat the cycle in a forward-moving, upward-spiraling progression.

Capacity building means developing the motivation, skills, knowledge and supportive climate for people to take charge of and responsibility for their professional actions and interactions. In the arts and education, it means that superintendents, principals, supervisors, teachers, specialists, artists, arts administrators, parents and the rest know and are able to administer, teach and support learning in the arts by all children. It implies teamwork, cooperation and, of course, partnerships.

Constituency building means making professional friends, allies and vocal advocates of everyone within the schoolhouse walls for the arts as educational basics. It means that through cooperation, collaboration and trust building, specialists, artists and classroom teachers, along with their supervisors and the parents, come to understand and value the important difference the arts can make to children's growth. It means that when the next round of cuts are threatened, an army beyond the usual suspects assembles to protest the cuts of the arts and arts specialists, and a chorus of voices from the entire faculty and all the parents insists that the arts are academics as important as mathematics, language arts, social studies and science. This chorus will swell and ring with conviction as more and more of the people who are making these claims experience the truth of them for themselves firsthand.

And then there is community building, the gradual, extensive and intensive process of creating a climate of awareness, acceptance and action by the entire local community in favor of the arts. This process is led by the local champions of change, arm in arm with the school, arts, business, philanthropic and political communities. Here the catalysts for community activism and commitment can make a critical difference.

In my work as well as in this book, I have begun to use these four themes as a framework and a filter. Once I have determined that a program has met the first acid test—it must have quality, integrity and equity of access—these themes become the critical standards by which I now take the measure of ongoing and prospective partnerships and programs and form the basis of my evaluation designs. I encourage you to do likewise, using these guiding questions as you proceed to build endurance and stability into your programs and your partnerships:

- How will you help to create a climate within your organization, your community and your school system that is receptive to the idea of institutional and instructional change?

- In what ways will your programs and services increase the instructional capacity of classroom and specialists teachers to teach the arts and to work with artists as resources for teaching and learning? What strategies can you offer for professional development, for curriculum design and integration, and for access to arts and cultural resources in the school, the district and the community?

- How will you help to ensure that the entire school, community or district is aware and understands the value of what happens to children and their families as a result of their formal and informal study in and through the arts? What methods will you use to get them personally involved so that they have firsthand and compelling knowledge of this information? How will you coordinate these campaigns with your school partners?

- What educational, marketing and public relations methods will you use to make sure that the entire community is aware of, understands and is willing to fight for the arts as basic education for all their children? How will you make sure they understand, firsthand, the significance and value of the arts to the intellectual, social, emotional and physical growth and development of all their children? How will you coordinate these campaigns with your school partners? With other arts and community organizations?

The Journey Beyond Enrichment

We have come to the end of our learning journey. This book has illustrated that the arts and cultural community have a distinct and critical role to play that will benefit school children and the arts community in the short and long run. The dynamic and interactive process is bound to improve the quality of education and community life. This, in turn should help to create a climate of acceptance and support for the arts within the community—one community at a time.

The arts community can help the schools to move the arts beyond enrichment and into the system—from the periphery to the heart of the learning process—by building effective partnerships among arts organizations, agencies, artists, schools and the community. By now, I hope many of you feel comfortable enough to consider the wisdom, value and practicality of working with schools in your locality. I think you understand, too, that plans must be made now to safeguard the progress you are making so that the arts have greater assurance of a permanent place in the curriculum of your local schools. I would imagine you are equipped to begin to construct a partnership with your local schools using the collected wisdom and specific information found within this book as well as from the various resources I refer to throughout.

I know that we have raised more questions, conundrums and dilemmas than we have answers, that each apparent solution quickly prompts another set of devilish questions, and that there is no one right way—no one right approach, right answer, philosophy or methodology—that will inevitably result in ideal partnerships with schools committed to education in, through and about the arts. In keeping with the Socratic approach, I will end on a note of inquiry.

Will Godot ever arrive? Will we somehow figure out how to deal with the conundrum of an impossible phenomenon: durable change in which the arts stay permanently woven into the instructional fabric of the curriculum while the world about us changes almost at the speed of light? I have no predictions. But I am either a cockeyed optimist or a perpetual Pollyanna because, despite all the forces beyond my ken and control, I always emerge from any Cassandra-like forecast of doom and gloom rededicated to the notion of "all the arts for all the children in entire schools and districts"—one school at a time. Over the years, and with all the setbacks—three steps forward, two steps back—I may have been discouraged and occasionally heartbroken, but I am rarely cynical when the change cycle, with little warning and no apparent explanation, takes another turn for the worse.

Oddly, I often take heart in the face of adversity because I have noticed that the arts-in-education idea can take advantage of conflicting messages in unsettled times—if people are prepared, focused, clear about their choices, steady on their feet and, as my great good friend and mentor Kathy Bloom used to say, ready for bear.

I hope this book has convinced you that you, too, can help to address some of the global questions and perhaps figure out 'where to?' and 'what next?', at least in your own backyard. I am convinced more than ever that your energy, commitment and precious arts and cultural resources can make a major difference in your schools, your communities and in the lives of all our children.

> The people have the say-so.
> Let the argument go on.
> Let the people listen.
> Tomorrow the people say Yes or No by one question:
>
> "What else can be done?"
> In the drive of faiths on the wind today the people know:
> "We have come far and we are going farther yet[...]"

Once having marched
Over the margins of animal necessity,
Over the grim line of sheer subsistence
    Then man came

To the deeper rituals of his bones,
To the lights lighter than any bones,
To the time for thinking things over,
To the dance, the song, the story,
Or the hours given over to dreaming,
    Once having so marched[...]

In the darkness with a great bundle of grief
    the people march.
In the night, and overhead a shovel of stars for
    keeps, the people march:
"Where to? what next?"

            —Carl Sandburg, "The People, Yes"[2]

Notes

1. "The National Arts Education Landscape: Past, Present, and Future," *Arts Education Policy Review*, July/August 1995, Vol. 96, No. 6, p. 13.

2. Carl Sandburg, *The People, Yes* (Harcourt Brace & Company, 1936, 1964; First Harvest Edition, 1990), pp. 281, 285, 286. Used by permission.

Appendices

Appendix A

Contributors and Other Voices

William Aguado, Executive Director, Bronx Council on the Arts, New York, NY—"Sharing Power in the Bronx: A Collaborative Work in Progress," Chapter 7

Anthony J. Alvarado, Superintendent of Community School District 2, New York, NY—"Building Professional Capacity for the Arts in Education" (interview), Chapter 2

Arnold Aprill, Executive Director, Chicago Arts Partnerships in Education (CAPE), Chicago, IL—"The Chicago Arts Partnerships in Education (CAPE): Building Bridges in the Tower of Babel," Chapter 4, Part I

ArtsConnection, New York, NY: Steven Tennen, Executive Director, and Joanne Bernstein-Cohen, Barry Oreck, Jessica Nicoll—Contributors to the case study in Chapter 4, Part I

Dr. Terry L. Baker, Senior Research Scientist, Education Development Center, New York, NY—"New Currency for the Arts in Education: From Change Theory into Promising Practice," Chapter 6

Richard Bell, National Executive Director, Young Audiences, New York, NY—"Building Continuity and Systemic Change: A Primer on the New Arts Partnerships," Chapter 4, Part I

Dr. Richard C. Benjamin, Superintendent of Schools, Nashville, TN—"The Arts, Artists, and Arts Specialists Can Transform Education" (interview), Chapter 2

John Bertles, educator/composer/founder of Bash the Trash, Hastings-on-Hudson, NY—"The Connective Process: A Partnership Between Artists and Teachers," Chapter 5, Part I

Dr. Ernest L. Boyer, former Chancellor of the State University of New York, U.S. Commissioner of Education and President of the Carnegie Foundation for the Advancement of Teaching, Princeton, NJ—A new version of Dr. Boyer's remarks to the NEA's Art-21 Conference in Chicago (April 1994) appear in the introduction to Chapter 2

Joan Boyett, Founder and Executive Director, Music Center Education Division, Los Angeles, CA—"Beyond Audience Development: Why Work with Schools?" Chapter 4, Part II

Deborah Brzoska, Fine Arts Coordinator, Vancouver Public Schools, Vancouver, WA—"Learning, Life and the Arts—Like Lunch," Chapter 5, Part I

Dr. Judith M. Burton, Professor and Chair, Arts and Humanities, Teachers College, Columbia University, New York, NY—"Natural Allies: A Trilogy," Chapter 5, Part II

Dr. Barbara Carlisle, Associate Professor of Theatre Arts, Virginia Tech University, Blacksburg, VA—"Speaking a Language We All Can Understand," Chapter 4, Part III

Leilani Lattin Duke, Director, Getty Center for Education in the Arts, Santa Monica, CA—"Staying the Course" (interview), Chapter 7

Dr. Elliot W. Eisner, Professor of Education and Art, Stanford University, Palo Alto, CA—"Standards for American Schools: Help or Hindrance?" Chapter 6

Dr. Carol Fineberg, Arts Education Consultant, C. F. Associates, New York, NY—"The Challenge and Promise of Integrated Curriculum and Transfer of Learning," Chapter 5, Part II

Ralph Flores, Arts Programming Director, Association House of Chicago, Chicago, IL—"CAPE Theater Artists Speak," Chapter 5, Part I

Dr. Charles B. Fowler, former arts writer, national consultant, and advocate, Washington, D.C.—Foreword, and cited by others

Phyllis Free, interdisciplinary artist/music educator, Louisville, KY—"Making Music Connect" (interview), Chapter 5, Part I

Mindy Richman Garfinkel, Congressional Liaison Specialist, National Endowment for the Arts, Washington, D.C.—"What Makes an Effective Partnership? Lessons Learned from the National Endowment for the Arts' Arts Plus Experience," Chapter 4, Part I

Dr. John I. Goodlad, Professor of Education and Director of the Center for Educational Renewal, University of Washington, Seattle, WA—Excerpts of Dr. Goodlad's work appear in the introductions to Chapters 2 and 3

Derek E. Gordon, Associate Managing Director for Education, John F. Kennedy Center for the Performing Arts, Washington, D.C.—"Making a Difference in the Community: Reflections on What Makes Good Partnerships," Chapter 4, Part III

Hollis Headrick, Director of Arts in Education, New York State Council on the Arts, New York, NY—"State Arts Agency Partnerships: Beyond Enrichment?" Chapter 7

Doug Herbert, Director for Arts in Education in the Division of Education and Access, National Endowment for the Arts, Washington, D.C.—"The National Policy Window for Arts Education," Chapter 7

Harold (Doc) Howe II, Senior Lecturer, Harvard Graduate School of Education, Cambridge, MA—"Beyond Footnotes: Building a Constituency for the Arts" (interview), Chapter 2

Jonathan Katz, Executive Director, National Assembly of State Arts Agencies (NASAA), Washington, D.C.—"The National Assembly of State Arts Agencies: Stimulating School Reform at the Federal, State, and Local Levels," Chapter 7

Mae Kennerly, Principal, Martin Luther King Jr. Elementary School, Louisville, KY—"The Arts, Manners and More" (interview), Chapter 2

Kentucky Center for the Arts, Louisville, KY: Marlow Burt, President; Michael Durham, Executive Vice President, and Susan Knight, Deborah Shannon, Jane Morgan Dudney—Contribute to "Creative Connections: Linking the Kentucky Center for the Arts' Resources to Statewide Reform—A Case Study," Chapter 3

Nancy Langan, Director of Education, National Assembly of Local Arts Agencies (NALAA), Washington, D.C.—Contributes to "The National Assembly of Local Arts Agencies: Catalysts for Community Building Through Local Arts Partnerships," Chapter 7

Reginald Lawrence and William S. Carroll, Founding Members, MPAACT (Ma'at Production Association of Afrikan Centered Theatre), Chicago, IL—"CAPE Theater Artists Speak," Chapter 5, Part I

Bella Lewitzky, Founder and Artistic Director, Lewitzky Dance Company, Los Angeles, CA—"Movement Thinking," Chapter 5, Part I

Robert Lynch, President and CEO, National Assembly of Local Arts Agencies (NALAA), Washington, D.C.—Contributes to "The National Assembly of Local Arts Agencies: Catalysts for Community Building Through Local Arts Partnerships," Chapter 7

Dr. John McLaughlin, Consultant, Arts and Education/Research and Evaluation, Lexington, KY—"Assessment, Evaluation and Research: Building Blocks for the Future in Arts Education," Chapter 6

Dr. John J. Mahlmann, Executive Director, Music Educators National Conference, Reston, VA—"The Arts: Who Shall Teach?" Chapter 6

Norma Moran, Teacher, New York City Public Schools, Bronx, NY—"Reflections of a Classroom Teacher on Working with Artists in the Classroom," Chapter 5, Part I

Scott Noppe-Brandon, Executive Director, Lincoln Center Institute, New York, NY—"The Role of the Arts and Aesthetic Education in the Classroom: Asking Questions, Seeking Answers" (interview), Chapter 5, Part II

Dr. David O'Fallon, Executive Director, Minnesota Center for Arts Education, Golden Valley, MN—"The Arts Organization and Public Education: A Guide to Conducting a Self-Audit," Chapter 4, Part II

Jane L. Polin, Program Manager and Comptroller, The GE Fund, Fairfield, CT—"Making Creative Connections Within a Business: Jane L. Polin Shares Some Lessons Learned," Chapter 7

Carol Ponder, Artist Design Consultant, Leonard Bernstein Center for Education Through the Arts, Nashville, TN—**Susan Standbrook** and **Karen Catignani**, Carol Ponder's cowriters, are teachers in the Nashville Public Schools—"Knowing the Place for the First Time: A Learning Journey," Chapter 5, Part I

Simon Richey, Education Director, UK Branch of the Gulbenkian Foundation, London, England—"Bridge Over Troubled Waters," Chapter 4, Part III

Sharon Ryan, Doctoral Candidate, Evaluator, Teachers College, Columbia University, New York, NY—"Arts Partnerships in the Classroom: Some Cultural Considerations," Chapter 5, Part II

Mark Schubart, Chairman, Lincoln Center Institute, New York, NY—"Teaching Kids to Listen" (interview), Chapter 4, Part I

Sam Shreyar, Doctoral Candidate, Evaluator, Teachers College, Columbia University, New York, NY—"Arts Partnerships in the Classroom: Some Cultural Considerations," Chapter 5, Part II

Dr. Robert Stake, Professor of Education and Director of the Center for Instructional Research and Curriculum Evaluation, University of Illinois, Urbana, IL—"Current Issues in Research and Evaluation of the Arts in Education" (interview), Chapter 6

Bennett Tarleton, Executive Director, Tennessee Arts Commission, Nashville, TN—"The ABCDs of Arts Partnerships," Chapter 4, Part II

Shirley Trusty-Corey, Executive Director, Arts Council of New Orleans, New Orleans, LA—"An Oasis in the Desert" (interview), Chapter 7

Jennifer Williams, Founder and Director, British American Arts Association, London, England—"The International Arts and Education Initiative," Chapter 7

Other Voices

Robert Cooper, Chairman, English Department, Martin Luther King, Jr. High School, New York, NY—Contributes to or appears in Chapter 4, Part III, the Introduction to Chapter 5 and Chapter 5, Part II, and Appendix G.

Dr. Craig Dreeszen, Executive Director, The Arts Extension Service, University of Massachusetts, Amherst—Contributes to Introduction to Chapter 4, Part I

Junius Eddy, writer, consultant; former Ford and Rockefeller Foundation officer, Little Compton, R.I.—Quoted in Chapter 5, Part II and Chapter 8

Dennis Horn, Assistant Director, Kentucky Arts Council—Quoted in and contributes to Chapters 4 and 5, Part II

Bethany Rogers, Associate, Annenberg Institute for School Reform, Providence, R.I.—Cited and contributes to Introduction, Chapter 6

Norma Rosenblum, History teacher, Fiorello H. LaGuardia High School for the Arts, New York, NY—Contributes to Chapter 4, Part III

Dr. Jerrold Ross, Dean, School of Education, St. John's University, New York, NY—Chapter 5, Part II

Dr. Theodore R. Sizer, Professor of Education, Brown University; Chairman, Coalition of Essential Schools, and Director, Annenberg Institute for School Reform, Providence, R.I.—Cited in Introduction to Chapter 6 and by many contributors

Louise K. Stevens, Director, ArtsMarket Consulting, Inc., Marion, MA—Contributes to section on National Assembly of Local Arts Agencies, Chapter 7

Appendix B

A Bird's-eye View of Arts and Education History

Jane Remer

1900-40s
Art and music in the public school curriculum taught largely by specialists. Museums, symphony orchestras and science/ecology centers (zoos, planetaria, aquaria) offer special children's programs and events, as well as adult education.

1950s
Performing arts centers, organizations and companies offer special programs, tickets and services at the host institution. Young Audiences and a few other nonprofit cultural organizations offer music programs as in-school assemblies.

1960s
Artist residencies in school classrooms, auditoria and the local community in the visual, performing, literary, design, architectural and folk arts gain support nationally. First Federal legislation supporting arts in (compensatory) education in the Johnson "Great Society" era. Formation of state arts agencies across the nation. Arts specialists in dance and theater are added to those in art and music in some localities. Lincoln Center for the Performing Arts establishes an Education Department with performances and services in the schools and at the Center.

1970s
First five years: Federal education and Arts and Humanities Endowments monies are awarded competitively and focus on the arts in education. J. F. Kennedy Center for the Performing Arts establishes national education program. John D. Rockefeller 3rd Fund Arts in Education Program introduces concept and practice of comprehensive programs and partnerships through two national city and state educational networks. State arts agencies introduce artist-in-schools coordinators. Formation of local arts agencies begins.

Second five years: Economic downturn and political changes begin reversal of trend to increase categorical support for the arts in public schools; Federal education funds are gradually converted from categorical support to bloc grants to the states; arts specialists are dismissed *en masse* in many urban centers. Publication in 1977 of *Coming to Our Senses: The Significance of the Arts for American Education*, which included findings and recommendations by a national panel of experts and researchers. Harvard University's Project Zero launched research into the arts and human cognition.

1980s

National Endowment for the Arts' emphasis shifts from artists in schools to artists in education and, with the 1988 *Toward Civilization* report, to arts in education and a significant increase of support for the field. *A Nation At Risk* in 1983 declares the public schools in dire straits and recommends reforms—the arts are not mentioned. The John Paul Getty Trust establishes the Getty Center for Education in the Arts focusing on discipline-based art education (DBAE) including study and practice of the disciplines of art history, aesthetics, criticism and studio art. *A Place Called School* (1983), the final volume of a comprehensive study of the nation's schools, indicates very little systemic and positive change in teaching the arts has occurred over the last 30 years. Comprehensive arts programs continue to grow.

1990s

First five years: Education reform reappears as "America 2000" and then "Goals 2000: Educate America Act" in 1994 in which the arts appear for the first time as a core subject. Voluntary National Standards in art, music, dance and theater are designed. Research and evaluation in the arts gain prominence and support. The National Assessment of Educational Progress will measure arts achievement at the eighth grade level in 1997. Arts partnerships gain favor as a modus operandi at the federal, national, state and local levels. At the same time, the Department of Education targets few funds for the arts and the Arts Endowment is drastically downsized as the national economy and political discontent prompt another swing away from arts and education support. State and local agencies attempt to pick up the slack as local efforts and leadership become critical. Stay tuned.

Note: For a complete chronology of the arts and education movement, see *Changing Schools Through the Arts: How to Build on the Power of an Idea* (New York: McGraw-Hill, 1982; ACA Books, 1990).

Interpretive Chronology of Major Events in the Arts in Education—Update: 1990 - 1995

The following borrows freely from "The National Policy Window for Arts Education," by Doug Herbert (Director for Arts in Education at the NEA), which appears in Chapter 7 of this book.

Seventies and Late Eighties

Harvard University's Project Zero, co-directed by Howard Gardner and David Perkins, was established in 1974 and has influenced arts education in recent years. Gardner's theory of multiple intelligences, put into practice in schools through Arts PROPEL and other projects, has fostered an increasing body of research and widespread discussion of the cognitive processes inherent in the creation of art. Gardner maintains that there are seven different intelligences through which people apprehend the world: linguistic, logical/mathematical, spatial, musical, kinesthetic, interpersonal and intrapersonal. An explanation of this theory can be found in Gardner's *Frames of Mind*.

Getty Center for Education in the Arts was formed in 1982 as a program of the J. Paul Getty Trust. It was launched as an initiative to support a comprehensive approach to the teaching of visual art. Called Discipline-Based Art Education, or DBAE, the approach proposed a balanced curriculum of history, critical analysis, and aesthetics in addition to art production and creation. The Getty has been active in developing comprehensive partnerships and significant advocacy efforts at the national, regional, state and local level. Its *Beyond Creating: The Place For Art in America's Schools* is an important document in arts education history.

Early to Mid-Nineties

America 2000 Arts Education Partnership with the National Endowment for the Arts was formed in 1992 by former Secretary of Education Lamar Alexander to implement several of the recommendations in the National Endowment for the Arts' 1988 report to the nation, *Toward Civilization*. Alexander also encouraged the formation of an independent task force, known as the Arts Education Partnership Working Group, to recommend further actions that could be taken to make the arts a more visible and vital part of national education reform.

The Arts Education Partnership Working Group, co-chaired by James Wolfensohn, then chairman of the Kennedy Center, and Harold Williams of the J. Paul Getty Trust, issued a report which declared that the arts had the power to help reshape elementary and secondary education. The report, *The Power of the Arts to Transform Education*, concluded that schools with strong arts programs evidence a range of benefits for students, teachers and the general learning environment:

- The arts are forms of understanding and ways of knowing that are fundamentally important to education;
- The arts are important to excellent education and to effective school reform;
- The most significant contribution of the arts to education reform is the transformation of teaching and learning;
- This transformation is best realized in the context of comprehensive, systemic education reform; and
- Art educators, artists, and arts organizations must be strongly encouraged to actively join in local, state, and national reform efforts.

The report was completed just as the Clinton administration took office. The new Secretary of Education, Richard Riley, embraced the findings and recommendations of the report, and he and President Bill Clinton inserted the arts into the National Education Goals as a core subject in the new administration's proposed Goals 2000: Educate America legislation. Moreover, the report's enunciation of the "transforming powers of the arts" was adopted, in some instances verbatim, in the **Improving America's Schools Act (IASA)**, the Clinton Administration's bill to reauthorize the **Elementary and Secondary Education Act** (since 1965, the nation's most heavily funded compensatory education legislation.)

Arts Education in Public Elementary and Secondary Schools is a nationwide survey of schools recently conducted by the U.S. Department of Education through funding from the National Endowment for the Arts. It was designed to determine the extent to which the arts are being taught in American schools at K-12, the characteristics and backgrounds of those teaching the arts, and the conditions that are associated with arts instruction. Copies are available from the National Center for Education Statistics at 202-219-1333.

Arts Education Research Agenda for the Future (NEA, 1994). The National Endowment for the Arts has worked in partnership with the Department of Education and the arts and education fields to support arts education research and to develop a national research agenda. More recently, the Arts Endowment commissioned a compilation of research studies which support the often-made claims of the benefits of arts education. The Morrison Institute for Public Policy (Arizona State University) report, *Schools, Communities and the Arts: A Research Compendium* (1995), summarizes research studies that have been determined to be sound in their methodologies and presents them in a lay person's language. It is available in both print and electronic formats from ARTSEDGE at the John F. Kennedy Center for the Performing Arts, 202-416-8871.

Goals 2000 Arts Education Leadership Fund was established in 1995 by the Arts Endowment and the National Assembly of State Arts Agencies with private-sector support from the Emily Hall Tremaine Foundation. The Leadership Fund is intended to assist states in implementing plans for ensuring that the arts are in state and local Goals 2000 reform plans. Matching grants are awarded to state agencies or their designees for projects that meet certain guidelines and criteria.

Goals 2000: Educate America Act: The passage of Goals 2000 in 1994 has begun a new era of federal-state-local relations in education that now holds great promise for arts education. The genesis of Goals 2000 can be traced to 1989, when the President and the 50 state governors devised the National Education Goals. For the first time in American history, there was an articulated national vision for education. Goal three of the National Education Goals called for all students to demonstrate competency in "challenging subject matter," for which the subjects of math, science, reading, writing and geography were specifically listed. The arts were originally omitted from this list but were added, along with foreign languages, as a result of the advocacy of leaders in the arts and education community.

National Assessment of Educational Progress (NAEP), known as "The Nation's Report Card" regularly assesses national samples of students to determine their proficiencies in basic subjects. The arts will be assessed in selected sites at the eighth-grade level in 1997; they have not been included in the NAEP subject schedule since the 1970s. With Arts Endowment funding, supplemented by support from the Getty Center for Education in the Arts, the first phase of the arts assessment—the development of a consensus framework of outcomes and the means of measuring their achievement—was completed in 1994. The efforts to develop the content standards in the arts and the assessment framework occurred simultaneously creating a common vision for arts education.

National Standards for Arts Education: *Dance, Music Theatre and Visual Arts: What Every Young American Should Know and Be Able to Do in the Arts* (1994). Led by the Music Educators National Conference, a consortium of national professional associations in arts education, with the financial support of the Department of Education and both the Arts and Humanities Endowments, undertook a two-year effort to develop a national consensus definition of what all students should know and be able to do in the arts by the end of grades 4, 8, and 12. This effort paralleled those in science, history, geography and the other core subjects listed in the National Education Goals. Whether in the arts or the sciences, these voluntary standards can help guide the states in devising their own content standards—a key component of the Goals 2000 legislation. Although the states are not required to develop standards in any subject, the arts are more firmly positioned in the national education policy framework than at any time in the past. Copies of the Standards are available from the MENC (1-800-828-0229), your state arts agency, or your state education agency.

The Arts and Education: Partners in Achieving Our National Education Goals was an action plan developed by a planning group formed under the sponsorship of the National Endowment for the Arts and the Department of Education. At the invitation of Chairman Jane Alexander and Secretary Richard Riley, representatives from more than 100 national organizations met in fall 1994 to affirm their belief that the arts are important to achieving the National Education Goals. More recently, with the support of the Arts Endowment and the Department of Education, the partners have established the **Goals 2000 Arts Education Partnership** as a permanent organization to implement the action plan and to maintain communications and coordinate advocacy and actions at the national, state, and local levels. The partnership is headquartered at the offices of the Council of Chief State School Officers (CCSSO) in Washington, D.C.

The National Assembly of Local Arts Agencies (NALAA) established an Institute for Community Development and the Arts. Begun in 1995, the mission is to promote additional government funding for the arts by researching 1,000 arts and community development programs from across the country and measuring the total local government support for the arts in 160 cities. Twenty-one publications will be produced describing these innovative programs, how to adapt them locally and the non-traditional ways being used to fund them. Arts education is one of the criteria for program participation. A handbook, *Working Relationships: The Arts, Education, and Community Development*, describes the partnerships developed by 11 communities and is available from the organization. Copies are available from NALAA at 202-371-2830.

The National Assembly of State Arts Agencies (NASAA), in addition to its partnerships with federal, national and local agencies and institutions, has recently published an important report on state arts agency activity in education. Titled, *The Education Commitment: An Overview of State Arts Agencies' Arts Education Activities*, by Kelly J. Barsdate (NASAA, February 1995), it is available from NASAA at 202-347-6352 for $12.00.

Appendix C

The Arts Institution's Commitment to Education

Checklist for the Courage to Change

Jane Remer

Thesis: *When arts organizations make a serious commitment to education, fundamental changes in the structure and operation of the organization are the inevitable outcome. Here are some of the characteristics that make up a profile for change. Use them as a checklist for your own organization. Feel free to add, revise or subtract to reflect your local realities.*

Evidence of Commitment

Staff
- has *at least a* half to full-time professional education staff person who holds a senior staff position, not subsumed under development, marketing, public relations, outreach, i.e. *not* a function of sales
- gives the education professional clear lines of command, responsibility and authority
- is physically integrated into the mainstream (office space and location)

Structure, Organization and Operation
The institution
- places education prominently in the mission statement where it is also closely related to artistic mission
- makes education a priority on the institutional agenda
- sets up board and advisory committees for education
- encourages the CEO and senior staff to provide direct support, leadership, presence and involvement in educational planning, meetings and key events
- establishes internal communication systems and collaborative working relationships between education and other departments
- collaborates with other local agencies and partners on educational ventures
- participates in local and national arts education networks, groups, alliances, associations

Programming
The institution
- integrates aspects of education programming into all departments and institutional activities
- maintains open discussion of the definitions of education, marketing and development; education is spoken of as a valuable and responsible resource and public service to the community, not a patronizing "give back"
- designs and designates specific performances and activities for students, teachers and parents
- commissions new works for its current repertory with an eye to its young audiences
- hires artists who agree to perform education and outreach services as part of their contractual duties
- (if a producing organization) uses its own artists (in addition to outside teaching artist consultants) in its education programs
- establishes Educational Advisory Boards of principals, teachers, supervisors, parents, business community and other local representatives to guide program design, development and financial support
- maintains ongoing internal and external documentation and evaluation of educational activities

Money
The institution
- aggressively raises funds for education programs
- allocates new or existing resources, especially money, for education
- commits a significant percentage of its budget to education

Appendix D

Program Design and Instructional Issues

Guiding Questions for Planning Meetings Among Schools and Their Arts Partners

Jane Remer

When arts organizations and schools agree to form a partnership, they first need to define program goals and instructional objectives. Once they determine which students will participate and settle on achievable learner outcomes, they can turn to issues about the content and form of instruction and assessment:

1. How do we best motivate, engage and sustain the interest of our students? What strategies do we use to capture their imaginations? How do we make the arts accessible and relevant to their daily concerns?

2. What themes are appropriate for the students in our age group? Should these be universal themes? Curricular? Social? Political? Aesthetic? How do we get our students involved in the decision-making process?

3. What is the design of our program? What are we going to teach? Will the program be "event-driven," "artist-driven," "theme-driven" or "discipline-driven"? Who will be responsible for curriculum design? Will it be a series of workshops, a course of study, a unit, a sequential curriculum? Where will instruction take place? In school? In the theater? In the museum? How will we engage both the schools and the arts partners in the instructional process?

4. Do we want to explicitly link the art form(s) and our themes to the rest of the curriculum? Or, do we want to teach only in and about the art form itself? Is this program concentrating on learning an arts discipline? About an arts discipline? How that discipline relates to other academic studies? How much emphasis will be placed on technical facts, skills and contextual information, e.g. this is a plié, dramatic exposition is...., an arpeggio sounds like this, the four vocal ranges are soprano/alto/tenor/bass, bel canto is..., Picasso was born in..., Richard Wright wrote *Native Son* at a time in American history when...?

5. What kinds of arts events will we include? Performances, workshops, lecture-demonstrations? Pre- and post-performance discussions or Q&A? Studio and museum visits and backstage tours? How many events will we offer? How should they be sequenced and over what period of time? Where and when do we offer them? During and/or after school, weekends, summers? Are these events for students, teachers, parents, the school community?

6. Who will be responsible for teaching what? Will artists and teachers work as a team in the classroom or will they take turns? What is the best use we can make of the artists' and the teachers' time, talents and skills? Who will identify the artists and the teachers, and by what criteria?

7. What training and professional development should be offered, and by whom? How else can we support artists and teachers whose students participate in our program? What are their roles and responsibilities? What about release time? Compensation? Credit? Recognition?

8. How can we best tap into the community's arts and cultural resources? Which ones seem most appropriate? What contributions and commitments do we expect of them? How formal should our arrangements be?

9. What resource and other materials do we need? If they don't exist, how should they be developed and used? Who is our audience?

10. How will we evaluate success? Of program operation? Of student performance? Of artist and teacher performance? What are our criteria? Who are our audiences? Who will be responsible for documentation, evaluation and assessment?

Appendix E

Partnerships in the Arts in Education

Guidelines and Criteria

Jane Remer

Criteria for Effective Partnerships

Key standard #1: Partnerships should equal more than the sum of their parts.

Partnerships are supposed to save time, improve the quality and increase the quantity of services. Ultimately, they should save money by eliminating duplication of effort. The partnership should also produce unique or unusual and exemplary benefits for the intended audience. If you and your partner cannot do the job significantly better, don't form the partnership.

Key standard #2: Partnerships should be based on true collaboration in which the operative pronoun "I" becomes "WE."

Many partnerships are superficial, representing collaborations by chief operating officers on paper only. A true collaboration is based on grassroots involvement of both arts and education personnel. Are the key players in the partnerships aware that this is a collaboration? Were all the stakeholders actively engaged in the planning and formation of the partnership in a timely fashion? Does everyone understand what they have agreed to and, most important, the expectations and consequences of working together? Can they answer the question, "Whose program is it, anyway?" with a quick and firm: "Ours." ?

Key standard #3: In healthy partnerships, each partner maintains an independent and separate identity.

In healthy arts and education partnerships, the primary institutional purposes of each collaborator overlap or converge. But partnership does not imply a blending of institutional personalities or distinctive characteristics. Quite the opposite, it takes advantage of the very different qualities that each can bring to the collaboration, thereby making it richer and more productive. Each partner works from institutional and professional strengths that are consistent with organizational missions and core values.

In effective partnerships, the collaborators work together to:

- Identify and define the problem to be solved and determine whether it can best be solved by a collaboration. In arts-in-education partnerships, it is always best to start from schools' goals and the needs of students since arts organizations are essentially educational resources to the schools in this relationship.

- Determine where their primary institutional purposes converge or overlap, agree on project goals and arrive at working definitions of artistic quality and integrity and educational authenticity and impact. These issues should be reviewed and revised throughout the partnership.
- Dedicate six months or more to planning and continue to plan throughout the venture.
- Identify and sustain resources so that successful programs can continue over time.
- Share the burden of both success and failure.

Guidelines for Evaluating Your Partnerships:

- Is there a written agreement signed by all parties? Does this agreement spell out leadership, decision-making processes, roles and functions, the workplan, the support systems/infrastructure, a timeline, money?
- What are the legitimate self-interests in collaboration (where do primary or secondary institutional purposes overlap or converge?)
- Who has the power and resources? How are these powers and resources shared? Who makes the decisions? How are they made? Are there checks and balances?
- Does each partner have the same understanding of the joint venture?
- What are the differences? What needs to be renegotiated? Who will mediate the process?
- How do partners communicate: face to face, in writing, by phone? Regularly? Is there an institutional language barrier? Are there different terms of art, acronyms, shorthand, or code being used? Has someone made a glossary of arts and education terminology and is there someone to interpret and facilitate the discussions?
- Who takes leadership and is it acknowledged? Is it rotating? Do both partners share equal responsibility for agreed-on roles and functions? Who is held accountable to whom, and by whom?
- How are decisions made? By consensus? By leader? By vote? When, why, how?
- Who implements the decisions? In cooperation with...? consultation with...?
- Are programs and instructional services evaluated formally? Informally? Collaboratively? By whom, and with what result? Who facilitates the process? How do the partners know when they are on course, off course, in need of mid-course corrections? Who supervises and coordinates the implementation of these recommendations?
- Is there a formal budget or financial agreement? Are there sufficient resources to support a cost-effective venture?

The Final, Telling Question for Each Partner

Ask yourself: Would I do this again? Regardless of your answer, examine your reasons, both pro and con, and discuss them with your partner(s). Successful collaborations take time to mature and benefit from frank discussions by all parties. They always benefit from continuing rounds of dialogue, discussion, action and evaluation which should be the cornerstone of the process.

Appendix F

The Conceptual Design and Agenda of New York City Opera's Artist Training Retreat[1]

Course Description

This course is designed to acquaint teaching artists with the idiosyncratic nature of large urban high schools and the accepted and recommended pedagogical methods and strategies used to deliver instruction. An overall view of school culture and issues of adolescent development will also be a focus of this course. Using writing as a tool for reflecting and processing experiences both past and present, members will engage in designing lessons and planning classroom activities that are relevant and useful. Current methodologies will be introduced and analyzed, i.e., cooperative learning, interdisciplinary connections, portfolio assessment, team teaching, etc. Methods familiar to the artists and common in the world of performance will be explored and included in the discussion.

General Course Objectives:
- How can the performing artist use his/her training and performing experience to form an effective collaboration with a school and a class?
- What are the skills a teacher must have to work successfully with a class of high school students?
- What pedagogical methods would work best in an interdisciplinary arts education program?

New York City Opera
Artist Training Retreat
A G E N D A

DAY ONE
Introduction: What Schools Are For—Mission, Philosophy and School Culture
- What is the purpose of school?
- What is the school's organizational chart?
- How does power work in a school?
- What is a school philosophy/mission?
- What is a school culture?
- How can I, the artist, work in congruence with a school culture?

Key Urban Teenage Issues
- What are the social, cultural, and political influences on teenagers?
- What are the common values and belief systems shared by teenagers?
- How can I, the artist, use these influences to further teaching and learning?

Journal Writing Assignments (Entries will be shared and discussed)
- Describe the culture of the high school you attended as a teenager.
- Compare that culture to the culture of the school you worked in this year.

- Discuss the most critical issue you faced as a teenager. Compare this to an issue faced by one of your students this year.

Aim
- Given the ideas noted in the earlier session, what classroom management techniques should be used to deliver instruction successfully? What pedagogical approaches will best motivate the students and allow for the most successful delivery of instruction?

Classroom Management Techniques
- seating students
- raising hands
- knowing names
- waiting
- other techniques that work
- (Activities: Role-play typical classroom situations)

Homework
- What classroom management techniques did you observe that you think you would like to emulate? Explain your reasons. Cite examples of management techniques you did not consider appropriate.
- Describe one lesson during your residency that you thought was very successful. Explain why.
- One that was unsuccessful and why.
- Compare and contrast the two lessons.

(end day one)

DAY TWO: Curriculum, Instruction and Age-Appropriate Classroom Practice
Discuss Homework Assignments
Pedagogical Methods
- What teaching strategies can I use to present material to students?
    - elements of a good developmental lesson plan; writing aims/objectives
    - motivation
    - cooperative learning strategies
    - interdisciplinary strategies/essential questions
    - portfolio assessment
    - team teaching
    - writing as a teaching and learning tool
    - student as teacher
    - journal writing/metacognition
  (Activities: Write a lesson using several of the methods described and discussed in class)

Teaching Strategies
- Present Lesson Strategies to the Group
- Feedback and Responses to Lesson Ideas
- Classroom Partnerships
- Role-Play the First Teacher and Artist Planning Meeting; the teacher is very negative about opera, partnerships, and the burden of the program

- Assessment and Evaluation

Final Remarks and Course Evaluation

(end day two)

Materials and References
- Detailed "script" of the two-day agenda
- An article on the developmental tasks appropriate for the adolescent
- Artistic developmental stages of children and adolescents
- An outline and a definition of terms in lesson plans
- Examples of lesson plans (traditional, unusual)
- Suggested writing techniques (descriptions)
- An outline of planning, implementing and evaluating interdisciplinary education: various concept models
- Portfolio assessment: definition, characteristics, examples
- Retreat evaluation form

Notes

1. Robert Cooper, Assistant Principal (Language Arts) of Martin Luther King, Jr. High School in Manhattan, is the principal author of this material. He and New York City Opera have granted permission for its inclusion in this book.

Appendix G

Artist Observation Checklist

Jane Remer

*Program:*_____ *Date:* _____

Artist(s): _____ *Location:* _____ *Time:*_____

*Discipline/Title of Workshop or Event:*_____ *Contact:*_____

Artist
- Description of Workshop or Event

Instruction
- Clarity of Purpose, Motivation and Lesson Plan
- Teaching Style and Age Appropriateness of Methodology
- Variety, Scope and Sequence of Activities
- Artistic Quality/Aesthetic Dimension (Imaginativeness, Creativity, Authenticity, Integrity)
- Educational Effectiveness/Relationship of the Parts to the Whole
- Degree of Student Initiative, Self-direction and Active Construction of Learning
- Nature of Student Response (Interest, Attention, Behavior, Focus, Attitude, Engagement)
- Artist/Teacher Partnership: Involvement, Role and Response of Classroom Teacher
- Classroom Atmosphere and Management

School Climate
- School Environment and Ecology
- Administrative Leadership, Awareness and Support
- Other comments

Appendix H
Evaluating Arts Partnerships
Jane Remer

I have assembled the following set of guidelines and criteria from the first and second editions of *Changing Schools Through the Arts: How to Build on the Power of an Idea* (New York: McGraw-Hill, 1982; ACA Books, 1990). They have been widely circulated and used by arts organizations and schools since the mid-seventies. I have since rethought the criteria for educational effectiveness and changed the construct from a hierarchical taxonomy to a horizontal, developmental range of intensity known as the Beyond Enrichment Continuum: Six Stages of Instructional Partnerships. The Role of the Artist in Arts Partnerships, and Joint Planning: Some Questions to Raise —"Whose Program Is It, Anyway?" are intact and are as valid today as when they were first written. Some things change, some things never do.

CRITERIA: Community Arts Programs and Educational Effectiveness in the Schools[1]

I. Highest Level of Educational Effectiveness
A. The form, content, and structure of the program grow out of a cooperative effort by school personnel (teachers, curriculum specialists, administrators), artists, and arts organization representatives and are related to and supportive of the content of teaching and learning in the schools.

B. Programs are planned as an ongoing series of related educational events.

C. The program includes the participation of artists who serve as resources to teachers and students in a variety of direct teaching and learning activities. These include creative experiences or demonstrations of the techniques, skills, and talents indigenous to their particular profession.

D. Preparatory and follow-up curriculum materials planned specifically for the program are provided to the schools. These materials result from work done jointly by school representatives, artists, and arts organization educational staff. Related visual and written materials and resources such as slides, recordings, tapes, films, reproductions, and teacher's guides are available in the schools and used by teachers in classrooms.

E. In-service training is available to teachers in order that they have general understanding of the arts organization, its purposes, its resources, and the nature of its services in terms of curriculum development.

F. Orientation and training are available to artists and arts organization educators so that they have an understanding of the nature of schools, the content of the educational program, and the learning characteristics of students at different age levels.

G. As a result of the foregoing, the arts event becomes part of the process of teaching and learning, not just a "field trip," time off from school work, or another assembly program.

II. Middle Level of Educational Effectiveness

A. The content of the program is planned by arts organization educators with some help from school personnel, but is not focused on the content of school studies.
B. Programs are isolated and sporadic events.
C. Contact with artists is limited.
D. Some preparatory materials are provided to the schools for the arts events. Few related materials are available in the schools.
E. No in-service training is available to teachers. Often they have no more information about the arts event or organization than the children they accompany.
F. No training is available to artists or arts organization educators. They assume an automatic interest or curiosity on the part of teachers and children. Capability to work with different age groups is learned on the job by trial and error.
G. The arts event is of some value to children and teachers but remains separate from the larger educational program of the schools.

III. Low Level of Educational Effectiveness

A. The content of the program is accidentally determined by the fact that the arts organization has a special event it feels has some significance for the schools, and the schools decide to send all fifth-grade classes and their teachers to it.
B. Programs are single, isolated, unrelated events or activities.
C. Artists are not involved as resources to teachers and students in the program.
D. No preparatory or follow-up materials are available.
E. No in-service training is available for teachers.
F. Arts organization representatives do not work with teachers and students since their regular responsibilities make very heavy demands on their time, or the schools have not made appointments for their classes in advance.
G. Educationally, the arts event is of dubious value to students and teachers.

The Role of the Artist in Arts Partnerships[2]

I. As Artists, They:

- Demonstrate their art form as a process and a product
- Stimulate curiosity about their professional trade and respect for the diligence and discipline required for excellence
- Provide role models and open new options for professional or amateur pursuit
- Help identify the artistically gifted and talented
- Work effectively with special populations using the art form as the language and medium for communication
- Bring normally isolated individuals together to work on group projects
- Generate community interest in the arts and the schools

II. As "Resource Teachers," They:

- Discuss, interpret, and illuminate the origin, history, and development of their field
- Develop basic artistic abilities and problem-solving skills
- Demonstrate how others can create their own activities or products using the arts

- Make connections between the arts process and the learning process and help find ways to relate the arts to each other and to mathematics, science, social studies, language arts, and so on
- Help build curriculum frameworks, guides, units of study, and other instructional and resource materials

III. As Trainers, They:
- Provide or participate in staff-development workshops and courses for entire or partial school faculties and community
- Orient and train other artists for school work

IV. As Administrators and Coordinators, They:
- Help schools establish linkages with arts organizations, community agencies, and vice versa
- Build bridges among schools and between a school and the central administration
- Organize arts resource teams and schedule visits and services
- Document activities and evaluate progress

Joint Planning: Some Questions to Raise
"Whose Program Is It, Anyway?"[3]

1. The main institutional purpose of arts organizations and school systems differs significantly. Where do interests and capabilities converge or coincide? Two linked rings provide a convenient metaphor for this concept if you shade in the overlap and agree to collaborate in that area.
2. Is this to be a partnership where both parties discuss and agree on mutual and limited goals, objectives, activities, and responsibilities in light of existing realities (resources, time, structure, organization), or will one side attempt to dictate all terms and conditions to the other?
3. Will the process used be one of negotiation and consensus to assure the best possible accommodation and compromise, or will one or each party make unilateral, arbitrary decisions without consulting the other?
4. Are the participants ready, able, and willing to spend the considerable time and energy necessary to plan, review, adjust, and assess mutual efforts?
5. If an effort falters or fails, who gets the blame, and if it succeeds, who gets the credit?
6. Who pays for what, directly or indirectly, and who seeks additional outside support from whom? Will support be secured by pooling scarce resources and collaborative fundraising?
7. Will a letter of agreement or some form of contract containing the terms and conditions of the collaboration help or hinder continuing efforts? If the former, who should draft, review and sign it?

Notes
1. Reprinted by permission, The JDR 3rd Fund ©1980. These criteria were originally written by Kathryn Bloom in consultation with Gene C. Wenner and myself in the mid-seventies.
2. Reprinted from *Changing Schools Through the Arts* (full citation).
3. Ibid.

Appendix I

Sources of Information about Research and Evaluation

Jane Remer

Through a Mirror: A Guide to Evaluating Programs. Louise K. Stevens. Marion, MA: ArtsMarket Consulting, Inc. Prepared under a National Endowment for the Arts Cooperative Agreement, 1993.

This is probably the best book of its kind for the general public. It discusses program evaluation, defines the elements of evaluation including a glossary of terms, provides guidance on how to shape and structure a project complete with charts, offers samples of research plans, questionnaires and focus group scripts, defines the different kinds of evaluation approaches and methods, and discusses the basics of reliable and accurate research. It also contains a planning guide and a pull-out section.

Available from the National Endowment for the Arts—limited number—or from ArtsMarket at 670 Front Street, Marion, MA 02738; phone: 508-748-1578.

Schools, Communities, and the Arts: A Research Compendium. Morrison Institute for Public Policy, School of Public Affairs, Arizona State University. Prepared under a Cooperative Agreement with the National Endowment for the Arts, 1995.

Prepared by Senior Research Analyst Nancy Welch and staff from the Institute for the National Endowment for the Arts, this is the most comprehensive and up-to-date collection of what is considered to be significant research and evaluation in the arts in education. It covers broad-based studies, targeted studies, compilations, attitudes and public opinion, and status studies. A "Quickscan" matrix in one of the appendices provides a handy overview.

Available from the Education Department, John F. Kennedy Center for the Performing Arts, Washington, D.C. 20566; phone: 202-416-8871; fax: 202-416-8876; e-mail: stoner@tmn.com. It is also available in PC-compatible and Macintosh formats via the World Wide Web at http://aspin.asu.edu/~rescomp.

Arts Education in Public Elementary and Secondary Schools. National Endowment for the Arts, Arts in Education Program, 1995.

This publication assesses the state of arts education in the nation, what is being taught, and by whom. Conducted by the U.S. Department of Education and funded by the Arts Endowment, it was designed to determine the extent to which the arts are being taught in American schools at the K-12 levels, the characteristics and backgrounds of those teaching the arts, and the conditions that are associated with arts instruction, such as the extent to which the arts are being taught in conjunction with other subjects and the presence of district curriculum specialists in the arts. It should provide policy makers and practitioners with important information.

Available from the National Center for Education Statistics, Office of Educational Research and Improvement, U.S. Department of Education, Washington, D.C. 20208-5651; phone: 202-219-1333.

Arts Education Research Agenda for the Future. National Endowment for the Arts and the U.S. Department of Education, Office of Educational Research and Improvement, Office of Research, February 1994.

This publication is an excellent overview of the field and contains the arts education research agenda that emerged from a national conference on arts education. The conference, cosponsored by the U.S. Department of Education and the National Endowment for the Arts, was attended by key researchers in each of the arts education disciplines, arts educators, artists and artist-teachers, representatives of arts institutions and organizations and educators, legislators and others who influence the priorities and development of research efforts. The agenda includes background, definitions and discussion of research questions about curriculum, instruction, assessment, evaluation, teacher education, media and technology, policy, funding and collaboration. Chapter 3, "Assessment and Evaluation," contains an intelligent and illuminating discussion about the role of assessment and evaluation in arts education and the constraints imposed on arts education by traditional methods. It proposes alternative models, methods and prototype tasks. It also lists 13 research questions for assessment and evaluation.

Available from the U.S. Government Printing Office, Order Desk: 202-783-3238.

Building A Case for Arts Education: An Annotated Bibliography of Major Research, 1990. John McLaughlin, Ed. The Kentucky Alliance for Arts Education & the Kentucky Arts Council.

This important monograph proposes an 11-point case statement for arts education based on current education concerns. The first section builds a case for arts education based on advocacy and current national, state and local trends, and also describes research trends and major issues in the arts education field. The second section lists bibliographic citations from the research literature that validate each of the 11 points of the case statement. The third section contains annotations of the 88 sources used, arranged by discipline. The sources include qualitative and quantitative research on dimensions of the arts and other variables; writings that are the accumulation of years of research by well-known education and arts researchers; and evaluations and assessments of arts projects and programs. This book was used as a resource for the 1995 publication by the Morrison Institute in Arizona.

Available from the Kentucky Alliance for Arts Education, P. O. Box 13280, Lexington, KY 40583; phone: 606-254-4358.

Toward Civilization: Overview from a Report on Arts Education. National Endowment for the Arts, May 1988.

This landmark report, prepared by then Chairman Frank Hodsoll of the National Endowment for the Arts for the United States Congress, contains thousands of hours of research and consultation on questions such as what is basic arts education, why is it important, what is the problem, the state of arts education, a conclusion and recommendations. It includes recommendations for an arts curriculum, the case for testing and evaluation in the arts, teachers of the arts, research priorities in arts education, leadership and the role of the Arts Endowment.

Available from the Superintendent of Documents, Government Printing Office, Washington, D.C. 20402-9325.

Evaluating the Arts in Education: A Responsive Approach. Robert E. Stake. Ohio: Charles E. Merrill Publishing Co., 1975.

Funded by the John D. Rockefeller 3rd Fund, this important book contains an introduction by Kathryn Bloom, director of the Fund's Arts in Education Program, essays by Robert Stake, Leslie D. McLean, Larry Braskamp and Robert Brown, and Jack Morrison, plus an interview with Stake on responsive evaluation. It also presents the first comprehensive annotated bibliography for evaluation of arts in education programs by Stake and Bernadine Evans Stake. The bibliography covers evaluation of the field in the two decades preceding publication. The book is written for the layperson in simple, vivid prose that makes the abstract concepts accessible.

Out of print. May be available from your local university library.

The Art of Case Study Research. Robert E. Stake. Thousand Oaks: Sage Publications, 1995.

This informative book contains an intensive study of case-study research methods. It is presented in textbook form with assignments based on an actual course outline. Topics include the unique case, research questions, the nature of qualitative research, data gathering, analysis and interpretation, case researcher roles, triangulation, writing the report, reflections and an actual case study of a school. There is a good bibliography and a glossary-index.

Available from Sage Publications, Inc., 2455 Teller Road, Thousand Oaks, CA 91320; phone: 805-499-0721; fax: 805-499-0871.

Bibliography

The Arts, Education and Americans Panel. *Coming to Our Senses: The Significance of the Arts for American Education*. New York: American Council for the Arts, 1988. (First edition, New York: McGraw-Hill, 1977).

The Association for Supervision and Curriculum Development. "A New Design for Education in the Arts" in *Educational Leadership: Journal of the Association for Supervision and Curriculum Development*, Vol. 45, No. 4, December 1987/January 1988.

Barsdate, Kelly J. *The Education Commitment: An Overview of State Arts Agencies' Arts Education Activities*. Washington, D.C. National Assembly for State Arts Agencies, 1995.

Baumol, William J., and William G. Bowen. *Performing Arts: The Economic Dilemma*. New York: The Twentieth Century Fund, 1966.

Bentzen, Mary M. *Changing Schools: The Magic Feather Principle* (I/D/E/A Reports on Schooling, a Charles F. Kettering Foundation Program). New York: McGraw-Hill, 1974.

Bloom, Benjamin. *Taxonomy of Educational Objectives, Book I: Cognitive Domain*. New York: Longman, 1956.

Bloom, Kathryn. *The Arts in Education Program: Progress and Prospects*. New York: The JDR 3rd Fund, 1976.

——. *Arts Organizations and Their Services to Schools: Patrons or Partners?* New York: The JDR 3rd Fund, 1974.

——, and Jane Remer. *A Rationale for the Arts in Education*. New York: The JDR 3rd Fund, 1975.

——, and Jane Remer. *Community Arts Programs and Educational Effectiveness in the Schools*. New York: The JDR 3rd Fund, 1975.

——, Junius Eddy, Charles Fowler, Jane Remer, and Nancy Shucker. *An Arts in Education Source Book: A View from the JDR 3rd Fund*, ed. Charles B. Fowler. New York: The JDR 3rd Fund, 1980. (Distributed by the American Council for the Arts, New York.)

Boyer, Ernest L. *The Basic School: A Community for Learning*. New Jersey: The Carnegie Foundation for the Advancement of Teaching, 1995.

Chapman, Laura H. *Instant Art, Instant Culture: The Unspoken Policy for American Schools*. New York: Teachers College Press, 1982.

——. *Approaches to Art in Education*. New York: Harcourt Brace Jovanovich, 1978.

The College Board. *Academic Preparation For College: What Students Need to Know and Be Able to Do*. New York: The College Board, 1983 (Known as The Green Book).

Consortium of National Arts Education Associations. "National Standards for Arts Education." Reston, VA: Music Educators National Conference, 1994.

Dewey, John. *Art as Experience*. New York: Capricorn Books, 1958. (First published in 1934.)

Dreeszen, Craig. *Intersections: Community Arts and Education Collaborations.* The Arts Extension Service, Division of Continuing Education, University of Massachusetts, Amherst, 1992.

Eddy, Junius. "A Review of Projects in the Arts Supported by ESEA's Title III," and "A Review of Federal Programs Supporting the Arts in Education." New York: The Ford Foundation, 1970.

———. *A Report on the Seattle School System's Arts for Learning Project.* Seattle: Seattle Public Schools, 1978.

———. *Arts Education 1977—In Prose and Print: An Overview of Nine Significant Publications Affecting the Arts in American Education.* Washington, D.C.: The Arts and Humanities Program, Office of Education, U.S. Department of Health, Education and Welfare, Publication 260-934/2044, 1978.

———. *The Music Came From Deep Inside: A Story of Artists and Severely Handicapped Children.* Cambridge, Mass.: Brookline Books, 1989 (First edition, New York: McGraw-Hill, 1982).

———. "Toward Coordinated Federal Policies for Support of Arts Education: A Position Paper of the Alliance for Arts Education." Washington, D.C.: The Alliance for Arts Education, 1977.

———. *The Upsidedown Curriculum.* Washington, D.C.: Alliance for Arts Education (J. F. Kennedy Center for the Performing Arts), 1981 (Revised reprint of the Ford Foundation booklet, Cultural Affairs, Summer 1970).

The Editors of "Education Week." *From Risk to Renewal: Charting a Course for Reform.* Editorial Projects in Education, Inc., 1993.

Eisner, Elliot W. *Cognition and Curriculum: Deciding What to Teach.* New York: Longman, 1982.

———. "Can Educational Research Inform Educational Practice?" in *The Art of Educational Evaluation: A Personal View.* London: The Falmer Press, 1985.

Fowler, Charles B. *The Arts Process in Basic Education.* Harrisburg, PA: Pennsylvania Department of Education, 1973.

———. *Dance as Education.* Washington, D.C.: the National Dance Association, an Association of the American Alliance for Health, Physical Education and Recreation, 1977.

———, ed. *An Arts in Education Source Book: A View from the JDR 3rd Fund,* with Kathryn Bloom, Junius Eddy, Jane Remer, Nancy Shuker, and Fowler (New York: The JDR 3rd Fund, 1980—available from ACA Books).

———. *Can We Rescue the Arts for America's Children?: Coming to Our Senses—10 Years Later.* New York: American Council for the Arts, 1988.

———. *Strong Arts, Strong Schools.* New York: Oxford University Press, in press.

Gardner, Howard. *Art, Mind, and Brain.* New York: Basic Books, 1982.

———. *The Arts and Human Development: A Psychological Study of the Artistic Process.* New York: Wiley, 1973.

———. *Frames of Mind: The Theory of Multiple Intelligences.* New York: Basic Books, 1983.

Getty Center for Education in the Arts. *Beyond Creating: The Place for Art in America's Schools.* Los Angeles: Getty Center for Education in the Arts, 1985.

Goodlad, John. *A Place Called School: Prospects for the Future.* Final report of the Study of Schooling in the United States. I/D/E/A Reports on Schooling, a Charles F. Kettering Foundation Program. New York: McGraw-Hill, 1984.

———. "Beyond the Rhetoric of Promise" in *Arts and the Schools,* ed. Jerome J. Hausman. New York: McGraw-Hill, 1980.

——. *What Schools Are For.* Phi Delta Kappa Educational Foundation, 1979.

——. *The Dynamics of Educational Change.* I/D/E/A Reports on Schooling, a Charles F. Kettering Foundation Program. New York: McGraw-Hill, 1975.

——, with M. Frances Klein and Associates. *Behind the Classroom Door.* Worthington, Ohio: Charles A. Jones Publishing Company, 1970.

Hausman, Jerome J., ed., assisted by Joyce Wright. *Arts and the Schools.* New York: McGraw-Hill, 1980.

Herbert, Douglas "The National Arts Education Landscape: Past, Present, and Future," Vol. 96, No. 6, page 13. —— July/August 1995 Arts Education Policy Review.

Hoffa, Harlan. *An Analysis of Recent Research Conferences in Art Education: Final Report.* Washington, D.C.: Bureau of Research, Office of Education, U.S. Department of Health, Education and Welfare. December 1970.

House, Ernest R. *The Politics of Educational Innovation.* Berkeley, Calif.: McCutchan Publishing Corporation, 1974.

Howe II, Harold. *Thinking About Our Kids: An Agenda for American Education.* New York: The Free Press/Macmillan, Inc., 1993.

The John F. Kennedy Center for the Performing Arts. *The Power of the Arts to Transform Education: An Agenda for Action—The Arts and Education Reform.* (Recommendations from the Arts Education Partnership Working Group). Washington, D.C. January 1993.

The JDR 3rd Fund. Annual Reports. New York: The JDR 3rd Fund, 1963-1977.

Joel, Lydia. "The Impact of Impact: Dance Artists as Catalysts for Change in Education" in *DanceScope*, Vol. 6, No. 2, Spring/Summer 1972.

Jones, Lonna. *The Arts and the U.S. Department of Education: A List of Funded Projects and Activities,* U.S. Department of Education, 1978. Washington, D.C.: U.S. Department of Education, 1979.

Katz, Jonathan, ed. *Arts and Education Handbook.* New York: American Council for the Arts, 1987.

——, ed. *Arts & Education Handbook: A Guide to Productive Collaborations.* Washington, D.C.: National Assembly of State Arts Agencies, 1988.

Koch, Kenneth. *Wishes, Lies and Dreams: Teaching Children to Write Poetry.* New York: Random House, 1971.

Langer, Susanne K. *Feeling and Form: A Theory of Art.* New York: Charles Scribner's, 1953.

——. *Philosophy in a New Key.* Cambridge, MA: Harvard University Press, 1957.

Laybourne, Kit, ed. *Doing the Media—A Portfolio of Activities and Resources.* New York: The Center for Understanding Media, 1972.

Loyacono, Laura L. *Reinventing the Wheel: A Design for Student Achievement in the 21st Century.* Denver, Colorado: National Conference of State Legislatures, 1992.

Lopate, Phillip. *Being With Children: A Highly Spirited Personal Account of Teaching Writing, Theater and Videotape.* New York: Doubleday & Co., 1975.

Madeja, Stanley S. *All the Arts for Every Child.* New York: The JDR 3rd Fund, 1973.

——, ed. *Arts and Aesthetics: An Agenda for the Future.* St. Louis, MO: CEMREL, Inc., 1977.

——, ed. *The Arts, Cognition, and Basic Skills.* St. Louis, MO: CEMREL, Inc., 1978.

———, ed. *Curriculum and Instruction in Arts and Aesthetic Education.* St. Louis, MO: CEM-REL, Inc., 1980.

McLaughlin, John, ed. *Toward a New Era in Arts Education: The Interlochen Symposium.* New York: American Council for the Arts, 1988.

———. *Building A Case for Arts Education: An Annotated Bibliography of Major Research.* Kentucky Alliance for Arts Education & the Kentucky Arts Council, 1990.

Mitchell, Ruth, ed. *Measuring Up to the Challenge: What Standards and Assessment Can Do for Arts Education.* New York: ACA Books, 1994.

Morrison Institute for Public Policy. *Schools, Communities, and the Arts: A Research Compendium.* School of Public Affairs, Arizona State University Prepared under a Cooperative Agreement with the National Endowment for the Arts, 1995.

Morrison, Jack. *The Rise of the Arts on the American Campus.* Carnegie Commission on Higher Education series. New York: McGraw-Hill, 1973.

———. *The Maturing of the Arts on the American Campus: A Commentary.* Los Angeles, CA.: University Press of America, 1985.

Murphy, Judith, and Lonna Jones. *Research in Arts Education: A Federal Chapter.* Washington, D.C.: Office of Education, U.S. Department of Health, Education, and Welfare Publication (OE) 76-02000, 1978.

———, and Ronald Gross. *The Arts and the Poor: New Challenge for Educators.* Washington, D.C.: Bureau of Research, Office of Education, U.S. Department of Health, Education and Welfare, June 1968.

Music Educators National Conference. "The Arts in General Education" in *Music Educators Journal,* Vol. 64, No. 5, January 1978.

———. *Try a New Face.* A Report on HEW-Supported Arts Projects in American Schools. Arts and Humanities Staff, Office of Education. Charles L. Gary, Projects Coordinator (in cooperation with the American Theatre Association, National Art Education Association, National Dance Association). Reporters include Sara A. Chapman, Junius Eddy, Charles B. Fowler, Charles L. Gary, Harlan Hoffa, Araminta Little. Washington, D.C.: U.S. Department of Health, Education and Welfare, 1979.

———, and CEMREL, Inc. *Toward an Aesthetic Education.* Reston, Va.: The Music Educators National Conference and CEMREL, Inc., 1970.

National Assembly of Local Arts Agencies. *Working Relationships: The Arts, Education and Community Development,* by Nancy Welch (Morrison Institute for Public Policy, Arizona State University) and Paul Fisher (Tucson/Pima Arts Council). Washington, D.C., 1995.

National Endowment for the Arts. *Report of the Task Force on the Education, Training and Development of Professional Artists and Arts Educators.* Washington, D.C.: December 1978.

———. *Toward Civilization: A Report on Arts Education.* Washington, D.C.: U.S. Government Printing Office, 1988.

———, and the U.S. Department of Education. Arts Education Research Agenda for the Future. Washington, D.C.: U.S. Government Printing Office, February 1994.

———, and the Coca Cola Foundation. *The Arts and Education: Partners in Achieving Our National Education Goals.* January 1995.

National School Boards Association. *The Arts in Education: Research Report 1978-2.* Digest of the report by the Arts, Education and Americans Panel. Washington, D.C.: NSBA, 1978.

Newsom, Barbara Y., and Adele Z. Silver. *The Art Museum as Educator: A Collection of Studies as Guides to Practice and Policy.* Berkeley, Calif.: University of California Press, 1977.

New York City Board of Education. *All the Arts for All the Children: A Report on the Arts in General Education, New York City, 1974-1977.* New York: New York City Board of Education, 1978.

——, Division of Curriculum and Instruction. *Architecture: A Design for Education.* New York: New York City Board of Education, 1979.

——, Division of Curriculum and Instruction. *Arts in General Education: An Administrator's Manual.* New York: New York City Board of Education, 1979.

The New York State Education Department. *RITA: Reading Improvement through the Arts.* Albany, N.Y.: The New York State Education Department, Division of Federal Educational Opportunity Programs, Title 1, ESEA, and the Division of Humanities and Arts Education, 1979.

Oklahoma State Department of Education. *A New Wind Blowing: Arts in Education in Oklahoma Schools.* Oklahoma City: Oklahoma State Department of Education, 1978.

Pankratz, David B., and Kevin V. Mulcahy. *The Challenge to Reform Arts Education: What Role Can Research Play?* New York: American Council for the Arts, 1989.

Pennsylvania State University. *Arts IMPACT: Curriculum for Change—A Summary Report.* Prepared by the Arts I(nterdisciplinary) M(odel) P(rograms) in the A(rts) for C(hildren) and T(eachers) Project Evaluation Team and submitted to the Arts and Humanities Program, Office of Education, U.S. Department of Health, Education and Welfare. University Park, PA: Pennsylvania State University, March 1973.

Read, Herbert. *Education Through Art.* (Third revision.) New York: Pantheon Books, 1956.

Reimer, Bennett. *A Philosophy of Music Education.* Englewood Cliffs, NJ: Prentice-Hall, 1970.

——. "Designing Effective Arts Programs" in *Arts and the Schools*, ed. Jerome J. Hausman. New York: McGraw-Hill, 1980.

Remer, Jane. *Networks, the Arts and School Change.* New York: The JDR 3rd Fund, 1975. (Revised and expanded for The National Elementary Principal, "The Ecology of Education: The Arts." Vol. 55, No. 3. January/February, 1976).

——. *The Identification Process for Schools Participating in the New York City Arts in General Education Project Network.* New York: The JDR 3rd Fund, 1975.

——. *Considerations for School Systems Contemplating a Comprehensive AGE Program.* New York: The JDR 3rd Fund, 1977.

——. *The League of Cities for the Arts in Education.* New York: The JDR 3rd Fund, 1977.

——. *Changing Schools Through the Arts: The Power of an Idea.* New York: McGraw-Hill, 1982.

——. "Arts Policy in Public Education" in *The Journal of Arts Management and Law*, Vol. 13, No. 1, Spring 1983.

——. "Quo Vadis Arts Education: A National Agenda" in *Design for Arts in Education*, Vol. 89, No. 2, November/December 1987.

——. *Changing School Through the Arts: How to Build on the Power of an Idea.* New York: ACA Books, 1990.

——. "Questioning the Educational Imperative" in *Dance/USA Journal*, Vol. 11, No. 3, Spring 1994.

Robinson, Dr. Ken, Researcher and Editor. *The Arts in Schools: Principles, Practice and Provision*, London: Calouste Gulbenkenian Foundation, 1982, 1989.

Rockefeller Panel. *The Performing Arts: Problems and Prospects.* New York: McGraw-Hill, 1965.

Sarason, Seymour B. *The Culture of the School and the Problem of Change.* Boston: Allyn and Bacon, Inc. 1971 (Seventh printing, 1974).

Shapiro, Stephen R., Richard Place, and Richard Scheidenhelm. *Artists in the Classroom.* Hartford, CT: Connecticut Commission on the Arts, 1973.

Shuker, Nancy, ed. *Arts in Education Partners: Schools and Their Communities.* Jointly sponsored by the Junior League of Oklahoma City, the Arts Council of Oklahoma City, Oklahoma City Public Schools, the Association of Junior Leagues and the JDR 3rd Fund, 1977 (Distributed by the American Council for the Arts, New York).

Silberman, Charles. *Crisis in the Classroom: The Remaking of American Education.* New York: Random House, 1970.

Sizer, Theodore R. *Horace's School*, Boston, Mass: Houghton Mifflin, 1992.

Sizemore, Judy. "Education Reform Opportunities for Artists and Craftspeople: A Handbook"; Editing and Layout by Dennis Horn. Frankfort, KY: Kentucky Arts Council, Summer, 1995.

Smith, Ralph A. *Aesthetic Concepts and Education.* Urbana, IL: University of Illinois Press, 1970.

Spolin, Viola. *Improvisation for the Theatre: A Handbook of Teaching and Directing Techniques.* Evanston, IL: Northwestern University Press, 1963 (Republished as the Theater Game File, consisting of index cards packaged in a box, CEMREL, St. Louis, MO, 1976).

Stake, Robert E. *Evaluating the Arts in Education: A Responsive Approach.* Columbus, Ohio: Charles E. Merrill, 1975.

——. *The Art of Case Study Research* (Thousand Oaks, CA: Sage Publications, Inc., 1995)

Stevens, Louise K. *Through A Mirror: A Guide to Evaluating Programs* (ArtsMarket Consulting, Inc. Marion, MA. Prepared under a National Endowment for the Arts Cooperative Agreement, 1993).

Tye, Kenneth A., and Jerrold M. Novotney. *Schools in Transition: The Practitioner as Change Agent.* I/D/E/A Reports on Schooling, A Charles F. Kettering Foundation Program. New York: McGraw-Hill, 1975.

U.S. Department of Education. *Arts Education in Public Elementary and Secondary Schools* (Office of Educational Research and Improvement, National Center for Education Statistics, 1995).

Weinstein, Gerald, and Mario D. Fantini. *Toward Humanistic Education, A Curriculum of Affect.* New York: Praeger University Series, 1970.

Wenner, Gene C. *Comprehensive [State] Arts Planning: The Ad Hoc Coalition of States for the Arts in Education*, ed. Kathryn Bloom. New York: The JDR 3rd Fund, 1975.

——. *Dance in the Schools: A New Movement in Education.* New York: The JDR 3rd Fund, The City Center of Music and Drama, and the National Endowment for the Arts, 1974.

Wilson, Brent, and Harlan Hoffa, eds. *The History of Art Education: Proceedings from the Penn State Conference.* University Park, IL: Pennsylvania State University, College of Arts and Architecture, School of Visual Arts, 1985.

Wolf, Dennis Palmer, and Thomas Wolf. *Academic Preparation in the Arts: Teaching for Transition from High School to College.* New York: College Entrance Examination Board, 1975 (Known as The Red Book).

Wolf, Thomas, ed. *The Arts Go To School: An Arts-in-Education Handbook.* New York: New England Foundation for the Arts and American Council for the Arts, 1983.

Index

About the American Council for the Arts

As the American Council for the Arts celebrates its 35th Anniversary Year in 1995-96, it marks three and a half decades of service to the arts. ACA is one of the oldest, continuously operating arts service organizations in the United States. Its mission is to promote public policies that advance and document the contribution of the arts and artists to American life. ACA's goals focus on: arts advocacy, the collection and dissemination of arts information, arts education and partnership building. For more than a decade, ACA has organized National Arts Advocacy Day, the Nancy Hanks Lecture on Arts and Public Policy, and other prestigious conferences and public forums. ACA's National Arts Policy Clearinghouse is one of the nation's leading, centralized resources of arts information. ArtsUSA, ACA's Internet site on the World Wide Web, provides electronic access to the Clearinghouse bibliographic database of arts research, arts education networks, ACA's book catalogue, advocacy updates, and other services. ACA also provides legislative information through its newsletter *ArtsUSA UpDate*, and is the publisher and distributor of more than 175 arts-related policy and career publications. ACA is currently active in partnerships promoting arts education within education reform efforts, and convenes national conferences on important arts education issues. The National Coalition of United Arts Funds has been administered by ACA as an affiliate program since 1988. The 67-member NCUAF is committed to fostering and promoting federated fundraising campaigns in the arts.

Board of Directors

Chair of the Board
Donald R. Greene

Vice Chairs
Jack Avrett
John Paul Batiste
Madeleine Berman
Willard L. Boyd
Elizabeth G. Christopherson
Richard S. Gurin
Howard S. Kelberg, Esq.
Fred Lazarus, IV
Mrs. Michael A. Miles
Jaime Oaxaca
Mrs. LeRoy Rubin

Secretary
Mrs. John R. Hall

Treasurer
Steven D. Spiess

Past Chairs
Mrs. Jack S. Blanton, Sr.
Gerald D. Blatherwick
Eugene C. Dorsey
Donald G. Conrad
Marshall S. Cogan
Louis Harris
David Rockefeller, Jr.
George M. Irwin

Members Emeriti
Donald G. Conrad

Eugene C. Dorsey
Louis Harris
John Kilpatrick

Members
Elaine Allen
Judith F. Baca
Harry Belafonte
Theodore Bikel
Winton Malcolm Blount
Raymond A. Boyce
John Brademas
Mrs. Martin Brown
Kathryn Murphy Burke
Nedda Casei
Marylouise Cowan
Stephanie French
Sonnai Frock-Rohrbeck
Jack Golodner
Mrs. Susan S. Goode
Michael Greene
Joan W. Harris
Rosario G. Holguin
A. William Holmberg, Jr.
Eleanor Holtzman
The Honorable Lonna R. Hooks
Richard Hunt
The Honorable Ruth E.
  Johnson, Esq.
Alexander Julian
Loretta E. Kaufman

Mrs. Donald M. Kendall
John A. Koten
Steven David Lavine
John J. Mahlmann
Bruce Marks
Cheryl McClenney-Brooker
Lee Kimche McGrath
Henry Moran
Velma V. Morrison
Thomas O. Muller, III
Mrs. John Nieto
Adolfo V. Nodal
Ervin R. Oberschmidt
Paul M. Ostergard
Jack Paden
Susan Pearce
Gerald Reiser
Milton Rhodes
Dr. James M. Rosser
Molly K. Sasse
Gerard Schwarz
Dick Scott
Jack R. Shultz
Mrs. David E. Skinner
John Straus
Dr. William Taylor
Mrs. James Thompson
Esther Wachtell
Mrs. Gerald H. Westby
Masaru Yokouchi

About the Author

Jane Remer is an author, editor and freelance consultant in the fields of education, the arts and the arts in education. She is also the Grants and Program Director for the Capezio/Ballet Makers Dance Foundation Inc. She has worked for over 30 years at the national, state and local levels with a variety of public and private agencies and organizations.

As Associate Director of the Arts in Education Program of the John D. Rockefeller 3rd Fund, Ms. Remer designed, coordinated and documented comprehensive arts-in-general-education programs operating in a network of six urban school districts around the country. She has been a panelist for the NEA's Challenge, Advancement, Arts in Education and Opera-Musical Theater programs. She has held senior administrative posts at the New York City Board of Education's Learning Cooperative, Lincoln Center for the Performing Arts, the Harkness School of Ballet, and New York University's La Maison Française.

In addition to writing for national publications, Ms. Remer is the author of *Changing Schools Through the Arts: How to Build on the Power of an Idea*, originally published by McGraw-Hill in 1982 and reissued in 1990 by the American Council for the Arts. A former dancer and arts professional in theater, music, and poetry, Ms. Remer holds a B.A. from Oberlin College, a Master of Arts in Teaching (French) from Yale University and credits towards a degree from Yale Law School. She lives on Manhattan's Upper West Side and is the mother of two children who are also Oberlin graduates and alumni of the New York City public schools.